Assessing Psychometric Fitness of Intelligence Tests

Assessing Psychometric Fitness of Intelligence Tests

Toward Evidence-Based Interpretation Practices

Edited by
Gary L. Canivez

ROWMAN & LITTLEFIELD
Lanham • Boulder • New York • London

Rowman & Littlefield
Bloomsbury Publishing Inc, 1385 Broadway, New York, NY 10018, USA
Bloomsbury Publishing Plc, 50 Bedford Square, London, WC1B 3DP, UK
Bloomsbury Publishing Ireland, 29 Earlsfort Terrace, Dublin 2, D02 AY28, Ireland
www.rowman.com

British Library Cataloguing in Publication Information Available

Library of Congress Cataloging-in-Publication Data Available

ISBN: 978-1-5381-4571-5 (cloth : alk. paper)
ISBN: 978-1-5381-4572-2 (pbk. : alk. paper)
ISBN: 978-1-5381-4573-9 (ebook)

For product safety related questions contact productsafety@bloomsbury.com.

∞™ The paper used in this publication meets the minimum requirements of American National Standard for Information Sciences—Permanence of Paper for Printed Library Materials, ANSI/NISO Z39.48-1992.

A Festschrift in Honor of Marley W. Watkins

Brief Contents

Contents

Preface

This book was inspired by former professors, colleagues, mentors, and friends who have greatly influenced me from my early training to my ongoing research and courses and continuing education workshop development. While my scholarship has concentrated on original research, book chapters, test reviews, and commentaries, I hadn't been motivated to create my own book project until now. This book is the culmination of a confluence of two main foci. The first, a career journey filled with serendipitous events and seized opportunities; the second, immense gratitude requiring a most public and enduring expression.

As an undergraduate psychology student at Bemidji State University (BSU), I was fortunate to have two advisors, Dr. Russell Bennett, professor of psychology (1978–2021), and Dr. James Rafferty, professor of psychology (1976–2016), who both encouraged me to be involved in undergraduate research experiences that would facilitate greater research competencies leading to graduate school admission and success. They also recommended I take a Psychology of Measurement course to obtain an introduction to measurement principles, one of the three scientific foundations of psychology (Measurement, Statistics, Research Methods/Experimental Design). This course was taught by Dr. Oscar Rouck, professor of psychology (1973–1982), who before his appointment at BSU was a research fellow at the Paderewski Foundation. While at the Paderewski Foundation, Dr. Rouck earned a Fulbright U.S. Scholar Award for a visiting lecturer position at the University of Dacca (Dhaka) from 1962 to 1963. He was involved in translation and adaptation of the Differential Aptitude Tests (DAT; Bennett, Seashore, & Wesman, 1947) into Urdu, and he supervised four thesis projects at the University of Dacca devoted to the translation, adaptation, and assessment of the psychometric properties of the Urdu-based DAT. To complement the Psychology of Measurement course, I concurrently enrolled in the measurement laboratory that accompanied the lecture to gain experience conducting measurement research. The laboratory project I conducted was a small concurrent validity study comparing the Self-Directed Search (SDS; Holland, 1977) and the Strong-Campbell Interest Inventory (SCII; Campbell & Hansen, 1981). It was in these classes that the critical importance of methods for assessing the reliability and validity of tests and measurements, as well as elements of test construction and norms, was introduced.

Drs. Rafferty and Bennett also were research supervisors for two undergraduate research studies I helped develop and conduct (one on effects of cold temperatures on altruism and one on effects of cold temperatures on aggression) and what better place could there be to study cold weather effects than Bemidji, Minnesota? Drs. Rafferty and Bennett combined these two small studies into a presentation we delivered at the 1983 Annual Convention of the Midwestern Psychological Association, Chicago, my first professional presentation.

Following graduation from Bemidji State, I circuitously ended up in graduate school at Southern Illinois University at Carbondale (SIUC), where the Department of Educational Psychology chairperson, Dr. John J. "Jack" Cody, asked what my interests were and what I ultimately wanted to do. With my interests in working with children and adolescents, measurement, and statistics, he helped me develop a plan for my graduate education. Because of my undergraduate research experiences, he awarded me a graduate assistantship that involved statistical analyses of ACT test scores of Illinois students during the 1970s and into the early 1980s that led to my first publication (Mouw, Cody, & Canivez, 1986). In combining the counseling and school psychology programs as several former students had done, I was able to craft a hybrid graduate program with courses from the Department of Educational Psychology and the Department of Psychology. Given my interests in statistics and measurement, one of the courses that I included in my program of study was the Principles of Measurement course taught by Dr. Patricia "Patti" Elmore, and it was the required paper in this class that ended up having quite a serendipitous outcome several years later. I chose to write my paper reviewing the topic of computerized and automated psychological testing and related applications. The Department of Educational Psychology had previously purchased a copy of the McDermott Multidimensional Assessment of Children (MMAC; McDermott & Watkins, 1985), which I reviewed and described as part of that paper, not knowing the future importance of its authors.

During the summer of 1987 I finished my internship in school psychology and my dissertation research and flew to Phoenix to interview for a school psychologist position with the Deer Valley Unified School District (DVUSD). Two of the district school psychologists, Dr. Joe Kush and Dr. Charles (Chuck) Heath, were part of the interview team along with Special Education Director Joann Martin. School psychology service delivery was described as a consultation-based model and use of pre-referral intervention (student-study) teams to address early student learning and behavioral concerns, which was a welcome departure from the special education refer-test-place model that was well engrained in special education cooperatives where I served in practica training and in my internship in southern Illinois. The interview went well, and I was offered the position the following morning. Within three weeks I had defended my dissertation, moved to Phoenix, and begun my first school psychologist position. As a new school psychologist I had much to learn, and I could not have been in a better place. It was while working for the DVUSD that I really learned what it meant to be a scientist-practitioner as this was modeled by many and strongly encouraged. At our first school psychologist meeting I was introduced to the full school psychology staff, and among them was Marley Watkins, who at the time I did not associate with the McDermott and Watkins MMAC program I had previously reviewed. However, shortly thereafter, I (and the other school psychologists) received article reprints in the district mail that served as discussion items at our regular school psychologist staff meetings, and some were authored or co-authored by Marley. It was then I realized the serendipity. Could this be the same Marley Watkins? Indeed, it was! It was in my first year as a school psychologist that my real education began as Marley provided me post-doctoral supervision.

My graduate school training as a school psychologist was quite typical for the times (and in many places yet today). In my Individual Measurement and Practice course at SIUC (intelligence test administration and interpretation) and subsequent practica, the *Intelligent Testing* (Kaufman, 1979) approach was emphasized in clinical assessment of children. During my practica, internship year, and in my first year as a school psychologist, my psychological evaluation reports often included two to three pages of descriptions of intelligence test performance, score comparisons, and interpretations of what they all might mean followed by recommendations supposedly informed by such comparisons and inferences. This included reporting and interpretation of the global Full-Scale IQ, Verbal and Performance IQs, factor-based scores, subtest scores, ipsative strengths and weaknesses, pairwise comparisons, and configural subtest combinations promoted in textbooks

(Sattler, 1982) and other interpretive guidebooks focused on the Wechsler Intelligence Scale for Children–Revised (WISC–R; Wechsler, 1974). Similar procedures were also applied to other intelligence or cognitive ability tests. However, the peer-reviewed research articles assessing the reliability, validity, and diagnostic utility of various intelligence test scores and score comparisons that I was then reading and discussing in our school psychologist staff meetings presented a tremendous amount of cognitive dissonance (if one were to ascribe to the scientist-practitioner model) as well as ethical challenges and dilemmas. The challenge I immediately faced was I could continue to interpret intelligence tests and write reports of intelligence test performance as I was previously trained *or* I could change my test interpretation practices to be consonant with the empirical evidence published in the peer-reviewed literature. That ethical dilemma was quickly resolved by my changing my test interpretation practices, focusing on reporting and interpreting scores and score comparisons that had strong empirical evidence for reliability and validity (i.e., evidence-based interpretation). Marley had a tremendous influence in this critical transformation not by proselytizing but by providing dissonant information from the extant literature. It was up to me to decide how best to proceed.

While I was a school psychologist for the DVUSD, several teachers at my schools were enrolled in a master's program in counseling through Northern Arizona University (NAU), and one came to me to ask some questions about her class in psychological testing and measurement. After I had answered her questions and illustrated on a whiteboard some of the measurement principles, she said that she better understood and that I should be teaching the class. She gave me the name of the regional director and when I called to inquire about possible adjunct teaching opportunities, I was invited to submit my CV, and I was hired as adjunct assistant professor to teach the next semester. I began teaching their graduate Tests and Measurement course but soon also taught a variety of other courses in counseling, human development, behavior management, and educational psychology. In addition to teaching for NAU in the Phoenix Region from 1988 to 1995 I was also asked to teach graduate courses as a faculty associate at the newly created Arizona State University, West Campus (ASU). From June 1989 to May 1991 I taught graduate courses in adolescent psychology, research and evaluation in education, and learning and instruction for ASU until they filled full-time faculty positions.

After working for the DVUSD for three years I was lured away to be a school psychologist for Tempe Elementary School District with better pay and an opportunity to supervise doctoral school psychologist interns. While I may have been working in a new district, I retained close collegial and personal relationships with Marley and Joe. Five years later, Marley and I followed Joe Kush into academia to teach in school psychology training programs. One year earlier, Joe began an assistant professor position teaching in the school psychology program at Duquesne University where he soon became its program director. During my years teaching as an adjunct assistant professor and later adjunct associate professor for NAU, year by year I was enjoying teaching graduate courses as much as being a school psychologist. In my later years at Tempe Elementary I started collecting data for research, presented research at conferences, and realized that I might enjoy being a university professor teaching in a school psychology program. I applied for various tenure-track school psychology assistant professor positions and was hired by Eastern Illinois University (EIU), whose psychology department chairperson at that time was Dr. Fred Yaffe. I learned just prior to interviewing for the EIU position that Fred was a psychology professor at Washburn University many years earlier when Joe Kush was an undergraduate psychology student there.

In 1995, the year I began as assistant professor of psychology at EIU to primarily teach in the school psychology program, Marley began as assistant professor at Pennsylvania State University also teaching in a school psychology program. Knowing scholarship was an integral part of earning tenure and promotion, Marley and I embarked on collaborative research projects that continue today even with Marley now in retirement.

When I started at EIU, my teaching assignments included the Individual Intellectual Assessment course, and in reviewing the curriculum, I saw there was no prerequisite course covering advanced measurement principles. Admission to the program did not require an undergraduate course in psychological measurement, although, like many programs, this was recommended. In a course dedicated to training students to administer, score, and interpret intelligence tests (and other tests as well), it is crucial for students to understand measurement principles related to reliability, validity, diagnostic utility, and norms to competently read and understand information and claims included in test technical manuals, clinical guidebooks, and the professional literature. Further, knowledge of theories of intelligence and cognitive abilities is also necessary to understand the constructs purportedly measured by various intelligence tests and what empirical support for their measurement with various tests existed. In the first years teaching the intellectual assessment course I needed to present a review of measurement and statistical methods to assess reliability, validity, diagnostic utility, and norms; followed by theories of intelligence; and finally training on administration, scoring, interpretation, and report writing. Needless to say, this was an impossible task and highly stressful for both student *and* instructor. I thus proposed and developed a course in advanced psychological measurement (first taught in 2000 as a seminar and beginning in 2003 as a specified course) provided in the first semester of graduate study to precede the intelligence assessment course in the second semester. The benefit of an advanced measurement course also meant that such principles could be applied to other assessment and intervention courses throughout the program and a foundation for evidence-based practice.

Further, when I talked with school, clinical, and other applied psychologists, it became obvious that their approaches to intelligence test interpretation were very like my previous graduate training but seemingly devoid of knowing the literature showing most of the interpretation methods promoted were based on scores or score comparisons that were inadequate in reliability, validity, and diagnostic utility and that also lacked treatment validity. Further discussions elucidated the problem that all admitted being inadequately trained in measurement and statistics—essential for understanding the professional literature as well as what was presented in technical manuals that might not sufficiently support score use, *or what might not be presented at all*, rendering judgments about score sufficiency impossible. This struck me as an enormous ethical problem in that test users might not have adequate information available in test technical manuals to determine which scores or score comparisons were sufficiently psychometrically supported. Inadequate training in measurement and statistics also poses an ethical problem when interpreting test scores and score comparisons lacking sufficient reliability, validity, and diagnostic utility. In my early international conference presentations, I asked practitioners and professors in other countries about these same concerns, and this appeared to be a universal problem. At my first attendance and presenting at the conference of the International Test Commission in Brussels, Belgium, in 2006, I discussed this problem with Tom Oakland, then professor at the University of Florida, and the possibility of developing a continuing education workshop to address these concerns based on my advanced measurement principles course, and he was not only in agreement but strongly encouraged me to develop such a workshop and present widely. I began with the creation of a workshop titled Measurement Matters: Basic Psychological Measurement Principles That Guide Test Selection, Use, and Interpretation and began presenting it to school psychologists in school districts as well as at state school psychology association conferences, national conventions, and international conferences. Because of the intersection of ethics, test standards, and measurement principles, I then expanded the content to cover ethical principles that impact test use and interpretation and standards for testing and test use. The resulting workshop title, Ethics, Test Standards, and Test Interpretation: Measurement Matters, now reflects this critical intersection.

In covering the various statistical methods for reliability, validity, and diagnostic utility research the workshop uses research and articles I and colleagues published as exemplars, and many examples come from research with intelligence tests. While numerous references to articles, chapters, and books were included in the workshop, I was often asked by workshop participants if I had a book covering the workshop content. This led to the creation of this book and the opening chapter: "Ethics, Test Standards, and Test Interpretation: Measurement Matters!" The remaining chapters focus on summarizing the psychometric fitness of specific intelligence tests and applications of psychometric and applied statistics to theory and issues of intellectual assessment and intelligence test scores.

The second focus of this book is that of publicly expressing my deep gratitude for the mentorship, collegiality, and friendship that Marley W. Watkins has so generously provided all these years and continues to provide. While this book serves as a vehicle to summarize and present important information covering ethics, test standards, measurement principles, and empirical evidence impacting intelligence test interpretation, it also serves as a *Festschrift* to honor the work and career of Marley W. Watkins. Marley has had a direct and career-long impact on my development as a scholar and school psychology professor, and he has also had direct and indirect impacts on the works of the other contributors in this volume. When planning this book, I sent out invitations to the vast array of Marley's colleagues and those who said they were influenced by his work, and many immediately and enthusiastically agreed to contribute chapters. Their contributions are a testament to Marley's extensive and unwavering influence advancing *evidence*-based test interpretation and railing against the *eminence*-based test interpretation all too prevalent in today's (and yesterday's) assessment practices. It is with profound admiration and infinite gratitude that I dedicate this book to the legacy of our esteemed colleague, Marley W. Watkins.

References

Bennett, G. K., Seashore, H. G., & Wesman, A. G. (1947). *Differential aptitude tests manual*. Psychological Corporation.

Campbell, D. P., & Hansen, J. C. (1981). *Manual for the SVIB-SCII: Strong-Campbell Interest Inventory* (3rd. ed.). Stanford University Press.

Holland, J. L. (1977). *The Self-Directed Search: A guide to educational and vocational planning* (Rev. ed.). Consulting Psychologists Press.

Kaufman, A. S. (1979). *Intelligent testing with the WISC–R*. Wiley.

McDermott, P. A., & Watkins, M. W. (1985). *Microcomputer systems manual for McDermott Multidimensional Assessment of Children*. Psychological Corporation.

Mouw, J. T., Cody, J. J., & Canivez, G. L. (1986). Decline in ACT mean scores: Alternative explanations. *Capstone Journal of Education*, 7(1), 3–14.

Sattler, J. M. (1982). *Assessment of children's intelligence and special abilities* (2nd ed.). Allyn & Bacon.

Wechsler, D. (1974). *Manual for the Wechsler Intelligence Scale for Children–Revised* (WISC–R). Psychological Corporation.

Acknowledgments

With any major project there are many who contribute to its success, and I am most grateful to you all. Your effort in helping me accomplish this book during the disruptive times of SARSCoV2 (COVID-19) and after is commendable.

I am indebted to the kindness and generosity of my esteemed friends and colleagues Drs. Ryan J. McGill, Stefan C. Dombrowski, Eric A. Youngstrom, and Cecil R. Reynolds for critical reviewing and sage suggestions for earlier drafts that helped to make the opening chapter a much stronger contribution. I am grateful for your enduring support, intellect, and encouragement.

I am grateful to the contributors for their recognition of the importance of this Festschrift to pay homage to the work and career of our esteemed colleague Dr. Marley W. Watkins, who has had a profound impact on each of us and the profession. This book would not have been possible without you.

To my mother, Carol Ann Canivez (née Busser), and father, Lynn Marino Canivez, for always encouraging and believing in me and modeling the hard work necessary to achieve goals, whatever they may be. You worked tirelessly in challenging times, never complained, and never let us kids know how challenging things really were so we could be kids without worry. In giving thanks, I am reminded of the story my mother told me, after I earned my PhD, of a parent-teacher conference when I was in elementary school where the teacher told my mother to steer me away from the sciences because I had no aptitude for it! Many thanks for *not* following that uninformed advice and allowing me the opportunity to discover and learn what I was interested in.

I would like to thank Mark Kerr for his initial encouragement and guidance for me to develop this project. While I thought it was a worthy cause, his enthusiasm for it made it seem more so.

Finally, to my wife, Mary, and children, Daniel, Sarah, and Hannah, many thanks for your support and patience of the countless hours I spent working on this book. Thanks for understanding.

Chapter 1

Ethics, Test Standards, and Test Interpretation

Measurement Matters!

Gary L. Canivez

Effective clinicians "(a) know what their tests can do and (b) act accordingly. Knowing what one's test can do—that is, what psychological functions they describe accurately, what diagnostic conclusions can be inferred from them with what degree of certainty, and what kinds of behavior they can be expected to predict—is the measure of a psychodiagnostician's competence. Acting accordingly—that is, expressing only opinions that are consonant with the current status of validity data—is the measure of his or her ethicality" (Weiner, 1989, p. 829).

This opening quote from Weiner is one of the most important statements reflecting the intersection of ethics, test standards, and measurement principles, all of which must be applied in competent test use, most importantly, test interpretation; and each of these topics is addressed in detail within this chapter. To follow Weiner's sage advice, psychologists must possess fundamental competencies in psychological measurement (test score reliability, validity, utility, and norms), which is one of the foundations of science. The importance of these competencies for ethical assessment and clinical practice cannot be overstated (Dawes, 2005; McFall, 1991, 1996, 2000).

Aiken et al. (1990) assessed graduate training in measurement, statistics, and methodology in North American PhD programs, finding inadequacies in measurement instruction; and Lambert (1991) echoed their concerns, pointing out the importance of measurement literacy and the need for more measurement experts in universities to provide increased instruction at both undergraduate and graduate levels. The American Psychological Association (APA) created a task force in 1996 to develop guidelines for test user qualifications, and the executive summary of the task force (Turner et al., 2001) defined test user qualifications as "the combination of knowledge, skills, abilities, training, experience, and, where appropriate, practice credentials that the APA considers desirable for the responsible use of psychological tests" (p. 1099). The guidelines would "inform test users as well as individuals involved with training programs, regulatory and credentialing bodies, and the public about the qualifications that promote high professional standards" (p. 1099). In a survey examining assessment training among APA–accredited clinical psychology doctoral programs, Childs and Eyde (2002), with a 46% survey return rate, found psychometrics reportedly *covered* in at least one course at a rate of 73% but only 24% offered a course *focused on* psychometrics. They further found 65% required at least one course covering psychometrics, but only 18% required a course focused on psychometrics; and topics of reliability and validity were covered in at least one course in 63% and 60% of programs, respectively, but none reported a course focused on reliability and validity. In a study of graduate training in research methods among APA–accredited professional programs with varying program orientations, Rossen and Oakland (2008) reported most required an introductory course in measurement (75% to 92%) but few required an advanced measurement course (17% to 44%). Accounting for differences in findings is difficult because of varying survey methods, survey foci, and types of programs examined.

Aiken et al. (2008) conducted a follow-up study to the Aiken et al. (1990) survey and commented that there was little change in doctoral training in measurement, concluding, "We find it deplorable that a dozen years later, the measurement requirement occupies a median of only 4.5 weeks in the PhD curriculum in psychology" (p. 43). They further lamented the inadequacies of measurement training that resulted in the situation "that most graduates lacked fundamental competency in measurement" (p. 43). Inadequate measurement training has its roots at the undergraduate level as Dahlman and Geisinger (2015) observed in reporting on the generally inadequate undergraduate instruction in measurement historically and presently. Such training inadequacy directly impacts *psychometric literacy* (Lambert, 1991) and competency, which is a crucial element for ethical clinical practice because incompetency is necessarily unethical. Further, psychometric illiteracy renders the clinician susceptible to pseudoscientific and unscientific practices (Dombrowski et al., 2022).

Use of psychological and educational tests is ubiquitous within professional psychological and educational practice (Dombrowski, 2020), and professional associations have developed and updated ethical principles, some directly or indirectly related to assessment and measurement, to guide professional practices to protect the public. As early as the 1950s, specialists in measurement and psychological assessment helped develop various standards and guidelines for tests and test use that informed test users and developers about critical features that also help protect the public (APA Committee on Test Standards, 1952; APA et al., 1954). Ethical standards and testing standards are not mutually exclusive, and there are many features that overlap. Influencing both are psychological measurement principles, research methods, and related applied statistics that provide the tools and procedures for test development and evaluation of test psychometric properties (psychometric fitness). Measurement principles provide the foundation for evidence-based assessment and are implicitly and explicitly addressed in professional ethics and test standards. Thus, one may see the crucial intersection of ethics, test standards, and measurement principles that impact test use and the focus of this chapter.

Ethical Principles Related to Measurement and Assessment

Ethical principles of the American Psychological Association (APA, 2017; www.apa.org/ethics/code/index) and the National Association of School Psychologists (NASP, 2020) are prominent ethics codes for psychologists in the United States, and other ethical codes exist for other contexts and countries such as the British Psychological Society (BPS, 2021), the International School Psychology Association (ISPA, 2021), and other associations in related helping professions. Ethical principles that directly or indirectly relate to test use are frequently included, and users of tests *must* understand and comply with such principles to guide professional practices. Critically, however, ethical principles and standards apply only to members of the professional association for whom the professional ethics were written.

American Psychological Association Ethical Principles

Ethical principles of psychologists and amendments (APA, 2017) include indirect and direct principles impacting test use (selection, administration, scoring, interpretation). Beneficence and nonmaleficence are cardinal principles of all ethical codes, and above all, practices must do no harm. In psychological assessment many practices have high-stakes impacts on clients, which require use of instruments with the highest psychometric qualities, and interpretations or inferences are qualified by psychometric properties reported in technical manuals and the extant literature. Research is also impacted by test scores as lower score reliability estimates reduce power and adequacy in hypothesis testing. Toward this is **Principle 2.01 Boundaries of Competence**, which states, "Psychologists provide services, teach, and conduct research with populations and in areas only within the boundaries of their competence, based on their education, training, supervised experience, consultation, study, or professional experience" (p. 5). Although *or* is used, it seems that more should be required than just professional experience. Initial training and preparation of psychologists, the foundation for competent clinical practice, is fundamentally guided by education, training, and supervised experiences through courses, practica, internship, and postdoctoral supervision. Recent publication of guidelines for education and training in psychological assessment for health care psychologists (Wright et al., 2021) provides numerous educational and training guidelines paralleling many test user qualifications outlined two decades earlier by Turner et al. (2001). Unfortunately, throughout this document, guidelines are stated in terms of "should learn" rather than "must [or shall] learn," and given the historically poor adoption and delivery of specific training in psychometrics and related applied statistics, one must continue to be concerned that inadequate training will continue to plague professional education and inadequate development of essential psychometric competencies. Time will tell if these training guidelines produce necessary adoption in graduate curricula and requirement of courses in psychometrics and applied statistics to address previously reported educational inadequacies (Aiken et al., 2008; Dahlman & Geisinger, 2015).

Principle 2.04 Bases for Scientific and Professional Judgments states, "Psychologists' work is based upon established scientific and professional knowledge of the discipline" (p. 5). In the context of test use, this would necessitate not just the knowledge of psychometric information provided in test manuals but also that reported in the extant literature. Some peer-reviewed studies may replicate and extend test technical manual preliminary findings, but some may substantially limit or contradict initial psychometric findings reported in the technical manual. This principle requires continued reading and applying findings from the peer-reviewed literature related to specific tests used by the professional because the knowledge base is ever changing and evolving. Additionally, there may be analyses or statistics not applied or reported (or inadequately reported) in test technical manuals that limit or prevent test users' ability to judge the psychometric adequacy of various scores or score comparisons (e.g., Canivez & Watkins, 2016; Canivez et al., 2021). Test interpretation practices need to change when evidence shows scores or score comparisons to be psychometrically inadequate. A complicating factor here is if the professional is inadequately educated in measurement and applied statistics related to understanding methods and procedures reported in the test technical manual and the extant literature, they may be incapable of judging the merits of what is claimed and thereby susceptible to what some might consider pseudoscientific approaches and claims (Farmer et al., 2021; Farmer et al., 2022; Lilienfeld et al., 2012). This is likely a factor in the perpetuation of interpretation practices not supported by evidence (e.g., Dombrowski et al., 2022; McGill et al., 2018; Watkins, 2000) suggestive of pathological science (Langmuir & Hall, 1989).

Ethical responsibilities of instructors, professors, and training programs are addressed by **Principle 7.01 Design of Educational and Training Programs**: "Psychologists responsible for education and training programs take reasonable steps to ensure that the programs are designed to provide the appropriate knowledge and proper experiences and to meet the requirements for licensure, certification, or other goals for which claims are made by the program" (p. 10). Based on past surveys of doctoral (Aiken et al., 1990, 2008) and undergraduate (Dahlman & Geisinger, 2015) instruction in measurement, this appears to be an area of considerable shortcoming in many, if not most, programs. For training professionals at the subdoctoral level (master's or specialist degree), common among school psychologists, this may be even more problematic for psychometric literacy and measurement competency. Relatedly, if those graduating from programs where such training was inadequate are later employed in teaching courses in training programs preparing future psychologists, they may lack the fundamental psychometric competencies required for providing necessary training, thereby perpetuating the problem.

Ethical principles directly impacting test use include **Principle 9.01 Bases for Assessments**: "Psychologists base the opinions contained in their recommendations, reports, and diagnostic or evaluative statements, including forensic testimony, on information and techniques sufficient to substantiate their findings" (pp. 12–13). Within this principle is the requirement to adequately know what information and techniques are sufficient as sufficiency depends on accumulated evidence of psychometric support for all scores and score comparisons. **Principle 9.02 Use of Assessments** states, "Psychologists administer, adapt, score, interpret, or use assessment techniques, interviews, tests, or instruments in a manner and for the purposes that are appropriate in light of the research on or evidence of the usefulness and proper application of the techniques" (p. 13). This requires full understanding of methods, procedures, and results presented in test manuals as well as those reported in the peer-reviewed literature, which is constantly evolving. Such evidence is required for all provided scores and for the variety of recommended score comparisons provided within test manuals or those promoted by others in clinical guidebooks. Another guideline states, "Psychologists use assessment instruments whose validity and reliability have been established for use with members of the population tested. When such validity or reliability has not been established, psychologists describe the strengths and limitations of test results and interpretation" (p. 13). Of particular importance is the general lack of information that may be available in a test technical manual regarding minority group members who, while proportionally sampled for norm development, may be too small for comparative or differential reliability and validity (bias) studies. Specifically, within the United States, Native American/First Nations/Indigenous populations and Asian Americans are subgroups in the population that are proportionally quite small and while proportionally sampled for developing representative norms, do not typically include sample sizes large enough to compare to the larger racial/ethnic groups (White/Caucasian, Black/African American, Latino(a)/Hispanic). Differential reliability, validity, and diagnostic utility are often unknown until such studies appear in the peer-reviewed literature, which may take many years or perhaps are never conducted or published. Oversampling such populations when conducting normative data collection would help to provide necessary data for such differential reliability and validity investigations, but rarely does this appear to be done or are such analyses reported in test technical manuals.

Principle 9.05 Test Construction is fundamentally important in specifying that "psychologists who develop tests and other assessment techniques use appropriate psychometric procedures and current scientific or professional knowledge for test design, standardization, validation, reduction or elimination of bias, and recommendations for use" (p. 13). While companies may not be obligated, psychologists in their employ may be. Documentation of test development procedures, psychometric assessments, and interpretive recommendations may be inadequate and in some cases may be obsolete or contrary to published psychometric evidence, yet the test authors or psychometricians within the company may not have editorial control over what is eventually published in manuals. Users of tests may recognize this conflict when comparing information in the test manuals (or lack of it) with peer-reviewed research in the extant literature. As such, test users should consider financial and other conflicts of interest when such discrepancies exist, and their test choice and interpretation decisions should be based on what scores and score comparisons warrant interpretation dictated by appropriate psychometric evidence available.

Principle 9.08 Obsolete Tests and Outdated Test Results includes three principles impacting test use: "Psychologists do not base their assessment or intervention decisions or recommendations on data or test results that are outdated for the current purpose" (p. 14). Thus, it is incumbent on the psychologist to know and understand research and evidence related to how long data and test results might be viable in a particular area. Variables such as age or developmental level of the individual, type of test and scores being used, and how the scores or score comparisons are being used should be considered. "Psychologists do not base such decisions or recommendations on tests and measures that are obsolete and not useful for the current purpose" (p. 14). The question of when a test or measure becomes obsolete and no longer useful is a complicated one that can relate to normative sample characteristics (representativeness), test content (items may be antiquated or their difficulty may have changed so inclusion or placement within the test may be suspect), or both. Also, it might be that some types of tests have shorter lifespans or shelf-lives than others. Test users must look to the peer-reviewed literature to understand such limitations and their effects on viability of scores for tests they use although such data may be limited. Finally, "psychologists retain responsibility for the appropriate application, interpretation, and use of assessment instruments, whether they score and interpret such tests themselves or use automated or other services" (p. 14). This is particularly important as technological advances allow for more computer or automated administration, scoring, and interpretation—including use of artificial intelligence (AI). However, while having a computer or automated system administer and score a test may reduce error associated with these tasks, given the many scores, score comparisons, and related "interpretations" or inferences emanating from various score comparisons, while intuitive or part of clinical tradition, may not be empirically supported. It is crucial that the test user be knowledgeable about which of the scores and score comparisons are empirically supported with replicated research and withhold interpretations of scores or comparisons not sufficiently supported. This is also crucial in evaluating the veracity of proposed new applications and uses of measures (including AI) with evidence published prior to recommendations for clinical application.

National Association of School Psychologists Ethical Principles

The National Association of School Psychologists Principles for Professional Ethics (NASP, 2020) also state the fundamental principle of beneficence (doing good, avoiding harm) and that "school psychologists must practice within the boundaries of their competence, use scientific knowledge from psychology and education to help clients and others make informed choices, and accept responsibility for their work" (p. 45). Like the APA ethical principles, the crucial element is recognizing what one's practice limits are based on one's education, training, and supervised experiences, and where deficiencies exist, seeking continuing education and supervision to remediate those deficiencies. This can be particularly difficult when one does not know what they do not know! **Principle II.1. Competence** states, "To benefit clients, school psychologists engage only in practices for which they are qualified and competent" (p. 45). Within the domain of test use and assessment this relates to psychometric literacy and competency in measurement and applied statistics to know which test scores and test score comparisons are sufficiently supported for use in individual clinical decision-making. Again, fundamental competencies of measurement must be applied to information provided in test technical manuals and the extant literature. **Standard II.1.3** states, "School psychologists engage in continuing professional development. They remain current regarding developments in research, continuing professional development, and professional practices that benefit children and youth, families, and schools" (p. 45). Of concern are the plethora of continuing education offerings presented by test publishers (or their representatives) or others with conflicts of interest. When direct instruction and development of psychometric literacy and measurement competency is insufficient, continuing professional development in the form of graduate courses and continuing education workshops may help to address such inadequacies. This was noted by Aiken et al. (2008), but they duly noted workshops could not supplant important fundamental coursework. However, availability of continuing education workshops devoted to psychometric literacy and measurement may be, and has been, quite limited, further complicating matters. It seems professional associations bear special responsibility to provide an abundance of such continuing education offerings related to measurement to help address the inadequacies of measurement training in graduate programs. Professional associations and accrediting bodies also bear a special responsibility to assure that psychometric literacy is sufficiently addressed in training programs through program and accreditation reviews.

    Principle II.2 Accepting Responsibility for Actions notes, "School psychologists accept responsibility for their professional work, monitor the effectiveness of their services, and work to correct ineffective recommendations" (p. 45). This suggests that when evidence in a test manual is absent or inadequately supports recommended interpretation practices the school psychologist amends their interpretation practices. Test score interpretations must be evidence based, particularly in individual clinical applications as these are often associated with high-stakes decisions. **Standard II.2.3** states, "School psychologists accept responsibility for the appropriateness of their professional practices, decisions, and recommendations" (pp. 45–46). Decisions and recommendations are often products of the tests and assessment procedures employed and responsibility for appropriate uses must be guided by empirical evidence supporting the practice. The quality of practices, decisions, and recommendations is dependent on scores and data produced by the tests or procedures, so knowledge of psychometric properties of test scores and their comparisons with other scores within the test, as well as comparisons with scores from other tests used in the clinical evaluation, is crucial and should reflect strong, evidence-based support. Appeals to theory or traditional practices are insufficient to support interpretation practices absent replicated supporting evidence.

Principle II.3 Responsible Assessment and Intervention Practices specifies, "School psychologists maintain the highest standard for responsible professional practices in educational and psychological assessment and direct and indirect interventions" (p. 46). Here, school psychologists must apply psychometric literacy and measurement principles in the selection of the most appropriate test or procedure for the situation, administer the test properly, and interpret only those scores and score comparisons shown to be sufficiently reliable, valid, and diagnostically accurate. **Principle II.3** specifies four standards specifically related to tests and assessment. **Standard II.3.2** specifies, "School psychologists use assessment techniques and practices that the profession considers to be responsible, research-based practice" (p. 46). The term *research-based* is perhaps a poor choice of terminology because it is not necessarily equivalent to *evidence-based*. Many interpretation practices are claimed to be research based yet many of the scores, score comparisons, or inferences made from them may not have been adequately or properly assessed for psychometric fitness, and in some instances the independent peer-reviewed literature has consistently shown various scores and score comparisons that form the basis of interpretations to be grossly inadequate (e.g., Canivez, 2013a; McGill et al., 2018; Watkins, 2000), yet their use continues. **Standard II.3.3** states, "School psychologists select assessment instruments and strategies that are reliable and valid for the examinee and the purpose of the assessment" (p. 46). In this situation, considerations of race/ethnicity, disability, language, culture, socioeconomic status, or other demographic features may have unknown differential reliability, validity, or diagnostic utility because such studies may not have been conducted to answer the question, and like APA ethical standards, this limitation may demand extremely cautious use of certain tests if at all. This is of particular concern regarding diversity, equity, and inclusion regarding assessment results. **Standard II.3.3** states, "If using norm-referenced measures, school psychologists choose instruments with norms that are representative, recent, and appropriate for the person being evaluated. School psychologists ensure that their supervisors are informed about the importance of using the most current version of published instruments" (p. 46). Generally speaking, recent norms are certainly critical for inferences made regarding the individual, and all things being equal, the most recent norms certainly are preferred. But, while norms may be recent in a newly released test, there may be unknown psychometric properties of scores and score comparisons when various analyses and information are not included in the test manual, thereby complicating the decision of whether or how to use the new version. Specifically, if a test with new norms is published but lacks crucial evidence showing that reliability, validity, and diagnostic utility are consistent across various normative subgroups, it may be impossible to know how well scores might work for someone from one of the smaller demographic subgroups. Further, as Beaujean (2015a) opined, immediate adoption of a new test version may be unwise until careful review of psychometric fitness has been conducted, and new editions of tests need to be scrutinized as a new test. Limitations may relate to an absence of analyses or results, inadequate examinations of subgroups within the normative sample, or psychometric properties less adequate than the previous edition. Psychologists must often wait for independent research to be published in the peer-reviewed literature to answer such questions. Further, analyses and results reported in test manuals need to be independently replicated for there to be confidence in reported psychometric properties. **Standard II.3.5** states, "When using digitally administered assessments (e.g., computers, tablets, virtual reality) and/or computer-assisted scoring or interpretation programs, school psychologists choose programs that meet professional standards for accuracy and validity" (p. 46). Assessing accuracy and validity of digital assessments, computer-assisted scoring, or interpretation programs may be difficult or impossible when the codes, algorithms, and formulae embedded in code are not made available due to proprietary and copyright claims. The same is true with the proliferation of AI.

Standard II.3.8 states, "School psychologists conduct valid and fair assessments. They actively pursue knowledge of the student's disabilities and developmental, cultural, linguistic, and experiential background and the select, administer, and interpret assessment instruments and procedures in light of those characteristics" (p. 47). Like the APA ethics, this relates to considerations of differential psychometric properties across these various variables, and typically such comparisons are not adequately examined or reported in test manuals. Independent studies may not answer such questions for some time after publication, if ever, so the clinician may not have the necessary information to make an informed judgment. Differential psychometric properties may result in test bias and may have discriminatory impacts that are also inconsistent with federal law in assessment of children with disabilities (U.S. Department of Education, 2006). When such information is unavailable, it is best to assume the test scores or comparisons are not sufficiently evidence based until research shows they are.

Test Standards

Concerns for the technical adequacy and documentation of psychological tests were recognized many decades ago, and a draft proposal for recommended disclosures of technical properties of psychological tests and diagnostic techniques was initially created by the American Psychological Association, Committee on Test Standards (APA, 1952), which sought broad public comment. Revisions through collaboration with representatives from the American Educational Research Association (AERA) and the National Council for Measurements Used in Education (NCMUE; now NCME) were later included and published in *Technical Recommendations for Psychological Tests and Diagnostic Techniques* (APA et al., 1954). Within the draft and in the final publication it was reported that an APA committee concerned with psychological measurement was formed in 1906 to standardize testing techniques, illustrating concerns about measurement from the earliest days of the profession. The overarching principle of the 1954 standards was that test manuals "should carry information sufficient to enable any qualified user to make sound judgments regarding the usefulness and interpretation of the test" (p. 2). This echoes Oscar Buros's earlier insistence that "test users have every right to demand that test authors and publishers present full particulars concerning the methods used in constructing and validating the tests which they place on the market" (1938, p. xiii). But again, the qualified user must possess psychometric literacy to make sound judgments regarding what is (or is not) included. *Technical Recommendations* was a forerunner of *Standards for Educational and Psychological Testing* (APA et al., 1974) and subsequent revisions (AERA et al., 1999, 2014), which have expanded greatly since the initial offering. These have also influenced other published standards and guidelines internationally.

Standards for Educational and Psychological Testing

Standards for Educational and Psychological Testing (AERA et al., 2014), hereafter referred to as *Standards*, provides "criteria for the development and evaluation of tests and testing practices and to provide guidelines for assessing the validity of interpretations of test scores for the intended test uses" in order to "promote sound testing practices and to provide a basis for evaluating the quality of those practices" (AERA et al., 2014, p. 1). These are so essential to quality assessment practices that every psychologist should have a copy and be well versed in its content. To facilitate this, a PDF version is now freely available for download from AERA (https://www.aera.net/Publications /Books/Standards-for-Educational-Psychological-Testing-2014-Edition). *Standards* applies to test authors and developers, publishers, and various users so that tests are appropriately used. "Uses of tests and testing practices are improved to the extent that those involved have adequate levels of assessment literacy" (AERA et al., 2014, p. 3). Presently the current *Standards* are in the process of revision.

The preface to *Standards* noted that a 2011 draft of a revised 1999 *Standards* was produced for public comment, and 35 professional associations, 10 test companies, and 13 academic or research institutions, credentialing organizations, or other institutions provided comments. The Joint Committee considered comments and produced the final revision, which was then approved by the three separate sponsoring organizations (AERA, APA, NCME). While *Standards* is prescriptive, there are no mechanisms for enforcement but it is consistent with each of the sponsoring organizations' code of conduct and ethical standards. Production of *Standards* is a monumental accomplishment and a tremendous benefit to all in the testing process. The introduction describes the purpose for *Standards* as well as the tests and uses where the standards apply.

Standards is organized around three parts. *Foundations* (Part I) includes three chapters concerned with validity (Chapter 1), reliability and errors in measurement (Chapter 2), and fairness in testing (Chapter 3), all of which begin with descriptions and background for the area followed by specific standards. *Operations* (Part II) includes six chapters concerned with the design and development of tests (Chapter 4); scores, scales, score linking, and cut-scores (Chapter 5); test administration, scoring, reporting, and interpretation (Chapter 6); documentation supporting tests (Chapter 7); test taker rights and responsibilities (Chapter 8); and test user rights and responsibilities (Chapter 9). *Testing Applications* (Part III) is concerned with applications specific to psychological testing and assessment (Chapter 10); testing and credentialing in workplaces (Chapter 11); educational testing and assessment (Chapter 12); and test uses in program evaluation, policy studies, and accountability (Chapter 13). Some of the information contained in *Standards* should be considered universally important for all psychologists such as *Foundations* and *Operations* whereas some might apply more specifically to work settings or tasks one is involved in. Within each of the chapters there are references to application of measurement and statistical indexes and procedures underpinning the standards and thus the importance of psychometric literacy.

International Test Commission Standards

The International Test Commission (https://www.intestcom.org) has published several important guidelines relating to tests including guidelines for translating and adapting tests, test use, technology-based assessment, quality control, test security, test disposal, and large-scale assessment of diverse populations. Recently published by the ITC are test adaptation reporting standards to facilitate transparent, accurate, and useful documentation of test adaptation procedures (Iliescu et al., 2024). While all are valuable and address specific contexts, *International Guidelines for Test Use* (ITC, 2001, 2013) is the most relevant here and parallels important features of *Standards* where the 1999 *Standards* (AERA et al., 1999) was influential in developing *International Guidelines*. *International Guidelines* was influenced by previous guidelines for test use published by professional associations in Australia, the UK, the United States, and Canada. Because of the numerous translations, adaptations, and publication of various versions of Wechsler scales of intelligence and other intelligence tests (e.g., RIAS [Reynolds & Kamphaus, 2003]), *International Test Commission Guidelines for Translating and Adapting Tests* also requires careful consideration in such contexts. These also apply to measures of personality, psychopathology, and other constructs.

International Guidelines details competencies necessary for appropriate and best practices in assessment and test use and most parallel those in *Standards*. *International Guidelines* also specifies that development and application of assessment competencies provided will lead to ethical test use. The primary focus is directed toward professional practices and thus applies to those purchasing and holding test materials, those selecting and determining test uses, those administering, scoring, or interpreting tests, those advising others using test scores, and those communicating test results to those who had been tested. These guidelines are also important for those conducting research. Additionally, *International Guidelines* is pivotal for those developing tests, those distributing or supplying tests, those involved in educating and training test users, test takers, professional associations and governing bodies, and legislators and policy makers.

Part 1 of *International Guidelines* focuses on test users' responsibility for ethical use of tests including acting in a professional and ethical manner, ensuring competency to use tests (i.e., practicing within scientific limits and substantiated experiences, establishing and maintaining high standards for competence and practicing within one's limits, and monitoring changes in test development and legal or policy changes impacting test use), and taking responsibility for test use (i.e., providing testing services and using tests qualified to use, assuming responsibility for test selection and recommendations based on them, avoiding harm or distress to those tested). Test users also have responsibilities for maintaining test material security (i.e., storing and controlling access, adhering to copyright law, preserving test integrity, refraining from publicly describing test materials or techniques) and maintaining test results confidentiality (i.e., limiting disclosure of test results only to those with right to know, disclosing information only with proper informed consents).

Part 2 of *International Guidelines* focuses on adhering to good test use practices including determining potential utility of testing in specific situations, choosing technically sound tests for specific situations, and considering issues of fairness in testing. Good test use practices also include providing necessary preparations for testing, administering tests properly, accurately scoring and analyzing test results, appropriately interpreting test results, communicating test results clearly and accurately, and reviewing appropriateness of tests and their uses.

What is abundantly clear from professional ethical standards, test standards and guidelines, and test user qualifications (Turner et al., 2001) is that test users must possess psychometric literacy as this is crucial for test users to follow ethical guidelines and test standards. Measurement and psychometric principles are the underpinnings of psychological science, and without competency in these it is impossible to judge the adequacy of tests, test scores, and test score comparisons that are used to make decisions about individuals in the assessment process. These competencies also impact research where statistical power will be influenced by the precision with which variables are measured, so these are not only for those clinically oriented. The final section presents the measurement principles and procedures that test users must understand and apply.

Measurement Principles and Procedures

Measurement is a fundamental element of any science because to scientifically study something, it must be observable (directly or indirectly) and quantified, and each scientific discipline studies specific objects or phenomena germane to that area. It is often said that if something exists then it exists in some amount that may be measured and therefore studied. Some have attributed this to Descartes, but an exact quote remains elusive. Thorndike (1914) wrote, "Whatever exists at all exists in some amount. To know it thoroughly involves knowing its quantity as well as its quality" (p. 16). While some sciences are concerned with and study physical objects that might be directly observed and measured, psychology largely involves the study of hypothetical constructs (e.g., intelligence, depression, anxiety) and related behaviors. Constructs (underlying unobservable theoretical entities) are not real things per se but an individual's behavior or responses to test questions are. That is, overt behavior and responses are observable and presumed to be a result of some underlying theoretical construct. An individual's performance on an abstract reasoning test is assumed to be a result of their intelligence (or perhaps some abstract reasoning ability). An individual's affirmative responses to, or endorsements of, test items regarding frenzied or increased activity, lack of need for sleep, euphoric mood, racing thoughts, and inflated self-esteem and self-confidence, might be assumed to be the result of underlying "mania." Based on an individual's observable behavior or responses to test questions, we infer some aspect or amount of the theoretical construct or attribute of interest.

Discoveries and advances in scientific understanding are directly related to the improving quality of measurement within a discipline. All sciences are concerned with relevant observations and the construction and improvement of tools or devices that improve observations that advances understanding. Astronomy began with observations by early astronomers simply using their unaided eyes, but the development of telescopes provided greater precision of observations (within the visible electromagnetic spectrum). Technological advances in better material to make glass, production of larger lenses, and more precise glass grinding led to better quality lenses, which improved optics. Using better materials for tubes holding lenses that were more rigid and less susceptible to distortion from heat, humidity, vibration, or other factors also improved observations. Other inventions such as use of mirrors for reflective telescopes and development of radio telescopes provided additional improvements and capabilities as well as observing and measuring beyond the visible light spectrum. Technological marvels such as the Hubble Space Telescope and the James Webb Space Telescope have produced observations unimaginable from Earth's surface. In the other direction, the creation of microscopes allowed for the discovery and description of microorganisms (i.e., bacteria, archaea, protozoa, viruses) and later experimentation that allowed for understanding and better explanation of beneficial microorganisms (i.e., those involved in making cheese, wine, beer, bread, etc.) as well as disease microorganisms (i.e., those causing amoebic or bacterial dysentery, cholera, syphilis, etc.). It may be said that better life comes from better science, but better science comes from better measurement!

In the development of psychology as a discipline, the earliest scientists were all interested in developing and improving measurement of psychological phenomena. In particular, Galton, Spearman, Cattell (James McKeen), and Binet were among early pioneers of psychological measurement and the field of psychometrics (Anastasi & Urbina, 1997). Galton (1879) defined psychometry as the "the art of imposing measurement and number upon operations of the mind" and he noted "that until the phenomena of any branch of knowledge have been subjected to measurement and number, it cannot assume the status and dignity of a science" (p. 149).

Within psychological measurement, measurement principles involve a variety theories or models (each with important assumptions) and approaches to quantify and assess reliability, validity, utility, and norms (for norm-referenced tests). *Reliability* relates to the consistency identified in observations or scores from a test or measurement procedure and reflects the degree of measurement precision (and error). *Validity* pertains to the appropriateness of inferences derived from test scores or observations, often reflecting some relationship to an underlying (latent) hypothetical construct and its nomological network (Cronbach & Meehl, 1955). *Utility* (diagnostic utility or diagnostic accuracy), sometimes referred to as *discriminative validity* (Haynes et al., 2018) or *diagnostic validity*, which distinguishes it from Campbell and Fiske's (1959) *discriminant validity*, is particularly important for tests, measures, or observations used in making individual decisions (individual prediction, diagnosis, classification, selection) and indicates the accuracy of decisions made from test scores (or their comparisons) applied to individuals (see Kraemer, 1992). Utility (i.e., the contribution of any measurement to a desired clinical outcome) is essential for both norm-referenced and criterion-referenced measures. Finally, *norms* reflect performance of some selected reference group on the test or measure and the normative sample characteristics provide an indication of the appropriateness of test use or generalizability for specific individuals adequately represented in the normative group. Much of psychological assessment and measurement is oriented toward a *nomothetic* understanding of the individual relative to a normal or typical population, so quality test norms are essential as they represent the reference anchor for these interpretations. There are numerous books devoted to detailed descriptions and explanations of measurement or psychometrics that are the basis for descriptions that follow. Notably among these are Furr (2022), Allen & Yen (2002), Raykov and Marcoulides (2011), Reynolds et al. (2021), Nunnally and Bernstein (1994), McDonald (1999), and Embretson and Reise (2000).

Classical Test Theory

Classical Test Theory (CTT) or Classical [Weak] True-Score Theory (Allen & Yen, 2002) is the predominant approach in assessing and understanding psychometric properties (psychometric fitness) of test scores and is frequently the focus of numerous analyses reported in standardized test technical manuals. Other theoretical approaches include Strong True-Score Theory/Latent Trait Theory/Item Response Theory (Allen & Yen, 2002; Embretson & Reise, 2000; Lord, 1965), which focuses on items within measures as variables of measurement, and Generalizability Theory (Cronbach et al., 1972), which examines various systematic variance sources. The Trinitarian Validity Model was the prevailing approach in organizing types of validity research evidence (Guion, 1980), dividing validity into three types (content validity [face validity and logical validity], criterion-related validity [concurrent validity and predictive validity], and construct validity [numerous methods relating test scores to theoretical elements or latent constructs]; Allen & Yen, 2002). The Trinitarian approach appears to have been supplanted by a more contemporary approach offered by Messick (1989, 1995). Messick's Unified Validity Theory organizes validity relative to the types of information or evidence provided to support construct validity (evidence based on test content, response processes, internal structure, association with other variables, consequences of use). Messick (1995) noted that other validity terms or descriptors were appropriate in their particular contexts, and these are used in the present chapter in addition to Messick's because of their descriptive and historical nature. Contemporary measurement textbooks (e.g., Furr, 2022; Reynolds et al., 2021) now parallel Messick's model as does *Standards* (AERA et al., 2014).

Classical Test Theory (CTT) assumptions of reliability may be expressed in the form of equations for individuals and groups and, as noted by Revelle and Condon (2019), originated with Spearman (1904). For elaborate presentation of all CTT assumptions and mathematical proofs or derivations, consult Allen and Yen (2002). When considering an individual, the formula $X_O = X_T + X_e$ (where X_O is an individual's obtained or observed test score, X_T is the individual's theoretical true score, and X_e is the amount of measurement error in the individual's obtained test score) expresses the contributions to an individual's observed score. Any observed score for an individual contains their true score and some amount of measurement error. The person's true score can be considered, in a practical sense, the theoretical value (test score) the person should obtain on a test based solely on their characteristics, knowledge, or competencies (Furr, 2022). But, because all measurement contains some measurement error a person's obtained score may be higher or lower than their true score. Thus the individual's observed score is an estimate of their true score, which cannot be directly measured.

For a group of individuals (a sample) we focus on the score variability within the sample and the formula $S_O^2 = S_T^2 + S_e^2$ (where S_C^2 is a sample's observed score variance, S_T^2 is the sample's theoretical true score variance, and S_e^2 is the error variance in the sample's observed scores) expresses the variability of observed scores in a sample that is composed of true score variance within the sample (true differences between individuals) and error variance within the sample. As in the case for individuals, the observed score variance is directly measured for a sample. While test scores and their variability are directly observed based on performance of individuals, true score variance and error variance cannot be directly observed or measured. These must be estimated through various reliability research methods and statistical analyses, each answering different questions.

Error variance and true score variance are both estimated through a variety of reliability methods that produce a reliability coefficient expressed as a correlation (r_{xx}). The reliability coefficient for test scores is a ratio of true score variance to total (observed) score variance expressed as $r_{xx} = \dfrac{S_T^2}{S_O^2}$. It is important to always remember that reliability coefficients are estimates in the same way that an individual's obtained score is an estimate of their true score. Like an individual's true score, we also do not know the true reliability of a test or procedure. In fact, reliability is a property of scores and not the test or procedure (Thompson & Vacha-Haase, 2000) so it is equally inappropriate to refer to a test (or procedure) as being reliable! Reliability coefficients are estimated using a particular method with a specific sample at a particular time. Each of the types of reliability estimation methods will produce varying (higher or lower) coefficients due to the nature of sources of error contributing to the scores, and some methods may only be appropriate for tests of certain constructs but not others. These are described in detail later

It is assumed that all measures have some amount of measurement error in observed scores and the major sources of error variance in test scores include (a) test construction, (b) test administration, and (c) test scoring. Error is assumed to be random, unsystematic variability introduced into test scores, and reliability estimates provide indications of measurement error. If a source of systematic variability is introduced into a set of test scores, this would not be considered error variance in CTT if it were identified and statistically removed.

Sources of Measurement Error

Test Construction

When a test is developed and constructed, there is a theoretically infinite number of items that could be created to measure the construct so choices must be made regarding the final test content. Also, if there are different ways to measure the construct, or if the construct is multidimensional, then there may be a variety of tasks or subtests that may be created to measure the construct, each having its own item content. Such selection is referred to as content sampling or domain sampling where subtests may be created or selected from a population of possible tasks from within the domain and test or subtest items are created or selected from a population of possible items from within the domain. As in other examples of sampling, there is sampling error when the entire population cannot be selected and the more tasks or items, the less sampling error there is likely to be. Error here may relate to the degree to which the person's score is affected by the content sampled with a hyperbolic example where some individuals may know answers to all *but* the questions on the test and some individuals may know answers to *only* the questions on the test.

Questions regarding what content is included, how items are worded, what and how instructions are worded and presented, and so forth point to elements that introduce error into the test when such factors affect test takers differently. No matter how test instructions are written, some individuals may find them instructive while others may find them more difficult, and this could introduce error. Relatedly, a test with more subtests or items may make the test longer and could introduce fatigue that for some individuals may more adversely affect their performance and introduce error to a greater extent than other individuals less susceptible to fatigue. A shorter test might not adequately sample from the domain and introduce error. Thus it appears that there is no escaping measurement error in test construction, but attempts are made to minimize it.

Test Administration

When a test is administered there are a variety of factors that may differentially influence the test taker's performance thereby affecting their obtained score. Some factors relate to examiner influences and some relate to physical and environmental conditions or psychological factors that impact attention, concentration, motivation, and so on when the individual is responding to questions or test materials. When the examiner deviates from the test standardization procedures, they may make the task more difficult or less difficult compared to what those in the standardization sample experienced. If instructions are not provided verbatim and elaboration provided, it might make the task easier and the test taker's performance better than it might have been under standard procedures. If some instructions are left out or inaccurately provided, the test taker's performance might be adversely affected. Other features of test administration that might introduce error include inappropriately arranging and placing test materials in proper, standardized orientation, timing incorrectly so more time or less time is provided, and verbally or nonverbally providing feedback or clues to response correctness. Maintaining strict adherence to standardization procedures is crucial to minimize error contributed by the examiner. Error contributed by an examiner could result in significant influences in obtained scores that could impact clinical decision-making (McDermott et al., 2014).

Elements of the test environment when the test is being administered may also interfere with test performance such as poor lighting, excessive heat and humidity, noise, and uncomfortable or inappropriate seating. Such factors influence the test taker's attention, concentration, and motivation so test environmental conditions must be optimal. There may also be factors within the test subject that may interfere with their optimal performance such as general carelessness, test anxiety, and drug or medication effects. Extended testing by adding more subtests to one's battery of tests lengthens the testing process and may create additional fatigue or if continuing testing another day may introduce additional sources of error by leading to less than adequate participation and effects on performance and scores. Aspects of guessing an answer when not knowing the correct answer or knowing an answer but marking the wrong response on an answer form also introduce error into observed scores.

Test Scoring

There are numerous possible scoring errors that test users may make that will contribute to measurement error. The only means of avoiding this is when the test is scored by a computer as under those conditions then there will be no error introduced as all responses will be scored the same way each time. One aspect of test scoring error is the examiner's judgment that may be involved in determining the correctness of an individual's item response. Relatedly, some tests have items that are scored in a non-binary way. Tests often contain scoring rubrics or guidelines and provide examples of item responses that are considered correct (1) or incorrect (0) and for non-binary item scores (one example, fully correct (2), marginally or partially correct (1), or incorrect (0). Anytime human judgment is involved there is likely to be some disagreement in judgments of item correctness, particularly for ambiguous responses, so the better the scoring rubric and response examples reflecting the scoring guidelines and the better the training and instruction in applying them, the less item scoring error. An aspect impacting proper application of scoring guidelines relates to the concept of drift[1] (Smith, 1986), whereby over time there is the increasing drift away from standardized procedures that were previously taught, including both administration and scoring.

Another element in test scoring errors may be the incorrect selection or placement of scoring templates on answer forms as the wrong template will surely provide incorrect scoring, and misalignment may result in different items or responses being counted or responses incorrectly highlighted for scoring. Relatedly, when scoring templates are used, the examiner must manually count the items indicated as endorsed because errors can result by counting incorrectly or failing to identify an endorsed item within the correctly placed template. Other scoring related errors include incorrectly summing item scores to generate a subtest total raw score. Errors may be made in transferring subtest totals from an answer page to a summary table either by writing the wrong number or writing the score in the incorrect place. Errors in summing may be made when adding several subtest scores to produce a composite score.

Finally, errors may be made when consulting normative tables for transforming raw scores into standard scores either by using the wrong conversion table based on age or some other characteristic or by misreading the corresponding standard score for the raw score. I am reminded of a situation several years ago when an examiner posted an inquiry on a popular email listserve about test scores from the Wechsler Intelligence Scale for Children–Fifth Edition (WISC–V; Wechsler, 2014) that did not make sense (i.e., the Full-Scale IQ [FSIQ] was many points higher than the factor-based index scores would suggest). Further inquiry indicated that they summed the scaled scores from all 10 primary subtests as had previously been done with the Wechsler Intelligence Scale for Children–Fourth Edition (WISC–IV; Wechsler, 2003), but in the WISC–V, the FSIQ is scaled based on the sum of scaled scores from only the first seven primary subtests. Thus the additional scores from three subtests greatly increased the FSIQ in the current version.

With respect to the three broad sources of error, the examiner has no control over errors emanating from the test construction process because the test they use already exists. However, errors emanating from test administration and test scoring is largely within their control (Mrazik et al., 2012; Styck & Walsh, 2016). In my school psychology graduate course on intelligence assessment I recall Dr. David Goh, professor and school psychology program director, noting that school psychologists are sometimes (perhaps often) asked to test children in less-than-optimal environments or conditions, and he described a situation when he was asked to test a child in a makeshift testing location in the school boiler room! As is typical of such environments, conditions were very warm, stuffy, humid, noisy, and not conducive to optimal testing and best child performance. We graduate students didn't quite believe the story and thought it was hyperbole to illustrate an important point. What I discovered as a school psychologist intern two short years later was that I too was asked to assess children in the school boiler room, on stairwell landings between floors, and in converted janitor closets with extremely confined space, poor lighting, no ventilation, and no climate control but complete with floor-level porcelain sinks for emptying mop buckets. While I refused to use such places for clinical evaluations of children and demanded that proper office space with satisfactory climate control, lighting, and privacy be provided, it was apparent that other school psychologists serving those schools apparently routinely used them with unknown but likely adverse effects. I admonish my students to reject such places for assessments, and they frequently return from internships or their first job to comment that they too did not believe my claim that school psychologists would be asked to evaluate children in such conditions until they too were asked to evaluate children in similar unacceptable places.

Reliability

Reliability pertains to the measurement precision of a test or procedure and is concerned with the assessment of consistency in test scores or observations. There are four frequently used reliability estimates (Test-Retest [Stability], Parallel/Alternate Forms [Equivalence], Interrater/Interscorer Agreement, Internal Consistency) in CTT, depending on the nature of the construct or method of measurement of the construct. Reliability estimates may be considered indexes of *consistency* (Furr, 2022) or a form of *agreement* (McDermott, 1988) and the statistical method employed depends on the type of data examined. Many standardized tests provide standardized scores that are scaled on a continuum and considered equal interval–based scores (scores on a continuum with equal unit intervals) that along with ratio-based scores (equal intervals and true, fixed, absolute zero) allow for use of parametric-based statistics such as Pearson product-moment correlations, *t*-tests, analysis of variance, and so forth. However, as McDermott pointed out, there may be test scores, score comparisons, or data that are nominal scale or ordinal scale metrics, and alternative, non-parametric statistical methods must therefore be used. For assessing reliability or agreement of ordinal data, Kendall's *W* (coefficient of concordance), Spearman's *rho*, linear or quadratic weighted kappa, or intraclass correlations (de Raadt et al., 2021) may be used; and in the case of nominal scale data, Cohen's (1960) *kappa* coefficient is frequently used to assess the agreement beyond chance. The *phi* coefficient may also be used.

Another important point McDermott made was that assessment of agreement (or consistency) for interval (or ratio) level data required a two-pronged test as a correlation coefficient (reliability index) is insufficient in fully determining agreement. The correlation coefficient (reliability index) provides an assessment of pattern agreement while dependent *t*-tests for mean differences provide assessment of level agreement (McDermott, 1988). The two-prong test requires the reliability coefficient to be statistically significant and high, while the test of mean differences is expected to be not statistically significant and/or the effect size trivial to small (Cohen, 1988). Effect size estimates are particularly necessary because psychometric studies typically include large samples that may produce statistically significant differences due to a large sample (overpowered), but differences may be trivial or small and not meaningful. Test scores are not sufficiently reliable when a high reliability coefficient is produced but a large, statistically significant mean difference exists in score comparisons and vice versa. Intraclass correlation coefficients are another alternative in testing agreement combining level and pattern agreement and providing options for modeling rater agreement (see McGraw & Wong, 1996a, 1996b; Shrout & Fleiss, 1979; Shrout et al., 1987; Streiner et al., 2015).

Reliability Procedures and Estimates

Test-Retest Reliability (Stability)

Test-retest reliability is concerned with the longitudinal or temporal stability (consistency) of test scores over some specified period of time (short-term, medium-term, long-term). Tests of psychological constructs that are theoretically stable over time (relatively unchanging), such as intelligence and personality traits (extraversion, neuroticism, etc.), must have scores on tests measuring or estimating those constructs that are also stable over time to be viable. The distinction between *traits* (relatively unchanging) and *states* (fluctuating moment by moment) is important both in measurement and assessment of reliability of test scores. Measurement of traits is expected to show acceptable temporal stability while measurement of states would not. As such, test-retest reliability is expected to be routinely assessed and reported for any test purporting to measure a psychological trait.

The procedure for assessing test-retest reliability (stability) is rather uncomplicated. A retest time interval is selected (short, medium, long) depending on research goals or constraints, and an appropriate, heterogeneous sample of test takers identified. The test is administered to the individuals in the sample at Time 1 and following the passage of the specified retest interval, the test is again administered to the same individuals at Time 2. This method produces pairs of scores on the test (Time 1 and Time 2) for all participants for statistical analyses. If the test includes a single score, the analysis will be for stability of that score, but for many tests there may be several subtests, factor-based composite scores, and perhaps an overall, total, or omnibus composite score, all of which require examination of stability. Statistically, most tests likely contain interval-based standard scores so assessment of pattern agreement would involve calculating Pearson product-moment correlations, which would be expected to be statistically significant and high. Dependent *t*-tests for mean differences would be used to assess level agreement and expected to be not statistically significant and have effect sizes that are trivial or small. Example applications of these methods with intelligence tests are provided in Wechsler (2014) for short-term stability and in Canivez and Watkins (1998) and Watkins et al. (2022) for long-term stability.

While intelligence test scores are frequently assessed for stability (at least short term) and results frequently included in test manuals (e.g., Wechsler, 2014), stability of various score comparisons or difference scores is not routinely reported but should be. In determining intra-individual (ipsative) strengths and weaknesses in intelligence subtest or factor score performance, long a staple of intelligence test clinical interpretation (e.g., Canivez, 2013a; McGill et al., 2018; Watkins, 2000), longitudinal instability would indicate inconsistent estimates of supposed cognitive strengths or weaknesses and render such comparisons inadequate for interpretation and judgments about the individual's performance and recommendations emanating from them (Cronbach & Snow, 1977). Such determinations of strengths or weaknesses are ideographic (person-centered) and may reflect nominal scale data for which Cohen's *kappa* is appropriately applied. Example applications of the stability of idiographic scoring of intelligence test subtest and composite score strengths and weaknesses are illustrated by Watkins and Canivez (2004) and Watkins et al. (2022) documenting substantial inadequacies.

In the test-retest method, several limitations exist including the possibility that there may be actual changes in individuals' true scores from Time 1 to Time 2 that affect reliability estimation. Also, the longer the retest interval the more likely random events occur that differentially affect individuals' characteristics (true scores) and that reduce the correlation coefficient estimating stability. Another factor is that, particularly with longer retest intervals, some participants may not be available for testing at Time 2 (sometimes referred to as subject *mortality*) which also impacts reliability estimates. Finally, it is possible that performance on the test at Time 1 may influence performance at Time 2, referred to as *carryover effects*, particularly for shorter retest intervals. Practice effects, memory effects, or changes in mood or attitude may be carryover effects and more likely to be present with shorter retest intervals.

Parallel/Alternate Forms Reliability (Equivalence)

For some tests (typically tests of academic achievement), the creation of multiple forms is useful when individuals may need to be assessed and reassessed on a regular basis for measuring performance and intervention effects where various alternate forms are to be used interchangeably. Particularly if a test is to be readministered within a short retest interval, exposure to the item content may result in items being remembered or in practice effects that might influence subsequent performance and scores. A different form of the test with different items yet measuring the same construct would help avoid, or at least minimize, such measurement problems. Use of alternate forms requires evidence that alternate (or parallel) forms of the same test produce equivalent scores and estimates of true scores. While it is typically not possible to know if tests are truly parallel due to very strict assumptions including equality of means, variances, covariances, and error variances (Allen & Yen, 2002; Furr, 2022), alternate-form reliability methods provide estimates of how equivalent measurement is among the various forms.

The procedure for assessing *alternate-form reliability* is also uncomplicated. First, one identifies an appropriate, heterogeneous sample to whom the multiple forms will be administered. Depending on test length and effort required, the multiple test forms might be administered in the same testing session, on the same day, or on multiple days but with a short interval. Because of possible order effects, it is necessary to randomly counterbalance order of administration to the individuals in the sample. As with the test-retest method, statistical treatment assesses pattern agreement by calculating Pearson product-moment correlations, which would be expected to be statistically significant and high. Dependent *t*-tests for mean differences is used to assess level agreement between the alternate forms and expected to be not statistically significant and have effect sizes that are trivial or small. An example of alternate forms reliability of this type is illustrated for the Peabody Picture Vocabulary Test, Fifth Edition (Dunn, 2019) and the Woodcock-Johnson IV (WJ IV; McGrew et al., 2014) speeded achievement tests (Sentence Reading Fluency, Math Facts Fluency, Sentence Writing Fluency), but the WJ IV also included IRT–based item difficulty comparisons for the other achievement subtests with alternate forms.

Interrater/Interscorer Agreement

Methods of assessing reliability that are not often discussed in basic measurement textbooks are those of *interrater agreement* (independent rater judgments on scales measuring the presence or absence [or estimated frequency] of a target individual's behaviors) and *interscorer agreement* (independent judgments regarding correctness of responses or applying a scoring rubric to responses in the item scoring process). In the assessment of child and adolescent problem behavior, psychopathology, personality, or adaptive skills (positive behavior), behavior rating scales and personality instruments have been developed where third-party raters (teachers, parents) intimately knowledgeable of the target individual, respond to item content as it relates to the target individual and are extremely popular (Benson et al., 2019). For scores from such scales to be viable as estimates of the target individual they must be representative of any competent rater who might provide ratings based on their observations of the target individual given the same context and conditions. If different raters produce vastly different ratings, then inferences about the target individual might relate more to the idiosyncratic ratings or judgments of the rater rather than the target individual rated, but it might also reflect raters observing the target individual in different settings and contexts where behavior might well be different (i.e., behavior is situation specific).

   To properly assess interrater agreement of scores from behavior rating scales or other instruments, it is necessary to identify two raters who observe the same target individual in the same setting, at the same time, over the observation period (e.g., Watkins & Canivez, 1997). In a school context, this might include rater pairs that include two teachers team teaching students in the same classroom at the same time, a regular education teacher and a special education teacher team teaching students in the same classroom at the same time, or even perhaps a teacher and a paraprofessional teacher assistant who work with students in the same classroom at the same time. The importance of rater pairs being in the same classroom (setting) at the same time is to be sure that the contexts influencing target individual behavior are the same for the rater pair observations. Teachers in different classrooms providing ratings of the same child might be considered interrater agreement observations, but there is a myriad of differences in different classrooms that may account for differences in the child's behavior (i.e., their true score) and a reduction in observed agreement. Teacher classroom behavior management practices and competencies; child ease, difficulty, interest, and preference of class subject matter; child–teacher personality conflicts, and so on, all influence child behavior in different settings thereby rendering such a comparison of ratings from the different settings a poor indicator of test score agreement among different independent raters. Differences in rater agreement when raters were in the same classroom versus different classrooms were illustrated by Schaefer et al. (2001) where correlations between raters in the same classroom were higher than those between raters in different classrooms. Other assessments comparing different raters in different settings (parent versus teacher), generally referred to as cross-informant agreement, also would not adequately assess interrater agreement for a scale given the very different contexts observations are made and influences on child behavior.

Once a minimum amount of observation time has passed (perhaps 1–2 months) based on the rating scale guidelines, children would be randomly selected as targets for ratings and both raters would then independently complete the rating scale. Obtaining a reasonable sample of children under such conditions is difficult because such team teaching is not very common. In deriving a sample of children, it would be important to limit the number of children rated by the rating pairs to one or two male and one or two female students (requiring more classrooms with pairs of raters) because results may be biased by specific rater pairs that rate large numbers of classroom children. Data analyses are the same as with test-retest and alternate forms reliability with expected large, statistically significant Pearson product-moment correlations providing evidence of pattern agreement and not statistically significant dependent t-tests for mean score differences with trivial or small effect sizes supporting level agreement. Intraclass correlations may also be applied in assessment of interrater agreement (McDermott, 1988; Shrout & Fleiss, 1979). Alternate methods with graphical advantages (i.e., Bland Altman analysis), popular in genetics, chemistry, and medicine, may be helpful too (Giavarina, 2015).

In the context of *interscorer agreement*, assessment of the agreement in applying scoring guidelines or rubrics must be conducted. Where human judgment is involved in the scoring of items, it is crucial that scoring criteria or rubrics are satisfactory for consistent scoring when a test is constructed and produced, and there is equal importance for consistent application of such scoring criteria or rubrics in training and later clinical practice. Test authors and publishers have the responsibility of creating adequate scoring guidelines while course instructors have the initial responsibility for developing competency in applying scoring guidelines and rubrics in trainees. Following training and supervised experiences the responsibility for competent application of scoring guidelines then rests with the clinician. An example of assessments of interscorer agreement is provided in *Wechsler Intelligence Scale for Children–Fifth Edition Technical and Interpretive Manual* (WISC–V; Wechsler, 2014). While such assessments by test companies are quite useful and informative, additional assessments for clinician application of scoring guidelines application are also important.

Internal Consistency

Internal consistency relates to the extent to which parts of a test are related to, or consistent with, other parts of the test and thus similarly measuring the latent dimension. Internal consistency is related to the content sampling error (Reynolds et al., 2021) and when parts of a test (items) are significantly related to other parts of a test (items), then that consistency indicates reliability and that they are measuring something the same. Methods of internal consistency are appropriate for tests that contain content that is homogeneous and measuring a singular dimension. There are several methods and estimates used to assess internal consistency, but unlike test-retest, alternate forms, and interrater agreement methods that require two test "administrations," internal consistency methods are estimable with a single administration of the test. Methods for estimating internal consistency include the split-half method (dividing the test into alternate or parallel forms), Kuder-Richardson Formula 20 (KR20, for dichotomously scored items), and Cronbach's coefficient α (a generalized KR20 formula for items scored on continuum). Another coefficient reflecting reliability is omega (ω; McDonald, 1999) and the various forms of omega (Watkins, 2017), which are discussed later as model-based reliability/validity coefficients.

The split-half method involves obtaining a heterogeneous sample and then administering the test to individuals in the sample. The test items are then divided into two equivalent parts (conceptually parallel or alternate forms) to generate total scores on each of the two halves, allowing the pairs of scores to be used in calculating the Pearson product-moment correlation. There are many ways to split the test into halves and the longer the test the more ways there are. Revelle and Condon (2019) provide the formula for calculating the number of unique combinations of splits and a 16-item test would have 6,435 possible unique splits! A frequent method of dividing a test into equivalent parts splits odd-numbered items into one half and even-numbered items into the other half. When a test is composed of items ordered by item difficulty (e.g., intelligence or achievement tests where item 1 is least difficult and subsequent items are progressively more difficult) then the two (odd and even) halves would include collections of items of roughly comparable difficulty overall, resulting in roughly equivalent (possibly parallel) parts (halves). Any other split would, in the case of items ordered by difficulty, produce less equivalent halves because each half would have an unequal number of items of lower or higher difficulty. When a test does not include items arranged by difficulty the split is effectively arbitrary and could be done randomly. However the split is made, each individual in the sample then has total scores for each half of the test. The pairs of total scores from the two halves then are used to calculate a Pearson product-moment correlation to estimate the relationship between the two halves. This, however, produces a correlation that is biased downward because the estimate is based on the alternate test forms half as long as the full test and must be adjusted with the Spearman-Brown Prophecy Formula (Brown, 1910; Spearman, 1910), shown below, to mathematically correct the estimate and produce the split-half reliability coefficient for the full-length test (Revelle & Condon, 2019).

Spearman-Brown Prophecy Formula (for correcting split-half estimate):

$$r_{SB} = \frac{2r_{x_1x_2}}{1 + r_{x_1x_2}},$$

where $r_{x_1x_2}$ = correlation between the two halves.

General Spearman-Brown Prophecy Formula:

$$r_{xx_{est}} = \frac{Nr_{xx}}{1 + (N-1)r_{xx}},$$

where $r_{xx_{est}}$ = estimated reliability of test with adjusted number of items from original,

$$N = \frac{\#\ of\ items\ in\ test\ producing\ r_{xx_{est}}}{\#\ of\ items\ in\ test\ r_{xx}\ is\ obtained}$$ (i.e., proportional test length change),

r_{xx} = original reliability coefficient.

The general Spearman-Brown prophecy formula allows for estimating the reliability coefficient if items (of equal quality and parallel content) are added to a test (increasing reliability coefficient estimate) and estimating the reliability coefficient if items are deleted from the test (decreasing reliability coefficient estimate). It may also be used to determine how many more or fewer items might be needed to achieve a pre-specified reliability coefficient (Allen & Yen, 2002, Furr, 2022).

While the split-half reliability method compares total scores from two equivalent halves, two other methods each focus on the test items and how they relate to all other items within the test (sum of item covariances or sum of item variances) and overall test variance. Cronbach's coefficient α (r_α) is a generalized version of the Kudar and Richardson (1937) Formula 20 (KR20 or r_{KR20}; specific for dichotomously scored items [0, 1]), it may be used with items containing non-binary (polytomous) response options. To illustrate the similarity, both formulae are presented below.

$$r_\alpha = \left(\frac{k}{k-1} \right)\left(1 - \frac{\sum s_i^2}{s_x^2} \right) \qquad r_{KR20} = \left(\frac{k}{k-1} \right)\left(1 - \frac{\sum pq}{s_x^2} \right),$$

where k = the number of test items,
$\sum s_i^2$ = the sum of item variances,
s_x^2 = total test variance,
$\sum pq$ = the sum of item products of the proportion scoring 1 (p) and the proportion scoring 0 (q).

Coefficient α is the average of all possible split-half estimates corrected for length and the preferred estimate of internal consistency (Reynolds et al., 2021) provided assumptions are met.

Factors Influencing Reliability Estimates

It bears repeating that all reliability coefficients are estimates of score reliability from a test or procedure that are based on a specific method, with a particular sample, at a particular time. Generally, internal consistency estimates will likely have the highest coefficients followed by alternate (parallel) forms reliability, then short-term test-retest reliability, then long-term test-retest reliability, and finally interrater agreement due to the sources of error in measurement and methods used to estimate reliability. Also, it is important to be mindful that some methods may not be appropriate for each test. If a test has no alternate forms, then obviously that method is irrelevant. If a test does not produce scores for a target individual based on third-party raters, then interrater agreement would not be a method used. Finally, if a test measures a construct that is not theoretically stable over time (states), then test-retest reliability (stability) would not be appropriate to assess score reliability.

Reliability estimates are affected by how many items there are in the test, the quality of items in the test, and the nature of the items. CTT indicates that increasing the number of items in a test will likely increase the reliability estimate provided the items are of equal or better quality and parallel to the others. Adding poor items that reduce the average interitem correlation for the total test will reduce estimates of reliability. Alternatively, removing poor items identified to have low item-total correlations could increase reliability even though the test would have fewer items. Items that have little or no variability also reduce reliability estimates and might be removed, modified, or replaced with better items to improve reliability. Related to this is the nature of the item. For example, there are a variety of behavior-rating scales that have items rated on a 4-point ordinal rating scale (Almost Never, Sometimes, Often, Almost Always) so item scores may range 0–3. Other behavior-rating scales might use an item rating that is binary (Absent, Present) so item scores may range 0–1. In estimating reliability, when items contain more rating options (and greater possible and observed variance), scales they belong to will tend to have higher reliability estimates compared to scales that have items rated in a binary manner (Reise et al., 2000) because variance is a primary factor in such estimates (Fife et al., 2012). While rating items in a dichotomous (Yes, No; Present, Absent) manner or indicating which behaviors are representative of a target individual may make such rating easier, it may come at the cost of lower item variance and lower scale reliability estimates.

Because reliability coefficients are correlation coefficients, anything that influences the magnitude of a correlation may influence the estimate of reliability. Restriction in range affects correlations, and there are implications for samples that are not sufficiently heterogeneous. Correlations, and thus reliability estimates, would be optimally estimated with a sample that was broad, diverse, and thus heterogeneous. By contrast, a narrow sample comprised of individuals with less variability and thus more homogeneous, would produce lower correlations and be less adequate estimates.

A final concern regarding reliability estimates relates to concerns that scales or tests may not satisfy assumptions required for the proper use of some reliability estimates. Cronbach's coefficient α and other internal consistency estimates may not be accurate estimates of reliability due to the test scores not meeting the assumptions for use. Gignac and Watkins (2013) pointed out potential problems related to traditional internal consistency estimates that relate to violations of assumptions such as tau-equivalence and multidimensionality. When scores are multidimensional, coefficient α will conflate multiple sources of systematic variance (Zinbarg et al., 2005). This has resulted in a call for greater use of the omega family of coefficients, which have fewer assumptions and address test complexities, such as multidimensionality, to assess unique measurement contributions to various variance sources within the test (Gignac & Watkins, 2013; Reise et al., 2013; Rodriguez et al., 2016a, 2016b; Watkins, 2017).

Applications of Reliability Estimates

Judging Adequacy of Tests

The first application of reliability estimates is in test selection. All things being equal, one should select the test or measure that has the highest test score reliability estimates (when compared in similar samples) as there will be less measurement error and greater precision in construct measurement. Wasserman and Bracken (2013) provided guidelines for acceptability of internal consistency reliability coefficients, which were similar to opinions of other experts and with other reliability estimates (e.g., Aiken, 2000; Bracken, 1987; Guilford & Fruchter, 1978; Nunnally & Bernstein, 1994; Reynolds et al., 2021). For individual decision-making related to diagnosis, classification, intervention, and placement (high-stakes decisions), Wasserman and Bracken recommended the minimum reliability coefficient of .90 (no more than 10% error), but as low as .80 in screening (low-stakes) decisions. For group assessments (and research) they indicated that reliability should be .60 or higher (see also Chapter 9 this volume). Reliability is also a limiting aspect for test validity estimates because greater measurement error (lower reliability) will reduce the magnitude of validity estimates. Of course, things are not always equal so other features of validity and utility play important roles in test use decisions and are explicated later. While a particular test may have somewhat lower estimates of score reliability, the measure may actually have validity and utility evidence superior to another test with somewhat higher estimates of reliability.

True Score Point Estimates

The most common test score point estimate is the observed score (or scores) from a test and is often a standard score based on some specified mean and standard deviation from the normative sample. The obtained score is an estimate of that individual's true score at that single point in time. As noted above, the observed score may be higher or lower than the person's true score due to some amount of measurement error. Another test score point estimate is the *estimated true score* (also referred to as the adjusted true score estimate [Furr, 2022]). The estimated true score provides an estimate of the true score accounting for the score reliability coefficient. An individual's estimated true score is given by the equation

$$\hat{T} = r_{xx}\left(X_O - \bar{X}_O\right) + \bar{X}_O \,,$$

where r_{xx} = test reliability coefficient,
X_O = individual's observed test score,
$\bar{X}_O$ = mean test score.

This equation adjusts the true score point estimate based on regression to the mean, which is directly related to the reliability estimate for the score. The higher the reliability estimate the less regression to the mean and the closer the observed score is to the person's true score. Alternatively, the lower the reliability estimate the more regression to the mean and the farther the observed score might be from the true score. If the test score reliability coefficient was 1.0 then the observed test score would equal the estimated true score (because there was no error in measurement). Regression to the mean is also larger the farther away from the population test mean the observed score falls.

Confidence Intervals

Test score reliability estimates also impact test score interpretation because professional ethics and test standards require consideration and presentation of the amount of measurement error present in obtained test scores. Here the application of the test score confidence interval (CI) indicates where the individual's theoretical true score might be, with some specified probability, and that the obtained score is not necessarily the person's true score. CIs help to illustrate the accuracy (or inaccuracy) of scores that qualify interpretations and judgments. Historically, the *obtained score* CI was routinely and customarily provided in test manuals, but more recently it is more likely that *estimated true score* CIs are provided (e.g., Wechsler, 2014). Glutting et al. (1987) examined several available methods and equations that produce CIs and indicated that if the clinician is interested in the measurement of the individual with a specific test *at the present time*, the obtained score CI is appropriate. In a clinical evaluation context that is likely the question of interest. If the assessment question is "What is the best long-run (stable) measure of an examinee's functioning in the performance area assessed by a specific test relative to other examinees in a particular reference group?" (Glutting et al., 1987, p. 613), then the estimated true score CI is most appropriate. While the obtained score CI is symmetrical around the obtained score, the estimated true score CI is asymmetrical around the obtained score (more points toward the test mean and fewer points in the extreme direction) with greater asymmetry the farther away the obtained score is from the normative test mean due to regression to the mean effects noted earlier. The estimated true score CI is, however, symmetrical around the estimated true score.

While observed score CIs may no longer be routinely reported they are quite easy to produce from the reliability estimates or standard errors of measurement reported in a test technical manual. Using a reliability estimate, the standard error of measurement is estimated by the equation

$$SE_M = S_x\sqrt{1 - r_{xx}} \,,$$

where S_x = standard deviation of test scores,
r_{xx} = reliability estimate for the test scores.

Once the standard error of measurement is obtained (or provided in a manual), it is then used in the equation for producing the CI using a specified probability indicating how "confident" one wishes to be (68%, 95%, 99%) in estimating where the true score might be. That confidence interval equation is

$$CI_p = X_O \pm (z_p)(SE_M),$$

where X_O = the observed test score,
z_p = z value for confidence probability (68% [z = 1.00], 95% [z = 1.96], 99% [z = 2.58],
SE_M = standard error of measurement for the test score.

For example, consider some test with a reported reliability (r_{xx} = .84) and standard deviation (S_x = 10) and an individual obtains a score of 50 on that test and you are interested in finding, with 95% confidence (probability = .95), where that person's true score is likely to fall.

$$SE_M = S_x \sqrt{1 - r_{xx}}$$

$$10\sqrt{1 - .84} = 10\sqrt{.16} = 10(.4) = 4.$$

$$CI_p = X_O \pm (z_p)(SE_M),$$

$$= 50 \pm (1.96)(4) = 50 \pm 7.84 \ (\cong 50 \pm 8).$$

We can thus state that there is a 95% chance that this individual's true test score is likely to be within the range of 42 to 58 points (rounding to whole test scores). The CI range will be smaller if one is willing to be less confident the true score is within the range (or if the reliability coefficient was higher) and the CI will be larger if one wishes to be more confident the true score is within the range (or if the reliability coefficient is lower). As the reliability estimate for a test score goes up, the SE_M goes down (i.e., less error variance and greater measurement precision), and the more confident we may be a person's true score is within a specified range. In keeping with CTT, if a test produced scores that were perfectly reliable then there would be no measurement error variance, the reliability estimate would be 1.0, and the estimated true score would equal the individual's obtained score (and the standard error of the measurement [SE_M] would be zero).

When confidence intervals are constructed for estimated true scores ($\hat{T}$) then the standard error of estimation would be used rather than the standard error of measurement and Stanley (1971) provided the equation,

$$SE_{est} = S_X (r_{xx}) \sqrt{1 - r_{xx}},$$

where S_X = standard deviation for score X,
r_{xx} = reliability estimate for score X.

Glutting et al. (1987) recommended the estimated true score confidence interval using a specified probability estimating where the true score might be given by the equation

$$CI_{\hat{T}} = \hat{T} \pm (z_p)(SE_{est})(r_{xx}),$$

where $\hat{T}$ = the estimated true score,
z_p = z value for confidence probability (68% [z = 1.00], 95% [z = 1.96], 99% [z = 2.58],
SE_{est} = standard error of estimation,
r_{xx} = reliability estimate for score X.

Score Comparisons

Another application of reliability coefficients is when there is interest in comparing two scores to determine if one is significantly higher. Some score comparisons are *intra-individual* where test scores from the same person are compared (change scores or discrepancy scores). For example, one might wish to determine if an individual's verbal score was significantly different from their nonverbal score. Furr (2022) presents several types of difference scores that might be of interest within an individual's test performance, which require examination of difference score reliability (see also Chapter 8 this volume). As Furr (2022) noted, the "psychometrically savvy researcher should know the reliability of differences scores for the same reasons that they should know the reliability of scores from any measure" (p. 220).

An alternate method applied to assessing intra-individual score differences relates to a comparison between an obtained score and the score that might be predicted from a related score (i.e., a regressed difference). While more complex than a simple difference score, it is conceptually more sound. This approach was discussed at length with an example related to properly estimating the significance of the difference between a child's obtained achievement test score (y) and the predicted (expected) achievement test score ($\hat{y}$) based on their general intellectual ability score (x; Reynolds, 1984). When determining if an individual's obtained score is significantly lower than what would be predicted then the *standard error of the estimate* (SE_{est}) would be the appropriate standard error to apply and not the standard error of the difference or the standard error of measurement. A benefit of such a comparison is that it accounts for regression to the mean.

Another consideration might be to determine significant *inter-individual* differences, for example, is Person A's test score is higher or lower than Person B's test score. If any conclusion were to be made regarding such score differences, it would at least need to be a statistically significant difference. These questions must consider the measurement error present in both test scores and the application of the *standard error of the difference* (SE_{diff}) to help determine if a significant difference between the scores exists or if the differences are just as likely due to measurement error. SE_{diff} is given by the formula

$$SE_{diff} = S_x\sqrt{2 - r_{xx_1} - r_{xx_2}} \text{ or } SE_{diff} = S_x\sqrt{1 - r_{xx_1} + 1 - r_{xx_2}}$$

where S_x = common standard deviation,
r_{xx_1} = reliability coefficient for test score 1,
r_{xx_2} = reliability coefficient for test score 2.

The formula for SE_{diff} should look somewhat familiar. The first formula is a simplification of the second but reflects standard errors of measurement for the two compared scores. An example helps illustrate. Consider two individuals who took the same test and Person A obtained a score of 38 and Person B obtained a score of 47. To determine if the two scores significantly differ (i.e.,

Person B scored higher), we need to know the reliability estimate for the scores and the standard deviation of test scores. Below is application of this information to the question where the standard deviation was 10 and the reliability estimate was $r = .88$.

$$SE_{diff} = S_x\sqrt{2 - r_{xx_1} - r_{xx_2}}$$

$$= 10\sqrt{2 - .88 - .88} = 10\sqrt{.24} = 10(.490) = 4.90$$

$$CV = (z_p)(SE_{diff}),$$

where CV = critical value for statistical significance,
z_p = z value for specified alpha ($z = 1.96$ for $\alpha = .05$ [95% confidence for two-tail test]).

$$CV = (1.96)(4.90) = 9.60$$

In this example, Person A's score of 38 and Person B's score of 47 reflects a 9-point difference, therefore $p > .05$ (difference *did not* exceed the CV) and the 9-point difference is likely the result of measurement error in Person A's score and measurement error in Person B's score rather than any real differences in the individuals. It is possible that Person A's true score was underestimated, and Person B's true score overestimated. In addition to a significance test Charter and Feldt (2009) presented a statistical significance test via the confidence interval with the formulae,

$$Lower = (X_1 - X_2) - (z_p)(S_x)\sqrt{2 - r_{x_1} - r_{x_2}},$$

$$Upper = (X_1 - X_2) + (z_p)(S_x)\sqrt{2 - r_{x_1} - r_{x_2}},$$

so, using the above example and information, the 95% confidence interval is -18.6 to 0.6. In a situation where the comparison is of two different scores with the same individual then the reliability coefficients may differ and the two scores would need to have the same standard deviation, which for standardized tests would likely be the case.

Research Applications

In addition to clinical applications, reliability also has important implications for research. In research situations, dependent variables must have satisfactory reliability because adequacy of results depends on it. If a dependent variable has poor reliability (large measurement error), then the effect would be to decrease statistical power, making it less likely to yield statistically significant results, and poor reliability also attenuates effect sizes. Greater statistical power and likelihood to detect statistically significant results is provided by dependent variables with higher reliability and produces more accurate effect sizes. As such researchers should routinely assess and present the score reliability of their dependent variables (Furr, 2022; see also Chapter 9 this volume).

Reliability of scores from a test are foundational to the integrity of the measure and much like the base of a pyramid. Test scores cannot be valid if they lack sufficient reliability. Without sufficient reliability, observations or measurements contain too much error to be of value, but while reliability is necessary, it is not sufficient. The next level of measurement adequacy is validity, which includes numerous research methods and approaches to assess adequacy of inferences made from test scores (and test score comparisons). The next section details these methods and approaches and the various questions they answer.

Validity

Validity is often simplistically defined as the extent to which a test measures what it purports to measure. It is better defined by evidence supporting various inferences or interpretations made about test performance from the scores on the measure. As Furr (2022) noted, and like reliability, validity is not a property of a test, so tests are neither valid nor invalid. *Standards* defines validity as "the degree to which evidence and theory support the interpretations of test scores for proposed uses of tests" (AERA et al., 2014, p. 11), and its importance is reflected in placement of validity as the first chapter. This is a more nuanced approach, and it may be that some test scores or score comparisons allow for appropriate and well-supported inferences or uses while others do not. Thus, it is better to think about validity in the context of valid for what purpose. Crucially, it is important to know which scores and score comparisons have sufficient empirical evidence for interpretive use and under what conditions and to consider that validity evidence is not static but ever evolving through the life cycle of the measure's use.

Validity is dependent on strong reliability, and like reliability, validity includes several theoretical perspectives and approaches. Reliability sets limits for validity (Bandalos, 2018), and when considering validity coefficients there is a formula that specifies the relationship between test score reliability coefficients and validity coefficients:

$$r_{xy} \leq \sqrt{r_{xx}r_{yy}}$$

r_{xy} = validity coefficient,
r_{xx} = reliability estimate for test x,
r_{yy} = reliability estimate for test y.

Given that a validity coefficient contains measurement error from both tests or measures in comparison, it seems obvious (and a mathematical necessity) that such coefficients will be lower than separate reliability coefficients because of the multiple sources of error. It should also be noted that diagnostic and classification accuracy (presented and discussed later) are affected by reliability and validity estimates.

Finally, *Standards* (AERA et al., 2024) and Furr (2022) present validity as the most important aspect of a test or procedure's psychometric quality and provide standards and examples related to the test interpretation in a study and for decisions about individuals. In the present chapter, these are separated hierarchically. As will be explained later in detail, there are many instances where test scores (or score comparisons) possess evidence for validity within research situations or in assessment of constructs they purport to measure. However, these are necessary, but not sufficient, for clinical decision-making as applied to individuals, which are often high-stakes situations. It is argued here that utility (diagnostic utility or diagnostic validity) and the related aspect of treatment validity (Burns et al., 2016) are even more important given the consequences for individuals. Many tests or measures contain scores or score comparisons that while providing strong evidence for various elements of validity are not sufficiently useful for accurate individual clinical (diagnostic) decision-making.

Validity Procedures and Estimates

Historically, the prevailing conceptualization of validity was referred to as the Trinitarian Model (Content Validity, Criterion Related Validity, Construct Validity) and this section is organized using these headings and subheadings for descriptive purposes. However, Messick's Unified Theory (1989, 1995) is a more contemporary approach where all validity is construct validity but based on various sources of evidence and integrated into *Standards* (AERA et al., 2012) and other major measurement texts (e.g., Furr, 2022) so simultaneously included. More important than the names are the methods used and what they tell us about validity support.

Content Validity/Evidence from Test Content

Evidence for test validity emanating from test content is based on judgments about the adequacy of what is included in the test (Allen & Yen, 2002; Furr, 2022), and such evidence is based on rational rather than empirical methods, so subjective. Haynes et al. (1995) defined content validity as "the degree to which elements of an assessment instrument are relevant to and representative of the targeted construct for a particular assessment purpose" (p. 238) and provided a rubric for considerations of relevancy of content coverage elements in questionnaire, observation, psychophysiological, and self-monitoring measures. This offers a useful way to review test content and minimize subjectivity.

Face Validity. Face validity isn't really validity but the mere appearance that the item content and tasks contained in the test measure the intended construct and is subjectively applied by experts or novices (nonexperts) in judging acceptability. The examinee may form an opinion regarding the content of the test they are taking that might influence their participation and performance. Most psychological tests seem to have tasks and items that appear relevant for the constructs they purport to measure (intelligence, personality, psychopathology, academic achievement, etc.) but some might intentionally eschew such face validity (e.g., projective tests) based on philosophical or theoretical perspectives.

Sampling Validity/Logical Validity. Sampling validity is a more sophisticated approach to considering test content and relies on experts to provide judgments regarding adequacy. Here, as noted above in the discussion of domain sampling related to reliability, the concern is with the extent to which the tasks (subtests) and their items adequately cover or sample the construct purported to be measured. This also involves consideration of the theory the test is based upon because there may be different theoretical perspectives regarding a construct (and how it is measured), and different theories might suggest different content and thus coverage.

Two important concepts relate to test content and sampling validity are *construct underrepresentation* and *construct irrelevant content (variance)*. If a test of some theoretical construct does not include tasks (subtests) or items that sufficiently measure (sample) all theoretical facets, then measurement of the construct might be incomplete or underrepresented. This denotes measurement that is too narrow (Messick, 1995) and might need to be expanded. Experts should be consulted to assess test content during the test construction process to provide such feedback before a test is completed and moved to the standardization phase thereby avoiding, or minimizing construct underrepresentation. Importantly there is also a tradeoff between test length and content sampling, and there is no definitive way to determine how much is sufficient. Too little content sampling risks underrepresentation but too much might produce a lengthy test that is cumbersome. Ad hoc committees of experts are often assembled to assess test content validity, but procedures are often only vaguely described if at all.

Construct irrelevant content relates to tasks (subtests) or items that are included in the test but are not indicators of the intended construct. There may be many factors contributing to construct irrelevant content and variance such as tasks or items that measure a different construct (e.g., items measuring fear or worry [items related to anxiety] in a depression scale), instructions that might be confusing to certain groups, or tasks that are irrelevantly too difficult or too easy for certain groups (Messick, 1995). Construct irrelevant content and variance may produce bias in measurement or introduce problems of test fairness.

Criterion-Related Validity/Associations With Other Variables

Criterion-related validity is concerned with comparing scores from a test in question to some existing criterion measure (i.e., a gold standard). The criterion must be a measure of the same construct or a substantively related one, the criterion must have sufficient evidence for score reliability and validity, and it must not contain identical items (uncontaminated). If the criterion contains identical content, then spurious results will be obtained. Criterion contamination is when performance on the test in question influences the criterion in some way. Anastasi and Urbina (1997) described a scenario where the criterion was provided by individuals rating examinees, but if they had knowledge of performance on the test in question, their ratings might be influenced by that knowledge and thereby affect correlations. The logic of criterion-related validity is that if there is a strong relationship between the test in question and some established criterion, then the test in question must be measuring that same construct or be substantively related. If results show weak relationships, then the problem is assumed to be with the test in question. This type of validity is virtually universal in test technical manuals to provide validity support. There are two types of criterion-related validity: concurrent validity and predictive validity. These two methods principally differ in terms of when the criterion is obtained.

Concurrent Validity. Concurrent validity is a correlational study where scores from the test in question and the criterion are obtained at the same time and scores from the test in question and the criterion produce a correlation coefficient (concurrent validity coefficient). Because the test in question and the criterion are often measures of the same construct collected at the same time, it is important to avoid order effects (carryover effects) by using random counterbalancing, so half the sample is administered the test in question first and the other half are administered the criterion first. Pearson product-moment correlations are typically used to quantify the relationship between scores on the two tests to assess the strength of the relationship of the test in question to the criterion. Additionally, the squared correlation coefficient (coefficient of determination) will index the proportion of shared variance between the two scores. Such examinations are available in virtually every test technical manual and also illustrated in Canivez (1995) where scores from the Kaufman Brief Intelligence Test (K–BIT; Kaufman & Kaufman, 1990), the test in question, were compared with scores from the Wechsler Intelligence Scale for Children–Third Edition (WISC–III; Wechsler, 1991), the criterion. The correlation between the K–BIT IQ Composite and the WISC–III FSIQ was .87 (r^2 = .76) so there was 76% shared variance between these two composite scores indicating considerable overlap of measurement and support of concurrent validity for the K–BIT IQ Composite.

Predictive Validity. Predictive validity is also a correlational study comparing scores from a test in question to scores from a criterion, but the criterion is obtained in the future to determine if the test in question can adequately predict future performance on the criterion. Thus, counterbalancing is not applied. Pearson product-moment correlations are typically used to quantify how well the test in question predicts future performance on the criterion. Such studies are common when examining criterion-related validity of college entrance examinations such as the ACT or SAT (test in question) where predicting future college performance (criterion) is important. Predictive validity studies are also important in assessing the criterion-related validity of individual and group intelligence tests as they should predict future performance on tests of academic achievement. One such study (Canivez, 2000) examined the predictive validity of the Developing Cognitive Abilities Test-Second Edition (DCAT; Wick et al., 1989) (test in question) administered to a large sample of 6th graders and the Iowa Tests of Basic Skills (ITBS; Hieronymus et al., 1990) (criterion) was administered to the sample when they were in 7th grade. The DCAT total score correlated .73 with the ITBS Vocabulary subtest, .72 with the ITBS Reading subtest, .69 with the ITBS Language Usage subtest, and .74 with the ITBS Mathematics Problem Solving subtest; providing support of predictive validity of the DCAT total score. These correlations indicate roughly 50% shared variance between the DCAT total score and academic achievement subtests which is the average relationship for intelligence and achievement tests (Naglieri & Bornstein, 2003). While such prediction is important, this should not be confused with the ability of a test's scores to be used in diagnostic or classification situations which requires more stringent methods to be discussed later (diagnostic utility).

With significant predictive validity, a linear regression formula can be produced to predict a score on test y given some value of test x and is expressed as follows:

$$\hat{Y} = b_1 X + b_0,$$

where $\hat{Y}$ is the predicted score on the criterion or outcome variable,
b_1 is the slope of the regression line ($b_1 = r_{xy}$ when variables x and y are standardized, and
b_0 is the *y-intercept* (where the regression line intersects the y-axis) and $b_0 = 0$ when variables x and y are standardized.

Incremental Validity. Related to predictive validity is incremental validity (Hunsley & Meyer, 2003), which is particularly useful and essential when a test provides scores that are hierarchically ordered. For example, intelligence tests typically contain subtest scores (Stratum I), factor-based composite scores composed of several related subtests (Stratum II), and an omnibus, full-scale score composed of all factors (Stratum III; Carroll, 1993). Assessing the relative importance of scores at the different levels is crucial to understand whether factor-based composite scores below the omnibus, full-scale score provide useful information above and beyond the full-scale score. Such comparisons are necessary because a variable that fails to add significant or meaningful improvement in prediction or explanation of an outcome should be discounted or considered redundant or unimportant. This is consistent with philosopher William of Ockham's (c. 1287–1347; alt., Occam) Law of Parsimony (Ockham's Razor; Jones, 1952). In tests or studies with multiple variables in linear combination, some variables may be more important than others and some may be redundant in explanation or prediction of an outcome so may be deemphasized or perhaps deleted. Incremental validity is important for assessing the importance of various scores from hierarchically oriented tests of intelligence in predicting performance on academic achievement tests which also may be hierarchically ordered. Also, if one is interested in prediction from the provided test scores (obtained scores) then use of hierarchical multiple regression (Pedhazur, 1997) will answer the question of incremental *predictive* validity, but if explanation of performance based on the theoretical constructs (latent construct scores) of a test is of interest, then hierarchical structural equation modeling would be needed to assess the latent constructs.

Glutting et al. (2006) provided both hierarchical multiple regression (HMR) analysis and structural equation modeling (SEM) results with the Wechsler Intelligence Scale for Children–Fourth Edition (WISC–IV; Wechsler, 2003) and Wechsler Individual Achievement Test–Second Edition (WIAT–II, Psychological Corporation, 2002) linking sample. Results showed that in both WISC–IV prediction (HMR) and WISC–IV explanation (SEM) of WIAT–II academic achievement, the FSIQ (or general intelligence factor) predicted or explained the largest portion of achievement score variance with little additional contribution from factor index scores or latent first-order factors. Thus interpretation of factor index scores was judged questionable. Oh et al. (2004) discussed differences in interpretation of latent abilities or constructs (SEM based) versus observed abilities or variables (HMR) and noted that SEM methods apply to theoretical explanations for performance of latent constructs that are pure measures without error while HMR methods apply to the prediction of external criteria by observed scores provided by a test. Observed test scores provided by tests and interpreted by practitioners include measurement error and variance from general and specific cognitive skills. Oh et al. (2004) illustrated that while SEM provided evidence for theoretical explanations there were no practical implications.

> First, even a cursory review of equations reveals that SEM constructs are not equivalent to observed scores. Second, constructs rank children differently than observed scores, and, as the correlation between observed scores increases, so does the change. Thus, children's relative position on constructs (e.g., VC) can be radically different than their standing on corresponding observed scores (the Verbal Comprehension Index). Third, as the appendix makes clear, construct scores are not readily available to psychologists. Fourth, it is possible to estimate construct scores. However, until the equations appear in computer interpretation programs, or unless psychologists are willing to engage in laborious calculations, they will have to rely on observed scores. (p. 169)

Another similar incremental predictive validity study examined incremental prediction of WIAT–II and WIAT–III (NCS Pearson, 2009) achievement test scores by the Wechsler Adult Intelligence Test–Fourth Edition (WAIS–IV; Wechsler, 2018) factor index scores beyond the FSIQ with the standardization sample linking samples where similar results were found (Canivez, 2013b). Incremental validity studies also pertain to groups and may set limits for clinical utility but do not directly assess clinical utility, an important feature that is discussed later in diagnostic utility.

Construct Validity

Construct validity includes numerous methods and approaches including evidence based on expected age or developmental changes, distinct (contrasting) group differences, convergent validity, divergent validity, discriminant validity, and factorial/structural validity. Each are illustrated below. While some would include diagnostic utility (efficiency)/diagnostic validity/discriminative validity in this area, diagnostic utility is presented as a method of higher-level importance and an approach separately presented.

Age/Developmental Changes. Constructs in psychology may follow a pattern of development or change over time within individuals that a test of that construct should mirror. When a test is constructed and normed there would not be sufficient time to examine longitudinal aspects for changes or development over time, but cross-sectional research designs might illustrate score differences of groups at different ages or developmental levels. When examining such differences in a norm-referenced test it is important to consider the changes or differences in raw scores because standardized scores would reflect the transformation of the raw score based on the sample mean and standard deviation for the age cohort which masks the developmental changes across the age groups. Examples of age or developmental changes may be reflected in graphs or growth curves, which often are not linear. Tests of cognitive development or intelligence, for example, often reflect quadratic relationships of test performance across age groups. Figure 1.1 illustrates smoothed quadratic trends for the four Wide Range Intelligence Test (WRIT; Glutting et al., 2000) subtests created by taking raw score means at each age level and applying a second-order polynomial to the cross-sectional groups. Consistent with theoretically purported and observed developmental changes, verbally oriented subtests of Vocabulary and Verbal Analogies (crystallized abilities [Cattell, 1963, Horn & Cattell, 1966]) more rapidly increase at early ages and then plateau in later ages whereas nonverbal/visually oriented subtests of Matrices and Diamonds (fluid abilities [Cattell, 1963; Horn & Cattell, 1966]) more rapidly increase at early ages, plateau, and then decline more rapidly in later ages compared to verbal/crystallized abilities. Similar mean subtest raw score changes across age groups illustrate these expected quadratic relationships of intellectual growth and development across the lifespan reported in the Reynolds Intellectual Assessment Scales–Second Edition (RIAS–2; Reynolds & Kamphaus, 2015a), thus providing construct validity evidence based on theoretically expected age/developmental changes.

Distinct Group Differences. Reporting of distinct group (contrasting group) differences is ubiquitous among virtually every psychological and educational test published. Compared to a random (and sometimes demographically matched) normal or typical sample one expects that a group of individuals with some characteristic measured by a test will significantly differ. A group of individuals diagnosed with a depressive disorder would be expected to have substantially higher scores on a measure of depression, a group of individuals diagnosed with an anxiety disorder would be expected to have substantially higher scores on a measure of anxiety, and a group of individuals diagnosed with intellectual disability would be expected to have substantially lower scores on an intelligence test when compared to a random and demographically matched sample of normal or typical individuals. Because tests are designed to measure specific constructs related to psychological conditions, groups of individuals who differ on the theoretical construct should differ on a test of that construct and if so, there is evidence that the test is indeed measuring that construct. Studies reported in test technical manuals often examine such distinct group differences as preliminary support for the construct validity of the measure, and the extant literature often includes such studies.

Distinct group differences studies are relatively easy to conduct. With focus on a particular test, one would think about the construct the test purports to measure and then identify a group of individuals who would be expected to obtain higher (or lower) scores than a group of individuals who would be considered normal or typical. Alternatively, if the construct measured by the test related to various groups who might score low, average, or high, then identifying three different groups might be a viable method (e.g., children with intellectual disability, normal or typical children, and children with giftedness to assess construct validity of an intelligence test). Unlike experimental research that might seek to determine whether various groups differ on some test, the focus in

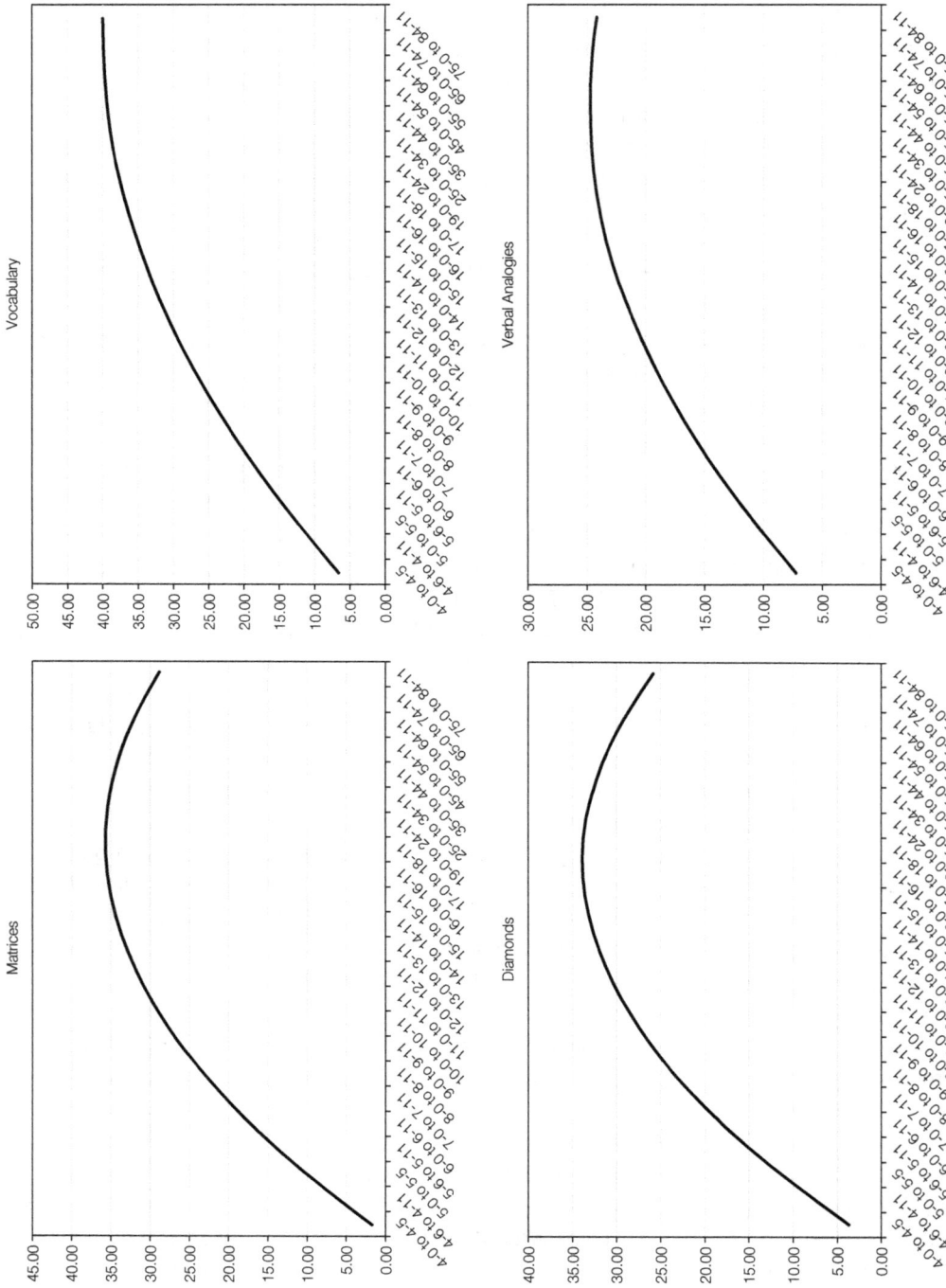

Figure 1.1. **Smoothed Mean Raw Scores by Age Group in Wide Range Intelligence Test (WRIT) Standardization Sample.** *Note.* Age group ranges on the *x*-axis are *not* equal. Raw score means obtained from Table 8.20 (Glutting et al., 2000, p. 121).

a construct validity study is to assume the groups differ on the construct the test in question purports to measure based on an independent method of classification or identification and to assess the adequacy of the test to measure the expected differences. Failure of distinct groups to substantially differ on the test would reflect poor construct validity of the test (i.e., the test isn't adequately measuring that purported construct). An example of such a study is illustrated in the first part of the Canivez and Sprouls (2005) study that determined the extent to which children meeting independent ADHD criteria differed from a sample of random and matched peers from the same classroom on various syndromes measured by the Adjustment Scales for Children and Adolescents (ASCA; McDermott, 1994; McDermott et al., 1993). Studies examining distinct group differences for a test with a single score and comparing two groups rely on an independent t-test for mean differences and an effect size estimate (e.g., Cohen's d; Cohen, 1988) to determine if, and to what extent, the groups differ on the test. Figure 1.2 illustrates a hypothetical example of score distributions for two groups on some hypothetical anxiety test (GAS) scaled in T score units ($M = 50$, $SD = 10$). As illustrated, the larger the effect size, the greater the group separation and less distribution overlap. If there are more than two groups being compared (e.g., Intellectual Disability, Normal/Typical, Intellectually Gifted; see Figure 1.3), then analysis of variance (ANOVA) with planned comparisons and/or post hoc comparisons would be used (Tabachnick & Fidell, 2019). When there are multiple dependent variables (several test scores within the test), then use of multivariate analysis of variance (MANOVA) is first used to determine if the groups differ on the combined test scores (dependent variables) followed by univariate analyses of variance (ANOVA) for the individual test scores (Tabachnick & Fidell, 2019).

While distinct group differences are useful to help provide construct validity support for test scores (i.e., the scores measure the purported construct), they are necessary, but not sufficient, for individual diagnostic uses of test scores. When research on group differences has shown statistically significant differences, it has been rare that such results translated to predictive power for individual use (Weiner, 2003). As will be detailed later, assessment of test score (or test score combinations) capability to correctly identify individuals with or without conditions the test should differentiate is a matter of diagnostic utility that must be separately examined and will be impacted by the effect sizes of group differences and the distributions overlap. Thus recommendations for diagnostic use of a test or its scores based on distinct group differences (or any other validity method) would be inappropriate absent examination of and strong support for diagnostic utility (and perhaps also treatment validity; e.g., Canivez, 2019; Hunsley & Mash, 2007; Kessel & Zimmerman, 1993; Youngstrom, 2014).

Convergent Validity. Convergent validity refers to the instance where two or more measures or tests designed to measure the same construct should produce high correlations and thus share a large amount of variance if measuring the same construct (see Figure 1.4a). Studies of convergent validity identify two or more tests or measures of the same construct, obtain a sufficiently large sample, and administer the tests to each of the individuals in random counterbalanced order. Counterbalancing administration of tests helps to reduce influences of one measure on the other(s) if the same order of administration was used (i.e., carryover effects). This approach and method is very similar to concurrent validity as described earlier in criterion-related validity, but in the case of convergent validity, there is no specification of a criterion measure assumed to adequately measure the intended construct or attribute. In convergent validity the study design assesses construct validity for both (or multiple) measures purporting to measure the same construct. The correlation between the two measures is an index of convergence and when high reflects large portions of shared variance, indicating they are measuring something the same. The correlation between the

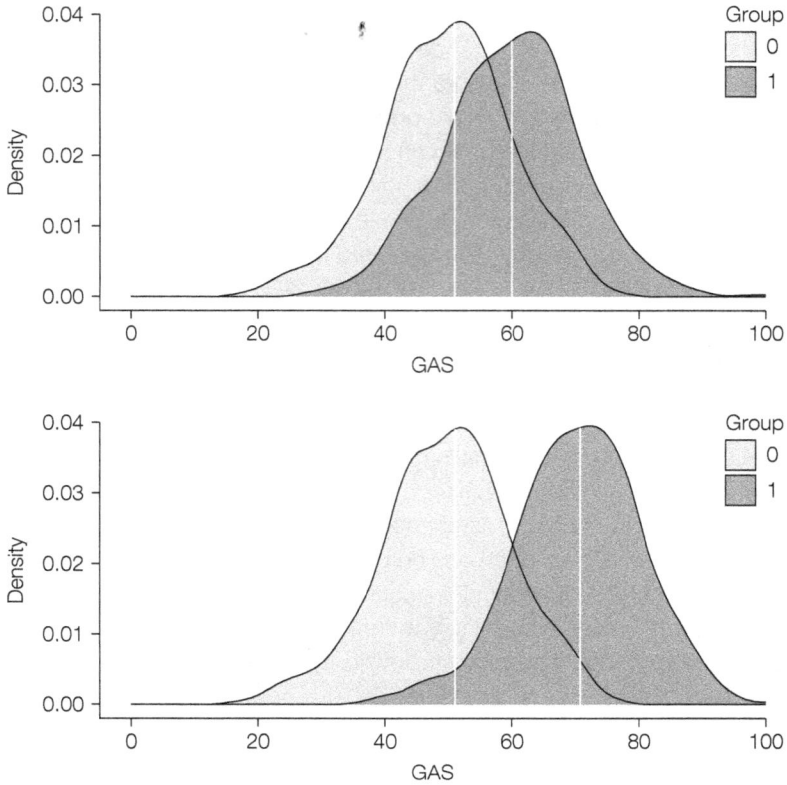

Figure 1.2. Illustrations of Score Distributions for Two Randomly Simulated Groups. *Note.* Illustrations of two randomly simulated group score distributions and means (0 = Random Normal Group [n = 500], 1 = Anxiety Disorder Group [n = 500]) on a hypothetical anxiety test (GAS = General Anxiety Scale) that was scaled as T scores (M_T = 50, SD_T = 10). The top density plots (Random Normal Group M = 49.76, SD = 10.21; Anxiety Disorder Group M = 59.80, SD = 10.57) effect size (Cohen's d = .97, equivalent to an Area Under the Curve [AUC] of .75) and the bottom density plots (Random Normal Group M = 49.76, SD = 10.21; Anxiety Disorder Group M = 70.49, SD = 9.87) effect size (Cohen's d = 2.06, or AUC of .93) illustrate greater group separation and less overlap as the effect size increases.

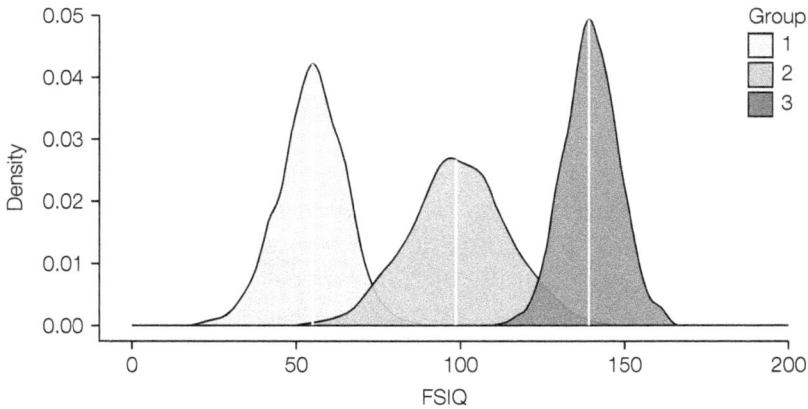

Figure 1.3. Illustration of Distributions of Three Randomly Simulated Groups. *Note.* Illustration of three randomly simulated groups (1 = Intellectual Disability [n = 1,000], 2 = Random Normal [n = 2,200], 3 = Intellectually Gifted [n = 1,000]) score distributions and means on a hypothetical intelligence test (FSIQ = Full-Scale Intelligence Quotient). Intellectual Disability (M = 54.81, SD = 9.94), Random Normal (M = 99.48, SD = 15.02), and Intellectually Gifted (M = 139.82, SD = 8.22) differed from one another on the FSIQ.

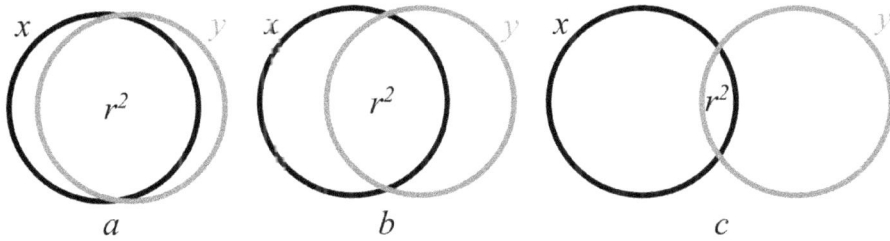

Figure 1.4. **Venn Diagrams Illustrating Convergent, Discriminant, and Divergent Validity.** *Note.* Venn diagrams of variance for test scores x and y illustrating a) Convergent Validity (variables x and y purportedly measure the same construct), b) Discriminant Validity (variables x and y measure different yet related constructs), and c) Divergent Validity (variables x and y measure very different constructs). r^2 is the proportion of shared variance of test x and test y.

K–BIT IQ Composite and the WISC–III FSIQ (r = .89) reported by Canivez et al. (2005) was very high with 79% shared variance, supporting strong convergent validity because these scores reflect measurement of the same construct (general intelligence). When convergent validity coefficients are low then it is not possible to determine which test is responsible for the poor relationship because a criterion was not specified a priori, and it is possible that both tests might be problematic.

Divergent Validity. Divergent validity is the linguistic and conceptual opposite of convergent validity where two or more measures designed to measure different constructs should produce low to near zero correlations and have little shared variance (see Figure 1.4c). Studies of divergent validity identify two or more tests or measures of very different constructs, obtain a sufficiently large sample, and administer the tests to each of the individuals in random counterbalanced order. For tests measuring different constructs there should be no relationship between performance on one test and performance on the other. In the Canivez et al. (2005) study, scores from the two intelligence tests (WISC–III and K–BIT) were compared to scores from the ASCA (McDermott et al., 1993), which measures syndromes related to child and adolescent psychopathology. Intelligence and psychopathology are very different constructs that should not share much, if any, variance. Canivez et al. reported the correlations between the WISC–III and the ASCA were low to near zero and ranged from -.18 to .07 (Mdn_r = -.10) and correlations between the K–BIT and the ASCA were also low to near zero and ranged from -.17 to .04 (Mdn_r = -.10). The two intelligence tests shared less than 5% measurement variance with ASCA syndromes and thus were measuring very different (divergent) constructs.

Discriminant Validity. With the publication of the seminal work of Campbell and Fiske (1959) on simultaneous examination of convergent and discriminant validity through the multitrait-multimethod (MTMM) matrix to assess construct validity for all included measures, the term *discriminant validity* has been routinely used to describe correlations between measures purportedly measuring different constructs that are lower than correlations between measures purportedly measuring the same construct (i.e., convergent validity). In discriminant validity the correlations do not necessarily have to be low to near zero as described above in divergent validity, they just need to be lower than hypothesized convergent validity coefficients (see Figure 1.4b). Campbell and Fiske (1959) pointed out that "tests can be invalidated by too high correlations with other tests from which they were intended to differ" (p. 81). Canivez et al. (2005) provided assessment of construct validity that also looked at correlations between the two intelligence tests (WISC–III and K–BIT) and scores from one of four measures of academic achievement, although this study was not an MTMM matrix study. Correlations between the K–BIT IQ Composite or WISC–III FSIQ with academic achievement subtests measuring basic reading, reading comprehension, mathematics calculation, mathematics reasoning, and writing ranged from .54 to .74. In comparison to the correlation between the two omnibus, global IQ scores ($r = .89$), these IQ-Achievement correlations are lower (so discriminant) but in comparison with the correlations between the two intelligence tests and the psychopathology syndromes (ASCA), these IQ-Achievement correlations are considerably higher (and so not divergent as they are not low to near zero). This illustrates how it might be useful to consider divergent and discriminant validity as different and important distinctions.

Multitrait-Multimethod Matrix. Construct validity by way of the multitrait-multimethod matrix was presented by Campbell and Fiske (1959) as an experimental design to examine construct validity of a group of measures differing in the traits measured and the methods used to measure the various traits. At a minimum, there must be at least two different traits and two different methods used to measure each trait (see Figure 1.5). As more traits and more methods are added, the number of tests administered to participants increases and makes for a more difficult study to conduct. In their description of the MTMM matrix, the main diagonal of correlations are individual test reliability coefficients (monotrait-monomethod), and these would be expected to be the highest correlations in the matrix. Convergent validity coefficients (monotrait-heteromethod) would be the next highest correlations because different methods measuring the same trait are expected to be high but likely not as high as reliability coefficients. Lowest correlations should be the remaining coefficients (heterotrait-monomethod and heterotrait-heteromethod) and provides evidence for how measures can (or should) differentiate constructs. When convergent validity correlations are too low or discriminant validity correlations are too high, it is not possible to point to a particular measure as the "problem" because either measure might be the cause of the lower or higher correlation or perhaps both are problematic. Unlike criterion-related validity where a criterion measure is selected, no such criterion measures are necessarily specified in the MTMM matrix.

Theory Consistent Intervention Effects. Various psychological and medical interventions have been developed to treat and ameliorate symptoms of specific psychological disorders that are quantified by certain tests. One example is the use of behavioral (or cognitive-behavioral) treatments (BT/CBT) to reduce symptoms of anxiety related to generalized anxiety disorder, panic disorder, obsessive-compulsive disorder, and specific phobias. Anti-anxiety medications may also show reduction of anxiety symptoms. Typical clinical research methods might evaluate the effectiveness

	Trait	Method 1		Method 2	
		A	B	A	B
Method 1	A	r_a			
	B	r_c	r_a		
Method 2	A	r_b	r_d	r_a	
	B	r_d	r_b	r_c	r_a

Note. Capital letters A and B refer to different traits.
r_a = Reliability coefficients (monotrait-monomethod)
r_b = Convergent validity coefficients (monotrait-heteromethod)
r_c = Divergent/Discriminant validity coefficients (monomethod-heterotrait)
r_d = Divergent/Discriminant validity coefficients (heterotrait-heteromethod)

Figure 1.5. **Example Multitrait-Multimethod Matrix for Two Traits and Two Methods.**

of such treatments to reduce such symptoms and use an anxiety test to quantify the amount of anxiety clients have before and after treatment. However, in assessing the construct validity of a test, the interest is in whether the test can measure the symptom reduction. While there is an element of circularity, for assessing the construct validity of a test, one method would be to find an intervention known to have substantial effects on the construct the test purports to measure (BT/CBT), find a sample of individuals diagnosed with the specific disorder (e.g., generalized anxiety disorder) related to the construct the test purports to measure (e.g., anxiety), randomly assign participants to the treatment (BT/CBT) and control groups, and administer the test to all participants when treatment is completed (between-subjects design). Support for construct validity of the test would be provided if the participants in the treatment group produced significantly lower scores on the test than those in the control group. It would also be possible to use a within-subjects design and administer the test in question before treatment (pretest) and after treatment (post-test) for all participants. The logic of this method is that the test must be measuring the purported construct if it is able to measure differences between those receiving a known powerful treatment that affects that construct and those not receiving the treatment (or if the test measures the post-test changes from pre-test scores following treatment).

Structural/Factorial Validity. A final method for examining construct validity of tests and their constituent scores relates to the test structure and the extent to which it adequately measures the purported construct. Examination of structural validity of tests is essential for evaluating interpretability of provided test scores (AERA et al., 2014; British Psychological Society [BPS], 2007, 2016; ITC, 2001, 2013). Constructs might be thought to be unidimensional (measuring a single dimension) or multidimensional (measuring several dimensions). If a test purports to measure a construct that is theoretically unidimensional, then the underlying structure should reflect measurement of a single dimension, and if the test purports to measure a multidimensional construct, then the underlying structure should reflect the measurement of the purported multiple dimensions and proper alignment of indicators or measured variables to the theoretically related dimensions (Dombrowski et al., 2020). Statistically, factor analysis is the method used to help determine how many and what dimensions are satisfactorily measured by the test. There are two primary methods of factor analysis: exploratory factor analysis (EFA), and confirmatory factor analysis (CFA). They serve somewhat different purposes and answer different questions, and while often considered a dichotomy, their use is more on a continuum with both being used for exploratory and confirmatory purposes (Bandalos & Gerstner, 2016). Bayesian structural equation modeling has also received increased attention (e.g., Dombrowski et al., 2018; Golay et al., 2013). Both EFA and CFA are large sample statistics so statistically significant findings in hypothesis testing might be unduly influenced by being over-powered. CFA is a special application of structural equation modeling (SEM) focused on the underlying measurement model of a test or measure (Brown, 2015; Kline, 2016; Byrne, 2013). Gorsuch (1983) and Carroll (1995) considered EFA and CFA complementary approaches with greater confidence in the structure of a test when EFA and CFA are in agreement. In both EFA and CFA the measured variables or indicators are observations made from test content, and for personality tests, behavior-rating scales, measures of psychopathology, or surveys of attitudes, the measured variables or indicators are *items*, whereas for tests of intelligence, academic achievement, or similar measures, the measured variables are the *subtest scores*. There are numerous outstanding and highly recommended books devoted to EFA (Gorsuch, 1983; Thompson, 2004; Watkins, 2021a, 2021b, 2022) and CFA (Brown, 2015; Kline, 2016; Thompson, 2004) as well as chapters within books (see Tabachnick & Fidell, 2019). These books and chapters provide extensive details of EFA and CFA well beyond the scope of this chapter. The Watkins books are particularly useful due to their breadth, annotation, references, and step-by-step approach with example data sets for practice using R and RStudio, SPSS, or Stata. Watkins (2018) also provides details on best practices in EFA.

EFA involves mathematically examining a correlation matrix of measured variables (items or subtest scores) to uncover a latent structure of the measure without constraints. A correlation matrix may contain convergent validity correlations and divergent (discriminant) validity correlations that provide the foundation for the underlying structure. To illustrate, a hypothetical (best case) correlation matrix for the 16 WISC–V primary and secondary subtests is presented in Table 1.1. Subtests within each of the five theoretical factors specified in the WISC–V are shaded the same and subtests within each of the five theoretical factors were specified to correlate .90 with each other (sharing 81% variance). Correlations between subtests from different factors were specified to correlate .10 (sharing 1% variance). This illustrates the artificially strong convergent validity correlations between subtests within the same factor and simultaneous artificially strong divergent (discriminant) validity correlations between subtests within different factors. This hypothetical example should be considered an idealized scenario to clearly illustrate a strong pattern and support for subtests within their theoretical factors, which while related to each other are not related to subtests from different factors. With coefficients like these, EFA would indeed produce five factors with properly aligned subtest indicators as highlighted, and given these hypothetical convergent and divergent (discriminant) validity coefficients, the five factors would be independent because their constituent subtest scores do not correlate well (share variance) with subtest scores outside the specific domain. Given subtest scores from tests such as intelligence are continuous variables, Pearson product-moment correlations are appropriately estimated and used in EFA. However, item level EFA for behavior rating scales or psychopathology measures likely requires use of correlations based on alternate correlation methods because items typically are categorical, dichotomous, or polytomous (ordinal), and the *phi* coefficient, tetrachoric correlation, or polychoric correlation may be more appropriate options (see Kline, 2011; Lorenzo-Seva & Ferrando, 2015; Watkins, 2021b).

EFA is theoretically agnostic, fundamentally guided by goals of parsimony, interpretability, and theoretical plausibility. Carroll (1995) opined that EFA allowed data to "speak for themselves" (p. 436) and both he and Reise (2012) noted that EFA results inform researchers of plausible models to later test in CFA rather than relying solely on theory. Of course, EFA is not entirely atheoretical as researchers often have some idea of the constructs expected to emerge. Thus, replication of EFA results should include examination with different samples. EFA results can be examined separately for various subgroups within a sample (sex/gender, race/ethnicity, etc.), or between different samples, with statistics such as the Coefficient of Congruence, Chi-Square Goodness of Fit, and Salient Variable Similarity Index (Cattell, 1949) indicating the extent to which resulting factor coefficients (based on the identical extraction and rotation method) are the same or similar (Watkins, 2020a).

Best practices in EFA as outlined by Watkins (2018, 2021a, 2021b, 2022) are delineated in 10 steps in the process. In considering variables to include (Step 1) it is recommended that 3–6 measured variables per factor be included, that variables well represent the domain, that variables are not dependent on each other, and that low reliability and low communality are avoided. The optimal number of participants to include and their characteristics (Step 2) depends on two constituent elements: the number of measured variables or indictors per factor included and communality (Watkins, 2021b), with fewer participants required when communality is high and factors overdetermined. Sample heterogeneity is desirable to maximize variability because

Table 1.1 *Hypothetical WISC–V Subtest Intercorrelation Matrix With Highlighted Convergent Validity Coefficients*

Wechsler Intelligence Scale for Children–Fifth Edition (WISC–V) Factors

	Verbal Comprehension				Visual Spatial		Fluid Reasoning			Working Memory				Processing Speed		
	SI	VC	IN	CO	BD	VP	MR	FW	PC	AR	DS	PS	LN	CD	SS	CA
SI	1.00															
VC	.90	1.00														
IN	.90	.90	1.00													
CO	.90	.90	.90	1.00												
BD	.10	.10	.10	.10	1.00											
VP	.10	.10	.10	.10	.90	1.00										
MR	.10	.10	.10	.10	.10	.10	1.00									
FW	.10	.10	.10	.10	.10	.10	.90	1.00								
PC	.10	.10	.10	.10	.10	.10	.90	.90	1.00							
AR	.10	.10	.10	.10	.10	.10	.10	.10	.10	1.00						
DS	.10	.10	.10	.10	.10	.10	.10	.10	.10	.90	1.00					
PS	.10	.10	.10	.10	.10	.10	.10	.10	.10	.90	.90	1.00				
LN	.10	.10	.10	.10	.10	.10	.10	.10	.10	.90	.90	.90	1.00			
CD	.10	.10	.10	.10	.10	.10	.10	.10	.10	.10	.10	.10	.10	1.00		
SS	.10	.10	.10	.10	.10	.10	.10	.10	.10	.10	.10	.10	.10	.90	1.00	
CA	.10	.10	.10	.10	.10	.10	.10	.10	.10	.10	.10	.10	.10	.90	.90	1.00

Note. Wechsler Intelligence Scale for Children–Fifth Edition (WISC–V) Subtests: SI = Similarities; VC – Vocabulary; IN = Information; CO = Comprehension; BD = Block Design; VP = Visual Puzzles; MR = Matrix Reasoning; FW = Figure Weights; PC = Picture Concepts; AR = Arithmetic; DS = Digit Span; PS = Picture Span; LN = Letter-Number Sequencing; CD = Coding; SS = Symbol Search; CA = Cancellation. These hypothetical values are intentionally more idealized than would be observed in actual data for illustrative purposes.

homogenous samples tend to attenuate correlations, which directly impacts factor analysis. Analyzing data (Step 3) should determine data accuracy, identify and address missing data, and address univariate and multivariate outliers. Analyses should also verify linearity of bivariate relationships and determine univariate and multivariate normality as some methods or procedures assume normally distributed data. Determining if EFA is viable (Step 4) involves inspection of the correlation matrix where some correlations should be ≥ .30 (i.e., there is covariance to support factors) and satisfactory results from Bartlett's Test of Sphericity and the Kaiser-Meyer-Olkin test of sampling adequacy. Selection of an EFA approach (Step 5), principal components analysis (which is not factor analysis but a data reduction method that generates linear composites of variables) or common factor analysis are options. Selection of a factor extraction method (Step 6) involves selecting a descriptive method (i.e., principal factors or image analysis) or an inferential method (i.e., maximum likelihood or alpha factoring) that depends on sample characteristics and data. Determination of how many factors should be retained (Step 7) involves consideration of multiple methods including the Kaiser (1960) criterion (eigenvalues > 1), visual scree test (Cattell, 1966), *SE* scree (Zoski & Jurs, 1996), parallel analysis (Horn, 1965), minimum average partials (Velicer, 1976), and theoretical convergence and parsimony. Often these different methods suggest different numbers of factors be retained so often it is useful to begin with extraction of the largest number of factors suggested as a starting point and the number of extracted factors iteratively reduced by one to compare plausibility (or problems) for each. When too many unsupported factors are extracted, the result may be that later factors do not include at least three salient factor coefficients (singlet or doublet factors), which likely are weak factors with low communality (Fabrigar et al., 1999), measured variables or indicators may have salient loadings on multiple factors (i.e., cross-loading); measured variables or indicators may not have any salient loadings on any factors as measured variable variance may be spread too thinly across too many factors; or communality estimates may exceed 1.0 (i.e., Heywood case). When too few factors are extracted, theoretically plausible factors may merge resulting in unsatisfactory results and limiting examination of second-order dimensions. Optimally, a viable solution will achieve simple structure (Thurstone, 1947) where salient indicators load on a single factor. A new method to supplement these factor extraction criteria is *exploratory graph analysis* (EGA; Golino & Epskamp, 2017), which Watkins et al. (2023) used with WISC–V primary subtest scores obtained from a large clinical sample and replicated the four-factor solution previously suggested by EFA with the standardization sample (Canivez & Watkins, 2016; Canivez et al., 2016). Once factors are extracted, they must be rotated (Step 8) to orient factor axes to the measured variables or indicators. Orthogonal rotation methods (varimax, quartimax, equimax) force the factors to be uncorrelated and factor axes perpendicular to each other. Given the ubiquitous observation of correlated factors and variables in the social sciences, oblique rotation is overwhelmingly recommended by measurement experts (see Watkins, 2021b for numerous references). Oblique factor rotation methods (promax, quartimin, oblimin) allow factors to be correlated to the extent that they are, and the more the factor axes deviate from perpendicular (orthogonal) the higher the factor correlation. When oblique rotation produces factor correlations < .33 then one may assume that the underlying factors are essentially uncorrelated and an orthogonal rotation method properly applied (Tabachnick & Fidell, 2019). When oblique rotation is required due to correlated factors, the correlated factors imply a higher-order (or bifactor) dimension that explains the correlated factors, and a second-order EFA should be examined (Gorsuch, 1983; Thompson, 2004; Watkins, 2018, 2021b). Interpretation of results follows (Step 9) noting desired simple structure, theoretical convergence and parsimony, and naming of factors. In the case of EFA for assessment of validity, obtaining the theoretically purported number of factors and the proper alignment of item or subtest indicators with the theoretically purported factors provides structural validity evidence. Finally, presentation of results (Step 10) is made, and in the context of validity, conclusions are reached as to how well the EFA matches the purported structure.

When first-order factors are meaningfully correlated ($r > .32$; Tabachnick & Fidell, 2019) this implies one (or more) factors explain those correlations and requires further explication (Carroll, 1995; Gorsuch, 1983; Thompson, 2004; Watkins, 2018) via second-order EFA. Additionally, results from second-order EFA may be further examined using the Schmid and Leiman (SL; 1957) transformation as used by and insisted on by Carroll (1993, 1995, 1997, 2003). It is a reparameterization of a higher-order model and an approximate bifactor solution (Reise, 2012) that disentangles the variance sources. While there are known problems with the SL transformation such as proportionality constraints in theoretically derived data (Mansolf & Reise, 2016; Yung et al., 1999), SL transformation with applied data has produced results indicating it is an accurate factor recovery method. Similarly, results have been recovered in statistical simulations (Giordano & Waller, 2020) so challenges of proportionality may be of greater concern for theoretical researchers than applied psychometricians. Several alternative methods to produce exploratory bifactor solutions have been proposed and examined (Dombrowski et al., 2019; Reise et al., 2023). Assessment of test structural validity requires this decomposition of variance in order for test users to judge how adequately the lower-order (first-order) factors measure constructs in comparison to higher-order factor(s) and decomposed variance estimates allow for model-based reliability and dimensionality estimates to be calculated for further explication (Bornovalova et al., 2020; Murray & Johnson, 2013; Reise, 2012; Reise et al., 2023; Watkins, 2017, 2021b), which is presented following presentation of CFA. Measured variables (items or subtests) variance is frequently a mixture of general construct variance, specific group factor variance, specific variance unique to the measured variable, and error variance, so estimating and disclosing those sources of variance is necessary.

Because EFA (and CFA) are used in test construction and assessment of test validity, some of the elements of best practices might not be possible. For example, a publisher may produce a test that includes only two measured variables to represent a latent construct (e.g., WISC–V Visual Spatial factor; Wechsler, 2014), which would fall short of the minimum of three suggested by best practices, but the researcher would still want to examine that structure to determine its adequacy based on the purported structure (and provided scores) despite the model underidentification while test users would be interested in how adequate such structures and resulting scores are.

CFA involves specifying a measurement model based on theory, hypothesized structure, or previous results (i.e., EFA) and mathematically testing that model with data to determine if the model adequately represents (or fits) data. CFA frequently specifies various plausible theoretical models that might explain data, and models are often compared to determine which might fit better or best. In specifying models, like in EFA, models may be specified with orthogonal factors or oblique factors, and if oblique models are specified, alternative higher-order and bifactor representations should also be specified and compared. Figure 1.6 illustrates these four different and potentially competing measurement models. The orthogonal model has independent (uncorrelated) factors so there are no double-headed arrows (covariances) connecting the first-order factors. The oblique model includes factors connected with double-headed arrows indicating covariances (correlations) between all specified factors. As in EFA, correlated factors imply higher-order or general bifactor constructs that may explain the factor correlations, which is obscured within an oblique structure and requires explication (Gorsuch, 1983; Reise et al., 2023; Thompson, 2004). The higher-order model includes paths from a general second-order factor to each of the first-order factors, which

Orthogonal

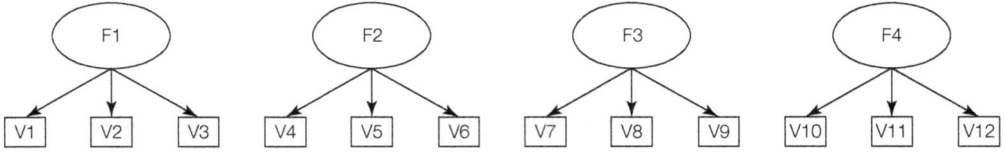

Oblique

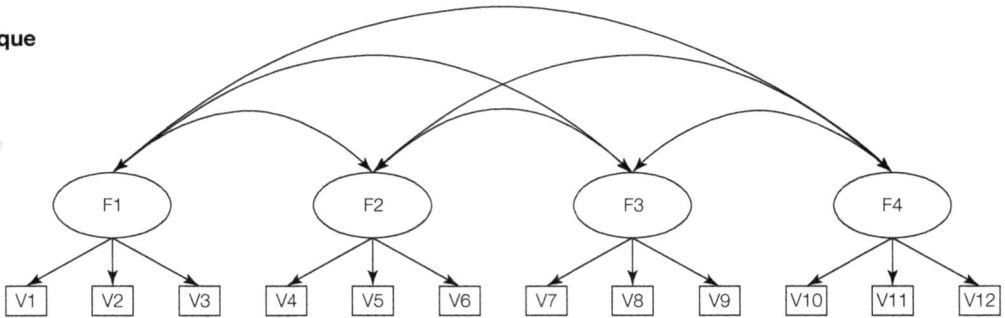

Higher-Order

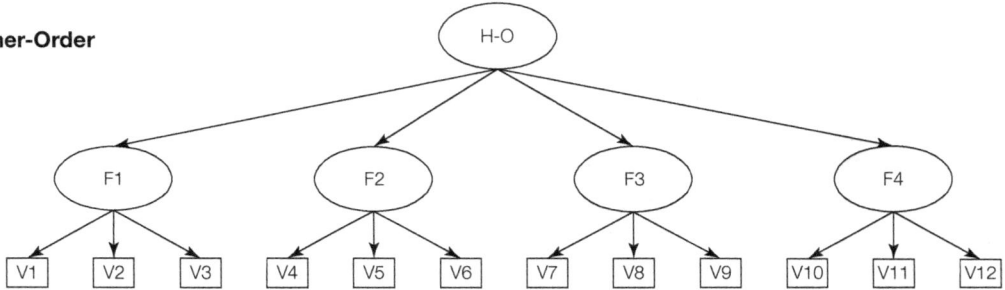

Bifactor

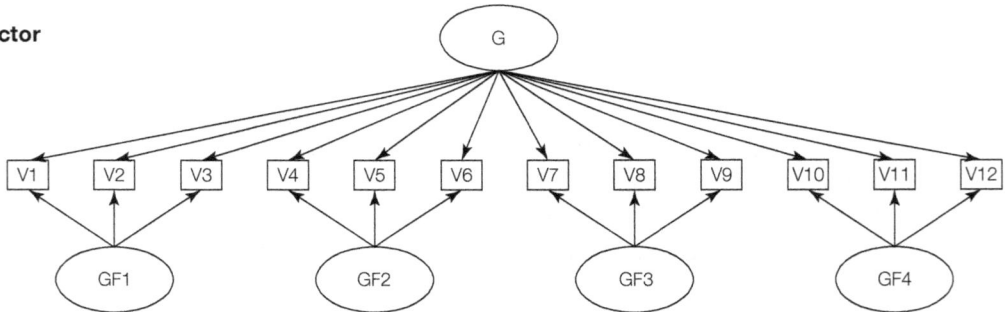

Figure 1.6. **Orthogonal, Oblique, Higher-Order, and Bifactor Measurement Models.** *Note.* Various structural measurement models (orthogonal, oblique, higher-order, bifactor) that might represent 12 measured variables/indicators.

in turn have paths leading to the measured variables. In the higher-order model the influence of the general second-order factor on the observed measured variables or indicators is indirect and the general second-order factor is fully mediated by the first-order group factors to influence the measured variables (Yung et al., 1999). McDonald (1999) referred to this model as the indirect hierarchical model, which is terminology that has occasionally been used by others (e.g., Canivez, 2014a; Gignac, 2008; Watkins, 2010). How much influence the second-order factor has on the observed indicators is obscured, and an important question regarding higher-order models is whether influences of a higher-order factor should be fully mediated by first-order factors (Gignac, 2005, 2006, 2008). The bifactor model (Holzinger & Swineford, 1937) is an alternative to the higher-order model and has a general factor (similar to the second-order factor in the higher-order model), that has direct paths to, and influences on, all the measured variables and has specific group factors with direct paths to and influences on the measured variables related to that specific factor; thus the specific group factors do not mediate the influence of the broad, general factor. The general factor in the higher-order (hierarchical) model is a superordinate dimension where first-order factors are abstractions from measured variables and the higher-order factor is an abstraction from first-order abstractions (Thompson, 2004). The general factor in the bifactor model is a breadth dimension (Gignac, 2008; Humphreys, 1982) with the general factor and specific group factors simultaneously abstractions from measured variables that are at the same level of inference and may be considered more parsimonious (Gignac, 2006). With respect to the construct of intelligence, Spearman's two-factor theory is one that conceptualizes intelligence from a bifactor perspective given the dominant role general intelligence appears to have on measured variables (and Spearman's [1927] indifference of the indicator), and Beaujean (2015b) argued that Carroll's perspective of intelligence was also of a bifactor nature despite the graphical representation that illustrates a higher-order model (see Canivez & Youngstrom, 2019).

CFA has various mathematical estimation methods (i.e., maximum likelihood, weighted least squares, unweighted least squares) depending on sample size and data characteristics (nominal, ordinal, or interval measured variables or indicators; non-normal versus multivariately normal distributions), and choice of estimator has consequences for parameter estimates and model fit (Lei & Wu, 2012). Because items are typically dichotomous or polytomous [ordinal], specification of measured variables as categorical in maximum likelihood estimation is typical for multivariate continuous data, but when data are not distributed with univariate and multivariate normality then weighted least squares or the robust maximum likelihood estimator (i.e., Satorra & Bentler, 1988) that adjusts for nonnormality can be used to calculate estimates and provide corrected fit indices (Brown, 2015; Byrne, 2013). Assessment of global model fit to data includes consideration of χ^2 tests, Comparative Fit Index (CFI), Tucker–Lewis Index (TLI), Standardized Root Mean Squared Residual (SRMR), and the Root Mean Square Error of Approximation (RMSEA). Higher CFI and TLI (model fit indicators) values indicate better fit whereas lower SRMR and RMSEA (model misfit indicators) values indicate better fit, and while there are no universally agreed upon criteria for approximate fit indices (McDonald, 2010), Hu and Bentler (1999) combinatorial heuristics are frequently applied and indicate adequate model fit with CFI and TLI ≥ .90 along with SRMR ≤ .09 and RMSEA ≤ .08. Good model fit requires CFI and TLI ≥ 0.95 with SRMR and RMSEA ≤ 0.06 (Hu & Bentler, 1999). Two other frequently used indicators of model fit are the Akaike Information Criterion (AIC; Akaike, 1987) and Bayesian Information Criterion (BIC; Raftery, 1995). Chen (2007) and Cheung and Rensvold (2002) indicated meaningful differences between well-fitting models were noted with ΔCFI > .01 and ΔRMSEA < .015. Burnham and Anderson (2004) indicated meaningful model differences could be identified with ΔAIC > 10, and Raftery (1995) suggested criteria for indications of superior model fit for ΔBIC values of 0 to -2 (weak), -2 to -6 (positive), -6 to -10 (strong), and > -10 (very strong). In addition to assessing global fit, assessment of local fit must be conducted as models should never be retained "solely on global fit testing" (Kline, 2016, p. 461). Examination of standardized path coefficients in models is also required because a model may have good global model fit but contain path coefficients that are not statistically significant or may be statistically significant (perhaps due to extremely high power from a very large sample) but low, challenging the validity of that model.

Structural equation modeling software often includes options for empirical suggestions for model modification (Lagrange Multiplier and Wald Test) for adding or dropping model parameters for improving model fit (Byrne, 2013; Kline, 2011) by testing significant χ^2 changes. Such modifications may (likely) capitalize on chance especially because CFA is a large sample statistic and may be overpowered particularly with test normative samples. Modifications are supposed to be theoretically and not just empirically viable, but as Watkins (2021b) pointed out there are many methodologists (see for example Bandalos & Finney, 2019; Gorsuch, 2003; Kline, 2011; Schreiber et al., 2006; Ullman, 2001) who are very skeptical about their use and warn about use of such model modification and respecification. Researchers also do not appear to find it difficult to come up with theoretical justifications for their inclusion even when there is no apparent connectivity in the specification of those parameters (i.e., utilization of those parameters in prior research). Such modifications should be treated very skeptically absent replications of superior model fit with different independent samples. Even greater skepticism should be applied when authors propose model modifications to improve fit in a single study but never use that model as a baseline or rival model with a subsequent independent sample. Examples of such model modifications can be found in two Wechsler scale articles (Weiss et al., 2013a, 2013b) and the critical commentary provided by Canivez and Kush (2013) challenging what was done and importantly, noting what was not done.

A final element of assessing model adequacy and the adequacy of resulting scores is the estimation of reliability provided by scores implied by models (model-based reliability) and assessment of model dimensionality. Watkins (2017) summarized reliability estimation problems with multidimensional measures and solutions offered by the Omega family of coefficients (McDonald, 1999). Model-based reliability/validity indexes and dimensionality indexes provide better estimates of reliability and dimensionality to guide interpretations of test scores. Because these indexes are proportions of variance contributed by latent constructs, they may be considered validity indexes (Brunner et al., 2012). Table 1.2 presents various model-based indices and their definitions. These indexes (and other statistical features) are crucial to the judgment of adequacy of scores provided by tests to determine which scores have sufficient reliability for interpretation but are, like variance estimates of test factors, absent in intelligence test technical manuals such as Wechsler scales (Wechsler, 2008, 2012; 2014) and WJ IV (McGrew et al., 2014) even when their absence and importance in earlier revisions has been pointed out so they could be included in newer versions (see Canivez, 2010, 2014b; Canivez & Kush, 2013). When such estimates are not provided in technical manuals (or when test users lack psychometric literacy to appreciate their meaning) it then is not possible for the test user to adequately judge score adequacy for clinical or research use and users must await peer-reviewed studies to provide them (see Canivez & Watkins, 2016; Canivez et al., 2016, 2017). Use of inadequately supported scores conflicts with professional ethical standards and testing standards.

Omega estimates (ω_H and ω_{HS}) may be obtained from CFA bifactor solutions or decomposed variance estimates from higher-order models produced by EFA or CFA and may be produced using the Omega program (Watkins, 2013), which is based on the tutorial by Brunner et al. (2012) and the work of Zinbarg et al. (2005) and Zinbarg et al. (2006). The Omega program also calculates construct reliability or replicability index (H), factor determinacy index (FDI), explained common variance (ECV), and percentage of uncontaminated correlations (PUC) indices. The Watkins and Canivez (2022) tutorial on assessing the psychometric utility of IQ test scores illustrates application

Table 1.2 Model-Based Reliability/Validity and Dimensionality Estimates

Estimate	Definition
Reliability/Validity Indexes	
Omega (ω)	ω is the proportion of variance in the unit-weighted total score attributable to all sources of common variance and a model-based estimate analogous to coefficient alpha extended to include more than one factor.
Omega Subscale (ω_s)	ω_s is the proportion of each subscale unit-weighted score's total variance attributed to the blend of general and the specific group factor variance.
Omega-Hierarchical (ω_H)	ω_H is the ratio of the general factor variance compared to the total test variance, reflecting the percentage of systematic variance in unit-weighted total scores attributable to the individual differences or the general factor. It is the model-based reliability estimate for the general factor with variability of specific group factors removed (i.e., unique variance of the general factor score).
Omega-Hierarchical Subscale (ω_{Hs})	ω_{Hs} is the proportion of subscale score variance accounted for by its intended group factor to the total variance of that subscale score, which indexes the reliable variance associated with that subscale after controlling for the effects of the general factor. It estimates the reliability of a unit-weighted group factor score after the influence of all other factors (general and other group factors) are removed (i.e., unique variance of the group factor score).
Index of Construct Reliability or Construct Replicability (H)	H is the correlation between a latent factor and an optimally weighted composite score and an indication of how well the latent construct is represented by its measured variables (Rodriguez et al., 2016b). H = FDI^2.
Factor Determinacy Index (FDI)	FDI is an estimate of how well factor scores estimate the latent factor and FDI = $\sqrt{H}$.
Dimensionality Indexes	
Explained Common Variance (ECV)	ECV indicates the proportion of common variance explained by the target construct.
Percentage of Uncontaminated Correlations (PUC)	PUC is the proportion of subtest correlations that are uncontaminated by multidimensionality and indexes the bias that could result from forcing multidimensional data into a unidimensional model.

Note. Definitions provided by Hancock and Mueller (2001), Rodriguez et al. (2016a, 2016b), Watkins (2013, 2017), and Watkins and Canivez (2022).

and judgments emanating from the various model-based reliability and dimensionality estimates provided by the Omega program. Although there are no universally accepted guidelines for acceptable or adequate levels of ω_H or ω_{Hs} for clinical decision-making, values less than .50 indicate the target factor accounts for less than 50% of the reliable score variance making meaningful interpretation unlikely (Gignac & Watkins, 2013). Thus, omega coefficients should at a minimum exceed .50, but .75 might be a preferable guideline for confident score interpretation (Canivez & Youngstrom, 2019; Reise, 2012; Reise et al., 2013; Watkins, 2017). H values lower than .80 suggest that the factor is not well defined and unlikely to replicate across studies or provide accurate path coefficients if included in statistical models (Ferrando & Lorenzo-Seva, 2018; Mueller & Hancock, 2019; Rodriguez et al., 2016a). The FDI is an index of how well a latent construct is estimated by a factor score and is related to H (H = FDI^2). As noted by Watkins (2013) in the Omega program, Grice (2001) provided an extensive presentation regarding varied methods of estimating factor scores and that varying methods of estimation produce different estimates and factor indeterminacy issues. Gorsuch (1983) recommended FDI ≥ .80, but Grice (2001) indicated that FDI > .90 "may be necessary if the factor score estimates are to serve as adequate substitutes for the factors themselves" (p. 436).

With respect to dimensionality, essential unidimensionality is supported by PUC values ≥ .80 (Rodriguez et al., 2016a, 2016b) and minimal bias would result from estimating a unidimensional factor from multidimensional data with ECV values ≥ .70 (Gu et al., 2017; Rodriguez et al., 2016a, 2016b; Sellbom & Tellegen, 2019). As PUC increases, ECV decreases in importance as an indicator of bias (Rodriguez et al., 2016b), so a test score might be considered essentially unidimensional when ECV and PUC are both ≥ .70 (Gu et al., 2017; Rodriguez et al., 2016a, 2016b; Sellbom & Tellegen, 2019).

To further emphasize the importance of model-based reliability estimates, Reise et al. (2023) concluded,

> In the development of new measures or the psychometric analysis of existing measures, there is no defensible reason for failing to report indices such as ω, ω_H, ω_{HS}, and ECV; if the data are consistent with a correlated factors model, they will also, in general, be consistent with a bifactor model[7]; those statistics are important to report so that researchers can judge whether the subscales provide any unique and reliable information once controlling for the general. (p. 343)

Reise et al. (2023) also concluded that "purveyors of subscales and 'multidimensional constructs' may not appreciate the implications of bifactor psychometric analysis, but full and fair reporting demands such models be considered" (p. 343), and they further opined that "a correlated factors model should not be an accepted 'default' unless careful theoretical consideration is given to explaining their redundancy and demonstrating their added value" (p. 344). This echoes suggestions of Murray and Johnson (2013) and Bornovalova et al. (2020). Test scores are likely to be multidimensional, but it is possible that they might be essentially unidimensional, or unidimensional enough so that the score may be interpreted as a measure of its purported construct without excessive bias (Rodriguez et al., 2016a, 2016b). Reise et al. (2013) described the assumption of unidimensionality as "a convenient fiction, sometimes useful in applied contexts" (p. 136).

Regarding both EFA and CFA, Kline (2023) pointed out an important error to avoid when considering factor names, constructs, or proxies they purportedly represent. The *naming fallacy* indicates "just because a proxy is named does not mean that the corresponding concept is understood or even correctly labeled" (p. 218). Kline (2016) also cautioned to avoid factor *reification*, which is "the belief that a hypothetical construct must correspond to a real thing" (p. 231). Further, all structures proposed or identified by EFA or CFA, no matter how well fitting, must be tested against external criteria to determine other elements of validity and incremental validity (Kline, 1994; Lubinski & Dawis, 1992). With respect to intelligence tests, the generally poor portions of unique variance provided by the first-order group factor scores is a foundational cause for poor incremental validity and diagnostic utility when controlling for the dominance of the general intelligence factor. Also, this further indicates that while first-order group factors may be located or identified in EFA or CFA, they may not contain acceptable portions of unique measurement variance and scores based upon them equally problematic and an indication that the hypothetical constructs they supposedly represent are not well measured. Thus, it isn't so much a question about what a test measures but how well it measures the purported constructs. This combined with poor longitudinal stability of intelligence test subtests and various ipsative subtest strengths and weaknesses and poor diagnostic utility of strengths and weaknesses renders interpretation primarily, if not exclusively, with the global, general intelligence score (see Canivez, 2013a; Kranzler & Floyd, 2020; McGill et al., 2018; Watkins et al., 2022). Sage advice is offered by Kranzler and Floyd (2020) in that test users should remember that "just because the test or its scoring system produces a score (and score profiles), examiners need not interpret these results or communicate these findings in their oral or written reports' (p. 203). This is consistent with both professional ethics and *Standards*.

Applications of EFA (Canivez & Watkins, 2016; Canivez et al., 2016) and CFA (Canivez & Watkins, 2016; Canivez et al., 2017) with the Wechsler Intelligence Scale for Children–Fifth Edition (Wechsler, 2014) illustrate applications of EFA and CFA principles and practices noted above (see also Chapter 2 this volume). For developing skills in use of model-based reliability and dimensionality, Watkins and Canivez (2022) provided a tutorial in using free software with application to the WISC–V as an example. Importantly, factor analytic methods are not simply abstract statistical procedures to reduce data to a more parsimonious explanation but methods to help understand and explain causal relationships that support a proposed scoring structure. Their importance should not be diminished or dismissed, and they are not merely esoteric exercises.

Diagnostic Utility

As previously discussed, reliability and its estimates help determine the consistency of observations and test scores and provide the foundation for all measurement. Validity methods involve research methods and findings that provide evidence that the test scores are satisfactorily measuring the intended construct. While test scores may have evidence supporting measurement of the intended construct, this does not necessarily mean that the scores are useful for clinical decisions as applied to individuals which frequently are high-stakes decisions. There may be many test scores and score comparisons that relate to a theoretical construct but do not have the necessary precision for correct classification or diagnostic accuracy when applied to individuals. This is the domain of *diagnostic utility* (sometimes referred to as *diagnostic validity* or *discriminative validity* (Haynes et al., 2018; [to differentiate it from discriminant validity]). As previously noted, distinct group differences validity is a necessary but not sufficient condition for tests, scores, or score comparisons when considering their utility for individual application. In distinct group differences there is often overlap in the score distributions for the control group (non-clinical comparison group) and the clinical group despite statistically significant mean differences. The larger the effect size for the mean difference between the two groups the greater the separation of the respective distributions and the less overlap there is (see Figure 1.2). The larger the effect size the greater the chances for use of a specified *cut-score* (cut-off score) to correctly differentiate individuals within each group. For individual application there are a variety of methods and procedures necessary to help determine the accuracy of individual decisions based on tests, scores, score comparisons, or score aggregation. An extremely useful primer on diagnostic utility and procedures is provided by Youngstrom (2014). Additionally, there are numerous well-crafted Wikipedia pages devoted to elements of diagnostic utility (e.g., https://en.wikipedia.org/wiki/Positive_and_negative_predictive_values)

Diagnostic Utility Procedures and Estimates

The starting point for assessing diagnostic utility is identical to distinct group differences where a sample of individuals with known characteristics that should be quantified by the target test scores or comparisons (clinical group) is identified using an independent criterion. Use of an independent criterion to create the groups helps avoid the circularity of using a test or scores to create the groups and then examine how well the test or scores worked in differentiating individuals in the groups. A comparison group comprised of individuals who do not have the condition or characteristics associated with the target test (control group) is identified and sometimes demographically matched, which is especially useful in small samples where random selection may not produce demographically equated groups. It is also possible to use a comparison group with a different but related disorder to assess differential diagnosis, a more difficult task than comparing those with disorders to those without. Participants in both groups are administered the test and analyses conducted to determine if test scores (or score comparisons) can correctly identify which group the individuals came from.

Univariate Classification

In the simplest example, consider the earlier illustration of an anxiety test (GAS) and a sample of individuals with an anxiety disorder that had significantly higher GAS scores than a sample of individuals without an anxiety disorder. Because classification, diagnosis, or selection is a binary decision, a decision threshold, criterion, or cut-score must be selected to decide which individuals demonstrate a score high enough to warrant classification of having the disorder or not. In Figure 1.7, three different cut-scores (scores at or above the cut-score results in classification as "anxiety disorder") are presented to illustrate effects on individual classifications. For a cut-score $T = 55$ (a liberal cut-score) approximately 2/3 of the individuals in the Anxiety Disorder group would be correctly classified (true positive) while approximately 2/3 of the individuals in the Random Normal group would also be correctly classified (true negative). But approximately 1/3 of the individuals in

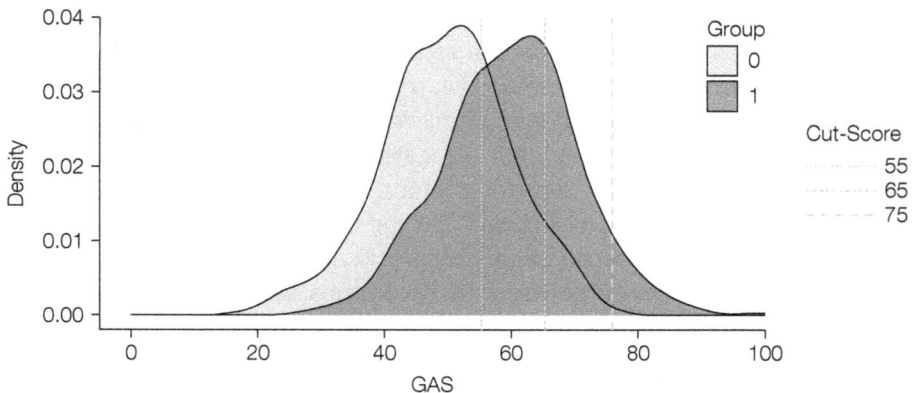

Figure 1.7. Illustration of Score Distributions for Two Randomly Simulated Groups with Various Cut Scores. *Note.* Score distributions for two randomly simulated groups (0 = Random Normal [$n = 500$], 1 = Anxiety Disorder [$n = 500$]) for a hypothetical anxiety test (GAS = General Anxiety Scale) that was scaled as T scores ($M_T = 50$, $SD_T = 10$). Random Normal ($M = 49.76$, $SD = 10.21$), Anxiety Disorder ($M = 59.80$, $SD = 10.57$), $t(998) = 15.29$, $p < .0001$, Cohen's $d = .97$, "Large" effect size, translating to an AUC of .75. Cut-scores illustrated reflect liberal ($T = 55$), moderate ($T = 65$), or conservative ($T = 75$) decision thresholds.

the Anxiety Disorder group would be incorrectly classified (false negative) while approximately 1/3 of individuals in the Random Normal group would be incorrectly classified (false positive). If increasing the cut-score to $T = 65$ (or $T = 75$), the result would be to increase the number of true negatives and reduce the number of false positives while simultaneously increasing the number of false negatives and reducing the number of true positives. Thus, decisions are affected by the selected cut-score, and one may choose a cut-score that guards against false negative or false positive decisions. Decisions are also affected by the effect size of the group mean differences, and as previously noted, as the effect size increases, the amount of overlap of the two distributions decreases. If the two distributions do not overlap at all then a cut-score placed between them would result in perfect classification with no false positive or false negative decisions. Thus, test scores or score comparisons that produce distinct group distributions that overlap very little will be more likely to be diagnostically useful.

Multivariate Methods for Classification

Two statistical methods are frequently used to initially assess differentiation of individuals within groups when a set of predictors is used: *discriminant function analysis* (DFA) and *logistic regression* (LR). The goals of DFA and LR are the same and results similar but they are based on different mathematical computations and assumptions. Tabachnick and Fidell (2019) provide separate chapters for DFA and LR with detailed explanations, assumptions, and examples for application. Because DFA and LR statistically maximize the separation of the groups and bias is associated with classifications when individual cases are used in creating DFA and LR classification coefficients that are also used to statistically reassign individuals to groups based on those coefficients, cross-validation of results with an independent sample is needed.

Discriminant Function Analysis. Discriminant function analysis (DFA) is multivariate analysis of variance (MANOVA) reversed. In MANOVA, the group variable is the independent variable and the set of test scores are the dependent variables to determine if the groups differ on the set of test scores. In DFA, the procedure uses the set of test scores as independent variables to predict group membership. For each group DFA produces a formula containing standardized coefficients (weights) applied to each independent variable (test score) and a constant, and these may later be used in evidence-based classification in determining to which group an individual being assessed more likely belongs. Larger weights indicate variables with a stronger association distinguishing individuals in the groups. An illustration for such classification formulae in a two-group comparison is provided below:

$$\text{Group 1} = b_{1_1} X_{1_1} + b_{2_1} X_{2_1} + b_{3_1} X_{3_1} + \ldots b_{k_1} X_{k_1} + b_{0_1}$$

$$\text{Group 2} = b_{1_2} X_{1_2} + b_{2_2} X_{2_2} + b_{3_2} X_{3_2} + \ldots b_{k_2} X_{k_2} + b_{0_2}$$

with unique coefficients b_j and test score predictors X_j ($j = 1, \ldots, k$), and unique constants (b_0) produced by DFA for each group.

In a three-group comparison there would be a Group 3 formula with its unique coefficients and constant. As provided in McDermott (1994), Canivez (1998), and Canivez and Sprouls (2005), an individual's test scores in a clinical evaluation may be entered into the classification formulae when studies provide the b coefficients, with the formula (Group 1 vs. Group 2) producing the higher score being the group the individual most resembles and should be so classified. Such application allows for an evidence-based and actuarial decision rather than a decision based on clinical judgment and will be more reliable among and between clinicians because it facilitates consistent use (McDermott, 1981; Meehl, 1954; Meehl & Rosen, 1955).

Logistic Regression. Logistic Regression (LR) is especially useful if independent variables (test scores) are nonlinear, if sample sizes are very unequal, or distributional assumptions are untenable and predictors (test scores) may be continuous, discrete, dichotomous, or a combination (Tabachnick & Fidell, 2019). The dependent variable (group) may be a binary outcome like diagnoses (0 [No], 1 [Yes]) or more than 2 outcomes so it is possible to attempt to differentiate more than two groups as in DFA. LR is relatively free of restrictions so it is a frequently used method. LR will produce coefficients (weights [b]) for each independent variable (test score [X]) and a constant (b_0) that when solved will produce a z value as illustrated below:

$$z = b_1 X_1 + b_2 X_2 + b_3 X_3 + \ldots b_k X_k + b_0$$

This z value is then used in a formula to estimate the probability of the condition or event (Glass & Hopkins, 1996) illustrated below:

$$Probability\,of\,event\,(1) = \frac{1}{1 + e^{-z}}$$

where e = base of natural log ($\cong 2.718$).

Coding the control group variable as 0 and the clinical group as 1 indicates this formula will be predicting the probability that an individual with test scores entered into the z formula above has the condition. Application of these formulae in clinical decision-making is another evidence-based approach that can facilitate consistent application and increased classification reliability.

Diagnostic Utility Statistics (Conditional Probabilities)

If DFA or LR is statistically significant then further assessment of classification accuracy is conducted. Using the DFA or LR formulae, each participant in the clinical group and control group is reclassified based on their individual scores entered into the formulae and then reassigned based on the statistical decision of which group they mathematically most resemble. These are then compared to the groups from which they came. A 2 X 2 matrix (in a 2-group comparison), sometimes referred to as a *confusion matrix*, will include the frequencies of correct classifications (true positive, true negative) and incorrect classifications (false positive, false negative) and allow for calculation of various conditional probabilities (see Figure 1.8) standardized by Kessel and Zimmerman (1993). Canivez and Watkins (1996) created an Excel spreadsheet template (see Figure 1.9) to automate calculation of conditional probabilities as well as calculation of the kappa coefficient and its statistical significance based on Kessel and Zimmerman's article although these are now available in numerous web-based calculators (e.g., Schwartz, 2006) and stand-alone programs (Watkins, 2020b). As noted above, DFA and LR studies need to be cross-validated (see Reynolds & Mason, 2009; Willson & Reynolds, 1982) with an independent sample (or multiple independent samples), which may take additional time and likely will result in lower accuracy estimates (shrinkage), but there is a statistical method for approximating cross-validation (the jackknife procedure) where the DFA or LR estimations are made holding one participant out while estimating DFA or LR classification coefficients and then applying those results to the held-out individual. This is iteratively repeated for each participant, and classification results compared to the original findings and shrinkage can thus be observed.

Conditional probabilities defined in Table 1.3 and formulae presented in Kessel and Zimmerman (1993) emerged from Bayes's theorem (Bayes & Price, 1763), and understanding the different estimates and their implications is crucial. Frequently there is much discussion about the sensitivity and specificity of tests, test scores, or diagnostic signs (markers). These probabilities relate to the

		Diagnostic Condition (True State)		
		Present	Absent	Total
Test Result	Positive	a (True Positive)	b (False Positive)	a+b
	Negative	c (False Negative)	d (True Negative)	c+d
	Total	a+c	b+d	a+b+c+d

a, b, c, and d are cell frequencies in applying selection criteria

Diagnostic Efficiency (Utility) Conditional Probabilities

Sensitivity (True Positive Rate = $a/(a+c)$
Specificity (True Positive Rate) = $d/(b+d)$
Positive Predictive Power (Value) = $a/(a+b)$
Negative Predictive Power (Value) = $d/(c+d)$
False Positive Rate = $b/(b+d)$
False Negative Rate = $c/(a+c)$
Overall Correct Classification (Hit) Rate = $(a+d)/N$

Observed Agreement P_o = $a+d)/N$
Chance Agreement P_c = $((a+b)(a+c)+(c+d)(b+d))/N^2$
Kappa = $(P_o-P_c)/(1-P_c)$

Figure 1.8. **2X2 Diagnostic Efficiency (Utility) Table (Confusion Matrix) With Conditional Probability Formulae.**

Diagnostic Efficiency Table

		Diagnosis		
		Present	Absent	Total
Test	Positive	65	5	70
	Negative	10	100	110
	Total	75	105	180

Results

Sensitivity (True Positive Rate) = 0.87
Specificity (True Negative Rate) = 0.95
Positive Predictive Power = 0.93
Negative Predictive Power = 0.91
False Positive Rate = 0.05
False Negative Rate = 0.13
Overall Correct Classification (Hit) Rate = 0.92

Observed Agreement Po = 0.92
Chance Agreement Pc = 0.52

Kappa = 0.83
Standard Error of Kappa = 0.07

Significance Test for Kappa Ho: k = 0   Z = 11.12
p < 0   two-tail test
p < 0   one-tail test

Figure 1.9. **Diagnostic Efficiency (Utility) Table Template Calculations From Canivez and Watkins (1996).**

positive test result or sign among those with the condition or a negative test result or sign among those without the condition. However, clinically, the more important conditional probabilities may be positive predictive power (PPP) and negative predictive power (NPP), which are probabilities that those with a positive test result or sign actually have the condition or those with a negative test result or sign actually do not have the condition (Landau et al., 1991; Milich et al., 1987). Clinical application of test scores for classification is particularly interested in distinguishing between those with and those without a disorder or condition. An illustration by Dawes (2001) related to smoking and lung cancer is instructive: the probability of being a chronic smoker among those with lung cancer is about .90 (sensitivity) but the probability of having lung cancer among those who were chronic smokers is about .10 (PPP). In psychology, clinicians are usually asked to determine if a client has or does not have a particular condition or disorder, which means the more important conditional probabilities are PPP to rule-in disorders and NPP to rule-out disorders (Swets et al., 2000; Treat & Viken, 2012; Youngstrom, 2014). Canivez and Sprouls (2005) and Canivez and Gaboury (2016) provide examples of studies using DFA and diagnostic utility statistics that go beyond simple distinct group differences comparisons. Figures 1.10 and 1.11 illustrate discriminant function density plots from Canivez and Gaboury (2016) and Canivez and Sprouls (2005) data, respectively, to illustrate the group separation and the greater diagnostic utility when distributions overlap less.

However, because PPP and NPP are affected by the base rate (prevalence) and the cut-score (decision threshold), consideration of the positive likelihood ratio (LR+) and negative likelihood ratio (LR-) are also valuable in application. These likelihood ratios, which are derived from the sensitivity and specificity estimates, are independent of the base rate so may be more likely to generalize beyond the sample where they were generated (Pepe, 2003). These methods have been long advocated in evidence-based medicine (Gray, 2004; Straus et al., 2019) and evidence-based psychological assessment (Garb & Wood, 2019; Youngstrom et al., 2017).

Table 1.3 Conditional Probability Definitions for Diagnostic Utility

Sensitivity (True Positive Rate)	Among those with the condition or disorder, the probability of having a positive test score or result.
Specificity (True Negative Rate)	Among those without the condition or disorder, the probability of having a negative test score or result.
Positive Predictive Power (Value)	Among those having a positive test score or result, the probability of having the condition or disorder.
Negative Predictive Power (Value)	Among those having a negative test score or result, the probability of not having the condition or disorder.
False Positive Rate	Among those without the condition or disorder, the probability of having a positive test score or result.
False Negative Rate	Among those with the condition or disorder, the probability of having a negative test score or result.
Overall Correct Classification (Hit) Rate	The proportion of those with and without the condition or disorder who were correctly identified by the test score or result.

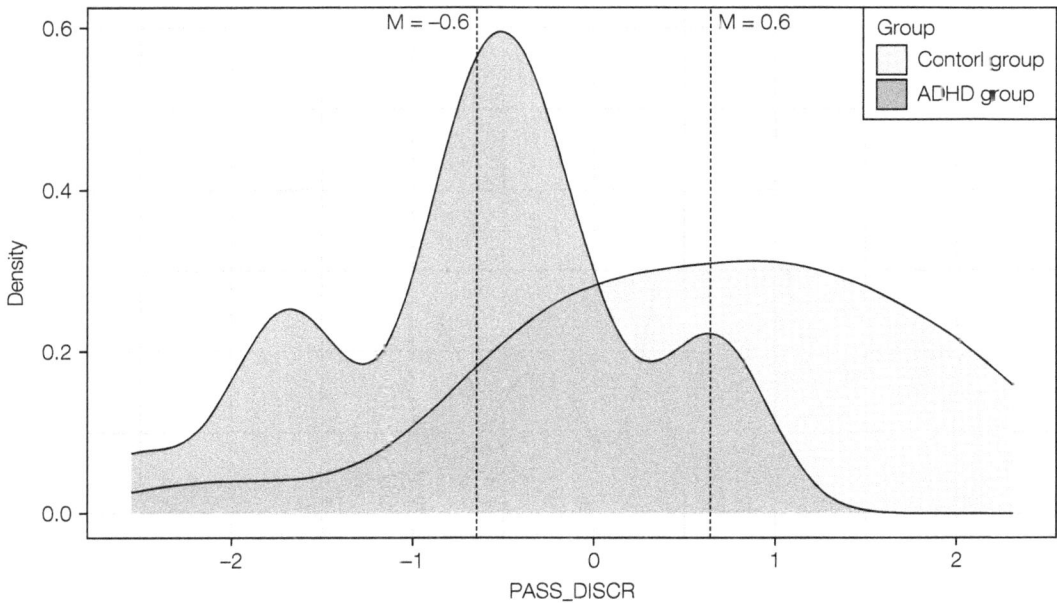

Figure 1.10. **Density Plots of the PASS Discriminant Function for the ADHD (*n* = 20) and Control (*n* = 20) Groups from Canivez and Gaboury (2016) Discriminant Function Analysis.**

LR+ is calculated by sensitivity/(1-specificity) to indicate how much a positive test result increases the odds of having the disorder or condition and is a statistic used to rule-in a disorder or condition. A LR+ value of 5.0 would indicate that a positive test result is five times more likely among those with the disorder or condition than those without the disorder or condition. LR+ values > 5 indicate strong evidence of diagnostic value while LR+ > 10 indicate convincing evidence (Deeks, 2001). LR- is calculated by (1-sensitivity)/specificity to indicate how much a negative test result decreases the odds of having the disorder or condition and is a statistic used to rule-out a disorder or condition. LR- values < .20 indicate strong evidence of diagnostic value while LR- < .10 indicate convincing evidence (Deeks, 2001). Thus, a general rule of thumb for minimal adequacy of diagnostic tests or scores is DLR+ ≥ 10 and DLR- ≤ .10. This information is easily obtained from studies that publish diagnostic utility statistics, and a low-tech method of application for use in individual clinical cases (and thus evidence based) is the probability nomogram that is illustrated in Figure 1.12 (e.g., Youngstrom, 2014). Jenkins et al. (2011) reported large improvements in accuracy when probability nomograms were used compared to traditional individual clinical judgment. There are now web-based nomogram calculators that allow one to select pretest probability and likelihood ratios (LR+ and LR-) and then the post-test probability is estimated. Schwartz (2006) created a very useful online calculator for DES (http://araw.mede.uic.edu/cgi-bin/testcalc.pl) that generates numerous statistics, including a probability nomogram.

As illustrated above, cut-scores will affect calculation of conditional probabilities, but estimation of overall accuracy and conditional probabilities (except sensitivity and specificity) is also affected by base rates of the condition (Treat & Viken, 2012; Youngstrom, 2014). Often, studies will have equal numbers of participants in the clinical group and in the control group, which means the base rate of disordered individuals is 50%. Clinical disorders, however, are not so prevalent, affecting perhaps 1%, 2%, 5%, or 10% of the overall population. Alternatively, clinics specializing in

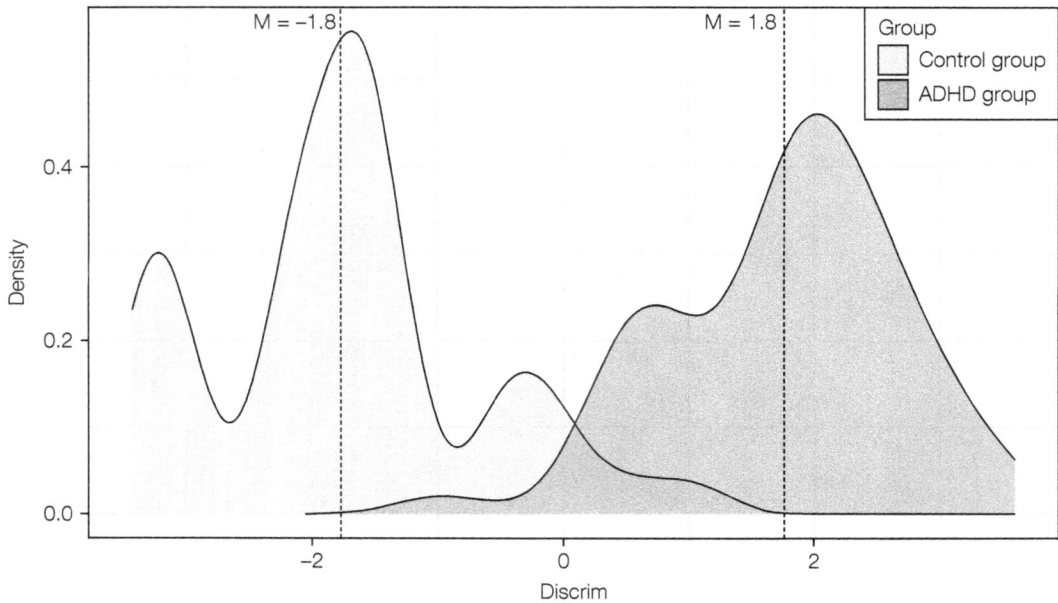

Figure 1.11. **Density Plots of the ASCA Discriminant Function for the ADHD (n = 53) and Control (n = 53) Groups from Canivez and Sprouls (2005) Discriminant Function Analysis.**

assessment and treatment of specific disorders might have base rates for the specialized disorder considerably higher than the population base rate; thus examination and assessment of diagnostic utility in specific settings is important, and results will likely vary (Youngstrom, 2014). Additional considerations relate to cut-scores and consequences for false positive or false negative decisions and the purpose for the assessment. If a false negative result is worse than a false positive result, then one may select a cut-score that protects against false negative decisions (at the expense of more false positives). In psychology and education, it may not be clear which is the worst type of error (false positive or false negative) so selecting a cut-score that balances the two errors may be appropriate. If the assessment is to be used for screening rather than diagnostic purposes, then it would be reasonable to select a cut-score that guards against false negatives, and while the screening may result in more false positives, the follow-up assessments (with more precise but more expensive [time and money] tests) will help identify which of the false positive results might be true positive cases (Kraemer, 1992). A method that assesses the diagnostic accuracy that is unaffected by cut-scores and base rates is the receiver operator characteristic (ROC) curve, which has been extensively used in assessing diagnostic systems in a variety of fields (Swets, 1988; Swets et al., 2000; Youngstrom, 2014).

Receiver Operator Characteristic (ROC) Curve Analysis

Receiver operator characteristic (ROC) curve analysis has its origins during World War II where it was used by the U.S. Army to assess the ability of radar receiver operators to accurately detect a radar signal of Japanese aircraft by separating the signal from the noise (Pierce, 1980). Later, ROC entered use in many diagnostic assessments in psychology, medicine, and engineering (Kraemer, 1992; Swets, 1988; Swets et al., 2000). The ROC analysis method plots the true positive rate (sensitivity) on the y-axis and the false negative rate (1-specificity) on the x-axis

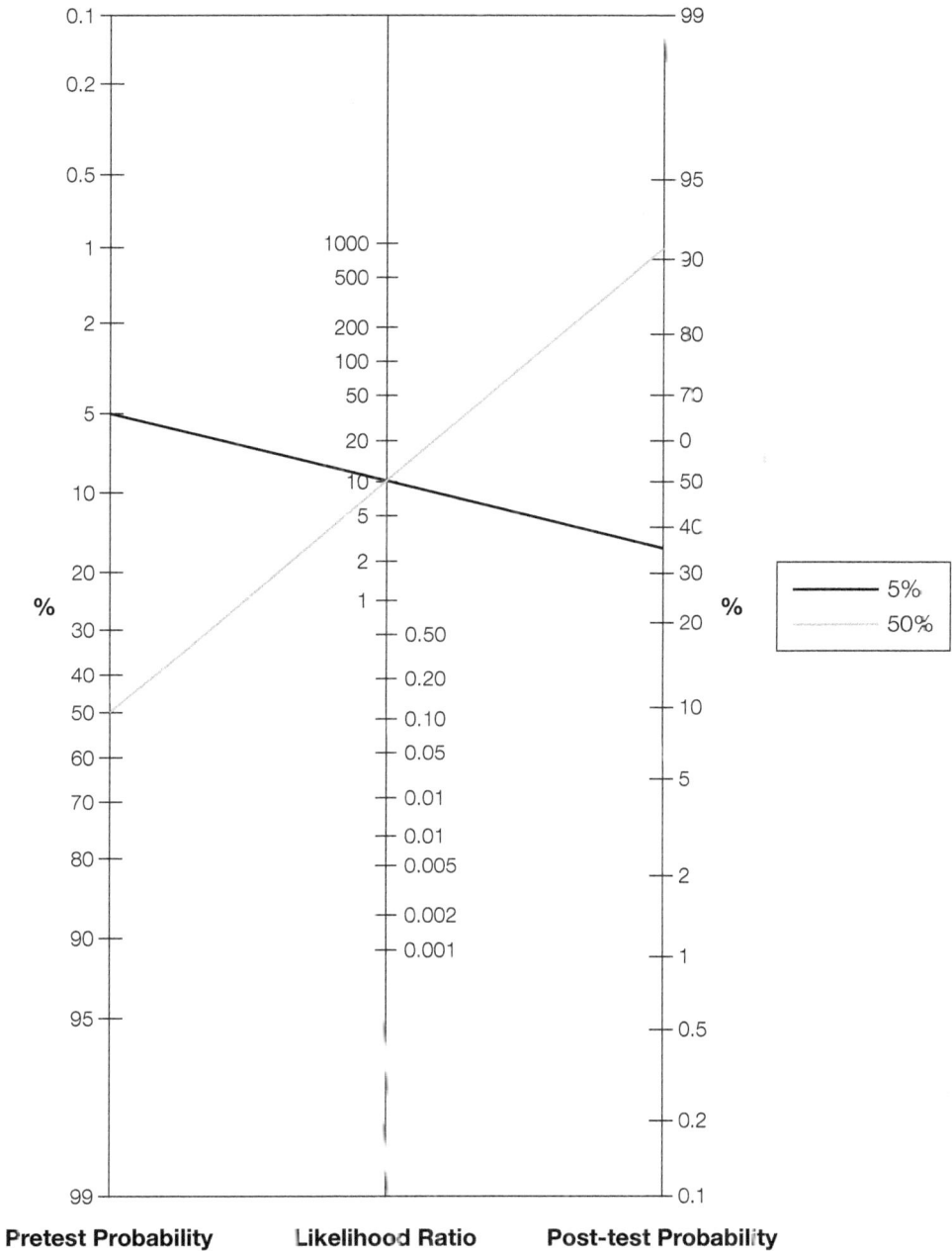

		5%
		50%

Pretest Probability   Likelihood Ratio   Post-test Probability

Figure 1.12. **Probability Nomogram Examples**. *Note.* With a diagnostic likelihood ratio (LR+) of 10 based on diagnostic utility statistics, a pretest probability of 50% (perhaps a base rate from a study with equal numbers of clinical and control participants) indicates a person testing positive would have a 91% post-test probability of matching the clinical group. However, if the pretest probability was 5% (perhaps a population base rate of a condition) then a person testing positive would have a 34% post-test probability of matching the clinical group. https://en.wikiversity.org/wiki/File:Probability_nomogram_--_useful_for_combining_probability_ and_new_information_that_changes_odds,_as_used_in_Evidence-Based_Medicine_and_Evidence-Based_ Assessment_01.pdf

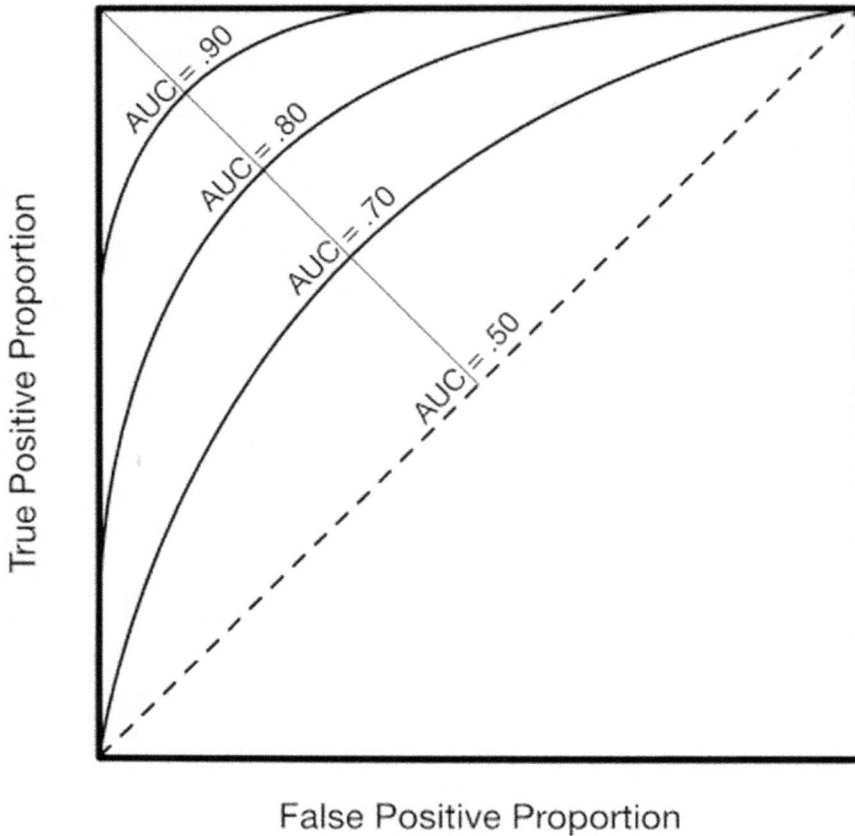

Figure 1.13. **Example ROC Curves with Varying Accuracy.**

for different cut-scores. In addition, the area under the curve (AUC) is estimated and provides a probabilistic meaning (Treat & Viken, 2012). Figure 1.13 illustrates various ROC curves. The diagonal line bisecting the ROC space is a line representing random classification accuracy, and the area under that line is .50. As diagnostic accuracy increases the ROC curve moves closer to the top-left corner and the amount of area underneath the curve increases. Application of ROC curves for the Canivez and Gaboury (2016) and Canivez and Sprouls (2005) data distinguishing individuals meeting ADHD criteria from random and matched normal (typical) children are illustrated in Figure 1.14. Benchmarks for area under the curve were provided by Swets (1996) with AUC between .50 and .70 indicating low accuracy, AUC between .70 to .90 reflecting medium accuracy, and AUC between .90 to 1.00 indicating high accuracy. Caution must be exercised when considering AUCs that exceed .90, particularly when the classifications are trivially easy such as differentiating "very ill" from "healthy controls" (see Youngstrom et al., 2019). Once ROC analyses show accuracy and functionality, an optimum cut-score needs to be selected and assessed using the conditional probabilities discussed above. Treat and Viken (2012) discuss several methods to assess optimum cut-scores from ROC analyses but also note the important consideration of the purpose of assessment and which decision error (false negative or false positive) is judged more problematic.

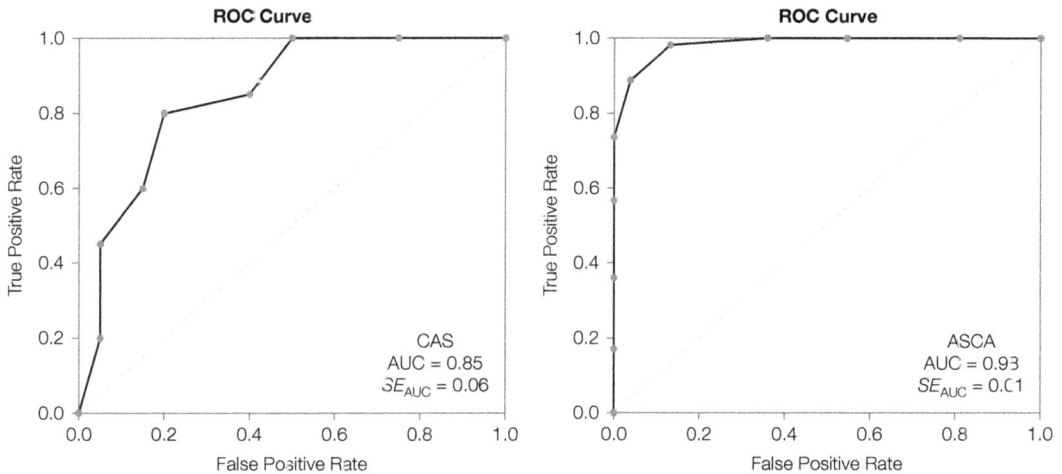

Figure 1.14. **Example ROC Curves Illustrating Diagnostic Utility.** *Note.* ROC curves illustrating diagnostic utility in classifying students meeting independent ADHD criteria for the Cognitive Assessment System (CAS; Naglieri & Das, 1997) from Canivez and Gaboury (2016) data (ADHD $n = 20$, Control $n = 20$) and Adjustment Scales for Children and Adolescents (ASCA; McDermott et al., 1993) from Canivez and Sprouls (2005) data (ADHD $n = 53$, Control $n = 53$). AUC = Area Under the Curve. $AUC_{CAS} < AUC_{ASCA}$, $z = -2.14$, $p < .0326$ (Hanley & McNeil, 1983).

Test Bias and Test Fairness

Bias in testing and test fairness are not just contemporary concerns as they have been a matter of concern (and debate) for many decades particularly within the area of intelligence (mental) testing (see Brown et al., 1999; Jensen, 1980a, 1980b; Reynolds, 1982; Reynolds & Brown, 1984; Reynolds & Kaiser, 1990; Reynolds et al., 1999; Reynolds & Suzuki, 2013). *Bias* and *fairness* are terms that require definition because they are not identical (Jensen, 1980a, 1980b). *Test bias* is a term that refers to the extent that test scores mean different things for members of different groups when bias is observed. It suggests differential interpretation of scores depending on what group an individual belongs to. That is, bias is present when there are systematic influences on test scores producing group differences not related to the construct being measured (Jensen, 1980a, 1980b). Bias is obviously problematic as a biased test would convey differential construct meaning depending on group membership. Test bias also refers to the extent to which test scores produce different outcomes or results so predictions or classifications may substantially differ by group. Jensen (1980a, 1980b) contextualized bias relative to features within the test (internal manifestations) and features related to test relationships with external variables (external manifestations). Zumbo (1999), Embretson and Reise (2000), and Furr (2022) also presented internal and external evaluation of bias in tests paralleling Jensen and referred to the internal methods as detecting *construct bias* and external methods detecting *predictive bias*. Thus test bias is empirically oriented and assessed by examination of various test psychometric properties (reliability, validity, utility) across various important subgroups (race/ethnicity, sex/gender, culture, nationality, socioeconomic status, age). A non-biased test would have equivalent (invariant) reliability, elements of validity, and diagnostic utility across the important subgroups with which the test is used.

Why is test bias important? Test bias is important because test scores should reflect the same construct for all test takers and not contain construct-irrelevant variance (Messick, 1989, 1995). Biased tests lead to erroneous inferences about individuals against whom the test is biased, and clinical decisions made with individuals may thus be biased. Much of the focus on test bias is on clinical applications and decisions regarding individuals and groups against whom the test is biased primarily because many such uses involve high-stakes decisions, but test bias will also impact research. When a biased test is used in research, study findings may be the result of test bias rather than the phenomenon being studied. While bias studies have focused primarily on intelligence and educational tests, assessment of bias in tests of personality, psychopathology, and other psychological constructs is also important (Walker, 2011). Test bias and its effects have ethical ramifications as pointed out earlier, and there are also legal considerations. For example, the Individuals with Disabilities Education Improvement Act of 2004 (IDEIA 2004; Public Law [P.L.] 108–446) continues "the longstanding requirement that procedures used for the evaluation and placement of children with disabilities not be discriminatory on racial or cultural basis" (p. 32). Thus, those using tests and procedures for identification of students with disabilities need to know if the tests or procedures they use are free from racial or cultural bias that could result in discriminatory impact. When such studies are unavailable, it will not be possible to know if or how a test is biased, and unbiased (or biased) measurement should not be assumed (Reynolds & Suzuki, 2013). *Standards* (AERA et al., 2014) also requires investigation of potential test bias.

Test fairness, however, differs from tests bias in that test fairness relates to judgments, opinions, and beliefs about test use and score adequacy (Jensen, 1980a, 1980b; Reynolds & Suzuki, 2013) but is not a psychometric property of test scores. Fairness is rooted in social, philosophical, political, or other perspectives but should not be dismissed outright simply because it is more subjective. At the same time, fairness is much more open to individual opinion or value judgments where agreement may be difficult. It is more likely that the lay public and those without psychometric literacy will have perspectives about test bias that are not empirically informed and likely reflects their judgments or beliefs about fairness yet use the term *bias*. Group differences in mean test scores are often used as de facto evidence of bias (Jensen, 1980a, 1980b; Reynolds & Suzuki, 2013), but as Furr (2022) and other measurement experts point out, mean score differences are not by itself evidence of test bias, and cannot directly inform us about fairness (Thorndike, 1971). Reynolds and Suzuki also point out that group mean differences may not be adequate indicators of bias because means are point estimates for an entire distribution, and distribution characteristics such as skewness, kurtosis, and variance or standard deviations may also vary between two groups possibly rendering the mean a poor indicator of central tendency of the underlying distribution. Alternatively, it is possible that two groups could differ on the measured characteristic and the test means may actually reflect true differences between the groups. However, attempts to discern causal mechanisms underlying observed group differences, particularly regarding ethnicity/race, is highly contentious and evokes strong opinions in such discussions. Thus, it is not surprising that many scholars are apprehensive and avoid such discussions or research in this area, resulting in emergence of more partisan perspectives.

Assessment of test bias is provided by the psychometric methods previously discussed (and some additional ones) but with an emphasis on comparisons between various population subgroups. Where test score reliability, validity, and diagnostic utility differ between various subgroups (frequently comparing a minority group [focal group] to a majority group [reference group]) such differential results may qualify score use and may reflect the influence of bias in measurement.

Assessing Internal Bias Indicators/Construct Bias

Differential Reliability

Assessment of differential internal consistency, test-retest (stability), alternate forms (equivalence), and interrater agreement reliability should be provided across all important subgroups a test is to be used with. While internal consistency estimates are typically the focus of comparison for bias research, other reliability estimates (stability, equivalence, interrater agreement) should also not differ between groups and should be examined (Jensen, 1980a, 1980b). When significant differences in reliability estimates are observed, a judgment about minimal adequacy needs to be made (i.e., ≥ .80), and while lower reliability estimates may be determined to be adequate, lower reliability estimates require adjustments to obtained score or true score confidence intervals because the confidence intervals provided for the overall sample will not be accurate for the subgroups. This also indicates that test scores may have greater precision for some groups than others. One complication is that some subgroups in standardization or research samples may be too small to provide adequate estimates for comparisons as is often the case for Indigenous/Native Americans and Asian Americans in the United States. In such cases it will not be possible to know if differential reliability exists. This is why it is crucial that test developers and publishers oversample smaller population subgroups so that such assessments may be conducted and reported to inform test users. Example studies that examined differential longitudinal stability of WISC–III (Wechsler, 1991) scores across race/ethnicity, sex, and age (Canivez & Watkins, 1999) and across disability (Canivez & Watkins, 2001) showed that long-term test-retest stability coefficients of WISC–III composite scores were very similar across the various groups and were not statistically different, indicating a lack of differential reliability (longitudinal stability) or bias across these demographic variables (Jensen, 1980a, 1980b). Differences in reliability coefficients can be statistically tested to aid in this determination (Feldt, 1969, 2006).

As just illustrated, some methods to assess potential test bias are conducted at the test score or composite score level (macro-statistical [Walker, 2011]), but methods to assess bias at the item level (micro-statistical [Walker, 2011]) are also of great value and essential in test development and evaluation of standardization and independent samples. What is now generally referred to as *differential item functioning* (DIF) was once referred to as *item bias* (Embretson & Reise, 2000; French & Finch, 2016; Zumbo, 2007). Zumbo (1999) noted that biased test items contain irrelevant or extraneous sources of variance that influence individuals' responses, which impacts performance and thus test scores. In test development, identification of such items allows test authors and developers to modify the item or discard the item in favor of alternate items. In the test development phase, expert review panels may be used to help determine if test item content contains items that appear to potentially be insensitive or biased, but this is a nonstatistical (judgmental) approach that is not a viable substitute for statistical approaches in identifying item bias. French and Finch (2016) provided a non-exhaustive variety of methods (nonstatistical; statistical but not accounting for ability; statistical and accounting for ability) frequently used to detect DIF and also provided very useful descriptions of DIF and applications (see also Walker, 2011; Zumbo, 1999, 2007).

What follows is a more general description of methods to assess item level bias, but more detailed elements, strengths, and limitations will require further study of referenced works.

Differential Rank Order

Jensen (1980a, 1980b) and Furr (2022) noted that differential rank orders of test item difficulties between different groups may be observed for tests containing items with different difficulty levels. The Spearman rank-order correlation coefficient (r_{rho}) of the ranked item difficulties could be compared between groups and if significantly lower for a specific group, then bias may be present as the lower correlation indicates the items do not perform similarly for the two groups. Jensen (1980a, 1980b) and Reynolds and Suzuki (2013) further indicated that when differential rank order is observed there is a need to assess why such differences were observed.

Differential Item Discrimination

Item discrimination is an index of the degree to which performance on an item is related to total test performance. That is, those scoring higher on a test (higher ability) would be more likely to answer an item correctly compared to those scoring lower on the test (lower ability). Assessment of differential item discrimination between groups can help identify if particular items have approximately equivalent item discrimination or not. Items not having approximately equal discrimination are probably biased and may require modification or removal to reduce bias.

Differential Item Functioning

Neither differential rank order nor differential item discrimination accounts for ability levels of individuals, which is problematic because item responses are expected to vary based on amounts of the latent construct. Thus methods not matching individuals (conditioning) based on level of the latent construct are no longer recommended (French & Finch, 2016). More sophisticated methods to assess item level differences between groups that may reflect DIF have been developed and extensively used. One early, well-tested, and effective method is the Mantel-Haenszel (MH) procedure (Mantel & Haenszel, 1959; Holland & Thayer, 1988), which is a χ^2 contingency table approach to compare item responses of a focal group (e.g., minority group [hypothesized disadvantaged group]) to item responses of a reference group (e.g., majority group [hypothesized advantaged group]). Three statistics are used in the MH procedure with the first being the $MH\chi^2$ for each item comparing item responses (correct or incorrect) by group (focal or reference) across the ability continuum divided into k intervals (conditioning). The second statistic used is the odds ratio (α_{MH}) reflecting the odds a reference group person responds correctly compared to the odds a focal group person responding correctly. Finally, a third statistic is created by multiplying the odds ratio (α_{MH}) by -2.35 to produce a Δ_{MH} (see French & Finch, 2016 for details).

Another DIF method uses logistic regression (LR) to identify DIF. Swaminathan and Rogers (1990) and Zumbo (1999) noted three advantages of LR over other methods like the MH procedure. Use of LR retains the continuous criterion variable, can model uniform and non-uniform DIF, and may be used with ordinal item scores. For ability and achievement tests where items are typically binary scores, items in personality or psychopathology tests often have items rated on an ordinal (graded response) rating scale. Ordinal logistic regression has the same modeling approach as that of binary logistic regression, simplifies the method by using a common statistical model, and has a test statistic with an effect size estimate (Zumbo-Thomas DIFF effect size; Zumbo, 1999). The formula below illustrates the LR for DIF:

$$y = b_0 + b_1 \mathbf{A}\text{biliy} + b_2 \mathbf{G}\text{roup} + b_3 \mathbf{AG}$$

where y (dependent variable) is the probability of answering an item correctly (the natural log of the odds ratio); b_0 is the intercept term; and b_1, b_2, and b_3, are the respective regression coefficients for the independent variable effects; $\mathbf{A}$bility is the conditioning independent variable and typically a total score; $\mathbf{G}$roup is the dummy coded (1 = reference, 2 = focal) independent variable representing the comparison groups; and $\mathbf{AG}$ is the interaction of $\mathbf{A}$bility X $\mathbf{G}$roup variables. LR thus assesses the relationship between item responses and the Ability (total score) variable, tests the Group effects indicating uniform DIF, and tests the interaction effect of Group X Ability indicating nonuniform DIF. DIF is identified when individuals matched on ability produce different item response probabilities (different LR curves). If LR curves do not differ then there is no DIF, and the tem is unbiased. Uniform DIF is indicated when groups have unequal intercepts and ability parameters, and nonuniform DIF is indicated when the interaction parameter is nonzero.

Item response theory based methods for DIF (French & Finch, 2016; Furr, 2022 Shealy & Stout, 1993; Swaminathan & Rogers, 1990; Walker, 2011; Zumbo, 1999, 2007) examine item characteristic curves (ICCs) between two groups to detect DIF. ICCs are logistic (S-curve) functions plotting the relationship between the probability of an item response across the continuum of the latent trait such that those with less of the latent attribute or trait have a lower probability of answering correctly and those with more of the latent attribute or trait have a higher probability of answering correctly (for binary items). If the ICCs of the two groups overlap, then the item functions similarly and does not appear to reflect bias or DIF. If the ICCs do not overlap, then there are three types of DIF that might be present: uniform DIF, nonuniform ordinal DIF, or nonuniform disordinal DIF. *Uniform DIF* is reflected when the ICCs of two groups significantly depart but are parallel and across the entire ability range one group has a consistently higher probability of answering the item correctly. This means that given equal levels of ability, individuals in one group have higher probabilities of correct item responses. In *nonuniform DIF* (ordinal or disordinal), the ICCs of two groups significantly depart and are not parallel, so the differences in the probability of correct item responses by the two groups is not consistent across ability level.

As Furr (2022) pointed out, IRT methods are more complex, and there are many issues regarding models (one-, two-, and three-parameter logistic [1PL, 2PL, 3PL] models), procedures, samples of items and people, and specialized software. What is presented here is merely introductory, and more details can be found in cited works. Zumbo (2007) indicated that with respect to samples of items and people, nonparametric IRT offers the advantage of not requiring as many items or people. Zumbo (2007) also indicated that in his view the third generation of DIF and future developments would address five purposes: "Fairness and equity in testing, Dealing with a possible threat to internal validity, Investigate the comparability of translated and/or adapted measures, Trying to understand item response processes, and Investigating lack of invariance" (pp. 230–231; see also Zumbo et al., 2015). An example of DIF analyses is provided in Reynolds and Kamphaus (2015b) in the reported use of Rasch-based (1PL model) DIF and the Mantel-Haenszel (MH) procedure to identify BASC–3 item bias across female and male, and African American, Hispanic, and White groups, but apparently not for Asian or "other" racial or ethnic groups. Reportedly "only a small number of items were removed" according to criteria "when a consistent pattern emerged across forms and levels" (Reynolds & Kamphaus, 2015b, p. 101). Measurement invariance at the item level is critical but can be examined beyond the test items.

Differential Factor Structure: Congruence and Measurement Invariance

Differential factor structure is critical for evaluating test validity in determining if a test measures the same constructs in the same way for various groups. As noted earlier, because the scoring of tests is reflected in the test structure, the structure of the test must be uniform across all important subgroups if the same scoring is to be used and the same inferences made. Further, different test structures for different groups might mean the composition of latent factors is different for different groups, which also complicates interpretation of the latent constructs. If a test has a different structure for various subgroups, then test scores may have different meanings and clinical inferences may be impacted. In research contexts, group comparisons may not be valid if the test structure differs for the groups to be compared. When a test has the same structure across different groups, we refer to this as *invariance*, which is highly desirable as it indicates a lack of construct bias and allows similar inferences and interpretations across groups.

As discussed previously, two general approaches to factor analysis are EFA and CFA, and both may be used to assess the extent to which test structure is the same for two or more groups. Also, as previously discussed, if the test items serve as measured variables (indicators), then EFA needs to begin with items and CFA needs to include items in proposed models. For EFA, when examining invariance, the focus will be on whether the factor pattern and/or structure coefficients produced in rotations of extracted factors differ between comparison groups. In such comparisons it is crucial that coefficients compared are based on identical extraction (maximum likelihood, principal factors, alpha factor extraction, etc.) and rotation (varimax, equimax, promax, etc.) methods. The Watkins (2020a) *Invariance* program includes three methods to assess factor invariance and calculates the Coefficient of Congruence (R_c; Burt, 1948; Lorenzo-Seva & ten Berge, 2006; Tucker, 1951; Wrigley & Neuhaus, 1955), Chi-Square Goodness of Fit, and Salient Variable Similarity Index (Cattell, 1949). The R_c ranges from -1 to 0 to +1 with .85–.94 reflecting fair similarity and ≥ .95 reflecting good similarity (Lorenzo-Seva & ten Berge, 2006) or "practical identity of the factors" (Jensen, 1998, p. 99). Thus, if the comparison groups' factors are congruent, this indicates the structure is not biased. Chi-Square Goodness of Fit "simultaneously tests for differences in pattern of loadings and size of loadings" (Jensen, 1980a, p. 449). Thus, statistically nonsignificant χ^2 values indicate the factors do not differ between the groups and indicates the factor structure is not biased. The Salient Variable Similarity Index (*s*) ranges from -1 (perfect negative congruence) to 0 (no congruence [chance agreement]) to +1 (perfect congruence [agreement]), and statistically significant *s* values > 0 (see Cattell, 1978) indicate factor structure match and the structure is not biased. The user must specify the factor coefficient salience, which is recommended to be .30 or .40 (Velicer et al., 1982; Watkins, 2020a). Example research using these EFA based invariance indexes can be found in Canivez (2006) comparing ASCA EFA of Ojibwe students to the ASCA normative sample; Canivez and Bohan (2006) comparing ASCA EFA of Yavapai Apache students to the ASCA normative sample; Canivez and Sprouls (2010) comparing ASCA EFA of Hispanic students to the ASCA normative sample and other varied samples; and Canivez and Beran (2009) comparing Canadian children to U.S. normative sample and U.S. Native American and Hispanic samples.

Use of CFA methods to assess factor structure invariance (factorial invariance) across various groups (sex/gender, race/ethnicity, etc.) utilizes multigroup CFA (MGCFA) procedures (Furr, 2022; Pendergast et al., 2017; Widaman & Olivera-Aguilar, 2023) to determine if model parameters are the same across the compared groups. When different groups have equivalent parameter estimates, measurement invariance is then assumed (not biased), but if not equivalent, then groups differ on that parameter and indicates construct bias. For measures where items are the measured variables or indicators (i.e., personality and psychopathology tests), model invariance should include item level data, but for some measures subtests are measured variables serving as the indicators (i.e., intelligence tests). The initial or baseline model is the starting point and includes the same factors and measured variables (indicators) associated with latent factors based on theory and past research. The baseline model also must specify the same fixed and free parameter estimates for each group. If the baseline model is a good fit for each of the comparison groups, then assessment of invariance may begin.

There are four successive and increasingly restrictive levels of factorial invariance. The first invariance level is *configural invariance* where the number of latent factors and the pattern of factor coefficients (loadings) are the same across comparison groups. This means that the measured variables (items or subtests) that load on specific latent factors are the same across the groups. The second invariance level is *metric invariance* (weak invariance) which includes the same number of factors and same measured variables loading on specific factors noted in configural invariance but adds the exact measured variable factor coefficients (loadings) are the same across the comparison groups. This indicates the units of measurement are the same for the different groups. The third invariance level is *scalar invariance* (strong invariance), which includes configural and metric invariance features (same measured variables load on the same number of factors with equivalent loadings across comparison groups) and adds equal measured variable (items or subtests) intercepts. When scalar invariance is met, two individuals from different groups who have the same level of the latent factor will obtain the same measured variable score (item or subtest); thus there is no systematic bias present. The final invariance level is *strict invariance* where in addition to all the other invariance elements it also includes equivalence of measured variable (item or subtest) error variance across comparison groups. Differences required to reject invariance include $\Delta CFI \leq .01$ and $\Delta RMSEA \leq .015$ for both factor loadings and intercepts and $\Delta SPMR \leq .03$ for factor loadings and $\leq .01$ for intercepts (Chen, 2007; Cheung & Rensvold, 2002). Nevertheless, strict invariance is rarely observed in the assessment literature, leading many methodologists to eschew this level of invariance.

Kush et al. (2001) provided an example of examination of WISC–III factor structure invariance comparing Caucasian/White and African American/Black children using both EFA and CFA methods and indicated that the WISC–III factor structure was quite similar. Dombrowski et al. (2021) published findings of WISC–V factorial invariance across sex, age, and clinical group using a very large clinical sample. Beaujean and McGlaughlin (2014) reported strict measurement invariance of RIAS subtests with a sample of Black and White students referred for special education evaluations, and Gygi et al. (2019) reported examination of RIAS invariance across four language groups.

Assessing External Bias Indicators/Test Use Bias

Differential Prediction: Predictive Validity Bias

One primary use of tests is to predict future performance on some criterion or outcome measure, which can be useful in selection, diagnosis, and placement. As such and presented earlier, a major method to assess validity is to examine how well the test predicts a criterion. In the context of test bias, a test that does not predict equally well across various groups may be biased, and test use may not be appropriate for some groups. Bias in prediction relates to the slope of the regression

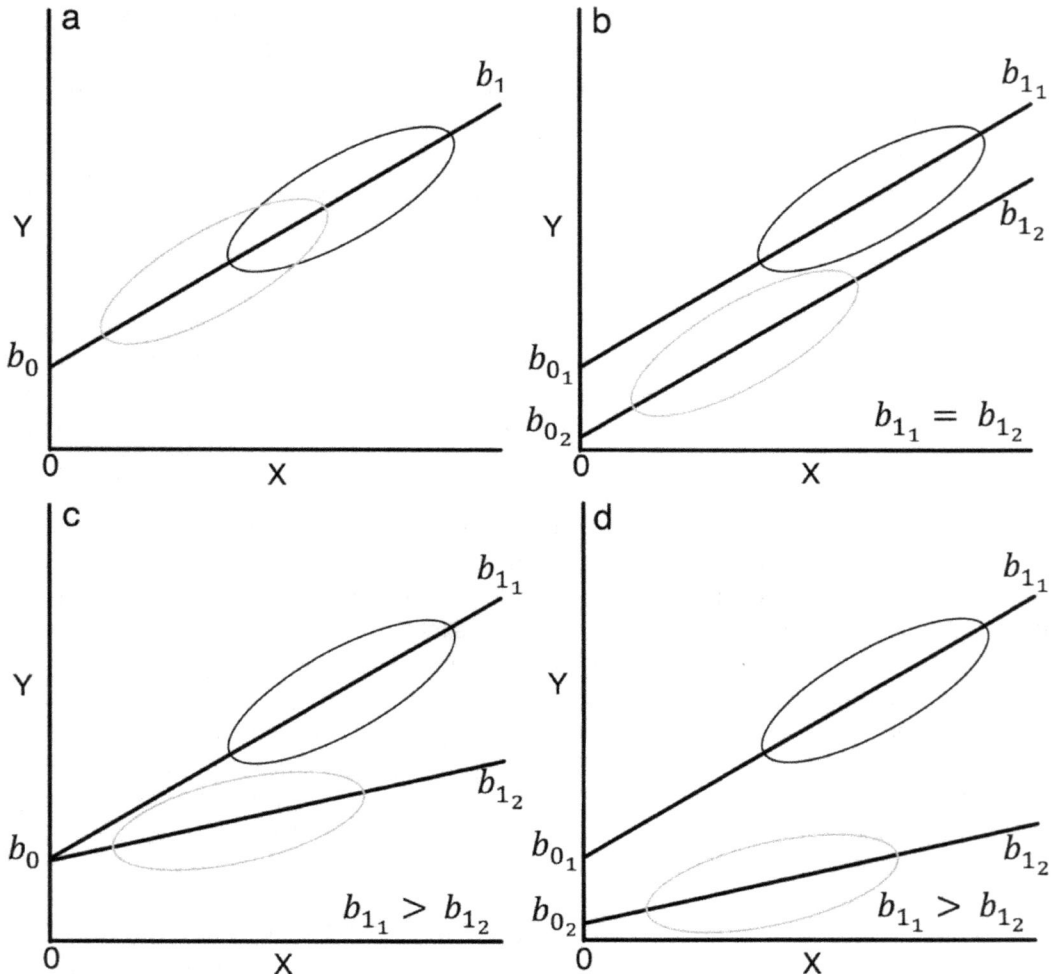

Figure 1.15. **Illustrations of Possible Predictive Validity and Indicators of Bias.** *Note.* Graph a illustrates no bias as both groups have the same regression line (same slope, same y-intercept). Graph b illustrates *intercept bias*. Graph c illustrates *slope bias*. Graph d illustrates *slope and intercept bias*. b_0 = regression line y-intercept, b_1 = regression line slope. Group 1 ellipse displayed in black, Group 2 ellipse displayed in grey.

line, which is directly related to the predictive validity coefficient (r_{xy}), and the *y*-intercept (where the regression line intersects with the y-axis (when X = 0). A test may be biased when various groups show differences in their separate regression line slopes, differences in *y*-intercepts, or both. Figure 1.15 illustrates four possible predictive validity alternatives where one group, on the average, scores higher on the predictor variable (X). Graph a illustrates there is no differential prediction because both groups have the same regression line (the same slope and *y*-intercept). Graph b illustrates what is referred to as *intercept bias* because the separate regression lines cross the *y* axis at different places. In this illustration, both regression lines have equivalent slopes, which means the predictive validity coefficients do not differ, which is good. This, however, means that for each value of X (Group 1 = Group 2) predicted Y scores will be higher for Group 1 than Group 2. Further, if a common regression line were used for Group 1 and Group 2, Group 1 predicted Y scores would be underestimated while Group 2 predicted Y scores were be overestimated. Graph c illustrates *slope bias* where the slope of the Group 1 regression line is higher than the slope of the Group 2 regression line. This also indicates that the predictive validity coefficient (r_{xy}) for Group 1 is higher than for Group 2. This is the most serious form of bias (Reynolds et al., 1999) because it relates to differential validity where the test is less valid for a group and errors of prediction will be larger as a result. Graph d illustrates both slope and intercept bias, which is a more complicated situation.

Differential criterion-related validity involves joint consideration of both *y*-intercept and slope differences among comparison groups. Assessment of differential prediction frequently uses Potthoff's (1966) procedure because it controls Type I error rates by providing a simultaneous *F* test for both *y*-intercept and slope differences (Canivez & Konold, 2001; Konold & Canivez, 2010; Weiss & Prifitera, 1995). Follow-up comparisons to detect whether differences exist between *y*-intercepts, slopes, or both are conducted for statistically significant omnibus *F* tests. In assessing predictive validity bias in the WISC–IV, Konold and Canivez (2010) found differential relationships in only 5 of the 30 omnibus comparisons but no differences were observed across race/ethnicity groups for WIAT–II and WISC–IV FSIQ scores. These results are consistent with other such assessments of intelligence tests and evidence for the equitable assessment of ability across groups differing by race/ethnicity (Reynolds, 2000) as well as sex/gender and parental education level. When the rare differential prediction is observed it is typically of *y*-intercept bias and operates in favor of the minority group (i.e., criterion performance was generally overpredicted for minority groups) rather than against them (Brown et al., 1999).

A related and well-known concern regarding differential prediction studies involves the problem of identifying a suitable criterion measure for use in assessing the validity and potential bias of a given predictor (Crocker & Algina, 1986; Furr, 2022). Some believe that the selection of a suitable criterion is often more difficult than selecting a good predictor (Nunnally & Bernstein, 1994). There is the possibility that criterion scores may also be biased, which complicates such assessment (Furr, 2022).

Nomological Network Considerations/Relationships with Other Variables

While assessment of differential prediction is important, studies examining other differential validity (i.e., convergent, discriminant, divergent) across important subgroups is also important. In order for a test score to be of value it should convey the same meaning across different subgroups the test is to be used with, which means that convergent validity, discriminant validity, and divergent validity coefficients for similar, related, or dissimilar constructs, repectively, ought not differ between the population subgroups. Structural equation modeling of such relationships could be used as well as multitrait-multimethod approaches. Such methods would help identify possible differential support of a hypothetical construct and its nomological network (Cronbach & Meehl, 1955).

Differential Diagnostic Utility

As described earlier, test validity supported by prediction, distinct group differences, latent factor structure, or other methods may provide evidence for test validity, but overlapping distributions might limit or even prohibit individual diagnostic use if satisfactory diagnostic utility is not obtained. In the context of assessing bias, one should expect that diagnostic utility of a score or collection of scores would be similar for different important subgroups. If diagnostic utility is found to be adequate for some groups but not others, the use of the test score or collection of scores in diagnostic use may be limited to only those groups for which acceptable diagnostic accuracy is provided. Thus, conducting separate diagnostic utility studies for specific population subgroups would further assess equity in measurement.

Norms

Most standardized tests include norms for score transformation based on a sample from the population of individuals for whom the test might be used. However, some tests or measures may focus on item endorsements and their relationships to diagnostic classification or disorder severity, or some level of performance compared to an established criterion of mastery or adequacy and thus may not be "norm-referenced." Because psychological test raw scores (i.e., subtest score based on sum of item responses or scores) do not typically convey meaning by themselves, standardized tests often provide *norm-based scores* by transforming the individual's raw score into a standardized score based on the mean and standard deviation of the reference (comparison) group. Thus the norm-based score provides an index that denotes the relative performance of the individual compared to the reference group. Characteristics of that reference group must be known to draw accurate inferences on how well the individual performed relative to the norm group. In psychological measurement, the unobserved construct or attribute is inferred from test scores, and norms provide a nomothetic comparison where an individual's test score is compared to the normative sample to provide a relative performance reflected in standardized scores (i.e., T, IQ) and percentile ranks.

Wasserman and Bracken (2013) and Kranzler and Floyd (2020) provide details on test norms, some of which are described here. There are several aspects of norms which need to be considered in judging their adequacy. One feature is the representativeness of the normative sample. If it were possible to measure each person in the population, for example, all children in the United States between the ages of 6 and 16, then it would be possible to report the population parameters and compare the individual child to the population parameters to know how well they performed. Obviously this is impossible so sampling from the population is the next best alternative.

Obtaining a normative sample is a costly and time-consuming process when done well, and ultimately the normative sample must reflect the population on key demographic variables. If one were to randomly select normative sample participants, it would likely require a very large sample to obtain a demographically representative sample so stratifying the norm sample on key variables in a manner that matches current population estimates from census data helps to target individuals matching those estimates to guarantee representation. Variables commonly used to stratify normative samples include sex, race, ethnicity, geographic region, community size, and socioeconomic status (SES). In child and adolescent tests, parent education level is frequently used as a proxy given the difficulty in obtaining other data indicating SES. Stratification allows for determination of how many individuals are needed within each of the stratification blocks. Because random selection is an important element for sampling, many of the best tests add random selection of individuals from a larger number of possible participants identified within the stratification blocks rendering a *stratified random sample*. Close inspection of the report of normative sample characteristics that should be detailed in the test technical manual will allow the user to determine how adequately the sample matches population demographics and it has been suggested that percentage differences between the normative sample and population estimates ±5% indicates undersampling or oversampling (Floyd & Bose, 2003). Wasserman and Bracken (2013) appropriately recommended that "test developers provide tables showing the composition of the standardization sample within and across all stratification criteria" (p. 56) as best practice because sampling inadequacies may not be revealed within single demographic variables. Another element relating to representation is that a normative sample may not include the demographic characteristics of a particular individual so the question of test bias may be invoked. Such a situation may or may not result in test bias and only empirical evidence can inform on this question.

Another feature requiring consideration is how current or recent the normative data are. In the context of intelligence testing, research by Flynn (1987) suggested that population estimates of IQ scores had increased at a rate of about 1/3 IQ points per year. This means that over time, norms of intelligence tests may provide overestimates of true IQ scores in the later years of the test. It has become customary for intelligence tests to be revised and/or norms updated roughly every 12–15 years. As noted in both APA and NASP ethical codes, clinicians are encouraged to use tests with contemporary, up-to-date norms so assessment decisions are made with the best available estimates. However, APA and NASP ethical codes also indicate that test selection and use reflect evidence for reliability and validity of scores and that the test is thus appropriate for the situation. All things being equal, a new version of a test with up-to-date norms would be preferred, but as Beaujean (2015a) noted, if available psychometric evidence for determining appropriate test score use is inadequate, it may be prudent to wait until supportive independent psychometric research is published, and use of an alternate test (or even, perhaps, the somewhat dated test) may be best. While intelligence tests are rather frequently revised and/or norms updated, tests of personality, psychopathology, and other psychological constructs may not be so frequently updated. Consideration of norm adequacy in these tests also should be of concern. Given the demographic changes that occur within the United States and other countries, at the very least normative representation may no longer be adequate.

The size of the normative sample is also of concern. In terms of sampling, larger samples reduce sampling error, and one may have greater confidence in the accuracy of test score estimates with larger normative samples. While larger normative samples are preferred, they come with an added expense in both time and money so cost benefit is likely considered. Wasserman and Bracken (2013) discussed normative sample size in the context of estimating population parameters, effect sizes, statistical significance testing, and power as well as the types of statistical analyses to be used. They also discussed suggested sample size minimums for pilot studies, intervention studies, and large-scale, group-administered tests. Of particular note, Wasserman and Bracken stated, "For individually administered tests, differential item function analyses require substantial oversampling of minorities" (p. 55), and such oversampling was pointed out earlier as necessary to assess psychometric adequacy of test scores, particularly for smaller minority groups (i.e., Indigenous/Native Americans, Asian Americans, etc.) who, while proportionally sampled, do not as a result yield sufficient numbers for differential reliability and validity analyses.

Normative sample size is also affected by age subgroups that reflect more rapid developmental changes early in life. In intelligence tests, it is common to divide each age group into four, 3-month age groupings from early childhood through late childhood or adolescence (see Wechsler, 2014). More rapid changes require norms so subdivided to estimate relative performance more adequately. Stratification of age for tests of behavior problems, personality, or psychopathology may not require such division so age might be based on one-year or larger intervals (i.e., ASCA). In the context of one-year age intervals, Kranzler and Floyd (2020) reported that a minimum of 100 individuals might be considered acceptable, but for smaller age intervals, they argued the "absolute low-end standard should be 30 children per norm block" (p. 61). Norfolk et al. (2015) examined 17 individually administered intelligence tests norm block sizes and nearly one-half (8 of 17) were judged insufficient with fewer than 30. Test users need to carefully review test technical manuals to ascertain the extent to which such norm blocks are satisfactory, but this becomes a serious challenge if the technical manual does not specify the sample sizes within each norm block (see Kranzler & Floyd, 2020).

Summary and Conclusion

Professional practice in psychology requires adherence to professional ethics with an overarching focus on beneficence and nonmaleficence. Within all codes of ethics for psychologists are direct and indirect principles that impact psychological assessment and use of tests or procedures guided by evidence for psychometric fitness. To buttress professional ethics, professional associations have created and regularly update test standards and test use guidelines that delineate methods and criteria that support responsible use of psychological tests. At the core of test standards, qualifications for test use, and professional ethics relating to assessment and test use are psychometric principles of measurement. Measurement principles addressing test score reliability, validity, diagnostic utility, and norms are crucial elements requiring knowledge and application reflecting competency and psychometric literacy. Without proficiency in measurement, it seems quite unlikely a professional would be capable of properly selecting specific tests for individuals and knowing which test scores or score comparisons possess satisfactory psychometric fitness that will allow for evidence-based interpretation and diagnostic use. Research regarding measurement training has indicated that there appears to be broad gaps in direct training that would lead to universal psychometric literacy, and lack of proficiency in this area leaves professionals vulnerable to pseudoscientific practices that impacts client care and research applications. To address this need, specific introductory and advanced coursework in measurement and applied statistics covering topics in reliability, validity, diagnostic utility, and norms presented above are necessary, starting at the undergraduate level and continuing at the graduate level so that psychometric literacy is sufficiently developed. Professional associations and accreditation bodies should require, no, *must* require, not just encourage, such coursework and proficiencies given the high-stakes decisions made in clinical use of tests and procedures. Absent such requirements it seems highly unlikely most test users will be able to abide Weiner's (1989) admonition for the ethical psychologist to "know what their test can do and act accordingly" (p. 829).

Note

1 The concept of drift in applied behavior analysis relates to observers who, over time, deviate from the original operational definition of a behavior, which leads to error in measuring an individual's behavior.

References

Aiken, L. R. (2000). *Psychological testing and assessment* (10th ed.). Allyn & Bacon.

Aiken, L. S., West, S. G., & Millsap, R. E. (2008). Doctoral training in statistics, measurement, and methodology in psychology: Replication and extension of Aiken, West, Sechrest, and Reno's (1990) survey of PhD programs in North America. *American Psychologist*, *63*(1), 32–50. https://doi.org/10.1037/0003-066X.63.1.32

Aiken, L. S., West, S. G., Sechrest, L., Reno, R. R., Roediger, H. L. III, Scarr, S., Kazdin, A. E., & Sherman, S. J. (1990). Graduate training in statistics, methodology, and measurement in psychology: A survey of PhD programs in North America. *American Psychologist*, *45*(6), 721–734 https://doi.org/10.1037/0003-066X.45.6.721

Akaike, H. (1987). Factor analysis and AIC. *Psychometrika*, *52*(3), 317–332. https://doi.org/10.1007/bf02294359

Allen, M. J., & Yen, W. M. (2002). *Introduction to measurement theory.* Waveland Press.

American Educational Research Association, American Psychological Association, and the National Council on Measurement in Education. (1999). *Standards for educational and psychological testing*. American Educational Research Association.

American Educational Research Association, American Psychological Association, & National Council on Measurement in Education. (2014). *Standards for educational and psychological testing.* American Educational Research Association.

American Psychological Association, Committee on Test Standards. (1952). Technical recommendations for psychological tests and diagnostic techniques: Preliminary proposal. *American Psychologist*, *7*(8), 461–475. https://doi.org/10.1037/h0056631

American Psychological Association, American Educational Research Association, & National Council for Measurements Used in Education. (1954). *Technical recommendations for psychological tests and diagnostic techniques.* American Psychological Association.

American Psychological Association, American Educational Research Association, National Council on Measurements Used in Education. (1954). Technical recommendations for psychological tests and diagnostic techniques. *Psychological Bulletin*, *51*(2, Part 2), 1–38. https://doi.org/10.1037/h0053479

American Psychological Association, American Educational Research Association, & National Council on Measurement in Education. (1974). *Standards for educational and psychological tests*. American Psychological Association.

American Psychological Association. (2017). *Ethical principles of psychologists and code of conduct* (2002, amended effective June 1, 2010, and January 1, 2017). https://www.apa.org/ethics/code/ethics-code-2017.pdf

Anastasi, A., & Urbina, S. (1997). *Psychological testing* (7th ed.). Prentice Hall.

Bandalos, D. L. (2018). *Measurement theory and applications in the social sciences*. Guilford Press.

Bandalos, D. L., & Finney, S. J. (2019) Factor analysis: Exploratory and confirmatory. In G. R. Hancock, L. M. Stapleton, & R. O. Mueller (Eds.), *The reviewer's guide to quantitative methods in the social sciences* (2nd ed., pp. 98–122). Routledge.

Bandalos, D. L., & Gerstner, J. J. (2016). Using factor analysis in test construction. In K. Schweizer & C. DiStefano (Eds.), *Principles and methods of test construction: Standards and recent advancements* (pp. 26–51). Hogrefe.

Bayes, T., & Price, R. (1763). An essay towards solving a problem in the doctrine of chance. By the late Rev. Mr. Bayes, communicated by Mr. Price, in a letter to John Canton, M. A. and F. R. S. *Philosophical Transactions of the Royal Society of London*, *53*, 370–418. https://doi.org/10.1098/rstl.1763.0053

Beaujean, A. A. (2015a). Adopting a new test edition: Psychometric and practical considerations. *Research and Practice in the Schools*, *3*(1), 51–57.

Beaujean, A. A. (2015b). John Carroll's views on intelligence: Bi-factor vs. higher-order models. *Journal of Intelligence*, *3*, 121–136. https://doi.org/10.3390/jintelligence3040121

Beaujean, A. A., & McGlaughlin, S. M. (2014). Invariance in the Reynolds Intellectual Assessment Scales for Black and White referred students. *Psychological Assessment*, *26*(4), 1394–1399. https://doi.org/10.1037/pas0000029

Benson, N. F., Floyd, R. G., Kranzler, J. H., Eckert, T. L., Fefer, S. A., & Morgan, G. B. (2019). Test use and assessment practices of school psychologists in the United States: Findings from the 2017 national survey. *Journal of School Psychology*, *72*, 29–48. https://doi.org/10.1016/j.jsp.2018.12.004

Bornovalova, M. A., Choate, A. M., Fatimah, H., Petersen, K. J., & Wiernik, B. M. (2020). Appropriate use of bifactor analysis in psychopathology research: Appreciating benefits and limitations. *Biological Psychiatry*, *88*(1), 18–27. https://doi.org/10.1016/j.biopsych.2020.01.013

British Psychological Society. (2007). Psychological testing: A user's guide. Author. https://www.bps.org.uk/guideline/psychological-testing-test-users-guide

British Psychological Society. (2016). Code of good practice for psychological testing. Author. https://cms.bps.org.uk/sites/default/files/2022-07/ptc09_code_of_good_practice_amended.pdf

British Psychological Society. (2021). *Code of ethics and conduct.* Author. https://doi.org/10.53841/bpsrep.2021.inf94

Brown, R. T., Reynolds, C. R., & Whitaker, J. S. (1999). Bias in mental testing since bias in mental testing. *School Psychology Quarterly*, *14*(3), 208–238. https://doi.org/10.1037/h0089007

Brown, T. A. (2015). *Confirmatory factor analysis for applied research* (2nd ed.). Guilford Press.

Brown, W. (1910). Some experimental results in the correlation of mental abilities. *British Journal of Psychology*, *3*(3), 296–322. http://doi.org/10.1111/j.2044-8295.1910.tb00207.x

Brunner, M., Nagy, G., & Wilhelm, O. (2012). A tutorial on hierarchically structured constructs. *Journal of Personality*, *80*(4), 796–846. https://doi.org/10.1111/j.1467-6494.2011.00749.x

Burnham, K. P., & Anderson, D. R. (2004). Multimodel inference: Understanding AIC and BIC in model selection. *Sociological Methods & Research*, *33*(2), 261–304. http://doi.org/10.1177/0049124104268644

Burns, M. K., Peterson-Brown, S., Haegele, K., Rodriguez, M., Schmitt, B., Cooper, M., . . . Hosp, J. (2016). Meta-analysis of academic interventions derived from neuropsychological data. *School Psychology Quarterly*, *31*(1), 28–42. https://doi.org/10.1037/spq0000117

Buros, O. K. (1938). Preface. In O. K. Buros (Ed.), *The 1938 mental measurements yearbook* (p. xiii). Rutgers University Press.

Burt, C. L. (1948). The factorial study of temperamental traits. *British Journal of Psychology* (Statistical Section), *1*(3), 178–203. https://doi.org/10.1111/j.2044-8317.1948.tb00236.x

Byrne, B. M. (2013). *Structural equation modeling with EQS: Basic concepts, applications, and programming* (2nd ed.). Routledge.

Campbell, D. T., & Fiske, D. W. (1959). Convergent and discriminant validation by the multitrait-multimethod matrix. *Psychological Bulletin*, *56*(2), 81–105. https://doi.org/10.1037/h0046016

Canivez, G. L. (1995). Validity of the Kaufman Brief Intelligence Test: Comparisons with the Wechsler Intelligence Scale for Children–Third Edition. *Assessment*, *2*(2), 101–111. https://doi.org/10.1177/107319119500200201

Canivez, G. L. (1998). Automated syndromic profile and discriminant classification analyses for the Adjustment Scales for Children and Adolescents. *Behavior Research Methods, Instruments, & Computers*, *30*, 732–734. https://doi.org/10.3758/bf03209496

Canivez, G. L. (2006). Adjustment Scales for Children and Adolescents and Native American Indians: Factorial validity generalization for Ojibwe youths. *Psychology in the Schools*, *43*(6), 685–694. https://doi.org/10.1002/pits.20179

Canivez, G. L. (2010). Review of the Wechsler Adult Intelligence Test-Fourth Edition. In K. F. Geisinger & R. A. Spies (Eds.), *The eighteenth mental measurements yearbook* (pp. 684–688). Buros Institute of Mental Measurements.

Canivez, G. L. (2013a). Psychometric versus actuarial interpretation of intelligence and related aptitude batteries. in D. H. Saklofske, C. R. Reynolds, & V. L. Schwean (Eds.), *The Oxford handbook of child psychological assessments* (pp. 84–112). Oxford University Press.

Canivez, G. L. (2013b). Incremental validity of WAIS–IV factor index scores: Relationships with WIAT–II and WIAT–III subtest and composite scores. *Psychological Assessment*, *25*(2), 484–495. https://doi.org/10 .1037/a0032092

Canivez, G. L. (2014a). Construct validity of the WISC–IV with a referred sample: Direct versus indirect hierarchical structures. *School Psychology Quarterly*, *29*(1), 38–51. https://doi.org/10.1037/spq0000032

Canivez, G. L. (2014b). Review of the Wechsler Preschool and Primary Scale of Intelligence–Fourth Edition. In J. F. Carlson, K. F. Geisinger, & J. L. Jonson (Eds.), *The nineteenth mental measurements yearbook* (pp. 732–737). Buros Institute of Mental Measurements.

Canivez, G. L. (2019). Evidence-based assessment for school psychology: Research, training, and clinical practice. *Contemporary School Psychology*, *23*, 194–200. https://doi.org/10.1007/s40688-019-00238-z

Canivez, G. L., & Beran, T. N. (2009). Adjustment Scales for Children and Adolescents: Factorial validity in a Canadian sample. *Canadian Journal of School Psychology*, *24*(4), 284–302. https://doi.org/10.1177 /0829573509344344

Canivez, G. L., & Bohan, K. (2006). Adjustment Scales for Children and Adolescents and Native American Indians: Factorial validity generalization for Yavapai Apache youths. *Journal of Psychoeducational Assessment*, *24*(4), 329–341. https://doi.org/10.1177/0734282906291397

Canivez, G. L., & Gaboury, A. R. (2016). Construct validity and diagnostic utility of the Cognitive Assessment System for ADHD. *Journal of Attention Disorders*, *20*(6), 519–529. https://doi.org/10.1177 /1087054713489021

Canivez, G. L., & Konold, T. R. (2001). Assessing differential prediction bias in the Developing Cognitive Abilities Test across gender, race/ethnicity, and socioeconomic groups. *Educational and Psychological Measurement*, *61*(1), 159–171. https://doi.org/10.1177/00131640121971022

Canivez, G. L., & Kush, J. C. (2013). WISC–IV and WAIS–IV structural validity: Alternate methods, alternate results. Commentary on Weiss et al. (2013a) and Weiss et al. (2013b). *Journal of Psychoeducational Assessment*, *31*(2), 157–169. https://doi.org/10.1177/0734282913478036

Canivez, G. L., Neitzel, R., & Martin, B. E. (2005). Construct validity of the Kaufman Brief Intelligence Test, Wechsler Intelligence Scale for Children–Third Edition, and Adjustment Scales for Children and Adolescents. *Journal of Psychoeducational Assessment*, *23*(1), 15–34. https://doi.org/10.1177 /073428290502300102

Canivez, G. L., & Sprouls, K. (2005). Assessing the construct validity of the Adjustment Scales for Children and Adolescents. *Journal of Psychoeducational Assessment*, *23*(1), 3–14. https://doi.org/10.1177 /073428290502300101

Canivez, G. L., & Sprouls, K. (2010). Adjustment Scales for Children and Adolescents: Factorial validity generalization with Hispanic/Latino Youths. *Journal of Psychoeducational Assessment*, *28*(3), 209–221. https://doi.org/10.1177/0734282909349213

Canivez, G. L., von der Embse, N. P., & McGill, R. J. (2021). Construct validity of the BASC–3 Teacher Rating Scales: Independent hierarchical exploratory factor analyses with the standardization sample. *School Psychology*, *36*(4), 235–254. https://doi.org/10.1037/spq0000444

Canivez, G. L., & Watkins, M. W. (1996). Automated calculation of diagnostic efficiency statistics. *Behavior Research Methods, Instruments, & Computers*, *28*, 132–133. https://doi.org/10.3758/bf03203650

Canivez, G. L., & Watkins, M. W. (1998). Long term stability of the Wechsler Intelligence Scale for Children–Third Edition. *Psychological Assessment*, *10*(3), 285–291. https://doi.org/10.1037/1040–3590.10.3.285

Canivez, G. L., & Watkins, M. W. (1999). Long term stability of the Wechsler Intelligence Scale for Children–Third Edition among demographic subgroups: Gender, race, and age. *Journal of Psychoeducational Assessment*, *17*(4), 300–313. https://doi.org/10.1177/073428299901700401

Canivez, G. L., & Watkins, M. W. (2001). Long term stability of the Wechsler Intelligence Scale for Children–Third Edition among students with disabilities. *School Psychology Review*, *30*(3), 361–376. https://doi .org/10.1080/02796015.2001.12086125

Canivez, G. L., & Watkins, M. W. (2016). Review of the Wechsler Intelligence Scale for Children–Fifth Edition: Critique, commentary, and independent analyses. In A. S. Kaufman, S. E. Raiford, & D. L. Coalson (Authors), *Intelligent testing with the WISC–V* (pp. 683–702, Appendix I). Wiley.

Canivez, G. L., Watkins, M. W., & Dombrowski, S. C. (2016). Factor structure of the Wechsler Intelligence Scale for Children–Fifth Edition: Exploratory factor analyses with the 16 primary and secondary subtests. *Psychological Assessment*, *28*(8), 975–986. https://doi.org/10.1037/pas0000238

Canivez, G. L., Watkins, M. W., & Dombrowski, S. C. (2017). Structural validity of the Wechsler Intelligence Scale for Children–Fifth Edition: Confirmatory factor analyses with the 16 primary and secondary subtests. *Psychological Assessment*, *29*(4), 458–472. https://doi.org/10.1037/pas0000358

Canivez, G. L., & Youngstrom, E. A. (2019). Challenges to the Cattell-Horn-Carroll Theory: Empirical, clinical, and policy implications. *Applied Measurement in Education*, *32*(3), 232–248. https://doi.org/10.1080/08957347.2019.1619562

Carroll, J. B. (1993). *Human cognitive abilities.* Cambridge University Press.

Carroll, J. B. (1995). On methodology in the study of cognitive abilities. *Multivariate Behavioral Research*, *30*(3), 429– 452. https://doi.org/10.1207/s15327906mbr3003_6

Carroll, J. B. (1997). The three–stratum theory of cognitive abilities. In D. P. Flanagan, J. L. Genshaft, & P. L. Harrison (Eds.), *Contemporary intellectual assessment: Theories, tests, and issues* (pp. 183–208). Guilford Press.

Carroll, J. B. (2003). The higher–stratum structure of cognitive abilities: Current evidence supports g and about ten broad factors. In H. Nyborg (Ed.), *The scientific study of general intelligence: Tribute to Arthur R. Jensen* (pp. 5–21). Pergamon Press.

Cattell, R. B. (1949). A note on factor invariance and the identification of factors. *British Journal of Psychology*, 2, 134–138.

Cattell, R. B. (1963). Theory of fluid and crystallized intelligence: A critical experiment. *Journal of Educational Psychology*, *54*(1), 1–22. https://doi.org/10.1037/h0046743

Cattell, R. B. (1966). The scree test for the number of factors. *Multivariate Behavioral Research*, *1*(2), 245–276. https://doi.org/10.1207/s15327906mbr0102_10

Cattell, R. B. (1978). *The scientific use of factor analysis in behavioral and life sciences.* Plenum.

Charter, R. A. & Feldt, L. S. (2009). A comprehensive approach to the interpretation of difference scores. *Applied Neuropsychology*, *16*(1), 23–30. https://doi.org/10.1080/09084280802644110

Chen, F. F. (2007). Sensitivity of goodness of fit indexes to lack of measurement invariance. *Structural Equation Modeling*, *14*(3), 464–504. https://doi.org/10.1080/10705510701301834

Cheung, G. W., & Rensvold, R. B. (2002). Evaluating goodness-of-fit indexes for testing measurement invariance. *Structural Equation Modeling*, *9*(2), 233–255. https://doi.org/10.1207/S15328007SEM0902_5

Childs, R. A., & Eyde, L. D. (2002). Assessment training in clinical psychology doctoral programs: What should we teach? What do we teach? *Journal of Personality Assessment*, *78*(1), 130–144. https://doi.org/10.1207/s15327752jpa7801_08

Cohen, J. (1960). A coefficient of agreement for nominal scales. *Educational and Psychological Measurement*, *20*(1), 37–46. https://doi.org/10.1177/001316446002000104

Cohen, J. (1988). Statistical power analysis for the behavioral sciences (2nd ed.). Lawrence Erlbaum Associates.

Cronbach, L. J., Gleser, G. C., Nanda, H., & Rajaratnam, N. (1972). *The dependability of behavioral measurements: Theory of generalizability for scores and profiles.* Wiley.

Cronbach, L. J., & Meehl, P. E. (1955). Construct validity in psychological tests. *Psychological Bulletin*, *52*(4), 281–302. https://doi.org/10.1037/h0040957

Cronbach, L. J., & Snow, R. E. (1977). *Aptitudes and instructional methods: A handbook for research on interactions.* Irvington Publishers.

Dahlman, K. A., & Geisinger, K. F. (2015). The prevalence of measurement in undergraduate psychology curricula across the United States. *Scholarship of Teaching and Learning in Psychology*, *1*(3), 189–199. https://doi.org/10.1037/stl0000030

Dawes, R. M. (2001). *Everyday irrationality: How pseudo-scientists, lunatics, and the rest of us systematically fail to think rationally.* Westview Press.

Dawes, R. M. (2005). The ethical implications of Paul Meehl's work on comparing clinical versus actuarial prediction methods. *Journal of Clinical Psychology*, *61*(10), 1245–1255. https://doi.org/10.1002/jclp.20180

de Raadt, A., Warrens, M. J., Bosker, R. J., & Kiers, H. A. L. (2021). A comparison of reliability coefficients for ordinal rating scales. *Journal of Classification*, *38*, 519–543. https://doi.org/10.1007/s00357-021 -09386-5

Deeks, J. J. (2001). Systematic reviews of evaluations of diagnostic and screening tests. *British Medical Journal, 323*(7305), 157–162. https://doi.org/10.1136/bmj.323.7305.157

Dombrowski, S. C. (2020). *Psychoeducational assessment and report writing* (2nd ed.). Springer Nature. https://doi.org/10.1007/978-3-030-44641-3

Dombrowski, S. C., Beaujean, A. A., Schneider, J. W. & McGill, R. J., & Benson, N. (2019). Using exploratory bifactor analysis to understand the latent structure of multidimensional psychological measures An applied example featuring the WISC–V. *Structural Equation Modeling: A Multidisciplinary Journal*, *26*(6), 847–860. https://doi.org/10.1080/10705511.2019.1622421

Dombrowski, S. C., Golay, P., McGill, R. J., & Canivez, G. L. (2018). Investigating the theoretical structure of the DAS–II core battery at school age using Bayesian structural equation modeling. *Psychology in the Schools*, *55*(2), 190–207. https://doi.org/10.1002/pits.22096

Dombrowski, S. C., McGill, R. J., Farmer, R. L., Kranzler, J. H., & Canivez, G. L. (2022). Beyond the rhetoric of evidence-based assessment: A framework for critical thinking in clinical practice. *School Psychology Review*, *51*(6), 771–784. https://doi.org/10.1080/2372966X.2021.1960126

Dombrowski, S. C., Watkins, M. W., McGill, R. J., Canivez, G. L., Holingue, C., Pritchard, A., & Jacobson, L. (2021). Measurement invariance of the WISC–V 10 subtest primary battery: Can index scores be compared across age, sex, and diagnostic groups? *Journal of Psychoeducational Assessment*, *39*(1), 89–99. https://doi.org/10.1177/0734282920954583

Dunn, D. M. (2019). *Peabody Picture Vocabulary Test, Fifth Edition manual*. NCS Pearson.

Embretson, S. E., & Reise, S. P. (2000). *Item response theory for psychologists*. Psychology Press.

Fabrigar, L. R., Wegener, D. T., MacCallum, R. C., & Strahan, E. J. (1999). Evaluating the use of exploratory factor analysis in psychological research. *Psychological Methods*, *4*(3), 272–299. https://doi.org/10.1037 /1082-989x.4.3.272

Farmer, R. L., McGill, R. J., Dombrowski, S. C., & Canivez, G. L. (2021). Why questionable assessment practices remain popular in school psychology: Instructional materials as pedagogic vehicles. *Canadian Journal of School Psychology*, *36*(2), 98–114. https://doi.org/10.1177/0829573520978111

Farmer, R. L., McGill, R. J., Lockwood, A. B., Dombrowski, S. C., Canivez, G. L., & Zaheer, I. (2022). Warning signs or hype in school-based assessment: Implications for training and pedagogy. *School Psychology: Training & Pedagogy*, *39*(1), 11–24. https://doi.org/10.31234/osf.io/ypcv7

Feldt, L. S. (1969). A test of the hypothesis that Cronbach's alpha or Kuder-Richardson coefficient twenty is the same for two tests. *Psychometrika*, *34*(3), 363–373. https://doi.org/10.1007/bf02289364

Feldt, L. S. (2006). Testing the difference between two alpha coefficients with small samples of subjects and raters. *Educational and Psychological Measurement*, *66*(4), 589–600. https://doi.org/10.1177 /0013164405282488

Ferrando, P. J., & Lorenzo-Seva, U. (2018). Assessing the quality and appropriateness of factor solutions and factor score estimates in exploratory item factor analysis. *Educational and Psychological Measurement*, *78*(5), 762–780. https://doi.org/10.1177/0013164417719308

Fife, D. A., Mendoza, J. L., & Terry, R. (2012). The assessment of reliability under range restriction: A comparison of α, ω, and test–retest reliability for dichotomous data. *Educational and Psychological Measurement*, *72*(5), 862–888. https://doi.org/10.1177/0013164411430225

Floyd, R. G., & Bose, J. E. (2003). Behavior rating scales for assessment of disturbance: A critical review of measurement characteristics. *Journal of Psychoeducational Assessment*, *21*(1), 43–78. https://doi.org /10.1177/073428290302100104

Flynn, J. R. (1987). Massive IQ gains in 14 nations: What IQ tests really measure. *Psychological Bulletin*, *101*(2), 171–191. https://doi.org/10.1037/0033-2909.101.2.171

French, B. F., & Finch, W. H. (2016). Detecting differential item functioning. In K. Schweizer & C. DiStefano (Eds.), *Principles and methods of test construction: Standards and recent advancements* (pp. 197–217). Hogrefe.

Furr, R. M. (2022). *Psychometrics: An introduction* (4th ed.). Sage Publications.

Galton, F. (1879). Psychometric experiments. *Brain*, *2*(2), 149–162. https://doi.org/10.1093/brain/2.2.149

Garb, H. N., & Wood, J. M. (2019). Methodological advances in statistical prediction. *Psychological Assessment*, *31*(12), 1456–1466. https://doi.org/10.1037/pas0000673

Giavarina, D. (2015). Understanding Bland Altman analysis. *Biochemia Medica*, *25*(2), 141–151. https://doi.org/10.11613/BM.2015.015

Gignac, G. E. (2005). Revisiting the factor structure of the WAIS–R: Insights through nested factor modeling. *Assessment*, *12*(3), 320–329. https://doi.org/10.1177/1073191105278118

Gignac, G. E. (2006). The WAIS–III as a nested factors model: A useful alternative to the more conventional oblique and higher-order models. *Journal of Individual Differences*, *27*(2), 73–86. https://doi.org/10.1027/1614-0001.27.2.73

Gignac, G. (2008). Higher-order models versus direct hierarchical models: *g* as superordinate or breadth factor? *Psychology Science Quarterly*, *50*, 21–43.

Gignac, G. E., & Watkins, M. W. (2013). Bifactor modeling and the estimation of model-based reliability in the WAIS-IV. *Multivariate Behavioral Research*, *48*(5), 639–662. https://doi.org/10.1080/00273171.2013.804398

Giordano, C., & Waller, N. G. (2020). Recovering bifactor models: A comparison of seven methods. *Psychological Methods*, *25*(2), 143–156. https://doi.org/10.1037/met0000227

Glass, G. V., & Hopkins, K. D. (1996) *Statistical methods in education and psychology* (3rd ed.). Allyn & Bacon.

Glutting, J. J., Adams, W., & Sheslow, D. (2000). *Wide Range Intelligence Test: Manual.* Wide Range.

Glutting, J. J., McDermott, P. A., & Stanley, J. C. (1987). Resolving differences among methods of establishing confidence limits for test scores. *Educational and Psychological Measurement*, *47*(3), 607–614. https://doi.org/10.1177/001316448704700307

Glutting, J. J., Watkins, M. W., Konold, T. R., & McDermott, P. A. (2006). Distinctions without a difference: The utility of observed versus latent factors from the WISC–IV in estimating reading and math achievement on the WIAI–II. *Journal of Special Education*, *40*(2), 103–114. https://doi.org/10.1177/00224669060400020101

Golay, P., Reverte, I., Rossier, J., Favez, N., & Lecerf, T. (2013). Further insights on the French WISC–IV factor structure through Bayesian structural equation modeling. *Psychological Assessment*, *25*(2), 496–508. https://doi.org/10.1037/a0030676

Golino, H. F., & Epskamp, S. (2017). Exploratory graph analysis: A new approach for estimating the number of dimensions in psychological research. *PLoS ONE*, *12*(6), 1–26. https://doi.org/10.1371/journal.pone.0174035

Gorsuch, R. L. (1983). *Factor analysis* (2nd ed.). Lawrence Erlbaum Associates.

Gorsuch, R. L. (2003). Factor analysis. In J. A. Schinka & W. F. Velicer (Eds.), *Handbook of psychology: Research methods in psychology* (vol. 2, pp. 143–164). Wiley. https://doi.org/10.1002/0471264385.wei0206

Gray, G. E. (2004). *Evidence-based psychiatry*. American Psychiatric Publishing, Inc.

Grice, J. W. (2001). Computing and evaluating factor scores. *Psychological Methods*, *6*(4), 430–450. https://doi.org/10.1037//1082-989x.6.4.430

Gu, H., Wen, Z., & Fan, X. (2017). Examining and controlling for wording effect in a self-report measure: A Monte Carlo simulation study. *Structural Equation Modeling: A Multidisciplinary Journal*, *24*(4), 545–555. https://doi.org/10.1080/10705511.2017.1286228

Guilford, J. P., & Fruchter, B. (1978). *Fundamental statistics in psychology and education* (6th ed.). McGraw–Hill.

Guion, R. M. (1980). On trinitarian doctrines of validity. *Professional Psychology: Research and Practice*, *11*(3), 385–398. https://doi.org/10.1037/0735-7028.11.3.385

Gygi, J. T., Ledermann, T., Grob, A., Rudaz, M., & Hagmann-von Arx, P. (2019). The Reynolds Intellectual Assessment Scales: Measurement invariance across four language groups. *Journal of Psychoeducational Assessment*, *37*(5), 590–602. https://doi.org/10.1177/0734282918780565

Hancock, G. R., & Mueller, R. O. (2001). Rethinking construct reliability within latent variable systems. In R. Cudeck, S. H. C. duToit, & D. F. Sorbom (Eds.). *Structural equation modeling: Present and future.* (pp. 195–216). Scientific Software.

Hanley, J. A., & McNeil, B. J. (1983). A method of comparing the areas under receiver operating characteristic curves derived from the same cases. *Radiology*, *148*, 839–843. https://doi.org/https://doi.org/10.1148/radiology.148.3.6878708

Haynes, S. N., Richard, D. C. S., & Kubany, E. S. (1995). Content validity in psychological assessment: A functional approach to concepts and methods. *Psychological Assessment*, *7*(3), 238–247. https://doi.org/10.1037/1040-3590.7.3.238

Haynes, S. N., Smith, G. T., & Hunsley, J. D. (2018). *Scientific foundations of clinical assessment* (2nd ed.). Routledge.

Hieronymus, A. N., Hoover, H. D., Oberley, K. R., Cantor, N. K., Frisbie, D. A., Dunbar, S. B., Lewis, J. C., & Lindquist, E. F. (1990). *Iowa Tests of Basic Skills*. Riverside Publishing.

Holland, P. W., & Thayer, D. T. (1988). Differential item performance and the Mantel-Haenszel procedure. In H. Wainer & H. I. Braun (Eds.), *Test validity* (pp. 129–145). Lawrence Erlbaum Associates.

Holzinger, K. J., & Swineford, F. (1937). The bi-factor method. *Psychometrika*, 2, 41–54. https://doi.org/10.1007/bf02287965

Horn, J. L. (1965). A rationale and test for the number of factors in factor analysis. *Psychometrika*, 30(2), 179–185. https://doi.org/10.1007/bf02289447

Horn, J. L., & Cattell, R. B. (1966). Refinement and test of the theory of fluid and crystallized general intelligences. *Journal of Educational Psychology*, 57(5), 253–270. https://doi.org/10.1037/h0023816

Hu, L.-T., & Bentler, P. M. (1999). Cutoff criteria for fit indexes in covariance structure analysis: Conventional criteria versus new alternatives. *Structural Equation Modeling*, 6(1), 1–55. http://doi.org/10.1080/10705519909540118

Humphreys, L. G. (1982). The hierarchical factor model and general intelligence. In N. Hirshberg & L. G. Humphreys (Eds.), *Multivariate applications in the social sciences* (pp. 223–239). Lawrence Erlbaum Associates.

Hunsley, J., & Mash, E. J. (2007). Evidence-based assessment. *Annual Review of Clinical Psychology*, 3, 29–51. https://doi.org/10.1146/annurev.clinpsy.3.022806.091419.

Hunsley, J., & Meyer, G. J. (2003). The incremental validity of psychological testing and assessment: Conceptual, methodological, and statistical issues. *Psychological Assessment*, 15(4), 446–455. https://doi.org/10.1037/1040-3590.15.4.446

Iliescu, D., Bartram, D., Zeinoun, P., Ziegler, M., Elosua, P., Sireci, S., Geisinger, K. F., Odendaal, A. Oliveri, M. E., Twing, J., & Camara, W. (2024). The Test Adaptation Reporting Standards (TARES): Reporting test adaptations. *International Journal of Testing*, 24(1), 80–102. https://doi.org/10.1080/15305058.2023.2294266

International School Psychology Association. (2021). *Code of ethics*. Author. https://www.ispaweb.org/wp-content/uploads/2021/07/ISPA-Code-of-Ethics-2021.pdf

International Test Commission. (2001). International guidelines for test use. *International Journal of Testing*, 1(2), 93–114. https://www.intestcom.org

International Test Commission. (2010). *International Test Commission guidelines for translating and adapting tests*. http://www.intestcom.org

International Test Commission. (2013). *International guidelines for test use* (Version 1.2). https://www.intestcom.org

Jenkins, M. M., Youngstrom, E. A., Washburn, J. J., & Youngstrom, J. K. (2011). Evidence-based strategies improve assessment of pediatric bipolar disorder by community practitioners. *Professional Psychology: Research and Practice*, 42(2), 121–129. https://doi.org/10.1037/a0022506

Jensen, A. R. (1980a). *Bias in mental testing*. Free Press.

Jensen, A. R. (1980b). Precis of bias in mental testing. *The Behavioral and Brain Sciences*, 3(2), 325–371. https://doi.org/10.1017/s0140525x00012334

Jensen, A. R. (1998). *The g factor: The science of mental ability*. Praeger.

Jones, W. T. (1952). *A history of western philosophy*. Harcourt, Brace. https://doi.org/10.1177/000271625228400172

Kaiser, H. F. (1960). The application of electronic computers to factor analysis. *Educational and Psychological Measurement*, 20(1), 141–151. https://doi.org/10.1177/001316446002000116

Kaufman, A. S., & Kaufman, N. L. (1990). *Manual for the Kaufman Brief Intelligence Test*. American Guidance Service.

Kessel, J. B., & Zimmerman, M. (1993). Reporting errors in studies of the diagnostic performance of self-administered questionnaires: Extent of the problem, recommendations for standardized presentation of results, and implications for the peer review process. *Psychological Assessment*, 5(4), 395–399. https://doi.org/10.1037/1040-3590.5.4.395

Kline, P. (1994). *An easy guide to factor analysis*. Routledge.

Kline, R. B. (2011). *Principles and practice of structural equation modeling* (3rd ed.). Guilford Press.

Kline, R. B. (2016). *Principles and practice of structural equation modeling* (4th ed.). Guilford Press.

Kline, R. B. (2023). *Principles and practice of structural equation modeling* (5th ed.). Guilford Press.

Konold, T. R., & Canivez, G. L. (2010). Differential relationships among WISC–IV and WIAT–II scales: An evaluation of potentially moderating child demographics. *Educational and Psychological Measurement*, *70*(4), 613–627. https://doi.org/10.1177/0013164409355686

Kraemer, H. C. (1992). *Evaluating medical tests: Objective and quantitative guidelines*. Sage Publications.

Kranzler, J. H., & Floyd, R. G. (2020). *Assessing intelligence in children and adolescents: A practical guide for evidence-based assessment* (2nd ed.). Rowman & Littlefield.

Kuder, G. R., & Richardson, M. W. (1937). The theory of the estimation of test reliability. *Psychometrika*, *2*, 151–160. https://doi.org/10.1007/bf02288391

Kush, J. C, Watkins, M. W., Ward, T. J., Ward, S. B., Canivez, G. L., & Worrell, F. C. (2001). Construct Validity of the WISC–III for White and Black students from the WISC–III standardization sample and for Black students referred for psychological evaluation. *School Psychology Review*, *30*(1), 70–88. https://doi.org/10.1080/02796015.2001.12086101

Lambert, N. M. (1991). The crisis in measurement literacy in psychology and education. *Educational Psychologist*, *26*(1), 23–35. https://doi.org/10.1207/s15326985ep2601_2

Landau, S., Milich, R., & Widiger, T. A. (1991). Predictive power methods may be more helpful for making a diagnosis than sensitivity and specificity. *Journal of Child and Adolescent Psychopharmacology*, *1*(5), 343–351. https://doi.org/10.1089/cap.1991.1.343

Langmuir, I., & Hall, R. N. (1989). Pathological science. *Physics Today*, *42*(10), 36–48. https://doi.org/10.1063/1.881205

Lei, P. W., & Wu, Q. (2012). Estimation in structural equation modeling. In R. H. Hoyle (Ed.), *Handbook of structural equation modeling* (pp. 164–180). Guilford Press.

Lilienfeld, S. O., Ammirati, R., & David, M. (2012). Distinguishing science from pseudoscience in school psychology: Science and scientific thinking as safeguards against human error. *Journal of School Psychology*, *50*, 7–36. https://doi.org/10.1016/j.jsp.2011.09.006

Lord, F. (1965). A strong true-score theory, with applications. *Psychometrika*, *30*, 239–270. https://doi.org/10.1007/BF02289490

Lorenzo-Seva, U., & Ferrando, P. J. (2015). POLYMAT-C: A comprehensive SPSS program for computing the polychoric correlation matrix. *Behavior Research Methods*, *47*(3), 884–889. https://doi.org/10.3758/s13428-014-0511-x

Lorenzo-Seva, U., & ten Berge, J. M. F. (2006). Tucker's congruence coefficient as a meaningful index of factor similarity. *Methodology: European Journal of Research Methods for the Behavioral and Social Sciences*, *2*(2), 57–64. https://doi.org/10.1027/1614-2241.2.2.57

Lubinski, D., & Dawis, R. V. (1992). Aptitudes, skills, and proficiencies. In M. D. Dunnette & L. M. Hough (Eds.), *Handbook of industrial and organizational psychology* (2nd ed., vol. 3, pp. 1–59). Consulting Psychology Press.

Mansolf, M., & Reise, S. P. (2016). Exploratory bifactor analysis: The Schmid-Leiman orthogonalization and Jennrich-Bentler analytic rotations. *Multivariate Behavioral Research*, *51*(5), 698–717. https://doi.org/10.1080/00273171.2016.1215898

Mantel, N., & Haenszel, W. (1959). Statistical aspects of the analysis of data from retrospective studies of disease. *Journal of the National Cancer Institute*, *22*(4), 719–748. https://doi.org/10.1093/jnci/22.4.719

McDermott, P. A. (1981). Sources of error in psychoeducational diagnosis of children. *Journal of School Psychology*, *19*(1), 31–44. https://doi.org/10.1016/0022-4405(81)90005-4

McDermott, P. A. (1988). Agreement among diagnosticians or observers: Its importance and determination. *Professional School Psychology*, *3*(4), 225–240. https://doi.org/10.1037/h0090563

McDermott, P. A. (1994). *National profiles in youth psychopathology: Manual of adjustment scales for children and adolescents*. Edumetric and Clinical Science.

McDermott, P. A., Marston, N. C., & Stott, D. H. (1993). *Adjustment scales for children and adolescents*. Edumetric and Clinical Science.

McDermott, P. A., Watkins, M. W., & Rhoad, A. (2014). Whose IQ is it?—Assessor bias variance in high-stakes psychological assessment. *Psychological Assessment*, *26*(1), 207–214. https://doi.org/10.1037/a0034832

McDonald, R. P. (1999). *Test theory: A unified treatment*. Lawrence Erlbaum Associates.

McDonald, R. P. (2010). Structural models and the art of approximation. *Perspectives on Psychological Science*, 5(6), 675–686. https://doi.org/10.1177/1745691610388766

McFall, R. M. (1991). Manifesto for a science of clinical psychology. *The Clinical Psychologist*, 44, 75–88.

McFall, R. M. (1996). Making psychology incorruptible. *Applied and Preventive Psychology*, 5(1), 9–15. https://doi.org/10.1016/S0962-1849(96)80021-7

McFall, R. M. (2000). Elaborate reflections on a simple manifesto. *Applied and Preventive Psychology*, 9(1), 5–21. https://doi.org/10.1016/S0962-1849(05)80035-6

McGill, R. J., Dombrowski, S. C., & Canivez, G. L. (2018). Cognitive profile analysis in school psychology: History, issues, and continued concerns. *Journal of School Psychology*, 71, 108–121. https://doi.org/10.1016/j.jsp.2018.10.007

McGraw, K. O., & Wong, S. P. (1996a). Forming inferences about some intraclass correlation coefficients. *Psychological Methods*, 1(1), 30–46. https://doi.org/https://doi.org/10.1037/1082-989X.1.1.30

McGraw, K. O., & Wong, S. P. (1996b). "Forming inferences about some intraclass correlations coefficients": Correction. *Psychological Methods*, 1(4), 390. https://doi.org/10.1037//1082-989x.1.4.390

McGrew, K. S., LaForte, E. M., & Shrank, F. A. (2014). *Technical manual. Woodcock Johnson IV*. Riverside Publishing.

Meehl, P. E. (1954). *Clinical versus statistical prediction: A theoretical analysis and review of the evidence*. University of Minnesota Press.

Meehl, P. E., & Rosen, A. (1955). Antecedent probability and the efficiency of psychometric signs, patterns, or cutting scores. *Psychological Bulletin*, 52(3), 194–216. https://doi.org/10.1037/h0048070

Messick, S. (1989). Validity. In R. L. Linn (Ed.), *Educational measurement* (3rd ed., pp. 13–103). American Council on Education and Macmillan

Messick, S. (1995). Validity of psychological assessment: Validation of inferences from person's responses and performances as scientific inquiry into score meaning. *American Psychologist*, 50(9), 741–749. https://doi.org/10.1037/0003-066x.50.9.741

Milich, R., Widiger, T. A., & Landau, S. (1987). Differential diagnosis of attention deficit and conduct disorders using conditional probabilities. *Journal of Consulting and Clinical Psychology*, 55(5), 762–767. https://doi.org/10.1037/0022-006x.55.5.762

Mrazik, M., Janzen, T. M., Dombrowski, S. C., Barford, S. W., & Krawchuk, L. L. (2012). Administration and scoring errors of graduate students learning the WISC–IV: Issues and controversies. *Canadian Journal of School Psychology*, 27(4), 279–290. https://doi.org/10.1177/0829573512454106

Mueller, R. O., & Hancock, G. R. (2019). Structural equation modeling. In G. R. Hancock, L. M. Stapleton, & R. O. Mueller (Eds.), *The reviewer's guide to quantitative methods in the social sciences* (2nd ed., pp. 445–456). Routledge.

Murray, A. L., & Johnson, W. (2013). The limitations of model fit in comparing the bifactor versus higher-order models of human cognitive ability structure. *Intelligence*, 41(5), 407–422. https://doi.org/10.1016/j.intell.2013.06.004

Naglieri, J. A., & Bornstein, B. T. (2003). Intelligence and achievement: Just how correlated are they? *Journal of Psychoeducational Assessment*, 21(3), 244–260. https://doi.org/10.1177/073428290302100302

Naglieri, J. A., & Das, J. P. (1997). *Cognitive Assessment System: Interpretive handbook*. Riverside Publishing.

National Association of School Psychologists. (2020). *The professional standards of the National Association of School Psychologists*. National Association of School Psychologists.

NCS Pearson. (2009). *Wechsler Individual Achievement Test–Third Edition technical manual*. Author.

Norfolk, P. A., Farmer, R. L., Floyd, R. G., Woods, I. L., Hawkins, H. K., & Irby, S. M. (2015). Norm block sample sizes: A review of 17 individually administered intelligence tests. *Journal of Psychoeducational Assessment*, 33(6), 544–555. https://doi.org/10.1177/0734282914562385

Nunnally, J. D., & Bernstein, I. H. (1994). *Psychometric theory* (3rd ed.). McGraw–Hill.

Oh, H.-J., Glutting, J. J., Watkins, M. W., Youngstrom, E. A., & McDermott, P. A. (2004). Correct interpretation of latent versus observed abilities: Implications from structural equation modeling applied to the WISC–III and WIAT linking sample. *The Journal of Special Education*, 38(3), 159–173. https://doi.org/10.1177/00224669040380030301

Pedhazur, E. J. (1997). *Multiple regression in behavioral research: Explanation and prediction* (3rd ed.). Harcourt Brace.

Pendergast, L. L., von der Embse, N., Kilgus, S. P., & Eklund, K. R. (2017). Measurement equivalence: A non-technical primer on categorical multi-group confirmatory factor analysis in school psychology. *Journal of School Psychology*, *60*, 65–82. https://doi.org/10.1016/j.jsp.2016.11.002

Pepe, M. S. (2003). *The statistical evaluation of medical tests for classification and prediction*. Wiley.

Pierce, J. R. (1980). *An introduction to information theory: Symbols, signals and noise* (2nd rev. ed.). Dover Publications.

Potthoff, F. R. (1966). Statistical aspects of the problem of bias in psychological tests (Institute of Statistics Mimeo Series No. 479). University of North Carolina Department of Statistics.

Psychological Corporation. (2002). *Wechsler Individual Achievement Test–Second Edition examiner's manual*. Author.

Public Law (P.L.) 108–446. *Individuals with Disabilities Education Improvement Act of 2004* (IDEIA). (20 U.S.C. 1400 et seq.). 34 CFR Parts 300 and 301. Assistance to States for the education of children with disabilities and preschool grants for children with disabilities; Final Rule. *Federal Register*, *71 (156)*, 46540–46845.

Raftery, A. E. (1995). Bayesian model selection in social research. *Sociological Methodology*, *25*, 111–163. https://doi.org/10.2307/271063

Raykov, T., & Marcoulides, G. A. (2011). *Introduction to psychometric theory*. Routledge.

Reise, S. P. (2012). The rediscovery of bifactor measurement models. *Multivariate Behavioral Research*, *47*(5), 667–696. https://doi.org/10.1080/00273171.2012.715555

Reise, S. P., Bonifay, W. E., & Haviland, M. G. (2013). Scoring and modeling psychological measures in the presence of multidimensionality. *Journal of Personality Assessment*, *95*(2), 129–140. https://doi.org/10.1080/00223891.2012.725437

Reise, S. P., Mansolf, M., & Haviland, M. G. (2023). Bifactor measurement models. In R. H. Hoyle (Ed.), *Handbook of structural equation modeling* (2nd ed., pp. 329–348). Guilford Press.

Reise, S. P., Waller, N. G., & Comrey, A. L. (2000). Factor analysis and scale revision. *Psychological Assessment*, *12*(3), 287–297. https://doi.org/10.1037//1040-3590.12.3.287

Revelle, W., & Condon, D. M. (2019). Reliability from α to ω: A tutorial. *Psychological Assessment*, *31*(12), 1395–1411. https://doi.org/10.1037/pas0000754

Reynolds, C. R. (1982). The problem of bias in psychological assessment. In C. R. Reynolds & T. B. Gutkin (Eds.), *The handbook of school psychology* (pp. 178–208). Wiley.

Reynolds, C. R. (1984). Critical measurement issues in learning disabilities. *Journal of Special Education*, *18*(4), 451–476. https://doi.org/10.1177/002246698401800403

Reynolds, C. R. (2000). Methods for detecting and evaluating cultural bias in neuropsychological tests. In F. Strickland & C. R. Reynolds (Eds.), *Handbook of cross-cultural neuropsychology* (pp. 249–285). Plenum.

Reynolds, C. R., Altman, R. A., & Allen, D. N. (2021). *Mastering modern psychological testing: Theory and methods* (2nd ed.). Springer.

Reynolds, C. R., & Brown, R. T. (1984). *Perspectives on bias in mental testing*. Plenum Press.

Reynolds, C. R., & Kaiser, S. M. (1990). Test bias in psychological assessment. In T. B. Gutkin & C. R. Reynolds (Eds.), *The handbook of school psychology* (pp. 847–525). Wiley.

Reynolds, C. R., & Kamphaus, R. W. (2003). *Reynolds Intellectual Assessment Scales: Professional manual*. PAR

Reynolds, C. R., & Kamphaus, R. W. (2015a). *Reynolds Intellectual Assessment Scales, Second Edition: Professional manual*. PAR.

Reynolds, C. R., & Kamphaus, R. W. (2015b). *Behavior Assessment System for Children, Third Edition: Manual*. Pearson.

Reynolds, C. R., Lowe, P. A., & Saenz, A. L. (1999). The problem of bias in psychological assessment. In T. B. Gutkin & C. R. Reynolds (Eds.), *The handbook of school psychology* (3rd ed., pp. 549–595). Wiley.

Reynolds, C. R., & Mason, B. A. (2009). Measurement and statistical problems in neuropsychological assessment of children. In C. R. Reynolds and E. Fletcher-Jansen (Eds.), *Handbook of clinical child neuropsychology*. Springer. https://doi.org/10.1007/978-0-387-78867-8_9

Reynolds, C. R., & Suzuki, L. A. (2013). Bias in psychological assessment: An empirical review and recommendations. In I. B. Weiner (Ed.), *Handbook of psychology* (2nd ed., pp. 82–113). Wiley.

Rodriguez, A., Reise, S. P., & Haviland, M. G. (2016a). Applying bifactor statistical indices in the evaluation of psychological measures. *Journal of Personality Assessment*, 98(3), 223–237. https://doi.org/10.1080/00223891.2015.1089249

Rodriguez, A., Reise, S. P., & Haviland, M. G. (2016b). Evaluating bifactor models: Calculating and interpreting statistical indices. *Psychological Methods*, 21(2), 137–150. https://doi.org/10.1037/met0000045

Rossen, E., & Oakland, T. (2008). Graduate preparation in research methods: The current status of APA-Accredited professional programs in psychology. *Training and Education in Professional Psychology*, 2(1), 42–49. https://doi.org/10.1037/1931-3918.2.1.42

Satorra, A., & Bentler, P. M. (1988). *Scaling corrections for chi-square statistics in covariance structure analysis*. In ASA 1988 Proceedings of the Business and Economic Statistics Section (pp. 308–313). American Statistical Association.

Schaefer, B. A., Watkins, M. W., & Carivez, G. L. (2001). Cross–context agreement of the Adjustment Scales for Children and Adolescents. *Journal of Psychoeducational Assessment*, 19(2), 123–136. https://doi.org/10.1177/073428290101900202

Schmid, J., & Leiman, J. M. (1957). The development of hierarchical factor solutions. *Psychometrika*, 22, 53–61. https://doi.org/10.1007/bf02289209

Schreiber, J. B., Nora, A., Stage, F. K., Barlow, E. A., & King, J. (2006). Reporting structural equation modeling and confirmatory factor analysis results: A review. *Journal of Educational Research*, 99(6), 323–337. https://doi.org/10.3200/JOER.99.6.323–338

Schwartz, A. (2006). Diagnostic test calculator (version 2010042101). http://araw.mede.uic.edu/cgi-bin/testcalc.pl?DT=69&Dt=1&dT=5&dt=69&2x2=Compute

Sellbom, M., & Tellegen, A. (2019). Factor analysis in psychological assessment research: Common pitfalls and recommendations. *Psychological Assessment*, 31(12), 1428–1441. https://doi.org/10.1037/pas0000623

Shealy, R., & Stout, W. F. (1993). A model-based standardization approach that separates true bias/DIF from group differences and detects test bias/DTF as well as item bias/DIF. *Psychometrika*, 58(2), 159–194. https://doi.org/10.1007/bf02294572

Shrout, P. E., & Fleiss, J. L. (1979). Intraclass correlations: Uses in assessing rater reliability. *Psychological Bulletin*, 86(2), 420–428. https://doi.org/10.1037/0033-2909.86.2.420

Shrout, P. E., Spitzer, R. L., & Fleiss, J. L. (1987). Quantification of agreement in psychiatric diagnosis revisited. *Archives of General Psychiatry*, 44(2), 172–177. https://doi.org/10.1001/archpsyc.1987.01800140084013

Smith, G. A. (1986). Observer Drift: A drifting definition. *The Behavior Analyst*, 9(1), 127–128. https://doi.org/10.1007/BF03391937

Spearman, C. (1904). The proof and measurement of association between two things. *The American Journal of Psychology*, 15(1), 72–101. https://doi.org/10.2307/1412159

Spearman, C. (1910). Correlation calculated from faulty data. *British Journal of Psychology*, 3(3), 271–295. http://doi.org/10.1111/j.2044-8295.1910.tb00206.x

Spearman, C. (1927). *The abilities of man: Their nature and measurement*. Macmillan.

Stanley, J. C. (1971). Reliability. In R. L. Thorndike (Ed.), *Educational measurement* (2nd ed., pp. 356–442). American Council on Education.

Straus, S. E., Glasziou, P., Richardson, W. S., & Haynes, R. B. (2019). *Evidence-based medicine: How to practice and teach EBM* (5th ed.). Churchill Livingstone.

Streiner, D. L., Norman, G. R., & Cairney, J. (2015). *Health measurement scales: A practical guide to their development and use* (5th ed.). Oxford University Press.

Styck, K. M., & Walsh, S. M. (2016). Evaluating the prevalence and impact of examiner errors on the Wechsler scales of intelligence: A meta-analysis. *Psychological Assessment*, 28(1), 3–17. https://doi.org/10.1037/pas0000157

Swaminathan, H., & Rogers, H. J. (1990). Detecting differential item functioning using logistic regression procedures. *Journal of Educational Measurement*, 27(4), 361–370. https://doi.org/10.1111/j.1745-3984.1990.tb00754.x

Swets, J. A. (1988). Measuring the accuracy of diagnostic systems. *Science*, 240(4857), 1285–1293. https://doi.org/10.1126/science.3287615

Swets, J. A. (1996). *Signal Detection Theory and ROC Analysis in psychological diagnostics: Collected Papers*. Lawrence Erlbaum Associates.

Swets, J. A., Dawes, R. M., & Monahan, J. (2000). Psychological science can improve diagnostic decisions. *Psychological Science in the Public Interest, 1*(1), 1–26. https://doi.org/10.1111/1529-1006.001

Tabachnick, B. G., & Fidell, L. S. (2019). *Using multivariate statistics* (7th ed.). Boston: Pearson.

Thompson, B. (2004). *Exploratory and confirmatory factor analysis: Understanding concepts and applications.* American Psychological Association.

Thompson, B., & Vacha-Haase, T. (2000). Psychometrics is datametrics: The test is not reliable. *Educational and Psychological Measurement, 60*(2), 174–195. https://doi.org/10.1177/0013164400602002

Thorndike, E. L. (1914). The nature, purposes, and general methods of measurements of educational products. In G. M. Whipple (Ed.), *The seventeenth yearbook of the National Society for Study of Education: Part II The measurement of educational products* (pp. 16–24). Public School Publishing.

Thorndike, R. L. (1971). Concepts of culture-fairness. *Journal of Educational Measurement, 8*(2), 63–70. https://doi.org/10.1111/j.1745-3984.1971.tb00907.x

Thurstone, L. L. (1947). *Multiple factor analysis.* University of Chicago Press.

Treat, T. A., & Viken, R. J. (2012). Measuring test performance with signal detection theory techniques. In H. Cooper, P. M. Camic, D. L., Long, A. T. Panter, D. Rindskopf, & K. J. Sher (Eds.), *Handbook of research methods in psychology: Volume 1 Foundations, planning, measures, and psychometrics* (pp. 723–744). American Psychological Association.

Tucker, L. R. (1951). *A method for synthesis of factor analysis studies.* Personnel Research Section Report No. 984. Department of the Army.

Turner, S. M., DeMers, S. T., Fox, H. R., & Reed, G. M. (2001). APA's guidelines for test user qualifications: An executive summary. *American Psychologist, 56*(12), 1099–1113. https://doi.org/10.1037/0003-066x.56.12.1099

Ullman, J. B. (2001). Structural equation modeling. In B. G. Tabachnick & L. S. Fidell (Eds.), *Using multivariate statistics* (4th ed.). Allyn & Bacon.

U.S. Department of Education. (2006). 34 CFR Parts 300 and 301 Assistance to States for the Education of children With Disabilities and Preschool Grants for Children with Disabilities; Final Rule. *Federal Register, 71* (156), 46540–46845.

Velicer, W. F. (1976). Determining the number of components form the matrix of partial correlations. *Psychometrika, 31*, 321–327. https://doi.org/10.1007/bf02293557

Velicer, W. F., Peacock, A. C., & Jackson, D. N. (1982). A comparison of component and factor patterns: A Monte Carlo approach. *Multivariate Behavioral Research, 17*(3), 371–388. https://doi.org/10.1207/s15327906mbr1703_5

Wasserman, J. D., & Bracken, B. A. (2013). Fundamental psychometric considerations in assessment. In I. B. Weiner, J. R. Graham, & J. A. Naglieri (Eds.), *Handbook of psychology: Assessment psychology* (2nd ed., vol. 10, pp. 50–81). John Wiley & Sons.

Walker, C. M. (2011). What's the DIF? Why differential item functioning analyses are an important part of instrument development and validation. *Journal of Psychoeducational Assessment, 29*(4), 364–376. https://doi.org/10.1177/0734282911406666

Watkins, M. W. (2000). Cognitive profile analysis: A shared professional myth. *School Psychology Quarterly, 15*(4), 465–479. https://doi.org/10.1037/h0088802

Watkins, M. W. (2010). Structure of the Wechsler Intelligence Scale for Children—Fourth Edition among a national sample of referred students. *Psychological Assessment, 22*(4), 782–787. https://doi.org/10.1037/a0020043

Watkins, M. W. (2013). *Omega* [Computer software]. Ed & Psych Associates.

Watkins, M. W. (2017): The reliability of multidimensional neuropsychological measures: From alpha to omega. *The Clinical Neuropsychologist 31*(6–7), 1113–1126. https://doi.org/10.1080/13854046.2017.1317364

Watkins, M. W. (2018). Exploratory factor analysis: A guide to best practice. *Journal of Black Psychology, 44*(3), 219–246. https://doi.org/10.1177/0095798418771807

Watkins, M. W. (2020a). *Invariance* [Computer software]. Ed & Psych Associates.

Watkins, M. W. (2020b). *Diagnostic Utility Statistics* [Computer software]. Ed & Psych Associates.

Watkins, M. W. (2021a). *A Step-by-Step Guide to Exploratory Factor Analysis with R and RStudio*. Routledge. https://doi.org/10.4324/9781003120001-3

Watkins, M. W. (2021b). *A Step-by-Step Guide to Exploratory Factor Analysis with SPSS*. Routledge. https://doi.org/10.4324/9781003149347

Watkins, M. W. (2022). *A Step-by-Step Guide to Exploratory Factor Analysis with Stata*. Routledge. https://doi.org/10.4324/9781003149286

Watkins, M. W., & Canivez, G. L. (1997). Interrater agreement of the Adjustment Scales for Children and Adolescents. *Diagnostique*, *22*(4), 205–213. https://doi.org/10.1177/073724779702200402

Watkins, M. W., & Canivez, G. L. (2004). Temporal stability of WISC-III subtest composite: Strengths and weaknesses. *Psychological Assessment*, *16*(2), 133–138. https://doi.org/10.1037/1040-3590.16.2.133

Watkins, M. W., & Canivez, G. L. (2022). Assessing the psychometric utility of IQ scores: A tutorial using the Wechsler Intelligence Scale for Children–Fifth Edition. *School Psychology Review*, *51*(5), 619–633. https://doi.org/10.1080/2372966X.2020.1816804

Watkins, M. W., Canivez, G. L., Dombrowski, S. C., McGill, R. J., Pritchard, A. E., Holingue, C. B., & Jacobson, L. A. (2022). Long-term stability of Wechsler Intelligence Scale for Children–Fifth Edition scores in a clinical sample. *Applied Neuropsychology: Child*, *11*(3), 422–428. https://doi.org/10.1080/21622965.2021.1875827

Watkins, M. W., Dombrowski, S. C., McGill, R. J., Canivez, G. L., Pritchard, A. E., & Jacobson, L. A. (2023). Bootstrap Exploratory Graph Analysis of the WISC–V with a clinical sample. *Journal of Intelligence*, *11*(137), 1–12. https://doi.org/10.3390/jintelligence11070137

Wechsler, D. (1991). *Manual for the Wechsler Intelligence Scale for Children-Third Edition*. Psychological Corporation.

Wechsler, D. (2003). *Wechsler Intelligence Scale for Children-Fourth Edition technical and interpretive manual*. NCS Pearson.

Wechsler, D. (2008). *Wechsler Adult Intelligence Scale–Fourth Edition: Technical and interpretive manual*. Pearson.

Wechsler, D. (2012). *Wechsler Preschool and Primary Scale of Intelligence-Fourth Edition: Technical and interpretive manual*. Pearson.

Wechsler, D. (2014). *Wechsler Intelligence Scale for Children-Fifth Edition technical and interpretive manual*. NCS Pearson.

Weiner, I. B. (1989). On competence and ethicality in psychodiagnostic assessment. *Journal of Personality Assessment*, *53*(4), 827–831. https://do.org/10.1207/s15327752jpa5304_18

Weiner, I. B. (2003). Prediction and postdiction in clinical decision making. *Clinical Psychology: Science and Practice*, *10*(3), 335–338. https://doi.org/10.1093/clipsy.bpg030

Weiss, L. G., Keith, T. Z., Zhu, J., & Chen, H. (2013a). WAIS–IV and clinical validation of the four- and five-factor interpretative approaches. *Journal of Psychoeducational Assessment*, *31*(2), 94–113. https://doi.org/10.1177/0734282913478030

Weiss, L. G., Keith, T. Z., Zhu, J., & Chen, H. (2013b). WISC–IV and clinical validation of the four- and five-factor interpretative approaches. *Journal of Psychoeducational Assessment*, *31*(2), 114–131. https://doi.org/10.1177/0734282913478032

Weiss, L. G., & Prifitera, A. (1995). An evaluation of differential prediction of WIAT achievement scores from WISC–III FSIQ across ethnic and gender groups. *Journal of School Psychology*, *33*(4), 297–304. https://doi.org/10.1016/0022-4405(95)00016-f

Widaman, K. F., & Olivera-Aguilar, M. (2023). Investigating measurement invariance using confirmatory factor analysis. In R. H. Hoyle (Ed.), *Handbook of structural equation modeling* (2nd ed., pp. 367–384). Guilford Press.

Wick, J. W., Beggs, D. L., & Mouw, J. T. (1989). *Developing Cognitive Abilities Test* (2nd ed.). American Testronics.

Willson, V. L., & Reynolds, C. R. (1982). Methodological and statistical problems in determining membership in clinical populations. *Clinical Neuropsychology*, *4*(3), 134–138.

Wright, A. J., Chavez, L., Edelstein, B. A., Grus, C. L., Krishnamurthy, R., Lieb, R., Mihura, J. L., Pincus, A. L., & Wilson, M. (2021). Education and training guidelines for psychological assessment in health service psychology. *American Psychologist 76*(5), 794–801. https://doi.org/10.1037/amp0000742

Wrigley, C. S., & Neuhaus, J. O. (1955). The matching of two sets of factors. *American Psychologist*, *10*(8), 418–419. https://doi.org/10.1037/h0049379

Youngstrom, E. A. (2014). A primer on receiver operating characteristic analysis and diagnostic efficiency statistics for pediatric psychology: We are ready to ROC. *Journal of Pediatric Psychology*, *39*, 204– 221. https://doi.org/10.1093/jpepsy/jst062

Youngstrom, E. A., Salcedo, S., Frazier, T. W., & Perez Algorta, G. (2019). Is the finding too good to be true? Moving from "More Is Better" to thinking in terms of simple predictions and credibility. *Journal of Clinical Child and Adolescent Psychology*, *48*(6), 811–824. https://doi.org/10.1080/15374416.2019.1669158

Youngstrom, E. A., Van Meter, A., Frazier, T. W., Hunsley, J., Prinstein, M. J., Ong, M.-L., & Youngstrom, J. K. (2017). Evidence-Based Assessment as an integrative model for applying psychological science to guide the voyage of treatment. *Clinical Psychology: Science and Practice*, *24*(4), 331– 363. https://doi .org/10.1111/cpsp.12207

Yung, Y. –F., Thissen, D., & McLeod, L. (1999). On the relationship between the higher-order factor model and the hierarchical factor model. *Psychometrika*, *64*(2), 113–128. https://doi.org/10.1007/bf02294531

Zinbarg, R. E., Revelle, W., Yovel, I., & Li, W. (2005). Cronbach's alpha, Revelle's beta, and McDonald's omega h: Their relations with each other and two alternative conceptualizations of reliability. *Psychometrika*, *70*(1), 123–133. https://doi.org/10.1007/s11336-003-0974-7

Zinbarg, R. E., Yovel, I., Revelle, W., & McDonald, R. P. (2006). Estimating generalizability to a latent variable common to all of a scale's indicators: A comparison of estimators for ωh. *Applied Psychological Measurement*, *30*(2), 121–144. https://doi.org/10.1177/0146621605278814

Zoski, K. W., & Jurs, S. (1996). An objective counterpart to the visual scree test for factor analysis: The standard error scree. *Educational and Psychological Measurement*, *56*(3), 443–451. https://doi.org/10 .1177/0013164496056003006

Zumbo, B. D. (1999). *A handbook on the theory and methods of differential item functioning (DIF): Logistic regression modeling as a unitary framework for binary and Likert-type (ordinal) item scores.* Directorate of Human Resources Research and Evaluation, Department of National Defense.

Zumbo, B. D. (2007). Three generations of differential item functioning (DIF) analyses: Considering where it has been, where it is now, and where it is going. *Language Assessment Quarterly*, *4*(2), 223–233. https:// doi.org/10.1080/15434300701375832

Zumbo, B. D., Liu, Y., Wu, A. D., Shear, B. R., Olvera Astivia, O. R., & Ark, T. K. (2015). A methodology for Zumbo's third generation DIF analyses and the ecology of item responding. *Language Assessment Quarterly*, *12*(1), 136–151. http://doi.org/10.1080/15434303.2014.972559

Zumbo, B. D., & Thomas, D. R. (1997). *A measure of effect size for a model-based approach for studying DIF* (Working paper of the Edgeworth Laboratory for Quantitative Behavioral Science). University of Northern British Columbia.

Chapter 2

Wechsler Intelligence Scale for Children–Fifth Edition

Psychometric Fitness and Evidence-Based Interpretation

Gary L. Canivez

Assessment of intelligence or cognitive abilities is an important component in educational, clinical, and psychoeducational evaluation of child and adolescent functioning, impairment, and psychopathology. Historically, Wechsler scales of intelligence have been the most frequently used intelligence tests in school and clinical psychology (e.g., Goh et al., 1981; Hutton et al., 1992; Pfeiffer et al., 2000; Stinnett et al., 1994; C. E. Watkins Jr. et al., 1995), and the Wechsler Intelligence Scale for Children–Fifth Edition (WISC–V; Wechsler, 2014a) continues that popularity as one of the most often used tests (and most frequently used intelligence test) among school psychologists (Benson et al., 2019; Groth-Marnat & Wright, 2016; L. T. Miller et al., 2021).

Interpretive recommendations for clinical use of the WISC–V (as with earlier editions) frequently follow a successive-level approach (e.g., Flanagan & Alfonso, 2017; Groth-Marnat & Wright, 2016; Kaufman et al., 2016; Sattler et al., 2024; Wechsler, 2014b) that incorporates presentation and description of obtained normative scores (FSIQ, Index Scores, Subtest Scores, pseudo-composites [i.e., Quantitative Reasoning, Auditory Working Memory, Nonverbal, etc.]) followed by within-person or *intra-individual* comparisons of scores (referred to by McDermott et al., 1992 as ipsative and by Freeman & Y.-L. Chen, 2019 as idiographic) to provide profile analyses. Profile analysis involves comparing factor level index scores to the individual's average performance, comparing subtest scores to the individual's average subtest performance, pairwise comparisons of factor index scores, pairwise comparisons of subtest scores, and comparisons of various pseudo-composites (ancillary index scores) to identify specious cognitive strengths and weaknesses thereby "going beyond the information contained in the FSIQ or the index scores" (Sattler et al., 2024, p. 343). Such putative cognitive strengths and weaknesses are then used to support a panoply of educational recommendations spanning remediation, classroom and instructional modifications or accommodations, and placement in special programs (Groth-Marnat & Wright, 2016; Kaufman et al., 2016; J. L. Miller et al., 2016; Sattler et al., 2024; Wechsler, 2014b).

While these methods and uses of score comparisons for clinical and educational recommendations have been used for many decades, their origins began with the Rapaport et al. (1945–1946) approach that not only interpreted score strengths, weaknesses, and profile shape in cognitive terms but also incorporated psychoanalytic interpretations (Kamphaus et al., 2012), which Kaufman et al. (2016) labeled "stupid testing" (p. 7). Kaufman (1979) attempted "to impose some empirical order on profile interpretation; to make sensible inferences from the data with full awareness of errors of measurement; and to steer the field away from the psychiatric couch" (p. 8) and should be applauded for his attempt in emphasizing interpretation of test score differences that were statistically significant and rare. However, empirical examinations of intelligence test profile interpretation methods have consistently produced negative findings in reliability, validity, and diagnostic utility of the basic scores used in profile interpretation as well as their comparisons (see Canivez, 2013a; McGill et al., 2018; Watkins, 2000). Despite the considerable adverse research and absence of replicated support, profile analysis still often forms the basis for professional training and clinical application in intelligence test interpretation (Farmer et al., 2021; Kranzler et al., 2020; Lockwood et al., 2022; Lockwood & Farmer, 2020; L. T. Miller et al., 2021; Sotelo-Dynega, & Dixon, 2014). In the face of negative findings for reliability, validity, and diagnostic utility of profile interpretation methods there seems to be a universal appeal to theory as though theory were sufficient to grant salvation to the method. When empirical evidence regarding basic measurement properties of test scores and comparisons contraindicates use, theory is no savior. All test scores, score comparisons, and interpretation methods require strong, replicated empirical evidence to support specific use (AERA, APA, NCME, 2014); however, such supportive evidence for profile interpretation remains elusive (Canivez, 2013a; McGill et al., 2018; Watkins, 2000).

Evidence-based test interpretation requires that test users consider the psychometric fitness of all provided scores and score comparisons (ipsative and pairwise), as well as evidence for diagnostic applications (or hypothesis generation) and treatment recommendations emanating from the scores and score comparisons. Importantly, the crucial questions are what evidence exists that supports diagnostic classification (or hypothesis generation) based on scores or score comparisons and what evidence exists that supports differential efficacy of interventions or program placements based on test-based strengths and weaknesses. As noted in Chapter 1, consideration of the psychometric properties of test scores and score comparisons allows the user to know what the test can do so that they may act accordingly (Weiner, 1989). As Kranzler & Floyd (2020) stipulated, "just because the test or its scoring system produces a score (and score profiles), examiners need not interpret these results or communicate these findings in their oral or written reports" (p. 203). Ethics and professional standards demand competency in test use, but often test users lack the training and competency to adequately understand and apply information regarding test psychometric properties. For those who do have such psychometric literacy, even if they read the technical manual, that manual may lack important and necessary details regarding methods used and lack full disclosure of results may not allow test users the ability to render appropriate judgments about psychometric support for the various scores, score comparisons, and interpretive suggestions (e.g., Canivez, 2010, 2014, 2017; Canivez & Watkins, 2016). Relatedly, test users must be mindful of financial conflicts of interest when considering information presented in workshops and literature (Beaujean et al., 2024). This chapter summarizes and reviews the available evidence for the psychometric fitness of the WISC–V based on the information provided in the *WISC–V Technical and Interpretive Manual* (Wechsler, 2014b) and studies identified in the extant peer-review literature.

Development of the WISC–V

Precursors

Groundwork for revision of the Wechsler Intelligence Scale for Children–Fourth Edition (WISC–IV; Wechsler, 2003) for the WISC–V was foreshadowed by an article promoting a possible five-factor structure for the WISC–IV related to the so-called Cattell-Horn-Carroll (CHC; McGrew, 2005) theory (model) based on re-analyses of the WISC–IV standardization normative and clinical samples (Weiss et al., 2013) and models suggested by Keith et al. (2006). The Weiss et al. (2013) article was the subject of several invited commentaries for a journal special issue, and Canivez and Kush (2013) reported numerous theoretical, methodological, and practical problems, many of which also appear to be present in the WISC–V (Canivez & Watkins, 2016). Of particular concern were the abandonment of simple structure (Thurstone, 1947) by including numerous subtest cross-loadings that produced miniscule global fit improvements, creating an intermediary "inductive reasoning" factor between the Fluid Reasoning (FR or G_f) factor and the subtest indicators (Picture Concepts and Matrix Reasoning) that may have been added to make the model work: retaining G_f despite the standardized path coefficient of higher-order g with G_f of 1.0 (rendering G_f empirically indistinguishable from g and thus redundant); failure to test rival bifactor models; failure to provide decomposed variance sources with the Schmid and Leiman transformation (SLT; 1957) procedure (something Carroll [1995] insisted upon); and failure to provide model-based reliability/validity and dimensionality estimates. The Weiss et al. speculations regarding primary and secondary interpretations of WISC–IV subtests delineated in their Table 6 that promoted first-order factors to primary interpretation while relegating general intelligence (g) to secondary interpretation based on the factor loadings was misguided. Without decomposing sources of subtest variance, the variance of g is obfuscated in their higher-order model, providing an illusion of first-order factor importance. Inspection of Weiss et al. Table 3 indicated that subtest g loadings (subtest relationships with the general factor) mostly reflected primary measurement of g. It is interesting that Keith et al. (2006) included fewer subtest cross loadings in their CHC model and did not introduce an intermediary inductive reasoning factor between G_f and subtest indicators but observed the standardized loading of 1.0 for g to G_f (rendering G_f empirically indistinguishable from g and thus redundant) and also failed to report decomposed variance estimates with the SLT, thereby obfuscating g variance and group factor variance.

Because of the WISC–IV and subsequent WISC–V link to the CHC model, there are additional unresolved problems (Canivez & Youngstrom, 2019; McGill & Dombrowski, 2019) that impact not only the WISC–V but other measures purporting to reflect the CHC model including the Woodcock-Johnson Tests of Cognitive Abilities, Fourth Edition (WJ IV Cognitive; Schrank et al., 2014) that was designed to be the CHC reference instrument. Major problems with the WJ IV Cognitive were identified by Canivez (2017), and independent assessments of the WJ IV (Dombrowski et al., 2017; Dombrowski et al., 2018) failed to replicate the purported structure reported in the *WJ IV Technical Manual* (McGrew et al., 2014). The same problems were previously identified in the Woodcock–Johnson III Tests of Cognitive Abilities (WJ III Cognitive; Woodcock et al., 2001), which was the first instrument constructed to represent the putative CHC model (McGill & Dombrowski, 2019). Independent assessments of the WJ III Cognitive factor structure (e.g., Dombrowski, 2013; Dombrowski & Watkins, 2013; Strickland et al., 2015) did not replicate the structure reported in the *WJ III Technical Manual* (McGrew & Woodcock, 2001). Whether this is a problem of the tests (WJ III and WJ IV), the CHC model, or both cannot be ascertained solely by structural validity studies, but there clearly are numerous problems (Canivez & Youngstrom, 2019; Wasserman, 2019). In the context of CHC constructs predicting reading and mathematics achievement, a meta-analysis indicated the largest effect of prediction was that of psychometric g, which accounted for more achievement variance than all CHC broad abilities combined (Zaboski et al., 2018), refuting the McGrew and Wendling (2010) narrative synthesis that de-emphasized interpretation of psychometric g in favor of CHC–based broad abilities. Zaboski et al. also noted the problem that many studies in the meta-analysis did not include g estimates, so ignoring psychometric g and emphasizing broad CHC abilities reflected by factor composite scores that conflate g variance and broad factor variance is a problem requiring more research assessing CHC *incremental validity* (e.g., Canivez, 2013b; Glutting et al., 2006).

WISC–V Development and Content

Historical features in WISC evolution were presented as introduction to the WISC–V although it seemed odd when development of the WISC–III was described to have "retained all of the subtests from the WISC–R and introduced a new subtest, Symbol Search, as a measure of processing speed" (Wechsler, 2014b, p. 5). This appears to be a bit of revisionist history given that the stated purpose for the creation and inclusion of their new Symbol Search subtest noted in the WISC–III *Manual* was so "abilities measured by the third factor could be better distinguished" (Wechsler, 1991, p. 4). The use of Symbol Search to strengthen the former Freedom from Distractibility (FD) factor (Little, 1992; Wechsler, 1991) did not have the desired effect of strengthening FD; rather, it pulled Coding away from FD and formed their newly specified factor termed Processing Speed (PS). The result then left Arithmetic and Digit Span as lone indicators of FD.

Excellent descriptions of the WISC–V content and its development from its predecessor, the WISC–IV, are provided in the *WISC–V Technical and Interpretive Manual* (Wechsler, 2014b). Among the changes, the WISC–IV Word Reasoning and Picture Completion subtests were eliminated and Visual Puzzles and Figure Weights (subtests introduced in the WAIS–IV; Wechsler, 2008) were added to improve measurement of visual spatial (VS) and fluid reasoning (FR) abilities, respectively; and Picture Span (adapted from WPPSI–IV Picture Memory subtest; Wechsler, 2012) was added to measure working memory (WM) with a visually oriented task. In their review of the WISC–V, Canivez and Watkins (2016) noted several positive elements including the large, demographically representative standardization sample with norm age block samples exceeding the recommended size (Kranzler & Floyd, 2020), adequate floor and ceiling levels of standardized scores for most clinical applications, overlap with the WPPSI–IV and WAIS–IV to allow appropriate selection depending on clinical questions and child characteristics, and numerous manual and technical supplements.

The WISC–V includes the FSIQ as an estimate of psychometric g, five factor-based Primary Index Scale scores (Verbal Comprehension Index [VCI], Visual Spatial Index [VSI], Fluid Reasoning Index [FRI], Working Memory Index [WMI], Processing Speed Index [PSI]) that purportedly measure broad abilities with combinations of primary and secondary subtests, and 16 intelligence-oriented subtests that purportedly measure narrow abilities. In addition to these factorially derived scores there are five contrived Ancillary Index Scale pseudo-composite scores (Quantitative Reasoning Index [QRI], Auditory Working Memory Index [AWMI], Nonverbal Index [NVI], General Ability Index [GAI], Cognitive Proficiency Index [CPI]) that were rationally created from primary and secondary subtests. A final set of three Complementary Index Scales were derived from newly created subtests that are not intelligence-oriented subtests so may not be substituted for primary or secondary subtests and are thus not included in subsequent psychometric review.

WISC–V score analyses and interpretation methods are described and annotated with examples in the *WISC–V Technical and Interpretive Manual* (Wechsler, 2014b), *Wechsler Intelligence Scale for Children–Fifth Edition Administration and Scoring Manual* (Wechsler, 2014c), and its supplement (Wechsler 2014d). Interpretation of WISC–V factor index scores as described in the manuals is, however, problematic. It was claimed that the WISC–V index scores were "reliable and valid measures of the primary cognitive constructs they intend to represent" (Wechsler, 2014b, p. 149) with the VCI measuring "the child's ability to access and apply acquired word knowledge," which involves "verbal concept formation, reasoning, and expression" (Wechsler, 2014b, p. 157); the VSI measuring "the child's ability to evaluate visual details and to understand visual spatial relationships to construct geometric designs from a model" (Wechsler, 2014b, p. 158); and the FRI measuring "the child's ability to detect the underlying conceptual relationship among visual objects and to use reasoning to identify and apply rules" (p. 158). Watkins and Canivez (2022) pointed out that the factor index scores are not pure measures of their intended constructs because they are complexly determined, including mixtures of *g* and group factor variance (empirical illustrations of this are presented later in this chapter). Beaujean and Benson (2019) noted that group factor scores "represent a collection of different attributes" (p. 129), and WISC–V users "will not know which attribute to invoke to account for a particular score" (Gustafsson & Åberg-Bengtsson, 2010, p. 97). While "each score obtained from a scale should reflect a single coherent psychological variable" (Furr, 2011, p. 26), multidimensionality of WISC–V factor index scores creates interpretation difficulties.

In addition to reporting subtest scaled scores (*M* = 10, *SD* = 3) that may be graphed for visual display of the scaled score profile, composite scores (*M* = 100, *SD* = 15), percentiles, and estimated true score confidence intervals (90% or 95%) are provided for the FSIQ, VCI, VSI, FRI, WMI, and PSI and composite scores may also be graphed for visual display of the index score profile. Primary analyses include ipsative (intra-individual) comparisons of the five index scores to either the mean index score or the FSIQ with user selected statistical significance critical value level (.15, .10, .05, .01) and reference group base rate of the total sample or by ability level. Subtest level ipsative (intra-individual) comparisons are suggested for the 10 primary subtests to either the mean of the 10 primary subtests or the seven FSIQ subtests with user selected statistical significance critical value level (.15, .10, .05, .01). These provide indications of index score or subtest score strengths and weaknesses. Pairwise comparisons of the five index scores with user selected statistical significance critical value level (.15, .10, .05, .01) and reference group base rate of the total sample or by ability level are next in primary analyses followed by pairwise subtest comparisons of the two primary subtests within each factor index score with user selected statistical significance critical value level (.15, .10, .05, .01). These are followed by derivation of ancillary and complementary analyses where the five Ancillary Index Scores (QRI, AWMI, NVI, GAI, CPI) and three Complementary Index Scores (NSI, STI, SRI) are generated and reported with percentiles and estimated true score confidence intervals (90% or 95%). Various ancillary and complementary index score pairwise comparisons and subtest pairwise comparisons with user selected statistical significance critical value level (.15, .10, .05, .01) are provided. Finally, a variety of process analysis pairwise comparisons may be conducted with user selected statistical significance critical value level (.15, .10, .05, .01) and reference group base rate of the total sample or by ability level. Each of these comparisons yielding intra-individual strengths and weaknesses or pairwise comparison differences is linked to possible interpretations impacting the assessed child. While difference scores are often examined in test score interpretations, Farmer and Kim (2020) found difference score reliability in the WISC–V to be generally inadequate and inconsistent across age especially among subtests so they recommended clinicians not use these difference scores in clinical decision-making.

As illustrated above and in Chapter 1, ethics and test standards dictate that clinical use of scores and inferences from scores and score comparisons require strong empirical evidence of psychometric support. That psychometric support must be provided by satisfactory estimates of test score (and score comparison) reliability, validity, and utility (diagnostic or treatment). Information regarding these WISC–V psychometric properties is presented below.

WISC–V Psychometric Properties

WISC–V Reliability

Internal Consistency

WISC–V internal consistency was estimated using the split-half method (except for speeded subtests [Coding, Symbol Search, Cancellation] where short-term test-retest reliability was used), and estimates for subtests and composite scores by age and for the total sample are provided (see Table 4.1, Wechsler, 2014b). Internal consistency estimates were good to excellent for subtests (ranging .81–.94), factor-based composites (ranging .88–.96), and ancillary composites (ranging .93–.96). Average internal consistency estimates across age met or exceeded the .90 criterion for high-stakes decisions and thus possible score interpretation (Kranzler & Floyd, 2020; Wasserman & Bracken, 2013) for Figure Weights, Arithmetic, and Digit Span subtests, all factor index scores (except PSI), all ancillary index scores, and the FSIQ. While encouraging, such estimates might be inaccurate estimates of reliability (Furr, 2022) in part due to not assessing all sources of measurement error (Hanna et al., 1981) as well as violation of assumptions for such estimates (score unidimensionality and *tau*-equivalence) where model-based reliability and dimensionality indexes provide more appropriate estimates (Cronbach & Shavelson, 2004; Gignac & Watkins, 2013; Revelle & Condon, 2019). While such model-based estimates are not presented in the *WISC–V Technical and Interpretive Manual* (Wechsler, 2014b), they are presented later in this chapter via independent analyses as well as in numerous independent WISC–V studies published in the extant peer-review literature (detailed and referenced later in this chapter). What is of considerable concern for WISC–V factor score interpretation is the poor amount of unique variance attributable to the factor index scores after removing the variance due to *g*!

Test-Retest Reliability (Stability)

As discussed in Chapter 1, assessment of test-retest reliability (stability) of test scores is critical for tests purporting to measure constructs that are theoretically stable over time. Intelligence is one such construct and thus test-retest stability of test scores is commonly provided in intelligence and cognitive ability test technical manuals. The WISC–V is no exception. To assess test-retest stability, the WISC–V was twice administered to a sample of 218 individuals from the normative sample with an average retest interval of 26 days (range 9–82 days), which assessed the short-term stability. The average uncorrected Pearson product-moment correlations (stability coefficients) across the five age groups for the FSIQ was .91 and ranged from .68 (FRI) to .91 (VCI) for primary index scores, ranged from .76 (QRI) to .89 (GAI) for ancillary index scores, and ranged from .63 (Picture Concepts) to .89 (Vocabulary) for primary and secondary subtests. Variability corrected stability coefficients were slightly higher. As with internal consistency, Wasserman and Bracken (2013) and Kranzler and Floyd (2020) recommended stability coefficients meet or exceed the .90 criterion for high-stakes decisions and thus possible score interpretation. Of the 16 primary and secondary subtests, only the corrected Vocabulary subtest short-term stability coefficient met that standard for possible score interpretation. Among composite scores, only the FSIQ, VCI, and GAI met that standard. Mean differences across the retest interval were mostly small or trivial in effect size but reflected somewhat higher scores at Time 2, particularly for PS subtests (and the PSI).

Canivez and Watkins (2016) noted the absence of short-term stability assessment for ipsative and pairwise composite and subtest score comparisons that form the basis of determination of cognitive strengths and weaknesses, which are crucial components of WISC–V interpretation (Wechsler, 2014a, 2014b), and to date it appears that such assessments have still not been conducted or reported by the publisher.[1] Neglect of assessment of stability of ipsative and pairwise composite and subtest score comparisons was also present in earlier versions of the WISC as well as other Wechsler scales such as the *Wechsler Adult Intelligence Scale–Fourth Edition* (WAIS–IV; Wechsler, 2008) and the *Wechsler Preschool and Primary Scale of Intelligence–Fourth Edition* (WPPSI–IV; Wechsler, 2012). Further, no peer-reviewed studies reporting stability of such cognitive strengths and weaknesses from the WISC–V normative sample could be located. If such differences and comparisons are to be recommended and used in clinical assessments to determine cognitive strengths and weaknesses, then assessment of their longitudinal stability is crucial to ascertain the extent to which such strengths and weaknesses are sufficiently reliable. If such strengths and weaknesses are not sufficiently reliable then interpretations and uses of them will be unreliable and misleading despite the intuitive appeal. The benefit of such an assessment would be that information about the stability of such cognitive strengths and weaknesses in a normative sample would help inform use, but to date there appears to be no such research.[2]

Watkins et al. (2022) examined and reported results of a long-term WISC–V test-retest stability study with a sample of 225 children and adolescents twice administered all 10 WISC–V primary subtests with an average retest interval of 2.6 years (*SD* = 0.9, range = 0.2–5.1 years). Archival data were obtained from a large outpatient clinic where the WISC–V was used in clinical neuropsychological evaluations. Examination of the long-term stability included nomothetic based scores (subtest scaled scores and composite scores) and idiographic based comparisons (intra-individual cognitive strengths and weaknesses using Kaufman et al., 2016 "intelligent rules of thumb" and scatter or score variability defined by Courville et al., 2016). Nomothetic based score stability found no statistically significant subtest or composite score changes across the retest interval and mean difference effect sizes were trivial reflecting *level agreement* (McDermott, 1988). Test-retest stability coefficients (Pearson *r*s) ranged from .50 (Picture Span) to .70 (Vocabulary) for subtests and ranged from .69 (FRI) to .86 (FSIQ) for composites and all were statistically significant (*p* < .05). While this generally supports *pattern agreement* (McDermott, 1988), none of the subtest or composite correlations met the .90 criterion (Kranzler & Floyd, 2020; Wasserman & Bracken, 2013), but three composite scores exceeded .80 (a more reasonable criterion for long-term stability [Bandalos, 2018; Schuerger & Witt, 1989]): FSIQ *r* = .86, VCI *r* = .84, VSI *r* = .82. Thus, it appears that only the FSIQ, VCI, and VSI are sufficiently stable across a long time interval.

Stability of intra-individual primary subtest differences (strengths and weaknesses) was poor with stability coefficients (*r*s) ranging from .06 (Matrix Reasoning) to .42 (Coding), primary subtest scatter *r* = .34, and kappa coefficients ranged from -.03 (Matrix Reasoning) to .49 (Digit Span) with scatter kappa = .33. Stability of composite score differences (strengths and weaknesses) were equally poor with stability coefficients (*r*s) ranging from .23 (WMI) to .43 (VSI & PSI), composite score scatter *r* = .34, and kappa coefficients ranged from .21 (FRI) to .41 (PSI) with scatter kappa = .35 (Watkins et al., 2022). These results indicated that presence or absence of intra-individual primary subtest or composite score differences or score scatter does not replicate across time and operated at chance levels. Using such cognitive strengths or weaknesses estimated by intra-individual performance differences from the WISC–V amounts to a method no better than the toss of a coin.

These WISC–V results, like those obtained with the WISC–IV (Ryan et al., 2010; Styck et al., 2019; Watkins & Smith, 2013), WISC–III (Canivez & Watkins, 1998, 1999, 2001; Watkins & Canivez, 2004), and WISC–R (Livingston et al., 2003; McDermott et al., 1992) continue to show good longitudinal stability for the FSIQ (a likely consequence of the power of aggregate scores) and verbal (VCI, VIQ) and nonverbal (VSI, PRI, PIQ) estimates, but the consistently observed unreliability of intra-individual cognitive strengths and weaknesses that form a primary method of intelligence test (WISC–V) analysis and interpretation renders such scores and resulting interpretations of dubious value. Such strengths and weaknesses that operate at chance levels cannot be informative (even for hypothesis generation), and "any long-term recommendations as to a strategy for teaching a student would need to be based on aptitudes that are likely to remain stable for months, if not years" (Cronbach & Snow, 1977, p. 161). Evidence-based WISC–V interpretation should not include intra-individual score comparisons despite the intuitive nature and decades of promotion without sufficient empirical evidence.

Interrater Agreement

Canivez and Watkins (2016) noted impressive interrater agreement for WISC–V subtest scoring was reported in the *WISC–V Technical and Interpretive Manual* (Wechsler, 2014b) with interscorer agreement ranging from .97–.99. This is, in part, due to the objective nature of item scoring for most subtests. Where some subjectivity exists for scoring Similarities, Vocabulary, Information, and Comprehension, excellent scoring rubrics and examples are provided in the *Wechsler Intelligence Scale for Children–Fifth Edition Administration and Scoring Manual* (Wechsler, 2014c) and resulted in high interscorer agreement (Wechsler, 2014b). Such evidence is important to show scoring guidelines result in scoring agreement with independent scorers, but whether such impressive WISC–V scoring agreement is replicable among clinicians not trained by or employed by the publisher is unknown. Also, while test scoring is an important source of possible error, test administration is another major source of error that may influence test scores, and while such research does not yet appear to have been conducted with the WISC–V, examiner sources of test score variance among clinicians have previously been found to be considerable (McDermott et al., 2014) although the exact source of examiner influences could not be specifically identified. Examiner errors on Wechsler scales appear quite frequent, and psychologists appear to make more errors than graduate students (Styck & Walsh, 2016). Canivez and Watkins (2016) noted the long history of examiner inaccuracy, particularly on verbally oriented subtests. Research regarding errors in WISC–V administration and scoring among clinicians is needed.

WISC–V Validity

Latent Factor Structure

One of the most consequential aspects of test validity is that of the latent factor structure because it influences the creation of scores and subsequent scoring and interpretation. The desired structure of the WISC–V was foreshadowed by earlier research with the WISC–IV (Weiss et al., 2013) where a five-factor structure that separated the former Perceptual Reasoning factor (PR) into two separate VS and FR dimensions was proposed but it appeared that several of the problems and concerns enumerated by Canivez and Kush (2013) were summarily dismissed and ignored in the *WISC–V Technical and Interpretive Manual* (Wechsler, 2014b). With the goal of WISC–IV revision into the WISC–V to include five distinct first-order factors by separating PR into two separate factors, Visual Puzzles and Figure Weights were added to help in the separation of the VS and FR dimensions, respectively. Analyses presented in the *WISC–V Technical and Interpretive Manual* (Wechsler, 2014b) provided the appearance of support for the five factors, but substantial problems exist with what was presented and perhaps greater problems about what was not presented or disclosed.

Since the publication of the WISC–V, its latent factor structure has been a source of contention and controversy. While Buros (1938) noted in the preface of the first *Mental Measurements Yearbook*, "Test users have every right to demand that test authors and publishers present full particulars concerning the methods used in constructing and validating the tests which they place on the market" (p. xiii), Canivez and Watkins (2016) delineated numerous crucial omissions, rendering an understanding of exactly what was done and why impossible even for those with relatively sophisticated psychometric skills. Despite claiming to be guided by the *Standards for Educational and Psychological Testing* (American Educational Research Association [AERA], American Psychological Association [APA], and National Council on Measurement in Education [NCME], 1999), there were many elements of methods and results that were not adequately described to allow readers of the *WISC–V Technical and Interpretive Manual* the ability to understand what exactly was done and why when assessing its structural validity (Boomsma, 2000). Beaujean (2016) did some psychometric detective work to discover what the publisher likely did in conducting WISC–V confirmatory factor analyses (CFA). Beaujean discovered that it appeared that scales were set using a relatively obscure method called *effects coding* (Little et al., 2006), and apparently a modified version of effects coding was used. Beaujean cautioned use of this modified effects coding method due to potential problems of

> parameterization of the latent variables that is not equivalent to more traditional scaling methods . . . it changes the interpretation of the latent variance's [*sic*] [variable's] scale to be the average of all variables' variances, not just the indicators for a specific latent variable . . . the *df* difference will cause a change in values of fit measures that use *df* (or number of estimated parameters) in their calculation. (p. 406)

Much more needs to be known and understood about this nontraditional method and its effects compared to traditional methods in CFA of intelligence tests like the WISC–V.

In addition to the matter of not disclosing use of effects coding, Canivez and Watkins (2016) noted the use of weighted least squares estimation that was only disclosed in the Table 5.4 footnote (Wechsler, 2014b, p. 82) with no explanation or justification, something Kline (2011) noted as essential for estimation methods other than maximum likelihood. Other problems, many identified by Canivez and Watkins, included the absence of exploratory factor analysis (EFA), cross-loading Arithmetic [AR] on *three* group factors thereby abandoning parsimony of simple structure (Thurstone, 1947), allowing the standardized path coefficient of 1.0 between *g* and the FR factor and thus retaining empirical redundancy of FR with *g*, degrees of freedom often did not comport to what was expected given freely estimated parameters of hypothesized models that suggested undisclosed fixing of parameters to not go beyond permissible bounds, an absence of consideration of rival bifactor models, failure to report decomposed variance sources between the higher-order *g* and lower-order group factors, and neglecting model-based reliability/validity and dimensionality estimates for *g* and the lower-order group factors. Some of these problems were identified by Canivez (2010, 2014) with other Wechsler scales, who implored the inclusion of variance estimates and model-based reliability/validity estimates to help test users determine adequacy of scores and score comparisons for interpretation—but to no avail. Due to these major problems, there is considerable doubt regarding the veracity of the publisher-promoted final measurement model (Model 5e); thus, Canivez and Watkins (2016) and Canivez et al. (2016, 2017) conducted and reported independent EFA and CFA with the total WISC–V standardization sample correlation matrices and descriptive statistics to provide users with the necessary evidence to guide evidence-based WISC–V interpretation. These independent studies utilized correlation matrices published in the *WISC–V Technical and Interpretive Manual* (Wechsler, 2014b) because the publisher denied access to the standardization sample data without rationale. As a result, only analyses of the WISC–V total standardization sample or with varying age groups were possible, and independent assessment of invariance across major demographic variables (sex/gender, race/ethnicity, SES, etc.) were not possible.

WISC–V Exploratory Factor Analyses

Because EFA was not reported by Wechsler (2014b), Canivez and Watkins (2016) and Canivez et al. (2016) conducted EFA using best EFA practices (Watkins, 2018; 2021). EFA and CFA are complementary methods for understanding the latent structure of a test, and there is greater confidence in a structure when EFA and CFA agree (Gorsuch, 1983). One of the virtues of EFA is that it is unrestricted, allowing data to "speak for themselves" (Carroll, 1995, p. 436), and both he and Reise (2012) argued that EFA results instruct researchers in plausible models that can be later tested in CFA. While EFA has been referred to as unrestricted factor analysis, CFA has been referred to as restricted factor analysis (Watkins, 2021; Widaman, 2012) because in EFA, all extracted factors are allowed to relate to all measured variables (and one may observe what those relations are) whereas in CFA, the researcher specifies which latent factors relate to specific measured variables (but not others), hence, restricted by some a priori model. Further, non-specified paths are set to zero although they may be small but non-zero values.

WISC–V Primary & Secondary Subtest EFA. In EFA applied to the 16 WISC–V primary and secondary subtests with the total standardization sample (Canivez & Watkins, 2016; Canivez et al., 2016), factor extraction criteria indicated that only the publisher-preferred "theory" suggested five factors, so to assess the adequacy of that preference, EFA began with forced extraction of five factors. Several problems were evident, substantially challenging the veracity of five first-order factors. The fifth factor included only one subtest with a salient pattern coefficient or loading (Figure Weights), and when extracting five factors and distributing the common variance across all five, Matrix Reasoning and Picture Concepts failed to saliently load on any factor. Also, Arithmetic had a salient loading only on WM, not saliently cross-loading multiple factors as imposed in Wechsler's preferred Model 5e (see Table I.1 in Canivez & Watkins, 2016; or Table 1 in Canivez et al., 2016). Because factors cannot be adequately defined by a single measured variable and it made no theoretical sense that Matrix Reasoning had no salient loading on any factor, the five-factor model was rejected as inadequate and four factors were then extracted and examined. In extracting four factors, all subtests (except Picture Concepts) had salient loadings on singular factors reflecting desired simple structure (Thurstone, 1947), and the four latent dimensions were identical to those previously observed with the WISC–IV. Block Design, Visual Puzzles, Matrix Reasoning, and Figure Weights all loaded on the same factor; thus, separate VS and FR factors did not emerge. Further, Arithmetic had a salient (although relatively low) loading on WM but did not saliently cross-load on other factors. Because the four-factor correlations from oblique rotation were moderate to large and statistically significant, ranging from .387 to .747, second-order EFA (Gorsuch, 1983; Thompson, 2004) and variance partitioning with the Schmid and Leiman transformation (SLT; 1957) was conducted as insisted on by Carroll (1995). Further, while Canivez and Watkins (2016) and Canivez et al. (2016) provided model-based reliability/validity estimates using omega-hierarchical (ω_h) and omega-hierarchical subscale (ω_{HS}) to assess the adequacy of unit-weighted scores based on the general factor and four group factors respectively, there are additional model-based indices that help assess reliability/validity and dimensionality that were not at that time included but were estimated for this chapter and are presented below to supplement earlier reported findings.

Table I.4 in Canivez and Watkins (2016) and Table 4 in Canivez et al. (2016) present results of the SLT of the higher-order WISC–V structure with 16 subtests and four group factors and include ω_h and ω_{HS} coefficients. Table 2.1 supplements these results by including additional model-based reliability/validity (omega [ω], omega-hierarchical [ω_h], omega-hierarchical subscale [ω_{HS}], construct reliability or replicability index [H]) and dimensionality (percentage of uncontaminated correlations [PUC] and explained common variance [ECV]) estimates as defined in Table 1.2 in Chapter 1 of this volume to more fully assess the structural adequacy of the 16 WISC–V primary and secondary subtests. These estimates were obtained using the Omega program (Watkins, 2013). While ω is provided, it estimates the proportion of variance in a unit-weighted composite score attributable to all modeled sources of common variance. As such, it is less important due to the conflation of variance sources from multiple attributes. Applying minimum versus preferred criteria for these estimates in Table 2.1 (Gu et al., 2017; Reise, 2012; Reise et al., 2013; Rodriguez et al., 2016a, 2016b; Sellbom & Tellegen, 2019; Watkins & Canivez, 2022), the general factor (PUC = .80) appeared essentially unidimensional (with ECV less important with PUC at this level). "The smaller the group factors, the more correlations there are that are influenced by only a single latent variable" (Rodriguez et al., 2016b, p. 145), and while the assumption of unidimensionality "is a convenient fiction, sometimes useful in applied contexts" (Reise et al., 2013, p. 136), in this case, the general factor appears unidimensional enough (Rodriguez et al., 2016b) for interpretation. ECV values for all four group factors indicated that they were not sufficiently unidimensional with values well below the suggested minimum (ECV ≥ .70). Reliability/validity estimates (ω_h and H) for the general factor exceeded preferred levels for interpretation of unit-weighted or optimally-weighted composite scores, respectively; but ω_{HS} and H indexes fell well below minimum levels for the group factors (except the PS ω_{HS} index), indicating unlikely meaningful interpretations of unique measurement of their hypothesized constructs. Figure 2.1 provides a visualization of WISC–V subtest and factor sources of variance illustrating the dominance of g variance and small portions of group factor variance for all but the PS dimension. Thus, evidence-based interpretation supports a composite score representing the general intelligence construct, but not the factor-based composites where ω_{HS}, H, and FDI failed to achieve preferred levels for confident interpretation.

WISC–V Primary Subtest EFA. Canivez and Watkins (2016) also reported preliminary EFA of the 10 WISC–V primary subtests (see Tables I.5 and I.6) to assess dimensionality and included second-order EFA, variance decomposition with the SLT, and provided model-based reliability/validity estimates (ω_h and ω_{HS}). Extraction of five factors with promax (oblique) rotation with only the 10 primary subtests, separation of VS and FR factors appeared and all 10 primary subtests properly aligned with their theoretical factors with simple structure. All subtests except Coding

Table 2.1 Model-Based Reliability/Validity and Dimensionality Estimates for the 16 Wechsler Intelligence Scale for Children–Fifth Edition (WISC–V) Primary and Secondary Subtests with the Total Standardization Sample (N = 2,200) According to an EFA Schmid and Leiman (1957) Orthogonalized Higher-Order Factor Model With Four First-Order Factors (Supplement to Table I.4 [Canivez & Watkins, 2016] and Table 4 [Canivez et al., 2016])

Model-Based Index	General	Verbal Comprehension	Visual Spatial[1]	Working Memory	Processing Speed	h^2	u^2
Total Variance	.363	.049	.029	.035	.064	.540	.460
ECV	.673	.090	.054	.064	.119		
ω	.926	.874	.802	.826	.694		
ω_H / ω_{HS}	.828	.251	.166	.185	.505		
Relative ω	.894	.287	.207	.224	.727		
Factor r	.910	.501	.408	.430	.710		
H	.904	.474	.339	.385	.608		
PUC	.800						
FDI	.951	.688	.582	.620	.780		

Note. h^2 = communality; u^2 = uniqueness; ECV = explained common variance; ω = Omega; ω_H = Omega-hierarchical (general factor); ω_{HS} = Omega-hierarchical subscale (group factors); H = construct reliability or replicability index; PUC = percentage of uncontaminated correlations; FDI = factor determinacy index. Due to the failure of Picture Concepts to achieve a salient factor pattern coefficient on any factor in EFA, it was not assigned to a group factor in model-based reliability and dimensionality estimations. Light shading indicates minimum level while dark shading indicates preferred level.
[1]Perceptual Reasoning (Perceptual Organization) is the former name of this dimension in previous WISC versions, but given the higher pattern and structure coefficients of Block Design and Visual Puzzles, this factor might alternatively be named Visual Spatial as in the WISC–V. Variance sources illustrated in Figure 2.1.

and Symbol Search had fair or good *g* loadings based on Kaufman's (1994) criteria ($\geq$ .70 = good, .50 –.69 = fair, < .50 = poor), showing that Coding and Symbol Search continue to be poor indicators of general intelligence. Factor correlations were moderate to high and statistically significant, ranging from .374 to .740, requiring second-order EFA, SLT, and model-based reliability/ validity and dimensionality estimates as previously conducted with all 16 primary and secondary subtests and are presented in Table I.6 (Canivez & Watkins, 2016). To supplement those omega coefficients, Table 2.2 includes ω, ω_H/ω_{HS}, H, PUC, ECV, and FDI estimates. The general factor was again observed to be essentially unidimensional (PUC = .889), and ECVs for the five group factors were very poor, ranging from .015 (FR) to .149 (PS). Model-based reliability/validity estimates indicated that ω_H and H for the general factor exceeded preferred levels for confident interpretation of unit-weighted or optimally-weighted composite scores, respectively, while ω_{HS} and H estimates for the five group factors fell below recommended minimum levels (except the PS ω_{HS}), indicating meaningful interpretations of unique measurement of factor index scores is likely not possible in the 10 WISC–V primary subtest higher-order model with five group factors. Figure 2.2 provides a visualization of the WISC–V primary subtest and factor variance sources illustrating the dominance

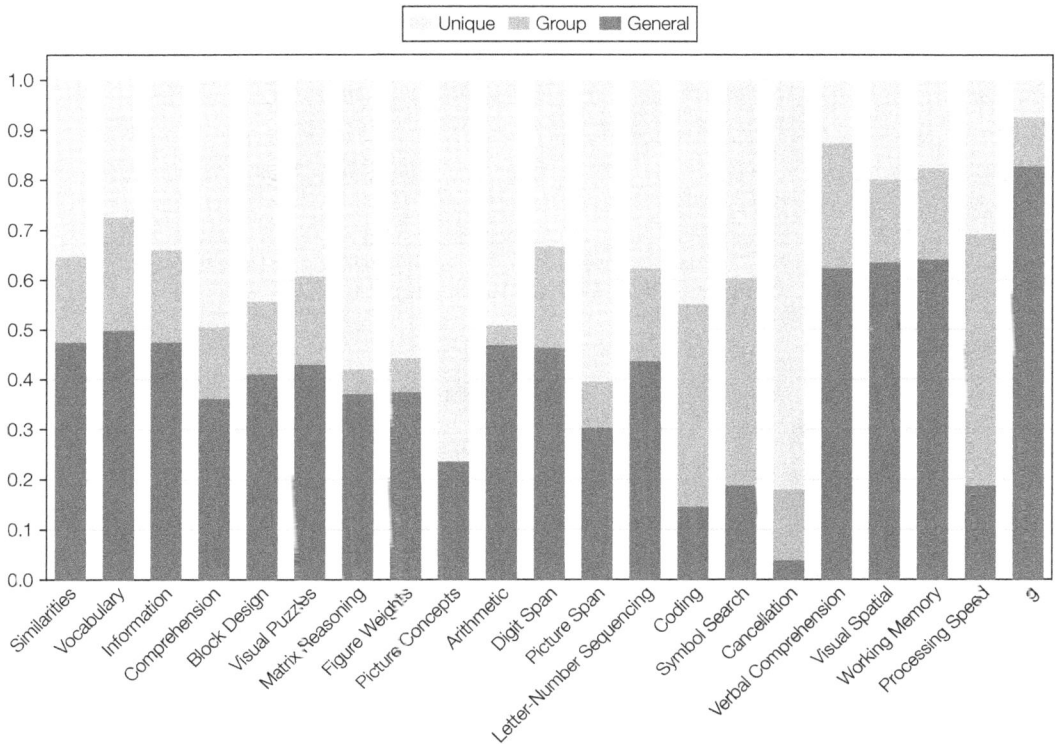

Figure 2.1. **Variance Sources (General, Group, Unique [Specific + Error) for the 16 WISC–V Primary and Secondary Subtests and Factors According to an EFA Schmid and Leiman (1957) Orthogonalized Higher-Order Factor Model with Four First-Order Factors.** *Note.* The *y*-axis displays total variance for subtests and explained common variance for factors. Due to the failure of Picture Concepts to achieve a salient factor pattern coefficient on any factor in EFA it was not assigned to a factor or included in model-based reliability and dimensionality estimations; thus, sources of variance are general or unique. Unique variance is subtest specificity and error variance combined.

of *g* variance and small or very small portions of group factor variance for all but the PS dimension. Matrix Reasoning and Figure Weights appear to be good measures of *g* but very poor indicators of FR. Thus, while FR may be identified or located in EFA with the 10 WISC–V primary subtests, FR is poorly indexed by its subtest indicators apart from *g*. The only viable score based on these results is a composite score representing *g* (i.e. FSIQ).

Because of the poor unique measurement of FR when five WISC–V first-order factors were extracted, Canivez and Watkins (2016) also conducted preliminary EFA with the 10 WISC–V primary subtests (see Tables I.7 and .8) extracting four first-order factors and rotating with promax (oblique). As with EFA of the 16 WISC–V primary and secondary subtests, extraction of four factors with the 10 WISC–V primary subtests yielded simple structure and subtests aligned with their theoretically related factors. Block Design, Visual Puzzles, Matrix Reasoning, and Figure Weights all loaded on the same factor (VS [or the former PR using WISC–IV terminology]) but given higher Block Design and Visual Puzzles pattern *and* structure coefficients, this factor might be appropriately labeled VS. As noted in Chapter 1, Kline (2016, 2023) cautions against both the naming fallacy and factor reification. Factor correlations ranged from .346 to .742 necessitating second-order EFA, SLT, and model-based reliability/validity and dimensionality estimates. Table 2.3

Table 2.2 Model-Based Reliability/Validity and Dimensionality Estimates for the 10 Wechsler Intelligence Scale for Children–Fifth Edition (WISC–V) Primary Subtests with the Total Standardization Sample (N = 2,200) According to an EFA Schmid and Leiman (1957) Orthogonalized Higher-Order Factor Model With Five First-Order Factors (Supplement to Table I.6 Canivez & Watkins [2016])

Model-Based Index	General	Verbal Comprehension	Visual Spatial	Fluid Reasoning	Working Memory	Processing Speed	h^2	u^2
Total Variance	.369	.043	.039	.009	.029	.086	.576	.424
ECV	.642	.075	.068	.015	.051	.149		
ω	.904	.811	.770	.628	.681	.740		
ω_H / ω_{HS}	.812	.257	.228	.059	.191	.538		
Relative ω	.899	.317	.296	.094	.280	.727		
Factor r	.901	.507	.477	.244	.437	.734		
H	.863	.358	.345	.083	.255	.612		
PUC	.889							
FDI	.929	.598	.587	.288	.505	.782		

Note. h^2 = communality; u^2 = uniqueness; ECV = explained common variance; ω = Omega; ω_H = Omega-hierarchical (general factor); ω_{HS} = Omega-hierarchical subscale (group factors); H = construct reliability or replicability index; PUC = percentage of uncontaminated correlations; FDI = factor determinacy index. Light shading indicates minimum level while dark shading indicates preferred level. Variance sources illustrated in Figure 2.2.

presents supplemental ω, ω_H / ω_{HS}, H, PUC, ECV, and FDI estimates. The general factor again appeared to be essentially unidimensional (PUC = .800), and ECVs for the four group factors were again poor, ranging from .047 (WM & PS) to .077 (Verbal Comprehension [VC]). Model-based reliability/validity estimates indicated that ω_H and H for the general factor exceeded preferred levels for interpretation of unit-weighted or optimally-weighted composite scores, respectively, while ω_{HS} and H estimates for the four group factors fell below recommended minimum levels, indicating meaningful interpretations of unique measurement of factor scores is likely not possible. Thus, there appears to be only viable confident interpretation for a *g*-based composite score (i.e., FSIQ) in the 10 WISC–V primary subtest higher-order model with four group factors. Figure 2.3 provides a visualization of WISC–V sources of primary subtest and factor variance in this model illustrating the dominance of *g* variance and small or very small portions of group factor variance for all but the PS dimension.

WISC–V Primary & Secondary Subtest EFA (4 Age Groups). Canivez et al. (2018) examined the factor structure of the 16 WISC–V primary and secondary subtest within four standardization sample age groups (6–8, 9-11, 12–14, 15–16) using hierarchical EFA identical to Canivez et al. (2016) and of the seven extraction criteria examined, only the publisher-preferred model suggested five factors. EFA began with extraction of five factors for all four age groups and as observed with the total sample, the fifth extracted factor included only a single subtest with salient loading

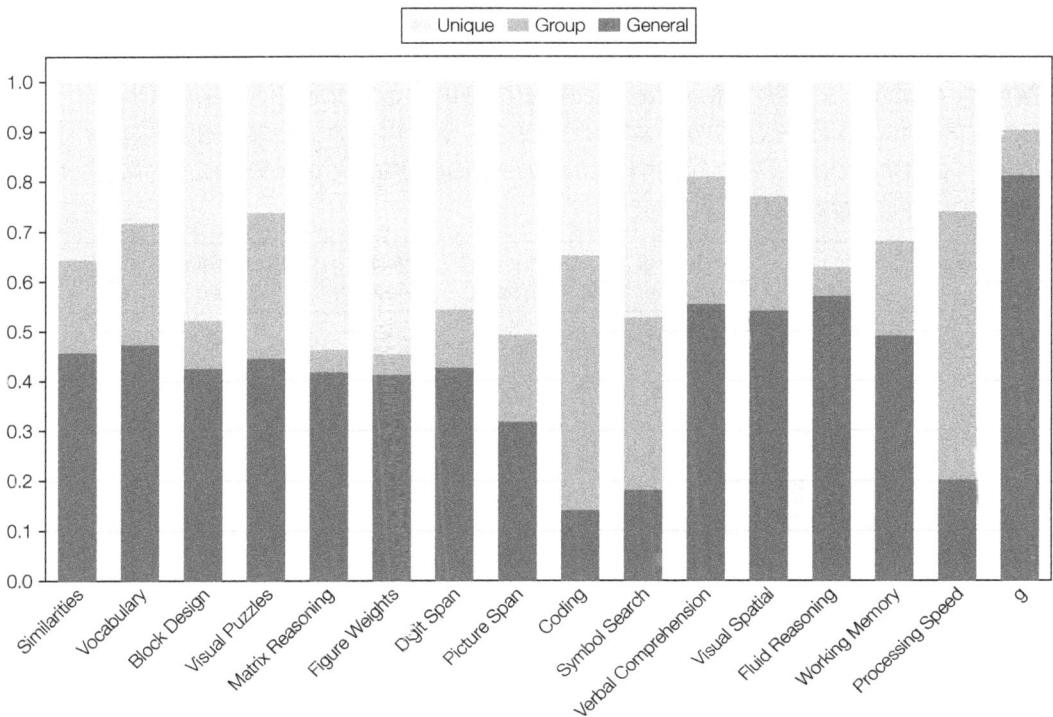

Figure 2.2. Variance Sources (General, Group, Unique [Specific + Error]) for the 10 WISC–V Primary Subtests and Factors According to an EFA Schmid and Leiman (1957) Orthogonalized Higher-Order Factor Model with Five First-Order Factors. *Note.* The *y*-axis reflects total variance for subtests and explained common variance for factors. Unique variance is subtest specificity and error variance combined.

(Cancellation [ages 6–8], Arithmetic [ages 9–11], Picture Concepts [ages 12–14 and ages 15–16]). Thus, four-factor EFAs were next assessed including second-order EFA of factor correlations, SLT based variance decomposition, and model-based reliability/validity estimates (ω_H and ω_{HS}). Results were virtually identical to those with the total sample with all VC, VS (PR), WM, and PS subtests properly aligned with their theoretically consistent factors except Picture Concepts, which had no salient loadings with any factors for ages 6–8 and 9–11 but saliently loaded on VC for ages 12–14 and 15–16. Block Design and Visual Puzzles had larger loadings with VS (PR) than Matrix Reasoning and Figure Weights except for ages 9–11 where Figure Weights loaded as high. Thus, with generally stronger loadings from Block Design and Visual Puzzles, VS might be a better name for that factor given the WISC–V content. SLT apportioned variance found most variance associated with the *g* factor and ω_H coefficients for all four age groups ranged .817 to .847, exceeding the preferred level for clinical interpretation of a unit-weighted composite score. The ω_{HS} coefficients for the four group factors in all four age groups were considerably lower (range of .131 to .280 for the VC, PR, and WM factors), falling far below the minimum threshold for confident clinical interpretation, but ω_{HS} coefficients for the PS factor ranged from .478 to .530 and approached or met the minimum standard. None of the group factors achieved ω_{HS} levels that would support confident interpretation of unit-weighted scores.

WISC–V Primary Subtest EFA (4 Age Groups). In a study examining the 10 WISC–V primary subtest structure within four standardization sample age groups (6–8, 9–11, 12–14, 15–16) using

Table 2.3 Model-Based Reliability/Validity and Dimensionality Estimates for the 10 Wechsler Intelligence Scale for Children–Fifth Edition (WISC–V) Primary Subtests with the Total Standardization Sample (N = 2,200) According to an EFA Schmid and Leiman (1957) Orthogonalized Higher-Order Factor Model With Four First-Order Factors (Supplement to Table I.8 Canivez & Watkins [2016])

Model-Based Index	General	Verbal Comprehension	Visual Spatial[1]	Working Memory	Processing Speed	h^2	u^2
Total Variance	.367	.043	.038	.026	.026	.560	.440
ECV	.655	.077	.069	.047	.047		
ω	.901	.811	.803	.676	.676		
ω_H / ω_{HS}	.800	.255	.142	.173	.173		
Relative ω	.888	.314	.177	.255	.255		
Factor r	.894	.505	.377	.415	.415		
H	.862	.356	.305	.231	.231		
PUC	.800						
FDI	.928	.597	.553	.481	.481		

Note. h^2 = communality; u^2 = uniqueness; ECV = explained common variance; ω = Omega; ω_H = Omega-hierarchical (general factor); ω_{HS} = Omega-hierarchical subscale (group factors); H = construct reliability or replicability index; PUC = percentage of uncontaminated correlations; FDI = factor determinacy index. Light shading indicates minimum level while dark shading indicates preferred level. [1]Perceptual Reasoning (Perceptual Organization) is the former name of this dimension in previous WISC versions, but given the higher pattern and structure coefficients of Block Design and Visual Puzzles, this factor might alternatively be named Visual Spatial as in the WISC–V. Variance sources illustrated in Figure 2.3.

hierarchical EFA as reported by Canivez et al. (2018), Dombrowski et al. (2018) observed that when attempting to extract five factors, only the 15–16 age group evidenced the viable fifth factor (FR) with salient loadings of Matrix Reasoning and Figure Weights. For the other age groups, the fifth factor (FR) was represented by a single subtest (Figure Weights [ages 6–8 and 9–11], Visual Puzzles cross-loaded [ages 12–14]). When extracting five factors, other anomalies were observed including Matrix Reasoning and Digit Span having no salient loadings on any factors (ages 6–8) and Matrix Reasoning having no salient loadings and Figure Weights loading on WM, and Visual Puzzles cross-loaded on VS and the fifth factor (ages 12–14), which are likely the result of overextraction. Most importantly, however, second-order EFA, variance decomposition using the SLT, and estimation of model-based reliability/validity coefficients ω_H and ω_{HS} replicated the findings from the total standardization sample that unit-weighted general factor scores exceeded preferred levels for interpretation and evidenced good measurement independent of the group factors. The five group factors for the 15–16 age group had ω_{HS} coefficients ranging from .201 to .249 and far below the .50 minimum criterion so unit-weighted composite scores possess too little unique variance to provide useful clinical interpretation. The same was true for group factors for ages 6–8, 9–11, and 12–14, except for the PS factor for ages 12–14, which met the minimum criterion. Results further indicated the WISC–V was an excellent measure of *g* within these four

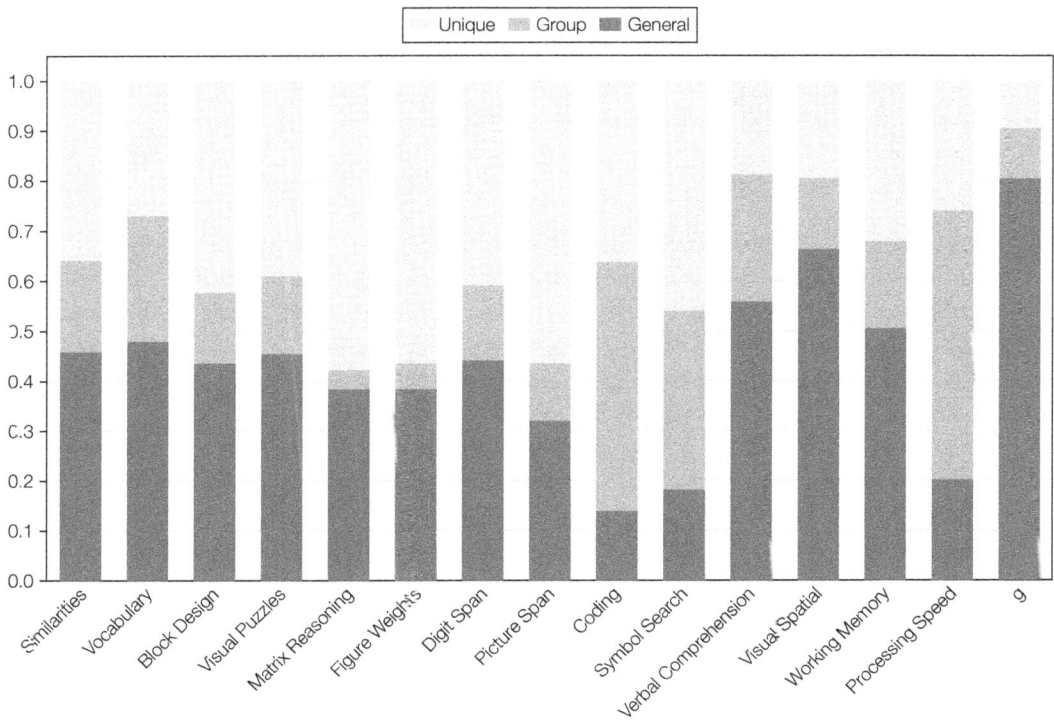

Figure 2.3. **Variance Sources (General, Group, Unique [Specific + Error]) for the 10 WISC–V Primary Subtests and Factors According to an EFA Schmid and Leiman (1957) Orthogonalized Higher-Order Factor Model with Four First-Order Factors.** *Note.* The *y*-axis reflects total variance for subtests and explained common variance for factors. Unique variance is subtest specificity and error variance combined.

age groups and worthy of clinical interpretation of a *g*-based score; however, the group factors were not.

WISC–V Primary Subtest EFA: Clinical Sample. Canivez et al. (2020) obtained a large clinical sample (*N* = 2,512) of children who were administered the WISC–V as part of neuropsychological assessments in a large outpatient neuropsychology clinic. Given the large sample Canivez et al. randomly bifurcated the sample (EFA Sample *n* = 1,256; CFA Sample *n* = 1,256) to conduct separate EFA and CFA. As with other WISC–V EFAs no factor extraction criterion suggested five factors other than publisher claim, so EFA began with extraction of five factors to assess results. None of the 10 primary subtests had a salient loading on the fifth factor rendering it inadequate. Further, even when allowing a fifth factor, Block Design, Visual Puzzles, Matrix Reasoning, and Figure Weights all loaded on the same factor although, like previous reviewed studies, Block Design and Visual Puzzles had larger pattern and structure coefficients/loadings so naming that factor VS is an acceptable alternative. No separate VS and FR factors emerged. Four-factor extraction, second-order EFA of factor correlations, SLT, and model-based reliability/validity and dimensionality estimates were used to assess factor adequacy. All subtests loaded on their theoretically appropriate factors and second-order EFA and SLT resulted in largest portions of subtest variance associated with the *g* factor. The general factor was essentially unidimensional with model-based dimensionality estimates PUC = .800 and ECV = .702, but ECVs for the four group factors were very poor, ranging from .026 (WM) to .118 (VS [PR]). Model-based reliability/validity estimates for the general factor exceeded preferred levels for interpretation of unit-weighted

(ω_H = .821) or optimally-weighted (H = .883) composite scores; while ω_{HS} (.083–.351) and H (.116–.505) estimates for the four group factors fell well below recommended minimum levels, indicating they were insufficiently indexed by the constituent subtests when g was removed and meaningful interpretations of factor index scores based on them is unlikely.

WISC–V Exploratory Bifactor Analyses

In EFA, decomposing variance sources using the Schmid and Leiman transformation (SLT; 1957) was insisted on by Carroll (1995) in understanding relative contributions of factors in second-order EFA. It has been the primary method to disclose variance apportioned to a higher-order dimension and to lower-order group factors and is an approximation of a bifactor solution (Canivez, 2016). The SLT is a reparameterization of the higher-order model and Yung et al. (1999), F. F. Chen et al. (2006), and Reise (2012) noted that the SLT includes a proportionality constraint of general and specific variance ratios, and Reise also indicated that nonzero cross-loadings are problematic. The larger the cross-loadings the greater the distortion of underestimating specific group factor loadings and overestimating general factor loadings. This led to the development of exploratory bifactor analysis (EBFA; Jennrich & Bentler, 2011) as an alternative to the second-order EFA based SLT and is "simply exploratory factor analysis using a bi-factor rotation criterion" (p. 2) to directly estimate bifactor model loadings. Exploratory bifactor modeling (EBFA) of the 16 WISC–V primary and secondary subtests with the standardization sample correlation matrix (Dombrowski et al., 2015) resulted in some similar EFA findings from traditional EFA methods such as the absence of separate VS and FR factors, dominance and well defined general intelligence factor, and poorly indexed group factors (Canivez & Watkins, 2016; Canivez et al., 2016, 2017) but also yielded some anomalous findings such as the absence of the VC factor. As discussed by Dombrowski et al., it may be that all that is common among the verbally oriented subtests was explained by g leaving insufficient residual variance for identifying the VC factor. Dombrowski et al. (2019) described and discussed the use of exploratory bifactor analysis (EBFA) as a methodological improvement for examining bifactor structure in EFA and re-analyzed the WISC–V standardization data correlation matrix to address the anomalous results of Dombrowski et al. (2015). Sensitivity analyses were used to identify causes for the anomalous results and reportedly, initial communality estimates/start values were important factors, especially for the six-factor model (g plus 5 group factors [publisher's preferred model]). It was noted that regardless, the six-factor model was inadequate and the model with g and four group factors (VC, VS, WM, PS [traditional Wechsler model]) was optimal. Matrix Reasoning, Figure Weights, and Picture Concepts subtests were good indicators of g but they were not indicators of a separate FR factor.

Dombrowski et al. (2022) compared application of EBFA to the SLT approach with an expanded clinical sample from the initial Canivez et al. (2020) EFA and CFA study (N = 5,359). The sample included children and adolescents who were subjects of neuropsychological assessments in a large outpatient clinic. Results were similar to past studies showing that the publisher's model including five group (first-order) factors is not adequately supported. Subtests that were supposed to form a separate FR factor were associated only with general intelligence in EBFA while in higher-order factor analysis Visual Puzzles, Block Design, Figure Weights, and Matrix Reasoning were associated with the same single factor (VS/PR). Further, Dombrowski et al. also reported model-based indicators of ω_H and H were at preferred levels for g in both EBFA and SLT, but ω_{HS} and H indexes for the four or five group factors were universally low, indicating that unit-weighted or optimally-weighted group factor scores are poorly indexed by their constituent subtests. In clinical practice, such results indicate interpretation of a FSIQ is strongly supported but factor index scores are not.

WISC–V Exploratory Graph Analysis

While factor analytic examinations of test structures has dominated construct validity research, particularly with intelligence tests, network psychometric approaches have been recently developed to offer an alternative approach for explaining correlation structures that might offer additional insights (Borsboom 2022; Isvoranu et al. 2022). Golino and Epskamp (2017) introduced a new method, *exploratory graph analysis* (EGA), where the number of latent dimensions are reflected by clusters of strongly connected nodes (or communities) and used the Gaussian graphical model (Lauritzen, 2006). Golino et al. (2022) illustrated that network models are presented in graphs where nodes that represent test scores are connected by edges that represent partial correlation coefficients between two scores after conditioning on all other test scores. McGrew et al. (2023) argued for the greater use of network analyses to aid in the understanding of the psychological structure of intelligence tests.

　　Watkins et al. (2023) applied a bootstrap EGA technique in examining the latent structure of the 10 WISC–V primary subtests with a large clinical sample (N = 7,149; M_{age} = 10.7 years, SD_{age} = 2.8 years). The observed EGA structure contained four subnetworks that reflected the frequently observed first-order WISC–V factor structure in EFA studies (Canivez & Watkins, 2016; Canivez et al., 2016) where VS and FR factors merged into a single dimension (VS/PR). The five-factor WISC–V structure promoted by the publisher did not emerge. As no EGA analyses of the WISC–V standardization sample has yet been published, it is unknown if five factors will emerge from the normative data.

WISC–V Confirmatory Factor Analyses

Because of the unusual and nonstandard methods used to conduct CFA with the standardization sample reported in the *WISC–V Technical and Interpretive Manual* (Wechsler, 2014b), inadequate descriptions of methods and results, and omissions of rival models and model-based reliability/validity and dimensionality estimates, several independent CFAs of the WISC–V with the standardization sample and clinical samples have been published in the peer-reviewed literature and an invited review. Summaries of these studies are presented below.

　　WISC–V Primary and Secondary Subtest CFA. Independent CFAs of the 16 WISC–V primary and secondary subtests with the total standardization sample by Canivez and Watkins (2016) using Mplus 7.3 (Muthén & Muthén, 2014) and by Canivez et al. (2017) using EQS 6.2 (Bentler & Wu, 2012) were reported with contradictory results to Wechsler (2014b) and extended results addressing omissions previously reported. These studies applied maximum likelihood estimation (rather than weighted least squares) and traditional setting of scales by fixing a latent factor variance to zero or fixing one factor path to 1.0 (not undisclosed effects coding discovered by Beaujean [2016]). All models proposed by Wechsler (2014b) were assessed and rival bifactor measurement models to the publisher's models 4a (Canivez & Watkins, 2016; Canivez et al., 2017) and 5a (Canivez et al., 2017) were also examined. All five of the publisher's specified higher-order measurement models with five group factors produced model specification errors reflecting negative FR variance and standardized path coefficients from higher-order g to FR > 1.0 and thus were inadequate. These models were judged unacceptable and like results from EFA did not support five first-order factors with the 16 primary and secondary subtests. While an equality constraint *could be* imposed on the variance of FR to be zero and model estimates obtained, this "only masks the underlying problem" (Hair et al., 1998, p. 610) and thus "should not be trusted" (Kline, 2016, p. 237) so global model fit statistics and parameter estimates were not reported. It is unknown if the publisher found these same results using maximum likelihood estimation and traditional scale setting and then decided to use weighted least squares estimation with effects coding to produce models that were presented as preferred, but use of nontraditional CFA methods without detailed explication as noted by Beaujean (2016) seemed odd. Even with nontraditional methods the standardized path coefficient from g to FR was reported to be 1.0 in Model 5e, the publisher's preferred model, which indicates a lack of consideration of local model misfit and a resulting problematic model.

Canivez et al. (2017) reported that the bifactor model with five group factors was a well-fitting and an admissible model (according to global model fit statistics), but inspection of Matrix Reasoning, Figure Weights, and Picture Concepts subtests indicated they did not have statistically significant FR loadings, which challenged model validity. Thus, these subtests appear to be indicators of g but not of a separate FR dimension. Thus, no further analyses of this model were conducted.

Canivez and Watkins (2016) and Canivez et al. (2017) reported the best-fitting (and preferred) model in their independent analyses was the bifactor model with four group factors, where Block Design, Visual Puzzles, Matrix Reasoning, Figure Weights, and Picture Concepts were associated with the same latent factor (VS [PR]). To supplement results and tables previously published and like EFA reported above, Table 2.4 also includes ω, H, PUC, ECV, and FDI estimates to further assess score adequacy. Like EFA results, the general factor showed model-based indices of ω_{H}, H, and FDI that met preferred standards indicating that a general factor score would be well indexed for confident interpretation and the PUC = .792 and ECV = .699 indices suggested the general factor appeared essentially unidimensional. The ω_{HS} coefficients for VC, VS, and WM were below minimum standards for confident interpretation while ω_{HS} for PS met the minimum for possible interpretation. None of the four group factors achieved minimum levels of H or FDI. Figure 2.4 illustrates sources of subtest and factor variances based on the bifactor model with four group factors and shows the large portions of general variance within most subtests and group factors.

While the focus of Canivez and Watkins (2016) and Canivez et al. (2017) was on the best-fitting model (bifactor model with 4 group factors), sources of variance and model-based reliability/validity and dimensionality estimates for the rival and also well-fitting higher-order model with four group factors (Model 4a) are presented here in Table 2.5. These results are virtually identical to the bifactor model with four group factors! As with the Model 4a Bifactor, model-based estimates for the higher-order Model 4a general factor were at preferred levels for ω_{H}, H, and FDI and indicated a unit-weighted or an optimally-weighted score would be well indexed, respectively. PUC was at the minimum level for the general factor and with PUC = .792 and ECV = .712, the general factor in the higher-order representation with four group factors was also essentially unidimensional. The ω_{HS} estimates for VC, VS, and WM were below the minimum standard while the ω_{HS} estimate for PS achieved the minimum standard for possible interpretation. H and FDI indices for all group factors were below the minimum standard, indicating that factor based scores are not well indexed by their indicators and likely not of interpretive value. Figure 2.5 illustrates the variance sources for the higher-order model with four group factors and illustrates large amounts of general variance in most subtests and factors

WISC–V Primary Subtest CFA. Canivez and Watkins (2016) and Canivez et al. (2017) also included independent CFA with the 10 WISC–V primary subtests with the total standardization sample

Table 2.4 Expanded Model-Based Reliability/Validity and Dimensionality Estimates in the WISC–V 16 Subtests for the Total Standardization Sample (N = 2,200) According to a CFA Bifactor Model With Four Group Factors (Supplement to Table I.10 Canivez & Watkins [2016]; Table 2 Canivez et al. [2017])

Model-Based Index	General	Verbal Comprehension	Visual Spatial[1]	Working Memory	Processing Speed	h^2	u^2
Total Variance	.372	.037	.027	.035	.062	.532	.468
ECV	.699	.069	.050	.065	.116		
ω	.929	.875	.809	.831	.693		
ω_H / ω_{HS}	.849	.200	.109	.182	.516		
Relative ω	.914	.229	.135	.218	.744		
Factor r	.921	.448	.330	.426	.718		
H	.914	.413	.344	.409	.623		
PUC	.792						
FDI	.956	.643	.587	.639	.789		

Note. h^2 = communality; u^2 = uniqueness; ECV = explained common variance; ω = Omega; ω_H = Omega-hierarchical (general factor); ω_{HS} = Omega-hierarchical subscale (group factors); H = construct reliability or replicability index; PUC = percentage of uncontaminated correlations; FDI = factor determinacy index. Due to the failure of Picture Concepts to achieve a salient factor pattern coefficient on any factor in EFA, it was not assigned to a factor in model-based reliability and dimensionality estimations. Light shading indicates minimum level while dark shading indicates preferred level.
[1]Perceptual Reasoning (Perceptual Organization) is the former name of this dimension in previous WISC versions, but given the higher pattern and structure coefficients of Block Design and Visual Puzzles, this factor might alternatively be named Visual Spatial as in the WISC–V. Variance sources illustrated in Figure 2.4.

and found that models with a single *g* factor and higher-order models with only two or three group factors did not produce adequate global model fit and were dismissed as inadequate explanations of WISC–V standardization sample data. Both the higher-order model and bifactor model with four group factors demonstrated good model fit with roughly equivalent CFI, TLI, SRMR, and RMSEA statistics, but the bifactor model was meaningfully better with a lower AIC estimate and selected as the preferred model as it was consistent with results from CFA and EFA with all 16 WISC–V subtests. Table 2.6 presents expanded model-based reliability/validity and dimensionality estimates that supplement Table 4 in Canivez et al. (2017). The ω_H, H, and FDI indices achieved preferred levels and indicate unit-weighted and optimally-weighted scores for the general factor would be well indexed and sufficient for confident interpretation. The PUC index of .800 met the preferred level suggesting the general factor was essentially unidimensional. ω_{HS} estimates for VC, VS, and WM group factors were below the minimum standard while the ω_{HS} estimate for PS met the minimum standard for possible interpretation. H and FDI indices for all four group factors were well below the minimum standard and indicated factor scores for these dimensions are not well indexed for confident interpretation. ECV indices for all four group factors were also quite low and indicated multidimensionality. Figure 2.6 illustrates variance sources for the 10 primary WISC–V subtest bifactor model with four group factors and illustrates large portions general variance in most subtests and factors.

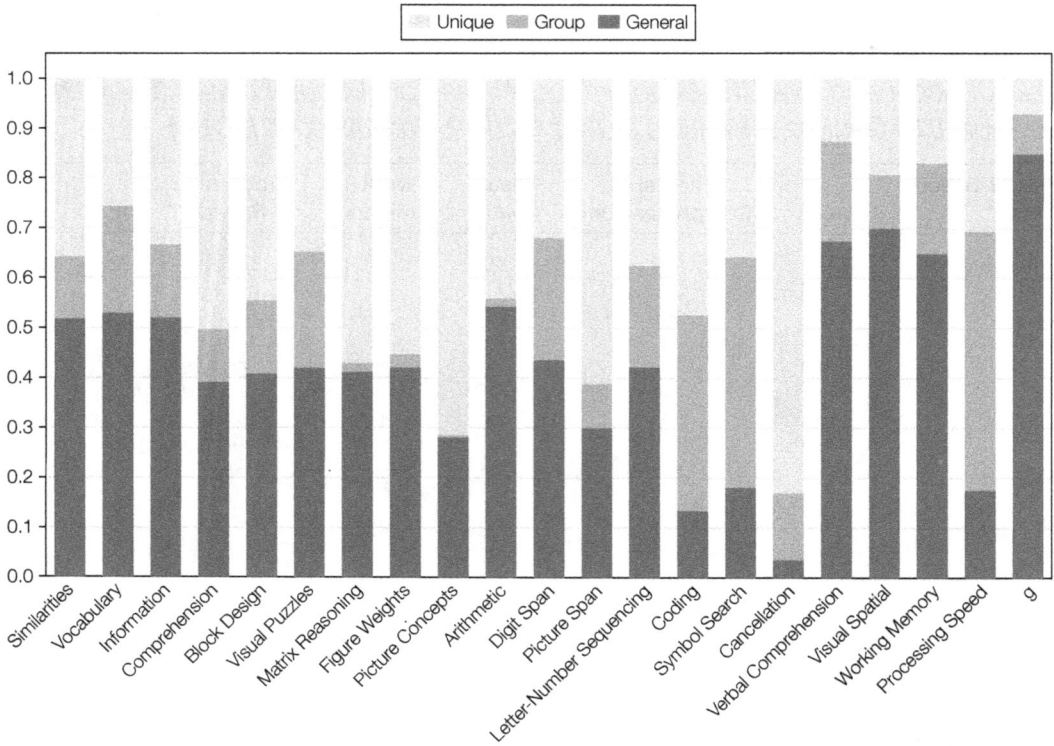

Figure 2.4. Variance Sources (General, Group, Unique [Specific + Error]) for the 16 WISC–V Primary and Secondary Subtests and Factors for the Total Standardization Sample According to a CFA Bifactor Model with Four Group Factors. *Note.* The *y*-axis reflects total variance for subtests and explained common variance for factors. Unique variance is subtest specificity and error variance combined.

The higher-order model with four group factors based on the 10 WISC–V primary subtests was also a well-fitting model so variance sources for this model are presented here in Table 2.7 to compare to the rival bifactor version. Table 2.7 also includes extended model-based reliability/validity and dimensionality estimates for further assessing scores based on latent dimensions. Standardized coefficients are similar to those in the bifactor model but not identical. Model-based reliability/validity estimates of ω_H, *H*, and FDI for the general factor met preferred standards for confident interpretation of either a unit-weighted score or an optimally-weighted score, respectively; and PUC = .800 was also at the preferred level indicating the general factor in the higher-order representation with four group factors was essentially unidimensional. ω_{HS} estimates for VC, VS, and WM were well below minimum standards while the ωHS estimate for PS achieved the minimum standard for possible interpretation. *H* indices for all group factors were below the minimum standard as were FDI estimates, suggesting group factor scores were inadequately indexed for confident interpretation. ECV values for all four group factors were also inadequate, indicating multidimensionality that complicates interpretation. Figure 2.7 illustrates the variance sources for the higher-order model with four group factors from the 10 primary subtests and illustrates, like the bifactor representation, large portions of general variance in most subtests and factors.

Watkins and Canivez (2022) published a tutorial on applying statistical analyses (SLT and model-based reliability/validity and dimensionality indices) to higher-order models using the publisher's preferred 10 WISC–V primary subtest higher-order model with five group factors (Wechsler, 2014b).

Table 2.5 Sources of Variance and Model-Based Reliability/Validity and Dimensionality Estimates in the WISC–V 16 Subtests for the Total Standardization Sample (N = 2,200) According to a Schmid and Leiman (1957) Orthogonalized CFA Higher-Order Factor Model With Four First-Order Factors

WISC–V Subtest	General		Verbal Comprehension		Visual Spatial[1]		Working Memory		Processing Speed		h²	u²	ECV
	b	S²	b	S²	b	S²	b	S²	b	S²			
Similarities	.707	.500	.393	.154							.654	.346	.764
Vocabulary	.741	.549	.412	.170							.719	.281	.764
Information	.715	.511	.397	.158							.669	.331	.764
Comprehension	.619	.383	.344	.118							.501	.499	.764
Block Design	.663	.440			.272	.074					.514	.486	.856
Visual Puzzles	.682	.465			.280	.078					.544	.456	.856
Matrix Reasoning	.622	.387			.255	.065					.452	.548	.856
Figure Weights	.630	.397			.259	.067					.464	.536	.855
Picture Concepts	.492	.242			.202	.041					.283	.717	.856
Arithmetic	.658	.433					.350	.122			.555	.445	.779
Digit Span	.690	.476					.367	.135			.611	.389	.779
Picture Span	.552	.305					.293	.086			.391	.609	.780
Letter-Number Sequencing	.676	.457					.360	.130			.587	.413	.779
Coding	.368	.135							.611	.373	.509	.491	.266

(Continued)

Table 2.5 (Continued)

WISC–V Subtest	General		Verbal Comprehension		Visual Spatial[1]		Working Memory		Processing Speed		h^2	u^2	ECV
	b	S^2	b	S^2	b	S^2	b	S^2	b	S^2			
Symbol Search	.421	.177							.699	.489	.666	.334	.266
Cancellation	.209	.044							.348	.121	.165	.835	.265
Total Variance		.369		.038		.020		.030		.061	.518	.482	
ECV		.712		.072		.039		.057		.119			
ω		.927		.874		.802		.821		.693			
ω_H/ω_{HS}		.845		.206		.116		.181		.509			
Relative ω		.912		.236		.144		.220		.734			
Factor r		.919		.454		.340		.425		.713			
H		.913		.415		.259		.350		.628			
PUC		.792											
FDI		.956		.644		.509		.591		.793			

Note. b = loading of subtest on factor, S^2 = variance explained, h^2 = communality, u^2 = uniqueness, ECV = explained common variance, ω = Omega, ω_H = Omega-hierarchical (general factor), ω_{HS} = Omega-hierarchical subscale (group factors), H = construct reliability or replicability index, PUC = percentage of uncontaminated correlations, FDI = factor determinacy index. Light shading indicates minimum level while dark shading indicates preferred level.

[1]Perceptual Reasoning (Perceptual Organization) is the former name of this dimension in previous WISC versions but given the higher pattern and structure coefficients of Block Design and Visual Puzzles, this factor might alternatively be named Visual Spatial as in the WISC–V. Variance sources illustrated in Figure 2.5.

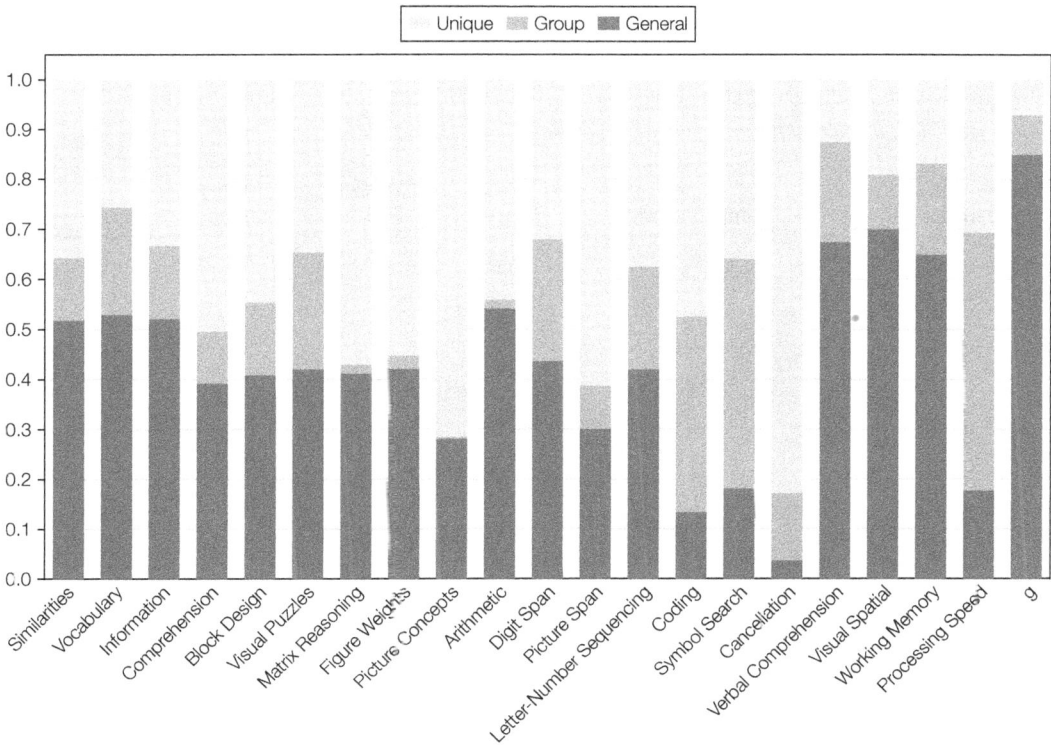

Figure 2.5. **Variance Sources (General, Group, Unique [Specific + Error]) for the 16 WISC–V Primary and Secondary Subtests and Factors According to an CFA Schmid and Leiman (1957) Orthogonalized Higher-Order Factor Model with Four First-Order Factors.** *Note.* The *y*-axis reflects total variance for subtests and explained common variance for factors. Unique variance is subtest specificity and error variance combined.

The tutorial was provided to instruct test users how to assess the adequacy of provided scores to promote evidence-based test interpretation when decomposed variance of a higher-order model is not provided by the publisher and when model-based reliability/validity and dimensionality estimates are not provided. Watkins and Canivez showed that like other representations of WISC–V structure from EFA and CFA, the general factor had preferred levels of ω_h, *H*, and FDI that indicated a unit-weighted or optimally-weighted factor score well indexed to provide confident interpretation. Also, the general factor had a PUC = .869 indicating essential unidimensionality. In contrast, ω_{hs}, *H*, and FDI estimates for all five group factors failed to achieve preferred levels indicating that factor scores based on them were not well indexed for confident interpretation. Further, all five group factors had extremely low ECV indicating multidimensionality and of particular note, FR accounted for a meager 0.3% of common variance and 0.2% total variance! Watkins and Canivez (2022) concluded that evidence-based interpretation of WISC–V was psychometrically restricted to only the general factor.

To contrast the results from the publisher's preferred higher-order model, variance sources and model-based reliability/validity and dimensionality indices for judging score adequacy of the 10 WISC–V primary subtest CFA bifactor model with five group factors are presented in Table 2.8. Like the higher-order WISC–V model with five group factors, the bifactor model with five group factors evidenced preferred levels of ω_h, *H*, and FDI, indicating a unit-weighted or optimally-weighted factor

Table 2.6 Expanded Model-Based Reliability/Validity and Dimensionality Estimates in the WISC–V 10 Primary Subtests for the Total Standardization Sample (N = 2,200) According to a CFA Bifactor Model With Four Group Factors (Supplement to Table 4 Canivez et al., 2017)

Model-Based Index	General	Verbal Comprehension	Visual Spatial[1]	Working Memory	Processing Speed	h^2	u^2
Total Variance	.381	.039	.034	.030	.086	.570	.430
ECV	.669	.068	.060	.053	.151		
ω	.904	.810	.813	.679	.736		
ω_H / ω_{HS}	.817	.230	.087	.199	.543		
Relative ω	.903	.285	.107	.293	.738		
Factor r	.904	.480	.294	.447	.737		
H	.870	.324	.300	.262	.600		
PUC	.800						
FDI	.933	.570	.548	.512	.775		

Note. h^2 = communality; u^2 = uniqueness; ECV = explained common variance; ω = Omega; ω_H = Omega-hierarchical (general factor); ω_{HS} = Omega-hierarchical subscale (group factors); H = construct reliability or replicability index; PUC = percentage of uncontaminated correlations; FDI = factor determinacy index. Light shading indicates minimum level while dark shading indicates preferred level. [1]Perceptual Reasoning (Perceptual Organization) is the former name of this dimension in previous WISC versions, but given the higher pattern and structure coefficients of Block Design and Visual Puzzles, this factor might alternatively be named Visual Spatial as in the WISC–V. Variance sources illustrated in Figure 2.6.

scores are well indexed for confident interpretation. As observed in the higher-order model with five group factors, the bifactor model general factor PUC = .889 indicated essential unidimensionality. All five group factors lacked preferred levels of ω_{HS}, H, and FDI estimates, indicating that factor scores based on them were not well indexed for confident interpretation. Like the higher-order model, FR accounted for miniscule portions of variance (0.5% of common variance, 0.3% total variance).

WISC–V Primary Subtest CFA: Clinical Sample. CFA of the 10 WISC–V primary subtests in the clinical sample reported by Canivez et al. (2020) with the CFA Sample (*n* =1,256) examined models with one to five first-order group factors and all models with two or more group factors also included a higher-order *g* factor. Bifactor alternatives to higher-order models with four or five group factors were also examined to illustrate differences between conceptualizations of *g* as a superordinate (higher-order) versus a breadth (bifactor) dimension. Four group factor models reflected a traditional Wechsler orientation while five group factors reflected a CHC orientation. CFA results indicated that models with one, two, or three group factors were inadequate based on global fit statistics. All models (higher-order and bifactor) with four (Wechsler) or five (CHC) group factors were well-fitting models based on global fit statistics. Assessment of standardized path coefficients indicated that all factor paths were statistically significant and there were no impermissible parameter estimates. One problem was identified in the CHC higher-order model where the standardized path coefficient from *g* to FR was .978 which was extremely high and

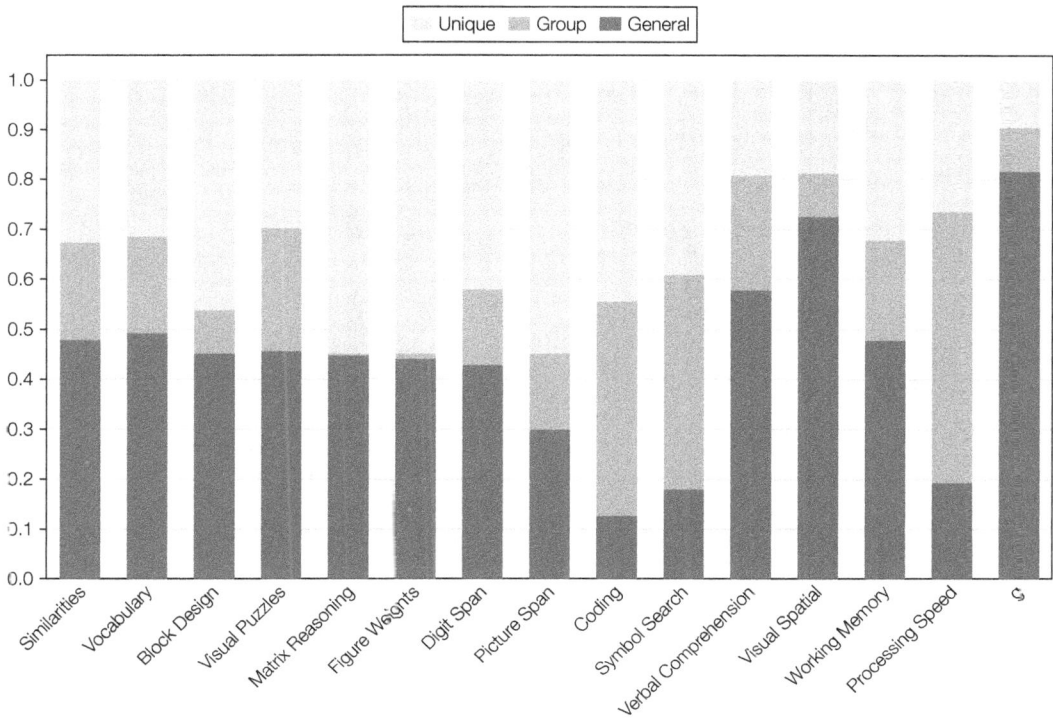

Figure 2.6. **Variance Sources (General, Group, Unique [Specific + Error]) for the 10 WISC–V Primary Subtests and Factors for the Total Standardization Sample According to a CFA Bifactor Model with Four Group Factors.** *Note.* The *y*-axis reflects total variance for subtests and explained common variance for factors. Unique variance is subtest specificity and error variance combined.

suggested a lack of discriminant validity. Also, because there are only 10 WISC–V primary subtests, most first-order factors are underidentified with only two subtest indicators and this means that the CHC higher-order and CHC bifactor models are mathematically equivalent. The Wechsler based bifactor model was judged as preferred and model-based reliability/validity and dimensionality estimates as provided in EFA were examined. As in EFA, the general factor was essentially unidimensional with model-based dimensionality estimates PUC = .800 and ECV = .704; but ECVs for the four group factors were again poor, ranging from .025 (WM) to .104 (VS [PR]). Model-based reliability/validity estimates for the general factor exceeded preferred levels for interpretation of unit-weighted (ω_H = .836) or optimally-weighted (*H* = .895) composite scores; but ω_{HS} (.100–.379) and *H* (.144–.484) estimates for the four group factors fell well below recommended minimum levels, indicating they were insufficiently defined by the subtests when *g* was removed and meaningful interpretations of factor index scores based on them is not recommended.

Another examination of the factor structure of the WISC–V was reported by Reynolds and Keith (2017) where they used CFA to examine the theoretical structure in comparison to a variety of plausible alternative higher-order and bifactor models in an attempt to better understand WISC–V structure. Unlike previously reported EFA and CFA studies by Canivez and colleagues who were forced to use correlation matrices and descriptive statistics from the manual, NCS Pearson provided Reynolds and Keith with the WISC–V standardization sample raw data for their analyses. The final model selected as the best-fitting WISC–V higher-order model produced by Reynolds and Keith was different from the publisher-preferred model (Model 5e) in that Arithmetic was given

Table 2.7 Sources of Variance and Model-Based Reliability/Validity and Dimensionality Estimates in the WISC–V 10 Primary Subtests for the Total Standardization Sample (N = 2,200) According to a Schmid and Leiman (1957) Orthogonalized CFA Higher-Order Factor Model With Four First-Order Factors

Subtest	General		Verbal Comprehension		Visual Spatial[1]		Working Memory		Processing Speed		h^2	u^2	ECV
	b	S^2	b	S^2	b	S^2	b	S^2	b	S^2			
Similarities	.699	.489	.427	.182							.671	.329	.728
Vocabulary	.708	.501	.433	.187							.689	.311	.728
Block Design	.685	.469			.262	.069					.538	.462	.872
Visual Puzzles	.697	.486			.267	.071					.557	.443	.872
Matrix Reasoning	.625	.391			.239	.057					.448	.552	.872
Figure Weights	.634	.402			.243	.059					.461	.539	.872
Digit Span	.656	.430					.422	.178			.608	.392	.707
Picture Span	.550	.303					.354	.125			.428	.572	.707
Coding	.359	.129							.599	.359	.488	.512	.264
Symbol Search	.427	.182							.713	.508	.691	.309	.264

Total Variance	.378	.037	.026	.030	.087	.558	.442
ECV	.678	.066	.046	.054	.155		
ω	.902	.809	.800	.681	.740		
ω_h/ω_{hs}	.811	.220	.102	.199	.545		
Relative ω	.899	.272	.128	.293	.736		
Factor r	.901	.469	.320	.447	.738		
H	.869	.312	.215	.265	.614		
PUC	.800						
FDI	.932	.559	.464	.514	.784		

Note. b = loading of subtest on factor; S^2 = variance explained; h^2 = communality; u^2 = uniqueness; ω = Omega; ω_h = Omega-hierarchical (general factor); ω_{hs} = Omega-hierarchical subscale (group factors); H = construct reliability or replicability index; ECV = explained common variance; PUC = percentage of uncontaminated correlations; FDI = factor determinacy index. Light shading indicates minimum level while dark shading indicates preferred level. [1]Perceptual Reasoning (Perceptual Organization) is the former name of this dimension in previous WISC versions, but given the higher pattern and structure coefficients of Block Design and Visual Puzzles, this factor might alternatively be named Visual Spatial as in the WISC–V. Variance sources illustrated in Figure 2.7.

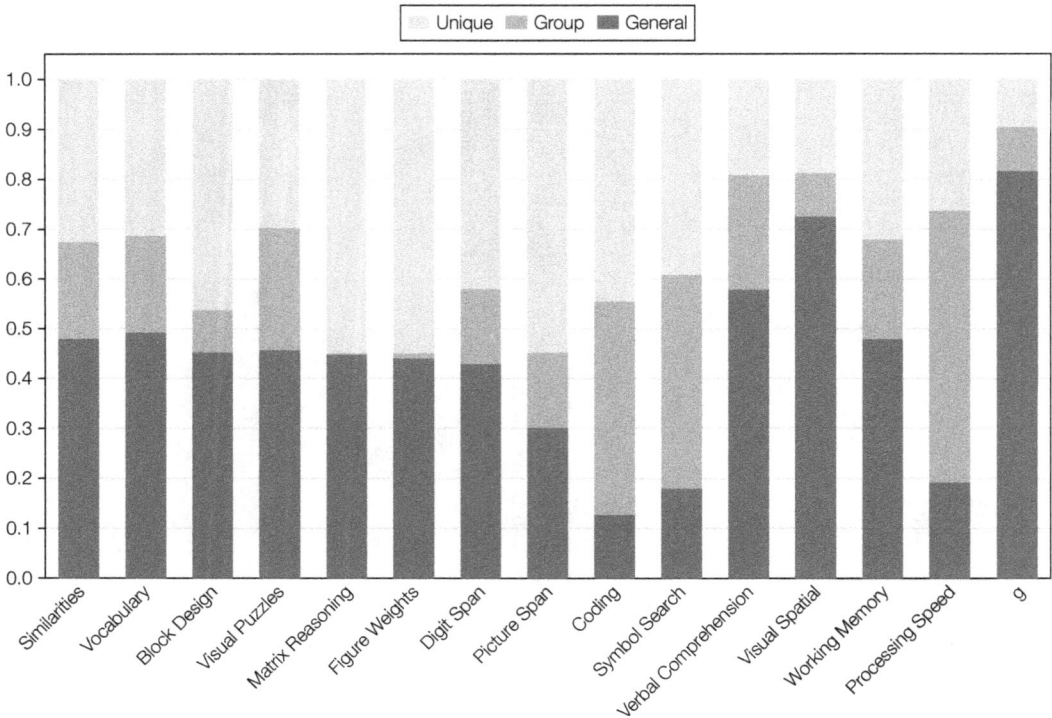

Figure 2.7. Variance Sources (General, Group, Unique [Specific + Error]) for the 10 WISC–V Primary Subtests and Factors According to a CFA Schmid and Leiman (1957) Orthogonalized Higher-Order Factor Model with Four First-Order Factors. *Note.* The *y*-axis reflects total variance for subtests and explained common variance for factors. Unique variance is subtest specificity and error variance combined.

a direct loading from *g*, and a WM cross-loading, and they also added correlated disturbances for the VS and FR group factors (.77) to represent an intermediate nonverbal general reasoning factor between the broad abilities and *g*. However, the model still produced a standardized path coefficient of .97 from *g* to FR suggesting inadequate discriminant validity and empirical isomorphism of FR and *g*. Nearly all alternative higher-order models examined were globally well fitting. The final WISC–V bifactor model selected included the five group factors, a singular path from *g* to Picture Concepts, and an added covariance (.62) between VS and FR. Like higher-order models nearly all were well fitting and few meaningful differences between models. Their Table 4 indicated that their final bifactor model was equivalent in global fit (CFI, RMSEA, AIC) to the bifactor model preferred in Canivez et al. (2017) that included only four group factors (VS and FR merged as single factor). Reliance on statistically significant χ^2 difference tests for model improvement despite the large sample and multiple comparisons but no meaningful differences in global fit may be concerning.

It was noted by Reynolds and Keith that a problem exists with bifactor models when there are only two subtest indicators for a factor as that factor is underidentified and one alternative to deal with this is to set initial factor loadings to equality (Little et al., 1999) to allow estimation (see Canivez and Watkins, 2006; and Canivez et al., 2017) or add a correlation between the two factors (Reynolds & Keith, 2017). This isn't so much a problem of the bifactor model as it is that the WISC–V VS factor only includes two subtest indicators (Block Design and Visual Puzzles). Further, the FR factor was supposed to be indexed by Matrix Reasoning, Picture Concepts, and Figure Weights; but as reported in both EFA and CFA, Picture Concepts does not load any factor in EFA

Table 2.8 Sources of Variance and Expanded Model-Based Reliability/Validity and Dimensionality Estimates in the WISC–V 10 Primary Subtests for the Total Standardization Sample (N = 2,200) According to CFA Bifactor Model With Five Group Factors

	General		Verbal Comprehension		Visual Spatial		Fluid Reasoning		Working Memory		Processing Speed		h^2	u^2	ECV
	b	S^2	b	S^2	b	S^2	b	S^2	b	S^2	b	S^2			
Similarities	.686	.471	.449	.202									.672	.328	.700
Vocabulary	.698	.487	.449	.202									.689	.311	.707
Block Design	.686	.471			.347	.120							.501	.409	.796
Visual Puzzles	.699	.489			.347	.120							.609	.391	.802
Matrix Reasoning	.672	.452					.123	.015					.467	.533	.968
Figure Weights	.677	.458					.123	.015					.473	.527	.968
Digit Span	.647	.419							.399	.159			.578	.422	.724
Picture Span	.542	.294							.399	.159			.453	.547	.649
Coding	.352	.124									.657	.432	.556	.444	.223
Symbol Search	.420	.176									.657	.432	.608	.392	.290

(Continued)

Table 2.8 (Continued)

	General		Verbal Comprehension		Visual Spatial		Fluid Reasoning		Working Memory		Processing Speed		h^2	u^2	ECV
	b	S^2	b	S^2	b	S^2	b	S^2	b	S^2	b	S^2			
Total Variance		.384		.040		.024		.003		.032		.086	.570	.430	.430
ECV		.674		.071		.042		.005		.056		.152			
ω		.904		.810		.750		.640		.679		.735			
ω_h / ω_{hs}		.822		.240		.151		.021		.211		.547			
Relative ω		.909		.296		.201		.032		.311		.743			
Factor r		.906		.490		.388		.143		.459		.739			
H		.873		.336		.215		.030		.275		.603			
PUC		.889													
FDI		.934		.579		.464		.173		.524		.777			

Note. b = loading of subtest on factor, S^2 = variance explained, h^2 = communality, u^2 = uniqueness, ECV = explained common variance, ω = Omega, ω_h = Omega-hierarchical (general factor), ω_{hs} = Omega-hierarchical subscale (group factors), H = construct reliability or replicability index, PUC = percentage of uncontaminated correlations, FDI = factor determinacy index. Light shading indicates minimum level while dark shading indicates preferred level. Variance sources illustrated in Figure 2.8.

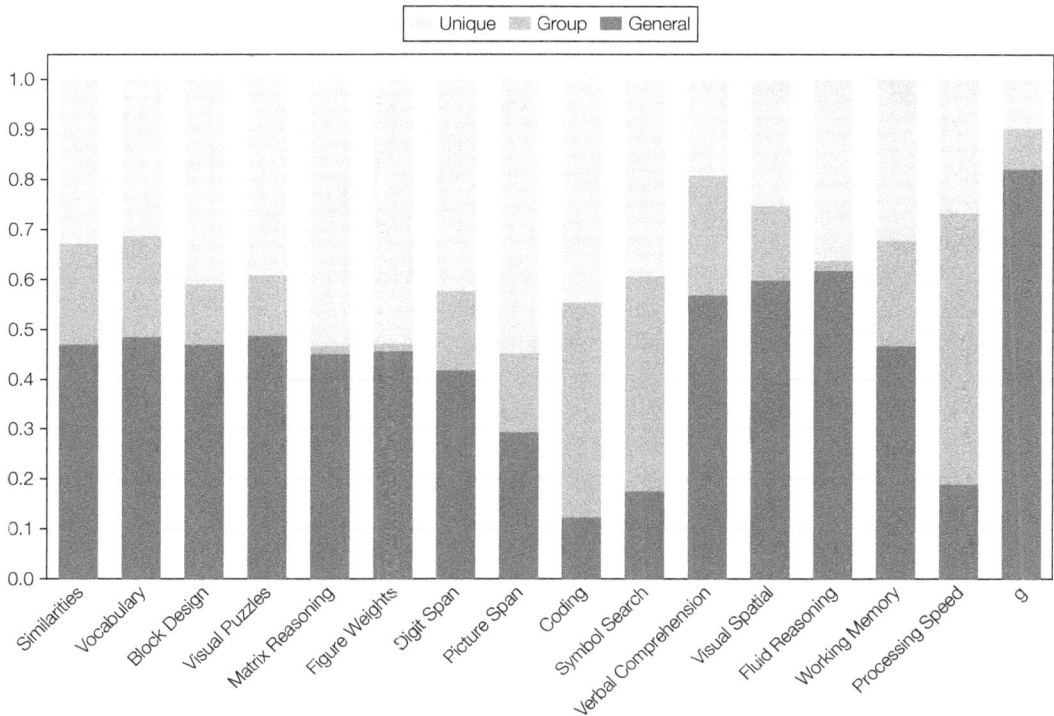

Figure 2.8. Variance Sources (General, Group, Unique [specific + error]) for the 10 WISC–V Primary Subtests and Factors for the Total Standardization Sample According to a CFA Bifactor Model with Five Group Factors. *Note.* The y-axis reflects total variance for subtests and explained common variance for factors. Unique variance is subtest specificity and error variance combined.

and is a poor or not statistically significant indicator of FR so functionally FR also seems to only be indexed by two subtests (Matrix Reasoning and Figure Weights) and also underidentified. Best practices in EFA note that latent variables should be measured by at least three measured variables (see Watkins, 2018, 2021) and the same principle also applies to CFA (Byrne, 2006) for model identification. Consistent with findings from Canivez and Watkins (2016), Canivez et al. (2017), and the extended model-based analyses presented earlier in this chapter, Reynolds and Keith found low unique variance of factor indexes when *g* variance was removed, with the exception of PS. Decomposed variance estimates from the Reynolds and Keith higher-order model showed that the WISC–V subtests primarily reflected variance from *g* with small portions of variance unique to the group factors. While different studies might suggest slightly different assignments of subtests to latent dimensions or adding or deleting various paths or covariances, the basic result of Reynolds and Keith (2017), like others, is that the WISC–V is a very good measure of *g* but there are measurement complications that limit confident interpretation of factor index scores as presented in the *WISC–V Administration and Scoring Manual* (Wechsler, 2014c) and the *WISC–V Technical and Interpretive Manual* (Wechsler, 2014b). While Reynolds and Keith focused on theoretical elements of what the WISC–V might measure, the added complexity of intermediary factors, empirical redundancy of *g* and FR, and cross-loading subtests limits clinical interpretation and replication of such models with independent samples necessary but absent. Further, as pointed out in Chapter 1, models suggested by EFA and CFA must be adjudicated by substantive research with criteria external to the test (Kline, 1994; Lubinski & Dawis, 1992; Oh et al., 2004).

Such research may include predictive validity, incremental validity, diagnostic utility, and ultimately treatment validity, all of which are crucial in determining adequacy of provided scores and score comparisons for clinical application.

Measurement Invariance and Subgroup Analyses

As discussed in Chapter 1, use of tests with various subgroups in a population, despite inclusion of representative samples, must show evidence that the constructs measured by a test are measured similarly. Thus, assessment of measurement invariance across important demographic variables (race, sex/gender, SES, etc.) is important. While such information is disappointingly absent from the *WISC–V Technical and Interpretive Manual* (Wechsler, 2014b), several studies are now available in the extant literature that reported examination of measurement invariance.

H. Chen et al. (2015) examined WISC–V measurement invariance across sex/gender with the WISC–V standardization sample. The baseline model was the publisher-preferred Model 5e that included three Arithmetic cross-loadings and a standardized path coefficient of 1.0 from g to FR. Perplexing was the mislabeling of latent factors as FSIQ, VCI, VSI, FRI, WMI, and PSI in their Figure 1 (similar to the mislabeling g as FSIQ in Wechsler [2014b] and in other international WISC–V versions). The IQ and Index scores refer to observed scores or measured variables, not the latent constructs of an SEM model. H. Chen et al. reported the univariate normality of subtest scores with all skewness and kurtosis estimates $< |1.0|$ that justified their use of maximum likelihood estimation rather than using the weighted least squares estimation used by Wechsler (2014b). While the proposed model demonstrated full invariance across sex/gender, there are problems with the baseline model as noted by Canivez and Watkins (2016) and Canivez et al. (2016, 2017). There was no consideration of the problem of the model containing the g–FR path of 1.0 continuing to disregard the empirical redundancy of FR with g as well as three cross-loadings of Arithmetic. There was no consideration of invariance of rival bifactor models or invariance of a model with only four first-order group factors (Wechsler model) which is likely a better conceptualization (see Canivez & Watkins, 2016; Canivez et al., 2016, 2017) given the extremely poor psychometric properties of FR in the WISC–V. Also, while the model may be invariant across sex/gender, this does not indicate how well the constructs are measured for each group. Decomposition of variance of g and the group factors (i.e., Schmid & Leiman, 1957) and application of model-based reliability/validity and dimensionality estimates would test how well each of the invariant constructs were measured but are absent.

Scheiber (2016) obtained WISC–V norming sample data ($N = 2,637$) from NCS Pearson to conduct invariance analyses across racial and gender/sex groups (Caucasian male [$n = 777$], Caucasian female [$n = 830$], African-American male [$n = 188$], African-American female [$n = 221$], Hispanic male [$n = 308$], Hispanic female [$n = 313$]). The model estimation method was not specified and *df* for freely estimated parameters did not match what was expected based on freely estimated parameters implied by the specified models so it is unknown if there were undisclosed model modifications resulting in fewer *df*. Standardized parameter estimates (path coefficients) were not provided so problems with path coefficients could not be assessed. Scheiber reported configural, metric, and intercept invariance across all six groups for the publisher-preferred model (Model 5e), but like H. Chen et al. (2015) did not include examination of alternate rival models such as a bifactor representation or Wechsler (4-factor) based higher-order or bifactor models that may also be invariant across these groups. Further, without additional variance decomposition and model-based reliability/validity and dimensionality estimates there is no assessment of how well the invariant factors are indexed across the six groups.

Graves et al. (2021) reported assessment of WISC–V invariance for the 10 primary subtests across race (Black, White) with a sample (N = 1,184) of children referred for special education services in Northwestern Pennsyvania and tested by school psychologists that was 55% Black and 60% male. CFA results for the oblique five-factor WISC–V model with the Black sample showed excellent global model fit but the latent factor correlation of .992 between VS and FR was excessively high and illustrated poor discriminant validity. CFA for an oblique four-factor WISC–V model also indicated good global model fit although it was reported the AIC favored the five-factor model. When retaining only the highest two subtest indicators of the PR factor AIC favored the oblique four-factor WISC–V model. Racial invariance was examined for the oblique five-factor WISC–V model for the Black and White participants and configural invariance (number and pattern of factors) was supported but metric invariance (factor loadings) was not. Partial metric invariance was then examined and showed that Figure Weights and Picture Span differed in measurement of FR and WM between Black and White students, respectively. The method of model estimation was not reported and only the invariance of the oblique first-order structure was examined.

Smith & Graves (2021) examined WISC–V invariance of the 10 primary subtests across gender/sex among the Black boys (n = 401) and Black girls (n = 246) with the subsample of Black children from the Graves et al. (2021) study. While global model fit for the oblique five-factor WISC–V structure was excellent, the latent variable correlation of .99 between VS and FR in their sample was deemed excessively large and lacking discriminant validity and indicated structural challenges. Thus, a four-factor model was also examined and also shown to have excellent global model fit, and AIC was noted to favor the oblique four-factor model. However, the oblique four-factor WISC–V measurement model illustrated did not include Block Design or Figure Weights as indicators of Perceptual Reasoning. Despite these findings, Smith and Graves focused on assessing invariance of the oblique five-factor WISC–V measurement model for Black boys and girls to assess adequacy of provided test scores. As with Graves et al. (2021), the method of model estimation was not reported and only the invariance of the oblique first-order structure was examined. Configural (number and pattern of factors) and metric (factor loadings) invariance was reportedly supported but scalar invariance (equivalent factor means and intercepts) was not. Black boys and girls both showed excessively high VS and FR correlations, 1.0 and .97, respectively. Partial scalar invariance was reported for VC, FR, and WM but not VS and PS. Figure captions for scalar invariance for Black boys and Black girls noted standardized estimates were reported; however, text indicated unstandardized estimates were reported but both included excessively high correlations between VS and FR and a lack of discriminant validity.

Stephenson et al. (2021) assessed the factor structure and measurement invariance of the 10 WISC–V primary subtests with a sample of 349 children ages 6–16 diagnosed with ASD at a large neurodevelopmental assessment center. Maximum likelihood estimation was reported in CFA and, in addition to examining model fit, they also applied model-based reliability/validity estimates (ω_H & ω_{HS}) to assess how well various factors were indexed. Results of CFA with the ASD sample indicated the best-fitting model was the four-factor bifactor model but only the g oriented FSIQ showed satisfactory ω_H (.86). The four group factors ω_{HS} coefficients ranged from .09 (WM) to .34 (VC) and were below the suggested minimum cutoff (.50). For comparison purposes in measurement invariance, Stephenson et al. obtained the WISC–V standardization sample normative data from the publisher and several models were tested for invariance between the ASD and standardization groups. The five-factor higher-order WISC–V model demonstrated configural and metric invariance across groups for first-order and higher-order levels with equivalent factor loadings; however, scalar invariance was not supported at the first-order level. A FSIQ model with correlated Similarities and Vocabulary subtests (based on modification indices) also demonstrated full configural and metric invariance and partial scalar invariance was reported with group differences observed on Coding and Digit Span subtests. The General Ability Index (GAI) model with correlated Similarities and Vocabulary subtests (based on modification indices) demonstrated full configural, metric, and scalar invariance. Finally, a Cognitive Proficiency Index (CPI) model was examined but the initial model showed only marginal fit for children with ASD and inadequate fit for the standardization sample so invariance was not examined.

Dombrowski et al. (2021) examined WISC–V structural invariance for the 10 primary subtests across age (6–8, 9–11, 12–14, 15–16), sex/gender, and diagnostic group (ADHD, Anxiety, encephalopathy) with a large clinical sample ($N = 5,359$). Archival data including WISC–V scores from clinical assessments were obtained from a large outpatient clinical psychology/neuropsychology clinic in a children's specialty hospital. Due to multivariate nonnormality of data, robust maximum likelihood estimation was used. Measurement invariance of the oblique five-factor measurement model was examined and reported. Configural invariance was observed across age, sex, and diagnostic groups as was metric invariance. Scalar invariance was observed for sex and diagnostic groups but was not supported across age groups. Fluid Reasoning subtests intercepts caused the lack of full scalar invariance reportedly also observed by Graves et al. (2021). Partial scalar invariance across age was observed by freeing the Figure Weights intercept.

While published studies examining invariance is helpful to understand adequacy of WISC–V measurement, basic invariance studies should be routinely conducted and reported in test technical manuals, especially for important population subgroups such as sex/gender, age, race/ethnicity, and socioeconomic status, which are all major stratification variables included in major tests of intelligence. Further, while test standardization samples include samples of White/Caucasian, Black/African American, and Hispanic/Latino(a) that would likely be sufficiently large for comparative invariance studies, other race/ethnicity groups such as Asian American and Native American or Indigenous groups are most likely not sufficiently large, and oversampling these groups to report such invariance (and other comparative studies) is important but unlikely to be provided. It may take many years following the publication of a test such as the WISC–V for invariance studies for these smaller groups to be conducted and reported in the extant literature, if ever. To date there appears to have been no such studies for Native American/Indigenous or Asian American groups so measurement invariance or equivalence for these groups is unknown 10 years following initial publication of the WISC–V.

Concurrent Validity/Convergent Validity

As presented in Chapter 1 (this volume), test validity may be supported by concurrent validity studies where another criterion test is used for comparison or by convergent validity studies where multiple tests of the same construct are compared with the expectation that similar test scores will provide high correlations. The *WISC–V Technical and Interpretive Manual* (Wechsler, 2014b) includes several such studies to provide evidence that various WISC–V scores have high correlations with similar scores from other intelligence tests. Evidence based on relations with other variables within the *WISC–V Technical and Interpretive Manual* (Wechsler, 2014b) includes four comparisons of the WISC–V with other measures of intelligence (WISC–IV, WPPSI–IV, WAIS–IV, Kaufman Assessment Battery for Children-Second Edition [KABC–II; Kaufman & Kaufman, 2004]).

Correlations between similar or the same composite scores from the WISC–V and the WISC–IV (n = 242) ranged from .59 (WMI) to .81 (FSIQ and VCI). Correlations between similar or the same composite scores from the WISC–V and the WPPSI–IV (n = 105) ranged from .34 (PSI) to .74 (FSIQ), while correlations between the WISC–V and the WASI–IV (n = 112) ranged from .56 (FRI, PR) and .84 (FSIQ). Correlations between similar composite scores from the WISC–V and the KABC–II (n = 89) ranged from .50 (FRI–G_f) to .81 (FSIQ–Fluid-Crystallized Index). Generally, comparisons of the WISC–V to other measures of intelligence show good correspondence with moderate to high correlations between similar composite scores. What was missing in tables comparing the WISC–V to the WISC–IV, WPPSI–IV, and WAIS–IV were correlations between dissimilar composite scores that should reflect lower correlations than respective convergent/concurrent correlations that would support discriminant validity. Some WISC–V composite score correlations with those from the KABC–II reflected discriminant validity but some correlations did not. For example, the correlation between the WISC–V VSI and KABC–II G_c (r = .55) did not differ from the correlation of WISC–V VSI and KABC–II G_v (r = .53), and the correlation between the WISC–V FRI and the KABC–II G_c (r = .52) did not differ from the correlation of the WISC–V FRI with the KABC–II G_f (r = .50). Thus, there seems to be a lack of adequate discriminant validity among some WISC–V composite scores, namely VSI and FRI.

Predictive Validity

The *WISC–V Technical and Interpretive Manual* (Wechsler, 2014b) also includes two studies within the area of relationships with other measures or variables to provide construct validity evidence by comparing performance on the WISC–V with performance on measures of academic achievement. One study compared the WISC–V to the Kaufman Test of Educational Achievement-Third Edition (KTEA–3; Kaufman & Kaufman, 2014) with a sample of 207, 6–16-year-olds with a testing interval of 0–52 days (M = 14 days). The second study compared the WISC–V to the Wechsler Individual Achievement Test-Third Edition (WIAT–III; Pearson, 2009) with a sample of 211, 6–16-year-olds with a testing interval of 0–59 days (M = 16 days). These studies could also be classified as predictive validity studies (albeit quite short-term), with achievement measures being administered a short time after administration of the WISC–V. Zero-order Pearson correlations between the WISC–V FSIQ and KTEA–3 and WIAT–III composite scores were typically in the .60s and .70s (and somewhat lower for KTEA–3 and WIAT–III subtest scores), similar to correlations reported in the extant literature (Brody, 1985; Jensen, 1998; Naglieri & Bornstein, 2003). Further, in both studies, the WISC–V VCI had correlations with achievement test composite and subtest scores reasonably similar to those produced by the FSIQ. While these results appear supportive, such correlations are problematic given that the WISC–V unit-weighted factor index scores conflate g variance and group factor variance identified earlier in this chapter, so the complexly determined factor index scores may owe their predictive validity to the rather large portion of g variance in the index score. This is why it has been recommended that hierarchical multiple regression (HMR) be conducted to assess *incremental validity* (Haynes & Lench, 2003; Hunsley, 2003; Hunsley & Meyer, 2003) so that the FSIQ could be included in the first block in predicting academic achievement and the factor index scores could be included in the second block. This would first allow for an assessment of how much achievement variance was accounted for by the FSIQ and then what additional achievement variance was accounted for by the factor index scores jointly and uniquely. In reviews of the WAIS–IV and WPPSI–IV, respectively, Canivez (2010, 2014) pointed out the absence of incremental validity in the respective test manuals and implored the publisher to include such analyses and results so test users would have necessary information for ethical and evidence-based test score interpretation.

Despite these earlier calls for incremental validity analyses to be included in Wechsler scales technical manuals (Canivez, 2010, 2014), the *WISC–V Technical and Interpretive Manual* (Wechsler, 2014b) is conspicuously devoid of these analyses and results, severely limiting test users ability to judge adequacy of provided scores. Also absent from the *WISC–V Technical and Interpretive Manual* (Wechsler, 2014b) are structural equation modeling (SEM) assessments of the theoretical explanations of academic achievement performance by the hierarchically ordered WISC–V latent factors (see Glutting et al., 2006; Oh et al., 2004), although, as pointed out in Chapter 1, such analyses do not provide practical implications when tests do not provide latent construct scores (Oh et al., 2024). The absence of these analyses means test users cannot know how much unique contribution WISC–V factor index scores provide in predicting or explaining WIAT–III or KTEA scores after accounting for the FSIQ or *g*.

Incremental Validity

As discussed in Chapter 1, when tests such as the WISC–V include hierarchically ordered scores, it is important to examine if lower-order (e.g., factor index) scores account for criterion score variance over and above the higher-order (e.g., FSIQ) score(s). This is another means to determine the viability of lower-order score interpretation. If lower-order scores provide substantive prediction over and above a higher-order score, then interpretation of the lower-order scores might be helpful. Numerous published structural validity studies and analyses of the WISC–V show that many subtests have large *g* saturation, and model-based indexes reported earlier in this chapter and elsewhere show little unique measurement of latent constructs represented by factor index scores so incremental validity of those scores seems unlikely. Incremental validity of intelligence tests in predicting academic achievement test performance (predictive validity) using hierarchical multiple regression (HMR) analyses has consistently found that after a global composite score (i.e., FSIQ) accounts for academic achievement score variability, the lower-order factor-based scores account for small portions of additional achievement score variability rendering them typically of little interpretive value (e.g., Canivez, 2013a; Canivez, 2013b; Canivez et al., 2014; Freberg et al., 2008; Glutting et al., 2006; Glutting et al., 1997; Ryan et al., 2002; Watkins et al., 2007). Test users may also want to understand what explanatory power lower-order factor scores have over and above the explanatory power of higher-order scores. This approach would use structural equation modeling to examine the latent constructs rather than observed scores (see Oh et al., 2004).

While not an incremental validity study, Kranzler et al. (2015) estimated latent factor scores based on the theoretical bifactor model for the adolescent standardization sample of the WAIS–IV using all 15 subtests (not just the 10 core subtests used in Canivez, 2013b). Then they estimated bifactor based factor scores as latent constructs for the small sample (*n* = 93) of sixteen 19-year-olds in the WAIS–IV and WIAT–II linking sample and examined predictive validity of the four WAIS–IV group factors and *g* using simultaneous regression (rather than HMR) to empirically test the method recommended by Hale et al. (2001) that was criticized by Schneider (2008), to examine unique effects of *g* and the group factors. A similar approach could be used with the WISC–V. While improving on the limitations present in the Canivez (2013b) study, overall results were quite similar with *g* accounting for substantial portions of WIAT–II achievement variance but illustrated that latent factor explanations had slightly less *g* and slightly more VC variance associated with

WIAT–II Word Reading, Reading Comprehension, Spelling, Listening Comprehension, and Total Achievement scores that needed to be considered in explanation. Kranzler et al. recommended that only the WAIS–IV FSIQ should be used in interpretation related to the other WIAT–II scores and concluded that replication with larger samples was needed before offering practice recommendations and that test publishers should begin providing latent construct scores to allow such interpretations.

Caemmerer et al. (2018) used a latent construct (SEM) approach (latent construct explanation) to examine WISC–V effects on the WIAT–III subtest scores using the publisher-provided standardization linking sample (N = 181) of 6- to 16-year-olds. The WISC–V measurement (structural) model used was *not* the same as the publisher-preferred Model 5e (Wechsler, 2014b) nor was it the same as the final preferred model produced by Reynolds and Keith (2017). General intelligence (g) was modeled as a higher-order dimension via a CHC model and despite numerous problems regarding the FR (G_f in CHC terminology) factor (little to no unique variance, empirically redundant with g) reported earlier in this chapter, it was retained as a latent factor. Within higher-order models the g factor is fully mediated by latent first-order CHC factors (higher-order model) but in bifactor models the g factor is *not* mediated by first-order factors and has direct effects independent of the group factors (CHC factors). A bifactor representation of the WISC–V was not directly examined. Results of Caemmerer et al. (2018) illustrated that when g was allowed as a direct explanation of the WIAT–III achievement subtests (see Caemmerer et al., 2018, Table 5), large effect sizes were observed for all nine WIAT–III achievement subtests (.42 [Essay Composition] to .76 [Math Problem Solving], Mdn = .58). Further, after g effects were removed, Gf provided *no* statistically significant effects on any achievement skill which further indicated its redundancy with g illustrated in numerous structural validity studies reviewed earlier. Also, direct effects of g dwarfed unique effects of CHC factors with g effects removed frequently observed in other examinations of Wechsler scales (e.g., Glutting et al., 2006; Kranzler et al., 2015; Parkin & Beaujean, 2012). Unique effects of first-order CHC broad factors were substantially less than g effects on most WIAT–III achievement subtests and composite scores. When modeling the five CHC first-order factors with g effects on the nine WIAT–III subtests, the statistically significant effects (see Caemmerer et al., 2018, Table 4) were mostly of large effect sizes but conflates g variance and CHC factor variance in such explanations. Interestingly, the CHC Gv (VS) dimension had no statistically significant effect in explaining any of the WIAT–III subtests with or without g. While an interesting study of the theoretical explanations of WIAT–III achievement subtests by WISC–V latent factors specified by the higher-order model, a major limitation is that the publisher does not provide latent construct scores for clinicians to use and interpret so there are no direct implications for results regarding the observed WISC–V test scores provided (Oh et al., 2004).

Caemmerer et al. (2024) recognized the practical limitations of latent construct explanation methods reported in Caemmerer et al. (2018) and using the same publisher supplied WISC–V and WIAT–III standardization linking sample data, examined WISC–V FSIQ and Factor Index scores prediction of WIAT–III subtest and composite scores. Their analysis method included the simultaneous multiple regression approach with the five WISC–V factor index scores to predict WIAT–III subtest and composite scores and reported statistically significant regression coefficients when controlling for the other four. They also examined the FSIQ as a separate univariate predictor of WIAT–III subtest and composite scores. This is not, however, a hierarchical multiple regression method to first examine the FSIQ prediction of WIAT–III achievement scores and then examine the five WISC–V factor index scores prediction of residual WIAT–III achievement scores. Thus, direct comparisons to past WISC incremental validity studies (e.g., Canivez, 2013b; Glutting et al., 2006) is not possible. Univariate predictions of WIAT–III achievement subtest and composite scores by the WISC–V FSIQ were reported to be statistically significant (except for Alphabet Writing Fluency), and all effect sizes were large. Relative contribution of WISC–V factor index scores in predicting academic achievement scores form the WIAT–III after accounting for the FSIQ is thus still unknown. Both Caemmerer et al. (2018) and Caemmerer et al. (2024) studies showed largest portions of achievement explanation by g and prediction by the FSIQ, respectively, with additional contributions by some first-order factors or factor index scores, particularly VC, but less contribution than that of global, general intelligence.

Discriminant/Divergent Validity

Two additional studies of WISC–V construct validity evidence based on relationships with other variables reported in the *WISC–V Technical and Interpretive Manual* (Wechsler, 2014b) include comparisons of the WISC–V with the Vineland Adaptive Behavior Scales-Second Edition (Vineland–II; Sparrow et al., 2005), a measure of adaptive behavior and the Behavior Assessment System for Children–Second Edition Parent Rating Scales (BASC–2 PRS; Reynolds & Kamphaus, 2004) Resiliency, Conduct Problems, Executive Functioning, and Attention Problems scales. Both studies reported using nonclinical samples for the Vineland–II ($n = 61$) and the BASC–2 ($n = 2,302$). Correlations between the WISC–V and Vineland–II subtest and composite scores were mostly low to near zero supporting divergent validity of tests measuring very different constructs. Correlations between the WISC–V and the reported BASC–2 scales were also low to near zero reflecting divergent validity of tests of very different constructs, although it would have been helpful to see correlations with the many other BASC–2 scales and composite scores that should also reflect divergent validity. Similar but more extensive comparisons and results were previously reported by Canivez et al. (2005) with the WISC–III.

Distinct Group Differences

Canivez and Watkins (2016) noted in their WISC–V review that a variety of clinical groups were obtained from independent researchers and examiners from clinical settings during WISC–V standardization to compare to matched samples of typical children and are reported under Special Group Studies in the *WISC–V Technical and Interpretive Manual* (Wechsler, 2014b). Special groups included generally small samples of children with Mild Intellectual Disability ($N = 74$), Moderate Intellectual Disability ($N = 37$), Specific Learning Disability–Reading ($N = 30$), Specific Learning Disability-Reading and Written Expression ($N = 22$), Specific Learning Disability–Math ($N = 28$), Attention Deficit Hyperactivity Disorder ($N = 48$), Gifted/Talented ($N = 95$), Traumatic Brain Injury ($N = 20$), Autism Spectrum Disorder–With Language Disorder ($N = 30$), Autism Spectrum Disorder–Without Language Disorder ($N = 32$). Each of the groups were compared to control groups composed of randomly selected and demographically matched typical children from the normative sample to provide preliminary validity evidence. Limitations of these preliminary studies were duly noted in the *WISC–V Technical and Interpretive Manual* (Wechsler, 2014b) and included small and nonrandom selection of special group participants who had classifications that might vary by different selection criteria. Also, data were collected by independent researchers and examiners. Such limitations are recognized to affect generalizability but are helpful upon initial publication.

WISC–V scores generally differed in expected ways between the special groups and their demographically matched control participants. In particular, the results of the preliminary distinct group differences comparisons showed that those identified as intellectually gifted scored significantly higher than children in the demographically matched control group while those identified with intellectual disability (ID; mild and moderate) scored significantly lower than those in the demographically controlled matched control group as expected. Effect sizes for subtest and composite score differences in these comparisons also far exceeded criteria for large effects (Cohen, 1988).

Using the publisher-provided special group data for the sample of children with intellectual disability (ID) and the matched typically developing children from the normative sample, Bergeron et al. (2023) extended WISC–V research by examining effects of using part scores (factor index scores [VCI, VSI, FRI, WMI, PSI]) compared to the FSIQ (and other global composites [GAI and NVI]) in classification of children with ID. They found relatively flat index score profiles in both groups but few individuals had index score profiles that matched their respective group profile. Classification accuracy was best for the FSIQ and conditional probabilities for all global composite scores (FSIQ, GAI, NVI) were best with criteria of ≤ .70 and ≤ .75 with minimal false positive classifications. The vast majority of those with ID had at least one statistically significant and meaningful factor index score that differed from their FSIQ and when assessing the number of those in the ID sample who would not meet the ID criterion with an index score exceeding 80, 37.8% would not! This excessively high false negative rate and other findings in their study and in the extant literature led Bergeron et al. to conclude that in assessment of intelligence for ID diagnosis, part scores (factor index scores) should not be used to supplant or supplement global composite IQ scores because of the numerous psychometric problems inherent in factor index scores and their comparisons.

A series of three WISC–V studies using the publisher-provided special group data for the sample of children diagnosed with ASD With Language Disorder (ASD-LI; $N = 30$) or ASD Without Language Disorder (ASD-NLI; $N = 32$) and the demographically matched, typically developing children from the normative sample (Control; $N = 62$) were conducted by Dale and colleagues (Dale et al., 2023; Dale et al., 2021, 2022). Dale et al. (2021) applied classification and regression tree (CART) analyses in an attempt to identify and assess profiles that might assist in ASD assessment. CART analyses were conducted at the subtest level and then the index score level for distinguishing two groups (ASD, Control) and at the subtest level and then index score level for distinguishing three groups (ASD-LI, ASD-NLI, Control). Several WISC–V subtests and index scores performance levels were noted to be associated with the group memberships. Kappa coefficients assessing prediction accuracy ranged from .468 (weak) to .654 (moderate) and only the three group comparison with subtests achieved moderate level of accuracy. Dale et al. (2022) used the same data set to compare performance on the WISC–V VCI (Similarities, Vocabulary) to the newly created Verbal Expanded Crystallized Index (VECI; Similarities, Vocabulary, Information, Comprehension). Repeated measures ANOVA (RMANOVA) was used to compare the ASD and Control groups and another RMANOVA compared the ASD-LI and ASD-NLI groups. The first RMANOVA had a statistically significant interaction where the control group VCI and VECI difference of 0.31 points was smaller than the difference of 7 points between the VCI and VECI for the ASD group (in favor of VCI), but that difference reflected a small effect size ($d = 0.36$). The second RMANOVA also contained a statistically significant interaction effect where the ASD-NLI group VCI and VECI means differed by 1.84 points while the ASD-LI group VCI and VECI means differed by 4.52 points (in favor of the VCI), but that difference also represented a small effect size ($d = 0.45$). Dale et al. (2023) again used this publisher-provided special group data set to assess group differences in ancillary index scales using MANOVA and linear discriminant analysis (LDA) of the five Ancillary Index Scores *and* the FSIQ (although the FSIQ is not an ancillary index). Also, ancillary index scores share several subtests so multicollinearity seems a problem.

MANOVA comparing ASD-LI, ASD-NLI, and Control groups was statistically significant as was LDA. Glass Δ effect sizes for all ancillary index scores and the FSIQ between the ASD-LI and control group and between the ASD-LI and ASD-NLI groups were large, while Glass Δ effect sizes between the ASD-NLI and control group ranged from trivial (GAI) to medium (AWMI, CPI). In all three studies Dale and colleagues came to conclusions and made recommendations that appeared to extend far beyond the recognized and significant limitations these data contain and also did not appear to consider the psychometric limitations reported earlier in this chapter regarding longitudinal stability (or instability) of WISC–V subtest and composite scores and score comparisons or sources of true score variance in complexly determined composite scores. As suggested, replication with larger, independent samples of children and adolescents with ASD are badly needed.

MacAllister et al. (2019) examined the WISC–V primary subtest and composite score performance with an independent sample of 80 predominantly Caucasian (n = 65) children and adolescents (41 male, 39 female) ranging in age from 6 to 15 years (M = 9.87) who had been diagnosed with epilepsy. They obtained from NCS Pearson a demographically matched sample from the WISC–V normative sample to serve as a control group for between group comparisons. Numerous independent t-tests for mean differences (rather than MANOVA/ANOVA) were conducted for comparisons between the Epilepsy and Control group (IQ, Index Scores, Subtest Scores) and no Bonferroni correction for Type I error rates were noted. Effect sizes for these comparisons were also absent. Results indicated statistically significant differences in means between the two groups with the Epilepsy group scoring lower on all composite and subtest scores. Effect sizes computed from descriptive statistics provided in the article indicated large effects for all composite score comparisons except VCI (medium). Effect sizes for primary subtests were either medium or large (BD, MR, DS, PS, SS). Within group (Epilepsy) composite score comparisons were also reported but missing effect size estimates. Effect sizes calculated from t values and sample size showed some statistically significant differences were small (FSIQ-CPI, VSI-WMI, FRI-PSI), some medium (FSIQ-GAI, GAI-CPI, VCI-WMI, VCI-PRI), and some large (VSI-PSI, FRI-WMI). While informative, there was a missed opportunity to provide more important comparisons with such a sample given the availability of the matched normative control group that would allow for assessment of diagnostic or classification accuracy of various WISC–V scores and comparisons (see Chapter 1 this volume).

WISC–V Diagnostic Utility and Treatment Utility

Generally, distinct group differences results illustrated in the *WISC–V Technical and Interpretive Manual* (Wechsler, 2014b) showed preliminary evidence with expected differences between various clinical groups and the specific matched control group from the normative sample with clinical groups scoring lower and the gifted group scoring higher. Such group differences do not necessarily mean that such differences allow for diagnostic or classification use of various WISC–V scores or score comparisons. Statements within the *WISC–V Technical and Interpretive Manual* indicating that results from such studies "demonstrate the differential sensitivity of the WISC–V to specific and general cognitive deficits exhibited by children commonly evaluated in clinical settings" (p. 112) and that information about group mean differences "provides evidence for the clinical utility and discriminant validity of the WISC–V subtests and composites" (p. 112) are not quite correct because group differences are necessary but they are not sufficient for individual decision-making. Sufficient evidence for clinical use of various scores and score comparisons for individuals must come from methods and analyses that test the classification or diagnostic accuracy or utility as illustrated in Chapter 1 of this volume. Use of logistic regression (LR) or discriminant function analysis (DFA) and use of conditional probabilities noted by Kessell and Zimmerman (1993) and receiver operator characteristic (ROC) curve analyses (Swets, 1996; Treat & Viken, 2012; Wasserman & Bracken, 2013) is necessary as is understanding clinical disorder base rates and cut-scores for individual decision-making (Meehl & Rosen, 1955). To date there appear to be no published studies in the extant literature attesting to the ability of the WISC–V scores or score comparisons for such individual diagnostic purposes although for some classifications or diagnoses (ID, Gifted/Talented, Epilepsy) the group differences studies appear to be promising given the very large effect sizes for some scores or comparisons.

Closely related to diagnostic utility or classification accuracy is *treatment utility*, which is another criterion that must be applied to intelligence tests like the WISC–V when authors or publishers of clinical guidebooks or test manuals offer suggestions or recommendations for interventions or programs to remediate identified problems based on specified test scores or score comparisons (i.e., idiographic/intra-individual cognitive strengths and weaknesses). Do specific WISC–V strengths and/or weaknesses provide sufficient information for differential treatment recommendations that work for some profiles/patterns but not others? This *aptitude by treatment interaction* (ATI) is the holy grail for clinical practice, but as yet, such ATIs have not been sufficiently supported (Braden & Shaw, 2009; Burns et al., 2016; Elliott & Resing, 2015; Floyd & Kranzler, 2019; Owen et al., 2010; Stuebing et al., 2015; Watkins & Glutting, 2000). Importantly, diagnostic and treatment recommendations linked to profiles/patterns of cognitive abilities should have replicated a priori evidence *before* encouraging clinicians to offer such recommendations and clinicians must consider such evidence before making such recommendations for ethical practice. When such evidence is absent or negative, such treatments or interventions should be offered only as an experimental procedure and systematically examined for efficacy with informed consent (see McFall, 1991, 1996, 2000).

Summary, Conclusions, and Recommendations

In the 10 years since publication of the WISC–V there have been reviews, critiques, and research to address its psychometric fitness for assessing intellectual abilities. As Canivez and Watkins (2016) noted, there are many positive elements of the WISC–V including a large and representative normative sample with good normative age block sample sizes, adequate floor and ceiling levels of standardized scores, overlap with the WPPSI–IV and WAIS–IV, and numerous manual and technical supplements. Canivez and Watkins also noted numerous problems of incomplete disclosure of key psychometric methods and results and addressed some shortcomings with independent analyses. This chapter has summarized and elaborated on some of the research presented in the *WISC–V Technical and Interpretive Manual* (Wechsler, 2014b) and studies in the extant literature assessing the reliability and validity of various WISC–V scores and score comparisons.

While short-term test-retest stability of WISC–V subtest and composite scores was included in the *WISC–V Technical and Interpretive Manual* (Wechsler, 2014b) and showed general support for most composite scores, there were no assessments of short-term test-retest stability of subtest or composite score strengths and weaknesses or scatter, a glaring omission given their suggested interpretations. Long-term WISC–V stability (Watkins et al., 2022) found acceptable stability only for the nomothetic oriented FSIQ, VCI, and VSI in a clinical sample. Long-term stability for all other subtests and composite scores was unacceptably low for individual decision-making. Long-term stability of all intra-individual (idiographic) subtest and composite score strengths and weaknesses and scatter was poor and indicated these metrics operate at chance levels and thus cannot be informative in diagnostic use or in generating hypotheses. Unfortunately, such analyses are absent with normative samples.

EFA with the 16 WISC–V primary and secondary subtests failed to identify or locate a viable fifth FR factor but VC, VS/PR, WM, and PS factors were reliably identified with their appropriate subtest indicators across various normative and clinical samples. The generally large factor correlations indicated presence of the robust g factor which was consistently shown to dominate measurement with dimensionality indexes indicating essential unidimensionality and model-based reliability/validity indexes that exceeded preferred levels, indicating composite scores for the general factor are well indexed. First-order group factors (VC, VS/PR, WM, [and FR when specified]) all had low dimensionality indexes suggesting they were not sufficiently unidimensional and their model-based reliability/validity indexes failed to achieve minimum levels and indicated scores based on them are poorly indexed for unique factor measurement after g variance is removed. Only the PS factor met minimum levels but confidence in PS is not strong. Identical results are observed in EFA of the 10 WISC–V primary subtests with the exception that the FR factor is identified or located with the full standardization sample, but it accounted for only 1.5% of unique WISC–V common variance so appears empirically redundant with g.

CFA results generally paralleled those from EFA with standardization and clinical samples. Both bifactor and higher-order WISC–V representations generally fit data well and both were generally plausible, but in both, the g factor dominated variance and explanation. As in EFA, model-based reliability/validity and dimensionality estimates showed the g factor to be essentially unidimensional and well indexed by its indicators. Like EFA, group/first-order factors were found to have low dimensionality estimates and low model-based reliability/validity indexes that fell below the suggested minimum value (except at times for PS) indicating scores representing them would be inadequately indexed. FR, when specified in CFA, accounts for poor amounts of variance and often produces model specification errors with negative error variance and relations with g at or exceeding 1.0 (i.e., Heywood cases). As such, the WISC–V does not appear to measure an FR factor independent of g so their empirical redundancy is a major interpretive problem.

Factor structure assessments of the WISC–V repeatedly show it measures general intelligence very well and clinicians may be confident in its measurement and use for individual decision-making. The factor based scores (WISC–V index scores) are conceptually complex given their conflation of g variance and group factor variance and therefore lack a univocal interpretation (F. F. Chen & Zhang, 2018; Ferrando & Lorenzo-Seva, 2019). This is not to say that the theoretical constructs do not exist, it is just that the WISC–V (and most intelligence tests) does not seem to adequately measure them apart from g. It may be that tests like the WISC–V, which were originally designed to principally measure general intelligence, cannot at the same time measure well the narrower, more specific ability constructs. Interpretive focus should concentrate on the FSIQ but interpretation of factor index scores should be done with extreme caution, if at all, and in consideration of detailed information presented here and in the peer-reviewed literature.

With respect to invariance studies currently published, there is some evidence for measurement invariance of tested models across sex/gender, age, race/ethnicity (White/Caucasian, Black/African American, and Hispanic/Latino), and clinical groups (ADHD, Anxiety, Encephalopathy), but more research must be conducted for other groups in the population (i.e., Asian Americans, Indigenous/ Native Americans). Invariance studies testing rival bifactor models as well as models containing only four group factors (no FR) must also be assessed and additional assessments of model-based dimensionality and reliability/validity to assess the adequacy of measurement of various constructs within the invariant model is needed. Model invariance does not address the question of how well the model works and given the poor model-based dimensionality and reliability/validity indexes observed for the five WISC–V group factors thus far, it may be that invariance simply means the inadequate unique measurement of group factors is equally inadequate across the compared groups.

Canivez and Watkins (2016) noted the "unbridled enthusiasm" (p. 692) in Fletcher-Jansen's (2014) *WISC–V Technical and Interpretive Manual Foreword* where the numerous scores and comparisons, new theoretical five-factor structure, and measurement of separate VS and FR dimensions would facilitate deconstructing the FSIQ for answering referral questions, and that "on a practical level, the WISC–V promises and delivers" (p. xv). Unfortunately, WISC–V research to date is considerably more sobering and has not provided the strong empirical support for the WISC–V score and score comparison interpretations envisioned. It would be nice if the WISC–V (or any test for that matter) lived up to the hype. Evidence-based assessment (Hunsley & Mash, 2007) requires using and interpreting scores and score comparisons that have replicated research support for specific applications, and this is fundamental to ethical (APA, 2017; NASP, 2020; Weiner, 1989) and legal (Reynolds & Milam, 2012) test use. Research reviewed here illustrates significant psychometric limitations for interpretations offered in the *WISC–V Technical and Interpretive Manual* (Wechsler, 2014b) and related interpretive guidebooks. All test users would do well to abide by the motto of the Royal Society, *Nullius in verba* [Take nobody's word for it], and base test interpretation and clinical judgments on scores that are consonant with replicated evidence in the peer-reviewed literature. Test users also must consider financial conflicts of interest in judging information they are given (Beaujean et al., 2024). This would greatly assist in proper interpretation of viable test scores and comparisons and in guarding against overinterpretation or misinterpretation of the many WISC–V scores and comparisons, thereby avoiding eminence-based assessment (Chapter 7, this volume).

Notes

1 There are currently no technical report supplements addressing this evidentiary lacuna on the Pearson WISC–V website.

2 This author submitted two federal grant research proposals—one to the National Institutes of Health/ National Institute of Mental Health and one to the U.S. Department of Education—to fund a large-scale project where the Psychological Corporation normative test examiners would have been paid to re-administer the WISC–IV and WIAT–III to participants (who would also have been paid) in the WISC–IV normative sample seven years following their initial testing to assess longitudinal stability of WISC–IV scores and intra-individual cognitive strengths and weaknesses in performance as well as longitudinal prediction of WIAT–III achievement from WISC–IV scores seven years earlier. Both proposals and their revisions were not funded with reviewers stating such research should be conducted by the test publisher (despite this author noting in the proposal that this had never been done previously and was

unlikely to ever be done by the publisher). Thus, all research on long-term stability of intelligence test scores and cognitive strengths and weaknesses are from clinical samples where reassessments have been more routinely conducted as a consequence of special education laws in the United States but with clinical sample limitations.

References

American Educational Research Association, American Psychological Association, and National Council on Measurement in Education. (1999). *Standards for educational and psychological testing*. Author.

American Educational Research Association, American Psychological Association, and National Council on Measurement in Education. (2014). *Standards for educational and psychological testing*. Author.

American Psychological Association. (2017). *Ethical principles of psychologists and code of conduct* (2002, amended effective June 1, 2010, and January 1, 2017). https://www.apa.org/ethics/code/ethics-code -2017.pdf

Bandalos, D. L. (2018). *Measurement theory and applications in the social sciences*. Guilford Press.

Beaujean, A. A. (2016). Reproducing the Wechsler Intelligence Scale for Children–Fifth edition Factor model results. *Journal of Psychoeducational Assessment*, *34*(4), 404–408. https://doi.org/10.1177 /0734282916642679

Beaujean, A. A., & Benson, N. F. (2019). Theoretically consistent cognitive ability test development and score interpretation. *Contemporary School Psychology*, *23*(2), 126–137. https://doi.org/10.1007/s40688-018 -0182-1

Beaujean, A. A., McGill, R. J., & Dombrowski, S. C. (2024). Financial conflicts of interest in school psychology: A continuing problem. *Contemporary School Psychology*, *28*, 109–119. https://doi.org/10 .1007/s40688-022-00435-3

Benson, N. F., Floyd, R. G., Kranzler, J. H., Eckert, T. L., Fefer, S. A., & Morgan, G. B. (2019). Test use and assessment practices of school psychologists in the United States: Findings from the 2017 national survey. *Journal of School Psychology*, *72*, 29–48. https://doi.org/10.1016/j. jsp.2018.12.004

Bentler, P. M., & Wu, E. J. C. (2012). *EQS for Windows*. Multivariate Software.

Bergeron, R., Floyd, R. G., McNicholas, P. J., & Farmer, R. L. (2023). Assessment of intellectual disability with the Wechsler Intelligence Scale for Children–Fifth Edition: Analysis of part score profiles and diagnostic outcomes. *School Psychology Review*, *52*(6), 747–762. https://doi.org/10.1080/2372966x .2022.2094284

Boomsma, A. (2000). Reporting analyses of covariance structures. *Structural Equation Modeling: A Multidisciplinary Journal*, *7*(3), 461–483. https://doi.org/10.1207/s15328007sem0703_6

Borsboom, D. (2022). Possible futures for network psychometrics. *Psychometrika*, *87*(1), 253–265. https:// doi.org/10.1007/s11336-022-09851-z

Braden, J. P., & Shaw, S. R. (2009). Intervention validity of cognitive assessment: Knowns, unknowables, and unknowns. *Assessment for Effective Intervention*, *34*(2), 106–115. https://doi.org/10.1177 /1534508407313013

Brody, N. (1985). The validity of tests of intelligence. In B. Wolman (Ed.), *Handbook of intelligence* (pp. 353–389). Wiley.

Burns, M. K., Petersen-Brown, S., Haegele, K., Rodriguez, M., Schmitt, B., Cooper, M., Clayton, K., Hutcheson, S., Conner, C., Hosp, J., & VanDerHeyden, A. M. (2016). Meta-analysis of academic interventions derived from neuropsychological data. *School Psychology Quarterly*, *31*(1), 28–42. https:// doi.org/10.1037/spq0000117

Buros, O. K. (1938). Preface. In O. K. Buros (Ed.), *The 1938 mental measurements yearbook* (p. xiii). Rutgers University Press.

Byrne, B. M. (2006). *Structural equation modeling with EQS* (2nd ed.). Lawrence Erlbaum Associates.

Caemmerer, J. M., Maddocks, D. L., Keith, T. Z., & Reynolds, M. R. (2018). Effects of cognitive abilities on child and youth academic achievement: Evidence from the WISC–V and WIAT–III. *Intelligence*, *68*, 6–20. https://doi.org/10.1016/j.intell.2018.02.005

Caemmerer, J. M., Young, S. R., Macdocks, D., Charamut, N. R., & Blemahdoo, E. (2024). Predicting achievement from WISC–V composites: Do cognitive-achievement relations vary based on general intelligence? *Journal of Psychoeducational Assessment*, 42(4), 390–408. https://doi.org/10.1177/07342829241240346

Canivez, G. L. (2010). Test review of the Wechsler Adult Intelligence Test–Fourth Edition. In R. A. Spies, J. F. Carlson, and K. F. Geisinger (Eds.), *The eighteenth mental measurements yearbook* (pp. 684–638). Buros Institute of Mental Measurements.

Canivez, G. L. (2013a). Psychometric versus actuarial interpretation of intelligence and related aptitude batteries. In D. H. Saklofske, C. R. Reynolds, & V. L. Schwean, (Eds.), *The Oxford Handbook of Child Psychological Assessments* (pp. 84–112). Oxford University Press. https://doi.org/10.1093/oxfordhb/9780199796304.013.0004

Canivez, G. L. (2013b). Incremental validity of WAIS–IV factor index scores: Relationships with WIAT–II and WIAT–III subtest and composite scores. *Psychological Assessment*, 25(2), 484–495. https://doi.org/10.1037/a0032092

Canivez, G. L. (2014). Test review of the Wechsler Preschool and Primary Scale of Intelligence–Fourth Edition. In J. F. Carlson, K. F. Geisinger, & J. L. Jonson (Eds.), *The nineteenth mental measurements yearbook* (pp. 732–737). Buros Center for Testing.

Canivez, G. L. (2016). Bifactor modeling in construct validation of multifactored tests: Implications for multidimensionality and test interpretation. In K. Schweizer & C. DiStefano (Eds.), *Principles and methods of test construction: Standards and recent advancements* (pp. 247–271). Hogrefe.

Canivez, G. L. (2017). Review of the Woodcock–Johnson IV. In J. F. Carlson, K. F. Geisinger, & J. L. Jonson (Eds.), *The twentieth mental measurements yearbook* (pp. 875–882). Buros Center for Testing.

Canivez, G. L., Dombrowski, S. C., & Watkins, M. W. (2018). Factor structure of the WISC–V in four standardization age groups: Exploratory and hierarchical factor analyses with the 16 primary and secondary subtests. *Psychology in the Schools*, 55(7), 741–769. https://doi.org/10.1002/pits.22138

Canivez, G. L., & Kush, J. C. (2013). WISC–IV and WAIS–IV structural validity: Alternate methods, alternate results. Commentary on Weiss et al. (2013a) and Weiss et al. (2013b). *Journal of Psychoeducational Assessment*, 31(2), 157–169. https://doi.org/10.1177/0734282913478036

Canivez, G. L., McGill, R. J., Dombrowski, S. C., Watkins, M. W., Pritchard, A. E., & Jacobson, L. A. (2020). Construct validity of the WISC–V in clinical cases: Exploratory and confirmatory factor analyses of the 10 primary subtests. *Assessment*, 27(2), 274–296. https://doi.org/10.1177/1073191118811609

Canivez, G. L., Neitzel, R., & Martin, B. E. (2005). Construct validity of the Kaufman Brief Intelligence Test, Wechsler Intelligence Scale for Children–Third Edition, and Adjustment Scales for Children and Adolescents. *Journal of Psychoeducational Assessment*, 23(1), 15–34. https://doi.org/10.1177/073428290502300102

Canivez, G. L., & Watkins, M. W. (1998). Long term stability of the Wechsler Intelligence Scale for Children–Third Edition. *Psychological Assessment*, 10(3), 285–291. https://doi.org/10.1037/1040-3590.10.3.285

Canivez, G. L., & Watkins, M. W. (1999). Long term stability of the Wechsler Intelligence Scale for Children–Third Edition among demographic subgroups: Gender, race, and age. *Journal of Psychoeducational Assessment*, 17(4), 300–313. https://doi.org/10.1177/073428299901700401

Canivez, G. L., & Watkins, M. W. (2001). Long term stability of the Wechsler Intelligence Scale for Children–Third Edition among students with disabilities. *School Psychology Review*, 30(3), 361–376. https://doi.org/10.1080/02796015.2001.12086125

Canivez, G. L., & Watkins, M. W. (2016). Review of the Wechsler Intelligence Scale for Children–Fifth Edition: Critique, commentary, and independent analyses. In A. S. Kaufman, S. E. Raiford, & D. L. Coalson (Authors), *Intelligent testing with the WISC–V* (pp. 683–702). Wiley.

Canivez, G. L., Watkins, M. W., & Dombrowski, S. C. (2016). Factor structure of the Wechsler Intelligence Scale for Children–Fifth Edition: Exploratory factor analyses with the 16 primary and secondary subtests. *Psychological Assessment*, 28(8), 975–986. https://doi.org/10.1037/pas0000238

Canivez, G. L., Watkins, M. W., & Dombrowski, S. C. (2017). Structural validity of the Wechsler Intelligence Scale for Children—Fifth Edition: Confirmatory factor analyses with the 16 primary and secondary subtests. *Psychological Assessment*, 29(4), 458–472. https://doi.org/10.1037/pas0000358

Canivez, G. L., Watkins, M. W., James, T., James, K., & Good, R. (2014). Incremental validity of WISC–IV^UK factor index scores with a referred Irish sample: Predicting performance on the WIAT–II^UK. *British Journal of Educational Psychology*, *84*(4), 667–684. https://doi.org/10.1111/bjep.12056

Canivez, G. L., & Youngstrom, E. A. (2019). Challenges to the Cattell-Horn-Carroll Theory: Empirical, clinical, and policy implications. *Applied Measurement in Education*, *32*(3), 232–248. https://doi.org/10.1080/08957347.2019.1619562

Carroll, J. B. (1995). On methodology in the study of cognitive abilities. *Multivariate Behavioral Research*, *30*(3), 429–452. https://doi.org/10.1207/s15327906mbr3003_6

Chen, F. F., West, S. G., & Sousa, K. H. (2006). A comparison of bifactor and second-order models of quality of life. *Multivariate Behavioral Research*, *41*(2), 189–225. http://doi.org/10.1207/s15327906mbr4102_5

Chen, F. F., & Zhang, Z. (2018). Bifactor models in psychometric test development. In P. Irwing, T. Booth, & D. J. Hughes (Eds.), *Wiley handbook of psychometric testing* (pp. 325–345). Wiley. https://doi.org/10.1002/9781118489772.ch12

Chen, H., Zhang, O., Raiford, S. E., Zhu, J., & Weiss, L. G. (2015). Factor invariance between genders on the Wechsler Intelligence Scale for Children–Fifth Edition. *Personality and Individual Differences*, *86*, 1–5. https://doi.org/10.1016/j.paid.2015.05.020

Cohen, J. (1988). *Statistical power analysis for the behavioral sciences* (2nd ed.). Lawrence Erlbaum Associates.

Courville, T., Coalson, D. L., Kaufman, A. S., & Raiford, S. E. (2016). Does WISC–V scatter matter? In A. S. Kaufman, S. E. Raiford, & D. L. Coalson (Eds.), *Intelligent testing with the WISC–V* (pp. 209–225). Wiley.

Cronbach, L. J., & Shavelson, R. J. (2004). My current thoughts on coefficient alpha and successor procedures. *Educational and Psychological Measurement*, *64*(3), 391–418. https://doi.org/10.1177/0013164404266386

Cronbach, L. J., & Snow, R. E. (1977). *Aptitudes and instructional methods: A handbook for research on interactions*. Irvington.

Dale, B. A., Finch, W. H., & Shellabarger, K. A. R. (2023). Performance of children with ASD on the WISC–V ancillary index scales. *Psychology in the Schools*, *60*(2), 431–440. https://doi.org/10.1002/pits.22688

Dale, B. A., Finch, W. H., Shellabarger, K. A. R., & Davis, A. (2021). Wechsler Intelligence Scale for Children–Fifth Edition profiles of children with autism spectrum disorder using a classification and regression trees analysis. *Journal of Psychoeducational Assessment*, *39*(7), 783–799. https://doi.org/10.1177/07342829211025924

Dale, B. A., Finch, W. H., Shellabarger, K. A. R., & Davis, A. (2022). Comparison of verbal performance of children with autism spectrum disorder on the WISC–V. *Journal of Psychoeducational Assessment*, *40*(7), 811–824. https://doi.org/10.1177/07342829221106

Dombrowski, S. C. (2013). Investigating the structure of the WJ–III Cognitive at school age. *School Psychology Quarterly*, *28*(2), 154–169. https://doi.org/10.1037/spq0000010

Dombrowski, S. C., Beaujean, A. A., McGill, R. J., Benson, N. F., & Schneider, W. J. (2019). Using Exploratory Bifactor Analysis to understand the latent structure of multidimensional psychological measures: An example featuring the WISC–V. *Structural Equation Modeling*, *26*(6), 847–860. https://doi.org/10.1080/10705511.2019.1622421

Dombrowski, S. C., Canivez, G. L., & Watkins, M. W. (2018). Factor structure of the 10 WISC–V primary subtests across four standardization age groups. *Contemporary School Psychology*, *22*, 90–104. https://doi.org/10.1007/s40688-017-0125-2

Dombrowski, S. C., Canivez, G. L., Watkins, M. W., & Beaujean, A. (2015). Exploratory bifactor analysis of the Wechsler Intelligence Scale for Children–Fifth Edition with the 16 primary and secondary subtests. *Intelligence*, *53*, 194–201. https://doi.org/10.1016/j.intell.2015.10.009

Dombrowski, S. C., McGill, R. J., & Canivez, G. L. (2017). Exploratory and hierarchical factor analysis of the WJ IV Cognitive at school age. *Psychological Assessment*, *29*(4), 394–407. https://doi.org/10.1037/pas0000350

Dombrowski, S. C., McGill, R. J., & Canivez, G. L. (2018). An alternative conceptualization of the theoretical structure of the WJ IV Cognitive at school age: A confirmatory factor analytic investigation. *Archives of Scientific Psychology*, *6*(1), 1–13. https://doi.org/10.1037/arc0000039

Dombrowski, S. C., McGill, R. J., Watkins, M. W., Canivez, G. L., Jacobson, L., & Pritchard, A. (2022). Will the *real* theoretical structure of the WISC–V please stand up? An exploratory factor analytic replication study. *Contemporary School Psychology*, *26*, 492–503. https://doi.org/10.1007/s40688-021-00365-6

Dombrowski, S. C., & Watkins, M. W. (2013). Exploratory and higher order factor analysis of the WJ–III full test battery: A school aged analysis. *Psychological Assessment*, *25*(2), 442–455. https://doi.org/10.1037/a0031335

Dombrowski, S. C., Watkins, M. W., McGill, R. J., Canivez, G. L., Holingue, C., Pritchard, A., & Jacobson, L. (2021). Measurement invariance of the WISC–V 10 subtest primary battery: Can index scores be compared across age, sex, and diagnostic groups? *Journal of Psychoeducational Assessment*, *39*(1) 89–99. https://doi.org/10.1177/0734282920954583

Elliott, J. G., & Resing, C. M. (2015). Can intelligence testing inform educational intervention for children with reading disability? *Journal of Intelligence*, *3*(4), 137–157. https://doi.org/10.3390/jintelligence3040137

Farmer, R. L., & Kim, S. Y. (2020). Difference score reliabilities within the RIAS-2 and WISC–V. *Psychology in the Schools*, *57*(8), 1273–1288. https://doi.org/10.1002/pits.22369

Farmer, R. L., McGill, R. J., Dombrowski, S. C., & Canivez, G. L. (2021). Why questionable assessment practices remain popular in school psychology: Instructional materials as pedagogic vehicles. *Canadian Journal of School Psychology*, *36*(2), 98–114. https://doi.org/10.1177/0829573520978111

Ferrando, P. J., & Lorenzo-Seva, U. (2019). On the added value of multiple factor score estimates in essentially unidimensional models. *Educational and Psychological Measurement*, *79*(2), 249–271. https://doi.org/10.1177/0013164418773851

Flanagan, D. P., & Alfonso, V. C. (2017). *Essentials of WISC-V assessment*. Wiley.

Fletcher-Janzen, E. (2014). Foreword. In D. Wechsler, *Wechsler Intelligence Scale for Children–Fifth edition technical and interpretive manual* (pp. xii–xv). Pearson.

Floyd, R. G., & Kranzler, J. H. (2019). Remediating student learning problems: Aptitude-by-treatment interaction versus skill-by-treatment interaction. In M. K. Burns (Ed.), *Introduction to school psychology: Controversies and current practice*. Oxford University Press.

Freberg, M. E., Vandiver, B. J., Watkins, M. W., & Canivez, G. L. (2008). Significant factor score variability and the validity of the WISC-III Full Scale IQ in predicting later academic achievement. *Applied Neuropsychology*, *15*(2), 131–139. https://doi.org/10.1080/09084280802084010

Freeman, A. J., & Chen, Y.-L. (2019). Interpreting pediatric intelligence tests: A framework from evidence-based medicine. In G. Goldstein, D. N. Allen, & J. DeLuca (Eds.), *Handbook of psychological assessment* (4th ed., pp. 65–101). Academic Press.

Furr, R. M. (2011). *Scale construction and psychometrics for social and personality psychology*. Sage Publications.

Furr, R. M. (2022). *Psychometrics: An introduction* (4th ed.). Sage Publications.

Gignac, R. E., & Watkins, M. W. (2013). Bifactor modeling and the estimation of model-based reliability in the WAIS–IV. *Multivariate Behavioral Research*, *48*(5), 639–662. https://doi.org/10.1080/00273171.2013.804398

Glutting, J. J., Watkins, M. W., Konold, T. R., & McDermott, P. A. (2006). Distinctions without a difference: The utility of observed versus latent factors from the WISC–IV in estimating reading and math achievement on the WIAI-II. *Journal of Special Education*, *40*(2), 103–114. https://doi.org/10.1177/00224669060400020101

Glutting, J. J., Youngstrom, E. A., Ward, T., Ward, S., & Hale, R. L. (1997). Incremental efficacy of WISC-III factor scores in predicting achievement: What do they tell us? *Psychological Assessment*, *9*(3), 295–301. https://doi.org/10.1037/1040-3590.9.3.295

Goh, D. S., Teslow, C. J., & Fuller, G. B. (1981). The practice of psychological assessment among school psychologists. *Professional Psychology*, *12*(6), 696–706. https://doi.org/10.1037/0735-7028.12.6.696

Golino, H., Christensen, A. P, & Garrido. L. E. (2022). Exploratory graph analysis in context. *Psicologia: Teoria e Prática*, *24*(3), 1–10. https://doi.org/10.5935/1980-6906/eptpic15531.en

Golino, H. F., & Epskamp, S. (2017). Exploratory graph analysis: A new approach for estimating the number of dimensions in psychological research. *PLoS ONE*, *12*(6), 1–26. https://doi.org/10.1371/journal.pone.0174035

Gorsuch, R. L. (1983). *Factor analysis* (2nd ed.). Lawrence Erlbaum Associates.

Graves, S. L., Smith, L. V., & Nichols, K. D. (2021). Is the WISC–V a fair test for Black children: Factor structure in an urban public school sample. *Contemporary School Psychology, 25*, 157–169 https://doi .org/10.1007/s40688-020-00306-9

Groth-Marnat, G., & Wright, A. J. (2016). *Handbook of psychological assessment.* (6th ed.). Wiley.

Gu, H., Wen, Z., & Fan, X. (2017). Examining and controlling for wording effect in a self-report measure: A Monte Carlo simulation study. *Structural Equation Modeling: A Multidisciplinary Journal, 24*(4), 545–555. https://doi.org/10.1080/10705511.2017.1286228

Gustafsson, J.-E., & Åberg-Bengtsson, L. (2010). Unidimensionality and interpretability of psychological instruments. In S. E. Embretson (Ed.), *Measuring psychological constructs: Advances in model-based approaches* (pp. 97–121). American Psychological Association.

Hair, J. F., Anderson, R. E., Tatham, R. L., & Black, W. C. (1998). *Multivariate data analysis* (5th ed.). Prentice Hall.

Hale, J. B., Fiorello, C. A., Kavanagh, J. A., Hoeppner, J.-A. B., & Gaither, R. A. (2001). WISC-III predictors of academic achievement for children with learning disabilities: Are global and factor scores comparable? *School Psychology Quarterly, 16*(1), 31–55. http://dx.doi.org/10.1521/scpq.16.1.31.19158

Hanna, G. S., Bradley, F. O., & Holen, M. C. (1981). Estimating major sources of measurement error in individual intelligence scales: Taking our heads out of the sand. *Journal of School Psychology, 19*(4), 370–376. https://doi.org/10.1016/0022-4405(81)90031-5

Haynes, S. N., & Lench, H. C. (2003). Incremental validity of new clinical assessment measures. *Psychological Assessment, 15*(4), 456–466. https://doi.org/10.1037/1040-3590.15.4.456

Hunsley, J. (2003). Introduction to the special section on incremental validity and utility in clinical assessment. *Psychological Assessment, 15*(4), 443–445. https://doi.org/10.1037/1040-3590.15.4.443

Hunsley, J., & Mash, E. J. (2007). Evidence based assessment. *Annual Review of Clinical Psychology, 3*, 29–51. https://doi.org/10.1146/annurev.clinpsy.3.022806.091419

Hunsley, J., & Meyer, G. J. (2003). The incremental validity of psychological testing and assessment: Conceptual, methodological, and statistical issues. *Psychological Assessment, 15*(4), 446–455. https:// doi.org/10.1037/1040-3590.15.4.446

Hutton, J. B., Dubes, R., & Muir, S. (1992). Assessment practices of school psychologists: Ten years later. *School Psychology Review, 21*(2), 271–284. https://doi.org/10.1080/02796015.1992.12085614

Isvoranu, A.-M., Epskamp, S., Waldorp, L., & Borsboom, D. (2022). *Network psychometrics with R: A guide for behavioral and social scientists.* Taylor & Francis. https://doi.org/10.4324/9781003111238

Jennrich, R. I., & Bentler, P. M. (2011). Exploratory bi-factor analysis. *Psychometrika, 76*, 537–549. https:// doi.org/10.1007/s11336-011-9218-4

Jensen, A. R. (1998). *The g factor: The science of mental ability.* Praeger.

Kamphaus, R. W., Winsor, A. P., Rowe, E. W., & Kim, S. (2012). A history of intelligence test interpretation. In D. P. Flanagan & P. L. Harrison (Eds.), *Contemporary intellectual assessment: Theories, tests, and issues* (3rd ed., pp. 56–70). Guilford.

Kaufman, A. S. (1979). *Intelligent testing with the WISC–R.* Wiley.

Kaufman, A. S. (1994). *Intelligent testing with the WISC–III.* Wiley.

Kaufman, A. S., & Kaufman, N. L. (2004). *Kaufman Assessment Battery for Children-Second Edition.* NCS Pearson.

Kaufman, A. S., & Kaufman, N. L. (2014). *Kaufman Test of Educational Achievement* (3rd ed.). NCS Pearson.

Kaufman, A. S., Raiford, S. E., & Coalson, D. L. (2016). *Intelligent testing with the WISC–V.* Wiley. https://doi .org/10.1002/9781394259397

Keith, T. Z., Fine, J. G., Taub, G., Reynolds, M. R., & Kranzler, J. H. (2006). Higher order, multi-sample, confirmatory factor analysis of the Wechsler Intelligence Scale for Children–Fourth Edition: What does it measure? *School Psychology Review, 35*(1), 108–127.

Kessel, J. B., & Zimmerman, M. (1993). Reporting errors in studies of the diagnostic performance of self-administered questionnaires: Extent of the problem, recommendations for standardized presentation of results, and implications for the peer review process. *Psychological Assessment, 5*(4), 395–399. https:// doi.org/10.1037/1040-3590.5.4.395

Kline, P. (1994). *An easy guide to factor analysis.* London: Routledge.

Kline, R. B. (2011). *Principles and practice of structural equation modeling* (3rd ed.). Guilford Press.

Kline, R. B. (2016). *Principles and practice of structural equation modeling* (4th ed.). Guilford Press.

Kline, R. B. (2023). *Principles and practice of structural equation modeling* (5th ed.). Guilford Press.

Kranzler, J. H., Benson, N., & Floyd R. G. (2015). Using estimated factor scores from a bifactor analysis to examine the unique effects of latent variables measured by the WAIS–IV on academic achievement. *Psychological Assessment*, 27(4), 1402–1416. https://doi.org/10.1037/pas0000119

Kranzler, J. H., & Floyd, R. G. (2020). *Assessing intelligence in children and adolescents: A practical guide for evidence-based assessment* (2nd ed.). Rowman & Littlefield.

Kranzler, J. H., Maki, K. E., Benson, N. F., Eckert, T. L., Floyd, R. G., & Fefer, S. A. (2020). How do school psychologists interpret intelligence tests for the identification of specific learning disabilities? *Contemporary School Psychology*, 24, 445–456. https://doi.org/10.1007/s40688-020-00274-0

Lauritzen, S. L. (2006). *Graphical models*. Oxford University Press. https://doi.org/10.1093/oso/9780198522195.001.0001

Little, S. G. (1992). The WISC–III: Everything old is new again. *School Psychology Quarterly*, 7(2), 136–142. https://doi.org/10.1037/h0088249

Little, T. D., Lindenberger, U., & Nesselroade, J. R. (1999). On selecting indicators for multivariate measurement and modeling with latent variables: When "good" indicators are bad and "bad" indicators are good. *Psychological Methods*, 4(2), 192–211. https://doi.org/10.1037/1082-989X.4.2.192

Little, T. D., Slegers, D. W., & Card, N. A. (2006). A non-arbitrary method of identifying and scaling latent variables in SEM and MACS models. *Structural Equation Modeling: A Multidisciplinary Journal*, 13(1), 59–72. doi:10.1207/s15328007sem1301_3

Livingston, R. B., Jennings, E., Reynolds, C. R., & Gray, R. M. (2003). Multivariate analyses of the profile stability of intelligence tests: High for IQs, low to very low for subtest analyses. *Archives of Clinical Neuropsychology*, 18(5), 487–507. https://doi.org/10.1016/s0887-6177(02)00147-6

Lockwood, A. B., Benson, N. F., Farmer, R. L , & Klatka, K. (2022). Test use and assessment practices of school psychology training programs: Findings from a 2020 survey of US faculty. *Psychology in the Schools*, 59(4), 698–725. https://doi.org/10.1002/pits.22639

Lockwood, A. B., & Farmer, R. L. (2020). The cognitive assessment course: Two decades later. *Psychology in the Schools*, 57(2), 265–283. https://doi.org/10.1002/pits.22298

Lubinski, D., & Dawis, R. V. (1992). Aptitudes, skills, and proficiencies. In M. D. Dunnette & L. M. Hough (Eds.), *Handbook of industrial and organizational psychology* (2nd ed., vol. 3, pp. 1–59). Consulting Psychology Press.

MacAllister, W. S., Maiman, M., Vasserman, M., Fay-Mcclymont, T., Brooks, B. L., & Sherman, E. M. S. (2019). The WISC–V in children and adolescents with epilepsy. *Child Neuropsychology*, 25(7), 992–1002. https://doi.org/10.1080/09297049.2019.1571181

McDermott, P. A. (1988). Agreement among diagnosticians or observers: Its importance and determination. *Professional School Psychology*, 3(4), 225–240. https://doi.org/10.1037/h0090563

McDermott, P. A., Fantuzzo, J. W., Glutting, J. J., Watkins, M. W., & Baggaley, A. R. (1992). Illusions of meaning in the ipsative assessment of children's ability. *The Journal of Special Education*, 25(4), 504–526. https://doi.org/10.1177/002246699202500407

McDermott, P. A., Watkins, M. W., & Rhoad, A. M. (2014). Whose IQ is it? Assessor bias variance in high-stakes psychological assessment. *Psychological Assessment*, 26(1), 207–214. https://doi.org/10.1037/a0034832

McFall, R. M. (1991). Manifesto for a science of clinical psychology. *The Clinical Psychologist*, 44, 75–88.

McFall, R. M. (1996). Making psychology incorruptible. *Applied and Preventive Psychology*, 5(1), 9–15. https://doi.org/10.1016/S0962-1849(96)80021-7

McFall, R. M. (2000). Elaborate reflections on a simple manifesto. *Applied and Preventive Psychology*, 9(1), 5–21. https://doi.org/10.1016/S0962-1849(05)80035-6

McGill, R. J., & Dombrowski, S. C. (2019). Critically reflecting on the origins, evolution, and impact of the Cattell-Horn-Carroll (CHC) model. *Applied Measurement in Education*, 32(3), 216–231. https://doi.org/10.1080/08957347.2019.1619561

McGill, R. J., Dombrowski, S. C., & Canivez, G. L. (2018). Cognitive profile analysis in school psychology: History, issues, and continued concerns. *Journal of School Psychology*, 71, 108–121. https://doi.org/10.1016/j.jsp.2018.10.007

McGrew, K. S. (2005). The Cattell–Horn–Carroll theory of cognitive abilities: Past, present, and future. In D. P. Flanagan, & P. L. Harrison (Eds.), *Contemporary intellectual assessment: Theories, tests, and issues* (2nd ed., pp. 136–181). Guilford Press.

McGrew, K. S., LaForte, E. M., & Shrank, F. A. (2014). *Technical manual: Woodcock–Johnson IV*. Riverside Publishing.

McGrew, K. S., Schneider, W. J., Decker, S. L., & Bulut, O. (2023). A psychometric network analysis of CHC intelligence measures: Implications for research, theory, and interpretation of broad CHC scores "beyond g." *Journal of Intelligence*, *11*(1), 19. https://doi.org/10.3390/jintelligence11010019

McGrew, K. S., & Wendling, B. J. (2010). Cattell-Horn-Carroll cognitive-ability achievement relations: What we have learned from the past 20 years of research. *Psychology in the Schools*, *47*(7), 651–675. https://doi.org/10.1002/pits.20497

McGrew, K. S., & Woodcock, R. W. (2001). *Technical manual: Woodcock-Johnson III*. Riverside Publishing.

Meehl, P. E., & Rosen, A. (1955). Antecedent probability and the efficiency of psychometric signs, patterns, or cutting scores. *Psychological Bulletin*, *52*(3), 194–216. https://doi.org/10.1037/h0048070

Miller, J. L., Saklofske, D. H., Weiss, L. G., Drozdick, L., Llorente, A. M., Holdnack, J. A., & Prifitera, A. (2016). Issues related to the WISC–V assessment of cognitive functioning in clinical and special groups. In L. G. Weiss, D. H. Saklofske, J. A. Holdnack, & A. Prifitera (Eds.), *WISC–V assessment and interpretation: Scientist-practitioner perspectives* (pp. 287–343). Academic Press.

Miller, L. T., Bumpus, E. C., & Graves, S. L. (2021). The state of cognitive assessment training in school psychology: An analysis of syllabi. *Contemporary School Psychology*, *25*, 149–156. https://doi.org/10.1007/s40688-020-00305-w

Muthén, B. O., & Muthén, L. K. (2014). *Mplus user's guide* (7th ed.). Los Angeles: Muthén & Muthén.

Naglieri, J. A., & Bornstein, B. T. (2003). Intelligence and achievement: Just how correlated are they? *Journal of Psychoeducational Assessment*, *21*(3), 244–260. https://doi.org/10.1177/073428290302100302

National Association of School Psychologists. (2020). *The professional standards of the National Association of School Psychologists*. National Association of School Psychologists.

Oh, H.-J., Glutting, J. J., Watkins, M. W., Youngstrom, E. A., & McDermott, P. A. (2004). Correct interpretation of latent versus observed abilities: Implications from structural equation modeling applied to the WISC–III and WIAT linking sample. *Journal of Special Education*, *38*(3), 159–173. https://doi.org/10.1177/00224669040380030301

Owen, A. M., Hampshire, A., Grahn, J. A., Stenton, R., Dajani, S., Burns, A. S., Howard, R. J., & Ballard, C. G. (2010). Putting brain training to the test. *Nature, 465*(7299), 775–779. https://doi.org/10.1038/nature09042

Parkin, J. R., & Beaujean, A. A. (2012). The effects of Wechsler Intelligence Scale for Children–Fourth Edition cognitive abilities on math achievement. *Journal of School Psychology*, *50*, 113–128. https://doi.org/10.1016/j.jsp.2011.08.003

Pearson. (2009). *Wechsler Individual Achievement Test* (3rd ed.). Author.

Pfeiffer, S. I., Reddy, L. A., Kletzel, J. E., Schmelzer, E. R., & Boyer, L. M. (2000). The practitioner's view of IQ testing and profile analysis. *School Psychology Quarterly*, *15*(4), 376–385. https://doi.org/10.1037/h0088795

Rapaport, D., Gill, M. M., & Schafer, R. (1945–46). *Diagnostic psychological testing*. Year Book.

Revelle, W., & Condon, D. M. (2019). Reliability from α to ω: A tutorial. *Psychological Assessment*, *31*(12), 1395–1411. https://doi.org/10.1037/pas0000754

Reise, S. P. (2012). The rediscovery of bifactor measurement models. *Multivariate Behavioral Research*, *47*(5), 667–696. https://doi.org/10.1080/00273171.2012.715555

Reise, S. P., Bonifay, W. E., & Haviland, M. G. (2013). Scoring and modeling psychological measures in the presence of multidimensionality. *Journal of Personality Assessment*, *95*(2), 129–140. https://doi.org/10.1080/00223891.2012.725437

Reynolds, C. R., & Kamphaus, R. W. (2004). *Behavior Assessment System for Children* (2nd ed.). Pearson.

Reynolds, C. R., & Milam, D. A. (2012). Challenging intellectual testing results. In D. Faust (Ed.), *Coping with psychiatric and psychological testimony* (6th ed., pp. 311–334). Oxford University Press.

Reynolds, M. R., & Keith, T. Z. (2017). Multi-group and hierarchical confirmatory factor analysis of the Wechsler Intelligence Scale for Children–Fifth Edition: What does it measure? *Intelligence*, *62*, 31–47. https://doi.org/10.1016/j.intell.2017.02.005

Rodriguez, A., Reise, S. P., & Haviland, M. G. (2016a). Applying bifactor statistical indices in the evaluation of psychological measures. *Journal of Personality Assessment*, *98*(3), 223–237. https://doi.org/10.1080/00223891.2015.1089249

Rodriguez, A., Reise, S. P., & Haviland, M. G. (2016b). Evaluating bifactor models: Calculating and interpreting statistical indices. *Psychological Methods*, *21*(2), 137–150. https://doi.org/10.1037/met0000045

Ryan, J. J., Glass, L. A., & Bartels, J. M. (2010). Stability of the WISC–IV in a sample of elementary and middle school children. *Applied Neuropsychology*, *17*(1), 68–72. https://doi.org/10.1080/09084280903297933.

Ryan, J. J., Kreiner, D. S., & Burton, D. E. (2002). Does high scatter affect the predictive validity of WAIS-III IQs? *Applied Neuropsychology*, *9*(3), 173–178. https://doi.org/10.1207/S15324826AN0903_5

Sattler, J. M., Dumont, R., & Coalson, D. L. (2024). Interpreting the WISC-V. In J. M. Sattler, *Assessment of children: Cognitive foundations and applications* (chapter 9, pp. 339–376). Jerome M. Sattler.

Schuerger, J. M., & Witt, A. C. (1989). The temporal stability of individually tested intelligence. *Journal of Clinical Psychology*, *45*(2), 294–302. https://doi.org/10.1002/1097-4679(198903)45:2<294::aid-jclp2270450218>3.0.co;2-n

Scheiber, C. (2016). Is the Cattell–Horn–Carroll-based factor structure of the Wechsler Intelligence Scale for Children–Fifth Edition (WISC–V) construct invariant for a representative sample of African–American, Hispanic, and Caucasian male and female students ages 6 to 16 years? *Journal of Pediatric Neuropsychology*, *2*, 79–88. https://doi.org/10.1007/s40817-016-0019-7

Schmid, J., & Leiman, J. M. (1957). The development of hierarchical factor solutions. *Psychometrika*, *22*, 53–61. https://doi.org/10.1007/bf02289209

Schneider, W. J. (2008). Playing statistical Ouija board with commonality analysis: Good questions, wrong assumptions. *Applied Neuropsychology*, *15*(1), 44–53. https://doi.org/10.1080/09084280801917566

Schrank, F. A., McGrew, K. S., & Mather, N. (2014). *Woodcock–Johnson IV Tests of Cognitive Abilities*. Riverside Publishing.

Sellbom, M., & Tellegen, A. (2019). Factor analysis in psychological assessment research: Common pitfalls and recommendations. *Psychological Assessment*, *31*(12), 1428–1441. https://doi.org/10.1037/pas0000623

Smith, L. V., & Graves, S. L. (2021). An exploration of gender invariance of the WISC–V among Black children in an urban school district. *Contemporary School Psychology*, *25*, 170–182. https://doi.org/10.1007/s40688-020-00307-8

Sotelo-Dynega, M., & Dixon, S. G. (2014). Cognitive assessment practices: A survey of school psychologists. *Psychology in the Schools*, *51*(10), 1031–1045. https://doi.org/10.1002/pits.21802

Sparrow, S. S., Cicchetti, D. V., & Balla, D. A. (2005). *Vineland Adaptive Behavior Scales* (2nd ed.). Pearson.

Stephenson, K. G., Beck, J. S., South, M., Norris, M., & Butter, E. (2021). Validity of the WISC–V in youth with autism spectrum disorder: Factor structure and measurement invariance. *Journal of Clinical Child & Adolescent Psychology*, *50*(5), 669–681. https://doi.org/10.1080/15374416.2020.1846543

Stinnett, T. A., Havey, J. M., & Oehler-Stinnett, J. (1994). Current test usage by practicing school psychologists: A national survey. *Journal of Psychoeducational Assessment*, *12*(4), 331–350. https://doi.org/10.1177/073428299401200403

Strickland, T., Watkins, M. W., & Caterino, L. C. (2015). Structure of the Woodcock-Johnson III Cognitive Tests in a referral sample of elementary school students. *Psychological Assessment*, *27*(2), 689–697. https://doi.org/10.1037/pas0000052

Stuebing, K. K., Barth, A. E., Trahan, L. H., Reddy, R. R., Miciak, J., & Fletcher, J. M. (2015). Are child cognitive characteristics strong predictors of responses to intervention? A meta-analysis. *Review of Educational Research*, *85*(3), 395–429. https://doi.org/10.3102/0034654314555996

Styck, K. M., Beaujean, A. A., & Watkins, M. W. (2019). Profile reliability of cognitive ability subscores in a referred sample. *Archives of Scientific Psychology*, *7*(1), 119–128. https://doi.org/10.1037/arc0000064

Styck, K. M., & Walsh, S. M. (2016). Evaluating the prevalence and impact of examiner errors on the Wechsler Scales of Intelligence: A meta-analysis. *Psychological Assessment*, *28*(1), 3–17. https://doi.org/10.1037/pas0000157

Swets, J. A. (1996). *Signal Detection Theory and ROC Analysis in psychological diagnostics: Collected Papers*. Lawrence Erlbaum Associates.

Thompson, B. (2004). *Exploratory and confirmatory factor analysis: Understanding concepts and applications.* American Psychological Association.

Thurstone, L. L. (1947). *Multiple factor analysis.* University of Chicago Press.

Treat, T. A., & Viken, R. J. (2012). Measuring test performance with signal detection theory techniques. In H. Cooper, P. M. Camic, D. L., Long, A. T. Panter, D. Rindskopf, & K. J. Sher (Eds.), *Handbook of research methods in psychology: Volume 1, Foundations, planning, measures, and psychometrics* (pp. 723–744). American Psychological Association.

Wasserman, J. D. (2019). Deconstructing CHC. *Applied Measurement in Education*, *32*(3), 249–268. https://doi.org/10.1080/08957347.2019.1619563

Wasserman, J. D., & Bracken, B. A. (2013). Fundamental psychometric considerations in assessment. In J. R. Graham & J. A. Naglieri (Eds.), *Handbook of psychology: Assessment psychology* (vol. 10, pp. 50–81). Wiley.

Watkins, C. E., Jr., Campbell, V. L., Nieberding, R., & Hallmark, R. (1995). Contemporary practice of psychological assessment by clinical psychologists. *Professional Psychology: Research and Practice*, *26*(1), 54–60. https://doi.org/10.1037/0735-7028.26.1.54

Watkins, M. W. (2000). Cognitive profile analysis: A shared professional myth. *School Psychology Quarterly*, *15*(4), 465–479. https://doi.org/10.1037/h0088802

Watkins, M. W. (2013). Omega [Computer software]. Ed & Psych Associates. https://edpsychassociates.com/Watkins3.html

Watkins, M. W. (2018). Exploratory factor analysis: A guide to best practice. *Journal of Black Psychology*, *44*(3), 219–246. http://doi.org/10.1177/0095798418771807

Watkins, M. W. (2021). *A step-by-step guide to exploratory factor analysis with SPSS*. Routledge. https://doi.org/10.4324/9781003149347

Watkins, M. W., & Canivez, G. L. (2004). Temporal stability of WISC–III subtest composite strengths and weaknesses. *Psychological Assessment*, *16*(2), 133–138. https://doi.org/10.1037/1040-3590.16.2.133

Watkins, M. W., & Canivez, G. L. (2022). Assessing the psychometric utility of IQ scores: A tutorial using the Wechsler Intelligence Scale for Children–Fifth Edition. *School Psychology Review*, *51*(5), 619–633. https://doi.org/10.1080/2372966X.2020.1816804

Watkins, M. W., Canivez, G. L., Dombrowski, S. C., McGill, R. J., Pritchard, A. E., Holingue, C. B., & Jacobson, L. A. (2022). Long-term stability of Wechsler Intelligence Scale for Children–Fifth Edition scores in a clinical sample. *Applied Neuropsychology: Child*, *11*(3), 422–428. https://doi.org/10.1080/21622965.2021.1875827

Watkins, M. W., Dombrowski, S. C., McGill, R. J., Canivez, G. L., Pritchard, A. E., & Jacobson, L. A. (2023). Bootstrap Exploratory Graph Analysis of the WISC–V with a clinical sample. *Journal of Intelligence*, *11*(137), 1–12. https://doi.org/10.3390/jintelligence11070137

Watkins, M. W., & Glutting, J. J. (2000). Incremental validity of WISC–III profile elevation, scatter, and shape information for predicting reading and math achievement. *Psychological Assessment*, *12*(4), 402–408. https://doi.org/10.1037/1040-3590.12.4.402

Watkins, M. W., Glutting, J. J., & Lei, P. -W. (2007). Validity of the full-scale IQ when there is significant variability among WISC-III and WISC-IV factor scores. *Applied Neuropsychology*, *14*(1), 13–20. https://doi.org/10.1080/09084280701280353

Watkins, M. W., & Smith, L. G. (2013). Long-term stability of the Wechsler Intelligence Scale for Children–Fourth Edition. *Psychological Assessment*, *25*(2), 477–483. https://doi.org/10.1037/a0031653

Wechsler, D. (1991). *Wechsler Intelligence Scale for Children—Third edition: Manual*. American Psychological Corporation.

Wechsler, D. (2003). *Wechsler Intelligence Scale for Children–Fourth Edition*. American Psychological Corporation.

Wechsler, D. (2008). *Wechsler Adult Intelligence Scale–Fourth Edition*. NCS Pearson.

Wechsler, D. (2012). *Wechsler Preschool and Primary Scale of Intelligence–Fourth Edition*. NCS Pearson.

Wechsler, D. (2014a). *Wechsler Intelligence Scale for Children–Fifth Edition*. Pearson.

Wechsler, D. (2014b). *Wechsler Intelligence Scale for Children–Fifth Edition technical and interpretive manual*. Pearson.

Wechsler, D. (2014c). *Wechsler Intelligence Scale for Children–Fifth Edition administration and scoring manual.* Pearson.

Wechsler, D. (2014d). *Wechsler Intelligence Scale for Children–Fifth Edition administration and scoring manual supplement.* London: Pearson.

Weiner, I. B. (1989). On competence and ethicality in psychodiagnostic assessment. *Journal of Personality Assessment, 53*(4), 827–831. https://doi.org/10.1207/s15327752jpa5304_18

Weiss, L. G., Keith, T. Z., Zhu, J., & Chen, H. (2013). WISC–IV and clinical validation of the four- and five-factor interpretative approaches. *Journal of Psychoeducational Assessment, 31*(2), 114–131. https://doi.org/10.1177/0734282913478032

Widaman, K. F. (2012). Exploratory factor analysis and confirmatory factor analysis. In H. Cooper (Ed.), *APA handbook of research methods in psychology: Data analysis and research publication* (vol. 3, pp. 361–389). American Psychological Association.

Woodcock, R. W., McGrew, K. S., & Mather, N. (2001). *Woodcock–Johnson III Tests of Cognitive Abilities.* Riverside Publishing.

Yung, Y.-F., Thissen, D., & McLeod, L. (1999). On the relationship between the higher-order factor model and the hierarchical factor model. *Psychometrika, 64*, 113–128. https://doi.org/10.1007/BF02294531

Zaboski, B. A., II, Kranzler, J. H., & Gage, N. A. (2018). Meta-analysis of the relationship between academic achievement and broad abilities of the Cattell-Horn-Carroll theory. *Journal of School Psychology, 71*, 42–56. https://doi.org/10.1016/j.jsp.2018.10.001

Chapter 3

Kaufman Assessment Battery for Children–Second Edition/ Normative Update (KABC–II/ KABC–II NU)

Clinical Interpretation From an Evidence-Based Perspective[1]

Ryan J. McGill and Stefan C. Dombrowski

The *Kaufman Assessment Battery for Children–Second Edition* (KABC–II; Kaufman & Kaufman, 2004a) measures the intellectual and processing abilities of children and adolescents ages 3:0 to 18:11 years and contains a total of 18 subtests.[2] The KABC–II was a major revision of the original K–ABC (Kaufman & Kaufman, 1983), which was a revolutionary addition to the suite of cognitive testing instrumentation available to practitioners at that time. The original K–ABC was designed principally from the standpoint of neuropsychological theory; in particular, Luria's depiction of cognitive processing (Luria, 1966). This model posits that the brain is composed of three functional units. The first unit is made up largely of older areas of the brain (i.e., the brain stem and reticular activation system) and is concerned with promoting alertness to external stimuli; the second unit is formed by the parietal, occipital, and temporal lobes and is responsible for storing and processing sensory information from the environment; and the third unit is formed by the frontal lobe, which is responsible for executive functions and planning behavior in response to external stimuli. For the K–ABC, Luria's model was repurposed in the form of a sequential-versus-simultaneous processing framework, and when combined with additional measures of academic functioning, it represented a significant departure from the traditional ability testing zeitgeist that had existed to that time (Keith, 1985). Additionally, the K–ABC was unique in that it established a new benchmark for the reporting of psychometric information in its technical manual and that several graduate students, who would go on to be considered luminaries in assessment psychology in their own right, participated in its development under Alan Kaufman's supervision at the University of Georgia (Kaufman, 2009).

Despite these achievements, questions were soon raised about the veracity of the instrument's theoretical structure. Most notably, Keith (1985) conducted exploratory and confirmatory analysis on the normative sample and produced results suggesting that the cognitive processing elements posited by the test publisher (i.e., sequential-simultaneous processing) was largely supported across age groups. However, it was suggested that those dimensions could potentially be alternatively conceptualized as Verbal Memory and Nonverbal Reasoning. More concerning, the measures of achievement did not cohere with the identified cognitive dimensions, thus calling into question the nature of the general factor thought to be measured by the omnibus full-scale score. Bracken (1985) further criticized the lack of alignment between the test and its presumed theoretical underpinnings, noting, "Faults may be found with the instrument, but commendably, most of the necessary data is made available in the K–ABC manual that enables one to find the faults" (p. 35).

The K–ABC was eventually revised with the publication of the KABC–II in 2004. The KABC–II underwent a major structural revision with eight subtests being eliminated and 10 indicators created and added to the new battery. The KABC–II is unique in that it is the only commercial ability measure to utilize a dual-interpretive structure: the Cattell-Horn-Carroll theory of human cognitive abilities (CHC; Schneider & McGrew, 2018) and Luria's theory of cognitive processing (Luria, 1966). This affords flexibility to the examiner in which approach to utilize for any examinee, though the technical manual (Kaufman & Kaufman, 2004b) stresses that an interpretive preference must be selected a priori so as to prevent an examiner from morphing from one battery to another to suit their preferences. Before elaborating on the differences between the CHC and Luria models, it is important to point out that the original K–ABC also employed a hybrid interpretive approach in which elements of Luria's theory were embedded within a more global Fluid-Crystallized, or Gf-Gc theory (Horn & Cattell, 1966) context, a linkage that does not appear to have been recognized in the literature concerning the instrument.

The CHC model features 10 core subtests that contribute to the measurement of five group-specific factors (Crystallized Ability [Gc], Fluid Reasoning [Gf], Visual Processing [Gv], Long-Term Storage and Retrieval [Glr], and Short-Term Memory [Gsm])[3] and an omnibus, full-scale score termed the *Fluid-Crystallized Composite* (FCI). By contrast, the Luria model employs a more parsimonious eight-core subtest configuration contributing to the measurement of four group-specific factors (Planning, Sequential Processing, Simultaneous Processing, and Learning) and a full-scale score termed the *Mental Processing Index* (MPI). An optional Delayed Recall index can also be calculated but is not structurally derived; therefore, its veracity is questionable. The hypothesized measurement models for these dueling interpretive structures at school age are depicted in Figures 3.1 and 3.2 respectively. As noted by McGill (2017), the only salient difference between the models is that the Luria model omits measures of acquired knowledge, also known as *Crystallized Ability* within the CHC nomenclature. It should also be noted that Fluid Reasoning was not able to be consistently located at preschool age; thus a more parsimonious scoring structure is employed across that age range. Additional supplementary subtests whose configurations differ according to the age of the child can also be administered but they do not contribute to the measurement of core global scales or indices.

Although users are advised in the manual (Kaufman & Kaufman, 2004b) to prioritize interpreting the test from the CHC perspective, the Luria model may be preferred in specific clinical situations including, but not limited to, examining children from culturally and linguistically diverse backgrounds or assessing individuals with known language impairments (Drozdick et al., 2018). It should also be noted that the KABC–II also provides users with an alternative nonverbal index of overall ability that is based on different configurations of core and supplementary measures that omit verbal responding from the examinee. As a result of this versatility, it is not surprising that surveys of the contemporary assessment practice of school psychologists consistently reveal that the KABC–II is one of the most often used instruments for the clinical assessment of intelligence and particularly among examiners assessing the cognitive abilities of culturally and linguistically diverse minorities (Benson et al., 2019; Sotelo-Dynega & Dixon, 2014).

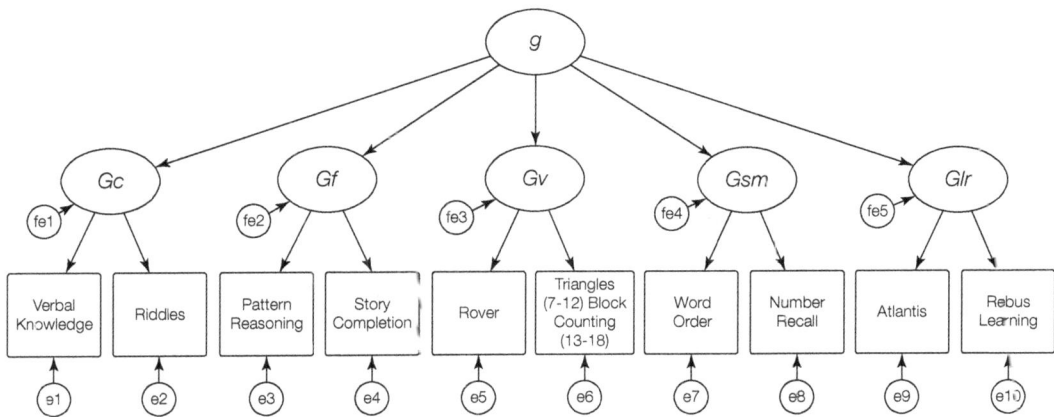

Figure 3.1. **Hypothesized KABC–II CHC Measurement Model.**

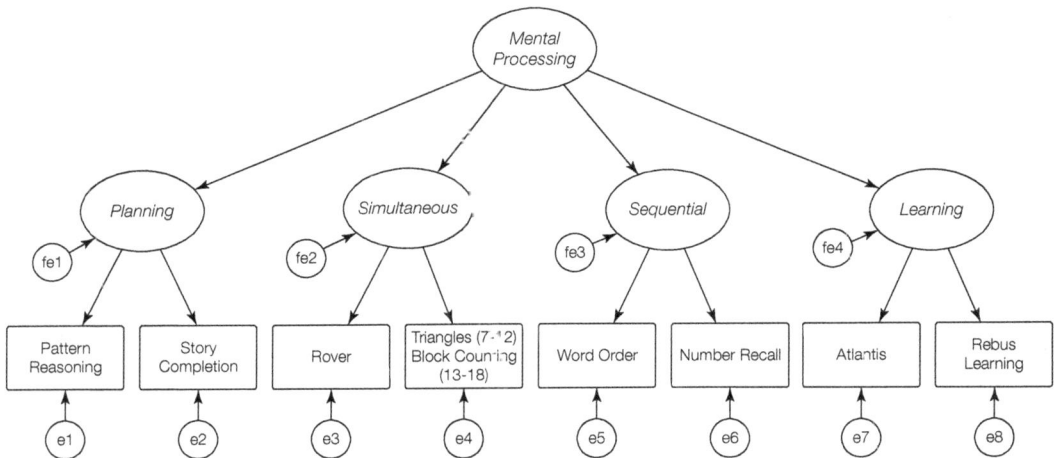

Figure 3.2. **Hypothesized KABC–II Luria Measurement Model.**

In the remainder of this chapter, the suggested KABC–II interpretive procedures will be outlined followed by a review of the validation evidence presented in the manual to support the use of those procedures. We will then conclude with a review of selected independent examinations of various aspects of construct validity for the instrument and its scores. For the sake of parsimony, particular attention will be paid to structural fidelity, predictive validity, and diagnostic utility (Keith & Kranzler, 1999). Our focus is limited to the version of the instrument normed for use in the United States.[4]

Suggested Interpretive Procedures for the Instrument

Like other commercial ability measures, a detailed step-by-step series of the interpretive procedures is outlined in the *KABC–II Technical Manual* (Kaufman & Kaufman, 2004b). As previously noted, users should have already selected the preferred interpretive model prior to administering the instrument to the examinee. Once those scores are obtained, users are encouraged to start by interpreting the omnibus full-scale score[5] before evaluating for index level strengths and weaknesses. However, "whether the FCI or MPI is used, before evaluating the global score you need to determine whether the global score is interpretable" (Kaufman et al., 2005). In doing so, examiners are invited to employ an intuitive rule of thumb that if the difference between the highest and lowest index score meets or exceeds 23 points then the global score should not be interpreted. Interpretability is also a consideration at the index level, and Kaufman and colleagues (2005) suggest that interpretation of an index score should only occur if "the child performed consistently on the Core subtests that compose that scale" (p. 89). There is no empirical evidence to support the use of these scatter heuristics in the technical manual or in the accompanying KABC–II interpretive literature.

While not required, examiners also have the option of conducting one or more of the plethora of planned clinical comparisons between index- and subtest-level scores that have been outlined in KABC–II interpretive resources (e.g., Drozdick et al., 2018; Kaufman et al., 2005), for example, combining different subtests to create pseudo-composites that compare a child's presumed performance across meaningful versus abstract stimuli. Finally, the KABC–II asks users to note relevant test session behaviors in the form of a qualitative checklist at the end of each subtest. These behaviors can be tabulated in the test record form, and users are invited to consider the potential clinical relevance of these tabulations.

Issues with the Development and Validation of the KABC–II

The *KABC–II Technical Manual* (Kaufman & Kaufman, 2004b) reports a wealth of reliability and validity evidence and provides a detailed description of the theoretical development of the instrument. Despite these strengths, several psychometric shortcomings and questions were noted in a recent factor analytic study by McGill (2020). Kaufman and Kaufman reported, "The KABC–II development process relied mostly on the technique of confirmatory factor analysis, used in an *exploratory* fashion[6] to evaluate subtests and decide how they should be grouped into scales" (p. 103). This is a curious disclosure given the fact that the theoretical rationale for the KABC–II appears to be well-established in the psychometric literature that was available at that time.

A major focus of the factor analyses conducted on the normative sample was to determine if Fluid Reasoning indicators could be separated from the Visual Processing measures. Whereas it is reported that EFA was used to identify possible alternative interpretive structures for the test, the EFA results "did not make a significant contribution to the overall analysis program" (p. 104) and were not reported in the technical manual. Instead, the test publisher relied exclusively on confirmatory factor analysis (CFA) employed across two stages. In stage one, CFA was used to examine various higher-order models ranging from a one-factor model to increasingly more complex correlated (oblique) factor models at each age range. The authors report checking at each step to verify that improvement in fit was statistically significant and that there was no evidence of local model misspecification (i.e., problematic loadings, out of bounds parameter estimates). Fit statistics for the models that were explored at this stage are not reported but the results for each age are described narratively. Nevertheless, it appears that there were issues getting all of the hypothesized CHC dimensions to emerge consistently across the age range if at all.

At age three, a one-factor (*g*) model was preferred even though it is reported that a Short-Term Memory dimension could be located that appeared to meet the stated inclusionary criteria in the manual. At age four, analyses supported the presence of Short-Term Memory and Long-Term Storage and Retrieval, but a Fluid Reasoning factor could not be located. As a result, hypothesized Fluid Reasoning measures were alternatively assigned to the Visual Processing factor. Although it can certainly be argued that it is likely that Fluid Reasoning could not be located at that age because of developmental differences in preschool children, it is not clear how the measures supposedly contributing to the measurement of Visual Processing morph to another dimension later in the developmental span. Interestingly, it was noted that the Crystallized Ability and Visual Processing factors were highly correlated, suggesting that they were likely isomorphic. Even so, a decision was made to retain both dimensions even though it is acknowledged that they were not statistically significant. Instead, the decision to retain them was based on consideration of their qualitative content. Nevertheless, the dimensional complexity of these measures raises the question of the discriminant validity of several of the hypothesized CHC dimensions.

At ages 5–7, the Fluid Reasoning and Visual Processing factors were not distinguishable, and all those measures were again assigned to the same factor. It was later reported that the latent factor correlations between Visual Processing and Fluid Reasoning exceeded .90 across the school age span (7–18), raising concern about whether Fluid Reasoning is a viable dimension for the instrument (Byrne, 2005). However, the authors noted that these abilities could be differentiated statistically, and the decision was made to retain Fluid Reasoning to better cohere with the presumed CHC interpretive model for the test. Additionally, different subtest configurations for the Visual Processing scale were explored to determine the most optimal combination of core tests that would help distinguish the abilities from each other. Results indicated that Triangles and Rover provided the most optimal differentiation in the younger portion of the school age range (7–12), and Block Counting and Rover was the best combination at ages 13 to 18.

In the next stage of the validation plan, a series of constrained CFAs were used to investigate hierarchical versions of the models retained at stage one containing a second-order general factor of intelligence. Those models are depicted visually in Figures 8.1 and 8.2 of the technical manual (pp. 106–107). It was believed that these models best aligned with the CHC interpretive structure for the test. Inspection of global fit statistics indicate that all the models fit the data well. However, at ages 7–18, all the models contain path loadings between *g* and Fluid Reasoning that suggest empirical redundancy.

As noted by Brown (2015), whereas standardized path loadings equal to 1.0 are technically permissible in CFA, they present an interpretive confound as they indicate that the lower-order dimension does not account for any meaningful variance that distinguishes it from general intelligence. When these problematic loadings are encountered, researchers are frequently advised in the methodological literature to delete the redundant variable(s) in accordance with the scientific law of parsimony. Values that exceed 1.0 are considered out-of-bounds estimates (i.e., Heywood cases) and indicate potential model misspecification. In sum, the factor analytic evidence reported in the technical manual (Kaufman & Kaufman, 2004b) raises concern about the veracity of the preferred CHC interpretive model. Additionally concerning are the correlations with similar CHC measures from the *Woodcock-Johnson IV Tests of Cognitive Abilities* (WJ IV) reported in that test's technical manual (McGrew et al., 2014). For example, the reported correlations between like Fluid Reasoning and Visual Processing scores was .46 and .37, respectively, which is relatively low. By contrast the correlation between like measures of Crystallized Ability was .82. If these indices from the KABC–II are *actually* measuring these abilities, then one would expect the alignment between what are purported to be estimates of the same latent dimension to be much stronger. Finally, the structural integrity of the Luria interpretive model was not explored in any meaningful way, which is problematic because it cannot be automatically assumed that a previously established higher-order solution will be maintained when the configuration of observed variables is altered.

Variance Partitioning and the Interpretive Relevance of Lower-Order Dimensions

Even if consensus is achieved with respect to ascertaining the correct number of first-order dimensions measured by the KABC–II, additional information is necessary for determining the interpretive relevance of the scores aligned with those dimensions. It is important to keep in mind that in a hierarchical measurement model, first-order factors are abstractions of measured variables; thus, extrapolating a higher-order general factor represents an abstraction from an abstraction (Beaujean, 2015). More importantly, a non-trivial portion (often the vast majority) of reliable variance in all subtests and first-order dimensions is attributable to general intelligence. Failing to consider this source of influence when interpreting first-order factors will lead to overestimating the effects of those attributes in explaining performance on the KABC–II (Carretta & Ree, 2001). As a result, Carroll (1995) insisted that it is necessary to decompose variance into components that can be sourced more appropriately to higher- and lower-order dimensions. To accomplish this task, he recommended second-order factor analysis of first-order factor correlations followed by a Schmid-Leiman (SL; Schmid & Leiman, 1957) procedure. When applied to factor analytic solutions, the SL procedure allows for the calculation of first-order subtest loadings that are independent of the influence of a higher-order general factor. According to Carroll (1995),

> I argue, as many have done, that from the standpoint of analysis and ready interpretation, results should be shown on the basis of orthogonal factors, rather than oblique, correlated factors. I insist, however, that the orthogonal factors should be those produced by the Schmid-Leiman (1957) orthogonalization procedure, and thus include second-stratum and possibly third-stratum factors. (p. 437)

More recently, methodologists have encouraged the use of bifactor modeling in CFA (Reise, 2012) to examine these effects. Although it has been argued that the SL procedure represents an approximate bifactor model in EFA, it is merely a reparameterization of the hierarchical model (Canivez, 2016). However, over the last decade, the two techniques have been used interchangeably in the psychometric literature to partition variance in cognitive tests (Dombrowski, McGill, Canivez et al., 2021).

Whether produced from a pure bifactor CFA model or SL procedure in EFA, orthogonalized factor loading estimates can also be used to produce various indices that evaluate dimensionality and aid in the evaluation of whether a particular score is clinically relevant. Although each of these estimates is important in its own right, Omega coefficients are often the focal point in determining whether a factor can be interpreted with confidence in clinical practice. Omega-hierarchical (ω_H) and omega-hierarchical subscale (ω_{HS}) estimate the unit-weighted portion of reliable variance in latent factors. The ω_H coefficient is the estimate for the general intelligence factor with variability of group factors removed, while the ω_{HS} coefficient is the estimate of a group factor with all other group and the general factor removed (Rodriguez et al., 2016). Although subjective, it has been suggested that omega coefficients should at a minimum exceed .50, but .75 is preferred (Reise et al., 2013). Additionally, it is important to consider explained common variance (ECV) and construct replicability (*H*). If the KABC–II factor or subtest scores fail to capture meaningful portions of true score variance they will likely be of limited clinical utility. Unfortunately this information is not reported in the technical manual.

Post-Publication KABC–II Psychometric Evidence

Given these limitations, the KABC–II has been the subject of numerous psychometric investigations. In particular, investigations that have sought to clarify its interpretive structure. Next we conduct a selected review of major KABC–II construct validity studies. Consistent with recent calls for advancing the cause of evidence-based practice to the practice of clinical assessment, we approach this evidence from an *evidence-based assessment* perspective (EBA; Dombrowski, 2020; Youngstrom, 2013).

Evidence-Based Assessment (EBA)

Practitioners and scholars have access to a plethora of information that may be useful for informing clinical assessment practice. Unfortunately, it is difficult to determine the specific sources of information that are most useful for informing the clinical bottom line. According to Hunsley and Mash (2007), "a truly evidence-based approach to assessment, therefore, would involve an evaluation of the accuracy and usefulness of this complex decision-making task" (p. 30) when considering the high degree of error endemic within this process. The EBA framework goes beyond traditional psychometric reliability and validity evidence and focuses more on the outcomes and utility of assessment processes. According to Youngstrom (2013), traditional approaches to scale validation remain important, but what really matters are the 3 *P*s of clinical assessment: prediction (assessment data's relationship to important external criteria); prescription (treatment utility of assessment); and process (identification of mediating variables for treatment). Essentially the goal of EBA is to subject our assessment method and clinical decision-making models to risky empirical tests (Meehl, 1978) to separate the proverbial wheat from the chaff in assessment science.

CHC Model Structural Validity

Most independent examinations of the latent structure of the KABC–II have focused on validating the preferred CHC interpretive model. For example, Reynolds and colleagues (2007) examined the measurement invariance of the KABC–II theoretical structure to ascertain the degree to which it was consistent across age and to verify the instrument's consistency with CHC theory. Results indicated the measurement model was invariant across age after imposing constraints to account for the fact that several subtests cannot be administered at certain ages. However, the model that was explicated is not described. A series of rival CHC models were then sequentially explored. Consistent with the CFA results reported in the technical manual, the baseline model contained evidence of a Heywood case and is not tenable for the data. The final validation model departed from publisher theory, most notably reporting a cross-loading for Pattern Reasoning on Visual Processing and Fluid Reasoning.

Later the KABC–II was included as one of five test batteries in a cross-battery (XBA; Flanagan et al., 2013) reference variable investigation of the CHC taxonomy featuring 423 participants ages 6 to 16 years (Reynolds et al., 2013). Results generally supported a three-stratum factor relatively consistent with a priori theory. However, despite attempts to apply post hoc constraints to the model, Fluid Reasoning could not be statistically distinguished from g though it was featured in the model figures that were reported and not eschewed as would be consistent with best practice (Brown, 2015). Additionally, the Pattern Reasoning cross-loading identified by Reynolds et al. (2007) was not modeled. The results were replicated in a more recent XBA study by Caemmerer et al. (2020).

Inexplicably, it took nearly 14 years before the KABC–II was subjected to EFA. In their analyses, McGill and Dombrowski (2018) examined both the core and supplementary subtest structures at school age (7–18) using the data obtained from normative participants. Core battery results supported a four-factor solution unifying the Fluid Reasoning and Visual Processing indicators and featuring a more accurately named Perceptual Reasoning factor. Inclusion of the supplementary measures provided support for a five-factor model that departed significantly from publisher theory. Whereas the Perceptual Reasoning factor was again supported, the addition of a fifth factor resulted in the theoretically preferred Long-Term Storage and Retrieval factor splitting into two different Glr dimensions. More concerning, ω_H coefficients for the general factor all exceeded .80 indicating that dimension possesses enough reliable variance to be interpreted. However, none of the ω_{HS} estimates for the group-specific factors exceeded .47 indicating that those dimensions cannot be interpreted with confidence.

In 2018 the KABC–II was subjected to a normative update, and the resulting *KABC–Second Edition Normative Update* (KABC–II NU; Kaufman & Kaufman, 2018) has supplanted the previous version of the instrument. Although the test was re-normed on 500 participants, the test publisher declined to report updated structural validity results. Instead, it was argued in the manual supplement (Kaufman et al., 2018) that because the content and organization of the test was not altered, users could consult the *KABC–II Technical Manual* (Kaufman & Kaufman, 2004b) to infer the structure of the NU. After noting several anomalies in the manual supplement, McGill (2020) subjected the reported summary data to CFA and multidimensional scaling (see Figure 3.3). Results of the core battery analyses across school age clearly preferred a hierarchical four-factor model, featuring a clean Perceptual Reasoning dimension. Models containing previously speculated cross-loadings were deemed inferior as were various bifactor model implementations, calling into question the viability of that model for the KABC–II NU (Bonifay et al., 2017).

However, Reynolds and Keith (2017) argue that the Perceptual Reasoning consolidation is reductionistic and fails to consider that the identification problems are specific to Fluid Reasoning and not Visual Processing. Therefore an alternative model where Visual Processing is retained, and the Fluid Reasoning indicators load directly onto g should also be considered. Unfortunately, McGill (2020) did not examine this model. Consequently, we used the same summary data employed in that study and conducted a constrained CFA analysis using Mplus version 8.0 (Muthén & Muthén, 2017) with maximum likelihood estimation. The resulting fit statistics across school-age indicated that the model is statistically inferior to the final model retained by McGill (2020) and thus is not tenable for the data.

Luria Model Structural Validity

Structural investigations of the Luria model have been less pervasive in the literature. McGill and Spurgin (2017) conducted the first Luria EFA using the KABC–II normative data, and results did not support the publisher-preferred four-factor model. At ages 7–12, the Planning dimension was

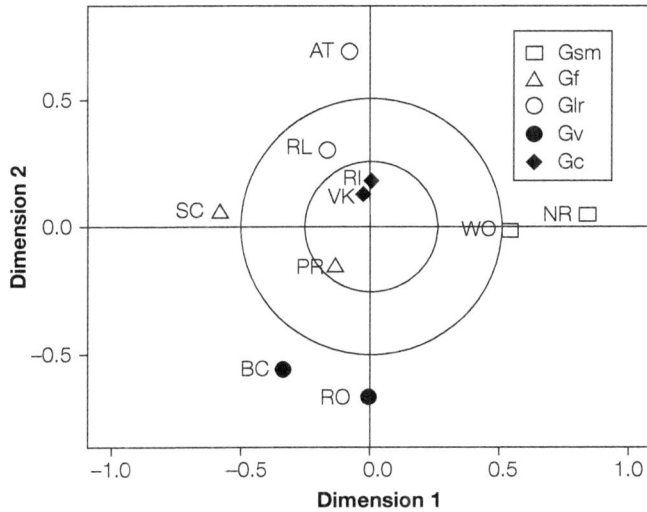

Figure 3.3. **Radex Model of the KABC–II CHC Core Battery for Ages 13–18.**

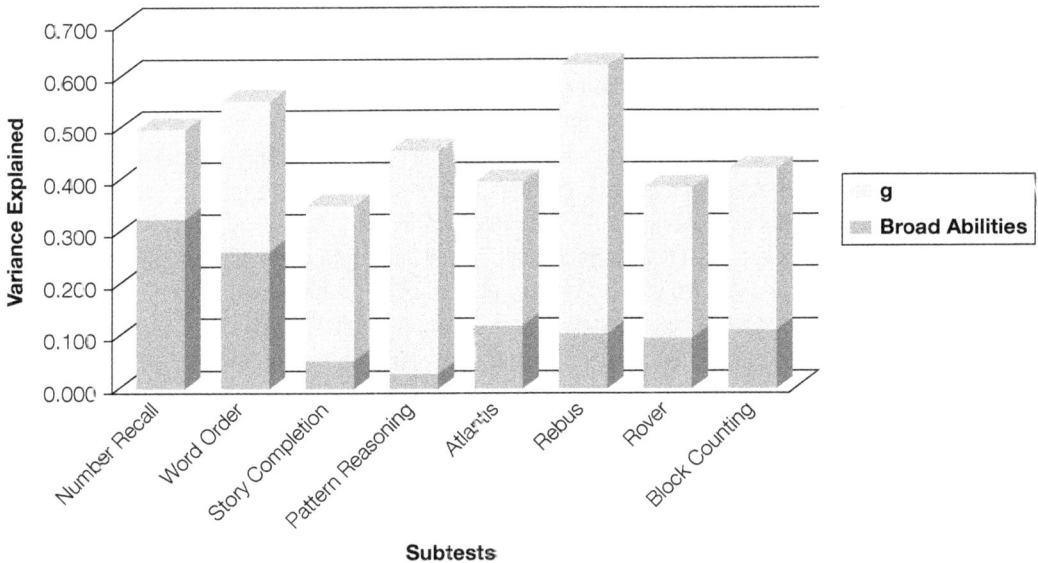

Figure 3.4. **Sources of Variance in KABC–II Luria Model Subtests.**

not mathematically viable, and Pattern Reasoning migrated to the Simultaneous Processing factor. At ages 13–18, Planning was again an impermissible factor and Pattern Reasoning did not load saliently on any factor. Figure 3.4 illustrates well the multidimensional nature of KABC–II measures and the dominance of g. Whereas general intelligence explained about 68% of subtest variance, no group-specific factors accounted for more than 16%. Although indices of clinical relevance were not calculated, these variance estimates leave no doubt that the unique contributions of the first-order dimensions are likely to be minimal.

McGill (2017) followed with an CFA investigation of the same data to further elucidate the Luria model structure. Results were more supportive of the four-factor publisher-preferred hierarchical four-factor model. However, the best-fitting model required the specification of a Pattern Reasoning cross-loading on both Planning and Simultaneous Processing consistent with Reynolds et al. (2007). Based upon the procedures articulated in Reynolds and Keith (2013), an approximation of the SL procedure was also conducted, and the results did not support primary interpretation at the Stratum II index-level of the test.

Incremental Predictive Validity

Once the structure of an instrument has been firmly established,[7] it is then important to examine relationships with external measures—in particular, predictive validity (Wiggins, 1973). Given the dimensional nature of KABC–II scores, it is especially important to assess the incremental validity of lower-order CHC/Luria scores in predicting achievement beyond the FCI/MPI. In fact, the joint test standards (American Educational Research Association, American Psychological Association, & National Council on Measurement in Education, 2014) specifically require that when a test provides users with multiple scores, the distinctiveness of the scores be firmly established. As per Hunsley and Meyer (2003), McGill (2015) investigated the incremental validity of the CHC index scores in predicting achievement outcomes beyond that accounted for by the omnibus FCI score. Across the school-age range, $R^2/\triangle R^2$ effect size indices indicated that the FCI accounted for 30% to 65% of the variance across achievement outcomes. By contrast, the CHC scores jointly failed to account for more than 8% of the variance among those measures. McGill and Spurgin (2016) replicated these results in their examination of the Luria interpretive model.

It is important to note that studies employing structural equation modeling as opposed to hierarchical multiple regression have furnished results largely supporting the findings reported above but have provided stronger evidence for the incremental validity of broad ability factors (e.g., Benson et al., 2016, Villeneuve et al., 2019). Nevertheless, in the latter study, Fluid Reasoning was again found to be redundant with the hierarchical general factor. Not surprisingly, a meta-analysis by Zaboski and colleagues (2018) examining the effects of CHC broad abilities on achievement (after controlling for g) found that the importance of the broad abilities was more circumspect and rarely did any individual dimension account for more than 10% of the variance in achievement.

Scatter and Diagnostic Utility

Perhaps the most controversial aspect of KABC–II assessment has been the procedures that have been advocated in various interpretive resources (e.g., Kaufman et al., 2005) for conducting scatter assessment amongst the hypothesized group-specific, factor-based indices. As previously noted, these guidelines do not appear to have been derived from any legitimate form of empirical evidence. Given this evidentiary lacuna, McGill (2016) conducted the first empirical examination of the potential iatrogenic impact of scatter on the structural or predictive validity of KABC–II scores. Put simply, no evidence was found to indicate that scatter had any meaningful effect on these outcomes. Subsequent investigations of the potential diagnostic value of scatter assessment on the KABC–II, which is a key principle undergirding emerging methods of specific learning disability (SLD) identification (i.e., PSW), have found that increasing levels of scatter predict SLD (McGill, 2018) and that intra-individual cognitive weaknesses discriminate between individuals with and without achievement weaknesses at no better than chance levels (McGill et al., 2018). In sum, practitioners engaged in these assessment practices would likely be better served flipping coins as an alternative (Meehl & Rosen, 1955).

Implications of Dimensional Complexity for Clinical Interpretation

To be fair, the test authors have fully acknowledged the dimensional complexity of KABC–II measures insofar as that clinicians need to consider that many of the subtests do not provide a pure measurement of the hypothesized CHC/Luria abilities that they are purported to assess (Drozdick et al., 2018). In this way, cognitive complexity is integrated purposefully into core aspects of KABC–II design to enhance the purported clinical utility of the instrument. From a technical standpoint, such default statements are less problematic as researchers are able to disentangle effects using many of the previously described procedures for variance partitioning to determine the actual portions of variance explained by various psychological dimensions and the degree that measurement error may confound confidant clinical interpretation of that score. However, from a conceptual vantage point, practitioners on the ground are not able to account for these effects at the level of the individual and risk committing a misattribution error when attempting to extract meaning from the scores that they obtain from an examinee (Canivez, 2013). As previously discussed, several independent KABC–II CFA studies have found that Pattern Reasoning (which is theoretically assigned to Fluid Reasoning) loads on both Visual Processing and Fluid Reasoning, a finding that is not surprising given the issues occurred in trying to separate these factors from each other during the development of the instrument, suggesting there is tremendous overlap between those dimensions as conceptualized on the KABC–II.

It is certainly possible that the Pattern Reasoning cross-loading could be a methodological artifact and not the true measurement model underlying the data. In a Monte Carlo simulation study of the plausible models that have been reported in the literature for popular commercial ability measures, Dombrowski et al. (2021) illustrated well the danger in relying on any one CFA study as prima facie evidence for determining the actual structure of a test. Some speculative models evade replication when subsequently examined again even when using the same methodological parameters. In reconciling these discrepancies, it is important to consider the degrees of freedom afforded to researchers in CFA programs (Dombrowski & McGill, 2024; Waller & Meehl, 2002). Assuming that the Pattern Reasoning cross-loading is in fact legitimate, what are the implications for clinical interpretation? Like all IQ tests, the KABC–II employs a scoring structure that assumes orthogonality among its latent dimensions. Core subtests linearly combine to form one and only one first-order index score. When departures from desired simple structure are observed (e.g., theoretically inconsistent subtest migration, cross-loading, etc.) in external research studies, it calls into question the integrity of the scoring structure of the test as these anomalies are rarely, if ever, accounted for by test publishers.

In sum, the mathematical hurdles introduced during the developmental phase of an instrument cannot be overcome by skilled detective work no matter how many times the loaded term *clinical judgment* is invoked as an intellectual safety blanket to discount negative research findings (Lilienfeld & Strother, 2020; McGill et al., 2018). Despite the intuitive appeal of such sentiments, the misguided idea that a practitioner can turn specious assessment information into clinical gold has been regarded in the EBA literature as a form of alchemist's fallacy (Lilienfeld et al., 2006). The fact that such contentions continue to undergird much assessment training in our business calls into question the idea that our field will ever engage in meaningful self-correction as a science.

Conclusion

In many respects the KABC–II/KABC–II NU is a fine instrument. Its materials and design at the time of its publication were innovative and its clinical versatility nonpareil. Nevertheless, as a result of the potential psychometric shortcomings noted in this chapter, a conflicting picture emerges as to how the instrument should be interpreted from an EBA perspective. On the one hand, there appears to be consensus that the KABC–II measures some of the hypothesized CHC dimensions that it purports to measure except for Fluid Reasoning and potentially Visual Processing. Whereas empirical evidence suggests that users can be reasonably confidant when interpreting the instrument at the global scale level (i.e., FCI, MPI, NVI), questions have been raised about the psychometric integrity of the first-order factors regardless of how they are theoretically conceptualized (i.e., CHC or Luria perspectives). This is not to say that practitioners should eschew interpretation of first-order factors as a matter of course. On the contrary, it is suggested that users engage in the interpretation of these indices with caution, considering unique contributions in measurement these indices afford beyond what is already known about the examinee from other available sources (Kranzler & Floyd, 2020). As compared to school age, limited examinations of preschool age structure support the more parsimonious interpretive model employed at that age range; however, more investigation is needed. It is unclear what, if any, clinical utility is afforded by the first-order indices with respect to treatment utility considerations.

Other matters discussed here appear to be more settled. For instance, the bulk of available research evidence does not provide support for the scatter assessment procedures that have previously been advocated for the instrument (e.g., Kaufman et al., 2005). More importantly, despite the intuitive appeal of the dual theoretical model, it remains unclear how a score can mysteriously morph from a CHC construct to a Luria dimension simply because the examiner elects to use one interpretive scheme rather than another (Braden & Ouzts, 2005). Simply put, the omission of measures of Crystallized Ability do not suddenly convert the Short-Term Memory index into a measure of Sequential Processing. Accordingly, users of the KABC–II are cautioned against committing the naming fallacy (Borsboom, 2005) when electing to use the Luria interpretive model.

Notes

1   Elements of this chapter were presented at the 2019 meeting of the National Association of School Psychologists, Atlanta, Georgia.

2   Specific subtests can only be administered at restricted age ranges and may not be administered across batteries.

3   The Visual Processing Index is produced from a different combination of subtests at different ages. Whereas Rover remains constant, Triangles is used at ages 7–12, and Block Counting is used at ages 13–18.

4   The KABC–II has been adapted and translated for use in several additional countries.

5   For examinees with limited verbal ability in English, an ancillary Nonverbal Index (NVI) is available using different combinations of subtests at different points in the age range. This index is thought to serve as an alternative estimate of general intelligence (g).

6   It is possible to use CFA programs in an exploratory manner; however, the number of closed-door analyses that appear to have been run raise concern as to whether the models that were ultimately retained for the instrument were obtained through capitalizing on chance (Byrne, 2005).

7   We would argue that there remain significant questions as to what the KABC–II/KABC–II NU measures.

References

American Educational Research Association, American Psychological Association, & National Council on Measurement on Education (2014). *Standards for educational and psychological testing*. American Educational Research Association.

Beaujean, A. A. (2015). John Carroll's views on intelligence: Bi-factor vs. higher-order models. *Journal of Intelligence*, 3(4), 121–136. https://doi.org/10.3390/jintelligence3040121

Benson, N. F., Floyd, R. G., Kranzler, J. H., Eckert, T. L., Fefer, S. A., & Morgan, G. B. (2019). Test use and assessment practices of school psychologists in the United States: Findings from the 2017 national survey. *Journal of School Psychology*, 72, 29–48. https://doi.org/10.1016/j.jsp.2018.12.004

Benson, N. F., Kranzler, J. H., & Floyd, R. G. (2016). Examining the integrity of measurement of cognitive abilities in the prediction of achievement: Comparisons and contrasts across variables from higher-order and bifactor models. *Journal of School Psychology*, 58, 1–19. https://doi.org/10.1016/j.jsp.2016.06.001

Bonifay, W., Lane, S. P., & Reise, S. P. (2017). Three concerns with applying a bifactor model as a structure of psychopathology. *Clinical Psychological Science*, 5(1), 184–186. https://doi.org/10.1177/2167702616657069

Borsboom, D. (2005). *Measuring the mind: Conceptual issues in contemporary psychometrics*. Cambridge University Press. https://doi.org/10.1017/CBO9780511490026

Bracken, B. A. (1985). A critical review of the Kaufman Assessment Battery for Children (K–ABC). *School Psychology Review*, 14(1), 21–36. https://doi.org/10.1080/02796015.1985.12085141

Braden, J. P., & Ouzts, S. M. (2005). Review of Kaufman Assessment Battery for Children, Second Edition. In R. A. Spies & B. S. Plake (Eds.), *The sixteenth mental measurements yearbook* (pp. 517–520). Buros Institute of Mental Measurements.

Brown, T. A. (2015). *Confirmatory factor analysis for applied research* (2nd ed.). Guilford Press.

Byrne, B. M. (2005). Factor analytic models: Viewing the structure of an assessment instrument from three perspectives. *Journal of Personality Assessment*, 85(1), 17–32. https://doi.org/10.1207/s15327752jpa8501_02

Caemmerer, J. M., Keith, T. Z., & Reynolds, M. R. (2020). Beyond individual intelligence test: Application of Cattell-Horn-Carroll theory. *Intelligence*, 79, 101433. https://doi.org/10.1016/j.intell.2020.101433

Canivez, G. L. (2013). Psychometric versus actuarial interpretation of intelligence and related aptitude batteries. In D. H. Saklofske, C. R. Reynolds, & V. L. Schwean (Eds.), *The Oxford handbook of child psychological assessment* (pp. 84–112). Oxford University Press.

Canivez, G. L. (2016). Bifactor modeling in construct validation of multifactored tests: Implications for understanding multidimensional constructs and test interpretation. In K. Schweizer & C. DiStefano (Eds.), *Principles and methods of test construction: Standards and recent advancements* (pp. 247–271). Hogrefe.

Carretta, T. R., & Ree, J. J. (2001). Pitfalls of ability research. *International Journal of Selection and Assessment*, 9(1), 325–335. https://doi.org/10.1111/1468-2389.00184

Carroll, J. B. (1995). On methodology in the study of cognitive abilities. *Multivariate Behavioral Research*, 30(3), 429–452. https://doi.org/10.1207/s15327906mbr3003_6

Dombrowski, S. C. (2020) A newly proposed framework and a clarion call to improve practice. In S. C. Dombrowski (Ed.), *Psychoeducational assessment and report writing* (2nd ed., pp. 9–59). Springer. https://doi.org/10.1007/978-3-030-44641-3_2

Dombrowski, S. C., & McGill, R. J. (2024). Clinical assessment in school psychology: Impervious to scientific reform? *Canadian Journal of School Psychology*, 39(4), 297–306. https://doi.org/10.1177/08295735231224052

Dombrowski, S. C., McGill, R. J., Canivez, G. L., Watkins, M. W., & Beaujean, A. A. (2021). Factor analysis and variance partitioning in intelligence test research: Clarifying misconceptions. *Journal of Psychoeducational Assessment*, 39(1), 28–38. https://doi.org/10.1177/0734282920961952

Dombrowski, S. C., McGill, R. J., & Morgan, G. B. (2021). Monte Carlo modeling of contemporary intelligence test (IQ) factor structure: Implications for IQ assessment, interpretation, and theory. *Assessment*, 28(3), 977–993. https://doi.org/10.1177/1073191119869828

Drozdick, L. W., Singer, J. K., Lichtenberger, E. O., Kaufman, J. C., Kaufman, A. S., & Kaufman, N. L. (2018). The Kaufman Assessment Battery for Children-Second Edition and KABC–II Normative Update. In D. P. Flanagan & E. M. McDonough (Eds.), *Contemporary intellectual assessment: Theories, tests, and issues* (4th ed., pp. 333–359). Guilford Press.

Flanagan, D. P., Ortiz, S. O., & Alfonso, V. C. (2013). *Essentials of cross-battery assessment.* John Wiley.

Horn, J. L., & Cattell, R. B. (1966). Refinement and test of the theory of fluid and crystallized general intelligences. *Journal of Educational Psychology, 57*(5), 253–270. https://doi.org/10.1037/h0023816

Hunsley, J., & Mash, E. J. (2007). Evidence-based assessment. *Annual Review of Clinical Psychology, 3,* 29–51. https://www.doi.org/10.1146/annurev.clinpsy.3.022806.091419

Hunsley, J., & Meyer, G. J. (2003). The incremental validity of psychological testing and assessment: Conceptual, methodological, and statistical issues. *Psychological Assessment, 15*(4), 446–455. https://doi.org/10.1037/1040-3590.15.4.446

Kaufman, A. S., & Kaufman, N. L. (1983). *Kaufman Assessment Battery for Children.* Circle American Guidance Service.

Kaufman, A. S., & Kaufman, N. L. (2004a). *Kaufman Assessment Battery for Children* (2nd ed.). American Guidance Service.

Kaufman, A. S., & Kaufman, N. L. (2004b). *Kaufman Assessment Battery for Children-Second Edition manual.* American Guidance Service.

Kaufman, A. S., & Kaufman, N. L. (2018). *Kaufman Assessment Battery for Children-Second Edition Normative Update.* NCS Pearson.

Kaufman, A. S., Kaufman, N. L., Drozdick, L. W., & Morrison, J. (2018). *Kaufman Assessment Battery for Children-Second Edition Normative Update manual supplement.* NCS Pearson.

Kaufman, A. S., Lichtenberger, E. O., Fletcher-Janzen, E., & Kaufman, N. L. (2005). *Essentials of KABC–II assessment.* John Wiley.

Kaufman, J. C. (Ed.). (2009). *Intelligent testing: Integrating psychological theory and clinical practice.* Cambridge University Press.

Keith, T. Z. (1985). Questioning the K–ABC: What does it measure? *School Psychology Review, 14*(1), 9–20, https://www.doi.org/10.1080/02796015.1985.12085140

Keith, T. Z., & Kranzler, J. H. (1999). The absence of structural fidelity precludes construct validity: Rejoinder to Naglieri on what the cognitive assessment system does and does not measure. *School Psychology Review, 28*(2), 303–321. https://doi.org/10.1080/02796015.1999.12085967

Kranzler, J. H., & Floyd, R. G. (2020). *Assessing intelligence in children and adolescents: A practical guide for evidence-based assessment* (2nd ed.). Rowman and Littlefield.

Lilienfeld, S. O., & Strother, A. N. (2020). Psychological measurement and the replication crisis: Four sacred cows. *Canadian Psychology, 61*(4), 281–288. https://doi.org/10.1037/cap0000236

Lilienfeld, S. O., Wood, J. M., & Garb, H. N. (2006). Why questionable psychological tests remain popular. *Scientific Review of Alternative Medicine, 10,* 6–15.

Luria, A. R. (1966). *Human brain and psychological processes.* Harper & Row.

McGill, R. J. (2015). Interpretation of KABC–II scores: An evaluation of the incremental validity of CHC factor scores in predicting achievement. *Psychological Assessment, 27*(4), 1417–1426. https://doi.org/10.1037/pas0000127

McGill, R. J. (2016). Invalidating the full scale IQ score in the presence of significant factor score variability: Clinical acumen or clinical illusion? *Archives of Assessment Psychology, 6*(1), 49–79.

McGill, R. J. (2017). Exploring the latent structure of the Luria model for the KABC–II at school age: Further insights from confirmatory factor analysis. *Psychology in the Schools, 54*(9), 1004–1018. https://doi.org/10.1002/pits.22037

McGill, R. J. (2018). Confronting the base rate problem: More ups and downs for cognitive scatter analysis. *Contemporary School Psychology, 22*(3), 384–393. https://doi.org/10.1007/s40688-017-168-4

McGill, R. J. (2020). An instrument in search of a theory: Structural validity of the Kaufman Assessment Battery for Children-Second Edition Normative Update at school-age. *Psychology in the Schools, 57*(2), 247–264. https://doi.org/10.1002/pits.22304

McGill, R. J., & Dombrowski, S. C. (2018). Factor structure of the CHC model for the KABC–II: Exploratory factor analyses with the 16 core and supplementary subtests. *Contemporary School Psychology*, 22(3), 279–293. https://doi.org/10.1007/s40688-017-0152-z

McGill, R. J., Dombrowski, S. C., & Canivez, G. L. (2018). Cognitive profile analysis in school psychology: History, issues, and continued concerns. *Journal of School Psychology*, 71, 108–121. https://doi.org/10.1016/j.jsp.2018.10.007

McGill, R. J., & Spurgin, A. R. (2016). Assessing the incremental value of KABC–II Luria model scores in predicting achievement: What do they tell us beyond the MPI? *Psychology in the Schools*, 53(7), 677–689. https://doi.org/10.1002/pits.21940

McGill, R. J., & Spurgin, A. R. (2017). Exploratory higher order analysis of the Luria interpretive model on the Kaufman Assessment Battery for Children-Second Edition (KABC–II) school-age battery. *Assessment*, 24(4), 540–552. https://doi.org/10.1177/1073191115614081

McGrew, K. S., LaForte, E. M., & Shrank, F. A. (2014). *Woodcock–Johnson IV: Technical Manual.* Riverside Publishing.

Meehl, P. E. (1978). Theoretical risks and tabular asterisks: Sir Karl, Sir Ronald, and the slow progress of soft psychology. *Journal of Consulting and Clinical Psychology*, 46(4), 806–834. https://doi.org/10.1037/0022-006X.46.4.806

Meehl, P. E., & Rosen, A. (1955). Antecedent probability and the efficiency of psychometric signs, patterns, or cutting scores. *Psychological Bulletin*, 52(3), 194–216. https://doi.org/10.1037/h0048070

Muthén, L. K., & Muthén, B. O. (2017). *Mplus* [Version 8.0]. Muthén & Muthén.

Reise, S. P. (2012). The rediscovery of bifactor measurement models. *Multivariate Behavioral Research*, 47(5), 667–696. https://doi.org/10.1080/00273171.2012.715555

Reise, S. P., Bonifay, W. E., & Haviland, M. G. (2013). Scoring and modeling psychological measures in the presence of multidimensionality. *Journal of Personality Assessment*, 95(2), 129–140. https://www.doi.org/10.1080/00223891.2012.725437

Reynolds, M. R., & Keith, T. Z. (2013). Measurement and statistical issues in child assessment research. In D. H. Saklofske, C. R. Reynolds, & V. L. Schwean (Eds.), *The Oxford handbook of child psychological assessment* (pp. 48–83). Oxford University Press.

Reynolds, M. R., & Keith, T. Z. (2017). Multi-group and hierarchical confirmatory factor analysis of the Wechsler Intelligence Scale for Children-Fifth edition: What does it measure? *Intelligence*, 62, 31–47. https://doi.org/10.1016/j.intell.2017.02.005

Reynolds, M. R., Keith, T. Z., Fine, J. G., Fisher, M. E., & Low, J. (2007). Confirmatory factor structure of the Kaufman Assessment Battery for Children-Second Edition: Consistency with Cattell-Horn-Carroll theory. *School Psychology Quarterly*, 22(4), 511–539. https://doi.org/10.1037/1045-3830.22.4.511

Reynolds, M. R., Keith, T. Z., Flanagan, D. P., & Alfonso, V. C. (2013). A cross-battery, reference variable, confirmatory factor analytic investigation of the CHC taxonomy. *Journal of School Psychology*, 51(4), 535–555. https://doi.org/10.1016/j.jsp.2013.02.003

Rodriguez, A., Reise, S. P., & Haviland, M. G. (2016). Applying bifactor statistical indices in the evaluation of psychological measures. *Journal of Personality Assessment*, 98(3), 223–237. https://doi.org/10.1080/00223891.2015.1089249

Schmid, J., & Leiman, J. M. (1957). The development of hierarchical factor solutions. *Psychometrika*, 22, 53–61. https://doi.org/10.1007/BF02289209

Schneider, W. J., & McGrew, K. S. (2018). The Cattell-Horn-Carroll Theory of Cognitive Abilities. In D. P. Flanagan & E. M. McDonough (Eds.), *Contemporary intellectual assessment: Theories, tests, and issues* (4th ed., pp. 73–163). Guilford Press.

Sotelo-Dynega, M., & Dixon, S. G. (2014). Cognitive assessment practices: A survey of school psychologists. *Psychology in the Schools*, 51(10), 1031–1045. https://doi.org/10.1002/pits.21802

Villeneuve, E. F., Hajovsky, D. B., Mason, B. A., & Lewno, B. M. (2019). Cognitive ability and math computation developmental relations with math problem solving: An integrated, multigroup approach. *School Psychology Quarterly*, 34(1), 96–108. https://doi.org/10.1037/spq0000267

Waller, N. G., & Meehl, P. E. (2002). Risky tests, verisimilitude, and path analysis. *Psychological Methods*, 7(3), 323–337. https://doi.org/10.1037/1082-989X.7.3.323

Wiggins, J. S. (1973). *Personality and prediction: Principles of personality assessment*. Addison-Wesley.

Youngstrom, E. A. (2013). Future directions in psychological assessment: Combining evidence-based medicine innovations with psychology's historical strengths to enhance utility. *Journal of Clinical Child & Adolescent Psychology*, *42*(1), 139–159. https://www.doi.org/10.1080/15374416.2012.736358

Zaboski, B. A., II, Kranzler, J. H., & Gage, N. A. (2018). Meta-analysis of the relationships between academic achievement and broad abilities of the Cattell-Horn-Carroll theory. *Journal of School Psychology*, *71*, 42–56. https://www.doi.org/10.1016/j.jsp.2018.10.001

Chapter 4

The Woodcock-Johnson IV Tests of Cognitive Abilities

A Paradox for Evidence-Based Assessment

Stefan C. Dombrowski, Ryan J. McGill, and Corinne J. Casey

The Woodcock-Johnson IV (WJ IV; Schrank et al., 2014a) comprises separate co-normed batteries of tests of cognitive ability (18 subtests; Schrank et al., 2014b), achievement (20 subtests; Schrank et al., 2014a), and oral language (12 subtests; Schrank et al., 2014b). The WJ IV authors report in the technical manual (McGrew et al., 2014) that the instrument's structure was guided by Carroll's (1993) Three Stratum Theory of Cognitive Ability (3S), the work of Horn and Cattell (1966), and contemporary neuroscience research on memory (e.g., McGrew et al., 2014). It has some very positive features including the linkage of its development with theory and the creation of three distinct yet symbiotic test batteries. The WJ IV Cognitive, Achievement, and Oral Language can be used independently or in any combination for selective testing. The Woodcock-Johnson Online Scoring and Reporting System (Schrank & Dailey, 2014) makes scoring easy and provides an array of composite, index scores, and other narrow ability and clinical cluster scores associated with the Cattel-Horn-Carroll Theory of Human Cognitive Abilities (CHC; Schneider & McGrew, 2018). Additionally, the WJ IV Interpretation and Instructional Interventions Program (WIIIP; Schrank & Wendling, 2015) is available and provides an online option for generating narrative interpretive text and related interventions, which the authors of this program claim are useful for linking assessment to intervention. The WJ IV, including the WJ IV Cognitive, is heavily featured in the cross-battery assessment (XBA; Flanagan et al., 2013) approach and other assessment approaches (e.g., patterns of strengths and weaknesses [PSW]) marketed to be useful for the identification of specific learning disabilities (SLDs) given its purported linkage to CHC theory. The various WJ battery of tests across the decades also have been used to make additional clinical and neuropsychological decisions (Miller et al., 2016).

Although this chapter focuses on the WJ IV Cognitive, it will be necessary to discuss the WJ IV full test battery due to the mutualism among the three independent batteries and the lack of information furnished by the test publisher regarding the independent psychometric structure of the WJ IV Cognitive. In fact, the WJ IV Cognitive was never separately evaluated for either standalone reliability or validity evidence. Instead, the evidence from the WJ IV full test battery was extrapolated from, and extended to, the WJ IV Cognitive. One other point deserves mention. The WJ IV is unique in its co-norming of three separate tests via imputation of missing data. In other words, not all participants were administered all 50 subtests. Instead, scores were imputed for participants who did not take a particular subtest. As a result of what the test publisher refers to as "planned missingness," test-retest results could not be calculated for many of the WJ IV tests. This information is commonly furnished in all tests of cognitive ability and permits an evaluation of the stability of the individual subtest and composite scores across repeated administrations.

The WJ IV Tests of Cognitive Abilities

The technical manual indicates that the WJ IV Cognitive was designed to measure a hierarchically ordered general intellectual ability factor (i.e., g) along with the lower-order CHC broad abilities of Comprehension-Knowledge (Gc), Fluid Reasoning (Gf), Short-Term Working Memory (Gwm), Cognitive Processing Speed (Gs), Auditory Processing (Ga), Long-Term Retrieval (Glr), and Visual-Processing (Gv). It is presently the only commercial ability measure to furnish composite scores for all of the seven consensus CHC broad abilities. The first ten subtests of the WJ IV Cognitive comprise the Standard Battery, and subtests 11–18 comprise the Extended Battery. There are numerous, additional scores that may be produced by the WJ IV scoring system using either selected subtests from the standard battery or a combination of standard and extended battery subtests. For instance, the first three subtests are used to produce the Brief Intellectual Ability composite score (BIA) while subtests 1–10 provide the General Intellectual Ability composite score (GIA; i.e., g; subtests 1–7) and the following three CHC index scores: Comprehension-Knowledge (Gc), Fluid Reasoning (Gf), and Short-Term Working Memory (Gwm). Additionally, a Cognitive Efficiency index and Gf-Gc composite scores may be produced from the standard 10 subtest battery. Subtests from the Extended Battery may be used to produce the additional four CHC index scores (e.g., Gs, Ga, Glr, and Gv) in addition to a Perceptual Speed (P), Quantitative Reasoning (RQ), and Number Facility (N) score. The WJ IV Cognitive subtest alignment with respective CHC theoretical factor scores and additional scores produced by the scoring system is presented in Table 4.1.

An Extrapolated Factor Structure

To comport with CHC theory, the publisher proposed a hierarchical seven-factor theoretical structure for the WJ IV Cognitive. However, that model was not directly investigated for the instrument by the test publisher or, if it was, those results were not disclosed. Instead, the test publisher extrapolated the structure from the WJ IV full test battery structure from analyses reported for its 47[1] subtests and extended the results to the WJ IV Cognitive as well as the other two remaining batteries (McGrew et al., 2014). It may be contended that this is acceptable practice; however, Cattell (1978) argued that it cannot be assumed that a previously identified latent variable will automatically be located by a smaller subset of variables. Nevertheless, this validation approach often occurs during the initial stages of theory building. However, the WJ IV Cognitive is more than a simple tool used to build theory.[2] It is used the world over to evaluate individuals for various clinical and educational

Table 4.1 Subtest Alignment by CHC Factor and Narrow Ability

Gc	Gf	Gwm
Oral Vocabulary (1) General Information (8)	Number Series (2) Concept Formation (9) Analysis-Synthesis (15)*	Verbal Attention (3) Numbers Reversed (10) Object-Number Sequencing (16)*

Gs	Ga	Glr
Letter-Pattern Matching (4) Pair Cancellation (17)	Phonological Processing (5) Nonword Repetition (12)	Story Recall (6) Visual-Auditory Learning (13)

Gv	**Quantitative Reasoning**	**Number Facility**
Visualization (7) Picture Recognition (14)	Number Series (2) Analysis-Synthesis (15)	Numbers Reversed (10) Number-Pattern Matching (11)

Perceptual Speed	**Cognitive Efficiency**	
Letter-Pattern Matching (4) Number-Pattern Matching (11)	Verbal Attention (3)* Letter-Pattern Matching (4) Numbers Reversed (10) Number-Pattern Matching (11)	

Note. Adapted from McGrew et al. (2014, p. 9).

*Additional tests are required to create an extended version of the cluster listed.

conditions some of which portend to change the trajectory of that individual's life by providing access to remedial services. Consequently, the instrument's factor structure would benefit from direct empirical validation.

For this reason, it is potentially inappropriate for the test publisher to claim that an instrument measures an attribute and then go on to produce various scores purporting to measure that attribute without furnishing empirical evidence in the form of factor analysis featuring the actual measured variables used to produce those scores. In the case of the WJ IV Cognitive, the test publisher claims that the WJ IV Cognitive measures attributes resembling a general factor, seven CHC factors, and additional cluster scores that are reported by the scoring system (see Table 4.1). The publisher's claims are based on the supposition that the structural alignment of an 18-subtest instrument nested within a 50-subtest battery will not be impacted when indicators are removed or added. However, the relationship among the variables (i.e., subtests) may change in the presence of a different subset of variables and so it is important to place greater emphasis on empirical evaluation (using factor analysis) than on theoretical conceptualization (Youngstrom & Van Meter, 2016; and see Dombrowski, McGill, Benson et al., 2019). Consequently, a case can be made that some of the CHC index scores and the myriad additional scores produced by the WJ IV scoring system for the WJ IV Cognitive lack appropriate evidentiary support.

Why is an understanding of the internal structure (i.e., structural or factorial validity) of an instrument critically important? The factor structure of an instrument provides the foundational validity evidence upon which all other validity evidence rests (e.g., incremental and diagnostic utility). Importantly, it also provides a statistical rationale for how an instrument should be scored and interpreted. Without full explication of, and factor analytical justification for, structural validity, a clinician or researcher will be less able to understand and properly interpret the scores provided by that instrument. Thus it is more than just the theoretical musing of an academic researcher; it provides the statistical rationale for an instrument's scores.

Put simply, even if it were acceptable to extrapolate the structure of an applied cognitive ability instrument from a broader psychoeducational assessment battery, concerns have been raised about the factor structure of the Woodcock-Johnson IV full test battery and its potential alignment with CHC theory. It is noted that some of these same concerns were raised previously during independent exploratory factor analyses (EFA) of the WJ III full test battery (Dombrowski & Watkins, 2013).

Lack of Regard for Prior WJ III Post-Publication Research?

One of the concerns surrounding the WJ IV relates to a lack of regard of prior independent factor analytic literature. When developing the WJ IV, the test authors did not appear to consider prior, relevant exploratory structural validity research on the Woodcock-Johnson III (WJ III; e.g., Dombrowski & Watkins, 2013). Several studies from the literature published around the same time as the WJ IV specifically analyzed the WJ III full battery (e.g., Dombrowski & Watkins, 2013) and WJ III Cognitive in isolation (e.g., Dombrowski & Watkins, 2013; Dombrowski, 2013, 2014a, 2014b, 2015).[3] For instance, Dombrowski and Watkins (2013) evaluated the structure of the WJ III full test battery and found that it did not fully align with hypothesized CHC theory. Specifically, the full test battery was determined to measure six factors at ages 9 to 13 (Gc, Grw, Gs, Combined Gf/Gq, Ga and Glr) and five factors at ages 14 to 19 (Gc, Ga, Gs, Gq and Glr), in contrast to the nine factors promoted by the publisher. An evaluation of the WJ III Cognitive by Dombrowski (2013) suggested that the instrument measured four factors (e.g., perceptual reasoning [combined Gf/Gv], verbal ability [Gc], processing speed [Gs], and memory [Glr]) at ages 9–13 and not the theoretically posited seven factors. Regardless of whether four or seven factors were uncovered, variance apportionment and subtest misalignment with theory raised concerns about whether and how to interpret the WJ III Cognitive group-specific factors.

In totality, the theoretically proposed structure was not adequately supported by independent exploratory factor analyses of the WJ III whether the full test battery or the cognitive was investigated. In addition to concerns about exploratory structure, the series of articles published by Dombrowski and colleagues raised concerns about the CFA analyses conducted by the test publisher and its linkage with CHC theory (Dombrowski & Watkins, 2013; Dombrowski, 2013; Dombrowski, 2014a, 2014b; Dombrowski, 2015). This included a lack of analysis of competing CFA models, an absence of important CFA fit statistics and standardized parameter estimates for the measurement model that was adopted (Dombrowski & Watkins, 2013).

Even so, post-publication CFA research conducted by Taub and McGrew (2004, 2014) have provided stronger support for the proposed theoretical structure of the WJ III Cognitive. For example, in the 2004 study, the proposed CHC model was found to be invariant across age using data obtained from the normative sample. Additionally, Taub and McGrew (2014) evaluated whether an additional hierarchy in the three-stratum model was plausible featuring elements of the Cognitive Performance Model proposed by Richard Woodcock. The retained model featured CPM dimensions atop the broad abilities mediating the influence of *g* to the previously second-order CHC broad abilities. However, Dombrowski, McGill, and Canivez (2018a) investigated this model using the normative sample from the WJ IV Cognitive and found that it was inferior to a seven-factor bifactor conceptualization and the four-factor model retained by these authors. Finally, Strickland et al. (2015) conducted an EFA and CFA of the WJ III Cognitive featuring a sample of referred elementary school participants. Whereas EFA results were consistent with the previous EFAs conducted by Dombrowski and colleagues, CFA results supported the seven-factor model posited by the test publisher. In sum, these conflicting WJ III Cognitive results and competing models in subsequent research suggest that any singular one-shot factor analysis, including those within tests' technical manuals, should be viewed cautiously until there is consistent replication across samples and contexts (Dombrowski, McGill, Farmer et al., 2022). Unfortunately, replication is something that is rarely undertaken in assessment psychology as there are few researchers with either the inclination or expertise to conduct such analyses (Dombrowski & McGill, 2024).

Recapitulation of CHC Structural Validity Concerns

Some of the same omissions evident in the WJ III Technical Manual were also evident in the WJ IV Technical Manual. First, there is an absence of information on the factor structure of the WJ IV Cognitive as the test publisher did not conduct a separate factor analysis of the WJ IV Cognitive. Additionally, there are concerns about the choice of both exploratory and confirmatory factor analytic (CFA) procedures used by the WJ IV test authors to examine the instrument's structure and its linkage with theory (Carivez, 2016; Dombrowski et al., 2017, 2018a, 2018b). Some of the more salient concerns are next addressed.

EFA Problems and Omissions

When analyzing the structure of the full WJ IV battery using principal axis factoring (PAF) with an oblique rotation, the test publisher stated that their analyses produced Heywood cases, impermissible factors, and a lack of convergence of the full test battery structure (McGrew et al., 2014). However, the technical manual did not report the details of these analyses, which may be attributable to overextraction (McGrew et al., 2014). The test publisher then proceeded to conduct a different yet what can be argued as a technically less appropriate method of analysis (i.e., principal components analysis [PCA]). Since the technical manual (McGrew et al., 2014) did not furnish the results of the PAF analysis, a determination of whether there was any practical difference in the patterns of loadings between the two analyses (i.e., PCA or PAF) was not possible.

Why would this comparison have been important? Some have argued that PCA is not a factor analytic procedure (Fabrigar & Wegener, 2012; Gorsuch, 1983) and thus it would have been useful to discern whether the choice of data analysis had any practical ramifications. Osborne (2015) explained, PCA is "not considered a true method of factor analysis and there is disagreement among statisticians about when it should be used, if at all" (p. 1). PCA is regarded as a mathematically simplified version of the general class of dimension reduction analyses. It computes the analysis without consideration of the underlying latent structure of the variables, using all the variance in the manifest variables, and therefore it does not discriminate between different dimensions of variance (e.g., shared and unique variance). Consequently, the components derived from PCA should not be interpreted as a reflection of latent dimensions such as a general factor or subordinate lower order factors (Bentler & Kano, 1990; Jensen, 1998; Preacher & MacCallum, 2003; Widaman, 1993). Instead, the measured variables in PCA are of interest rather than a hypothetical latent construct such as general intelligence or group-specific factors (i.e., Gc, Gf). Widaman (1993) noted that salient loadings tend to be higher in PCA than in factor analysis and that such inflation is magnified when the salient loadings are more moderate in value (e.g., 0.40 in the population) rather than high (e.g., 0.80). Fabrigar et al. (1999) explained that PAF removes random error from the factors so the relation among factors in a PAF analysis are more likely to approach the population values. Additionally, PAF includes only common variance whereas PCA includes common and specific variance, which can inflate factor loadings and give the misleading appearance of a stronger group factor structure (Snook & Gorsuch, 1989).

Representing a further possible problem with the EFA analyses undertaken, the test publisher used a type of rotation (e.g., varimax) following factor extraction that some consider less appropriate when evaluating tests of cognitive ability (Dombrowski, McGill, Canivez et al., 2021). Gorsuch (1983) commented that "varimax is inappropriate if the theoretical expectation suggests a general factor may occur" (p. 185). Indeed, the WJ IV was created with presumption of a general factor and specifically referenced 3S as the basis for its implementation of CHC theory (Beaujean, 2015) so the choice of varimax rotation is questionable (and possibly inappropriate) given the fact that rotation mathematically precludes identification of a general factor. Varimax rotation is also considered inappropriate when factors are highly correlated as in the case of tests of cognitive ability such as the WJ IV Cognitive. In these circumstances, an oblique rotation (e.g., promax) is considered necessary (Thompson, 2004). Although an oblique rotation is necessary, an additional step is often suggested. Gorsuch (1983) commented that higher-order factors are implicit in all oblique rotations so it is recommended that these factors be extracted and examined. The test publisher did not include this additional step (McGrew et al., 2014) because varimax rotation, as with all orthogonal rotations, does not produce correlations between rotated factors and therefore eliminates the option of undertaking a second-order factor analysis.

One elegant approach recommended for extracting and examining higher-order factors is through the Schmid-Leiman transformation (SL; Schmid & Leiman, 1957) procedure.[4] This procedure was used by Carroll (1993) when he created 3S. Because 3S was cited as being highly influential in the development of CHC theory and the WJ IV, it was surprising that the SL procedure was overlooked. The SL procedure involves making first-order factors orthogonal to second-order factors by first extracting the variance explained by the second-order factors. The next step in the procedure is to residualize the first-order factors of all the variance present in the second-order factors. Schmid and Leiman (1957) argued that this process "preserves the desired characteristics of the oblique solution" and "discloses the hierarchical structure of the variables" (p. 53). Carroll (1995) emphasized that "orthogonal factors should be those produced by the SL (1957) orthogonalization procedure" (Carroll, 1995, p. 437) noting in fact that this transformation produces "an orthogonal factor pattern very similar to the Spearman-Holzinger bi-factor pattern" (Carroll, 1993, p. 90). The SL procedure permits variance partitioning (i.e., determining the variance accounted for by higher and lower order factors), which assists when attempting to make interpretive decisions in clinical practice (Dombrowski, McGill, Canivez et al., 2021). The SL procedure was used to examine the structure of the WJ III Cognitive, Achievement, and full test battery (Dombrowski, 2014a, 2014b, 2015b; Dombrowski & Watkins, 2013) and the WJ IV Full test battery and Cognitive (Dombrowski, McGill, & Canivez, 2017, 2018b). It is a widely used and well-established procedure that has also been used in many other analyses of cognitive ability including the Cognitive Assessment System (e.g., Canivez, 2011), the Differential Abilities Scales–Second Edition (e.g., Dombrowski, McGill, Canivez et al., 2019), Reynolds Intellectual Assessment Scales (e.g., Dombrowski et al., 2009; Nelson & Canivez, 2012), the Stanford-Binet–Fifth Edition (e.g., Canivez, 2008; DiStefano & Dombrowski, 2006), and Wechsler scales (e.g., Canivez & Watkins, 2010; Canivez et al., 2016; Dombrowski, Canivez, & Watkins, 2018; Dombrowski, McGill, Watkins et al., 2021; Kush & Canivez, 2019). Finally, McGrew

(2012) indicated that he conducted the SL procedure on the 50 subtest WJ III battery but the results of those analyses have yet to be disclosed.

There are additional problems with the exploratory factor analyses (EFA) presented in the WJ IV Technical Manual (McGrew et al., 2014). The technical manual did not present rudimentary factor analytic statistics including percentage of variance accounted for by higher- and lower-order factors, communality estimates, and estimates of clinical relevance including omega-hierarchical (ω_H) and omega-hierarchical subscale (ω_{HS}; Canivez, 2016; Reise, 2012; Rodriguez et al., 2016). The body of literature on EFA methodology (e.g., Carroll, 1993, 1995, 2003; Dombrowski, McGill, Canivez et al., 2021; Gorsuch, 1983; Thompson, 2004) in concert with indices of clinical relevance (e.g., Reise et al., 2013; Rodriguez et al., 2016) recommends the inclusion of this information when evaluating instruments with higher- and lower-order dimensions as it can aid test users in determining how an instrument's scores should be scored and interpreted to make high-stakes decisions about individuals.

CFA Problems and Omissions

Along with problems with the EFA analyses undertaken, there were also problems associated with the confirmatory factor analytic (CFA) procedures reported (see Canivez, 2017 for a detailed review). First, the technical manual reported only testing a few competing CFA models (Model 1: single *g* factor; Model 2: 9 broad CHC higher-order model; and Model 3: broad plus narrow CHC higher-order factor model). It would seem to have behooved the test publisher to also examine rival models such as Woodcock's Cognitive Performance Model (e.g., Taub & McGrew, 2014) model and Dombrowski and Watkins's (2013) WJ III full test battery SL models. Second, best-fitting initial models and cross-validation models across each age group had comparative fit indexes (CFI; .603–.700), Tucker–Lewis Indexes (TLI; .607–.684), or root mean square errors of approximation (RMSEA; .115–.123) that did not approach levels considered to be adequate in the psychometric literature (CFI, TLI > .90; Hu & Bentler, 1999; RMSEA ≤ .08; Hu & Bentler, 1999). Thus the WJ IV structural models tested were not well-fitting. Third, the WJ IV data were multivariate non-normal (Mardia's 1970 multivariate kurtosis estimate was 27.6) and produced Heywood cases. Consequently, maximum likelihood (ML) estimates should not have been relied upon and robust ML estimates should instead have been used (Byrne, 2006, 2012). Although the test publisher claimed that they "left no stone unturned" (McGrew et al., 2014; p. 179), the scholarly evidence presented in the technical manual does not seem to match this claim. The omission of a separate examination of the structure of the WJ IV Cognitive is a major problem. Likewise, the less-than-optimal choice of EFA methodology, the lack of inclusion of rudimentary EFA statistics, the omission of clinical relevance estimates, the omission of variance partitioning, the poor CFA results, and the incomplete review of the WJ III structural validity literature suggests that simple extrapolation of the factor structure from the WJ IV full test battery to the WJ IV Cognitive is problematic. For users of the instrument who wish to consider the information in the technical manual alongside independent factor analytic results, there is research available that will help guide an evidence-based approach to interpretation of the WJ IV Cognitive.

Independent Factor Analytic Research Findings

Dombrowski, McGill, and Canivez (2017) examined the factor structure of the WJ IV Cognitive across two standardization sample age ranges (9–13; 14–19) using EFA (i.e., principal axis factoring with an oblique [promax] rotation) followed by the SL procedure. The results generally yielded a recommendation of four factors. Additionally, the seven-factor solution proposed by the test publisher was investigated using these same procedures and found untenable as three of the factors had only a single salient subtest loading indicating they were mathematically impermissible. Across both age ranges there was significant subtest migration to theoretically different factors from that proposed by the test publisher. This rendered the seven-factor solution across both age ranges nonviable. When extracting four factors across both age ranges, the WJ IV Cognitive was found to have a hierarchical (*g*) factor with four first-order group factors (presumably working memory, verbal ability, processing speed, and perceptual reasoning) at both age ranges (Dombrowski et al., 2017). However, the composition of the four factors deviated from that proposed by the test publisher with the exception of the verbal ability factor (Gc), processing speed (Gs), and working memory (Gwm) factors at ages 9–13 and working memory and processing speed factors at ages 14–19. Interestingly, the four-factor solution located by Dombrowski and colleagues (2017) was reminiscent of the prior WISC–IV factor structure that contained verbal ability, working memory, processing speed, and perceptual reasoning factors.

In a second study, Dombrowski, McGill, and Canivez (2018a) used CFA to compare a variety of structural models including the publisher proposed seven-factor structure, Woodcock's Cognitive Processing three-factor model, and the four-factor EFA/SL structure suggested by Dombrowski and colleagues (2017). The results of the CFA study found most evidentiary support for the four-factor EFA structural solution suggested by Dombrowski et al. (2017) (e.g., Gc, Gwm, Gs and Perceptual Reasoning [Gf/Gv]) across the 9 to 19 age range). The CFA results also suggested that when modeling seven first-order factors and the higher-order *g* factor with all 18 WJ IV Cognitive subtests, as presented in the technical manual, inadmissible results were produced including a Heywood case (1.02 loading of Ga on *g*) and a negative variance estimate (-0.04) for the Ga factor within both age groups. Modeling an oblique seven-factor structure also yielded an inadmissible solution. The Ga factor produced a Heywood case and was linearly dependent upon the Gwm factor (1.041 loading at ages 9–13; 1.006 loading at ages 9–14). Oral Vocabulary was essentially isomorphic with the Gc factor (loading of .989 at ages 9–13; .991 at ages 14–19). All of these results are suggestive of possible over factoring and model misspecification (Kline, 2016). A bifactor representation of the WJ IV Cognitive with general intelligence (*g*) and seven group factors produced admissible results, but the fit indices were inferior to most of the four-factor structures (oblique, higher order, bifactor), largely replicating the four-factor structure presented in the EFA-SL study by Dombrowski et al. (2017). The resulting four-factor structure found with the WJ IV Cognitive is similar to structural models found in independent WISC–V research (Canivez et al., 2016, 2017; Canivez, McGill, Dombrowski et al., 2020; Dombrowski, Canivez, & Watkins, 2018; Dombrowski, McGill, Watkins et al., 2022). These findings were also replicated by Dombrowski, McGill, & Morgan (2021) who used Monte Carlo simulation to study the structure of the WJ IV Cognitive for the 9–13 age range.

The conclusion from several independent factor analytic studies suggests that the WJ IV Cognitive may not fully align with CHC theory with respect to the identification of separate Gf, Gv, Gltr, and Ga factors. There was modest evidence for Gc, Gwm, Gs, and a fused Gf/Gv factor. However, it should be noted that the composition of subtests under a four-factor model does not comport with the publisher-proposed subtest composition as many subtests migrated away from their theoretically posited factors. The Glr subtests of Story Recall and Visual Auditory Learning loaded together with the Gf and Gv subtests to form a Perceptual Reasoning factor. The Ga subtests of Phonological Processing and Nonword Repetition paired with the Gwm subtests. The Gs subtests loaded together along with Number Series. Number Series, a newly added subtest to the WJ IV, appears to be heavily *g* loaded leaving little residual variance for group factor alignment. Finally, the Gc factor contained the two theoretically proposed factors but Oral Vocabulary loaded .97 on the Gc factor in the age 9 to 13 analysis and .99 in the age 14 to 19 analysis suggesting that it captured a large percentage of the Gc factor variance entirely. It is noted that most of the research regarding the WJ IV Cognitive focuses on the extended battery. However, when CFA was used to evaluate the 10-subtest standard battery from the WJ IV Cognitive across the 9-13 and 14-19 age ranges—the only study to date to investigate the standard battery's factor structure— the results provided support for the scoring structure posited by the test publisher (e.g., a general ability factor [GAI] and three group factors [Gc, Gf & Gwm]; McGill, 2023).

Evidence-Based Interpretation in the Face of Multidimensional Complexity

There is an abundance of interpretive books, manuals, and book chapters available for the WJ IV battery of tests, and there are frameworks (e.g., school neuropsychological assessment Miller & Maricle, 2019) that use the WJ IV battery of tests to make additional interpretative and diagnostic decisions. For the sake of parsimony, we will not provide further explication of how to use these interpretive procedures as they are adequately explained elsewhere (e.g., Flanagan et al., 2013); rather, this section will provide a discussion of whether to engage in these practices given the available empirical evidence outlined to this point in the chapter.

As previously discussed, the structural validity of the WJ IV Cognitive has been questioned (Sattler, 2018). As a result, a case can be made that users should interpret the panoply of composite and cluster scores produced by the WJ scoring system with caution. Despite these evidentiary shortcomings, this chapter will forge ahead and consider additional aspects of validity and issues that might influence use of the instrument in clinical practice.

Predictive Validity

Intelligence test scores have been used to predict relationships with other outcomes such as academic achievement. This aspect of construct validity is associated more broadly with predictive validity. It is important to be aware that the establishment of structural validity is a necessary prerequisite to these evaluations. If there is evidence that the factor structure of an instrument does not measure what it claims to measure then the promoted scoring structure is likely nonsensical and using that scoring structure to study other aspects of validity will arguably produce specious outcomes.

The results of three recent WJ IV Cognitive multiple regression studies contend that selected CHC cluster scores account for significant portions of academic achievement across early lifespan and thus should be the focal point of interpretation on the test (e.g., Cormier et al., 2016; Cormier, Bulut, et al., 2017; Cormier, McGrew, et al., 2017). However, some of these studies de-emphasize the influence of *g* (Cormier, Bulut, et al., 2017; Cormier, McGrew, et al., 2017) or omit its influence altogether (Cormier et al., 2016).

The Cormier et al. (2016) article used a series of multiple regression analyses to examine the linear relationship between the seven WJ IV broad CHC cluster scores and the two WJ IV ACH writing clusters at each of the 14 age groups (ages 6–19, inclusively). The regression models incorporated all seven broad CHC cluster scores (i.e., Gc, Gf, Gwm, Gs, Ga, Glr, and Gv) as predictor variables with the WJ IV ACH writing clusters of Basic Writing Skills (two subtests: Spelling and Editing) and Written Expression (two subtests: Writing Samples and Sentence Writing Fluency) as criterion variables. Although the article claims the results are useful for predicting the relationship of selected CHC cognitive clusters with basic writing skills and written expression, the methodological approach used within this study may be questioned. The analyses used simultaneous multiple regression to investigate the influence of all seven CHC cognitive factors but did not consider the effects of the general factor (as measured by the GIA). Additionally, the CHC factors were not investigated separately to determine the R-squared change for each factor. Without these additional analytical steps (i.e., investigation of g only; g plus seven CHC factors; g plus each CHC factor separately), the article's conclusion that Gc, Gs, and Gf are "especially important predictors of basic writing skills and written expression" (p. 787) may be questioned. While it is acknowledged that the authors have found an association, it is contended that the importance of that association is better investigated using an incremental rather than simultaneous approach to regression.

In the other two studies (e.g., Cormier, Bulut, et al., 2017; Cormier, McGrew, et al., 2017), the influence of g was considered against the backdrop of the seven CHC factors simultaneously entered into the regression models in the respective prediction of reading and writing. In both studies the incremental inclusion of each separate CHC factor in the regression analyses was not investigated but would have permitted a more granular examination of the predictive capacity of the factors and whether they contained sufficient variance to warrant further interpretive consideration (Keith, 2015; Pedhazur, 1997). Instead, it is noted that the change in R-squared reflects that of the seven CHC factors in combination. Moreover, the presentation of additional statistical information (e.g., F ratios, significance level, degrees of freedom, unstandardized beta weights, and standard errors) commonly found in multiple regression studies would have been helpful. Since both studies omitted participants without complete cognitive and achievement data, a comparison to the imputed standardization sample would have also been worthwhile. In fairness, it is recognized that the authors undertook a significant number of analyses and perhaps had to be selective in their reporting of the results.

The Cormier, McGrew et al. (2017) reading prediction study reported that the variance accounted for by the general factor ranged from 29% to 60% depending upon the age range. The results further indicated a medium effect and that the broad CHC clusters account for a moderate amount of additional variance in Reading Rate and Reading Fluency with the broad CHC cluster R-squared change values of .13 and .08, respectively. Following these findings, the authors moved to an investigation of the standardized regression coefficients to make the case that the Gf, Gc, and Gs clusters have interpretive relevance because their standardized regression coefficients were sufficiently high (> .10 = moderate; > .30 = strong). As mentioned, the authors' case for this position would have been better supported had they actually investigated and presented the R-squared change values following the incremental addition of each factor (i.e., Gc, Gf, Gs, etc.).

In the Cormier, Bulut, et al. (2017) math achievement predictive study, the authors noted that the broad CHC abilities of Gf, Gc, and Gs demonstrate significant relations above and beyond those accounted for by general intelligence. Specifically, the authors concluded that Gf, Gc, and Gs appear to have significant relations with math calculation skills throughout the school years.[5] In addition, Gf and Gc also demonstrate consistent relations with math problem solving throughout the school years. However, it is important to consider the results of the analysis furnished in the study. First, unlike Cormier, McGrew et al. (2017), the variance accounted for by the GIA was not presented. The degree of variance accounted for by the GIA would have been worthwhile to understand. Second, and as with the Cormier, McGrew et al. (2017) study, the authors did not present the individual CHC factor R-squared change and instead used the R-squared change for the seven CHC factors in combination. The reported change in R-squared value was .05 to .10 for math calculation skills and .04 to .13 for math problem solving across 14 age groups. However, a review of the R-squared change values revealed that, with the exception of ages 6 and 12 for Math Problem Solving and age 9 for Math Computation, the variance accounted for by the CHC clusters in the prediction of both math clusters was generally below .08 suggesting a small but non-trivial incremental addition of variance. Following this finding, the authors inspected the standardized regression coefficients of each of the CHC clusters, which led them to the assertion that Gf, Gc, and Gs appear to provide additional contribution of variance above that accounted for by the general factor. Again, an appropriate approach to determine the predictive relevance of the specific CHC factors would have been to investigate the R-squared change with each specific CHC factor singularly, something that was not done in any of the Cormier studies.

When looking to predictive validity studies on instruments aligned with CHC theory, including the WJ III, the empirical evidence suggests that the general factor's predictive relevance exceeds that of any group factor for an outcome such as academic achievement (Zaboski et al., 2018). And incremental predictive studies that account for the influence of general intelligence mostly find that the residual predictive influence of CHC factors is generally trivial with the exception of Gc predicting Oral Expression (e.g., change in R-squared Gc = .23, McGill & Busse, 2015).

What does this all mean in terms of applied interpretive relevance? The conclusions produced by the Cormier et al. (2016) analyses should be given less emphasis when making generalizations regarding the predictive relevance regarding the writing clusters given that the analysis contained the analytical omissions described previously. The other two Cormier et al. (2017) studies demonstrated that while it is technically correct that there is an additional contribution of variance (when all the CHC clusters are included) for reading rate, reading fluency, math calculation, and math problem solving, it appears that this incremental amount of variance is generally small in comparison to that provided by the GIA. However, it remains less clear whether and which factors actually make an incremental contribution as each CHC cognitive factor was not investigated separately for its incremental variance contribution. Even if it is assumed that there is non-trivial incremental variance attributable to Gc, Gf, and Gs—which should only tentatively be concluded because this analysis was not undertaken—it may not be worthwhile to move to a consideration of these factors as targets for the interpretive prediction of achievement. What does it actually mean to say that all seven CHC factors in combination offer a nominal amount of additional predicative variance? Ultimately this is a value judgment. However, considering the small amount of variance attributable to all seven CHC factors in combination, it appears that these factors are less important in comparison to the general factor and may not be worth the time, effort, and expense to administer and interpret.

Of course, the Cormier and colleagues series of studies are predicated upon evidence for the structural validity of the WJ IV Cognitive; yet, the results of independent examinations of both the full battery (Dombrowski et al., 2018a) and the WJ IV Cognitive (Dombrowski et al., 2017; 2018b) demonstrate that evidence for the publisher posited structural model is questionable. Even if independent factor analytic results for the myriad scores on the WJ IV suggested the attainment of simple structure and a hierarchical regression analysis is employed, it is possible that the predictive validity of the lower-order factors would follow the same pattern of results from the extended cognitive ability literature where the general factor variance accounts for the majority of variance in predicting a specific outcome such as achievement. Unfortunately, the results from Dombrowski et al. (2017; 2018a; 2018b) suggest a lack of simple structure and that the factors proposed by the technical manual should be considered empirically fragile. Simply put, the veracity of the publisher-proposed CHC factors and the other composites for the WJ IV Cognitive (and achievement [Dombrowski, McGill, Benson et al., 2019]) has yet to be definitively established so using them as a basis for predictive validity is problematic and prone to producing specious clinical outcomes.

Diagnostic Utility

Diagnostic utility (DU) is another consideration. It is likewise predicated upon the attainment of structural validity. DU employs a type of analysis that determines whether, and how much greater than chance, a score or combination of scores will be when making diagnostic decisions. In the case of tests of cognitive ability, combinations of index level scores have been used to make diagnostic decisions such as SLD. For instance, Flanagan et al. (2013) extensively used the WJ IV battery of tests (and other batteries aligned with CHC theory) as part of their cross-battery assessment SLD diagnostic approach. There are other approaches as well that use a type of PSW approach for diagnosing SLD (e.g., Hale & Fiorello, 2004; Schultz & Stevens, 2015), but the empirical foundation for these interpretative algorithms have been called into question (Benson et al., 2019a, 2019b; Dombrowski, Benson, & Maki, 2024; McGill et al., 2018). Most of the evidence for the viability of PSW comes from studies that show the association of a specific CHC factor with an academic achievement area (see Fenwick et al., 2016; Fiorello et al., 2006 for examples). Although these types of associative studies may be an important first step toward the understanding of a linkage between cognitive and academic achievement within a PSW model, a more authoritative approach would be to employ diagnostic utility methodology. As mentioned, this procedure will permit an understanding of whether these group differences are diagnostic (i.e., how much more accurate the procedure is in offering a diagnosis than a simple coin flip). Although presently accumulating, the available diagnostic utility statistics for permutations of these approaches featuring the WJ III/WJ IV suggest that diagnostic decisions rendered in these models, featuring these data, operate at chance and in some cases less than chance levels (Kranzler et al., 2016, 2019; Maki et al., 2022). For instance, a recently published systematic review details the lack of evidentiary support for the diagnostic accuracy of the various PSW models and suggests the field should abandon the procedures (Dombrowski, Benson, & Maki, 2024).

Additionally, it is important to consider the lack of research regarding the longitudinal stability of PSW profiles. If the stability of these profiles is unknown or inadequate, then this creates problems for their use for diagnostic utility purposes. As previously noted, the utilization of the scores undergirding the PSW profiles are predicated upon structural validity evidence so there could be a cascading problem with validity and then diagnostic utility. Future research regarding the longitudinal stability of the various PSW profiles is clearly necessary but only after issues with the structural validity of the WJ IV Cognitive are addressed.

Direct Subtest, Index, and Cluster Level Interpretation

Direct subtest, index, and cluster level interpretation is likely the most commonly used approach to interpretation of the WJ IV Cognitive. Although there is consensus within the scientific community that subtest level interpretation in its various forms for diagnostic purposes should be eschewed (McGill et al., 2018; Watkins, 2000), there are still calls to engage in clinically astute detective work (Kaufman & Lichtenberger, 2006) or to use clinical judgment to guide this practice (Sattler, 2018). It is surprising that we still need to invoke this admonition after more than 30 years of empirical rebuke of this practice. At best this suggests that clinical assessment is slow to self-correct; at worst, but perhaps too Draconian, it raises concern about whether clinical assessment should be regarded as a pathological science (Michell, 1999) and may be impervious to scientific reform (Dombrowski & McGill, 2024). Nonetheless, training and subsequent practice are generally guided by the available assessment texts, which may well be responsible for promoting practices that can be regarded as low-value (Dombrowski, McGill, Farmer et al., 2022; Farmer et al., 2021).

As mentioned throughout, even in some of the factors that have been located for the WJ IV Cognitive, they often contained a different subtest composition than what was proposed by the publisher. These findings would preclude interpretation of the index for any of the factors that did not attain concordance between the structure proposed by the test publisher and that found within factor analysis.

Even if the WJ IV Cognitive attained simple structure (i.e., subtests clearly load theoretically proposed factors without any cross loading), which it does not, there are several metrics of interpretability that ought to be considered before engaging in index level interpretation (see Dombrowski, 2020 for a discussion and example). These metrics have not been incorporated into the technical manuals of commercial ability measures or in interpretive guides that foster contemporary test interpretation (e.g., Flanagan & McDonough, 2018). They include explained common variance (ECV), explained total variance (ETV), omega coefficients, and H (an index of factor replicability). Omega-hierarchical (ω_H) and omega-hierarchical subscale (ω_{HS}) estimate the unit-weighted portion of reliable variance in latent factors. The ω_H coefficient is the estimate for the general intelligence factor with variability of group factors removed while the ω_{HS} coefficient is the estimate of a group factor with all other group and the general factor removed (Rodriguez et al., 2016). Although subjective, it has been suggested that omega coefficients should at a minimum exceed .50, but .75 is preferred (Reise et al., 2013). Additionally, it is important to consider ECV, ETV, and construct replicability (H). If the WJ IV factor or subtest scores fail to capture meaningful portions of true score variance they will likely be of limited clinical utility. The technical manual for the WJ IV battery of tests would have benefited from this information although in fairness the WJ IV was published before the widespread dissemination of these metrics.

Omega-hierarchical estimates for Dombrowski et al.'s (2018a) CFA study (see Table 4.2) indicate that while the broad g factor contained sufficient target construct variance to permit individual interpretation (18 subtest ω_H = .80 for age 9–13), the ω_{HS} estimates for the four WJ IV Cognitive group factors were generally low (< .50), suggesting that the group factors should be cautiously interpreted if at all (Brunner et al., 2012; Reise, 2012). Similarly, the H index (Hancock & Mueller, 2001) furnished evidence for individual interpretation of the general factor (H = .89 for ages 9–13) but not the respective group factors (i.e., H < .65 across all group factors with most < .50).[6] Similarly, ECV and ETV scores indicate that the general factor contains approximately five to seven times more variance than the respective group factors. Put simply, it appears that the WJ IV Cognitive is likely overfactored and contains insufficient target construct variance at the group-factor level for confidant clinical interpretation of those indices (Frazier & Youngstrom, 2007).

Table 4.2 Sources of WJ IV Subtest Variance According to a Bifactor CFA (Ages 9–13)

Subtest	General *g* *b*	Working Memory (Gwm) *b*	Perceptual Reasoning (Gf/Gv) *b*	Processing Speed (Gs) *b*	Verbal Ability (Gc) *b*
	General	First Order Factors			
Verbal Attention (Gwm)	.59	**.45**			
Memory for Words (Aud Mem)	.52	**.48**			
Object Number Sequence (Gwm)	.63	**.36**			
Nonword Repetition (Ga)	.46	**.37**			
Phonological Processing (Ga)	.62	**.24**			
Numbers Reversed (Gwm)	.57	**.16**			
Visualization (Gv)	.51		**.51**		
Visual-Auditory Learning (Glr)	.43		**.38**		
Picture Recognition (Gv)	.35		**.43**		
Analysis-Synthesis (Gf)	.62		**.31**		
Concept Formation (Gf)	.63		**.21**		
Story Recall (Glr)	.52		**.19**		
Letter-Pattern Matching (Gs)	.50			**.60**	
Number-Pattern Matching (PerSpd)	.49			**.60**	
Pair Cancellation (Gs)	.41			**.61**	
Number Series (Gf)	.66			**.13**	
Oral Vocabulary (Gc)	.67				**.61**
General Information (Gc)	.50				**.61**
Explained Common Variance	.61	.09	.09	.13	.09
Explained Total Variance	.30	.04	.04	.06	.04
ω_H/ω_{HS}	.80	.22	.24	.39	.44
H	.89	.48	.48	.64	.55

Note. b = factor loading; ω_H = Omega-hierarchical (*g*); ω_{HS} = Omega-hierarchical subscale (group factors); *H* = construct replicability. Alignment of subtests with respective CHC stratum I or II factors posited in the WJ IV Technical Manual is indicted following each subtest name. Adapted from Dombrowski et al. (2018).

Conclusion

Although the publisher proposed a theoretical linkage of the WJ IV Cognitive with seven CHC factors, the research evidence provided at the 9 to 19 age range does not fully support this proposed linkage at the present time. Instead, results suggest a more parsimonious four-factor solution and offers a different theoretical conceptualization for the WJ IV Cognitive, one more consistent with the prior four-factor-based Wechsler models (i.e., general ability along with verbal ability, working memory, processing speed, and perceptual reasoning). Additionally, the panoply of additional scores, which were created by the test publisher by simply combining subtests without structural validity evidence, are to be questioned until they are afforded adequate empirical support.

One final point deserves consideration. If the structure proposed within an instrument's technical manual is not established and, further, cannot be consistently replicated by independent studies then engaging in accurate CHC–based profile analytic interpretive procedures (e.g., XBA, PSW analyses) will be challenging if not potentially contraindicated (Beaujean et al., 2018). The foundation for such practice rests upon a theoretical/factor structure that has consistent and replicated empirical support. The evidence presented in this chapter suggests that this support is not as strong as is frequently conveyed in the non-empirical literature and challenges the interpretive practices posed within the commercially marketed literature, test technical manuals, or workshops claiming to be evidence based.

Therefore, the field is advised to exercise caution when attempting to interpret the various CHC broad factor indices or when engaging in interpretive approaches such as XBA and PSW using the WJ IV until more consistent, empirical support for these approaches appears (Cucina & Howardson, 2017). Consequently, users are encouraged to interpret the scores provided by the WJ Cognitive circumspectly to ensure that interpretive practice is guided by the presently available empirical evidence (Dombrowski et al., 2007; Dombrowski et al., 2006) rather than theoretical or intuitive considerations. Although calls to use to clinical judgment in regard to cognitive ability test interpretation within technical manuals and other interpretive guidebooks are intuitively appealing,[7] they often offer little additional insight leading to diagnosis at better than chance levels. To persist with interpretation based upon intuitive considerations thinking that one has the capacity to make clinically astute decisions using myriad IQ test profiles (despite the empirical evidence contraindicating this practice) should be considered a form of interpretive hubris. By contrast, the extant empirical literature suggests that there is no pot of clinical gold at the end of these interpretive practices. Continuing to interpret the WJ IV Cognitive (or, for that matter, any test of cognitive ability) without consideration of the totality of the empirical evidence risks characterizing assessment psychology as a pathological discipline (Langmuir & Hall, 1989) and little more than a professional granfalloon.[8]

Notes

1 The WJ IV Technical Manual reports 50 subtests yet only the 47-subtest correlation matrix was furnished.

2 Dombrowski and Watkins (2013) noted that there is an element of circularity—a psychometric tautology, if you will—as it was used to initially provide evidence for CHC Theory and subsequently serve as the main reference instrument for making future refinements to the theory.

3 In fairness, the test authors may have been in the final stages of developing the WJ IV and could have understandably overlooked this body of research that, incidentally, represented the first independent examination of the factor structure of the WJ III battery of tests 10 years after the instrument was published.

4 It is noted that the variance apportioned to higher- and lower-order dimensions may be accomplished in other ways as well and regardless of whether a higher-order or bifactor conceptualization of intelligence is presumed (see Dombrowski, Golay et al., 2018, Table A4 for an example).

5 It should be noted that in some PSW workshops, it is suggested that Gc cannot be the primary weakness identified in a confirmatory pattern associated with a learning disability.

6 Metrics of interpretability are similarly available in Dombrowski et al. (2017) and consistent with those reported herein.

7 The value of clinical judgment is not to be discounted as part of the broader psychological/psychoeducational assessment process. There are times when this is necessary and important. Extreme caution is suggested when using clinical judgment to decipher the myriad IQ test profile analytic scores. The history of this practice has not yielded meaningful clinical insight (see Dombrowski, McGill, Farmer et al., 2022; McGill et al., 2018; Watkins, 2000; Watkins et al., 2005) and is prone to a phenomenon known as the alchemist's fallacy.

8 Adapted from Vonnegut (1976). Dombrowski, McGill, Farmer et al. (2022) expand on his conceptualization by describing a professional granfalloon as a group of individuals who share an identity organized around a common cause that is potentially meaningless and scientifically unsupported. Pratkanis (1995) discusses one of the ways in which a pseudoscience may be marketed via the creation of a granfalloon.

References

Beaujean, A. A. (2015). John Carroll's views on intelligence: Bi-factor vs. higher-order models. *Journal of Intelligence, 3*(4), 121–136. https://doi.org/10.3390/jintelligence3040121

Beaujean, A. A., Benson, N., McGill, R. J., & Dombrowski, S. C. (2018). A misuse of IQ Scores: Using the dual discrepancy/consistency model for identifying specific learning disabilities. *Journal of Intelligence, 6*(3), 1–25. https://doi.org/10.3390/jintelligence6030036

Benson, N. F., Beaujean, A., McGill, R. J., & Dombrowski, S. C. (2018). Critique of the core-selective evaluation process. *The DiaLog, 47*(2), 14–18.

Benson, N. F., Beaujean, A. A., McGill, R. J., & Dombrowski, S. C. (2019). Rising to the challenge of SLD identification: A rejoinder. *The DiaLog, 48*(1), 17–18.

Bentler, P. M., & Kano, Y. (1990). On the equivalence of factors and components. *Multivariate Behavioral Research, 25*(1), 67–74. http://doi.org/10.1207/s15327906mbr2501_8

Brunner, M., Nagy, G., & Wilhelm, O. (2012). A tutorial on hierarchically structured constructs. *Journal of Personality, 80*(4), 796–846. https://doi.org/10.1111/j.14676494.2011.00749.x

Byrne, B. M. (2006). *Structural equation modeling with EQS: Basic concepts, applications, and programming* (2nd ed.). Routledge.

Byrne, B. M. (2012). *Structural equation modeling with Mplus: Basic concepts, applications, and programming.* Routledge.

Canivez, G. L. (2008). Orthogonal higher-order factor structure of the Stanford-Binet Intelligence Scales-Fifth Edition for children and adolescents. *School Psychology Quarterly, 23(4),* 533–541. https://doi.org/10.1037/a0012884

Canivez, G. L. (2011). Hierarchical factor structure of the Cognitive Assessment System: Variance partitions from the Schmid–Leiman (1957) procedure. *School Psychology Quarterly, 26*(4), 305–317. http://doi.org/10.1037/a0025973

Canivez, G. L. (2016). Bifactor modeling in construct validation of multifactored tests: Implications for understanding multidimensional constructs and test interpretation. In K. Schweizer & C. DiStefano (Eds.), *Principles and methods of test construction: Standards and recent advancements* (pp. 247–271). Hogrefe.

Canivez, G. L. (2017). Review of the Woodcock-Johnson IV. In J. F. Carlson, K. F. Geisinger, & J. L. Jonson (Eds.), *The twentieth mental measurements yearbook* (pp. 875–882). Buros Center for Testing.

Canivez, G. L., McGill, R. J., Dombrowski, S. C., Watkins, M. W., Pritchard, A. E., & Jacobson, L. A. (2020). Construct validity of the WISC–V in clinical cases: Exploratory and confirmatory factor analyses of the 10 primary subtests. *Assessment*, *27*(2), 274–296. https://doi.org/10.1177/1073191118811609

Canivez, G. L., & Watkins, M. W. (2010). Investigation of the factor structure of the Wechsler Adult Intelligence Scale–Fourth Edition (WAIS–IV): Exploratory and higher-order factor analyses. *Psychological Assessment, 22*(4), 827–836. http://doi.org/10.1037/a0020429

Canivez, G. L., Watkins, M. W., & Dombrowski, S. C. (2016). Factor structure of the Wechsler Intelligence Scale for Children–Fifth Edition: Exploratory factor analyses with the 16 primary and secondary subtests. *Psychological Assessment, 28*(8), 975–986. https://doi.org/10.1037/pas0000238

Canivez, G. L., Watkins, M. W., & Dombrowski, S. C. (2017). Structural validity of the Wechsler Intelligence Scale for Children-Fifth Edition: Confirmatory factor analyses with the 16 primary and secondary subtests. *Psychological Assessment, 29*(4), 458–472. http://doi.org/10.1037/pas0000358

Carroll, J. B. (1993). *Human cognitive abilities: A survey of factor-analytic studies.* Cambridge University Press. https://doi.org/10.1017/CBO9780511571312

Carroll, J. B. (1995). On methodology in the study of cognitive abilities. *Multivariate Behavioral Research*, *30*(3), 429–452. http://doi.org/10.1207/s15327906mbr3003_6

Carroll, J. B. (2003). The higher-stratum structure of cognitive abilities: Current evidence supports g and about ten broad factors. In H. Nyborg (Ed.), *The scientific study of general intelligence: Tribute to Arthur R. Jensen* (pp. 5–21). Pergamon Press. http://doi.org/10.1016/B978–008043793-4/50036-2

Cattell, R. B. (1978). *The scientific use of factor analysis in behavioral and life sciences*. Plenum.

Cormier, D. C., Bulut, O., McGrew, K. S., & Frison, J. (2016). The role of Cattell–Horn–Carroll (CHC) cognitive abilities in predicting writing achievement during the school-age years. *Psychology in the Schools*, *53*(8), 787–803. https://doi.org/10.1002/pits.21945

Cormier, D. C., Bulut, O., McGrew, K. S., & Singh, D. (2017). Exploring the relations between Cattell–Horn–Carroll (CHC) cognitive abilities and mathematics achievement. *Applied Cognitive Psychology*, *31*(5), 530–538. https://doi.org/10.1002/acp.3350

Cormier, D. C., McGrew, K. S., Bulut, O., & Funamoto, A. (2017). Revisiting the relations between the WJ-IV measures of Cattell-Horn-Carroll (CHC) cognitive abilities and reading achievement during the school-age years. *Journal of Psychoeducational Assessment*, *35*(8), 731–754. https://doi.org/10.1177/0734282916659208

Cucina, J. M., & Howardson, G. N. (2017). Woodcock-Johnson-III, Kaufman Adolescent and Adult Intelligence Test (KAIT), Kaufman Assessment Battery for Children (KABC), and differential ability scales (DAS) support Carroll but not Cattell-Horn. *Psychological Assessment*, *29*, 1001–1015. doi:10.1037/pas0000389

DiStefano, C., & Dombrowski, S. C. (2006). Investigating the theoretical structure of the Stanford-Binet, Fifth Edition. *Journal of Psychoeducational Assessment, 24*(2), 123–136. https://doi.org/10.1177%2F0734282905285244

Dombrowski, S. C. (2013). Investigating the structure of the WJ–III Cognitive at school age. *School Psychology Quarterly*, *28*(2), 154–169. https://doi.org/10.1037/spq0000010

Dombrowski, S. C. (2014a). Exploratory bifactor analysis of the WJ–III Cognitive in adulthood via the Schmid-Leiman procedure. *Journal of Psychoeducational Assessment, 32*(4), 330–341. https://doi.org/10.1177/0734282913508243

Dombrowski, S. C. (2014b). Investigating the structure of the WJ III Cognitive in early school age through two exploratory bifactor analysis procedures. *Journal of Psychoeducational Assessment*, *32*(6), 483–494. https://doi.org/10.1177%2F0734282914530838

Dombrowski, S. C. (2015). Exploratory bifactor analysis of the WJ–III Achievement at school age via the Schmid-Leiman orthogonalization procedure. *Canadian Journal of School Psychology*, *30*(1), 34–50. https://doi.org/10.1177%2F0829573514560529

Dombrowski, S. C. (2020). A newly proposed framework and a clarion call to improve practice. In S. C. Dombrowski, *Psychoeducational assessment and report writing* (2nd. ed., pp. 9–59). Springer Nature.

Dombrowski, S. C., Ambrose, D. A., & Clinton, A. (2007). Dogmatic insularity in learning disabilities diagnosis and the critical need for a philosophical analysis. *International Journal of Special Education*, *22*(1), 3–10.

Dombrowski, S. C., Beaujean, A. A., Schneider, J. W., McGill, R. J., & Benson, N. (2019). Using exploratory bifactor analysis to understand the latent structure of multidimensional psychological measures: An applied example featuring the WISC-V. *Structural Equation Modeling: A Multidisciplinary Journal, 26*(6), 847–860. https://doi.org/10.1080/10705511.2019.1622421

Dombrowski, S. C., Benson, N. F., & Maki, K. E. (2024). A systematic review of the PSW diagnostic accuracy evidence for SLD Identification: Is it time to abandon PSW? *School Psychology Review*, 1–19. https://doi.org/10.1080/2372966X.2024.2369494

Dombrowski, S. C., Canivez, G. L., & Watkins, M. W. (2018). Factor structure of the 10 WISC–V primary subtests across four standardization age groups. *Contemporary School Psychology, 22*, 90–104. https://doi.org/10.1007/s40688-017-0125-2

Dombrowski, S. C., Golay, P., McGill, R. J., & Canivez, G. L. (2018). Investigating the theoretical structure of the DAS–II core battery at school age using Bayesian structural equation modeling. *Psychology in the Schools, 55*(2), 190–207. https://doi.org/10.1002/pits.22096

Dombrowski, S. C., Kamphaus, R. W., et al. (2006). The Solomon Effect in learning disabilities diagnosis: Have we not yet learned from history? *School Psychology Quarterly, 21*(3). 359–373. https://doi.org/10.1037/h0084128

Dombrowski, S. C., & McGill, R. J. (2024). Clinical assessment in school psychology: Impervious to scientific reform? *Canadian Journal of School Psychology, 39*(4), 297–306. https://doi.org/10.1177/08295735231224052

Dombrowski, S. C., McGill, R. J., Benson, N., & Beaujean, A. A. (2019). The Woodcock-Johnson IV Tests of Achievement provides too many scores for clinical interpretation. *Journal of Psychoeducational Assessment, 37*(7), 819–836. https://doi.org/10.1177/0734282918800745

Dombrowski, S. C., McGill, R. J., & Canivez, G. L. (2017). Exploratory and hierarchical factor analysis of the WJ IV Cognitive at school age. *Psychological Assessment, 29*(4), 394–407. https://doi.org/10.1037/pas0000350

Dombrowski, S. C., McGill, R. J., & Canivez, G. L. (2018a). An alternative conceptualization of the theoretical structure of the Woodcock-Johnson IV Tests of Cognitive Abilities at school age: A confirmatory factor analytic investigation. *Archives of Scientific Psychology, 6*(1), 1–13. https://doi.org/10.1037/arc0000039

Dombrowski, S. C., McGill, R. J., & Canivez, G. L. (2018b). Hierarchical exploratory factor analyses of the Woodcock-Johnson IV full test battery: Implications for CHC application in school psychology. *School Psychology Quarterly, 33*(2), 235–250. https://doi.org/10.1037/spq0000221

Dombrowski, S. C., McGill, R. J., Canivez, G. L., & Peterson, C. H. (2019). Investigating the theoretical structure of the Differential Ability Scales-Second Edition through hierarchical exploratory factor analysis. *Journal of Psychoeducational Assessment, 37*(1), 94–104. http://dx.doi.org/10.1177/0734282918760724

Dombrowski, S. C., McGill, R. J., Canivez, G. L., Watkins, M. W., & Beaujean, A. A. (2021). Factor analysis and variance partitioning in intelligence research: Clarifying misconceptions. *Journal of Psychoeducational Assessment, 39*(1), 28–38. https://doi.org/10.1177/0734282920961952

Dombrowski, S. C., McGill, R. J., Farmer, R. L., Kranzler, J. H., & Canivez, G. L. (2022). Beyond the rhetoric of evidence-based assessment: A framework for critical thinking in clinical practice. *School Psychology Review, 51*(6), 771–784. https://doi.org/10.1080/2372966X.2021.1960126

Dombrowski, S. C., McGill, R. J., & Morgan, G. B. (2021). Monte Carlo modeling of contemporary Intelligence Test (IQ) factor structure: Implications for IQ assessment, interpretation, and theory. *Assessment, 28*(3), 977–993. https://doi.org/10.1177/1073191119869828

Dombrowski, S. C., McGill, R. J., Watkins, M. W., Canivez, G. L., Jacobson, L., & Pritchard, A. (2022). Will the *real* theoretical structure of the WISC–V please stand up? An exploratory factor analytic replication study. *Contemporary School Psychology, 26*, 492–503. https://doi.org/10.1007/s40688-021-00365-6

Dombrowski, S. C., & Watkins, M. W. (2013). Exploratory and higher order factor analysis of the WJ-III full test battery: A school-aged analysis. *Psychological Assessment, 25*(2), 442–455. https://doi.org/10.1037/a0031335

Dombrowski, S. C., Watkins, M. W., & Brogan, M. J. (2009). An exploratory investigation of factor structure of the Reynolds Intellectual Assessment Scales (RIAS). *Journal of Psychoeducational Assessment, 27*(6), 279–286. https://doi.org/10.1177/0734282909333179

Fabrigar, L. R., & Wegener, D. T. (2012). *Exploratory factor analysis*. Oxford University Press.

Fabrigar, L. R., Wegener, D. T., MacCallum, R. C., & Strahan, E. J. (1999). Evaluating the use of exploratory factor analysis in psychological research. *Psychological Methods, 4*(3), 272–299. http://doi.org/10.1037/1082-989X.4.3.272

Farmer, R. L., McGill, R. J., Dombrowski, S. C., & Canivez, G. L. (2021). Why questionable assessment practices remain popular in school psychology: Instructional materials as pedagogic vehicles. *Canadian Journal of School Psychology*, *36*(2), 98–114. https://doi.org/10.1177/0829573520978111

Fenwick, M. E., Kubas, H. A., Witzke, J. W., Fitzer, K. R., Miller, D. C., Maricle, D. E., ... & Hale, J. B. (2016). Neuropsychological profiles of written expression learning disabilities determined by concordance-discordance model criteria. *Applied Neuropsychology: Child*, *5*(2), 83–96. https://doi.org/10.1080/21622965.2014.993396

Fiorello, C. A., Hale, J. B., & Snyder, L. E. (2006). Cognitive hypothesis testing and response to intervention for children with reading problems. *Psychology in the Schools*, *43*(8), 835–853. https://doi.org/10.1002/pits.20192

Flanagan, D. P., & McDonough, E. M. (Eds.). (2018). *Contemporary intellectual assessment: Theories, tests, and issues* (4th ed.). Guilford Press.

Flanagan, D. P., Ortiz, S. O., & Alfonso, V. C. (2013). *Essentials of cross-battery assessment* (3rd. ed.). John Wiley & Sons.

Gorsuch, R. L. (1983). *Factor analysis* (2nd ed.). Erlbaum.

Hale, J. B., & Fiorello, C. A. (2004). *School neuropsychology: A practitioner's handbook.* Guilford Press.

Hancock, G. R., & Mueller, R. O. (2001). Rethinking construct reliability within latent variable systems. In R. Cudeck, S. du Toit, & D. Sorbom (Eds.), *Structural equation modeling: Present and future—A festschrift in honor of Karl Joreskog* (pp. 195–216). Scientific Software International.

Horn, J. L., & Cattell, R. B. (1966). Refinement and test of the theory of fluid and crystallized general intelligences. *Journal of Educational Psychology*, *57*(5), 253–270. http://doi.org/10.1037/h0023816

Hu, L. T., & Bentler, P. M. (1999). Cutoff criteria for fit indexes in covariance structure analysis: Conventional criteria versus new alternatives. *Structural Equation Modeling, 6*(1), 1–55. https://doi.org/10.1080/10705519909540118

Jensen, A. R. (1998). *The g factor: The science of mental ability.* Praeger.

Kaufman, A. S., & Lichtenberger, E. O. (2006). *Assessing adolescent and adult intelligence* (3rd ed.). John Wiley.

Keith, T. Z. (2015). *Multiple regression and beyond: An introduction to multiple regression and structural equation modeling* (2nd ed.). New York: Routledge.

Kline, R. B. (2016). Methodology in the social sciences. *Principles and practice of structural equation modeling* (4th ed.). Guilford Press.

Kranzler, J. H., Floyd, R. G., Benson, B., Zaboski, B., & Thibodaux, L. (2016). Classification agreement analysis of Cross-Battery Assessment in the identification of specific learning disorders in children and youth. *International Journal of School & Educational Psychology, 4*(3), 124–136. https://www.doi.org./10.1080/21683603.2016.1155515

Kranzler, J. H., Gilbert, K., Robert, C. R., Floyd, R. G., & Benson, N. F. (2019). Further examination of a critical assumption underlying the Dual-Discrepancy/Consistency approach to specific learning disability identification. *School Psychology Review*, *48*(3), 207–221. htpps://www.doi.org./10.17105/SPR-2018-0008.V48-3

Kush, J. C., & Canivez, G. L. (2019). The higher order structure of the WISC-IV Italian adaptation using hierarchical exploratory factor analytic procedures. *International Journal of School & Educational Psychology*, *7*(Sup1), 15–28. https://doi.org/10.1080/21683603.2018.1485601

Langmuir, I., & Hall, R. N. (1989). Pathological science. *Physics Today*, *42*(10), 36–48. https://doi.org/10.1063/1.881205

Maki, K. E., Kranzler, J. H., & Moody, M. E. (2022). Dual discrepancy/consistency pattern of strengths and weaknesses method of specific learning disability identification: Classification accuracy when combining clinical judgment with assessment data. *Journal of School Psychology*, *92*, 33–48. https://doi.org/10.1016/j.jsp.2022.02.003

Mardia, K. V. (1970). Measures of multivariate skewness and kurtosis with applications. *Biometrika, 57*(3), 519–530. https://doi.org/10.1093/biomet/57.3.519

McGill, R. J. (2018). Confronting the base rate problem: More ups and downs for cognitive scatter analysis. *Contemporary School Psychology, 22*(3), 384–393. https://doi.org/10.1007/s40688-017-0168-4

McGill, R. J. (2023). Confirmatory factor analysis of the WJ IV Cognitive: What does the standard battery measure at school age? *Journal of Psychoeducational Assessment, 41*(4), 461–468. https://doi.org/10.1177/07342829231159440

McGill, R. J., & Busse, R. T. (2015). Incremental validity of the WJ III COG: Limited predictive effects beyond the GIA-E. *School Psychology Quarterly, 30*(3), 353–365. https://doi.org/10.1037/spq0000094

McGill, R. J., Dombrowski, S. C., & Canivez, G. L. (2018). Cognitive profile analysis in school psychology: History, issues, and continued concerns. *Journal of School Psychology*, 71, 108–121. https://doi.org/10.1016/j.jsp.2018.10.007

Michell, J. (1999). *Measurement in psychology: A critical history of a methodological concept.* Cambridge University Press.

Miller, D. C., & Maricle, D. E. (2019). *Essentials of school neuropsychological assessment* (3rd ed.). John Wiley.

Miller, D. C., McGill, R. J., & Johnson, W. L. B. (2016). Neurocognitive applications of the Woodcock-Johnson IV. In D. P. Flanagan & V. C. Alfonso (Eds.), *WJ IV clinical use and interpretation: Scientist-practitioner perspectives* (pp. 355–388). Academic Press. https://doi.org/10.1016/B978-0-12-802076-0.00013-X

Nelson, J. M., & Canivez, G. L. (2012). Examination of the structural, convergent, and incremental validity of the Reynolds Intellectual Assessment Scales (RIAS) with a clinical sample. *Psychological Assessment, 24(1),* 129–140. https://doi.org/10.1037/a0024878

Osborne, J. W. (2015). What is rotating in exploratory factor analysis? *Practical Assessment, Research & Evaluation*, 20(2). https://doi.org/10.7275/hb2g-m060

Pedhazur, E. J. (1997). *Multiple regression in behavioral research: Prediction and explanation* (3rd ed.). New York, NY: Holt, Rinehart & Winston.

Pratkanis, A. R. (1995). How to sell a pseudoscience. *The Skeptical Inquirer*, 19, 19–25.

Preacher, K. J., & MacCallum, R. C. (2003). Repairing Tom Swift's electric factor analysis machine. *Understanding Statistics, 2*(1), 13–43. https://doi.org/10.1207/S15328031US0201_02

Reise, S. P. (2012). The rediscovery of bifactor measurement models. *Multivar. Behav. Res., 47*, 667–696. 10.1080/00273171.2012.71555

Reise, S. P., Bonifay, W. E., & Haviland, M. G. (2013). Scoring and modeling psychological measures in the presence of multidimensionality. *Journal of Personality Assessment*, 95(2), 129–140. https://doi.org/10.1080/00223891.2012.725437

Rodriguez, A., Reise, S. P., & Haviland, M. G. (2016). Evaluating bifactor models: Calculating and interpreting statistical indices. *Psychological Methods*, 21(2), 137–150. https://doi.org/10.1037/met0000045

Sattler, J. M. (2018). *Assessment of children: Cognitive foundations and applications* (6th ed.). Sattler Publishing.

Schmid, J., & Leiman, J. M. (1957). The development of hierarchical factor solutions. *Psychometrika, 22*, 53–61. https://doi.org/10.1007/ BF02289209

Schneider, W. J., & McGrew, K. S. (2018). The Cattell-Horn-Carroll model of intelligence. In D. P. Flanagan & E. M. McDonough (Eds.), *Contemporary intellectual assessment: Theories, tests, and issues* (4th ed., pp. 73–163). Guilford Press.

Schrank, F. A., & Dailey, D. (2014). Woodcock–Johnson online scoring and reporting [Online format]. Riverside.

Schrank, F. A., McGrew, K. S., & Mather, N. (2014a). *Woodcock-Johnson IV.* Riverside.

Schrank, F. A., McGrew, K. S., & Mather, N. (2014b). *Woodcock–Johnson IV Tests of Cognitive Abilities.* Riverside.

Schrank, F. A., & Wendling, B. J. (2015). WJ IV Interpretation and Instructional Interventions Program (WIIIP). Riverside.

Schultz, E. K., & Stephens, T. L. (2015). Core-Selective Evaluation Process: An efficient and comprehensive approach to identify students with SLD using the WJ IV. *The DiaLog, 44*(2), 5–12.

Snook, S. C., & Gorsuch, R. L. (1989). Component analysis vs. common factor analysis: A Monte Carlo study. *Psychological Bulletin, 106*(1), 148–154. https://doi.org/10.1037/0033-2909.106.1.148

Strickland, T., Watkins, M. W., & Caterino, L. C. (2015). Structure of the Woodcock-Johnson III cognitive tests in a referral sample of elementary school students. *Psychological Assessment, 27*(2), 689–697. https://doi.org/10.1037/pas0000052

Taub, G. E., & McGrew, K. S. (2004). A confirmatory factor analysis of Cattell-Horn-Carroll Theory and cross-age invariance of the Woodcock-Johnson Tests of Cognitive Abilities III. *School Psychology Quarterly, 19*(1), 72–87. https://doi.org/10.1521/scpq.19.1.72.29409

Taub, G. E., & McGrew, K. S. (2014). The Woodcock-Johnson Tests of Cognitive Abilities Cognitive Performance Model: Empirical support for intermediate factors within CHC theory. *Journal of Psychoeducational Assessment, 32*(3), 187–201. https://doi.org/10.1177/0734282913504808

Thompson, B. (2004). *Exploratory and confirmatory factor analysis: Understanding concepts and applications.* American Psychological Association. https://doi.org/10.1037/10694-000

Vonnegut, K. (1976). *Wampeters, Foma & Granfalloons (opinions).* Dial Press.

Watkins, M. W. (2000). Cognitive profile analysis: A shared professional myth. *School Psychology Quarterly, 15*(4), 465–479. https://doi.org/10.1037/h0088802

Watkins, M. W., Dombrowski, S. C., & Canivez, G. L. (2018). Reliability and factorial validity of the Canadian Wechsler Intelligence Scale for Children–Fifth Edition. *International Journal of School and Educational Psychology, 6(4),* 252–265. https://doi.org/10.1080/21683603.2017.1342580

Watkins, M. W., Glutting, J. J., & Youngstrom, E. A. (2005). Issues in subtest profile analysis. In D. P. Flanagan & P. L. Harrison (Eds.), *Contemporary intellectual assessment: Theories, tests, and issues* (pp. 251–268). Guilford Press.

Widaman, K. F. (1993). Common factor analysis versus principal component analysis: Differential bias in representing model parameters? *Multivariate Behavioral Research, 28*(3), 263–311. https://doi.org/10.1207/ s15327906mbr2803_1

Youngstrom, E. A., & Van Meter, A. R. (2016). Empirically supported assessment of children and adolescents. *Clinical Psychology: Science and Practice, 23*(4), 327–347. https://doi.org/10.1111/cpsp .12172

Zaboski, B. A., II, Kranzler, J. H., & Gage, N. A. (2018). Meta-analysis of the relationship between academic achievement and broad abilities of the Cattell-Horn-Carroll theory. *Journal of School Psychology, 71,* 42–56. https://doi.org/10.1016/j.jsp.2018.10.001

Chapter 5

Utility of Intelligence Tests for the Determination of Eligibility for Special Education and Related Services

John H. Kranzler and Randy G. Floyd

Many medical conditions (i.e., diseases, illnesses, and injuries) share the same or similar symptoms, and some present in different ways. To differentiate between two or more possible causes of an individual's condition, medical doctors and other clinicians (e.g., licensed psychologists) engage in a process known as *differential diagnosis*. The goal of this process is to narrow down the list of possible causes to arrive at a diagnosis. Diagnoses are essentially hypotheses that organize and explain an array of clinical data. They facilitate communication among those providing patient care, provide an understanding of a condition's etiology and prognosis, guide treatment selection, and, in some cases, are useful for prevention. The *Diagnostic and Statistical Manual of Mental Disorders* (DSM–5; American Psychiatric Association [APA], 2013) is the nosological system used by mental health professionals and researchers to classify mental disorders.

The Individuals with Disabilities Education Act (IDEA) is the nation's federal special education law that ensures that public schools provide a free and appropriate education (FAPE) to all children and youths with disabilities. To qualify, a student must be found to have a disability that requires special education and related services (e.g., counseling or speech therapy) designed to meet their unique educational needs. Schools do not diagnose the causes of learning and other difficulties, however. Rather, they determine whether a student is eligible or ineligible based on the criteria for each of the following 12 categories of disability under IDEA: intellectual disability, hearing impairment (including deafness), speech or language impairment, visual impairment (including blindness), serious emotional disturbance, orthopedic impairment, autism, traumatic brain injury, other health impairment, specific learning disability, deaf-blindness, and multiple disabilities. These disability categories tend to be more general than medical diagnoses, and only a few specific diagnoses are listed under the definitions of disabilities covered by IDEA (e.g., Tourette's Syndrome under the other health impairment category). In addition to establishing criteria for disability determination, IDEA also outlines the required procedures for evaluation and eligibility determination. It is important to note that these provisions do not delineate specific tests, criteria, or decision procedures. Instead, they maintain that the evaluation must use a variety of assessments that are valid, reliable, and non-discriminatory; that the eligibility determination cannot be made based on a sole criterion; and that eligibility determination must be decided by a qualified team of educational professionals.

To receive federal funding for special education and related services, states must develop rules and regulations that are consistent with IDEA and its implementation within each state. States are mandated to have regulations that provide all of the protections contained in IDEA (e.g., FAPE, procedural due process). In addition, IDEA defines the term *child with a disability* according to disability categories at the federal level but that term is also operationally defined by each state. While each state's definition must be consistent with IDEA's, disability definitions and, more importantly, the specific rules and regulations used for determining eligibility for special education and related services are developed by individual states. This has resulted in considerable variability in state policies and practices governing the identification of disabilities in the schools (e.g., Maki & Adams, 2019; McNicholas et al., 2018). Regardless of the specific rules and regulations used for eligibility determination in each state, the identification of children and youths with disabilities must be done with a high degree of classification accuracy.

Aims of This Chapter

The main focus of this chapter is the utility of tests of intelligence for the identification of students with disabilities covered by IDEA. According to results of a recent survey of over 1,300 school psychologists, tests of intelligence are the second-most-administered psychological instrument in the field (Benson et al., 2019). Approximately 95% of practitioners reported administering an intelligence test during the past year ($M = 3.5$ per month). Despite the widespread administration of these tests, controversy and disagreement have long surrounded their interpretation and use (e.g., McGill et al., 2018).

We begin by briefly discussing what intelligence tests measure and the ways in which they can be interpreted. We then discuss research on intra-individual, or profile, analysis of intelligence tests. In this section, we emphasize the contributions of one particular scholar—Dr. Marley W. Watkins—whose seminal research over the past several decades has been instrumental in the on-going examination of the validity of intelligence test interpretive practices. Dr. Watkins's scholarly contributions have contributed significantly to improvements in the quality of psychological services delivered to children and youth, families, and schools. Following this, we examine empirical evidence supporting the utility of different contemporary approaches to intelligence test use and interpretation for the determination of eligibility for special education and related services.

Intelligence Test Interpretation

What Do Intelligence Tests Measure?

The Cattell-Horn-Carroll (CHC) theory of intelligence is a taxonomy of human cognitive abilities that specifies the number of cognitive abilities and their arrangement (see Schneider & McGrew, 2018). In CHC theory, intelligence is multidimensional and consists of three levels, or strata, of cognitive abilities with varying degrees of referent generality. *Referent* generality refers to "the variety of behaviors or mental activities to which [a construct] relates and the degree to which it relates to them" (Coan, 1964, p. 138). The ability with the most referent generality, *psychometric g*, is located at the top of the three-stratum hierarchy, at Stratum III (see Jensen, 1998). All cognitive abilities are related to *g* to some degree. Stratum II consists of eight or more broad cognitive abilities (e.g., Fluid Reasoning, Comprehension-Knowledge, Short-Term Memory) that reflect different kinds of test content (e.g., verbal, numerical, and spatial) or cognitive processes (e.g., visual processing, short-term memory, and perceptual speed). At Stratum I, there are over 80 narrow cognitive abilities (e.g., spatial scanning, phonetic coding, and memory for sound patterns). On intelligence tests, individual subtests generally correspond to Stratum I abilities. Two or more subtests can be combined to derive broader scores at Strata II and III of CHC theory, which are called composite, index, or cluster scores.

Which CHC abilities are measured by intelligence tests? Due to practical limitations (e.g., time), standardized tests of intelligence tend to measure psychometric *g* and only a handful of broad and narrow cognitive abilities. In addition to *g*, most intelligence tests measure three to five broad abilities at Stratum II of CHC theory (see Kranzler & Floyd, 2020, pp. 155–189). Intelligence tests also measure a number of narrow Stratum I abilities generally corresponding to the number of subtests on any particular instrument. For example, Benson et al. (2019) found that the most widely used intelligence test in schools today is the Wechsler Intelligence Scale for Children–Fifth Edition (WISC–V; Wechsler, 2014a). The WISC–V is a standardized, norm-referenced instrument that was developed to assess the intellectual abilities of children and youths ages 6 to 16 years.[1] Intellectual ability on the WISC–V is measured by 10 primary subtests. These subtests are used to derive five primary index scores (Verbal Comprehension, Visual Spatial, Fluid Reasoning, Working Memory, and Processing Speed). These index scores are "factor-based and recommended for a comprehensive description and evaluation of intellectual ability" (Wechsler, 2014b, p. 7). The overall score, the Full-Scale Intelligence Quotient (FSIQ), is a hierarchical factor-based score that is derived from 7 of the 10 primary subtests. Thus the WISC–V measures the psychometric *g* at Stratum III, five broad cognitive abilities at Stratum II, and as many as 10 narrow abilities at Stratum I (cf. Canivez et al., 2018; Dombrowski et al., 2018).

How Are Intelligence Tests Interpreted?

Intelligence test results can be analyzed in terms of their elevation, scatter, or shape (Cronbach & Gleser, 1953). *Elevation* refers to interpretation of the level of a score on an intelligence test. Age-based norm-referenced (i.e., population-relative) subtest and composite scaled scores are the most common means for examining an individual's level of performance. *Scatter* refers to the interpretation of the amount of variability in an individual's test scores, usually defined as the range or variance of a person's subtest scores. Last, *shape* refers to the profile, or shape, of an individual's test scores. Disagreement over intelligence test interpretation has evolved over time and has largely surrounded the question of whether to focus on the elevation of an individual's test scores or their shape or pattern (e.g., McGill et al., 2018).

According to Kamphaus et al. (2018), the interpretation of intelligence tests has evolved over time in four distinct waves. The first wave focused solely on interpretation of the level of the overall intelligence quotient (IQ) score and its assignment to a descriptive category (e.g., Dull, Normal, Superior). Given that the first intelligence test developed for use in the United States, the Stanford-Binet Intelligence Scale (Terman, 1916), yielded only an overall IQ, this was the only kind of interpretation possible. The second wave of test interpretation was ushered in with the publication of the first intelligence test to produce age-based standard scores for different composites and subtests in addition to an overall score, the Wechsler-Bellevue Intelligence Scale (WBIS; Wechsler, 1939). Because the WBIS measured a number of different cognitive abilities, during the second wave of intelligence test interpretation, psychologists emphasized analysis of the shape of an individual's subtest and composite test scores rather than level of the overall score. As Watkins (2003) stated, "psychologists speculated that the variability (scatter) or profile (shape) of an individual's scaled scores across the subtests of an intelligence battery might be a sign of neurological dysfunction (Mitrushina et al., 1994), learning disability (McLean et al., 1990), or emotional disability (Kaufman, 1990)" (p. 118). Rapaport et al. (1945–1946) proposed the first method of intra-individual, or ipsative (i.e., person-relative), analysis, which involved the visual inspection of an individual's intelligence test score profile and a clinical judgment to determine the presence of psychological pathology. However, because it was based on the subjective inspection of test scores and not substantiated by empirical research, this method was criticized for its lack of scientific rigor (Brown, 1946).

Publication of Kaufman's *Intelligent Testing with the WISC–R* in 1979 revolutionized the interpretation of intelligence tests and led to the third wave (Kaufman, 1979, 1994). The intelligent testing (IT) approach combines clinical judgment, statistics, and psychometrics. By conducting statistical tests between an individual's scores, one can differentiate between random variability and variability that is statistically significant to identify ipsative cognitive strengths and weaknesses. In the IT method, there are successive levels of analysis starting with examination of the elevation of the overall score but then proceeding with ipsative analysis of the composite and subtest scores. At these levels, intra-individual cognitive strengths and weaknesses are identified when a composite or subtest score is statistically significantly higher or lower than the average of those scores. Interpretation of the overall score is discouraged, despite being the most reliable and valid score, when there is statistically significant variability among the composite scores; and interpretation of composite scores is discouraged when there are statistically significant differences among the subtests that are summed to derive them. When significant differences are observed, base-rate data are then examined to determine the prevalence of those score differences in the normative (i.e., non-clinical) sample. An individual's profile of specific cognitive abilities is deemed to be of more clinical importance for diagnosis and treatment planning than the elevation of those scores when the observed differences are both statistically significant and relatively uncommon and supported by other clinical data. Although the initial version of the IT approach recommended the interpretation of individual subtests, the most recent iteration recommends analysis of "clinical clusters" instead (Flanagan & Kaufman, 2004).[2] In contrast, Sattler's (2018) successive-level approach to intelligence test interpretation is quite similar to the IT approach but espouses additional successive levels of analysis involving inter-subtest comparisons and intra-subtest analyses (i.e., examination of patterns and noteworthy qualitative features of responses).

Although the first three waves of intelligence test interpretation differed in important ways, all three were susceptible to the criticism that they were not based on psychological theory. Until only about 20 years ago, standardized tests of intelligence were criticized on the grounds that they were not derived from explicit theories of intelligence (e.g., Brody, 1994). Moreover, the methods of ipsative analysis in the second wave were driven by the results of statistical tests of test score differences that were then confirmed by other assessment data in the formation of clinical hypotheses (e.g., Groth-Marnat, 1997), rather than being guided by theory of intelligence or research on psychopathology.

According to Kamphaus et al. (2018), the field is presently in a fourth wave wherein intelligence theory, research, and test development have been combined to guide the interpretation of intelligence tests. At present, CHC theory is the most widely used framework for both designing and interpreting intelligence tests. Many contemporary tests of intelligence tests are explicitly based on CHC theory (e.g., Kaufman Assessment Battery for Children, Second Edition Normative Update [KABC–II NU]; Kaufman & Kaufman, 2018), while the development of others, such as the WISC–V, were strongly influenced by it. CHC theory also provides the framework for popular test interpretation methods such as cross-battery assessment (Flanagan et al., 2018) and use of the Culture-Linguistic Interpretative Matrices (Ortiz et al., 2018).

With regard to test interpretation practices in the fourth wave, many experts and test developers now recommend that the primary level of clinical interpretation be done at the composite score level with a focus on the pattern of Stratum II cognitive abilities rather than the level of the overall score (e.g., Wechsler, 2014a). Flanagan and Alfonso (2017), for example, stated that "analysis of the primary index scores is a critical, and arguably necessary, component of WISC–V interpretation" (p. 209). Their approach to intelligence test interpretation emphasizes interpretation of the normative strengths and weaknesses of an individual's composite scores. Thus, since the inception of intelligence testing in the early 1900s, their interpretation has shifted from a focus on the elevation of general ability in the early 1900s to an emphasis on shape, scatter, or both in the mid-1900s to the early 2000s and then back to a focus on elevation today.

Although one might reasonably assume that the merging of theory, research, and test development in the fourth wave would result in a consensus on best practices, results of a recent survey by Kranzler et al. (2020a) suggest that there may be more disagreement today among school psychologists about how to interpret tests of intelligence than ever before. Today, some experts argue for an emphasis on the interpretation of normative strengths and weaknesses of composite scores as measures of broad cognitive abilities (e.g., Flanagan & Alfonso, 2017). Others contend that the focus of interpretation should be on ipsative analysis (e.g., Fiorello & Wycoff, 2018; Sattler, 2018), and still others call for a return to an emphasis on the interpretation on the elevation of the overall score (e.g., Benson et al., 2019; Kranzler & Floyd, 2020; McGill et al., 2018; Zaboski et al., 2018).

Research on Intra-Individual (Ipsative) Analysis

Since the beginning of the second wave of intelligence test interpretation more than 75 years ago, a considerable amount of research has been conducted on the validity and utility of the intra-individual interpretation of scatter and profiles of specific cognitive ability test scores. We briefly summarize research in each of these areas (for more in-depth reviews, see Watkins, 2003; Watkins et al., 2005).

Scatter

Binet and Simon (1916) were among the first to hypothesize that the variability of intelligence test performance was an indication of pathology. As Harris and Shakow (1937) stated, "scatter beyond the normal amount has been suggested as a means of distinguishing feebleminded, mentally superior, and psychopathic subjects from normal individuals" (p. 137). Scatter has been operationalized in four different ways. The first method involves calculation of an individual's range of subtest scores by subtracting the lowest score from the highest. In the second, the variance of an individual's subtest scores is computed. Referred to as the profile variability index (PVI), this method is superior to the range because it is based on all subtests instead of only the two most extreme scores. The third method consists of the multivariate analysis of scatter with the Mahalanobis distance statistic (e.g., Crawford & Allan, 1994). The advantage of this method over univariate methods is that it can take into account subtests' means and variances and the inter-correlations among them. The fourth method is an ipsative approach that involves calculating the number of an individual's subtests that are greater than 1 standard error or measurement from their mean subtest scaled score (i.e., $\pm$ 3).

Research using all four methods of scatter analysis has failed to demonstrate that it is useful for differentiating clinical and non-clinical groups of children and youth. For example, Watkins and Worrell (2000) examined the variability of subtest scores on the Wechsler Intelligence Scale for Children–Third Edition (WISC–III; Wechsler, 1991) with 2,200 children and youths from the normative sample and 684 students identified with specific learning disability (SLD) ages 6 to 16 years. For each participant they calculated the number of subtests that deviated more than $\pm$ 3 from the mean of the subtests used to derive the Verbal and Performance IQ indexes and the FSIQ. Diagnostic utility was examined using Receiver Operating Characteristic (ROC) Area Under the Curve (AUC). ROC is a probability curve, and AUC represents the degree of separability at various threshold settings. Values of AUC indicate how well the model distinguishes between two groups, such as non-SLD and SLD. An excellent model has an AUC near 1, and a poor model has an AUC near 0. When the AUC is .50, the model has no class separation capacity whatsoever. Results of their analysis revealed that the AUC ranged from .50 to .53, thereby indicating that subtest scatter differentiated between the SLD and non-SLD groups at or near chance levels.

Watkins (2005) replicated and extended these findings by examining the diagnostic utility of all four operational definitions of subtest scatter on the WISC–III. Participants were 2,200 children and youths from the normative sample and 1,592 students with SLD ages 6 to 16 years. Subgroups of children and youths with specific reading disability (n = 600) and low achievement in reading (n = 846) were also identified. Although the SLD and low achievement groups had lower mean scores than the normative sample, only the range and PVI were statistically significantly different from the normative sample, with small effect sizes. In addition, the four measures of scatter were highly inter-correlated for all groups (rs > .80). To examine the classification accuracy of each measure of scatter, Watkins calculated ROC AUC and found that AUC statistics for the normative-clinical group scatter comparisons ranged from .50 to .55. The results of Watkins's and colleagues research, which were consistent with the findings of other studies, further substantiated the inability of scatter analysis on intelligence tests to differentiate between clinical and non-clinical groups (for a review, see Watkins et al., 2005).

Subtest Profile Analysis

As Watkins and Kush (1994) noted, clinicians have long "attempted to find unique patterns of subtest scores that could differentially diagnose children as suffering from learning disability, emotional disabilities, and [intellectual disability]" (p. 640). Indeed, McGrew and Wendling (2010) more recently opined that "less emphasis should be placed on the overall full-scale IQ and that cognitive assessment should be more selective and focused. For example, there should be selective testing of key markers for screening at-risk children" (p. 651). At the current time, according to the results of a recent survey by Kranzler et al. (2020a), nearly 70% of practicing school psychologists interpret subtest profiles although most also interpret the level of the overall score.

More than 75 specific subtest patterns based on ipsative analysis have been identified for the Wechsler scales alone (McDermott et al., 1992). One of the profiles that has attracted the most research attention is the so-called SCAD profile, which is short for the Symbol Search (S), Coding (C), Arithmetic (A) and Digit Span (D) subtests on the WISC–III (e.g., Watkins, 2005). According to its proponents, a marker of clinical significance is observed when an individual's scores on these subtests are substantially lower than their scores on an estimate of general ability (based on the four subtests of the Perceptual Organization [PO] Index). Evidence for the SCAD profile is based on group difference research showing that a significantly greater proportion of children and youths with disabilities (e.g., SLD and attention-deficit hyperactivity disorder) have larger differences between the SCAD and PO subtests than non-clinical samples. In *Intelligent Testing with the WISC–III*, Kaufman (1994) stated that the SCAD profile, "when interpreted in the context of other relevant information and test data, becomes an important piece of evidence for diagnosing a possible abnormality" (p. 221). However, it is important to note that statistically significant differences between clinical and non-clinical groups do not provide prima facie evidence demonstrating that a particular subtest profile has sufficient diagnostic accuracy for clinical decision-making.

Watkins et al. (1997) conducted the first study of the diagnostic utility of the SCAD profile. Participants included 363 school-age children and youths who had been identified with either SLD (91%) or emotional disability (9%) and had been administered 12 subtests of the WISC–III The non-clinical comparison group consisted of 2,158 children and youths ages 6 to 16 years in the normative sample of the WISC–III with FSIQs greater than 70. SCAD-PO differences of 7, 9, and 12 points were used as decision thresholds. Results of ROC AUC analyses indicated that the AUC across all of these thresholds between groups was .59, which is only slightly better than chance diagnostic accuracy. Watkins et al. also examined the relationship between the SCAD profile and academic achievement for the clinical group after controlling for general ability. Results of these analyses revealed that the SCAD profile does not add importantly to the incremental predictive validity of general ability on the WISC–III for reading, math, and written expression. Results of Watkins's and colleagues study, which are consistent with other investigations on the utility of the SCAD and other profiles of specific cognitive abilities for differential diagnosis, have been consistently negative over the past 30 years (e.g., see McGill et al., 2018).

Why do subtest profiles lack diagnostic utility? One of the main reasons has to do with the temporal stability of intra-individual cognitive strengths and weaknesses identified with ipsative analysis. Research has shown that the overall score on intelligence tests is very stable after school age (e.g., Kranzler & Floyd, 2020). Because subtest scores are used to derive the overall score on intelligence, if the overall score is relatively stable over time but subtest scores are not, this can only mean that subtests contain a great deal of error. In other words, the random error associated with the measure of one subtest cancels out in another when summed to derive the overall score. Watkins and colleagues have conducted a number of studies to examine the reliability of cognitive ability subtest and composite scores over time (Borsuk et al., 2006; Canivez & Watkins, 1998; Styck et al., 2019; Watkins & Canivez, 2004). Watkins and Canivez (2004), for example, examined the temporal stability of 54 subtest composite score strengths and weaknesses derived from the profile analysis literature (e.g., Groth-Marnat, 1997; Kaufman, 1994). Participants were 579 students receiving special education and related services who had been administered the WISC–III twice. The average test-retest interval was 2.80 years (*SD* = 0.55). Results of their study indicated that none of the subtest composites were stable across time. On average, agreement between the cognitive strengths and weaknesses on these subtest composites occurred at chance levels.

Similar results were obtained by Styck et al. (2019), who examined within- and between-person reliability for a sample of 296 children and youths receiving special education and related services. All participants were tested twice on the Wechsler Intelligence Scale for Children–Fourth Edition (WISC–IV; Wechsler, 2003) with an average test-retest interval of 2.84 years. Results of their analyses indicated that within-person reliability was substantially lower than between-person reliability for both subtest and index scores. They concluded that "subscore profiles using subtest and index scores from the WISC–IV do not appear to provide reliable information" (p. 124). In sum, because the results of research on subtest score profile analyses over the past two decades have repeatedly found them to lack clinical utility for differential diagnosis, Watkins (2000) referred to these practices as "shared professional myth."

Utility of Intelligence Tests in the Schools

As Braden and Shaw (2009) stated, "test users administer cognitive tests to students who are experiencing academic difficulties in school under the assumption that doing so will help stakeholders (e.g., educators, support services personnel, and parents) find ways to help students overcome their difficulties" (p. 106). In the schools today, individually administered intelligence tests are primarily used for identifying the causes underlying a student's learning difficulties and for determining eligibility for special education and related services. Toward this end, intelligence tests are commonly administered as a rule-in criterion for the identification of SLD and intellectual disabilities (ID) but are also administered to rule out ID as an explanation of under achievement. In the next section, we examine the empirical evidence supporting the utility of intelligence tests for determining eligibility for special education and related services for children and youths with learning difficulties.

Specific Learning Disability

In 2018–2019, 4.7% of all students enrolled in public schools in the United States—more than 2.3 million students—received special education and related services with specific learning disability (SLD) as their primary disability category (National Center for Education Statistics [NCES], 2020). The largest disability category under IDEA is SLD, comprising approximately 33% of all students with disabilities education. Not surprisingly, Benson et al. (2019) found that school psychologists spend about 25% of their time conducting comprehensive assessments for suspected SLD. Given its prevalence, it is imperative that school psychologists and other school-based professionals reliably distinguish between children and youths with and without SLD.

What Is a Learning Disability?

The term *learning disability* can be defined in different ways. In a broad sense, it refers to a general difficulty with learning that does not meet the criteria for ID. These children and youths are sometimes referred to as *slow learners* because they take longer to grasp concepts as their same-age peers and often do not have the same depth of understanding. In other words, these students are therefore learning *dis-abled* in general. Because academic progress tends to be commensurate with below-average general cognitive ability, their underachievement is expected. In contrast, the narrow sense definition of learning disability refers to *unexpected underachievement*. These are individuals who experience difficulty learning in some areas of academic achievement (e g., reading, writing, or mathematics) but not all. Because their learning difficulties are typically specific to particular achievement domains, IDEA uses the disability category label of SLD. The narrow sense definition is what most people mean when they refer to SLD. At the heart of this definition is the concept of *discrepancy* from expected academic achievement (Grigorenko et al., 2020).

Methods of SLD Eligibility Determination

At the current time, there are three different general approaches for the identification of SLD: (a) IQ–Achievement Discrepancy (IAD), (b) Response-to-Intervention (RtI), and (c) Patterns of Strengths and Weaknesses (PSW). Despite the fact that no consensus definition of SLD exists, at the core of each of these general approaches is the concept of *discrepancy in academic functioning*. All three methods share some core features such as the need to rule out exclusionary criteria (e.g., inadequate educational background, sensory impairment, and ID) but differ markedly in how they define discrepancy in academic functioning and whether intelligence tests are used for identification and how they are interpreted when they are administered. In a recent survey, Benson et al. (2020) found that all three SLD identification approaches are widely used and that state regulations tend to have stronger effects on the identification practices of school psychologists than do such demographic characteristics as age, highest degree obtained, and years of experience. At present more than 37% of school psychologists reported using the IAD framework, 51% reported using the RtI framework, and 53% reported using the PSW framework. Many school psychologists also indicated that they used more than one approach.

   IAD approach. When the precursor to IDEA, the Education for All Handicapped Children Act (P.L. 94-142), was first passed in 1975, the federal definition of SLD required the identification of a "severe discrepancy" between the overall score on an intelligence test (IQ) and at least one domain of academic achievement for eligibility for special education and related services. In the IAD approach, SLD is typically identified when an individual's level of academic achievement in a particular academic domain is substantially below what one would predict based on their IQ. In this approach, IQ is essentially used as a benchmark against which to compare achievement, and a student's academic achievement is assumed to be commensurate with it. Although exclusionary criteria must be ruled out in this approach, discrepancy between IQ and achievement is the primary inclusionary criterion for SLD identification. Over the next three decades, virtually every state used the IAD approach for identifying SLD (Mercer et al., 1996).

   The simplest and most straightforward way to determine the presence of IAD is to determine whether a large difference exists between scores on IQ and achievement tests when scores are expressed in the same metric such as standard-score (e.g., *z*-score) units. One criticism of the IAD approach is that it precludes the identification of low-performing students (without ID) who have serious educational needs for special education and related services. However, given that these children and youths are performing at a level that is commensurate with their IQ, their levels of IQ and achievement are not sufficiently discrepant to warrant identification as SLD. In addition, because it is often difficult to observe a severe enough discrepancy until as late as the third grade, the IAD approach has been referred to as a wait-to-fail model (e.g., Vaughn & Fuchs, 2003).

   The simple discrepancy model, however, has also been criticized on psychometric grounds primarily because it does not account for *regression toward the mean*. Regression toward the mean refers to the fact that when two variables are correlated (imperfectly), as general intelligence and achievement are, an individual's score on the predicted variable tends to be not as extreme as their score on the predictor. Also, the more extreme the score on the predictor is, the more that score is subject to regression. Because of regression, some degree of academic underachievement is predictable for students with high IQs, and the opposite is true for individuals scoring near the bottom of the IQ distribution. When regression to the mean is not taken into account in the identification of SLD in the IAD approach, the result is the over-identification of children with above-average IQs and the under-identification of children with below-average IQs.

IAD regression models, therefore, are generally seen as an improvement over the simple discrepancy model for determining significant IQ-achievement discrepancies. In IAD regression models, an individual's obtained level of achievement is compared with their predicted level, which is calculated by regressing IQ on achievement. In this way, real achievement is compared with expected achievement. If the obtained achievement score is significantly below the level of achievement one would predict based on the student's IQ, then a discrepancy is said to exist. Thus a regression model of SLD identification is actually an *expected-actual achievement discrepancy model* and not an IAD model.

Nevertheless, regardless of the model used, research has shown that the identification of disability using the IAD approach tends to have poor diagnostic accuracy and does not reliably identify SLD (e.g., Fletcher & Miciak, 2017). The poor decision accuracy in the IAD approach stems largely from measurement error due to the use of difference scores. Although the overall score on every major intelligence test tends to have excellent internal reliability and stability, difference scores are notoriously unreliable. Consequently, the diagnostic accuracy of the IAD approach is rather poor even when using a regression model because eligibility determination involves making a dichotomous decision based on the determination of a severe discrepancy that is calculated using standard scores on continuous variables that are measured imperfectly at one point in time. As Francis et al. (2005) asserted, "a single assessment at a single point of time is not psychometrically adequate for determinations that have a significant long-term impact on a child's development" (p. 104).

RtI approach. To encourage the use of SLD identification procedures that are more relevant to classroom instruction, a provision was added during reauthorization of IDEA in 2004 that allows the use of RtI. RtI refers to "a process that determines if the child responds to scientific, research-based intervention as a part of the evaluation procedures" (IDEA, 2004, see Section 614[b][6]). In the RtI approach, there are different methods used for the determination of SLD. After ruling out exclusionary criteria, eligibility determination in the RtI approach is based on the presence of an academic performance discrepancy, inadequate rate of progress, or both. Thus, in this approach SLD is identified when an individual's level of achievement in a particular academic area falls substantially below what one would predict based on their age- or grade-peers rather than on general cognitive ability. Because intelligence tests are not pertinent to the rule-in criteria for SLD in the RtI approach, they are typically not used for identification but they may be included to rule out ID as a cause of under-achievement (e.g., Kranzler & Floyd, 2020).

In the RtI approach, SLD is best conceptualized as an inadequate response to intervention (Fletcher & Miciak, 2017). At the current time there are three main ways to identify inadequate response to intervention and resultant unexpected under-achievement in the RTI literature. The first method involves examination of the rate of academic growth as measured by the slope of curriculum-based measures (CBM) of basic academic skills scores over time. In the second, level of academic achievement to a final benchmark at the end of instruction is measured either by a standardized achievement test or CBM. The third method involves examination of a dual-discrepancy based on CBM slope over time and comparison to an achievement benchmark at the end of instruction. In each of these methods, under-achievement is defined by performance that falls significantly below a predetermined cut-point in comparison to same age- or grade-peers using either school, district, or national norms. One advantage of RtI over other SLD identification approaches is that it is based on more than one assessment at more than one point in time, which is the Achilles' heel of the IAD approach.

Does the RtI approach identify the same children and youths as SLD as the IAD approach? Shinn (2007) asserted that "using a RtI model, it is not expected that different students will be identified as SLD than those identified historically" (p. 601). Reynolds (2009), however, contended that the RtI approach will result in the over-identification of children and youths with below average general cognitive ability (i.e., slow learners). As he stated, "if intellectual functioning is related to learning rate or complexity (and it is), this outcome is mathematically inevitable" (p. 18). In an examination of this hypothesis, Kranzler et al. (2020b) found that the overall IQ score on the Kaufman Brief Intelligence Test–Second Edition (KBIT–2; Kaufman & Kaufman, 2004b) for a group of students with SLD ($n = 30$) who had been identified in an RtI model was statistically significantly lower than that for a group of same-age peers ($n = 249$) in general education, with a large effect size. For the SLD group, almost three-fourths (73.3%) had IQ scores that were below the mean of the normative sample of the KBIT–2 and almost half (43.3%) were below 90. Results of their study, therefore, support Reynolds's (2009) contention that use of the RtI approach will result in the over-identification of children and youths with below-average IQs.

Thus use of the current RtI approach alters the conceptualization of SLD from the traditional narrow sense (unexpected underachievement) to the broad sense (expected underachievement). Kranzler et al. (2020b), however, proposed the use of a modified RtI approach in which SLD is identified when an individual's level of academic achievement in a particular academic domain is substantially below the level one would predict based on their general cognitive ability after ruling out exclusionary criteria. The primary rule-in criterion in their model is inadequate response to intervention within the current RtI framework, but in their model expected achievement is based not on comparison with same age- or grade-peers but on comparison CBM slopes or benchmarks after being regressed on IQ. In their modified model, therefore, unexpected achievement is achievement that is discrepant from that expected based on an individual's level of psychometric *g*. Use of this model would circumvent the measurement issues that plague IAD approach while enabling the identification of children and youths displaying unexpected underachievement at all levels of cognitive ability. Further research is needed to examine the viability of the modified RtI model before its implementation, however

PSW Approaches. An important development since the reauthorization of IDEA in 2004 is the advancement of new approaches for the identification of SLD based on the analysis of patterns of strengths and weaknesses (PSW) in specific cognitive abilities measured by intelligence tests. Although not explicitly outlined in federal law, PSW approaches are permitted under the provision of alternative research-based practices in IDEA. At the current time, the three most prominent PSW approaches are the Concordance-Discordance model (C/D; Fiorello et al., 2012), the Dual Discrepancy/Consistency model (DD/C; Flanagan et al., 2018), and the Discrepancy/Consistency model (D/C; Naglieri & Feifer, 2018). PSW proponents argue that SLD identification must include tests of cognitive ability to measure basic psychological processes to be consistent with the federal definition of SLD. In contrast to the IQ–achievement and RtI discrepancy approaches, the PSW methods define SLD as unexpected academic underachievement (i.e., general intelligence in the average range or above and academic weakness in one or more areas) and corresponding weakness in one or more specific cognitive abilities. Thus in PSW models, SLD results from deficits in cognitive processing that are held to be importantly related to different academic areas.

In a recent survey, Maki and Adams (2022) found that of the school psychologists who reported using of the PSW framework, the DD/C model is by far the most widely used. Flanagan et al. (2010) asserted that it "stems in large measure from the research on the relations between cognitive abilities and processes and academic outcomes. That is, the collected data should demonstrate meaningful and empirically supported relations between specific cognitive and academic deficits" (p. 742). In their model, the identification of SLD involves examination of achievement and cognitive data to determine whether an individual displays a PSW characterized by dual discrepancy-consistency within an otherwise normal cognitive ability profile. After ruling out exclusionary criteria, in the DD/C model PSW criteria for SLD are met when (a) general intelligence falls in the average range or higher (standard score of $\geq$ 90); (b) a weakness is found for at least one broad cognitive ability (standard score < 90); (c) a statistically significant difference is observed between general ability and one or more cognitive weaknesses; (d) a weakness is found for at least one academic achievement area (standard score < 90); and (e) a statistically significant difference is observed between general intelligence and one or more academic weaknesses.

What evidence supports the utility of the DD/C PSW model? As Fletcher and Miciak (2017) stated, the following five arguments have been presented in support of the use of the PSW approach for SLD identification: (a) federal legislation mandates cognitive assessments for SLD identification; (b) clinicians using tests of cognitive ability make better diagnostic decisions; (c) examination of PSW effectively discriminates between SLD and slow learners; (d) tests of cognitive ability have treatment utility; and (e) cognitive abilities are importantly correlated with achievement domains (also see McGill et al., 2016). Although Fletcher and Miciak effectively discredited the first four of these arguments, broad and narrow cognitive abilities of CHC theory are positively correlated with different domains of academic achievement (e.g., Kranzler & Floyd, 2020). Results of a recent meta-analysis by Zaboski et al. (2019) on the relations between general and specific cognitive abilities of CHC theory and academic achievement, however, revealed that only one broad cognitive ability, Comprehension-Knowledge, had a medium-to-large effect size for the prediction of basic reading, reading comprehension, basic math, and math calculation with the largest effects for reading with older students. The amount of variance predicted by other broad cognitive abilities was less than 10%. In contrast, psychometric g had by far the strongest relation to achievement across all academic domains and for all age groups often accounting for more variance than all of the broad cognitive abilities combined.

It is also important to note that "demonstrating that cognitive measures and achievement are correlated does not establish that such measures are related to intervention outcomes or provide value-added information to identification" (Fletcher & Miciak, 2017, p. 3). A number of studies have examined whether the PSW methods are capable of reliably grouping children and youths with and without SLD (e.g., Kranzler et al., 2016, 2019, Miciak et al., 2014, 2018; Stuebing et al., 2012; Taylor et al., 2017). Results of these studies have consistently found that the PSW methods do not reliably identify SLD. In fact, in the DD/C method, Kranzler et al. (2019) found that the odds of observing a weakness in an area of academic achievement and a corresponding weakness in a cognitive ability that is supposedly meaningfully and empirically related to that area of achievement is worse than flipping a coin. Taken as a whole, research suggests that use of the PSW methods have a very low probability of accurately identifying true SLD.

Grigorenko et al. (2020) stated,

> It has been difficult to agree on the best way to identify SLDs, although there is consensus that their core is unexpected underachievement. A source of active research and controversy is whether "unexpectedness" is best identified by applying solely exclusionary criteria (i.e., simple low achievement), inclusionary criteria based on uneven cognitive development (e.g., academic skills lower than IQ or another aptitude measure, such as listening comprehension), or evidence of persisting difficulties . . . despite effective instruction. (p. 39)

The diagnosis of SLD is made by multidisciplinary teams in schools. IDEA (2004) provides a definition of SLD and the legal underpinnings for the identification process. At the state and district levels, however, local rules and regulations define the required steps in the assessment process within individual schools. Regardless of the regulations used to diagnose SLD, it is important to follow best-practice recommendations for the identification of SLD such as those by the National Association of School Psychologists (2010) and the National Joint Committee on Learning Disabilities (2010) whether intelligence tests are administered or not.

Intellectual Disability

In contrast to SLD, students with ID as their primary disability category compose only 6% of those receiving special education services in the United States. That is 0.8% of students (about 100,000 students) in the public schools (NCES, 2020). This rate of cases is consistent with and slightly lower than the proportion of the population affected by ID, which appears to be around 1% (McKenzie et al., 2016). As the rate from the NCES reflects only the primary eligibility category and not multiple disability categories, this lower rate is understandable. Even with ID's lower prevalence than SLD, school psychologists and other school-based professionals should be able to determine when the condition exists and when other conditions better account for school-based learning problems.

What Is an Intellectual Disability?

The disability condition now known as ID stands in stark contrast to SLD in that there is little debate—and in fact general consensus—regarding how it should be defined. ID is a developmental disability that surfaces early in development and continues to be associated with limitations in functioning in society (or risk of such) throughout adulthood. All the most prominent definitions of ID highlight (a) deficits in intellectual functioning, (b) deficits in adaptive functioning, and (c) onset during the developmental period (APA, 2013; IDEA, 2004; Schalock et al., 2021). For example, the United States federal definition, supporting special education law, defines ID as significantly subaverage general intellectual functioning, existing concurrently with deficits in adaptive behavior and manifested during the developmental period, that adversely affects a child's educational performance (IDEA, 2004). In comparison, the most recent and most prominent definition of ID across the globe (Schalock et al., 2021) stated that it is

> characterized by significant limitations both in intellectual functioning and in adaptive behavior as expressed by conceptual, social, and practical adaptive skills. The disability originates during the developmental period, which is defined operationally as before the individual attains age 22. (p. 13)

Despite these commonalities across definitions of the condition, the terminology used to describe ID has evolved substantially throughout the past century and not been standard across special education guidelines across states. For example, terms such as *mental retardation*, *cognitive disability*, *cognitive impairment*, *mental disability*, *cognitive delay*, and *intellectual impairment* have all been employed. Only during the past 10 to 15 years has the consensus term emerged in ID (McNicholas et al., 2018; Schalock et al., 2010).

Methods of ID Eligibility Determination

Assessments designed to identify ID require that multiple methods be employed. Following the definition of ID, intelligence tests are typically administered to produce a measure of intellectual function, and adaptive behavior rating scales and interviews are typically given to produce measures of conceptual, social, and practical adaptive skills. In contrast to SLD, achievement tests may be administered but their results are rarely considered central in determining the presence or absence of ID. Additional methods may include interviews with parents and caregivers to identify the history of the condition (to meet the onset during the developmental period criterion) and other related health and mental health conditions and behavior problems. A medical evaluation and observations in naturalistic settings (e.g., classrooms) may also be conducted.

Definitions of ID uniformly require that evidence of the limitations in intellectual functioning be revealed through an IQ equal to or more than two standard deviations below the normative mean, which is typically an IQ of approximately 70 or below. Although the federal definition of ID does not specify exactly what "significantly subaverage" means, McNicholas et al. (2018) and Polloway et al. (2017) found that the vast majority of states specify an IQ threshold of approximately 70 or below as a marker of ID. There is also increasing recognition that measurement error affects all applied measurements. As the most prominent rule-in criterion for ID, almost half of all state special education regulations require consideration of flexible cut-offs for IQ scores (McNicholas et al., 2018).

Although a low IQ has long been the pathognomonic feature of ID and prominent definitions and special education regulations have delineated both IQ (versus index or subtest scores) and its threshold in indicating deficits (approximately 70), there is greater variation in the scores employed used to identify adaptive behavior deficits and fewer specific parameters to follow. As noted previously, Schalock et al. (2010), Schalock et al. (2021), and the APA (2013) described adaptive behaviors as falling into three domains. Conceptual skills include higher-order thinking and achievement-oriented skills such as expressive and receptive language skills as well as reading, math, and writing. Social skills pertain to those competencies necessary for interpersonal interactions with others in school and community settings and also include personal responsibility, self-esteem, and rule following. Practical skills are evident in activities of daily living, including self-care and personal safety. However, few states are specific in recommending consideration of these three domains. In fact, most states refer only in general terms to deficits in adaptive behaviors.

Differential Diagnosis and Comorbidities

With three criteria for ID (the third being age of onset during the developmental period) and their assessment in mind, the process of differential diagnosis of ID can be undertaken. A thorough assessment helps to ensure that other recognized conditions are eliminated as the primary causes of the symptoms of ID. Both Farmer and Floyd (2018) and Floyd et al. (2021) addressed this process. In particular, Farmer and Floyd highlighted SLD, autism spectrum disorder (ASD), and language disorder, among other conditions, because of their strong similarities. As such, it is important for clinicians to be well versed in a variety of educational and behavioral problems of infancy, childhood, and adolescence in order to determine when other conditions better explain a deficit in intellectual functioning and adaptive behavior.

Exclusionary Criteria

In a manner consistent with the exclusionary factors considered during assessment of SLD, the process of identifying ID must also consider exclusionary factors. Some factors overlap with SLD whereas others better explain the intellectual and adaptive deficits seen primarily in ID. Linguistic and cultural differences should be examined as influences. Limited English proficiency might depress both scores from most intelligence tests as well as ratings of conceptual skills, especially language skills, and limited acculturation might lead to lower scores from such tests and diminished displays of adaptive behaviors in school and community settings. Vision and hearing deficits as well as motor impairment should also be eliminated as potential causes of ID. McNicholas et al. (2018) determined that 76% to 86% of state regulations describing ID explicitly stated that these exclusionary conditions should be considered before concluding special education services for ID are needed. It follows that tests can be selected to eliminate or at least drastically reduce the effects of these influences on test scores (Kranzler & Floyd, 2020).

Other Considerations Not Due to ID Criteria but Clinical Lore in Intelligence Tests Interpretation

As noted earlier in this chapter, the third-wave IT approach (Kaufman, 1979, 1994) to intelligence test interpretation had a very strong influence on the practice of assessment of children and youths for well more than a quarter of a century. Even considering the long-standing consensus definition of the condition now called ID, some of the central practices of the IT approach have compounded the complexity of ID assessment and likely undermined the accuracy of interpretations drawn from the most prevalent intelligence tests administered to those suspected of having ID. In particular, in cases in which there were statistically significant differences between the scores used to derive the overall score for an individual, the validity of the IQ was questioned and the interpretation of the IQ was discouraged. Farmer and Floyd (2018) noted that this practice likely had profound negative effects on countless numbers of individuals with ID as it affected generations of "intelligent testers" and even influenced some guidelines for identifying ID around the turn of the millennium (e.g., National Research Council, 2002).

Three studies conducted by Watkins and colleagues have shown that variability across composite scores associated with IQ do not undermine the IQ's predictive power. For example, using large data sets that included children and youths with and without disabilities, Watkins et al. (2007) revealed that the relations between IQs and concurrent reading and mathematics scores did not differ across groups of children and youths formed based on the extent of variation in composite score profiles and matched on IQs. Applying the same design, Kotz et al. (2008) offered similar conclusions after examining relations between IQs and two co-normed achievement subtests. More importantly, Freberg et al. (2008) extended these findings with similarly defined groups while considering IQs and achievement test scores obtained across a three-year interval. Again, these predictive relations were not attenuated by variability in composite score profiles.

Across these studies and numerous analyses within them, one might have anticipated, by chance, that composite score profile variability would attenuate (or accentuate) some relation between IQs and academic achievement scores that would suggest that this variation was meaningful. However, there appears to be no evidence supporting this claim—as well as plenty of counterevidence.

Inspired by the sophisticated analyses and skepticism made manifest in publications from Watkins and his colleagues (e.g., Watkins & Kush, 1994; Watkins et al., 2005), Bergeron and Floyd (2006, 2013) examined the intelligence test score profiles of children and youths with ID in order to critically evaluate common assumptions stemming from the IT approach. Driving this evaluation was an existing assumption that most individuals with ID have flat score profiles (i.e., without substantial variation). Furthermore, they endeavored to shed light on whether such presumed lack of variation across scores would be prototypical and potentially diagnostically useful when considering ID.

Bergeron and Floyd (2006) targeted composite score profiles of children and youths with ID receiving special education services as well as their matched comparisons. Although almost every participant obtained an IQ of 70 or below on the Woodcock-Johnson III Tests of Cognitive Abilities (Woodcock et al., 2001), the composites formed from the same subtests varied substantially. In particular, composite score scatter (i.e., relative strengths and weaknesses as defined by the IT approach; Kaufman, 1994) was far more common among those with ID (in 80% of cases) compared to matched comparisons (57%). Furthermore, 77% of participants produced at least a single composite score in the Low Average range (deviation IQ scores from 80 to 89) or higher on at least one part score and more than 37% produced a composite in the Average range (90 to 110) or higher. Clearly both groups demonstrated significant profile variability and something other than a flat profile.

In a follow-up study, Bergeron and Floyd (2013) advanced understanding of the effects of the IT approach on ID eligibility. They employed samples of children and youths with ID who completed the Wechsler Intelligence Scale for Children–Fourth Edition (WISC–IV; Wechsler, 2003), the Kaufman Assessment Battery for Children–Second Edition (KABC–II; Kaufman & Kaufman, 2004a), or the Differential Abilities Scales–Second Edition (DAS–II; Elliott, 2007). Results revealed that a substantial number of cases (although not as many as in Bergeron and Floyd 2006) produced composites scores in the Low Average range or higher: WISC–IV (45%), KABC–II (52%), and DAS–II (33%). The number producing scores in the Average range or higher was up to 17% of cases in one data set. Despite this lower score variation than in their prior study, these results indicate that if profile variation (at least in the form of normative scores in the Low Average range or higher) signaled the need to invalidate IQ, a third or more of individuals with ID (and up to 52%) would not be diagnosed with the condition. This is an unacceptably high number of false negatives.

More recently, analyses completed by W. Joel Schneider using the WISC–V norming sample data and reported in Floyd et al. (2021) revealed that the typical person with an IQ of 70 has at least one WISC–V index score in the Average range of 90 or higher. It is clear that the practice of invalidating IQs when their components are discrepant is particularly problematic when applied to cases of ID. This fact was noted in the most recent guidelines for the identification of ID offered by the American Association on Intellectual and Developmental Disabilities (Schalock et al., 2021) as Freberg et al. (2008), Watkins et al. (2007), and Bergeron and Floyd (2013) were cited as evidence of the problematic nature of this practice.

A Final Word on the Utility of Intelligence Tests for ID Identification

As we reiterated above, the definition of ID and recommendations for how to identify the condition are generally invariant across professional groups and special education regulations. When the basic criteria for ID are met, most would conclude that ID has been identified and other conditions, like SLD, can be ruled out. However, some conditions like ASD and ID commonly co-occur (Matson & Shoemaker, 2009) so the task must shift from differential diagnosis to consideration of comorbidities. Research by Watkins and colleagues and others has revealed that variation in score profiles does not invalidate the central score in ID identification, the IQ, and it should in no way contribute to a differential diagnosis. Alternately, bigger threats to the accurate identification of ID include (a) the Flynn effect, which inflates the scores produced by older tests (Flynn, 1984); and (b) psychometric sampling error, which may lead scores to be lower or higher than a person's true general intelligence due to systematic error stemming from sampling only a subset of specific abilities across items or subtests (Jensen, 1998). Furthermore, it is certain that cultural and linguistic differences noncompliance during testing, and deliberate faking can undermine valid testing (Floyd et al., 2021).

Conclusion

The measurement of intelligence is viewed by many to be one of psychology's greatest contributions to society (Nisbett et al., 2012). Not only is the overall score on tests of intelligence one of the most reliable and valid of all psychological variables, it is more predictive of many important social outcomes, including academic achievement, than any other measurable psychological trait (Jensen, 1998). Originally created for use in the schools to identify children and youths who were at risk for educational failure based on their general cognitive ability, intelligence tests have remained a cornerstone of practice in school psychology (e.g., Wasserman, 2018). The overall score on intelligence tests has been robustly substantiated for the identification of disabilities under IDEA. The utility of the interpretation of specific cognitive ability strengths and weaknesses, however, either through the analysis of ipsative profiles or the normative examination of index scores, is currently without empirical support for the identification of disabilities.

Notes

1 Information on the development of the WISC–V and the reliability and validity evidence supporting its use can be found in *Technical and Interpretive Manual* (Wechsler, 2014b) and in reviews (e.g., Canivez & Watkins, 2016).

2 Clinical clusters consist of two or three subtests that are grouped based on theory and relevant research that go beyond the full-scale and index scores.

References

American Psychiatric Association. (2013). *Diagnostic and statistical manual of mental disorders* (5th ed.). Author.

Benson, N. F., Floyd, R. G., Kranzler, J. H., Eckert, T. L., Fefer, S. A., & Morgan, G. B. (2019). Test use and assessment practices of school psychologists: Findings from the 2017 National Survey of Assessment Practices in School Psychology. *Journal of School Psychology, 72*, 29–48. https://doi.org/10.1016/j.jsp.2018.12.004

Benson, N. F., Maki, K. E., Floyd, R. G., Kranzler, J. H., Eckert, T. L., & Fefer, S. A. (2020). A national survey of school psychologists' practices in identifying specific learning disabilities. *School Psychology, 35*, 146–157. https://doi.org/10.1037/spq0000344

Bergeron, R., & Floyd, R. G. (2006). Broad cognitive abilities of children with mental retardation: An analysis of group and individual profiles. *American Journal on Mental Retardation, 111*, 417–432. https://doi.org/10.1352/0895-8017(2006)111[417:bcaocw]2.0.co;2

Bergeron, R., & Floyd, R. G. (2013). Individual part score profiles of children with intellectual disability: A descriptive analysis across three intelligence tests. *School Psychology Review, 42*, 22–38. https://doi.org/10.1080/02796015.2013.12087489

Binet, A., & Simon, T. (1916). *The intelligence of the feebleminded*. Williams and Wilkins.

Borsuk, E. R., Watkins, M. W., & Canivez, G. L. (2006). Long-term stability of membership in a Wechsler Intelligence Scale for Children-Third Edition (WISC–III) subtest core profile taxonomy. *Journal of Psychoeducational Assessment, 24*(1), 52–68. https://doi.org/10.1177/0734282905285225

Braden, J. P., & Shaw, S. R. (2009). Intervention validity of cognitive assessment: Knowns, unknowables, and unknowns. *Assessment for Effective Intervention, 34*(2), 106–115. https://doi.org/10.1177/1534508407313013

Brody, N. (1994). Cognitive abilities. *Psychological Science, 5*(2), 63–68. https://doi.org/10.1111/j.1467-9280.1994.tb00632.x

Brown, A. W. (1946). Review of Diagnostic Psychological Testing. Vol. 1. [Review of the book Diagnostic Psychological Testing. Vol. I. D. Rapaport, M. M. Gill, R. Schafer & R. R. Holt]. *Psychological Bulletin, 43*(5), 477–479. https://doi.org/10.1037/h0049564

Canivez, G. L., Dombrowski, S. C., & Watkins, M. W. (2018). Factor structure of the WISC–V for four standardization age groups: Exploratory and hierarchical factor analyses with the 16 primary and secondary subtests. *Psychology in the Schools, 55*(7), 741–769. https://doi.org/10.1002/pits.22138

Canivez, G. L., & Watkins, M. W. (1998). Long-term stability of the Wechsler Intelligence Scale for Children-Third Edition. *Psychological Assessment, 10*(3), 285–291. https://doi.org/10.1037//1040-3590.10.3.285

Canivez, G. L., & Watkins, M. W. (2016). Review of the Wechsler Intelligence Scale for Children—Fifth edition: Critique, commentary, and independent analyses. In A. S. Kaufman, S. E. Raiford, & D. L. Coalson (Eds.), *Intelligent testing with the WISC–V* (pp. 683–702). Wiley.

Coan, R. W. (1964). Facts, factors, and artifacts: The quest for psychological meaning. *Psychological Review, 71*(2), 123–140. https://doi.org/10.1037/h0043231

Crawford, J. R., & Allan, K. M. (1994). The Mahalanobis distance index of WAIS–R subtest scatter: Psychometric properties in a healthy UK sample. *British Journal of Clinical Psychology, 33*(1), 65–69. https://doi.org/10.1111/j.2044-8260.1994.tb01094.x

Cronbach, L. J., & Gleser, G. C. (1953). Assessing similarity between profiles. *Psychological Bulletin, 50*(6), 456–473. https://doi.org/10.1037/h0057173

Dombrowski, S. C., Canivez, G. L., & Watkins, M. W. (2018). Factor structure of the 10 WISC–V primary subtests across four standardization age groups. *Contemporary School Psychology, 22*, 90–104. https://doi.org/10.1007/s40688-017-0125-2

Elliott, C. D. (2007). *Differential Ability Scales-Second Edition*. Harcourt Assessment.

Farmer, R. L., & Floyd, R. G. (2018). Use of intelligence tests in the identification of children and adolescents with intellectual disability. In D. P. Flanagan & E. M. McDonough (Eds.), *Contemporary intellectual assessment: Theories, tests, and issues* (4th ed., pp. 643–661). Guilford Press.

Fiorello, C. A., Hale, J. B., & Wycoff, K. L. (2012). Cognitive hypothesis testing: Linking test results to the real world. In D. P. Flanagan & P. L. Harrison (Eds.), *Contemporary intellectual assessment: Theories, tests, and issues* (3rd ed., pp. 484–496). Guilford Press.

Fiorello, C. A., & Wycoff, K. L. (2018). Cognitive hypothesis testing: Linking test results to the real world. In D. P. Flanagan & E. M. McDonough (Eds.), *Contemporary intellectual assessment: Theories, tests, and issues* (4th ed., pp. 715–730). Guilford Press.

Flanagan, D. P., & Alfonso, V. C. (2017). *Essentials of WISC–V assessment*. Wiley.

Flanagan, D. P., Costa, M., Palma, K., Leahy, M. A., Alfonso, V. C., & Ortiz, S. O. (2018). Cross-battery assessment, the cross-battery assessment software system, and the assessment-intervention connection. In D. P. Flanagan & E. M. McDonough (Eds.), *Contemporary intellectual assessment: Theories, tests, and issues* (4th ed., pp. 731–776). Guilford Press.

Flanagan, D. P., Fiorello, C. A., Ortiz, S. O. (2010). Enhancing practice through application of Cattell-Horn-Carroll theory and research: A "third" approach to specific learning disability identification. *Psychology in the Schools, 47*(7), 739–760. https://doi.org/10.1002/pits.20501

Flanagan, D. P., & Kaufman, A. S. (2004). *Essentials of WISC–IV assessment.* Wiley & Sons.

Flanagan, D. P., Ortiz, S. O., & Alfonso, V. C. (2013). *Essentials of cross-battery assessment* (3rd ed.). Wiley.

Fletcher, J. M., & Miciak, J. (2017). Comprehensive cognitive assessments are not necessary for the identification and treatment of learning disabilities. *Archives of Clinical Neuropsychology, 32*(1), 2–7. https://doi.org/10.1093/arclin/acw103

Floyd, R. G., Farmer, R. L., Schneider, W. J., & McGrew, K. S. (2021). Theories and measurement of intelligence. In L. M. Glidden (Ed.), *APA handbook of intellectual and developmental disabilities* (Vol. 1, pp. 386–424). American Psychological Association.

Flynn, J. R. (1984). The mean IQ of Americans: Massive gains 1932 to 1978. *Psychological Bulletin, 95*(1), 29–51. https://doi.org/10.1037//0033-2909.95.1.29

Francis, D. J., Fletcher, J. M., Stuebing, K. K., Lyon, R. L., Shaywitz, B. A., & Shaywitz, S. E. (2005). Psychometric approaches to the identification of LD: IQ and achievement scores are not sufficient. *Journal of Learning Disabilities, 38*(2), 98–108. https://doi.org/10.1177/00222194050380020101

Freberg, M. E., Vandiver, B. J., Watkins, M. W., & Canivez, G. L. (2008). Significant factor score variability and the validity of the WISC–III full scale IQ in predicting later academic achievement. *Applied Neuropsychology, 15*(2), 131–139. https://doi.org/10.1080/09084280802084010

Grigorenko, E. L., Compton, D. L., Fuchs, L. S., Wagner, R. K., Willcutt, E. G., & Fletcher, J. M. (2020). Understanding, educating, and supporting children with specific learning disabilities: 50 years of science and practice. *American Psychologist, 75*(1) 37–51. https://doi.org/10.1037/amp0000452

Groth-Marnat, G. (1997). *Handbook of psychological assessment* (3rd ed.). Wiley.

Harris, A. J., & Shakow, D. (1937). The clinical significance of numerical measures of scatter on the Stanford-Binet. *Psychological Bulletin, 34*(3), 134–150. https://doi.org/10.1037/h0058420

Individuals with Disabilities Education Improvement Act of 2004, Pub. L. No. 108-446 (2004).

Jensen, A. R. (1998). *The g factor: The science of mental ability*. Praeger.

Kamphaus, R. W., Winsor, A. P., Rowe, E. W., & Kim, S. (2018). A history of intelligence test interpretation. In D. P. Flanagan & E. M. McDonough (Eds.), *Contemporary intellectual assessment* (4th ed., pp. 56–70). Guilford Press.

Kaufman, A. S. (1979). *Intelligent testing with the WISC–R*. Wiley.

Kaufman, A. S. (1990). *Assessing adolescent and adult intelligence.* Allyn & Bacon.

Kaufman, A. S. (1994). *Intelligent testing with the WISC–III*. Wiley.

Kaufman, A. S., & Kaufman, N. L. (2004a). *Kaufman Assessment Battery for Children, Second Edition*. American Guidance Service.

Kaufman, A. S., & Kaufman, N. L. (2004b). *Kaufman Brief Intelligence Test, Second Edition*. American Guidance Service.

Kaufman, A. S., & Kaufman, N. L. (2018). *Kaufman Assessment Battery for Children, Second Edition Normative Update*. Pearson.

Kotz, K. M., Watkins, M. W., & McDermott, P. A. (2008). Validity of the general conceptual ability score from the Differential Ability Scales as a function of significant and rare interfactor variability. *School Psychology Review, 37*(2), 261–278. https://doi.org/10.1080/02796015.2008.12087899

Kranzler, J. H., & Floyd, R. G. (2020). *Assessing intelligence in children and adolescents: A practical guide for evidence-based assessment* (2nd ed.). Rowman & Littlefield.

Kranzler, J. H., Floyd, R. G., Benson, N., Zaboski, B., & Thibodaux, L. (2016). Classification agreement analysis of cross-battery assessment in the identification of specific learning disorders in children and youth. *International Journal of School & Educational Psychology, 3*(3), 124–136. https://doi.org/10.1080/21683603.2016.1155515

Kranzler, J. H., Gilbert, K., Robert, C. R., Floyd, R. G., & Benson, N. (2019). Further examination of a critical assumption underlying the dual discrepancy/consistency approach to SLD identification. *School Psychology Review, 48*(3), 207–221. https://doi.org/10.17105/spr-2018-0008.v48-3

Kranzler, J. H., Maki, K. E., Benson, N. F., Floyd, R. G., & Fefer, S. A. (2020a). How do school psychologists interpret intelligence tests for the identification of specific learning disabilities? *Contemporary School Psychology*, *24*, 445–456. https://doi.org/10.1007/s40688-020-00274-0

Kranzler, J. H., Yaraghchi, M., Matthews, K., & Otero-Valles, L. (2020b). Does the response-to-intervention model fundamentally alter the traditional conceptualization of specific learning disability? *Contemporary School Psychology*, *24*, 80–88. https://doi.org/10.1007/s40688-019-00256-x

Maki, K. E. & Adams, S. R. (2019). A current landscape of specific learning disability identification: Training, practices, and implications. *Psychology in the Schools*, *56*(1), 18–31. https://doi.org/10.1002/pits.22179

Maki, K. E., & Adams, S. R. (2022). Special education evaluation practices and procedures: Implications for referral and eligibility decision-making. *Contemporary School Psychology*, *26*, 350–358. https://doi.org/10.1007/s40688-020-00335-4.

Matson, J. L., & Shoemaker, M. (2009). Intellectual disability and its relationship to autism spectrum disorders. *Research in Developmental Disabilities*, *30*(6), 107–1114. https://doi.org/10.1016/j.ridd.2009.06.003

McDermott, P. A., Fantuzzo, J. W., Glutting, J. J., Watkins, M. W., & Baggaley, A. R. (1992). Illusions of meaning in the ipsative assessment of children's ability. *The Journal of Special Education*, *25*(4), 504–526. https://doi.org/10.1177/002246699202500407

McGill, R. J., Dombrowski, S. C., & Canivez, G. L. (2018). Cognitive profile analysis in school psychology: History, issues, and continued concerns. *Journal of School Psychology*, *71*, 108–121. https://doi.org/10.1016/j.jsp.2018.10.007

McGill, R. J., Styck, K. M., Palomares, R. S., & Hass, M. R. (2016). Critical issues in specific learning disability identification: What we need to know about the PSW model. *Learning Disability Quarterly*, *39*(3), 159–170. https://doi.org/10.1177/0731948715618504

McGrew, K. S., & Wendling, B. J. (2010). Cattell-Horn-Carroll cognitive-ability achievement relations: What we have learned from the past 20 years of research. *Psychology in the Schools*, *47*(7), 651–675. https://doi.org/10.1002/pits.20497

McKenzie, K., Milton, M., Smith, G., & Oullette-Kuntz, H. (2016). Systematic review of the prevalence and incidence of intellectual disabilities: Current trends and issues. *Current Developmental Disorders Reports*, *3*, 104–115. https://doi.org/10.1007/s40474-016-0085-7

McLean, J. E., Reynolds, C. R, & Kaufman, A. S. (1990). WAIS-R subtest scatter using the profile variability index. *Psychological Assessment: A Journal of Consulting and Clinical Psychology*, *2*(3), 289–292. https://doi.org/10.1037/1040-3590.2.3.289

McNicholas, P. J., Floyd, R. G., Woods, I. L., Singh, L. J., Manguno, M. S., & Maki, K. E. (2018). State special education criteria for identifying intellectual disability: A review following revised diagnostic criteria and Rosa's Law. *School Psychology Quarterly*, *33*(1), 75–82. https://doi.org/10.1037/spq0000208

Mercer, C. D., Jordan, L., Allsopp, D. H., & Mercer, A. R. (1996). Learning disabilities definitions and criteria used by state education departments. *Learning Disability Quarterly*, *19*(4), 217–232. https://doi.org/10.2307/1511208

Miciak, J., Fletcher, J. M., Stuebing, K. K., Vaughn, S., & Tolar, T. D. (2014). Patterns of cognitive strengths and weaknesses: Identification rates, agreement, and validity for learning disabilities identification. *School Psychology Quarterly*, *29*(1), 21–37. https://doi.org/10.1037/spq0000037

Miciak, J., Taylor, W. P., Stuebing, K. K., & Fletcher, J. M. (2018). Simulation of LD identification accuracy using a pattern of processing strengths and weaknesses method with multiple measures. *Journal of Psychoeducational Assessment*, *36*(1), 21–33. https://doi.org/10.1177/0734282916683287

Mitrushina, M., Drebing, C., Satz, P., Van Gorp, W., Chervinsky, A., & Uchiyama, C. (1994). WAIS-R intersubtest scatter inpatients with dementia of Alzheimer's type. *Journal of Clinical Psychology*, *50*(5), 753–758.

Naglieri, J. A., & Feifer, S. G. (2018). Pattern of strengths and weaknesses made easy: The discrepancy/consistency method. In V. C. Alfonso & D. P. Flanagan (Eds), *Essentials of specific learning disability identification* (4th ed., pp. 431–474). Wiley.

National Association of School Psychologists. (2010). *Position statement on identification of students with specific learning disabilities.* Author. www.nasponline.org/profdevel/online-learning.aspx

National Center for Education Statistics. (2020). *Children and youths with disabilities.* http://nces.ed.gov/programs/coe/indicator_cgg.asp

National Joint Committee on Learning Disabilities. (2010, June). *Comprehensive assessment and evaluation of students with learning disabilities.* www.ldanatl.org/pdf/NJCLD%2520Comp%2520Assess%2520Paper%2520

National Research Council. (2002). *Mental retardation: Determining eligibility for Social Security benefits.* Washington, DC: National Academy Press.

Nisbett, R., E., Aronson, J., Blari, C., Dickens, W., Flynn, J., Halpern, D. F, & Turkheimer, E. (2012). Intelligence: News findings and theoretical developments. *American Psychologist, 67*(2), 130–159. https://doi.org/10.1037/a0026699

Ortiz, S. O., Piazza, N., Ochoa, S. H., & Dynda, A. M. (2018). Testing with culturally and linguistically diverse populations: New directions in fairness and validity. In D. P. Flanagan & E. M. McDonough (Eds.), *Contemporary intellectual assessment: Theories, tests, and issues* (4th ed., pp. 684–712). Guilford Press.

Polloway, E. A., Auguste, M., Smith, J. D., & Peters, D. (2017). An analysis of state guidelines for intellectual disability. *Education and Training in Autism and Developmental Disabilities, 52,* 332–339.

Rapaport, D., Gil, R., & Schafer, R. (1945–1946). *Manual of psychological testing-I: Diagnostic testing of intelligence and concept formation.* Macy Jr. Foundation.

Reynolds, C. R. (2009). RTI, neuroscience, and sense: Chaos in the diagnosis and treatment of learning disabilities. In E. Fletcher-Janzen & C. R. Reynolds (Eds.), *Neuropsychological perspectives on learning disabilities in the era of RTI: Recommendations for diagnosis and intervention* (pp. 14–27). Wiley.

Sattler, J. M. (2018). *Assessment of children: Cognitive foundations and applications* (6th ed.). Author.

Schalock, R. L., Buntinx, W. H. E., Borthwick-Duffy, S., Bradley, V., Craig, E. M., Coulter, D. L., . . . Yeager, M. H. (2010). *Intellectual disability: Definition, classification, and system of supports* (11th ed.). American Association on Intellectual and Developmental Disabilities.

Schalock, R. L., Luckasson, R. A., & Tassé, M. J. (2021). *Intellectual disability: Definition, classification, and system of supports* (12th ed.). American Association on Intellectual and Developmental Disabilities.

Schneider, W. J., & McGrew, K. S. (2018). The Cattell-Horn-Carroll theory of cognitive abilities. In D. P. Flanagan & E. M. McDonough (Eds.), *Contemporary intellectual assessment: Theories, tests, and issues* (4th ed., pp. 73–162). Guilford Press.

Shinn, M. R. (2007). Identifying students at risk, monitoring performance, and determining eligibility within response to intervention: Research on educational need and benefit from academic intervention. *School Psychology Review, 36*(4), 601–617. https://doi.org/10.1080/02796015.2007.12087920

Stuebing, K. K., Fletcher, J. M., Branum-Martin, L., & Francis, D. J. (2012). Evaluation of the technical adequacy of three methods for identifying specific learning disabilities based on cognitive discrepancies. *School Psychology Review, 41*(1), 3–22. https://doi.org/10.1080/02796015.2012.12087373

Styck, K. M., Beaujean, A. A., & Watkins, M. W. (2019). Profile reliability of cognitive ability subscores in a referred sample. *Archives of Scientific Psychology, 7*(1), 119–128. https://doi.org/10.1037/arc0000064

Taylor, W. P., Miciak, J., Fletcher, J. M., & Francis, D. J. (2017). Cognitive discrepancy models for specific learning disabilities identification: Simulations of psychometric limitations. *Psychological Assessment, 29*(4), 446–457. https://doi.org/10.1037/pas0000356

Terman, L. M. (1916). *The measurement of intelligence.* Houghton Mifflin.

Vaughn, S., & Fuchs, L. S. (2003). Redefining learning disabilities as inadequate response to instruction: The promise and potential problems. *Learning Disabilities Research and Practice, 18*(3), 137–146. https://doi.org/10.1111/1540-5826.00070

Wasserman, J. D. (2018). *A history of intelligence assessment: The unfinished tapestry.* In D. P. Flanagan & E. M. McDonough (Eds.), Contemporary intellectual assessment: Theories, tests, and issues (4th ed., pp. 3–55). Guilford Press.

Watkins, M. W. (2000). Cognitive profile analysis: A shared professional myth. *School Psychology Quarterly, 15*(4), 465–479. https://doi.org/10.1037/h0088802

Watkins, M. W. (2003). IQ subtest analysis: Clinical acumen or clinical illusion? *The Scientific Review of Mental Health Practice, 2,* 118–141.

Watkins, M. W. (2005). Diagnostic validity of Wechsler subtest scatter. *Learning Disabilities: A Contemporary Journal, 3*(1), 20–29. https://doi.org/10.1177/082957359901500102

Watkins, M. W., & Canivez, G. L. (2004). Temporal stability of WISC-III subtest composite: Strengths and weaknesses. *Psychological Assessment, 16*(2), 133–138. https://doi.org/10.1037/1040-3590.16.2.133

Watkins, M. W., Glutting, J. J., & Lei, P.-W. (2007). Validity of the Full Scale IQ when there is significant variability among WISC–III and WISC–IV factor scores. *Applied Neuropsychology, 14*(1), 13–20. https://doi.org/10.1080/09084280701280353

Watkins, M. W., Glutting, J. J., & Youngstrom, E. A. (2005). Issues in subtest profile analysis. In D. P. Flanagan & P. L. Harrison (Eds.), *Contemporary intellectual assessment: Theories, tests, and issues* (p. 251–268). Guilford Press.

Watkins, M. W., & Kush, J. C. (1994). Wechsler subtest analysis: The right way, the wrong way, or no way? *School Psychology Review, 23*(4), 640–651. https://doi.org/10.1080/02796015.1994.12085739

Watkins, M. W., & Worrell, F. C. (2000). Diagnostic utility of the number of WISC-III subtests deviating from mean performance among students with learning disabilities. *Psychology in the Schools, 37*(4), 303–309. https://doi.org/10.1002/1520-6807(20002)37:4<311::aid-pits1>3.0.co;2-x

Wechsler, D. (1939). *The measurement of adult intelligence.* Williams & Wilkins.

Wechsler, D. (1991). *Wechsler Intelligence Scale for Children* (3rd ed.). Psychological Corporation.

Wechsler, D. (2003). *Wechsler Intelligence Scale for Children* (4th ed). Psychological Corporation.

Wechsler, D. (2014a). *Wechsler Intelligence Scale for Children* (5th ed.). Pearson Assessment.

Wechsler, D. (2014b). *Wechsler Intelligence Scale for Children technical and interpretive manual* (5th ed.). Pearson.

Woodcock, R. W., McGrew, K. S., & Mather, N. (2001). *Woodcock-Johnson III.* Riverside Publishing.

Zaboski, B. A., II, Kranzler, J. H., & Gage, N. A. (2018). Meta-analysis of the relationship between academic achievement and broad abilities of the Cattell-Horn-Carroll theory. *Journal of School Psychology, 71,* 42–56. https://doi.org/10.1016/j.jsp.2018.10.001

Chapter 6

From Spearman to Watkins

The Never-Ending Fight Against Faculty Psychology[1]

A. Alexander Beaujean

Marley Watkins made an indelible contribution to psychology through his work criticizing the popular practice of interpreting score profiles from intelligence instruments. Watkins's critique resembles Charles Spearman's critique of score profiles made nearly three-quarters of a century earlier. Yet neither historians of psychology nor critics of score profiles discuss this part of Spearman's research program. This omission is strange considering that Spearman believed it was interconnected with all the other parts of the program (e.g., two-factor theory, noëgenesis). To begin correcting this oversight, in this chapter I provide an overview of Spearman's critique as well as some concepts and history necessary to understand his critique.

Marley Wayne Watkins (1949–) has made many contributions to the discipline of psychology, one of which is his scholarship concerning score profiles from intelligence instruments (e.g., Glutting et al., 1997; McDermott et al., 1992; Styck et al., 2019; Watkins, 2003; Watkins et al., 2005). Throughout this scholarship, Watkins has granted that intellective profiles have psychological allure but has also insisted that allure is insufficient grounds for interpretation. If psychology is to be a scientific field, then there needs to be robust empirical evidence supporting its practices. Yet the evidence supporting profile interpretation seldom goes beyond clinical conjecture and personal anecdote. As such, the belief that intellective profile interpretation is a scientific practice is currently little more than a "shared professional myth" (Watkins, 2000, p. 465).

Watkins conducted his work on score profiles around the turn of the 20th century, but his conclusions bear close resemblance to what the British psychologist Charles Edward Spearman (1863–1945) wrote nearly three-quarters of a century earlier (Spearman, 1927e, 1937d). Watkins does not reference Spearman, but that is understandable since reference to Spearman's work is absent in nearly all discussions of score profiles. Instead, most discussions of Spearman's scholarship only focus on his two-factor theory or, much less frequently, noëgenesis (Stephenson, 1977). The neglect of Spearman's critique of score profiles is strange, however, considering that he believed it was interconnected with his other work (Spearman, 1937c). Before discussing Spearman's critique of score profiles, however, it will be beneficial to first discuss some core score profile concepts because psychologists tend to use them imprecisely and inconsistently (Manson, 1944).

Score Profiles

The term *profile* comes from combining the Latin words *pro* (supporting) and *filo* (line or thread). It originally denoted the concept of an outline of some physical object such as land features, buildings, or the side of a person's face (Bernard, 2019). Later, the term was used to denote a description of the same object (e.g., biography), and in the 19th century, psychologists used it to denote scores produced from psychological instruments. A *score profile* is the presentation of at least two score values for a particular person or group qua group (Spearman, 1927a, p. 27). One of the first published psychological score profiles is shown in Figure 6.1.

The values in a score profile are assumed to come from measurement and so represent attributes that meet the requirements to be a quantity or ordinal quantity (Joint Committee for Guides in Metrology, 2012). If the attributes only meet the requirements for non-ordinal qualities, then the set of values is called a *configuration* (von Eye, 2002). Profiles and configurations share a common origin and some features, but their interpretations differ. As neither Watkins nor Spearman discussed configurations, I limit my discussion in this chapter to score profiles.

Score profiles have no meaning in and of themselves but attain meaning through our interpretation of them. Interpreting score profiles requires a *person-orientation*, which is an approach to psychology wherein persons are the primary interest, while their attributes are secondary (Stern, 1911). It contrasts with an *attribute-orientation*, which is an approach where attributes are the primary interest and persons are secondary. Whereas psychologists taking an

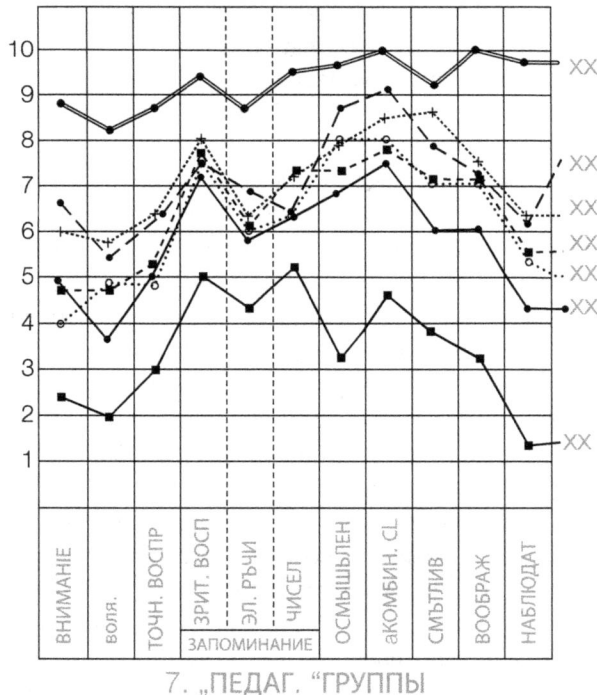

Figure 6.1. **Example Score Profile of Intellective Attributes.** *Note.* From left to right the attributes are attention, volition, memorization, visual memory, auditory memory, numerical memory, comprehension, construction, intelligence, imagination, observation. From "Psikhologicheskie profili," by Rossolimo, G., 1910b, *Ezhegodnik Eksperimental'noi Pedagogiki*, 3(1), p. 48.

attribute-oriented approach focus on how one or more attributes differ across multiple persons, psychologists taking a person-oriented approach focus on how one or more persons differ across multiple attributes (Asendorpi, 2015; Lundh, 2015). In principle, the results from person- and attribute-orientations can converge, but this requires some assumptions that are typically either unexamined or not met when examined (Molenaar & Campbell, 2009; but see Adolf & Fried, 2019). Even if the assumptions are not met, however, the two approaches can still be complementary (Bergman, 1998; Horn, 2006). After all, "breaking up the mind even into the smallest pieces or finest elements does not in the least preclude eventually putting it together again" (Spearman, 1937e, p. 98).

Varieties of Score Profiles and Interpretations

There is no single way to interpret score profiles because instruments can produce different kinds of scores. We can classify most profiles using a few basic criteria, however, which can help understand them better. These criteria are shown in Figure 6.2.

Profile Components

All score profiles consist of elevation, scatter, and shape, so profile interpretation can involve one, two, or all three components (Cronbach & Gleser, 1953; Skinner, 1978). *Elevation* is a summary value for a person across the profile, while *scatter* is the spread of score values in reference to the elevation. Very roughly, elevation and scatter are analogous to the statistical concepts of central tendency and dispersion, respectively. *Shape* is the pattern of the scores and indicates a person's relative strengths (i.e., profile peaks) and weaknesses (i.e., profile depressions).

Profile Metric

A score's *metric* concerns the meaning of its values. The values in a score profile can be in any metric as long as it is used for all the scores. A common metric is necessary because it allows for direct comparison of the scores in the profile (Manson, 1944; Hollingworth, 1922). We can classify most score metrics that psychologists use as raw, contentual, normative, or ipsative.

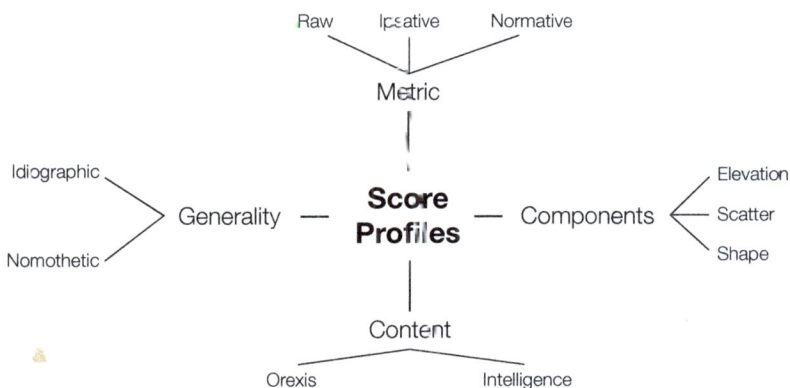

Figure 6.2. **Classes of Psychological Score Profiles.**

Raw scores are untransformed values. In the physical sciences, raw scores typically have measurement units (e.g., second, meter), but in psychology, raw scores are usually units of behavior (e.g., number of times talked) or behavior products (e.g., number of items correctly answered).[2] Contentual, normative, and ipsative metrics are all transformations of raw scores. *Contentual* scores are transformations of raw scores that incorporate the content of particular outcomes or criteria (e.g., developmental milestones, professional knowledge) so the score values are typically reported by referencing those outcomes or criteria (e.g., pass/fail, present/absent/emerging).

Normative means pertaining to a *norm* (i.e., a rule or authoritative standard). Much in psychology does not have norms for what is good or desirable, so psychologists tend to use what is typical for particular population as the norm (Stigler, 1996; Stigler & Kruskal, 1999; Spearman, 1930b). Psychologists often use statistics to describe typicality, in which case normative scores are transformations of raw scores that incorporate statistical units (e.g., standard deviation, percentile rank). *Ipsative* comes from the Latin word *ipse* (oneself), so *ipsative scores* are transformations of raw scores that incorporate within-person comparisons (Cattell, 1944). There is no single way to create ipsative scores (Boverman, 1962). Historically, psychologists tended to create ipsative scores by subtracting a set of raw scores for a given person from the average of those scores for the same person (i.e., elevation value). Currently, it is more common to convert raw scores to normative scores and then ipsatize them.

Profile Generality

Something's *generality* is its scope of applicability—the extent to which it goes beyond, or is independent of, something else. The generality of a score profile concerns the purpose of creating the profile, which ranges from idiographic to nomothetic (Robinson, 2011). *Idiographic* means pertaining to a unique instance or individual, so the idiographic purpose of creating score profiles is to understand a particular person. When used for an idiographic purpose, score profiles are sometimes called a *psychogram* or *psychograph*, and the study of psychograms and psychographs is called *psychography* (Stern, 1911). *Psychography* is a play on the term *biography* because like a biography, the purpose of a psychography is to describes a unique person (Roback, 1952). Unlike a biography, however, psychography is limited to describing a person's unique set of psychological attributes. In addition, biography has an artistic and empathetic component that is absent from psychography. Thus, psychography can provide a basis for biography, but they are not interchangeable endeavors.

Nomothetic means pertaining to laws or something general, so the nomothetic purpose of creating score profiles is to go beyond a particular person in order to understand something more general. That something is usually a population to which a person with a given profile belongs, in which case all persons with the same (or similar enough) score profiles are treated as being psychically similar with respect to the attributes captured by the scores (Zubin, 1938).

We can divide work in the nomothetic approach into either bottom-up or top-down work (Caprara & Cervone, 2000). *Bottom-up* work involves studying persons one at a time in order to find generalities that apply to a particular population distributively (i.e., apply to every member of the population). With respect to score profiles, this involves creating a psychogram for each person and determining those that belong to the same population (Lamiell, 2003). *Top-down* work involves studying samples of persons in order to find generalities that apply to a particular population collectively (i.e., to the population as whole or in aggregate). With respect to score profiles, this usually involves collecting information on the same set of attributes from a relatively large sample of persons and determining the profiles statistically (Asendorpf, 2015). Thus, in top-down work, score profiles are often as much statistical concepts as psychological.

Typology

Both bottom-up and top-down work with score profiles are forms of *typology*, which is the study of types.[3] The term *type* comes from a Greek term for marking or impressing upon, but over time and geography it came to mean the result of the marking or impressing and then a general kind of something akin to a class or population. With the latter meaning, sometimes it is used to refer to a model or exemplar (e.g., prototype, archetype) while other times it is used to refer to a possibly imperfect realization or copy of the model (e.g., ectype). Either way, scholars often engage in typology in order to create type-based classification schemes (i.e., typification schemes) or place objects into one of the types of an already-created typification scheme (Marradi, 1990).[4] I will call the former process *typifying* and the latter *typing*.

Psychologists studying types are concerned with *psychical typification schemes*, which are schemes with membership based on psychical criteria as manifested in behavior. In principle, psychical typing is possible without using score profiles. For example, the history of psychiatry is replete with psychical typification schemes that use physicians' clinical observations as criteria (e.g., Diefendorf & Kraepelin, 1907). At the same time, these alternative criteria often seem to function as if they are just implicit score profiles rather than explicit ones (Cattell, 1950).[5] In any case, the criteria for most modern psychical typification schemes are explicit score profiles or configurations.

Profile Content

The *content* of a score profile concerns the aspect of the psyche to which the attributes represented by the scores belong. For psychography, ideally the content involves the entire personality sphere (Allport, 1937). This can become unwieldy for nomographic investigations, however, so psychologists tend to focus on just a portion of the sphere—either orexis (i.e., affection and conation) or noesis (i.e., intellection). While Spearman's critique concerned score profiles with both orectic and noetic content, Watkins focused only on profiles with noetic content. Consequently, I constrain my discussion to *intellective profiles* (i.e., profiles comprised of scores representing attributes involving knowledge creation or use) and *intellective profile analysis* (i.e., interpretation of intellective profiles).

Early History of Intellective Profiles

Psychologists often credit publication of the Bellevue Intelligence Scales (BIS; Wechsler, 1939) as the event that catalyzed intellective profile analysis in psychology (e.g., Payne, 1961; Rabin, 1965). While it is true that the popularity of intellective profile analysis in the United States increased with publication of the BIS, psychologists were engaging in the practice long before (Beaujean & Benson, 2019; Kamphaus et al., 2012; McGill et al., 2018). In fact, Spearman's work had nothing to do with the BIS as the intellective profile analysis he critiqued was the form that was prevalent in the 19th century before mass publication of commercial intelligence instruments. Thus, understanding his critique requires understanding the historical context in which he made it.

The First Forms of Intellective Profiles

It is difficult to trace the history of intellective profile analysis because it is intertwined with, yet distinct from, the history of intellective types. Societies have a long history of creating intellective typification schemes, a tradition that antedates the development of score profiles by millennia (Roback, 1952). Most early schemes were literary in that they were based on word portraits, often of well-known historical persons (MacKinnon, 1944). Thus, the schemes differed substantially from one author to the next.

Physicians and legal philosophers helped create somewhat more technical typification schemes, but they were for practical purposes (e.g., diagnoses, criminal sentencing) and focused on extremes (e.g., idiocy, lunacy, genius). As such, score profiles were more or less synonymous with syndromes (Cattell, 1950). The focus on extremes was partly because of the lack of technics for measuring the psyche with fidelity, so typification schemes were either based on anatomy or physiology (e.g., skull size, humors) or behavior qua behavior. For both, it is much easier to observe unusual forms than variations of what is typical. Unfortunately, the criteria for many of these early typification schemes were based on the developers' unique experiences or what the developers believed would be commercially successful, so the schemes rarely had much empirical or theoretical support (Leahey & Leahey, 1983; Shuey, 1937).

The version of psychology as we currently know it began to emerge sometime in the 19th century (but see Hatfield, 1994). Much like their modern counterparts, scholars operating in this "new psychology" viewed science as requiring measurement of quantities so their typification schemes focused on variations of so-called normal persons rather than exclusively on so-called abnormal persons (James, 1890). The criteria for the typification schemes were often intellective, with particular interest in *psychical imagery*, which involves having an experience that resembles perception without direct sensory stimulation (Satran, 2005; Thomas, 2020). The types in these schemes went by various terms (e.g., imagery types, memory types, speech types, cognitive types; Titchener, 1916; Vernon, 1973), but I will use the term *ideational type* because the criteria concerned ideas as they manifested in sensations, memory, and speech.

The investigation of ideational types was not really a shared research program as psychologists often disagreed with each other about core concepts and methods (Griffitts, 1927). Nonetheless, the study of ideational types was predicated on two shared assumptions. First, the psyche is compensatory, meaning that doing something well precludes doing something else equally well. Consequently, determining a person's ideational type involved having the person complete a variety of similar tasks different ways—often accompanied by having the person describe the completion process—and then figuring out those for which the person performed best or was most prominent (Sully, 1910). The second assumption is that the methods for capturing a particular way of doing something were more or less interchangeable (for a description of common methods, see Colvin, 1909). Thus, typifying a person using one set of instruments and techniques would result in the same outcome (i.e., produce the same type) as typifying the person using any other set of instruments and techniques. An example may clarify things.

The French psychologist Alfred Binet (1857–1911) conducted multiple investigations on ideational types before turning his attention to the Binet-Simon instrument (Binet, 1894, 1899). He believed his work showed there were three distinct ideational types: visual, auditory, and indifferent. *Visual type* persons do things visually and self-describe their psychical activity by employing visual images. Thus they respond to tasks involving visual stimuli better (e.g., quicker, more accurately) than tasks involving auditory stimuli. By contrast, *auditory type* persons do things auditorily, describe their psychical activity as using sounds, and respond to auditory stimuli better. Distinct from the visual and auditory types are *indifferent type* persons who do just as well with tasks involving visual stimuli as those involving auditory stimuli.

Neither Binet nor his contemporaries explicitly discussed their typification methods in terms of profiles. Nonetheless, we can see primitive forms of intellective profiles and intellective profile analysis in their techniques. They administered a variety of instruments, the scores from which had values in some comparable metric (e.g., seconds, percent correct). Subsequently, they created implicit or explicit score profiles and then used the profile shapes as criteria for typing persons.

Intellective Profiles of Naomi Norsworthy and Grigory Rossolimo

Psychologists moved from the primitive forms of score profiles to more modern forms at the beginning of the 20th century. Edward Lee Thorndike (1874–1949) presaged these modern forms (Thorndike, 1903), which his student Naomi Norsworthy (1877–1916) carried out. Norsworthy was the first female graduate student in psychology at Columbia University's Teachers College and later became the first female faculty member at the same institution (Cautin & Benjamin, 2012). Norsworthy's primary interests were in intellectual disability (ID), so for her dissertation she examined different physical attributes (e.g., height, weight) and psychical attributes (e.g., visual perception, memory, language) in children with and without an ID (Norsworthy, 1906, 1907).[6]

Although the analysis of variance technique had yet to be invented at the time Norsworthy was working on her dissertation, some approximations to it were available (Stigler, 1986). They all required computing averages (e.g., mean, median) within each group, however, which posed a problem for the attributes Norsworthy captured. Specifically, she knew the attributes were strongly related to chronological age and biological sex but she did not control for either in her sampling design. Consequently there would be substantial confounding if she compared raw score averages across groups with and without an ID. One possible solution was to split her sample into separate age or sex subgroups. Her sample of children with an ID was relatively large for the time ($n = 157$) but was not large enough to be split into subgroups. Thus the solution she chose was to convert all the raw scores to standard scores.[7]

Standard scores all have the same general form, which is shown in Equation 1.

$$\text{Standard Score} = \frac{Raw - \overline{Raw}}{D_{Raw}},\tag{1}$$

where *Raw* is the raw score value for a specific person, $\overline{Raw}$ is a central tendency index value for the raw score values within a norm group, and D_{Raw} is an index of dispersion value for the raw score values in the same norm group. A *norm group* is a set of persons sampled from a population of interest in order to represent that population. Norsworthy created multiple norm groups by splitting her sample of children without an ID into age- and sex-based subgroups. She calculated $\overline{Raw}$ values by using the median for particular norm groups, and she calculated the D_{Raw} values by using the probable error for the same norm groups.[8] For the *Raw* values, she used the scores of children with an ID.

Norsworthy believed that using standard scores had two important implications for her investigation (Norsworthy, 1906, p. 50). First, since her norm groups were stratified by age and sex, the resulting standard score values already accounted for these extraneous attributes. Thus the resulting values allowed her to compare the performance of all the persons with an ID to those without an ID. Second, the metric for all standard scores appears to be identical, which she believed allowed her to compare all the attributes for a given person. That is, she believed it allowed her to compare score values regardless of what attributes the scores represented. It was this second implication that she believed was original to her method.

Norsworthy's work is notable for being one of the first—if not *the* first—to involve constructing intellective profiles in a way that resembles modern practice, yet it is seldom cited.[9] When psychologists do reference her, it is usually in passing as someone who studied ID empirically (e.g., Juni & Trobliger, 2009; Peterson, 1925). Some historians have surmised that the lack of credit is because Norsworthy's instrument battery captured attributes that were too basic rather than capturing the complex attributes that Binet captured with the Binet-Simon (Flugel & West, 1963). This is doubtful, however, because she designed her battery to capture both basic and complex intellective attributes although she did so under the constraint of being able to administer most of the instruments to groups of children simultaneously. A more likely reason for the neglect of her work is her interpretation of the score profiles. Before discussing her interpretation, however, it will be useful to introduce an alternative interpretation of score profiles.

Psychologists typically credit Grigory Ivanovich Rossolimo (1860–1928) with instigating the modern interpretation of score profiles (e.g., Kohs, 1923; Stern, 1914). Rossolimo was an early-20th-century Russian physician interested in the mind.[10] Russian psychology before the 1917 revolution was largely dominated by physicians like Rossolimo who studied the methods of European experimental psychology (Leopoldoff, 2014). Rossolimo believed the standardization of these experimental procedures could be applied to diagnosing psychopathology and, consequently, could improve diagnostic reliability and accuracy (Byford, 2020). The way to do this was through psychological testing.

In many ways, Rossolimo's creation of the profile method parallels Binet's creation of the Binet-Simon (Nicolas et al., 2013). First, both disliked the subjectivity of making diagnoses based on clinical interview and observation, so believed that the standardization within psychological testing provided a better alternative. Second, both believed that in order for testing to be accepted, instrument administration and interpretation would need to be relatively simple and directly tied to clinical applications (Leopoldoff, 2014; Mikhno, 2020). Third, both believed that accurately capturing the intelligence sphere required focusing more on complex intellective attributes (e.g., memory, comprehension) than basic ones. As Rossolimo and Binet both believed the instruments available in their respective countries did not capture complex intellective attributes well, they both created their own (Rossolimo, 1910a,b; for English translations, see Parker, 1916; Rossolimo, 1911).

Although initially Binet wanted instruments that would produce measurement values, he eventually focused on an instrument (the Binet-Simon) that would produce scores with values useful for distinguishing between certain types of persons (Michell, 2012). He accomplished this by requiring the administration of items covering a hodgepodge of content and then summarizing performance by a single score (i.e., mental age). Rossolimo appears to have had the same goal for his instruments. They required administering items covering a hodgepodge of content as well, but Rossolimo created separate scores for each content area. The score values for each content area ranged from 0 to 10, which he believed made the score values directly comparable.[11] To simplify the interpretation, he presented all the score values for a person simultaneously on a graphic profile (see Figure 6.1).

Rossolimo interpreted performance on his instrument based on the respondents' profile shape. A straight line indicated a balanced intelligence sphere while zigzags indicated relative strengths and weaknesses that could be indicative of underlying psychopathology. To determine whether a particular score profile was pathological, he compared its shape to the shape of profiles from persons already diagnosed with a certain psychopathological conditions (Byford, 2020). Thus, like Binet, Rossolimo employed "dust bowl empiricism" (Schoenfeldt, 1999) to interpret performance on his instrument rather than a particular psychological theory (Luria, 1969).

Superficially, Rossolimo's work was similar to Norsworthy's work. They both were interested in extreme forms of psychical attributes and argued that understanding exceptional persons' intelligence spheres required going beyond a single score. Nonetheless, they markedly differed in how they interpreted score profiles.

Norsworthy's interpretation both reflected Thorndike's then-current views (e.g., Thorndike 1903, 1906) as well as presaged some of his later writings (e.g., Thorndike, 1911, 1913). On the one hand, the profiles she examined were relatively clear in indicating that children with an ID were more likely to lag behind their peers in developing more complex intellective attributes but not so with simpler intellective attributes or physical attributes. On the other hand, she did not believe that ID constituted a particular intellective type because there was too much score profile variability (Norsworthy, 1906, p. 91). Instead, understanding a particular person's intelligence sphere required measuring multiple intellective attributes and determining the person's relative strengths and weaknesses. This is because she believed—like Thorndike (Michell, 2020)—the attributes she captured were quantities and the standard scores in her profiles were measurement values that accurately represented the quantities. Thus it made sense to her that psychologists could meaningfully interpret score differences within a profile (Norsworthy, 1906, p. 83).

It is unclear whether Rossolimo believed the attributes he assessed were quantities, but it is somewhat irrelevant because he represented the attributes as raw behavior counts. Some psychologists criticized Rossolimo's choice of score metric, arguing that a value of 8 for attention did not necessarily indicate the same attribute strength as a value of 8 for comprehension (e.g., Claparède, 1916). The metric was unimportant for Rossolimo, however, because his purpose was to understand and diagnose particular persons, not to measure attributes. Thus his profiles were more psychological than statistical (Byford, 2014) and served a purpose distinct from those of Norsworthy.

Spearman's Critique

Spearman criticized psychologists' use of profiles early in his career (Hart & Spearman, 1912) but did not expound upon it until later in his career. He devoted two chapters to the issue in *The Abilities of Man* (Spearman, 1927a), but his discussion was truncated. It was not until the end of his career that he elaborated on it in more depth (e.g., Spearman, 1935, 1937a,b,d, 1939).

Understanding Spearman's criticism requires understanding the Rossolimo and Norsworthy approaches to profiles within the broader context of the two distinct approaches to differential psychology that were dominant in the early 20th century (see Table 6.1). There is no consensus on the terms to use for these approaches, with some suggestions: *clinical-statistical* (Cattell, 1950); *Continental European–Anglo-American* (Allport, 1957); and *German-American* (Toomela, 2007; Vernon, 1933). There is a kernel of truth to all of these bifurcations, but the meanings are all excessively wide. Spearman called the two approaches *psychometric* and *intuitionist* (Spearman, 1934; see also Cattell, 1937; Wenzl, 1928), although he noted the terms were somewhat misleading and that the approaches were not necessarily mutually exclusive (Spearman, 1935). Lacking a better set of terms, however, these are the ones I use in this chapter.

Table 6.1 Two Approaches to Score Profiles

Intuitionist	Psychometric
Continental Europe (particularly Germany)	America and Britain
Persons	Attributes
Types	Traits
General	Aggregate
Single cases	Populations
Wholes	Parts
Understanding	Explanation

The Psychometric and Intuitionist Approaches to Individual Differences

The so-called psychometric approach was an outgrowth of empiricist and positivist approaches to psychology, which held that psychologists should treat their subject matter no differently than the subject matter of natural sciences (Harré, 1999; MacKinnon, 1944). Consequently, the primary aim of psychological research is to search for explanations in terms of general laws and causal mechanisms, and the methods for achieving this aim need to involve instruments and techniques that can mimic the natural sciences in terms of precision and objectivity. When applied to differential psychology, this requires first describing persons' distinct psychical attributes. Experiments usually take the form of finding correlations among a variety of distinct attributes, while interpretation involves attempting to explain the correlations in terms of interactions among psychological, physiological, or environmental mechanisms.

As an outgrowth of empiricist and positivist approaches, the psychometric approach is predicated on psychical attributes represented in score profiles being measurable and relatively universal quantities (e.g., Thorndike, 1904, 1911). Thus, describing the attributes requires naming them, operationalizing them, and developing measurement instruments to capture them. Inasmuch as scores from these instruments are based on standard scores, score values are tied to statistical distributions. As such, creating a psychometric score profile requires investigating a relatively large sample or applying the results from a large-sample investigation to particular persons. Either way, the major aim of using a score profile is to describe a particular person's strengths and weaknesses along relatively universal attributes. Thus, psychical typification schemes are typically not created or, if created, the types are interpreted as shorthand for particular patterns of attribute strengths and weaknesses.

Although the psychometric approach has a philosophical basis, it prizes empirical work much more than philosophy. The opposite is the case for the intuitionist approach (Misiak, 1961). One of the major philosophical influences on the intuitionist approach was Wilhelm Dilthey (1833–1911), who claimed that psychology's subject matter entailed employing unique methods (Wenzl, 1928). The distinction was not one of nomothetic versus ideographic because psychologists could study their subject matter either nomothetically or idiographically (Wolman, 1981). Instead, the distinction was between *Naturwissenschaften* (natural science) and *Geisteswissenschaften* (science of the spirit, or human science). Natural scientists attempt to analyze and explain the natural world, but human scientists attempt to understand lived human experiences (Harré, 1999). The only way to do this is through *Verstehen* (understanding or intuition; Allport, 1929). It means grasping something as meaningful only as a whole and not through its parts (Holt, 1962). Thus psychologists can only understand persons by capturing their histories and subjective understandings of how they interact with the world around them.

Steeped deep within *Geisteswissenschaften*, the intuitionist approach to score profiles holds that the total configuration represents something distinct from the individual scores. Not only is the whole greater than the sum of the parts, but any combination of the attributes is insufficient to understanding the person. Thus persons are not a multitude of attributes but a unitary whole in their multiple attributes — a *unitas multiplex*.

The intuitionist approach did not eschew empirical inquiry, but such inquiry typically took the form of case studies. Likewise, measuring was viewed as an intermediary step toward understanding a person's more fundamental qualities. As such, any objective information obtained from psychometric techniques needed to be supplemented with subjective information from biographical techniques (e.g., interviews, diaries). Consequently, score profiles are interpreted in terms of psychography and types, with the types being more a phenomenological entity than a statistical one (MacKinnon, 1944).

Oligarchic Doctrine

Spearman was dissatisfied with the psychrometric and the intuitionist approaches to score profiles because he believed both were based on what he called the *oligarchic doctrine* (Spearman, 1927a, 1937d).[12] The term *oligarchic* means governed by a few, and Spearman employed the *doctrine* concept more or less synonymously with theory or meta-theory (e.g., Spearman, 1927b). Thus the oligarchic doctrine was a theory that privileged a few dominant attributes.

Spearman believed the oligarchic doctrine was "nothing less than an intensification of that old 'faculty psychology'" (Spearman, 1927a, p. 28). *Faculty psychology* (or facultism) is a set of beliefs about how the psyche is organized that can be traced back to antiquity (Commins, 1933; Perler, 2015). Originally, the word *faculty* meant a power, which some philosophers interpreted as particular attributes (typically activities) while others interpreted as classes of attributes (Schmitt, 1946). Either way, faculties were qualities common among persons and involved in making persons alike. Over time the concept became more of an ordinary-language concept, and in doing so it took on another meaning as a more or less quantitative psychical ability that could describe and explain how persons differed. This ordinary-language meaning eventually became the meaning with which British psychologists in the late 19th and early 20th century tended to employ the term, including Spearman.

The oligarchic doctrine held that the psyche consists of a set of faculties that directly impinge on what persons do. Each faculty is (a) a quantity; (b) unitary within itself (i.e., autonomous); and (c) independent of other faculties (Burt, 1924). This had implications for psychological measurement (for similar implications concerning psychological interventions, see Sleight, 1915; Spearman, 1914). As quantities, faculties can be measured. The unity of a faculty means that any instrument or procedure that measures it does so completely. Some instruments or procedures may be more accurate or tractable than others, but they are all equivalent in the sense that they capture the same faculty (e.g., Binet, 1909). Since the faculties are independent of each other, however, a comprehensive psychological assessment requires capturing information about each unique faculty. This information can then be integrated by creating a score profile (e.g., Hollingworth, 1922).

Research programs adhering to the oligarchic doctrine largely focus on determining the catalog of faculties. In early history the catalog was small because there were some criteria, however flawed, for determining a faculty's existence (Maher, 1921). The criteria gradually eroded as the faculty concept became part of ordinary language, and eventually the catalog came to consist of thousands of faculties—most of which were ordinary language terms (e.g., Allport & Odbert, 1936; Partridge, 1910). Thus psychologists in Spearman's time could select "some half a dozen traits . . . more or less arbitrarily to constitute the whole 'profile' of an individual. Profiles of the sort can be constructed in literally millions; and without any definite grounds for preferring one to another" (Spearman, 1930a, p. 361).

Spearman did not believe the faculty concept was necessarily bad or that faculties necessarily had fictional extensions. To the contrary, he was explicit that some faculties may be open to scientific inquiry (Spearman, 1937e).[13] As such, his criticism of faculties was that psychologists adopted faculty concepts as psychical attributes based on inadequate forms of inquiry. Thus, the particular faculties *cum* attributes that interested psychologists could easily be inappropriate concepts for scientific work.

Spearman outlined his solution to the faculty problem in two seminal papers he published before completing graduate school (Spearman, 1904a,b). This solution had two parts. First, "we needs must know, What goes with What" (Spearman, 1937d, p. 39)—that is, rigorously determine how different aspects of a particular attribute relate to each other via calculating their correlations. Finding correlations is insufficient, however, because the correlation values could have been produced artificially (e.g., as methodological artifacts). Consequently, the second part is to determine if the attribute components go together because they have functional unity.[14] Spearman broadly defined *functional unity* as all the different manifestations of a particular attribute being interlocked (Spearman, 1937d, p. 191; see also Lumsden & Ross, 1973). Making a strong argument that an attribute has function unity can be difficult because there is not a single cause of it or technique for determining it (for more information, see Cattell, 1943a, 1950; Hearnshaw, 1941). As such, before examining whether an attribute has functional unity it is usually advisable to rule out what can look like functional unity, but is not.

First, functional unity is not what I will call titular unity. *Titular unity* involves unity in concepts' names. By contrast, functional unity involves unity in concepts' extensions. Confusion arises when one kind of unity exists without the other (Johnson, 1928). Titular unity without functional unity results in treating two or more different concepts as equivalent because they have the same name—an error sometimes called the *jingle fallacy* (Thorndike, 1904). Conversely, functional unity without titular unity results in treating a single concept as being two or more distinct concepts because it has different names—an error sometimes called the *jangle fallacy* (Kelley, 1927).

Psychological concepts are particularly susceptible to the jingle and jangle fallacies because, by design, psychology's jargon largely comes from ordinary language (White, 2000). On the one hand, this is somewhat necessary because much of what interests psychologists was part of ordinary language long before psychology became a knowledge field. On the other hand, this is troublesome because there tends to be substantial disagreement among psychologists about concepts—even the most basic ones (Zagaria et al., 2020). Scientists in other disciplines address the problem of ordinary language concepts by refining them to be technical concepts or by inventing neologisms, but psychologists have largely eschewed both. Consequently, having a lexicon of psychological concepts that have functional and titular unity requires an iterative process of conceptual and empirical investigations (Machado et al., 2000; McDougall, 1932).

Second, functional unity is not statistical unity. *Statistical unity* is typically captured through factor analysis or related procedures. Strictly speaking, factors in a factor analysis are just numbers that, when combined using certain rules, reproduce the original variance and covariances (Maraun, 2003). They are statistical concepts that may be more or less useful but do not necessarily represent anything that exists in the world. Determining whether a factor represents something in the world requires extensive work that goes beyond factor analysis—something Spearman noted multiple times (e.g., Spearman, 1905, 1934). Spearman's protégé Raymond Bernard Cattell (1905–1998) expounded on the distinction between statistical and functional unity through his concepts of surface and source traits (Cattell, 1946). *Source traits* are those that have functional unity, while *surface traits* are those that result from the interaction of source traits or other kinds of attributes.[15] Both may show up as factors in a factor analysis, but only source traits represent something that has psychical meaning and is irreducible.

Spearman warned of some of the troubles that would arise by confusing source and surface traits (Spearman, 1930a, 1930b), but psychologists largely ignored him. Armed with a variety of factor extraction and rotation techniques along with an ever-increasing arsenal of psychometric instruments, psychologists were able to invent a multiplicity of intelligence-related constructs at will.[16] By the middle of the 20th century, it was "widely accepted that factors can be fractionated and proliferated almost without end" (Ferguson, 1965, p. 47). This would not necessarily be troublesome if psychologists treated the factors as conjectures, but this is not what they did (Coan, 1964). Instead, they named the factors using familiar terms (e.g., reason, memory, visual perception) and subsequently confused the factors with the concepts bearing the same name. Factors are not the same as concepts, however, as factors are statistical while concepts are linguistic (Maraun et al., 2009). Confusing the two has led to a century of illegitimate concept equating (Maraun & Gabriel, 2013). Currently, there are hundreds—maybe thousands—of factor analysis–based constructs related to intelligence (e.g., Carroll, 1993; Schneider & McGrew, 2018), but relatively little is known about whether they are statistical chimera or represent meaningful concepts with functional unity (Slaney & Garcia, 2015).

Application to Intuitionists

Spearman was not the first to criticize the oligarchic doctrine; many psychologists before him had also denounced various forms of facultism. What was novel to Spearman was realizing that intuitionists employed the type concept in a manner that strongly resembled how psychometrists employed the faculty concept (Spearman, 1927a, 1937d). They create types using a variety of criteria, name the types using ordinary language terms, and then later come to believe of the names given to the types as representing something existing in the world. In other words, they assume that within a psychical typification scheme each type is independent from other types and unitary. Consequently, the same critique Spearman leveled at the faculty form of the oligarchic doctrine he also leveled at the type form. "Above all, these 'types'—as previously, the faculties, temperaments, and so forth—have failed to supply just what constitutes an irreducible minimum for science in general—namely, a proven account of *what goes with what*" (Spearman, 1937e, p. 205, emphasis in original).

Seeing the relation between faculties and types comes from understanding the parallels between the two ways of describing persons (Cattell, 1950). Describing persons using attributes requires

(a) defining the attribute concepts; (b) establishing that the attributes exist in more than name (i.e., have extensions in the world); and (c) determining how to capture persons' manifestation of the attributes (e.g., measuring). Likewise, describing persons using types requires (a) defining the type concept, (b) establishing the type exists in more than name, and (c) determining how to place persons into the type (i.e., typing).

Just as establishing that an attribute exists requires determining its essence, so too does establishing a type. There are two major kinds of types: continuous and species (for others, see Cattell, 1952, p. 502). *Continuous types* are those in which the attributes that comprise the type vary together across extremes (Cattell, 1946). For example, shortness and tallness are two extremes of a continuous typification scheme that consists of multiple physical attributes (e.g., leg length, torso length, shoulder breath). In nearly any population there is a continuous grading of statures from a tall type to a short type with many other intermediate types in between.

From a slightly different perspective, we can think of continuous types as a multivariate extension of the bipolar attribute concept (Cattell, 1943b, 1946). In many areas of psychology, psychologists assume that attributes are bipolar in that they (a) are continuous; (b) have two poles (i.e., positive extreme and negative extreme); and (c) the space in between the two extremes is more or less neutral (Paunonen & Hong, 2015). Consequently, describing persons using a continuous typification scheme versus describing them using a set of continuous attributes will look very similar and, in some situations, be indistinguishable.

Species types are those in which the pattern of attributes that comprise one type does not overlap with the pattern of attributes for any other type (Cattell, 1950). Particular attributes may overlap across types, but the patterns are distinct and there are few or no intermediary types in between. For example, pure dog breeds are species types because the pattern of attributes that comprise, say, a golden retriever have little overlap with the pattern of attributes that comprise a malamute. Psychical attributes seldom separate distinctly so species types are rare in psychology (but see Eysenck, 1952).

Some difficulties with employing the type concept are illustrated with the history of ideational types (Fernald, 1912; Griffitts, 1927). In early history, psychologists implicitly assumed the types were of the species variety and that all persons could be placed into one distinct type. Yet there was (a) no consensus about the type definitions, (b) no work done to establish that the types represented a functional unity, and (c) no consensus about how to go about determining if a person belonged to a particular type. Thus, confusion reigned.

During the first part of the 20th century, multiple experiments failed at typifying persons as particular types. Instead, they found that typically developing persons can employ multiple forms of imagery depending on the stimuli involved. For example, we tend to employ more visual images for concrete, nonverbal stimuli and more auditory/motor images for abstract, verbal stimuli. Some psychologists responded to these studies by denouncing the type concept, with Thorndike being one the most vocal proponents of this position (Thorndike, 1914). He contended every person belongs to one and the same type: mediocrity. Consequently, psychologists should focus on quantitative differences in attributes instead of types.

Other psychologists responded to the studies quite differently than Thorndike. Some adjusted their meaning of the type concept (Griffitts, 1927). This took different forms, but often involved interpreting typification schemes as consisting of continuous types rather than species types. There was no consensus about the meaning change, however, which produced a situation in which psychologists employed the same terms to mean different things (i.e., the jingle fallacy) as well as created their own idiosyncratic techniques for typifying persons.

Yet still other psychologists—particularly European intuitionists—took an entirely different tack (Vernon, 1973). They rejected the idea that typifying persons as the same type ever implies the persons will behave the same. Instead, types were just generalizations about how persons' attributes dynamically interact that could help psychologists understand how persons differ. In addition, the intuitionists rejected the idea that types could be investigated statistically. While they agreed that it was important to study types empirically, the qualitative nature of types required an entirely different inquiry approach (e.g., Wellek, 1957).

It is in this context that Spearman made his critique of the intuitionists in general, and types specifically (e.g., Spearman, 1937a,b,e). He did not go to Thorndike's extreme and call for the expulsion of psychical types. To the contrary, Spearman claimed that just as some faculties could be legitimate scientific concepts, so too could some types. Determining this, however, required more than simply constructing typification schemes from general impressions as the intuitionists tended to do.

> Here, again, then, we find that any genuine science of individual differences must needs depend upon ascertaining what correlations exist. Nothing else can avail instead. Beneath the flowers of literature that we have quoted there may indeed lie mines of scientific gold. But until these have been actually discovered—which can only be done by the light of correlations—the preceding doctrine of types can at most be taken as a hope, not as an achievement. (Spearman, 1927a, p. 54)[17]

At the same time, basing type concepts solely on statistics (e.g., correlations, factor analysis) would also be troublesome (Spearman, 1935). Instead, it takes a combination of conceptual and philosophical work along with empirical investigations to determine what concepts are legitimate ones for psychologists to employ (Spearman, 1934).

Conclusion

Throughout much of psychology's history there have been psychologists who advocated for intellective profile analysis. Early on it was the so-called intuitionists whose ideas were then elaborated on by psycho-diagnosticians in the mid-20th century (e.g., Rapaport et al., 1945). This was transformed in the later part of the century as the intelligent testing approach (Kaufman, 1979), which is still popular although in a more elaborate form (McGill et al., 2018).

For as long as there have been advocates of intellective profile analysis, there have also been critics. Spearman's critique targeted the intuitionist era, while Watkins was one of the more formidable critics during the intelligent testing era. Unfortunately, little seems to have changed across these periods. To see this, compare the following two quotes.

> The "oligarchic" doctrine, which takes ability to fall into some few great faculties each functioning in a unitary manner; which would claim to measure each faculty by a single value; which puts together a set of such measurements into the so-called mental "profiles"; which on the strength of these would dispose of the fate of thousands of persons—this doctrine would seem on closer scrutiny to be wholly devoid of foundation. (Spearman, 1927a, p. 40)

> Although it is appropriate for researchers to continue investigating complex patterns of [intellective attributes], scientific psychological practice cannot be sustained by clinical conjectures

and personal anecdotes that have consistently failed empirical validation. Consequently, psychologists should eschew interpretation of cognitive test profiles and must accept that they are acting in opposition to the scientific evidence if they engage in this practice. (Watkins, 2000, p. 476)

We can only hope as the second century of scientific psychology continues that either the practice of interpreting score profiles will cease or psychologists will create a much stronger evidence base to support it.

Notes

1 Work for this chapter was supported by the National Science Foundation under grant no. 1920730.

2 The terms *absolute score*, *physical score*, *objective score*, or *interactive score* are sometimes used instead of *raw score* to denote score values that have a measurements unit (Cattell, 1946).

3 In modern psychology the term *style* is as likely or more likely to be used when discussing intelligence or cognition rather than type. The history of the change as well as the distinction between the style and type concepts is beyond the scope of this chapter (for an introduction see Vernon, 1973) so I only employ the term *type* throughout this chapter.

4 The term *typology* is often used in place of *typification scheme*, but in this chapter I use the former term only to denote the study of types.

5 A so-called criminal profile is another example of a psychical typological scheme that does not consist of score profiles (Bernard, 2019). They are distinct from all other psychical typological schemes; however, because they involve trying to identify unknown persons rather than placing known persons into types.

6 Although the term *intellectual disability* is relatively recent (Wehmeyer et al., 2008), the concepts of interest to Norsworthy are consistent with those captured by the modern term.

7 Norsworthy did not cite any literature to support her use of standard scores but she almost assuredly learned about them from Thorndike (1904), who in turn got the idea from Sir Francis Galton (1889).

8 *Probable error* is the half-range of an interval about some average value for a distribution such that half of the values from the distribution will lie within the interval and half outside. If the distribution of values is symmetric, then the probable error is the same as the semi-interquartile range.

9 As of January 2024, Google Scholar listed 91 citations for her dissertation (Norsworthy, 1906) and 6 citations for an article she published that summarized her dissertation (Norsworthy, 1907).

10 Rossolimo was trained as a neurologist, but psychiatry and neurology were not as distinct in the 19th and early 20th centuries as they are in the 21st century. At the time, neurologists often studied, classed, diagnosed, and treated what we would currently consider psychiatric conditions. Some authors of older psychology texts describe Rossolimo using the now-archaic term *alienist* (e.g., Stern, 1914). Derived from a French word for a person with mental deficits (*aliéné*), an alienist was a professional in medicine or related discipline who worked with mentally alienated persons (Berrios, 1999).

11 Rossolimo created different versions of the instruments in his battery (Byford, 2020). The short version consisted of 10 items and was designed for use by persons without medical training. The complete version was limited to use in medical contexts. While it had more items, it also produced scores out of 10 through a more complex calculation algorithm (Parker, 1916).

12 In previous work, Spearman used the term *multi-focal* instead of *oligarchic*. For discussion of the change in terms, see Burt (1949).

13 Spearman's obituary states faculty psychology "was rescued from its disrepute and given a sure scientific foundation through the study of correlations between various abilities and character traits—

though the new factors that Spearman and his people discovered were often very different from the old 'faculties'" (Obituary, 1945).

14 Spearman used the word *functional uniformity* in his original work but then switched to *functional unity* (e.g., Hart & Spearman, 1914). Both capture more or less the same concept as the term *unitary trait* (Holzinger, 1936).

15 Cattell makes another similar distinction when he distinguishes between univocal and unitractic instruments (Cattell, 1973). *Univocal instruments* are those in which the items form a single factor, while *unitractic* instruments are those in which the items capture a single attribute.

16 Constructs and concepts are distinct; the former are empirical while the latter are parts of language. For a discussion of the differences see Markus (2008).

17 One of Spearman's last students, William Stephenson (1902–1989), developed the Q technique for factor analysis, which factors persons instead of attributes (Stephenson, 1936a,b). It was one of the first techniques for statistically capturing psychical types (Stephenson, 1953).

References

Adolf, J. K., & Fried, E. I. (2019). Ergodicity is sufficient but not necessary for group-to-individual generalizability. *Proceedings of the National Academy of Sciences*, *116*(14), 6540–6541. https://doi.org /10.1073/pnas.1818675116

Allport, G. W. (1929). The study of personality by the intuitive method. An experiment in teaching from *The Locomotive God*. *The Journal of Abnormal and Social Psychology*, *24*(1), 14–27. https://doi.org/10.1037 /h0072160

Allport, G. W. (1937). *Personality: A psychological interpretation*. Holt.

Allport, G. W. (1957). European and American theories of personality. In H. P. David & H. von Bracken (Eds.), *Perspectives in personality theory* (pp. 3–26). Basic Books.

Allport, G. W., & Odbert, H. S. (1936). Trait-names: A psycho-lexical study. *Psychological Monographs*, *47*(1), i–171. https://doi.org/10.1037/h0093360

Asendorpf, J. B. (2015). Person-centered approaches to personality. In M. Mikulincer, P. R. Shaver, M. L. Cooper, & R. J. Larsen (Eds.), *APA handbook of personality and social psychology, vol. 4: Personality processes and individual differences* (pp. 403–424). American Psychological Association. https://doi.org /10.1037/14343-018

Beaujean, A. A., & Benson, N. F. (2019). The one and the many: Enduring legacies of Spearman and Thurstone on intelligence test score interpretation. *Applied Measurement in Education*, *32*(3), 198–215. https://doi.org/10.1080/08957347.2019.1619560

Bergman, L. R. (1998). A pattern-oriented approach to studying individual development: Snapshots and processes. In R. B. Cairns & L. R. Bergman (Eds.), *Methods and models for studying the individual.* (pp. 83–122). Sage Publications.

Bernard, A. (2019). *The triumph of profiling: The self in digital culture*. Polity Press.

Berrios, G. E. (1999). Classifications in psychiatry: A conceptual history. *Australian & New Zealand Journal of Psychiatry*, *33*(2), 145–160. https://doi.org/10.1046/j.1440-1614.1999.00555.x

Binet, A. (1894). *Psychologie des grands calculateurs et joiers d'échecs [Psychology of great mental calculators and chess players]*. Hachette.

Binet, A. (1899). *The psychology of reasoning: Based on experimental researches in hypnotism*. Open Court.

Binet, A. (1909). *Les idées modernes sur les enfants [Modern ideas about children]*. Flammarion.

Boverman, D. M. (1962). Normative and ipsative measurement in psychology. *Psychological Review*, *69*(4), 295–305. https://doi.org/10.1037/h0045573

Burt, C. L. (1924). Historical sketch of the development of psychological tests. In Consultative Committee of the Board of Education (Ed.), *Report of the consultative committee on psychological tests of educable capacity and their possible use in the public system of education* (pp. 1–61). H. M. Stationery Office.

Burt, C. L. (1949). The two-factor theory. *British Journal of Statistical Psychology*, *2*(3), 151–179. https://doi.org/10.1111/j.2044-8317.1949.tb00277.x

Byford, A. (2014). The mental test as a boundary object in early-20th-century Russian child science. *History of the Human Sciences*, *27*(4), 22–58. https://doi.org/10.1177/0952695114527598

Byford, A. (2020). *Science of the child in late imperial and early Soviet Russia*. Oxford University Press.

Caprara, G. V., & Cervone, D. (2000). *Personality: Determinants, dynamics, and potentials*. Cambridge University Press. https://doi.org/10.1017/CBO9780511812767

Carroll, J. B. (1993). *Human cognitive abilities: A survey of factor-analytic studies*. Cambridge University Press.

Cattell, R. B. (1937). Measurement versus intuition in applied psychology. *Journal of Personality*, *6*(2), 114–131. https://doi.org/10.1111/j.1467-6494.1937.tb02245.x

Cattell, R. B. (1943a). The description of personality. I. Foundations of trait measurement. *Psychological Review*, *50*(6), 559–594. https://doi.org/10.1037/h0057276

Cattell, R. B. (1943b). The description of personality. II. Basic traits resolved into clusters. *The Journal of Abnormal and Social Psychology*, *38*(4), 476–506. https://doi.org/10.1037/h0054116

Cattell, R. B. (1944). Psychological measurement: Normative, ipsative, interactive. *Psychological Review*, *51*(5), 292–303. https://doi.org/10.1037/h0057299

Cattell, R. B. (1946). *Description and measurement of personality*. World Book.

Cattell, R. B. (1950). *Personality: A systematic theoretical and factual study*. McGraw-Hill. https://doi.org/10.1037/10773-000

Cattell, R. B. (1952). The three basic factor-analytic research designs–their interrelations and derivatives. *Psychological Bulletin*, *49*(5), 499–520. https://doi.org/10.1037/h0054245

Cattell, R. B. (1973). *Personality and mood by questionnaire*. Jossey-Bass.

Cautin, R. L., & Benjamin, L. T. (2012). Columbia University, history of psychology at. In R. W. Rieber (Ed.), *Encyclopedia of the history of psychological theories* (pp. 188–210). Springer. https://doi.org/10.1007/978-1-4419-0463-8_417

Claparéde, E. (1916). Profils psychologiques gradués d'après l'ordination des sujets: Avec quelques mots sur l'utilité des profils en psychologie légale [Graduated psychological profiles according to the order of subjects: With a few words on the usefulness of profiles in forensic psychology]. *Archives de Psychologie, 16*, 70–81.

Coan, R. W. (1964). Facts, factors, and artifacts: The quest for psychological meaning. *Psychological Review*, *71*(2), 123–140. https://doi.org/10.1037/h0043231

Colvin, S. S. (1909). Methods of determining ideational types. *Psychological Bulletin*, *6*(7), 223–237. https://doi.org/10.1037/h0075187

Commins, W. D. (1933). What is "faculty psychology"? *Thought: A Journal of Philosophy*, *8*(1), 48–57. https://doi.org/10.5840/thought19338170

Cronbach, L. J., & Gleser, G. C. (1953). Assessing similarity between profiles. *Psychological Bulletin*, *50*(6), 456–473. https://doi.org/10.1037/h0057173

Diefendorf, A. R., & Kraepelin, E. (1907). *Clinical psychiatry: A textbook for students and physicians, abstracted and adapted from the 7th German edition of Kraepelin's "Lehrbuch der Psychiatrie"* (Rev. ed.). MacMillan. https://doi.org/10.1037/13656-000

Eysenck, H. J. (1952). *The scientific study of personality*. Routledge & Kegan Paul.

Ferguson, G. A. (1965). Human abilities. *Annual Review of Psychology*, *16*(1), 39–62. https://doi.org/10.1146/annurev.ps.16.020165.000351

Fernald, M. R. (1912). The diagnosis of mental imagery. *The Psychological Monographs*, *14*(1), i–169. https://doi.org/10.1037/h0093065

Flugel, J. C., & West, D. J. (1963). *A hundred years of psychology* (3rd ed.). Methuen.

Galton, F. (1889). *Natural inheritance*. Macmillan & Company.

Glutting, J. J., McDermott, P. A., Watkins, M. W., Kush, J. C., & Konold, T. R. (1997). The base rate problem and its consequences for interpreting children's ability profiles. *School Psychology Review*, *26*(2), 176–188. https://doi.org/10.1080/02796015.1997.12085857

Griffitts, C. H. (1927). Individual differences in imagery. *Psychological Monographs*, *37*(3), i–91. https://doi.org/10.1037/h0093250

Harré, R. (1999). The rediscovery of the human mind: The discursive approach. *Asian Journal of Social Psychology*, *2*(1), 43–62. https://doi.org/10.1111/1467-839X.00025

Hart, B., & Spearman, C. (1912). General ability, its existence and nature. *British Journal of Psychology*, *5*(1), 51–84. https://doi.org/10.1111/j.2044-8295.1912.tb00055.x

Hart, B., & Spearman, C. E. (1914). Mental tests of dementia. *The Journal of Abnormal Psychology*, *9*(4), 217–264. https://doi.org/10.1037/h0074835

Hatfield, G. (1994). Psychology as a natural science in the eighteenth century. *Revue de synthese*, *115*(3), 375–391. https://doi.org/10.1007/BF03181250

Hearnshaw, L. S. (1941). Psychology and operationism. *Australasian Journal of Psychology and Philosophy*, *19*(1), 44–57. https://doi.org/10.1080/00048404108541506

Hollingworth, H. L. (1922). *Judging human character*. D. Appleton.

Holt, R. R. (1962). Individuality and generalization in the psychology of personality. *Journal of Personality*, *30*(3), 377–404. https://doi.org/10.1111/j.1467-6494.1962.tb02312.x

Holzinger, K. J. (1936). Recent research on unitary mental traits. *Journal of Personality*, *4*(4), 335–343. https://doi.org/10.1111/j.1467-6494.1936.tb02038.x

Horn, J. L. (2006). Comments on integrating person-centered and variable-centered research on problems associated with the use of alcohol. *Alcoholism: Clinical and Experimental Research*, *24*(6), 924–930. https://doi.org/10.1111/j.1530-0277.2000.tb02074.x

James, W. (1890). *The principles of psychology* (Vol. 2). Holt.

Johnson, H. M. (1928). Some fallacies underlying the use of psychological "tests." *Psychological Review*, *35*(4), 328–337. https://doi.org/10.1037/h0070345

Joint Committee for Guides in Metrology. (2012). *JCGM 200:2012. International vocabulary of metrology— basic and general concepts and associated terms (VIM)* (3rd ed.). Author. https://www.bipm.org/utils/common/documents/jcgm/JCGM_200_2012 pdf

Juni, S., & Trobliger, R. (2009). Codification of intratest scatter on the Wechsler intelligence scales: Critique and proposed methodology. *Canadian Journal of School Psychology*, *24*(2), 140–157. https://doi.org/10.1177/0829573509333456

Kamphaus, R. W., Winsor, A. P., Rowe, E. W., & Kim, S. (2012). A history of intelligence test interpretation. In D. P. Flanagan & P. L. Harrison (Eds.), *Contemporary intellectual assessment* (3rd ed., pp. 56–70). Guilford.

Kaufman, A. S. (1979). *Intelligent testing with the WISC-R*. Wiley.

Kelley, T. L. (1927). *Interpretation of educational measurements*. World Book.

Kohs, S. C. (1923). *Intelligence measurement: A psychological and statistical study based upon the block design tests*. Macmillan.

Lamiell, J. T. (2003). *Beyond individual and group differences: Human individuality, scientific psychology, and William Stern's critical personalism*. Sage Publications. https://doi.org/10.4135/9781452229317

Leahey, T. H., & Leahey, G. E. (1983). *Psychology's occult doubles: Psychology and the problem of pseudoscience*. Nelson-Hall.

Leopoldoff, I. (2014). A psychology for pedagogy: Intelligence testing in USSR in the 1920s. *History of Psychology*, *17*(3), 187–205. https://doi.org/10.1037/a0035954

Lumsden, J., & Ross, J. (1973). Validity as theoretical equivalence. *Australian Journal of Psychology*, *25*(3), 191–197. https://doi.org/10.1080/00049537308255845

Lundh, L.-G. (2015). The person as a focus for research—The contributions of Windelband, Stern, Allport, Lamiell, and Magnusson. *Journal for Person-Oriented Research*, *1*(1–2), 15–33. https://doi.org/10.17505/jpor.2015.03

Luria, A. R. (1969). The neuropsychological study of brain lesions and restoration of damaged brain functions. In M. Cole & I. Maltzman (Eds.), *A handbook of contemporary Soviet psychology: Abnormal and social psychology* (pp. 277–301). Basic Books.

Machado, A., Lourenço, O., & Silva, F. J. (2000). Facts, concepts, and theories: The shape of psychology's epistemic triangle. *Behavior and Philosophy*, *28*(1/2), 1–40.

MacKinnon, D. W. (1944). The structure of personality. In J. M. Hunt (Ed.), *Personality and the behavior disorders* (vol. 1, pp. 3–48). Ronald Press.

Maher, M. (1921). *Psychology: Empirical and rational* (9th ed.). Longmans, Green and Company.

Manson, M. P. (1944). The concepts of the profile, psychograph, and evalograph. *Journal of Educational Psychology*, *35*(3), 145–156. https://doi.org/10.1037/h0054428

Maraun, M. D. (2003). *Myths and confusions: Psychometrics and the latent variable model* [Unpublished book]. http://www.sfu.ca/~maraun/myths-and-confusions.html

Maraun, M. D., & Gabriel, S. M. (2013). Illegitimate concept equating in the partial fusion of construct validation theory and latent variable modeling. *New Ideas in Psychology*, *31*(1), 32–42. https://doi.org/10.1016/j.newideapsych.2011.02.006

Maraun, M. D., Slaney, K. L., & Gabriel, S. M. (2009). The Augustinian methodological family of psychology. *New Ideas in Psychology*, *27*(2), 148–162. https://doi.org/10.1016/j.newideapsych.2008.04.011

Markus, K. A. (2008). Constructs, concepts and the worlds of possibility: Connecting the measurement, manipulation, and meaning of variables. *Measurement*, *6*(1/2), 54–77. https://doi.org/10.1080/15366360802035513

Marradi, A. (1990). Classification, typology, taxonomy. *Quality and Quantity*, *24*(2), 129–157. https://doi.org/10.1007/BF00209548

McDermott, P. A., Fantuzzo, J. W., Glutting, J. J., Watkins, M. W., & Baggaley, A. R. (1992). Illusions of meaning in the ipsative assessment of children's ability. *The Journal of Special Education*, *25*(4), 504–526. https://doi.org/10.1177/002246699202500407

McDougall, W. (1932). Of the words character and personality. *Journal of Personality*, *1*(1), 3–16. https://doi.org/10.1111/j.1467-6494.1932.tb02209.x

McGill, R. J., Dombrowski, S. C., & Canivez, G. L. (2018). Cognitive profile analysis in school psychology: History, issues, and continued concerns. *Journal of School Psychology*, *71*, 108–121. https://doi.org/10.1016/j.jsp.2018.10.007

Michell, J. (2012). Alfred Binet and the concept of heterogeneous orders. *Frontiers in Psychology*, *3*(261), 1–8. https://doi.org/10.3389/fpsyg.2012.00261

Michell, J. (2020). Thorndike's credo: Metaphysics in psychometrics. *Theory & Psychology*, *30*(3), 309–328. https://doi.org/10.1177/0959354320916251

Mikhno, O. (2020). Characteristic of a student in experimental pedagogy by O. Nechaev and G. Rossolimo. *Continuing Professional Education: Theory and Practice*, *1*(1), 61–67. https://doi.org/10.28925/1609-8595.2020.1.9

Misiak, H. (1961). *The philosophical roots of scientific psychology*. Fordham University Press. https://doi.org/10.1037/11150-000

Molenaar, P. C. M., & Campbell, C. G. (2009). The new person-specific paradigm in psychology. *Current Directions in Psychological Science*, *18*(2), 112–117. https://doi.org/10.1111/j.1467-8721.2009.01619.x

Nicolas, S., Andrieu, B., Croizet, J.-C., Sanitioso, R. B., & Burman, J. T. (2013). Sick? Or slow? On the origins of intelligence as a psychological object. *Intelligence*, *41*(5), 699–711. https://doi.org/10.1016/j.intell.2013.08.006

Norsworthy, N. (1906). *The psychology of mentally deficient children*. Science Press.

Norsworthy, N. (1907). Suggestions concerning the psychology of mentally deficient children. *Journal of Psycho-asthenics*, *12*(1), 3–17.

Obituary: Prof. C. E. Spearman: A pioneer of modern psychology. (1945, September 20). *The Times*, 7.

Parker, B. (1916). The psychograph of Rossolimo. *American Journal of Psychiatry*, *73*(2), 273–293. https://doi.org/10.1176/ajp.73.2.273

Partridge, G. E. (1910). *An outline of individual study*. Sturgis & Walton.

Paunonen, S. V., & Hong, R. Y. (2015). On the properties of personality traits. In M. Mikulincer, P. R. Shaver, M. L. Cooper, & R. J. Larsen (Eds.), *APA handbook of personality and social psychology, vol. 4: Personality processes and individual differences* (pp. 233–259). American Psychological Association. https://doi.org/10.1037/14343-011

Payne, R. W. (1961). Cognitive abnormalities. In H. J. Eysenck (Ed.), *Handbook of abnormal psychology* (pp. 193–261). Pitman Medical.

Perler, D. (Ed.). (2015). *The faculties: A history*. Oxford University Press.

Peterson, J. (1925). *Early conceptions and tests of intelligence*. World Book Company.

Rabin, A. I. (1965). Diagnostic use of intelligence tests. In B. B. Wolman (Ed.), *Handbook of clinical psychology* (pp. 477–497). McGraw-Hill.

Rapaport, D., Gil, M., & Schafer, R. (1945). *Diagnostic psychological testing* (Vol. 1). Year Book Publishers.

Roback, A. A. (1952). *The psychology of character: With a survey of personality in general* (3rd ed.). Routledge. https://doi.org/10.4324/9781315010274

Robinson, O. C. (2011). The idiographic/nomothetic dichotomy: Tracing historical origins of contemporary confusions. *History & Philosophy of Psychology*, *13*(2), 32–39. https://doi.org/10.53841/bpshpp.2011.13.2.32

Rossolimo, G. I. (1910a). *Profili psikhicheski nedostatochnykh detei: Opyt eksperimental'nopsikhologich eskogo kolichestvennogo issledovaniia stepenei odarennosti* [Profiles of mentally defective children: A quantitative experimental-psychological study of levels of intelligence]. *Sovremennaia Psikhiatriia* [Modern Psychiatry] *9–10*, 377–412.

Rossolimo, G. I. (1910b). *Psikhologicheskie profili* [Psychological profiles]. *Ezhegodnik Eksperimental'noi Pedagogiki* [Yearbook of Experimental Pedagogy] *3*(1), 87–133.

Rossolimo, G. I. (1911). Mental profiles: A quantitative method of expressing psychological processes in a normal and pathological cases. *Journal of Experimental Pedagogy*, *1*, 211–214.

Satran, R. (2005). Chekhov and Rossolimo. *Careers in Medicine and Neurology in Russia 100 Years Ago* *64*(1), 121–127. https://doi.org/10.1212/01.wnl.0000148605.03751.d9

Schmitt, D. E. (1946). *Modern criticism of the Thomistic concept of faculty* [Unpublished master's thesis]. Loyola University Chicago. https://ecommons.luc.edu/luc_theses/362

Schneider, W. J., & McGrew, K. S. (2018). The Cattell–Horn–Carroll theory of cognitive abilities. In D. P. Flanagan & E. M. McDonough (Eds.), *Contemporary intellectual assessment* (4th ed., pp. 73–163). Guilford.

Schoenfeldt, L. F. (1999). From dust bowl empiricism to rational constructs in biographical data. *Human Resource Management Review*, *9*(2), 147–167. https://doi.org/10.1016/S1053-4822(99)00016-9

Shuey, H. (1937). The fundamental principles of typology. *Psychological Review*, *44*(2), 170-182. https://do .org/10.1037/h0053764

Skinner, H. A. (1978). Differentiating the contribution of elevation, scatter and shape in profile similarity. *Educational and Psychological Measurement*, *38*(2), 297–308. https://doi.org/10.1177 /001316447803800211

Slaney, K. L., & Garcia, D. A. (2015). Constructing psychological objects: The rhetoric of constructs. *Journal of Theoretical and Philosophical Psychology*, *35*(4), 244–259. https://doi.org/10.1037/teo0000025

Sleight, W. G. (1915). *Educational values & methods: Based on the principles of the training process*. Clarendon Press.

Spearman, C. E. (1904a). "General intelligence" objectively determined and measured. *American Journal of Psychology*, *15*(2), 201–293. https://doi.org/10.2307/1412107

Spearman, C. E. (1904b). The proof and measurement of association between two things. *American Journal of Psychology*, *15*(1), 72–101. https://doi.org/10.2307/1412159

Spearman, C. E. (1905). Proof and disproof of correlation. *American Journal of Psychology*, *16*(2), 228–231. https://doi.org/10.2307/1412129

Spearman, C. E. (1914). Qualified and unqualified "formal training." *Journal of Experimental Pedagogy and Training College Record*, *2*(1), 247–254.

Spearman, C. E. (1927a). *The abilities of man: Their nature and measurement*. Macmillan.

Spearman, C. E. (1927b). The mathematics of intelligence. *Nature*, *120*, 690. https://doi.org/10.1038 /120690a0

Spearman, C. E. (1930a). "G" and after—A school to end schools. In C. Murchison (Ed.), *Psychologies of 1930* (pp. 339–366). Clark University Press. https://doi.org/10.1037/11017-018

Spearman, C. E. (1930b). Normality. In C. Murchison (Ed.), *Psychologies of 1930* (pp. 444–459). Clark University Press. https://doi.org/10.1037/11017-024

Spearman, C. E. (1934). The battle between "intuitionists" and "psychometrists." *British Journal of Psychology*, *24*(4), 403–407. https://doi.org/10.1111/j.2044-8295.1934.tb00714.x

Spearman, C. E. (1935). The old and the young sciences of character. *Journal of Personality*, *4*(1), 11–16. https://doi.org/10.1111/j.1467-6494.1935.tb02021.x

Spearman, C. E. (1937a). German science of character, Part I: Approach from experimental psychology. *Journal of Personality*, *5*(3), 177–1. https://doi.org/10.1111/j.1467-6494.1937.tb02218.x

Spearman, C. E. (1937b). German science of character, Part II: Approach and typology. *Journal of Personality*, *6*(1), 36–50. https://doi.org/10.1111/j.1467-6494.1937.tb02237.x

Spearman, C. E. (1937c). *L'examen de l'intelligence* [Measurement of intelligence]. *Le Travail Humain*, 5(4), 385–391.

Spearman, C. E. (1937d). *Psychology down the ages* (vol. 1). Macmillan.

Spearman, C. E. (1937e). *Psychology down the ages* (vol. 2). Macmillan.

Spearman, C. E. (1939). *Personnalité volontaire, personnalité intellectuelle* [Willful personality, intellectual personality]. Hermann et Cie.

Stephenson, W. (1936a). The foundations of psychometry: Four factor systems. *Psychometrika*, 1(3), 195–209. https://doi.org/10.1007/BF02288366

Stephenson, W. (1936b). The inverted factor technique. *British Journal of Psychology*, 26(4), 344–361. https://doi.org/10.1111/j.2044-8295.1936.tb00803.x

Stephenson, W. (1953). *The study of behavior: Q-technique and its methodology*. University of Chicago Press.

Stephenson, W. (1977). Factors as operant subjectivity. *Operant Subjectivity*, 1(1), 3–16.

Stern, W. (1911). *Die differentielle psychologie in ihren methodischen grundlagen* [Differential psychology and its methodological foundations]. Barth.

Stern, W. (1914). *The psychological methods of testing intelligence*. Warwick & York.

Stigler, S. M. (1986). *The history of statistics: The measurement of uncertainty before 1900*. Harvard University Press.

Stigler, S. M. (1996). Statistics and the question of standards. *Journal of research of the National Institute of Standards and Technology*, 101(6), 779–789. https://doi.org/10.6028/jres.101.074

Stigler, S. M., & Kruskal, W. H. (1999). Normative terminology. In S. M. Stigler (Ed.), *Statistics on the table: The history of statistical concepts and methods* (pp. 403–430). Harvard University Press.

Styck, K. M., Beaujean, A. A., & Watkins, M. W. (2019). Profile reliability of cognitive ability subscores in a referred sample. *Archives of Scientific Psychology*, 7(1), 119–128. https://doi.org/10.1037/arc0000064

Sully, J. (1910). *The teacher's handbook of psychology* (5th ed.). D. Appleton.

Thomas, N. J. T. (2020). Mental imagery. In E. N. Zalta (Ed.), *Stanford encyclopedia of philosophy* (fall 2020 ed.). Stanford University Press. https://plato.stanford.edu/archives/fall2020/entries/mental-imagery/

Thorndike, E. L. (1903). *Educational psychology: An introduction to the theory of mental and social measurements*. Science Press.

Thorndike, E. L. (1904). *An introduction to the theory of mental and social measurements*. Science Press.

Thorndike, E. L. (1906). *The principles of teaching: Based on psychology*. Mason-Henry Press.

Thorndike, E. L. (1911). *Individuality*. Houghton Mifflin.

Thorndike, E. L. (1913). Educational diagnosis. *Science*, 37(943), 133–142. https://doi.org/10.1126/science.37.943.133

Thorndike, E. L. (1914). *Educational psychology, vol. 3: Mental work in fatigue and Individual differences in the causes*. Teachers College, Columbia University.

Titchener, E. B. (1916). *Experimental psychology: A manual of laboratory practice. Vol 1. Qualitative Experiments. Part I: Student's manual*. Macmillan. https://doi.org/10.1037/10606-000

Toomela, A. (2007). Culture of science: Strange history of the methodological thinking in psychology. *Integrative Psychological and Behavioral Science*, 41(1), 6–20. https://doi.org/10.1007/s12124-007-9004-0

Vernon, P. E. (1933). The American v. the German methods of approach to the study of temperament and personality. *British Journal of Psychology*, 24(2), 156–177. https://doi.org/10.1111/j.2044-8295.1933.tb00693.x

Vernon, P. E. (1973). Multivariate approaches to the study of cognitive styles. In J. R. Royce (Ed.), *Multivariate analysis and psychological theory* (pp. 125–148). Academic Press.

von Eye, A. (2002). *Configural frequency analysis: Methods, models, and applications*. Erlbaum.

Watkins, M. W. (2000). Cognitive profile analysis: A shared professional myth. *School Psychology Quarterly*, 15(4), 465–479. https://doi.org/10.1037/h0088802

Watkins, M. W. (2003). IQ subtest analysis: Clinical acumen or clinical illusion? *Scientific Review of Mental Health Practice*, 2(2), 118–141.

Watkins, M. W., Glutting, J. J., & Youngstrom, E. A. (2005). Issues in subtest profile analysis. In D. P. Flanagan & P. L. Harrison (Eds.), *Contemporary intellectual assessment: Theories, tests, and issues* (pp. 251–268). Guilford Press.

Wechsler, D. (1939). *The measurement of adult intelligence*. Williams & Wilkins.

Wehmeyer, M. L., Buntinx, W. H. E., Lachapelle, Y., Luckasson, R. A., Schalock, R. L., Verdugo, M. A., . . . Yeager, M. H. (2008). The intellectual disability construct and its relation to human functioning. *Intellectual and Developmental Disabilities*, *46*(4), 311–318. https://doi.org/10.1352/1934-9556(2008)46[311:TIDCAI]2.0.CO;2

Wellek, A. (1957). The phenomenological and experimental approaches to psychology and characterology. In H. P. David & H. von Bracken (Eds.), *Perspectives in personality theory* (pp. 278–299). Basic Books.

Wenzl, A. (1928). Contemporary German psychology. *Monist*, *38*(1), 120–157.

White, S. H. (2000). Conceptual foundations of IQ testing. *Psychology, Public Policy, and Law*, *6*(1), 33–43. https://doi.org/10.1037/1076-8971.6.1.33

Zagaria, A., Andó, A., & Zennaro, A. (2020). Psychology: A giant with feet of clay. *Integrative Psychological and Behavioral Science*, *54*(3), 521–562. https://doi.org/10.1007/s12124-020-09524-5

Zubin, J. (1938). A technique for measuring like-mindedness. *Journal of Abnormal and Social Psychology*, *33*(4), 508–516. https://doi.org/10.1037/h0055441

Chapter 7

From Eminence to Evidence

Bridging the Research-to-Practice Gap in Intelligence Testing

Nicholas Benson

Intelligence is a construct, an abstraction that cannot be directly observed. Intelligence is commonly defined as a general mental capability that supports mental functions such as planning, reasoning, thinking abstractly, learning, comprehending one's surroundings, and responding adaptively (Gottfredson, 1997). As a construct, intelligence is defined implicitly by a network of propositions explaining empirical relations among its indicators (Cronbach & Meehl, 1955). The corpus of published empirical research supports the proposition that a general factor of intelligence (g) accounts for much of the variation in cognitive test performance across individuals (Carroll, 1993; Jensen, 1998; McGill et al., 2018). This finding is consistent with Spearman's (1927) Two-Factor Theory. Spearman grouped factors into two categories: general and specific. The general category is appropriately operationalized using a group of diverse mental tasks, with the common variance among these tasks representing g. In accordance with his theorem of indifference of the indicator, Spearman proposed that when measuring "the amount of g possessed by a person, any test will do. . . . The most ridiculous 'stunts' will measure the self-same g as will the highest exploits of logic or flights of imagination" (p. 197). Although interpretive emphasis is placed on g, Spearman included a specific category in Two-Factor Theory because he did not view intelligence as unidimensional. Nevertheless, the specific category could aptly be described as a catchall for poorly measured, nondescript factors as Spearman surmised that these factors could not be measured with adequate precision.

Spearman's concern about measurement precision notwithstanding, factor analysts have consistently demonstrated the existence of multiple factors. Thurstone, a factor analyst and theorist who pioneered efforts to identify important abilities other than g, believed that multiple abilities must be considered when attempting to understand the structure of human intelligence. In his Theory of Primary Mental Abilities, Thurstone (1941) specified subsets of mental operations grouped based on sharing a factor. Accordingly, such groupings are commonly referred to as *group factors*. Thurstone viewed these groupings as unifying factors, each of which provides cohesiveness and functional unity to a respective subset of mental operations. The assertion of functional unity implies that these subsets of operations work together as an integrated unit to accomplish mental tasks. As such, he believed that factors represent abilities. Thurstone's work has been instrumental to the development of subsequent theories that include multiple factors either in addition to or in lieu of *g*. Subsequent factor analytic theories have followed the Thurstonian tradition of referring to factors as abilities (e.g., Carroll, 1993; Horn & Blankson, 2005; Horn & Cattell, 1966; Schneider & McGrew, 2018). At present, most theorists stratify abilities based on dimensions of breadth and abstraction. Abilities at the most psychologically transparent dimension are referred to as *narrow abilities*. The ability with the greatest breadth and greatest degree of abstraction is *g* although this ability is not recognized in some theories (e.g., Extended *Gf-Gc* Theory; Horn & Cattell, 1966). Abilities at the intermediate stratum are referred to as *broad abilities*.

Evidence of validity is needed to support intended interpretations and uses of test scores, and tests should not be administered in the absence of sufficient evidence to support these intended interpretations and uses (American Educational Research Association et al., 2014). Although factor analytic research has consistently revealed the multidimensionality of data obtained via administration of a diverse set of mental tasks to human samples, the mere emergence of multiple factors does not justify reification of these factors into abilities. Rather, empirical evidence is needed to establish the interpretive relevance and clinical utility of test scores reflecting these factors. Few of the group factors that have been proposed provide adequate representations of distinct cognitive abilities that replicate across data sets and methods (Benson et al., 2018). Further, test derived scores reflecting these factors rarely have sufficient unique, reliable variance to be statistically distinguishable from scores purported to measure conceptually similar constructs. As variation in performance is finite, it is exceedingly difficult to measure general and specific abilities using the same set of mental tasks (Beaujean & Benson, 2019a). The bulk of variance tends to be common to these tasks as positive intercorrelations among mental tasks (i.e., the positive manifold) "is arguably both the best established and the most striking phenomenon in the psychological study of intelligence" (Van der Mass et al., 2006, p. 855). Consequently, intelligence tests tend to be good measures of *g* and relatively poor measures of other abilities.

Despite evidentiary limitations, the prominence of broad and narrow cognitive abilities in clinical practice is undeniable. Applied psychologists have a long-standing interest in inter-individual and intra-individual comparisons of test scores reflecting these abilities. It is rarely the case that patterns of test scores are perfectly consistent, yet scatter is often presumed to be indicative of psychopathology. Intra-individual comparisons (i.e., ipsative analysis, scatter analysis) examine within-person differences from some reference point, most commonly the mean of a set of scores. Inter-individual comparison, also known as configural analysis, focuses on identifying score patterns presumed to be characteristic of diagnostic groups.

In a recent survey, 64% of practicing school psychologists reported that they routinely interpret profiles of index scores reflecting broad abilities, while 70% reported that they routinely interpret profiles of individual subtest scores reflecting narrow abilities (Kranzler et al., 2020). Relatedly, 62% of practitioners reported that they eschew interpretation of the overall score, the best estimate of *g*, when there is one or more statistically significant difference between index scores. In a survey of practices in identifying specific learning disabilities, 53% of practicing school psychologists reported using a processing strengths and weaknesses approach that involves measurement and interpretation of multiple broad and sometimes narrow abilities to make a determination regarding the presence or absence of a cognitive weakness that correlates with an observed academic deficit (Benson et al., 2020). Although most practicing school psychologists (80%) regularly interpret an overall score reflecting *g*, evidence clearly indicates that practitioners routinely interpret scores purported to reflect broad and narrow cognitive abilities.

Given practitioners' interest in index and subtest interpretation, it is not surprising that their interpretation is encouraged in the manuals of most tests of intelligence. Authors and publishers develop and market intelligence tests that measure several abilities and often produce a greater number of scores than the number of abilities posited in the underlying theory (Beaujean & Benson, 2019a). Thus the interpretive relevance and clinical utility of some scores is seemingly inferred from mere covariation among tasks. Likewise many tests of intelligence are developed to facilitate interpretation of scores from individual subtests. It appears that school psychologists are rarely dissuaded from such practices during their professional preparation. Past (Alfonso et al., 2000; Oakland & Zimmerman, 1986) and recent (Lockwood & Farmer, 2019) surveys of instructors who teach the cognitive assessment course in school psychology programs have found that it is commonplace to emphasize interpretation of scores reflecting broad and narrow abilities.

Pfeiffer and colleagues (2000) proposed that critics "extend an invitation to the practitioner to learn why practitioners—operating in the complexity of the clinical world—find considerable value in using clinical interpretive techniques such as profile analysis" (p. 384). Watkins (2000) astutely pointed out the futility of studying practitioners' perspectives as a means of validating clinical practices. Attempts to better understand practitioners' perspectives might, however, shed light on their long-standing propensity to rely upon practices that have repeatedly failed to hold up under empirical scrutiny. As most practitioners utilize similar practices, their adoption of assessment practices is seemingly influenced by authoritative voices. I hypothesize that the adoption and sustained use of poorly supported practices can be explained, in large part, by a shared propensity to engage in eminence-based practice. In other words, many in the profession readily accept arguments made from authority or based upon conventional wisdom even when these arguments conflict with empirical evidence.

The purpose of this chapter is to propose a shift from eminence-based to evidence-based practice with the aim of reducing the research-to-practice gap in applied assessment. This chapter begins with a review of historical trends favoring clinical judgment and the art of assessment over empirical evidence and the science of assessment. This historical review focuses on the tradition of interpreting intra-individual and inter-individual differences in performance with tests of intelligence, a topic chosen because it aligns closely with the theme of this edited book. Next, the promise of evidence-based practice for improving assessment practices is discussed. The chapter concludes with a discussion of scientific attitudes and strategies that can be used to promote evidence-based assessment.

Historical Trends: The More Things Change, the More They Remain the Same

Interest in extending the interpretation of performance on tests of intelligence beyond a single score has been around since the onset of clinical use of these tests. In addition to interest in interpreting multiple cognitive abilities, irregularity in relations among these scores, or even in the responses to individual test items, has long been presumed to be indicative of psychopathology. For example, Binet and colleagues (1916) opined that "general paralytics," a term used to describe patients who displayed symptoms of dementia in tandem with muscle incoordination and paralysis, respond inconsistently to items and tasks, which differentiates them from intellectually disabled individuals who tend to display consistent patterns of errors and pervasive difficulties with mental tasks. Numerous studies were conducted to investigate the meaningfulness of scattering on the Stanford Revisions of the Binet-Simon Scale. While scatter was operationalized somewhat differently by the various research teams who completed these studies, Harris and Shakow concluded that "research up to now has failed to demonstrate clearly any valid clinical use for numerical measures of scatter" (1937, p. 148).

Harris and Shakow's admonition failed to constrain interest in scatter. In fact, interest in interpreting scores reflecting multiple cognitive abilities, as well as the scatter among these scores, increased exponentially due to a trinity of events: (a) the influence of L. L. Thurstone, (b) the aspirations of applied psychologists to move beyond the roles of administering and scoring tests to interpreting them for diagnostic and treatment planning purposes, and (c) the publication of the Wechsler-Bellevue Intelligence Scale (Beaujean & Benson, 2019b). As previously noted, Thurstone's work influenced subsequent theorists and appears to be the genesis of the belief that practitioners must assess multiple cognitive abilities to acquire an accurate and comprehensive understanding of a person's intellectual functioning. John Carroll is often cited as an authoritative voice in support of interpretation of scores reflecting broad and narrow abilities. Carroll was an eminent scholar who aspired to "identify, catalog, and interpret the known abilities, without regard for their importance or validity" (Carroll, 1993, p. 693). Based on his life's work, Carroll (2003) concluded that intelligence is multifactorial, that subtest scores tend to be strongly influenced by g, and that there existed a consistent bias in some of the tests and test manuals he reviewed whereas the existence of g was not acknowledged and its role on subtest performance discounted. While he recognized the existence of broad and narrow abilities, he believed that research was needed to determine which of these abilities were important to administer and interpret in various clinical situations. Despite his acknowledgment regarding the need for evidence to support the interpretation and use of scores reflecting these abilities, practitioners have been called to administer a multitude of tasks toward the goal of assessing "the total range of cognitive and academic abilities and neuropsychological processes" (Flanagan et al., 2012, p. 459).

With respect to applied psychologists, interpretation of scatter provided a means to move beyond the role of technician whose work was limited to administering and scoring tests under the supervision of psychiatrists to the role of diagnostician whose work involved interpreting assessment data and engaging in extrapolation to provide diagnostic and treatment decisions (Benjamin, 2005). In tandem with projective testing, scatter interpretation helped establish the status of applied psychologists as professionals who could practice independently. As Rosenzweig (1946) opined, this new role allowed psychologists to be a "diagnostician who uses whatever objective instruments are available but relies heavily upon his experience, upon interview procedures, upon projective techniques" to understand the whole personality, not just its intellectual component (p. 94). Work by David Rapaport and his colleagues at the Menninger Clinic provided the dominant framework for diagnostic psychological testing (e.g., Rapaport, et al., 1945; Schafer, 1946; Schafer & Rapaport, 1944). This framework included administration of a standard test battery including a Wechsler scale and various projective tests, a standard that stood for decades as the primary assessment strategy in clinical settings (e.g., Lubin et al., 1984; Weiner, 1983). To facilitate interpretation, Rapaport and colleagues developed scattergrams, a technique used to study performance across a variety of tests. An underlying assumption of this technique was that "the deviation of some of an individual's subtest scores from his central tendency of general position relative to the total population—reveals some characteristic of his intellectual functioning and personality organization, whether this characteristic be an impairment or an uneven development of function" (Rapaport et al., 1945, p. 49). Statistical and clinical criteria for operationalizing scatter, and explicit instructions for making diagnoses from profiles (e.g., schizophrenia, depression, neuroses), were developed and proffered to practitioners.

These practices ascended to prominence in clinical practice despite scathing criticism in an early review.

> The experienced clinician, upon a superficial first glance at *Diagnostic Psychological Testing*, is likely to hail it with enthusiasm. He will probably exclaim, "Here is something really important, something which will enable individual psychological testing to contribute something worth while." Upon more careful examination, however, he will be sadly disappointed. If he reads carefully and stops for a moment to analyze some of the concepts, he will find them quite meaningless. It is unfortunate that such a prodigious amount of work and effort should produce so little of real significance. (Brown, 1946, p. 478)

The third major event was the development of the Wechsler-Bellevue. The absence of support for scatter in previous research was attributed to psychometric shortcomings of the Stanford-Binet, a situation that many hoped could be remedied by the relative advantages of the Wechsler-Bellevue. As noted in his review of Rapaport and colleagues' first volume of *Diagnostic Psychological Testing*, Brown (1946) lamented that just when most psychologists had been convinced that scatter was the norm and occurred, in large part, as a function of the test, the advent of the new test renewed interest in scatter so that "now it seems the same line of arguments must be presented all over again for the Wechsler-Bellevue. Let us hope that it will be more fruitful. This volume does not give much ground, however, for optimism in this direction" (p. 478). Chief among its advantages, the Wechsler-Bellevue featured a point scale, consisting of eleven subtests of comparable weighted scores, that facilitated profile analysis and afforded "a better opportunity for clear-cut, quantitative and statistical treatment" (Rabin, 1945, p. 413).

Despite these apparent advantages, research identified patterns of subtest scatter that while characteristic of groups were of little or no value when making diagnostic decisions at the level of individuals. In summarizing the lack of evidence supporting the utility of subtest scores for individual diagnosis, Rabin and Guertin (1951) concluded that this line of research did not represent a meaningful theoretical or practical contribution to psychology and expressed doubt that "the continued clogging of the periodical literature with testimonials pro and con, based on scanty and uncontrolled evidence, will be of further benefit" (p. 241). Additional cautions followed in the form of Cohen's (1952) factor analytic study of the Wechsler-Bellevue:

> Much of the test rationales of Wechsler and Rapaport is not supported in the present factor-analytic rationale. These authors imply a specificity of measurement for each of the subtests which is untenable in the light of the appreciably high order of subtest intercorrelation. The latter leads to test communalities whose magnitude, together with the relatively low reliabilities, precludes the possibility of the subtests measuring specific factors to any significant degree, at least in patient populations. (p. 277)

The one-two combo delivered by these authors did little to dissuade interest in scatter. Wechsler rationalized that such unflattering findings resulted from the wide age range of the Wechsler-Bellevue, a problem remedied by the development of separate versions for children and adults, namely the Wechsler Intelligence Scale for Children and the Wechsler Adult Intelligence Scale. The development of separate versions proved to make little difference with respect to the usefulness of scatter. Cohen (1957, 1959) factor analyzed the new versions, replicating his findings from his previous study and invalidating arguments in support of subtest interpretation. Guertin and colleagues (1956, 1962, 1966,

1971) published periodic summaries of ongoing research on scatter and found that publications on the topic continued unabated despite the consistency with which researchers failed to identify useful diagnostic profiles. In recognition of this irony, they expressed wonderment and pondered if "it should not be said that there are no positive results instead of leaving an open crack in the door, implicitly indicating a still-tenacious clinging to an overworked hypothesis" (1956, p. 252).

Many continued to cling to this overworked hypothesis, and profile analysis flourished. This likely relates, in large part, to the authoritative voice of David Wechsler. Wechsler is viewed as one of the 100 most eminent psychologists of the 20th century (Haggbloom et al., 2002), and his influence, through multiple revisions of the Wechsler scales, has continued since his death in 1981. Evidence supporting scatter interpretation continued to be illusive despite these revisions. Hirshoren and Kavale (1976) suggested that while research regarding profile analysis should not be abandoned, its use remains unvalidated and thus should be viewed as malpractice. Likewise, Kavale and Forness (1984), added that "profile and scatter analysis is not defensible" (p. 136).

In the midst of these admonishments, Kaufman (1979) developed his intelligent testing approach. In this approach, a score reflecting g is interpreted first then scatter is examined among scores reflecting broad and narrow abilities to determine if g is "ineffectual as an explanation of the child's mental functioning" (p. 21). Wechsler served as a mentor to Kaufman, which seemingly solidified the latter's unwavering belief that scatter has meaning and profile analysis is beneficial. Like his mentor, Kaufman is an eminent scientist-practitioner. In addition to his own accomplishments as a scholar and test author, Kaufman mentored some of the most prominent scientist-practitioners in school psychology. It is possible that Wechsler, Kaufman, and their proteges are more likely than most to spin gold out of the straw that is patterns of index and subtest scores. Nevertheless, practices should be based on evidence rather than eminence. In 2013, Kaufman opined that a "wait-and-see attitude for profile interpretation is fine for a laboratory, but not for the real world of diagnosis and intervention" (p. 227). While this pragmatic approach may seem reasonable at face value, it belies numerous failed attempts to support profile interpretation.

Proponents of profile analysis eventually recognized that scatter is typical rather than atypical, and thus research began to focus on the magnitude of scatter and the frequency with which discrepancy scores of various magnitudes appear in normative groups (e.g., Kaufman, 1976; Reynolds & Gutkin, 1981; Matarazzo et al., 1988). This line of research led to the now common practice of publishing normative tables (i.e., base-rate tables) that practitioners are encouraged to use to evaluate the frequency with which score differences of various magnitudes occur in a representative sample of peers. A score discrepancy is presumed to be more clinically meaningful when it has a low base rate, meaning score differences of this magnitude or greater occur infrequently. Although base-rate tables help to temper over-interpretation of small score differences, the rarity criterion does not provide direct evidence of diagnostic or treatment utility.

Research on scatter continued in the 1990s. Evidence supporting profile analysis continued to be illusive while evidence negating its use continued to amass. McDermott and colleagues advised psychologists to "just say no" to subtest analysis (McDermott et al., 1990, p. 299), publishing follow-up studies to drive home this point (McDermott et al., 1992; McDermott & Glutting, 1997). Macmann and Barnett (1997) conducted a simulation study that examined interpretations from Kaufman's intelligent testing approach, and results indicated that his proposed interpretations could not be interpreted with confidence. While the methods for interpreting scatter had become more sophisticated, the results remained the same (Watkins, 2003; McGill et al., 2018). Practices for interpreting scatter continued to change, and new proponents stepped up to provide authoritative guidance on how to implement new and improved methods presumed to be highly informative when integrated with data from other tests and assessment techniques using clinical judgment (e.g., Flanagan, Alfonso et al., 2018a; Flanagan, Costa et al., 2018b).

Beaujean and Benson (2019b) referred to this trend of revising and recycling wishful hypotheses regarding cognitive profiles as the Voorhees Phenomenon, a reference to the immortal Jason Voorhees character from the Friday the 13th movies. There continues to be negligible evidence to support such practices after more than a century's worth of research, and thus it is unreasonable to view the interpretation of scatter as evidence based. As noted by Meehl (1997), the tradition of administering tests and proffering score interpretations despite negligible evidence of validity is "the most scandalous example of practitioners ignoring large bodies of consistent research data" (p. 95).

The Promise of Evidence-Based Practice

Evidence-based practice movements have formalized in the past few decades, originating in medicine (Evidence Based Medicine Working Group, 1992) and later expanding to other professions such as psychology (American Psychological Association, 2006). Evidence-based assessment (EBA) refers specifically to evidence-based practices involving assessment. In other words, EBA involves the use of assessment practices that are empirically supported and have demonstrably positive effects on diagnosis and treatment. Canivez (2019) recently commented on the definition, history or roots forms, and importance of EBA. Further, he discussed implications of EBA for research, training, and clinical practice. Thus I refer interested readers to his article rather than restating these matters here.

It is well past time for a shift from eminence-based to evidence-based practice in the applied assessment of intelligence. The research-to-practice gap continues to be large, with clinical judgment and the art of assessment frequently taking precedence over empirical evidence and the science of assessment. Meehl (1997) noted that clinical judgment relies upon experience and anecdotal evidence, which "is unavoidably a mixture of truths, half-truths, and falsehoods" (p. 91). Although most practitioners value clinical judgment, inherent limitations can be exposed through comparison with the history of medicine. As pointed out by Meehl (2002), there were over 800 drugs listed in the Merck Manual at the end of the 19th century, and most of them were inefficacious. In fact, most practices at the time were either useless or harmful. Thankfully, medicine adopted the scientific method, and tremendous progress has been made in the last 120 years. Like medicine, advances in applied psychological assessment will be modest until researchers and practitioners adopt higher scientific standards and insist that interpretations and uses of assessment data be evidence based. Such support requires evidence of diagnostic and treatment utility in addition to evidence of structural fidelity as evidenced by factor analytic findings.

The profession must do more to discourage uncritical adoption of innovative but unvalidated practices. Publishers and test authors have a financial interest in marketing tests with commercial appeal (Frazier & Youngstrom, 2007). Progressive ideas are relatively more appealing to most in comparison to conservative caveats that limit practice to empirically supported interpretations and uses of test scores. In the words of a Nobel Prize winning economist, "Many people have made money selling magic potions and Ponzi schemes, but few have gotten rich selling the advice, 'Don't buy that stuff'" (Thaler, 2015, p 60). Given the appeal of innovative ideas, the profession must demand that authorities promoting these ideas prove their contentions like everybody else. Pretensions of certitude must be challenged. As an example, Schneider and Kaufman (2017) contended that "it is not irrational to believe that comprehensive cognitive assessment is more beneficial than can be supported by current evidence" (Schneider & Kaufman, 2017, p. 18). Given that more than a century's worth of research has not established the importance of scatter, the rational conclusion is that practitioners should not use profile analysis. While such practices may very well be more beneficial than indicated by empirical research, this is a hypothesis that must be supported empirically rather than accepted based on an argument from authority.

Scientific Attitudes and the Promotion of Evidence-Based Assessment

Epistemic humility has been proposed as an overarching educational philosophy for applied psychology programs (Lilienfeld et al., 2017). The goals of this philosophy are to diminish resistance to evidence-based practice and reduce the gap between research and practice. It is believed that these goals can be addressed through the development of a scientific attitude featuring modesty about one's knowledge claims and an ethical responsibility to develop awareness of what one does not know. A scientific attitude provides safeguards against biases that all humans are prone to regardless of their status in academic and professional circles and thus helps to ensure high quality services. Moreover, a scientific attitude begets the selection of assessment practices and interventions based on empirical evidence rather than on clinical lore or recommendations from charismatic proponents.

Developing a scientific attitude is no mean accomplishment. Intuitive reasoning (i.e., commonsense) comes naturally while scientific reasoning "is unnatural: it must be learned, practiced, and maintained as a habit of mind" (Lilienfeld et al., 2012, p. 13). People differ with respect to their attitudes about science. As illustrated in Figure 7.1, scientific attitudes exist on a continuum from pro-science to anti-science. A pro-science attitude involves a fervent commitment to science and the promotion of scientific findings as the basis for theory and practice. At the extreme of this attitude is scientism (i.e., the veneration of science and excessive belief in its techniques and findings).

A pseudoscience attitude is characterized by tolerance of weak scientific standards. Individuals with this attitude tend to be easily swayed by claims that have the superficial appearance of science but lack its substance. At the extreme of this attitude are charlatans who advocate for unsupported practices although calculated deception is presumed to be the exception among proponents of pseudoscience (Lilienfeld et al., 2012). Rather, most individuals with this attitude view themselves as having a scientific attitude, but this view belies their propensity to accept viewpoints, findings, and practices that are not supported or are only marginally supported by empirical evidence. Some individuals with this attitude may have knowledge deficits, while others are strongly influenced by factors such as group identity, allegiance to mentors, relationships with colleagues, ideological

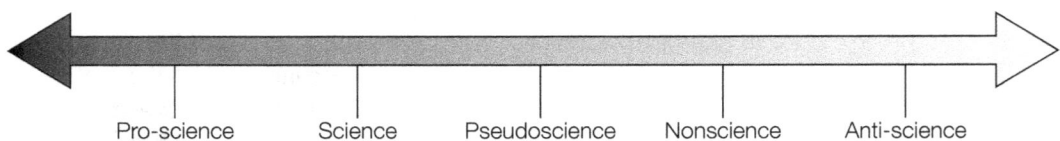

Pro-science   Science   Pseudoscience   Nonscience   Anti-science

Figure 7.1 **Continuum of Scientific Attitudes.**

stances, financial interests, and other personal attributes. A propensity toward pseudoscience may cut across science in general or be specific to issues that conflict with core values and beliefs.

A nonscience attitude is characterized by neglect or even deliberate rejection of scientific methods. Consistent with findings from graduates of clinical and counseling doctoral programs (Zachar & Leong, 2000), it is likely that many graduates of school psychology programs have little interest in topics such as research design and statistics. Thus it is possible that many in the profession of school psychology possess a nonscience attitude. An anti-science attitude involves negative views of science and at its extreme includes active efforts to suppress empirical findings and promote alternative, albeit bogus, viewpoints. Many individuals with this attitude associate with organized anti-science movements. Anti-science movements denigrate scientific findings, harass individual scientists, manufacture uncertainty, publish fraudulent research, and fund the promotion of alternative views that are unsupported by scientific evidence (Hotez, 2020). Anti-science movements are less likely to influence those who have adopted a scientific attitude and engage in scientific reasoning as a habit of mind.

A scientific attitude is integral to the development of scientific competence. Those with strong scientific interests and values are more likely to invest their time developing measurement literacy, knowledge of research designs and methods, and statistical expertise. Also, engaging in mutual skepticism with those who hold different perspectives can help to identify and correct biases that hinder scientific reasoning (von Hippel et al., 2020). When engaging with those who hold similar perspectives, it is important to point out scientific and clinical errors instead of remaining silent out of fear of being viewed as a pompous curmudgeon. In contexts that involve important issues such as psychological distress, physical health, and social justice, allowing others to "persist in egregious mistakes . . . is not only foolish, it is downright immoral" (Meehl, 1973, p. 299).

While scientific attitudes can and should be honed throughout a career, it is important that future school psychologists establish a solid foundation during graduate school. As noted by Lilienfeld and colleagues (2017), university faculty have a responsibility to foster scientific attitudes and reasoning skills. Students should be taught how to detect exaggerated claims in the assessment literature (Farmer et al., 2021). Also, faculty should consider consistency with empirical research when making decisions about the adoption of textbooks and other course materials. Based on their review of cognitive assessment textbooks, Farmer and colleagues (2021) found that poorly supported assessment practices are routinely recommended in major textbooks despite a preponderance of contrary evidence. To address this limitation, Farmer and colleagues suggest that students should be required to read peer-reviewed articles featuring studies that contribute to the evidence base. Asking students to read original research and discuss findings in class provides opportunities for them to hone their scientific reasoning skills. This practice will help students establish scientific reasoning as a habit of mind, which in turn will help to increase the likelihood that they will rely on evidence, rather than eminence, as the basis for their practices.

Although the history of intelligence testing reveals that authoritative voices have often trumped empirical research as a guide to practice, the evidence-based practice movement may ultimately bridge the research-to-practice gap. An indispensable requirement in medicine is that the efficacy of a drug must be established in clinical trials before a pharmaceutical company can obtain approval to sell the drug. This requirement helps to ensure advances in treatment outcomes. In contrast, in psychology we accept authoritative proclamations (e.g., that practices are "more beneficial than can be supported by current evidence" [Schneider & Kaufman, 2017, p.18]) and proceed with business as usual. Professionals who consider themselves scientists should not blindly trust authoritative arguments. As Carl Sagan (1996) cautioned, "Too many such arguments have proved too painfully wrong. Authorities must prove their contentions like everybody else. This independence of science, its occasional unwillingness to accept conventional wisdom, makes it dangerous to doctrines less self-critical, or with pretensions of certitude" (p. 28).

Scatter interpretation has been a part of practice for more than a century and yet there is little supporting evidence and ample evidence demonstrating its shortcomings. There have been many iterations of this practice, from early strategies for interpreting performance with the Stanford Revisions of the Binet-Simon Scale to modern processing strengths and weaknesses models. None of these iterations has withstood empirical scrutiny. Thus it is time to act on evidence and put a moratorium on the interpretation of cognitive profiles "pending radical changes to measurement instruments that may reasonably be expected to produce different results" (Beaujean & Benson, 2019b, p. 27). More generally, it is long past time for the profession to insist that interpretations and uses of assessment data be evidence based.

References

Alfonso, V. C., LaRocca, R., Oakland, T. D., & Spanakos, A. (2000). The course on individual cognitive assessment. *School Psychology Review*, *29*(1), 52–64.

American Educational Research Association, American Psychological Association, & National Council on Measurement in Education. (2014). *Standards for educational and psychological testing.* American Educational Research Association.

American Psychological Association, Presidential Task Force on Evidence-Based Practice. (2006). Evidence-based practice in psychology. *American Psychologist*, *61*(4), 271–285. https://doi.org/10. 1037/0003-066X.61.4.271.

Beaujean, A. A., & Benson, N. F. (2019a). Theoretically-consistent cognitive ability test development and score interpretation. *Contemporary School Psychology*, *23*, 126–137. https://doi.org/10.1007/s40688 -018-0182-1

Beaujean, A. A., & Benson, N. F. (2019b). The one and the many: Enduring legacies of Spearman and Thurstone on intelligence test score interpretation. *Applied Measurement in Education*, *32*(3), 198–215. https://doi.org/10.1080/08957347.2019.1619560

Benjamin, L. T., Jr. (2005). A history of clinical psychology as a profession in America (and a glimpse at its future). *Annual Review of Clinical Psychology*, *1*, 1–30. https://doi.org/10.1146/annurev.clinpsy.1.102803 .143758

Benson, N. F., Beaujean, A. A., McGill, R. J., & Dombrowski, S. C. (2018). Revisiting Carroll's survey of factor-analytic studies: Implications for the clinical assessment of intelligence. *Psychological Assessment*, *30*(8), 1028–1038. https://doi.org/10.1037/pas0000556

Benson, N. F., Maki, K. E., Floyd, R. G., Eckert, T. L., Kranzler, J. H., & Fefer, S. A. (2020). A national survey of school psychologists' practices in identifying specific learning disabilities. *School Psychology*, *35*(2), 146–157. https://doi.org/10.1037/spq0000344

Binet, A., Simon, T., & Kite, E. S. (1916). *The intelligence of the feeble-minded*. Williams & Wilkins. https://doi .org/10.1037/11070-000

Brown, A. W. (1946). Review of Diagnostic Psychological Testing Vol I. *Psychological Bulletin*, *43*(5), 477–479. https://doi.org/10.1037/h0049564

Canivez, G. L. (2019). Evidence-based assessment for school psychology: Research, training, and clinical practice. *Contemporary School Psychology*, *23*(2), 194–200. https://doi.org/10.1007/s40688-019 -00238-z

Carroll, J. B. (1993). *Human cognitive abilities: A survey of factor-analytic studies.* Cambridge University Press.

Carroll, J. B. (2003). The higher–Stratum structure of cognitive abilities: Current evidence supports *g* and about ten broad factors. In H. Nyborg (Ed.), *The scientific study of general intelligence: Tribute to Arthur R. Jensen* (pp. 5–21). Pergamon.

Cohen, J. (1952). A factor-analytically based rationale for the Wechsler-Bellevue *Journal of Consulting Psychology, 16*(4), 272–277. https://doi.org/10.1037/h0060803

Cohen, J. (1957). A factor-analytically based rationale for the Wechsler Adult Intelligence Scale. *Journal of Consulting Psychology, 21*(6), 451–457. https://doi.org/10.1037/h0044203

Cohen, J. (1959). The factorial structure of the WISC at ages 7–6, 10–6, and 13–6. *Journal of Consulting Psychology, 23*(4), 285–299. https://doi.org/10.1037/h0043898

Cronbach, L. J., & Meehl, P. E. (1955). Construct validity in psychological tests. *Psychological Bulletin, 52*(4), 281–302. https://doi.org/10.1037/h0040957

Evidence Based Medicine Working Group (1992). Evidence based medicine: A new approach to teaching the practice of medicine. *JAMA, 268*, 2420–2425.

Farmer, R. L., McGill, R. J., Dombrowski, S. C., & Canivez, G. L. (2021). Why questionable assessment practices remain popular in school psychology: Instructional materials as pedagogic vehicles. *Canadian Journal of School Psychology, 36*(2), 98–114. https://doi.org/10.1177/0829573520978111

Flanagan, D. P., Alfonso, V. C., & Ortiz, S. O. (2012). The cross-battery assessment approach: An overview, historical perspective, and current directions. In D. P. Flanagan & P. L. Harrison (Eds.), *Contemporary intellectual assessment: Theories, tests, and issues* (3rd ed., pp. 459–483). Guilford Press.

Flanagan, D. P., Alfonso, V. C., Sy, M. C., Mascolo, J. T., McDonough, E. M., & Ortiz, S. O. (2018a). Dual discrepancy/consistency operational definition of SLD: Integrating multiple data sources and multiple data-gathering methods. In V. C. Alfonso & D. P. Flanagan (Eds.), *Essentials of specific learning disability identification* (pp. 329–430). Wiley.

Flanagan, D. P., Costa, M., Palma, K., Leahy, M. A., Alfonso, V. C., & Ortiz, S. O. (2018b). Cross-battery assessment, the cross-battery assessment software system, and the assessment-intervention connection. In D. P. Flanagan & E. M. McDonough (Eds.), *Contemporary intellectual assessment: Theories, tests, and issues* (4th ed., pp. 731–776). Guilford Press.

Frazier, T. W., & Youngstrom, E. A. (2007). Historical increase in the number of factors measured by commercial tests of cognitive ability: Are we overfactoring? *Intelligence, 35*(2), 169–182. https://doi.org/10.1016/j.intell.2006.07.002

Gottfredson, L. S. (1997). Mainstream science on intelligence: An editorial with 52 signatories, history and bibliography. *Intelligence, 24*(1), 13–23. https://doi.org/10.1016/S0160-2896(97)90011-8

Guertin, W. H., Frank, G. H., & Rabin, A. I. (1956). Research with the Wechsler-Bellevue Intelligence Scale: 1950–1955. *Psychological Bulletin, 53*(3), 235–257. https://doi.org/10.1037/h0047957

Guertin, W. H., Ladd, C. E., Frank, G. H., Rabin, A. I., & Hiester, D. S. (1966). Research with the Wechsler Intelligence Scales for Adults. *Psychological Bulletin, 66*(5), 385–409. https://doi.org/10.1037/h0020410

Guertin, W. H., Ladd, C. E., Frank, G. H., Rabin, A. I., & Hiester, D. S. (1971). Research with the Wechsler Intelligence Scales for Adults: 1965–1970. *The Psychological Record, 21*, 289–339. https://doi.org/10.1007/BF03394023

Guertin, W. H., Rabin, A. I., Frank, G. H., & Ladd, C. E. (1962). Research with the Wechsler Intelligence Scales for Adults: 1955–60. *Psychological Bulletin, 59*(1), 1–26. https://doi.org/10.1037/h0040560

Haggbloom, S. J., Warnick, R., Warnick, J. E., Jones, V. K., Yarbrough, G. L., Russell, T. M., Borecky, C. M., McGahhey, R., Powell, J. L., III, Beavers, J., & Monte, E. (2002). The 100 most eminent psychologists of the 20th century. *Review of General Psychology, 6*(2), 139–152. https://doi.org/10.1037/1089-2680.6.2.139

Harris, A. J., & Shakow, D. (1937). The clinical significance of numerical measures of scatter on the Stanford-Binet. *Psychological Bulletin, 34*(3), 134–150. https://doi.org/10.1037/h0058420

Hirshoren, A., & Kavale, K. (1976). Profile analysis of the WISC-R: A continuing malpractice. *Exceptional Child, 23*(2), 83–87. https://doi.org/10.1080/0156655760230202

Horn, J. L., & Blankson, N. (2005). Foundations for better understanding of cognitive abilities. In D. P. Flanagan & P. L. Harrison (Eds.), *Contemporary intellectual assessment: Theories, tests, and issues* (pp. 41–68). Guilford Press.

Horn, J. L., & Cattell, R. B. (1966). Refinement and test of the theory of fluid and crystallized general intelligences. *Journal of Educational Psychology, 57*(5), 253–270. https://doi.org/10.1037/h0023816

Hotez, P. J. (2020). Combating antiscience: Are we preparing for the 2020s? *PLoS Biology*, *18*(3), 1–6. https://doi.org/10.1371/journal.pbio.3000683

Jensen, A. R. (1998). *The g factor*. Praeger.

Kaufman, A. S. (1979). *Intelligent testing with the WISC–R*. Wiley.

Kaufman, A. S. (2013). Intelligent testing with Wechsler's fourth editions: Perspectives on the Weiss et al. Studies and the eight commentaries. *Journal of Psychoeducational Assessment*, *31*(2), 224–234. https://doi.org/10.1177/0734282913478049

Kavale, K. A., & Forness, S. R. (1984). A meta-analysis of the validity of Wechsler Scale profiles and recategorizations: Patterns or parodies? *Learning Disability Quarterly*, *7*(2), 136–156. https://doi.org/10.2307/1510314

Kranzler, J. H., Maki, K. E., Benson, N. F., Eckert, T. L., Floyd, R. G., & Fefer, S. A. (2020). How do school psychologists interpret intelligence tests for the identification of specific learning disabilities? *Contemporary School Psychology*, *24*, 445–456. https://doi.org/10.1007/s40688-020-00274-0

Lilienfeld, S. O., Ammirati, R., & David, M. (2012). Distinguishing science from pseudoscience in school psychology: Science and scientific thinking as safeguards against human error. *Journal of School Psychology*, *50*, 7–36. https://doi.org/10.1016/j.jsp.2011.09.006

Lilienfeld, S. O., Lynn, S. J., O'Donohue, W. T., & Latzman, R. D. (2017). Epistemic humility: An overarching educational philosophy for clinical psychology programs. *The Clinical Psychologist*, *70*(2), 6–14.

Lockwood, A. B., & Farmer, R. L. (2019). The cognitive assessment course: Two decades later. *Psychology in the Schools*, *57*(2), 265–283. https://doi.org/10.1002/pits.22298

Lubin, B., Larsen, R. M., & Matarazzo, J. D. (1984). Patterns of psychological test usage in the United States: 1935–1982. *American Psychologist*, *39*(4), 451–454. https://doi.org/10.1037/0003066x.39.4.451

Macmann, G. M., & Barnett, D. W. (1997). Myth of the master detective: Reliability of interpretations for Kaufman's "intelligent testing" approach to the WISC–III. *School Psychology Quarterly*, *12*(3), 197–234. https://doi.org/10.1037/h0088959

Matarazzo, J. D., Daniel, M. H., Prifitera, A., & Herman, D. O. (1988). Inter-subtest scatter in the WAIS–R standardization sample. *Journal of Clinical Psychology*, *44*(6), 940–950. https://doi.org/10.1002/1097-4679(198811)44:6<940::AID-JCLP2270440615>3.0.CO;2-A

McDermott, P. A., Fantuzzo, J. W., & Glutting, J. J. (1990). Just say no to subtest analysis: A critique on Wechsler theory and practice. *Journal of Psychoeducational Assessment*, *8*(3), 290–302. https://doi.org/10.1177/073428299000800307

McDermott, P. A., Fantuzzo, J. W., Glutting, J. J., Watkins, M. W., & Baggaley, A. R. (1992). Illusions of meaning in the ipsative assessment of children's ability. *The Journal of Special Education*, *25*(4), 504–526. https://doi.org/10.1177/002246699202500407

McDermott, P. A., & Glutting, J. J. (1997). Informing stylistic learning behavior, disposition, and achievement through ability subtests: Or more illusions of meaning? *School Psychology Review*, *26*(2), 163–175. https://doi.org/10.1080/02796015.1997.12085856

McGill, R. J., Dombrowski, S. C., & Canivez, G. L. (2018). Cognitive profile analysis in school psychology: History, issues, and continued concerns. *Journal of School Psychology*, *71*, 108–121. https://doi.org/10.1016/j.jsp.2018.10.007

Meehl, P. E. (1973). Why I do not attend case conferences. In P. E. Meehl (Ed.), *Psychodiagnosis: Selected papers* (pp. 225–302). University of Minnesota Press.

Meehl, P. E. (1997). Credentialed persons, credentialed knowledge. *Clinical Psychology: Science and Practice*, *4*(2), 91–98. https://doi.org/10.1111/j.1468-2850.1997.tb00103.x

Meehl, P. E. (2002). Cliometric metatheory: II Criteria scientists use in theory appraisal and why it is rational to do so. *Psychological Reports*, *91*(2), 339–404. https://doi.org/10.2466/PR0.91.6.339-404

Oakland, T. D., & Zimmerman, S. A. (1986). The course on individual mental assessment: A national survey of course instructors. *Professional School Psychology*, *1*(1), 51–59. https://doi.org/10.1037/h0090497

Pfeiffer, S. I., Reddy, L. A., Kletzel, J. E., Schmelzer, E. R., & Boyer, L. M. (2000). The practitioner's view of IQ testing and profile analysis. *School Psychology Quarterly*, *15*(4), 376–385. https://doi.org/10.1037/h0088795

Rabin, A. I. (1945). The use of the Wechsler-Bellevue scales with normal and abnormal persons. *Psychological Bulletin*, *42*(7), 410–422. https://doi.org/10.1037/h0053835

Rabin, A. I., & Guertin, W. H. (1951). Research with the Wechsler-Bellevue test: 1945–1950. *Psychological Bulletin*, *48*(3), 211–248. https://doi.org/10.1037/h0059554

Rapaport, D., Gil, M., & Schafer, R. (1945) *Diagnostic psychological testing* (Vol. 1). Year Book Publishers.

Reynolds, C. R., & Gutkin, T. B. (1981). Test scatter on the WPPSI: Normative analyses of the standardization sample. *Journal of Learning Disabilities*, *14*(8), 460–464. https://doi.org/10.1177/002221948101400805

Rosenzweig, S. (1946). Clinical psychology as a psychodiagnostic art. *Journal of Personality*, *15*(2), 94–100. https://doi.org/10.1111/1467-6494.ep8926390

Sagan, C. (1996). *The demon-haunted world: Science as a candle in the dark*. The Random House Publishing Group.

Schafer, R. (1946). Ability patterns and personality the expression of personality and maladjustment in intelligence test results. *Annals of the New York Academy of Sciences*, *46*, 609–624. https://doi.org/10.1111/j.1749-6632.1946.tb31691.x

Schafer, R., & Rapaport, D. (1944). The scatter: In diagnostic intelligence testing *Journal of Personality*, *12*(4), 275–284. https://doi.org/10.1111/j.1467-6494.1944.tb01963.x

Schneider, W. J., & Kaufman, A. S. (2017). Let's not do away with comprehensive cognitive assessments just yet. *Archives of Clinical Neuropsychology*, *32*(1), 8–20. https://doi.org/10.1093/arclin/acw104

Schneider, W. J., & McGrew, K. S. (2018). The Cattell–Horn–Carroll theory of cognitive abilities. In D. P. Flanagan & E. M. McDonough (Eds.), *Contemporary intellectual assessment: Theories, tests, and issues* (4th ed., pp. 73–163). Guilford Press.

Spearman, C. E. (1927). *The abilities of man: Their nature and measurement.* Blackburn Press.

Thaler, R. H. (2015). *Misbehaving: The making of behavioral economics*. W. W. Norton & Co.

Thurstone, T. G. (1941). Primary mental abilities of children. *Educational and Psychological Measurement*, *1*(1), 103–115. https://doi.org/10.1177/001316444100100110

von Hippel, W., Buss, D. M., & Richardson, G. B. (2020). Science progresses through open disagreement: Rejoinder to Fine (2020). *Archives of Scientific Psychology*, *8*(1), 11–14. https://doi.org/10.1037/arc0000073

Watkins, M. W. (2000). Cognitive profile analysis: A shared professional myth. *School Psychology Quarterly*, *15*(4), 465–479. https://doi.org/10.1037/h0088802

Watkins, M. W. (2003). IQ subtest analysis: Clinical acumen or clinical illusion? *The Scientific Review of Mental Health Practice: Objective Investigations of Controversial and Unorthodox Claims in Clinical Psychology, Psychiatry, and Social Work*, *2*, 118–141.

Weiner, I. B. (1983). The future of psychodiagnosis revisited. *Journal of Personality Assessment*, *47*(5), 451–461. https://doi.org/10.1207/s15327752jpa4705_1

Zachar, P., & Leong, F. T. (2000). A 10-year longitudinal study of scientists and practitioner interests in psychology: Assessing the Boulder model. *Professional Psychology: Research and Practice*, *31*(5), 575–580. https://doi.org/10.1037//0735-7028.31.5.575

Chapter 8

Unreliable Differences

Considering the Reliability of Discrepancy Scores

Ryan L. Farmer and Samuel Y. Kim

One of the most important roles of a psychologist is to identify mental health conditions in children, adolescents, and adults, and much of that work relies on scores from psychological tests. In making these decisions, psychologists frequently compare a person's test score to a specific cut-off, or criterion, score. For intelligence tests, when a score is below a certain value, we often argue that the individual has an intellectual deficit or disability. In clear cases, it is often easier to identify. However, there are instances where the scores are close to the criterion score. For example, a score that is only 3 points off a criterion score can make it difficult to make a claim of a deficit or disability. Now if the score on the measure had a confidence interval of 5 points versus 15 points, would that change the perspective of the diagnosis? Precision of an instrument plays a critical role in substantiating claims from the scores.

Aside from diagnosis, psychological assessment informs several decision-making processes such as treatment and educational placement. With such high-stakes decisions, the reliability of a measure is critical. In the above example, a test with a narrower confidence interval of a person's ability is more useful than one with a wider range and especially when a score is near a criterion or cut-off. These confidence intervals are calculated using reliability estimates; thus, reliability is an important concept with far reaching consequences. Consistent with *The Standards* (AERA et al., 2014), the conceptualization of reliability has much to do with precision.[1] In a classroom, an instructor may grade student essays according to grammar and syntax and at other times primarily on content. While both of these evaluation foci are reasonable qualities on which to grade, flipping between the two evaluation methods on a single assignment will lead to increased error in the grading process—that is, the *variance* in grades is not consistently coming from the same source. Some students may pass while others fail when submitting essays of similar quality. This inconsistency can ultimately hinder learning for the students.

Error in measurement has long been an issue in psychology and other fields,[2] with one of the first attempts in psychology likely being Spearman's (1904) correction for correlation coefficients used when the measures of the constructs included accidental variance—what we might call construct-irrelevant influences. The first use of the term *reliability coefficient* was by Brown

(1910), though his use is more akin to the contemporary test-retest reliability concept and was the correlation coefficient between two administrations of the same instrument taken at different time points. In this sense, Brown's conceptualization of reliability coefficients was something of a measure of replicability of measurement. The importance of reliability is due to most psychological measurement today being undergirded by Classical Test Theory (CTT; see Lord et al., 1968). In CTT, the score obtained is thought to be comprised of the person's true ability and measurement error. In this model, it is crucial to estimate measurement error to better understand a person's true ability. When an intelligence test is administered to a young child, an IQ score is obtained, and though it isn't perfect, it's a fairly good indicator of general intelligence (e.g., Farmer et al., 2014). It appears to be made up of three distinguishable sources of variances: true score variance, specific variance, and error variance. As discussed, variance stemming from a child's general intelligence—the true score variance—is the variance of interest. Finally, variance stemming from random error is also observed. Both specific and random error variance are grouped together as error and can come either from construct-irrelevant influences or imprecision inherent to the instrument. Because of error, any score that is obtained on a psychological measure is clouded and, at best, just a rough estimate of the actual score.

Reliability: A Brief Overview

Generally speaking, *reliability* concerns itself with consistency of test scores between forms of a test (i.e., alternate forms reliability) and stability of test scores over time (i.e., test-retest reliability). From the perspective of CTT, reliability is thought of as the ratio of true score variance to total score variance and represents the precision of the scores or, more formally, the extent to which an observed score is free of measurement error (Furr, 2017; Price, 2016). From the perspective of replication, "reliability is the measure of the degree of consistency in examinee scores over replications of a measurement procedure" (Brennan, 2001, pp. 295–296). Reliability coefficients typically range from 0 to 1 with lower values indicating a lower amount of true score variance to total score variance and values closer to 1 representing the opposite. For those interested in a general overview of reliability, see Furr (2017); those interested in a technical overview of reliability should see Price (2016); those looking for a historical perspective of reliability should see Brennan (2001); and those interested in a conceptual perspective of internal consistency reliability should review (Henson, 2001). The purpose of this chapter is to focus on the calculation of *difference score reliability*, a type of internal consistency reliability, which is an indirect estimate of the reliability of scores based on CTT. Given this focus, we begin by providing context regarding (a) types of scores in intelligence tests, (b) how those scores are formed, and (c) the typical reliability of scores from intelligence tests. Next, (d) we discuss difference scores, their uses, and their reliability. Finally, (e) we address implications and interpretation of difference scores.

Reliability in Intelligence Tests

IQ tests produce a number of test scores and types including (a) subtest scores, (b) stratum II composite scores, (c) stratum III composites, (d) ancillary scores (i.e., scores that are not based on an attribute's theory; Beaujean & Benson, 2019), and (e) difference scores. In addition, a number of sources encourage clinicians to interpret profiles of cognitive abilities (e.g., Kaufman et al., 2016).

Given the clinical and educational decisions that stem from the interpretation of test scores from intelligence tests (e.g., Kranzler et al., 2020) and the effect those decisions may have on services and treatment, the internal consistency and stability of those scores and profiles becomes imperative. Consistent with *The Standards* (AERA et al., 2014), many publishers often report test score reliability in test manuals. However, this reporting is often selective (e.g., McGill et al., 2018); publishers regularly report internal consistency reliability of subtests, stratum II composite scores, and stratum III composites but do not consistently report reliability estimates of ancillary scores. Worse, publishers often do not report the reliability of difference scores or profiles, which frequently appear in training material (Farmer et al., 2021) and undergird popular cognitive profile analysis strategies (McGill et al., 2018). In the following sections, we will discuss reliability estimates for each type of score produced by IQ tests as well as for profiles, using the scores from the *Kaufman Assessment Battery for Children–Second Edition, Normative Update* (KABC–II NU; Kaufman & Kaufman, 2018); *Woodcock Johnson IV Tests of Cognitive Abilities* (WJ IV COG; Schrank et al., 2014); *Wechsler Intelligence Scale for Children–Fifth Edition* (WISC–V; Wechsler, 2014), and *Reynolds Intellectual Assessment Scale–Second Edition* (RIAS–2; Reynolds & Kamphaus, 2015). Due to recent updates and frequent uses (Benson et al., 2019), however, our focus will be on difference scores, their calculation, interpretation, and properties.

One of the most commonly reported characteristics by test publishers is internal consistency, but there is variability in how the scores are calculated. Untimed subtests are often calculated using split-half reliability, which evenly divides the items on a subtest and examines the relationship (via correlation coefficient) between the two halves. Alternatively, when subtests are scored using a multi-point system (e.g., 0, 1, or 2 points are awarded), Rasch-based methods for calculating reliability may be used (see Gustafsson, 1980). Finally, subtests that include smaller tests (e.g., multi-test subtests such as the WJ IV Oral Vocabulary test) may use a composite score reliability approach (e.g., Mosier, 1943). In another variation, timed tests are often estimated using test-retest reliability due to challenges with the rate-based nature of the tests having such a limited number of scores. Thus, the reliability of timed tests during a single testing session are interpreted as estimates of consistency rather than stability, and standards typically provided for internal consistency are applied as opposed to those for test-retest methods.

Composite scores, on the other hand, are often calculated based on the inter-correlations and individual internal consistencies of their constituent parts and may use any number of approaches including those offered by Mosier (1943) and Nunnally and Bernstein (1994). While it is outside of the scope of this chapter to provide formulae for each of these approaches, interested readers may wish to explore Larry Price's (2016) recent textbook *Psychometric Methods*, which describes and discusses a number of these statistical procedures.

Reliability of Primary Scores (Stratum I, II, and III)

Primary scores from IQ tests include subtests (stratum I), composite scores stemming from a small number of subtests that are intended to represent broad cognitive abilities (stratum II), and composite scores stemming from a (typically) larger number of subtests that are intended to represent general intelligence (stratum III). Generally speaking, the more items that are aggregated, the less impact measurement error has on the derived score because fewer items generally have greater measurement error. As test developers have learned to maximize consistency between items, to lengthen subtests, and to include two or more smaller tests as part of a single subtest, these differences have been minimized. For instance, the WJ IV COG (Schrank et al., 2014) features several tests with testlets that are intended to measure stratum II domains. Generally these composites are reliable. For instance, the median total sample reliabilities reported in the WJ IV COG technical manual was 0.89 [range 0.74 to 0.97]. Despite using fewer composite subtests, the median of the average subtest reliability reported in the WISC–V (Wechsler, 2014) was a respectable 0.86 [range 0.81 to 0.94]. The KABC–2 NU (Kaufman & Kaufman, 2018) median total sample subtest reliability reported for ages 3 to 6 was 0.87 [range 0.83 to 0.97] and for ages 7 to 18 was 0.91 [range 0.79 to 0.96]. Finally, the RIAS–2 (Reynolds & Kamphaus 2015) median total sample subtest reliability was 0.86 [range 0.81 to 0.99]. Across the 73 subtests from the four tests, the median subtest reliability was 0.88 [bootstrapped 95% CI 0.86 to 0.90] with a minimum observed reliability coefficient of 0.74 and a maximum observed reliability coefficient of 0.99 (see Figure 8.1).

Composite scores that are intended to represent stratum II are typically computed from three or more subtests, and this increase in items leads generally to an increase in reliability coefficient estimates. For instance, the WJ IV COG has 17 composites, excluding variants of general intelligence (e.g., Gf-Gc Composite), and the median reliability coefficient was 0.93 [range 0.86 and 0.97]. The five primary composites from the WISC–V (e.g., Verbal Comprehension Index) had a median reliability of 0.92 [range 0.88 to 0.93]. Similarly, the five primary composites from the RIAS–2 had a median reliability coefficient of 0.91, ranging between 0.90 and 0.99. Finally, the four primary composites from the KABC–2 NU for children ages 3 to 7 was 0.95 [range 0.91 to 0.98], and the five primary composites from the KABC–2 NU for people ages 8 to 18 was also 0.95 [range 0.91 to 0.97]. Across 34 primary composites from the four tests, the median primary composite reliability was 0.93 [bootstrapped 95% CI 0.92 to 0.94], with a minimum observed reliability coefficient of 0.86 and a maximum observed reliability coefficient of 0.99 (see Figure 8.1).

Finally, the primary scores representing general intelligence have the highest reliability coefficients. The increase in items contributing to these global composites tends to increase the internal consistency of these scores. For the WJ IV COG, the median reliability coefficient for the total sample was 0.97 for General Intellectual Ability, 0.94 for Brief Intellectual Ability, and 0.96

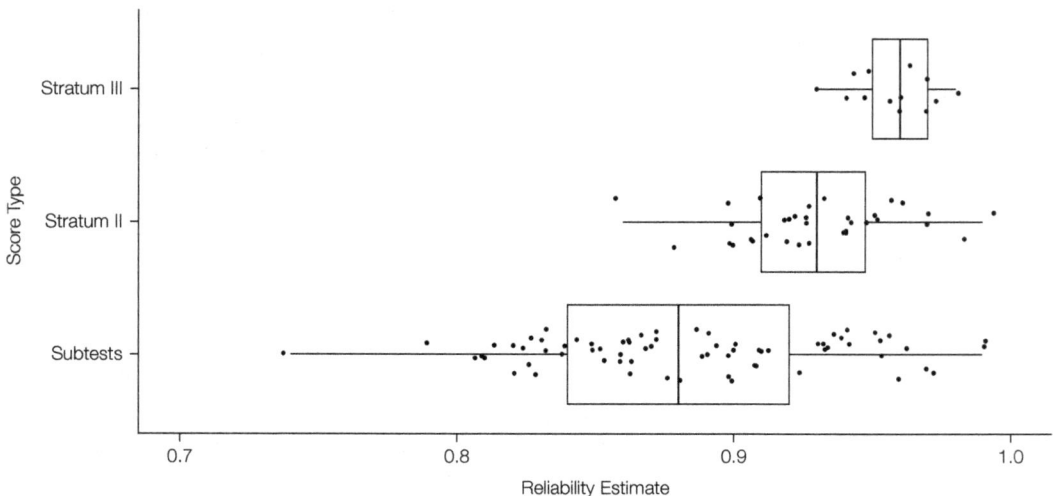

Figure 8.1. **Reliability Estimates by Score Type Across the KABC–2 NU, RIAS–2, WISC–V, and WJ IV COG.**

for the Gf-Gc Composite. For the WISC–V, the median reliability coefficient for the total sample was 0.96 for the Full-Scale IQ, 0.96 for the General Ability Index, and 0.95 for the Nonverbal Index. For the KABC–2 NU 3–7 age group, the Fluid-Crystallized Index (FCI) was 0.97, the Mental Processing (MPI) was 0.96, and the Nonverbal Index (NVI) was 0.94. For the 8–18 age group, the FCI was 0.98, the MPI was 0.97, and the NVI was 0.95. Finally, for the RIAS–2, the median reliability coefficient for the total sample was 0.93. Across the 13 primary global composites from the four tests, the median reliability coefficient was 0.96 [bootstrapped 95% CI 0.95 to 0.97], with a minimum observed reliability coefficient of 0.93 and a maximum observed reliability coefficient of 0.98 (see Figure 8.1). The observant reader might notice the reduction in range of reliability scores from subtest to composite to global composite reliability coefficients, which (a) corroborates the Spearman-Brown prophecy, and (b) suggests a soft ceiling for reliability on IQ tests. Indeed, these data make it clear that primary composites (e.g., stratum II) are typically more consistent than subtests, and global composites (stratum III) are typically more consistent than both composites and subtests.

Ancillary composites, or pseudo-composites, are linear or weighted combinations of various subtests to form face valid but otherwise atheoretical scores. While the interpretation of such scores is not well supported by theory, several tests provide ancillary composites for clinicians to use (e.g., Quantitative Reasoning Index [QRI] from the WISC–V). Beaujean and Benson (2019) contend that due to the atheoretical development of the WISC–V and overreliance on factor analytic (cf. theoretical) techniques for identifying the instrument's model, primary composites such as Processing Speed Index qualify as pseudo-composites. While this is a gray area (i.e., while theory generation following observed data is not inadmissible, and factor analytic techniques are an excellent example of existential abduction [Haig, 2018]), inadequate effort has been made to understand the nature of the underlying trait. This chapter will avoid identifying composites identified by publishers as primary in this category and focus on clear cases of pseudo-composites. However, because ancillary composites pull from several subtests like primary composites, their reliability coefficient estimates are typically acceptable. From the WISC–V, the reliability coefficients for the QRI, Auditory Working Memory Index, and Cognitive Processing Index were 0.95, 0.93, and 0.93, respectively. From the WJ IV COG, the reliability coefficients for the Cognitive Efficiency was 0.93 and for the Cognitive Efficiency–Extended was 0.95. Finally, from the KABC–2 NU Delayed Recall for ages 3 to 7 was 0.92 and for ages 8 to 18 was 0.95. Across these seven ancillary composites from the four tests, the median reliability coefficient was 0.93.

Reliability of Difference Scores

Difference scores—or discrepancy scores—are unique in that they are not directly derived from a student's normative standing but are the result of subtracting one norm-referenced score from another (e.g., Verbal Comprehension Index–Fluid Reasoning Index). These differences are often interpreted as strengths and weaknesses between cognitive abilities (Canivez, 2013). For instance, if a student obtains a score of 100 on the Verbal Comprehension Index and a score of 80 on the Fluid Reasoning Index, they are said to have a relative strength in Comprehension Knowledge over Fluid Reasoning. Notable differences are said to be indicative of learning or processing disorders, and using difference scores may be clinically useful for classification or treatment selection (Flanagan et al., 2013; cf. McGill et al., 2018). Furthermore, difference scores provide the quantitative components of cognitive profile analysis strategies (McGill et al., 2018).

Cognitive profile analysis strategies are varied in their specific criteria and processes but share the investigation of differences between cognitive abilities represented by scores from IQ tests (e.g., Fiorello & Wycoff, 2018; Flanagan et al., 2013). From this perspective, the computation of difference scores supports clinicians in making quantitative arguments that such differences between cognitive abilities are present.

Difference scores can be calculated from subtest pairings, composite pairings, or by ipsative comparison (i.e., the difference between a single score [subtest or composite] and an anchor score such as the average of similar scores). Difference scores from subtests and ipsative comparisons were prominent in the 1980s and 1990s, with concerns over their reliability and validity leading to a reduction in use at the end of the century (Bray et al., 1998; McDermott et al., 1990, 1992; Watkins, 2000). However, as Cattell-Horn-Carroll–based IQ tests and interpretation rose in prominence, this led to a shift from subtest and ipsative comparison to composite comparisons. Despite substantial critical discourse in the 1990s and inadequate evidence of their utility (McGill et al., 2018), subtest- and composite-level difference scores are still found in interpretation guidelines (Kaufman et al., 2016; Sattler, 2018), are a foundational element of cognitive profile analysis based approaches (see McGill et al., 2018), and continue to be recommended in test manuals (e.g., Reynolds & Kamphaus, 2015; Wechsler, 2014) and other instructional materials (Farmer et al., 2021). Relatedly, these strategies continue to be taught in graduate programs (Lockwood & Farmer, 2020) and used in practice (Kranzler et al., 2020).

To the casual observer, the ubiquitous nature of using difference scores seems to be without issue, but a careful examination of the reliability calculations demonstrates a flaw in the logic. Thorndike and Hagen (1969) reported a formula for calculating the reliability of difference scores when the two component scores have equivalent *SD*s, as is often the case when comparing one subtest to another, or one composite to another.

$$(1)\ r = r_a + r_b 2\text{-}r_{ab}(1\text{-}r_{ab})$$

In this frequently used formula, r is the reliability of the difference score, r_a and r_b are the reliabilities of the two comparison scores, and r_{ab} is the correlation between the comparison scores. Difference score reliability, then, is a function of the reliability of the comparison scores and the extent to which those scores covary. The most reliable difference scores are those that stem from very reliable components and that have a low-to-moderate correlation with one another. Given two scores with equal standard deviation with reliabilities of .92 and .93 respectively and for which their correlation is .35, the equation is solved thus:

$$(1.1)\ r = .92 + .932\text{-}.35(1\text{-}.35)$$

$$(1.2)\ r = .925\ \text{-}.35(1\text{-}.35)$$

$$(1.3)\ r = .575(.65)$$

$$(1.4)\ r = .88$$

Inversely, component scores with low-to-moderate reliability or scores with a high correlation with one another lead to lower difference score reliability. This time, consider two other scores with equal standard deviation that have reliabilities of .80 and .89 respectively with correlation held constant.

$$(2.1)\ r = .80 + .892\text{-}.35(1\text{-}.35)$$

$$(2.2)\ r = .845\ \text{-}.35(1\text{-}.35)$$

$$(2.3)\ r = .495(.65)$$

$$(2.4)\ r = .76$$

Certainly scores with reliability of .80 and .89 are fairly common and it would be difficult to describe these scores as unreliable; however, this small reduction in component score reliability has notable impact on the result of the difference score's reliability. In this example, the correlation between the two scores is increased from .35 to .80.

$$(3.1)\ r = .80 + .892\text{-}.80(1\text{-}.80)$$

$$(3.2)\ r = .845\ \text{-}.80(1\text{-}.80)$$

$$(3.3)\ r = .045(.20)$$

$$(3.4)\ r = .23$$

The effect of the correlation on the difference score reliability is palpable, leading to a sizable decrease in reliable variance. While the values above were selected for demonstration purposes, scores with reliability above .80 and high correlation with other scores are common due to the focus of making intelligence tests more reliable along with the positive manifold of intelligence tests.

In a different example, when the correlation between the component scores is higher than the average reliability of the component scores (e.g., r_a = .80; r_a = .82; $\bar{x}_{r(ab)}$ = .81; r_{ab} = .82), the solution is ultimately negative (-0.06). Given the theoretical bounds of reliability, 0.00 to 1.00, this result is untenable and its interpretation unclear. Take for instance the difference score reliability obtained for the WISC–V FSIQ-GAI comparison. The FSIQ and GAI are very reliable, both with coefficient alpha estimates of .96. Furthermore, they both serve as indexes of general intelligence and covary substantially with an observed correlation of .97. This results in a difference score reliability coefficient of -.33, which should likely be interpreted as reliability of 0.00. Again, difference in methods (e.g., the presence or absence of timed processing speed subtests) are no doubt accounted for by this difference score though this is not well captured due to the inconsistency of the indicator. Arguably, comparing the FSIQ to the GAI is effectively asking whether a student's general intelligence is significantly different from their general intelligence, and users of such strategies should question whether such strategies are theoretically consistent regardless of their psychometric fitness.

Considering its broad use, evaluating the reliability of various difference scores is necessary for assessing whether or not they are fit for interpretation. Hacherl (2020), Stinson (2020), and Farmer and Kim (2020) completed analyses of difference score reliabilities from the KABC–II NU, WJ IV COG, WISC–V, and RIAS–2 using the methods described above. Bootstrapping with 10,000 replications was used via the rcompanion package (v.2 3.26; Mangiafico, 2020) to estimate medians and 95% confidence intervals of subtest and composite difference score reliabilities from each of the available contemporary tests. Those data are available by test and score type in Table 8.1.

Across tests, the median reliability estimate for subtests was .85 (.83 to .86) and for composite scores was .85 (.84 to .86). These data are visualized in Figure 8.2, and it is worth noting that there is significant overlap between the two distributions at the upper end though a considerable

Table 8.1 Median and 95% Confidence Interval of Difference Score Reliabilities by Test and Type

Test	Subtest (95% CI)	Subtest *n*	Composites (95% CI)	Composite *n*
KABC–2 NU (3–6)	.89 (.87 to .90)	153	.91 (.89 to .93)	28
KABC–2 NU (7–18)	.90 (.87 to .90)	150	.91 (.88 to .92)	32
RIAS–2	.84 (.81 to .90)	28	.79 (.46 to .89)	10
WISC–V	.77 (.74 to .77)	120	.80 (.77 to .83)	56
WJ IV COG	.81 (.79 to .83)	153	.83 (.80 to .84)	55

Note. KABC–2 NU = Kaufman Assessment Battery for Children–Second Edition Normative Update; RIAS–2 = Reynolds Intellectual Assessment Scales–Second Edition; WISC–V = Wechsler Intelligence Scale for Children–Fifth Edition; WJ IV COG = Woodcock Johnson IV Tests of Cognitive Abilities. The notations *3–6* and *7–18* represent the KABC–2 NU battery age-range. CI = confidence interval. Data from the KABC–2 NU and WJ IV COG come from Hacherl (2020) and Stinson (2020). Data from the RIAS–2 and WISC–V come from Farmer and Kim (2020).

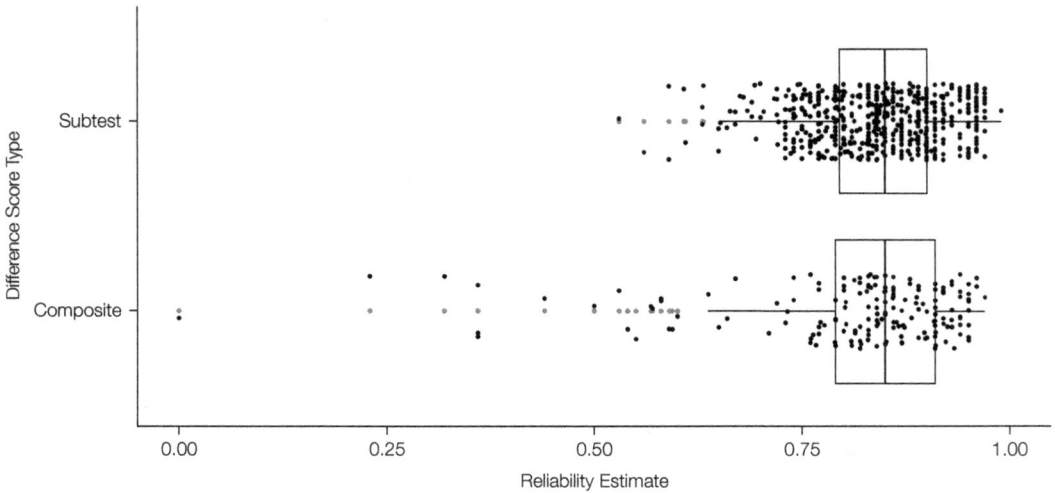

Figure 8.2. **Boxplot of Difference Score Reliability Estimates by Score Type.**

number of reliability estimates fall below *r* = .75 for both subtests and composites. One interesting phenomenon here is that subtest-based difference score reliabilities are much less variable and are clustered about the median (minimum = 0.53, p.25 = .79, median = .85, p.75 = .90, maximum = .99) whereas composite-based difference score reliabilities have several values well below *r* = .50 (minimum = 0, p.25 = .79, median = .85, p.75 = .91, maximum = .97).

Thus the argument that composite-level difference scores have higher reliability than subtest-level difference scores is likely untrue, and in fact there may be more composite-level difference scores well below *r* = .50. One possible reason for presence of composite-level difference scores with reliability coefficients below .50 is shared variance. That is, we have demonstrated that the subtest reliability varies more so than stratum II and stratum III reliabilities and so cannot solely explain that stratum II and stratum III composite-level difference scores will have lower reliability coefficients. Indeed, if this were the only deciding factor, this finding would be anomalous as lower reliability of component parts would always lead to lower reliability of different scores from those component parts.

The intercorrelation of those component parts plays a significant role. Subtests have been historically selected to represent more abstract abilities such as Comprehension Knowledge or General Intelligence; however, they also have substantial unique variance—that is, variance that is attributed to the unique characteristics of a given subtest (e.g., analogy skill in tests like Similarities, motor control in tests like Coding and Symbol Search) and not shared with other subtests even those selected to represent the same abstract ability. For instance, consider the unique qualities of the Similarities and Information subtests. Similarities emphasizes a child's unique skill related to analogies, requires some vocabulary knowledge, requires vocal reporting, and so forth. On the other hand, the Information subtest requires more specific and arguably more culturally bound knowledge, with considerably less emphasis on analogy and still a sizable emphasis on vocabulary skill. What is the same across these subtests that is carried forward into the Verbal Comprehension Index?

As subtests are aggregated, unique variance plays a smaller role, and shared variance plays a more considerable role. At stratum II, scores are a combination of variance attributable to (a) subtest unique characteristics, (b) the stratum II ability they aim to represent, (c) the general factor, and (d) error. Given the often sizable and reliable contribution of the general factor to the variance makeup of various composite scores, subtracting one composite from another is likely to remove a portion of shared variance as well as differentiate those variance components that are unique to the two scores. This leads to a question of how to successfully interpret these types of scores.

Interpretation of Difference Scores

While test manuals recommend a relatively straightforward approach to interpreting difference scores, Charter (1999) and Charter and Feldt (2009) suggest determining whether a difference score should be interpreted by evaluating the 95% confidence interval of the score itself, which is calculated using a relatively straightforward formula for the width (Schneider, 2014).

$$\text{CI Width} = 2Z_{CI\%}\sigma_x(r_{xx}-r_{xx}^2)$$

Herein, the z-score associated with 95% confidence intervals, 1.96, is represented by $Z_{CI\%}$; the standard deviation of the test score (e.g., 15 for standard scores) is represented by σ_x; and the difference score reliability is represented by r_{xx}. While it is feasible to substitute alternative z-scores, Charter (1999) and Charter and Feldt (2009) recommend the use of the 95% CI to increase the severity of the test to be performed. Once the CI have been calculated, the clinician can then apply two non-inferiority tests where the boundary conditions are set by 0 (i.e., no difference) and the significance criteria described by test publishers for a given alpha criteria (e.g., a difference of 11 points when alpha is set at .05). Charter and Feldt (2009) describe four different possible outcomes, each with different implications for interpretation, as depicted in Figure 8.3.

Effectively, Charter and Feldt (2009) recommend that considering confidence intervals in relation to 0 (no difference) and the critical value (minimum difference for a change in decision-making) gives the practitioner information about whether those differences are meaningful and whether they should be interpreted. In Type 1 and Type 2, Charter and Feldt discourage interpretation of difference scores as they are either not meaningfully different from 0 or because they are entirely below the

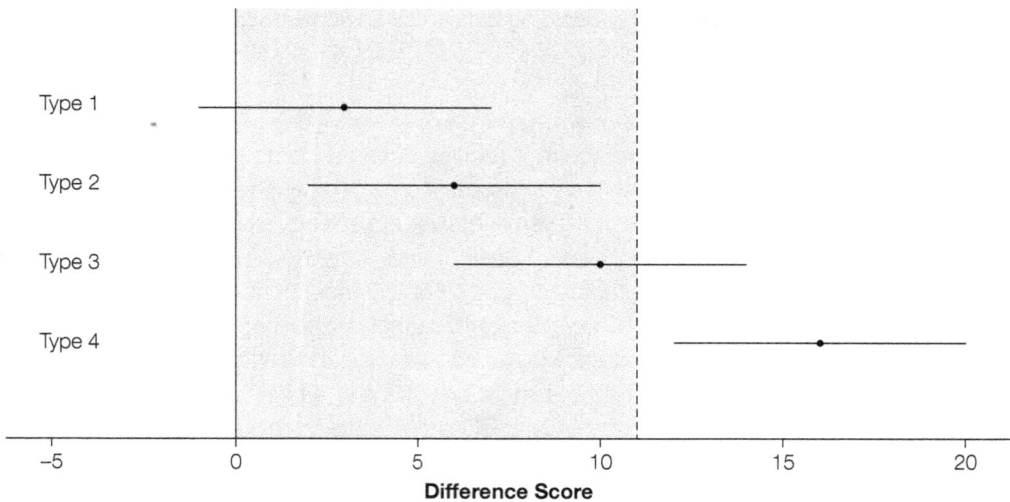

Figure 8.3. Visualization of Difference Scores and Their Confidence Intervals in Relation to a Difference of 0 and a Critical Value. *Note.* Difference score interpretation guidelines as recommended by Charter and Feldt (2009).

critical threshold. The situation in Type 3, that the score is entirely above zero and partially above and below the critical threshold, is more ambiguous and the authors argue that practitioners can choose to interpret the difference or not but also that they should collect additional information related to any decisions. They recommend that in Type 4, when the confidence interval is entirely above the critical value, practitioners should have more confidence in decision-making related to difference scores.

Charter and Feldt's (2009) approach to interpreting difference scores is more conservative than what seems to be recommended by most test manuals but it is still vulnerable to false positives. Relying too heavily on difference scores and critical values can lead to inaccurate pathologizing (i.e., false positives). One frequent argument is that difference scores are not diagnostic nor are they used in treatment selection but are used to generate hypotheses for further testing. As such, proponents will argue, lower reliability is acceptable. This reasoning is flawed. While use of an abductive (i.e., reasoning from observed data to a causal mechanism) approach for clinical reasoning is altogether defensible, beginning with heavily confounded data is not. As Vertue and Haig (2008) explain, the data from which a clinician abduces an explanation must be reliable to control for confounds, increase the potential of replicability, and so forth. It seems that various interpretation guidelines (confirmatory and exploratory) blur reliability and validity by asserting that if the difference is clearly above the critical value after considering the score's reliability (vis-á-vis confidence intervals), then it may warrant action (Charter & Feldt, 2009). While it is true that reliability is a crucial psychometric concept, reliability is necessary but insufficient for score interpretation. Even with the most permissive review of these data, the data available from Hacherl (2020), Stinson (2020), and Farmer and Kim (2020) should warrant caution and can in no way promote the use of difference scores alone without clear evidence of utility.

Conclusion

In this chapter, we briefly reviewed basic principles of reliability; provided descriptive information about the reliability of intelligence test scores by type; and discussed the calculation and interpretation of difference score reliability. The available data suggest that most subtest-level difference scores fall below reasonable standards of reliability (e.g., .70, .80) and that composite-level differences only intermittently meet these standards. We reason that if interpreting difference scores in isolation warrants individual evaluation of reliability estimates at minimum, then more complex interpretive systems that are undergirded by quantitative differences between cognitive abilities will warrant the same precautions. Perhaps most important, we remind readers that having adequate reliability is not sufficient for interpretation, and we know of no compelling evidence for the diagnostic or treatment utility of difference scores. Much more research is necessary to justify the use of difference scores as part of an evidence-based interpretive framework.

Notes

1   *Precision* is not to be confused with its common-language synonym, *accuracy*. Accuracy has to do with how well a score—given a specific cut-score—correctly identifies people with a disease and people without a disease. Accuracy is a function of test sensitivity, test specificity, and disease prevalence and is typically reserved for evaluation of diagnostic utility. Further discussion of accuracy is beyond the scope of this chapter.
2   For a contextual-historical review of reliability, see Brennan (2001).

References

American Educational Research Association, American Psychological Association, & National Council on Measurement in Education. (2014). *Standards for educational and psychological testing.* American Educational Research Association.

Beaujean, A. A., & Benson, N. F. (2019). Theoretically-consistent cognitive ability test development and score interpretation. *Contemporary School Psychology*, 23(2), 126–137. https://doi.org/10.1007/s40688-018 -0182-1

Benson, N. F., Floyd, R. G., Kranzler, J. H., Eckert, T. L., Fefer, S. A., & Morgan, G. B. (2019). Test use and assessment practices of school psychologists in the United States: Findings from the 2017 National Survey. *Journal of School Psychology*, 72, 29–48. https://doi.org/10.1016/j.jsp.2018.12.004

Bray, M. A., Kehle, T. J., & Hintze, J. M. (1998). Profile analysis with the Wechsler scales: Why does it persist? *School Psychology International*, 19(3), 209–220. https://doi.org/10.1177/0143034398193002

Brennan, R. L. (2001). An essay on the history and future of reliability from the perspective of replications. *Journal of Educational Measurement*, 38(4), 295–317. https://doi.org/10.1111/j.1745-3984.2001 .tb01129.x

Brown, W. (1910). Some experimental results in the correlation of mental abilities. *British Journal of Psychology*, 3(3), 296–322. https://doi.org/10.1111/j.2044-8295.1910.tb00207.x

Canivez, G. L. (2013). Psychometric versus actuarial interpretation of intelligence and related aptitude batteries. In D. H. Saklofske, C. R. Reynolds, & V. L. Schwean, (Eds.), *The Oxford handbook of child psychological assessments* (pp. 84–112). Oxford University Press. https://doi.org/10.1093/oxfordhb/ 9780199796304.013.0004

Charter, R. A. (1999). Testing for true score differences using the confidence interval method. *Psychological Reports*, 85(3), 808–808. https://doi.org/10.2466/pr0.1999.85.3.808

Charter, R. A., & Feldt, L. S. (2009). A comprehensive approach to the interpretation of difference scores. *Applied Neuropsychology*, 16(1), 23–30. https://doi.org/10.1080/09084280802644110

Farmer, R. L., Floyd, R. G., Reynolds, M. R., & Kranzler, J. H. (2014). IQs are very strong but imperfect indicators of psychometric g: Results from joint confirmatory factor analysis. *Psychology in the Schools*, 51(8), 801–813. https://doi.org/10.1002/pits.21785

Farmer, R. L., & Kim, S. Y. (2020). Difference score reliabilities within the RIAS–2 and WISC–V. *Psychology in the Schools, 57*(8), 1273–1288. https://doi.org/10.1002/pits.22369

Farmer, R. L., McGill, R. J., Dombrowski, S. C., & Canivez, G. L. (2021). Why questionable assessment practices remain popular in school psychology: Instructional materials as pedagogic vehicles. *Canadian Journal of School Psychology, 36*(2), 98–114. https://doi.org/10.1177/0829573520978111

Fiorello, C. A., & Wycoff, K. L. (2018). Cognitive hypothesis testing: Linking test results to the real world. In D. P. Flanagan & E. M. McDonough (Eds.). *Contemporary intellectual assessment* (4th ed., pp. 715–730). Guilford Press.

Flanagan, D. P., Ortiz, S. O., & Alfonso, V. C. (2013). *Essentials of cross-battery assessment*. John Wiley & Sons.

Furr, R. M. (2017*). Psychometrics: An introduction* (3rd ed.). Sage Publications.

Gustafsson, J.-E. (1980). *An Introduction to Rasch's Measurement Model*. ERIC Clearinghouse on Tests, Measurement, and Evaluation; National Institute of Education (ED); National Swedish Board of Education; Swedish Council for Research in the Humanities and Social Sciences. ERIC-TM-79. https://eric.ed.gov/?id=ED211594

Hacherl, G. (2020). Reliability of index and subtest discrepancy scores from the KABC–II NU. *Masters Theses & Specialist Projects*. https://digitalcommons.wku.edu/theses/3174

Haig, B. D. (2018). *Method matters in psychology: Essays in applied philosophy of science*. Springer.

Henson, R. K. (2001). Understanding internal consistency reliability estimates: A conceptual primer on coefficient alpha. *Measurement and Evaluation in Counseling and Development, 34*(3), 177–189. https://doi.org/10.1080/07481756.2002.12069034

Kaufman, A. S., & Kaufman, N. L. (2018). *Kaufman Assessment Battery for Children, Second Edition*. Pearson.

Kaufman, A. S., Raiford, S. E., & Coalson, D. L. (2016). *Intelligent testing with the WISC–V*. John Wiley & Sons.

Kranzler, J. H., Maki, K. E., Benson, N. F., Eckert, T. L., Floyd, R. G., & Fefer, S. A. (2020). How do school psychologists interpret intelligence tests for the identification of specific learning disabilities? *Contemporary School Psychology, 24*(4), 445–456. https://doi.org/10.1007/s40688-020-00274-0

Lockwood, A. B., & Farmer, R. L. (2020). The cognitive assessment course: Two decades later. *Psychology in the Schools, 57*(2), 265–283. https://doi.org/10.1002/pits.22298

Lord, F. M., Novick, M. R., & Birnbaum, A. (1968). *Statistical theories of mental test scores*. Addison-Wesley.

Mangiafico, S. (2020). rcompanion: Functions to Support Extension Education Program Evaluation (2.3.26) [Computer software]. https://CRAN.R-project.org/package=rcompanion

McDermott, P. A., Fantuzzo, J. W., & Glutting, J. J. (1990). Just say no to subtest analysis: A critique on Wechsler theory and practice. *Journal of Psychoeducational Assessment, 8*(3), 290–302. https://doi.org/10.1177/073428299000800307

McDermott, P. A., Fantuzzo, J. W., Glutting, J. J., Watkins, M. W., & Baggaley, A. R. (1992). Illusions of meaning in the ipsative assessment of children's ability. *The Journal of Special Education, 25*(4), 504–526. https://doi.org/10.1177/002246699202500407

McGill, R. J., Dombrowski, S. C., & Canivez, G. L. (2018). Cognitive profile analysis in school psychology: History, issues, and continued concerns. *Journal of School Psychology, 71*, 108–121. https://doi.org/10.1016/j.jsp.2018.10.007

Mosier, C. I. (1943). On the reliability of a weighted composite. *Psychometrika, 8*, 161–168. https://doi.org/10.1007/BF02288700

Nunnally, J. C., & Bernstein, I. H. (1994). *Psychometric theory* (3rd ed). McGraw-Hill.

Price, L. R. (2016). *Psychometric methods: Theory into practice*. Guilford Press.

Reynolds, C. R., & Kamphaus, R. W. (2015). *Reynolds Intellectual Assessment Scales, Second Edition*. PAR.

Sattler, J. M. (2018). *Assessment of children: Cognitive foundations and applications* (6th ed.). Jerome M. Sattler.

Schneider, W. J. (2014, January 16). Reliability coefficients are for squares. Confidence interval widths tell it to you straight. *Assessing Psyche, Engaging Gauss, Seeking Sophia*. https://assessingpsyche.wordpress.com/2014/01/16/reliability-is-for-squares/

Schrank, F. A., McGrew, K. S., & Mather, N. (2014). *Woodcock-Johnson IV Tests of Cognitive Abilities*. Riverside.

Spearman, C. (1904). Correlation calculated from faulty data. *British Journal of Psychology, 3*(3), 271–295. https://doi.org/10.1111/j.2044-8295.1910.tb00206.x

Stinson, K. (2020). Reliability of index and subtest discrepancy scores on The WJ-IV Cognitive. *Masters Theses & Specialist Projects*. https://digitalcommons.wku.edu/theses/3194

Thorndike, R. L., & Hagen, E. (1969). *Measurement and evaluation in psychology and education* (3rd ed.). Wiley & Sons.

Vertue, F. M., & Haig, B. D. (2008). An abductive perspective on clinical reasoning and case formulation. *Journal of Clinical Psychology, 64*(9), 1046–1068. https://doi.org/10.1002/jclp.20504

Watkins, M. W. (2000). Cognitive profile analysis: A shared professional myth. *School Psychology Quarterly, 15*(4), 465–479. https://doi.org/10.1037/h0088802

Wechsler, D. (2014). *Wechsler Intelligence Scales for Children–Fifth Edition*. Pearson.

Chapter 9

Nunnally Got It Right the First Time

Internal Consistency Reliability of .55 Is Acceptable for Research Purposes

Gilles E. Gignac

Nunnally's (1978) minimum internal consistency reliability recommendations of .70 and .80 for exploratory and basic research, respectively, are well known and well cited. Less well known is that Nunnally (1967) originally recommended internal consistency reliability between .50 and .60 as minimally acceptable. Based on a review of the literature, Nunnally's (1978) revised guidelines for internal consistency reliability are found to be unjustifiably stricter than published guidelines for other types of test score reliability. Furthermore, Nunnally did not provide thorough theoretical or practical reasons for considering .70 as the minimally acceptable level of internal consistency reliability. His primary justification was the simple notion that this reliability level corresponds to a standard error of measurement more than half ($\approx$ .55) of a test score's standard deviation, a consideration more pertinent to practical applications of psychological assessments than research contexts.

Consequently, the purpose of this investigation was to develop a minimum internal consistency reliability guideline based on criterion-based considerations. On the basis of the outcomes of three proposed approaches to evaluating a minimum internal consistency reliability guideline, I recommend that researchers consider it acceptable to conduct exploratory and basic research on a sample of data where internal consistency reliability is .55 or greater. By contrast, data for which internal consistency reliability is less than .50 should be analyzed only with serious caution. It is concluded that Nunnally's (1978) revised recommendation for a minimum internal consistency reliability of .70 may be a more appropriate aim for test developers rather than typical researchers employing a previously published measure.

Part of the motivation for writing this chapter is derived from an experience I had with a reviewer of a manuscript I submitted for potential publication at a journal. Briefly, the scores from one of the tests included in the research project's battery had internal consistency reliability clearly less than .70. However, all of the key estimated effects associated with that test were significant statistically.

Furthermore, the sample size on which the analyses were based was relatively respectable ($N \approx$ 220). Nonetheless, the reviewer had a problem with the study because of what was perceived as unacceptably low level of internal consistency reliability, that is, it was lower than Nunnally's (1978) minimum guideline of .70, a guideline now apparently sacrosanct and part of psychometric lore.

Few seem to be aware that Nunnally (1967) originally recommended a minimum internal consistency reliability of ".60 or .50" (p. 226) but later shifted the minimum guideline upward (i.e., to .70) in his second edition (1978; see also Nunnally & Bernstein, 1994). No reason was provided by Nunnally for the shift. Furthermore, Nunnally appears never to have provided any thorough justifications for the selection of a minimally acceptable internal consistency reliability guideline, and yet the guideline appears to have been entirely accepted by many without question. Naturally there are exceptions. For example, Pedhazur and Pedhazur Schmelkin (1991) questioned "the wisdom of proposing specific values as standards of reliability, because they tend to develop a life of their own and are frequently applied without concern to the ideas that led to them" (p. 109).

In this chapter, I will propose three criterion-based (i.e., non-normative) approaches to the development of a minimum internal consistency reliability guideline. To foreshadow, based on the outcomes of the three approaches, I will conclude that Nunnally's (1967) originally recommended minimum guideline of between .50 and .60 (i.e., specifically .55) was a more appropriate minimum internal consistency reliability guideline with respect to conducting exploratory and basic research in comparison to the more widely cited .70 minimum guideline (Nunnally, 1978).

Background on Internal Consistency Reliability

Theoretically, test score reliability may be described as the correspondence between the observed scores obtained from a particular test and the true scores underlying the test (Lord & Novick, 1968). In its simplest conceptualization, test score reliability refers to the correspondence between the test scores obtained from cases on one occasion and the scores obtained from the same test on another occasion (Cronbach, 1990). In practical terms, test score reliability refers to consistency of measurement. For example, when a person steps on a scale to measure their weight, a scale that provides reliable scores will yield the same weight estimate across two occasions, assuming the time between measurements is relatively short.

In the context of psychological measurement, however, there are well-known problems associated with estimating test score reliability with simple methods such as a test-retest correlation, including practice and memory effects, which may be expected to inflate estimates of test score reliability (Nunnally & Bernstein, 1994). Consequently, psychometricians and researchers tend to focus on internal consistency reliability. One popular method of estimating internal consistency reliability is coefficient α, or Cronbach's α.[1] Coefficient α can be formulated in various ways. For example, it can be formulated as the ratio of number of items (squared) multiplied by the mean inter-item covariance to the sum of the square variance/covariance matrix (i.e., total variance; Cortina, 1993).

$$\alpha = \frac{k^2 * \overline{COV}}{\sum S^2, COV} \tag{1}$$

The above formulation is a ratio of true score variance to total variance, a commonly specified definition of internal consistency reliability (Nunnally & Bernstein, 1994).

Another commonly seen formulation of internal consistency reliability is known as standardized coefficient α (Crocker & Algina, 1986), which is based on Pearson correlations rather than Pearson covariances. As can be seen in equation (2), the number of items (k) and the average inter-item correlation are in the numerator of the standardized coefficient α formulation.

$$\alpha = \frac{k * \bar{r}}{1+(k-1)\bar{r}} \tag{2}$$

Coefficient α is known as a lower-bound to internal consistency reliability as it underestimates slightly the internal consistency reliability of test scores when the assumption of essential tau-equivalence is violated (i.e., coefficient α assumes that all items measure the dimension with equal strength; Graham, 2006). In practice, coefficient ω is a more accurate estimate of internal consistency reliability as it does not assume essential tau-equivalence and can be extended to multidimensional data (McNeish, 2018). Arguably researchers should use coefficient ω rather than coefficient α. However, the work in this chapter will be based on coefficient α as it is still useful and more familiar among researchers (see Raykov & Marcoulides, 2019). Additionally, coefficient α and coefficient ω can be expected to yield similar results. In fact, based on simulation work, Raykov (1997) found that coefficient α will underestimate internal consistency reliability by at most .02 for scales with five items or more (measuring a single dimension). Thus, although it is accurate to describe coefficient α as a lower-bound estimate, it may be regarded as an overall good estimate in most cases (Savalei & Reise, 2019). Ultimately, the work presented in this chapter should be considered to apply equally to both coefficient α and coefficient ω.

Reliability Guidelines

Researchers and clinicians have been recommended to take into consideration the reliability of test scores when considering the use of those test scores (Kaplan & Saccuzzo, 2005; Nunnally & Bernstein, 1994). However, how high internal consistency reliability must be to use the test scores justifiably has arguably not been resolved convincingly beyond some authors providing opinions or recommendations.

In this context, there are at least two approaches to the contemplation of statistical guidelines: (a) normative, and (b) criterion-based. Normative guidelines could be ascertained by collating comprehensively many internal consistency reliability estimates reported broadly in the literature. For example, Peterson (1994) conducted a meta-analysis of coefficient α based on a review of eight psychology and marketing journals, covering the years 1960 to 1992. A total of 4,286 coefficient α were harvested. Peterson (1994) found that the median coefficient α was .79. Thus a researcher who obtained an internal consistency reliability of approximately .80 could contextualize such an estimate as typical. Importantly, Peterson (1994) reported that 25% of published internal consistency reliability estimates were less than .70. Thus a value less than .70 may not be regarded as rare or entirely unusual (see also Shepperd et al., 2016). Although normative guidelines may help contextualize whether an estimate of coefficient α may be unusual or not, normative guidelines cannot be expected to provide a guideline for a minimally required level of internal consistency reliability as such a guideline would presumably be required to take into consider psychometric/statistical issues (i.e., criterion-based considerations).

It is widely known that Nunnally (1976) recommended that test scores should achieve a minimum internal consistency reliability of .70. However, consistent with Lance and colleagues (2006), I will note that Nunnally (1976) distinguished early-stage research from basic research and suggested that a minimum of .70 was appropriate for early-stage research and .80 for basic research. Values closer to .90, and preferably .95 were required for situations in which important decisions were to be made (Nunnally, 1976). In contrast to Nunnally (1976), Cronbach appears to have never published guidelines for coefficient α, per se; however, he did state, "Reliabilities of the main scores in standard ability tests used for important decisions often are (and should be) 0.90 or higher. A lower reliability is entirely acceptable in many situations" (Cronbach, 1990, p. 209). Cronbach (1990) did not provide any further details in this context.

To my knowledge, Nunnally (1976) never provided any thorough justifications for why .70 should be considered the minimum level of internal consistency reliability for early-stage research. Despite this, I believe Nunnally's guidelines for internal consistency reliability may be best described as criterion-based as there was no suggestion that they were normative. The absence of any reasoning behind the development of Nunnally's internal consistency reliability guidelines might help explain why Nunnally wavered between the first (1968) and second editions (1976) of his famous book *Psychometric Theory*, where he initially recommended ".60 or .50" (1968, p. 226) and then .70 (1976) for early-stage research.

In addition to the above, Nunnally (1978) stated, "If, for example, coefficient α for a 40-item test is only .30, the experimenter should reconsider the measurement problem, perhaps by choosing different types of items" (p. 230). It is noteworthy that Nunnally (1978) did not specify "only .60" or even "only .50" as a coefficient α value that should cause sufficient alarm in a researcher to take action. Evidently Nunnally (1978) took into consideration other factors when evaluating a potentially worrisomely low level of internal consistency reliability in the context of research. Thus, given the absence of any reason to require .70 as the minimum coefficient α for research purposes and the suggestion that a coefficient value of .30, rather than .60 or .50, should be considered so low as to require some action on the part of the researcher, I believe that Nunnally would have been open to an argument that the observation of a coefficient α less than .70 for a set of test scores should not preclude a researcher from carrying on with analyzing those data to test hypotheses.

In addition to Nunnally's published guidelines (1968; 1976; see also Nunnally & Bernstein, 1994), other psychometricians and researchers have published criterion-based guidelines for internal consistency reliability. For example, Kaplan and Saccuzzo (1982) recommended a minimum of .70 for basic research. Murphy and Davidshofer (1988) suggested that .70 was a low level of internal consistency reliability and .80 to .90 was a moderate to high level. Thus these guidelines are largely consistent with those reported by Nunnally (1976).

However, there are some internal consistency reliability guidelines that diverge from the widely cited minimum expectation of .70. For example, Davis (1964) suggested that for research predicting more than 50 cases, an internal consistency reliability as low as .50 may be considered acceptable. Additionally, Wasserman and Bracken (2003) recommended a minimum internal consistency reliability of .60 or greater for scenarios not involving screening, diagnosis, intervention, placement, or selection, which the reader may perhaps interpret as research scenarios. Finally, Clark and Watson (1995) noted that some researchers considered internal consistency reliability of .60 as adequate for research purposes, again in apparent contradistinction to Nunnally (1978) although consistent with Nunnally (1968).

As I argue later, it is my view that Nunnally (1968) got it right the first time: internal consistency reliability of between .50 and .60 (i.e., .55) should be considered minimally acceptable for research purposes. Prior to providing some rationale for choosing a minimum internal consistency reliability guideline, I will review guidelines for other types of test score reliability to help build the case that internal consistency reliability less than .70 may be considered acceptable for research.

Comparisons With Other Reliability Guidelines

As documented widely, internal consistency reliability is not the only type of reliability for which guidelines have been published. For example, Cohen's *kappa* (Cohen, 1960) is a standardized measure of reliability that represents the degree of agreement in the scores provided by two raters (i.e., inter-rater reliability). Landis and Koch (1977) recommended interpreting *kappa* values between .40 and .60 as "moderate," Cicchetti and Sparrow (1981) suggested "fair," and Fleiss (1971) suggested "fair to good," implying that reliability of between .40 and .60 would be acceptable for research purposes. Obviously reliability values of between .40 and .60 are lower than Nunnally's (1978) commonly cited minimum of .70 for internal consistency reliability.

Consider also the intra-class correlation (Bartko, 1976), a more versatile inter-rater reliability coefficient than *kappa* (i.e., it can handle more than two raters and data scored on more than a dichotomous scale). Values between .50 and .75 have been suggested to be considered moderate levels of reliability as estimated via the intra-class correlation (Koo & Li, 2016; Portney & Watkins, 2009), again suggesting values non-trivially less than .70 may be considered acceptable for research purposes. It is noteworthy that the mixed-model intra-class correlation with fixed indicators or measures and random cases is equivalent to coefficient α (Bravo & Potvin, 1991). Consequently, the reliability guidelines published for the intra-class correlation and Nunnally's (1978) guidelines for coefficient α may be argued to be inconsistent.

Cicchetti (1994) outlined test-retest reliability guidelines, categorizing them as "excellent" for reliability scores of .75 and above, "good" for those between .60 and .74, and "fair" for a range of .40 to .59. Somewhat stricter, del Rosario and White (2005) interpreted test-retest correlations greater than .80 as "high," .70 to .80 as "moderate," and .60 to .70 as "low-moderate." A value of .57 was described as "just below the low moderate range" (p. 1078), suggesting a value that was not impressive but not unacceptably low either.

The above review of test score reliability guidelines in areas broader than internal consistency reliability suggest that application of the Nunnally (1978) minimum .70 guideline for internal consistency reliability is stricter than what is expected for other types of test score reliability. To my knowledge, no justification has been provided for why the standards for internal consistency reliability should be higher than those for other types of reliability. A challenge in this area, as alluded to above, is that no rationale has been provided to help yield criterion-based guidelines for test score reliability. Next I provide a logical and rational explanation for why the Nunnally (1978) widely cited .70 minimum guideline may be too strict for research purposes.

On What Basis Might Criterion-Based Reliability Guidelines Be Provided?

At least three criterion-based (i.e., non-normative) approaches may be contemplated in the generation and evaluation of internal consistency reliability guidelines: (a) impact of reliability on observed score correlations and statistical power, (b) estimated lower-bound confidence interval for coefficient α, and (c) meaningful interpretation of observed composite scores. Although no single approach may be expected to provide an entirely convincing rationale for choosing a minimum amount of test score internal consistency reliability, if all three methods were to converge on the same approximate value, it may be considered relatively compelling evidence for a suggested minimum criterion-based guideline for internal consistency reliability.

Reliability Impact on Observed Score Correlations and Power

Based on a meta-analysis of differential psychology meta-analyses, Gignac and Szodorai (2016) found that relatively small, typical, and relatively large observed correlations corresponded to .10, .20, and .30, respectively. However, it is well established that the magnitude of a correlation is impacted negatively by the presence of measurement error (Baugh, 2002; Nunnally & Bernstein, 1994). According to classical test theory (Crocker & Algina, 1986), the maximum possible observed correlation between two composite scores is equal to the square root of the product of their reliabilities (i.e., r_{max}):

$$r_{max} = \sqrt{r_{xx} * r_{yy}} \tag{3}$$

Thus if the scores from two composites are associated with internal consistency reliabilities of .70 and .85, the maximum possible observed correlation between those two variables will be .77. As test scores in psychology are almost always associated with some level of measurement error (Peterson, 1994), the observed score correlations reported by Gignac and Szodorai (2016) are undoubtedly smaller than the corresponding true score correlations (i.e., not impacted by measurement error). Correspondingly, based on the meta-analyses that reported correlations disattenuated for measurement error in the test scores, Gignac and Szodorai (2016) found that relatively small, typical, and relatively large true score correlations corresponded to .15, .25, and .35, respectively. Thus, arguably, differential psychology researchers are typically aiming to estimate an effect in the population at the true score level equal to .25. In the hypothetical case of perfect measurement, the sample size required to detect an observed score correlation of .25 as significant statistically ($p < .05$) with 80% probability is equal to 122.[2]

Given the true score population correlation of .25, and r_{max} values calculated across various levels of internal consistency reliability for a particular variable's scores, the impact on sample size requirements to detect an observed effect across various levels of internal consistency can be calculated. A large increase in required sample size would be a contra indicator for a particular minimum internal consistency reliability recommendation. Consequently, I calculated the sample sizes required to detect the corresponding attenuated observed score correlation as statistically significant with 80% probability across 16 levels of internal consistency reliability (ranging from .25 to 1.0) where the population true score correlation was equal to .25 (i.e., typical for differential psychology; Gignac & Szodorai, 2016).

As can be seen in Figure 9.1, the association between internal consistency reliability and power was nonlinear. Specifically, reductions in internal consistency reliability across the .00 to .50 continuum were more substantially impactful on sample size requirements in comparison to changes in internal consistency reliability across the .50 to 1.0 segment of the reliability continuum. Specifically, the sample size cost of analyzing data associated with internal consistency reliability of .80 in comparison to perfect reliability was relatively trivial as a sample size of 153 was found to be associated with power of 80% to detect the attenuated correlation of .224 (i.e., r_{max}) as significant statistically ($p < .05$), which was only 31 more cases than that required to identify the corresponding

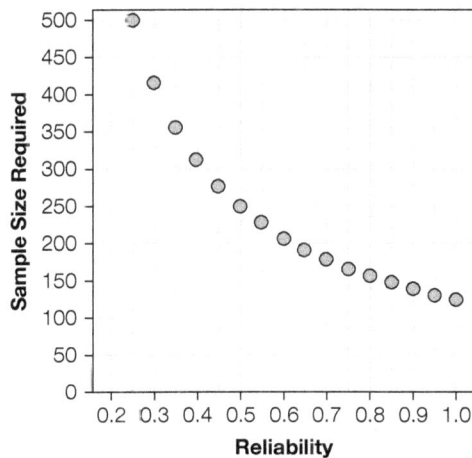

Scatter Plot Depicting the Association Between Internal Consistency Reliability in a Set of Composite Scores (e.g., Dependent Variable) and the Sample Size Required to Detect a True Score Effect in the Population of .25 as Significant Statistically (p < .05) with 80% Probability.

non-attenuated correlation of .25 as significant statistically with 80% probability (i.e., 123 cases).[3] Additionally, the sample size required for the condition in which internal consistency reliability was .70 corresponded to 177—again, a relatively trivial increase. Finally, at the .60 and .55 internal consistency reliability levels, the sample sizes required to detect the corresponding observed score correlations of .194 and .185 as significant statistically (with 80% probability) corresponded to 205 and 226, respectively. Finally, beyond an internal consistency reliability of approximately .50 to .55, the increases in sample sizes required to detect the corresponding observed score correlation as significant statistically (with 80% probability) accelerated non-negligibly (see Figure 9.1), suggesting that values of internal consistency reliability less than .55 may be considered problematic with respect to recommending a minimum level of internal consistency reliability in composite scores. Thus, based on these results, a criterion-based rationale for recommending a minimum internal consistency reliability of .55 may be advanced, a value somewhere between the Nunnally (1967) original minimum recommendation of between ".60 or .50" (p. 226).

Estimated α Lower-Bound Confidence Interval

A second approach to the consideration of a criterion-based minimum internal consistency reliability guideline is based on an examination of the 95% confidence intervals associated with a point-estimate of coefficient α: interval ranges that would be expected to be impacted by sample size. Several psychometricians have recommended minimum sample sizes for the purpose of estimating internal consistency reliability. On the relatively more permissive side, Kline (1986) recommended a minimum sample size of 200. By comparison, Nunnally (1967) suggested a minimum sample size of 300 (see also Nunnally & Bernstein, 1994); however, Segall (1994) described a sample size of 300 as relatively small. Finally, Charter (2003) recommended a sample size of 400 for internal consistency reliability estimation. Based on this short review, a minimum sample size between 200 and 400 may be considered minimally acceptable: a fairly wide range.[4]

In my view, previously published sample size recommendations for internal consistency reliability fail to acknowledge an important consideration: test score reliability is sample specific, i.e., not a property of the test (Thompson & Vacha-Haase, 2000). Consequently, all empirical studies that use composite scores should report the internal consistency reliability of those scores irrespective of sample size as it is the internal consistency reliability associated with the composite scores of the study that will impact the magnitude of the estimated effect sizes and not the internal consistency reliability reported in a test manual or a previously published paper with a large sample size (Fan & Thompson, 2001; Vacha-Haase et al., 1999).

Because test score reliability is a property of data not a property of a test (Thompson & Vacha-Haase, 2000), a test may be found to yield respectable internal consistency reliability in one sample of data but substantially less respectable reliability in another. For example, based on a reliability generalization study (i.e., a meta-analysis of reliability coefficients; see Vacha-Haase, 2000), Beretvas et al. (2002) found that the internal consistency reliability of test scores derived from the Marlowe-Crowne Social Desirability Scale (Crowne & Marlowe, 1960) could be predicted to be .80 for adult women and .53 for adolescent boys. Therefore, to the question "Is the Marlowe-Crowne Social Desirability Scale a sufficiently reliable test?" the best one could answer would be "It depends on the sample." For this reason, researchers are encouraged to report the internal consistency reliability associated with the test scores for their sample (Fan & Thompson, 2001; Vacha-Haase et al., 1999).

In addition to the systematic influences on the reliability of test scores that can be uncovered through a reliability generalization investigation, test score reliability can be expected to vary from sample to sample because of sampling fluctuations—much like any other point-estimate in statistics (Harding et al., 2014; Thompson, 2007). It is well established and arguably well known that across smaller samples, the variability in point-estimates tends to be larger in comparison to point-estimates derived from larger samples (Altman & Bland, 2005; Henry, 2013). Perhaps less well known is that coefficient α has a corresponding standard error from which confidence intervals can be estimated.

Feldt et al. (1987) published some of the earlier work on the development of a standard error (and confidence interval) for coefficient α. Since Feldt et al. (1987), other work has been developed to improve the accuracy of coefficient α confidence interval estimation (e.g., Bonett & Wright, 2015; Iacobucci & Duhachek, 2003); however, the practical improvements in estimation accuracy are not large for most cases. Based on my review of the literature, Feldt et al.'s (1987) standard error will be respectably accurate when the scale has five items or more and the sample size is 50 or more—conditions that I believe would be the case in the vast majority of research scenarios. Therefore, I used Feldt et al.'s coefficient α standard error for the remainder of this chapter, as it is more widely implemented in readily available software.

Arguably researchers should report the confidence intervals associated with a coefficient α estimate in the same way they have been recommended to report confidence intervals for effect sizes, that is, the Pearson correlation and Cohen's d (Cumming et al., 2012). Confidence intervals can be estimated for coefficient α with R ("cocron" package), which includes an easy to use R web interface (Diedenhofen & Musch, 2016). Additionally, as there is a direct correspondence between coefficient α and the two-way mixed intra-class correlation coefficient (items or measures are fixed; people effects are random; see Bravo & Potvin, 1991), confidence intervals can be easily estimated for coefficient α via the intra-class correlation utility in SPSS (see Baumgartner & Chung, 2001).

In order to examine systematically the confidence intervals associated with coefficient α, an examination that may shed light on the minimum internal consistency reliability question, I estimated the 95% confidence intervals associated with coefficient α values of .70, .80, and 90 across eight sample sizes: 50, 100, 150, 200, 400, 600, 800, and 1000. As the number of items that comprise a scale is related slightly negatively with the standard error of coefficient α (i.e., larger numbers of items yield slightly narrower confidence intervals up to about 10 items; Iacobucci & Duhachek, 2003), I chose a relatively small number of items for the hypothetical scale (i.e , 5) in order to capture a large percentage of research scenarios (i.e., only a small percentage of tests have fewer than 5 items). For the following analyses, I used the cocron package in R (Diedenhofen & Musch, 2016) to estimate the coefficient α 95% confidence intervals.

As can be seen in Figure 9.2 (left-side), with a sample size of 50, the lower-bound 95% confidence interval associated with a point-estimate of internal consistency reliability of .70 corresponded to a coefficient α of .54 and the upper-bound confidence interval corresponded to a coefficient α of .81. Even with a sample size of 200, the lower-bound 95% confidence was less than .65 (i.e., .63), which would be expected to cause concern in researchers and reviewers who adhere to Nunnally's (1978) minimum coefficient α guideline strictly. Thus a dimension measured by a scale for which coefficient α is .70 in the population would yield a substantial amount of variability in point-estimates across samples ranging from relatively low ($N = 50$) to a size that would be considered respectable for individual differences research (i.e., $N = 200$). Stated alternatively, what some would consider a "reliable psychometric measure" (i.e., $\alpha = .70$) can be expected to yield conventionally considered low levels of internal consistency reliability across a non-negligible number of samples simply due to sampling fluctuations, underscoring the fact that reliability is a property of data, not a measure (Thompson & Vacha-Haase, 2000). In particular, it will be noted that for a small but still respectable sample of 50 cases,[5] the lower-bound coefficient α was essentially .55. Thus coefficient α values appreciably lower than .70 should be expected to occur just by chance, and such an observation should not curtail the possibility of analyzing data or require some defense or extraordinary explanation for why the data were analyzed to test a hypothesis.

As can be seen in Figure 9.2, it will be noted that the degree of confidence in coefficient α estimation increased across the magnitude of the coefficient α point-estimates (i.e., .70, .80 and .90).

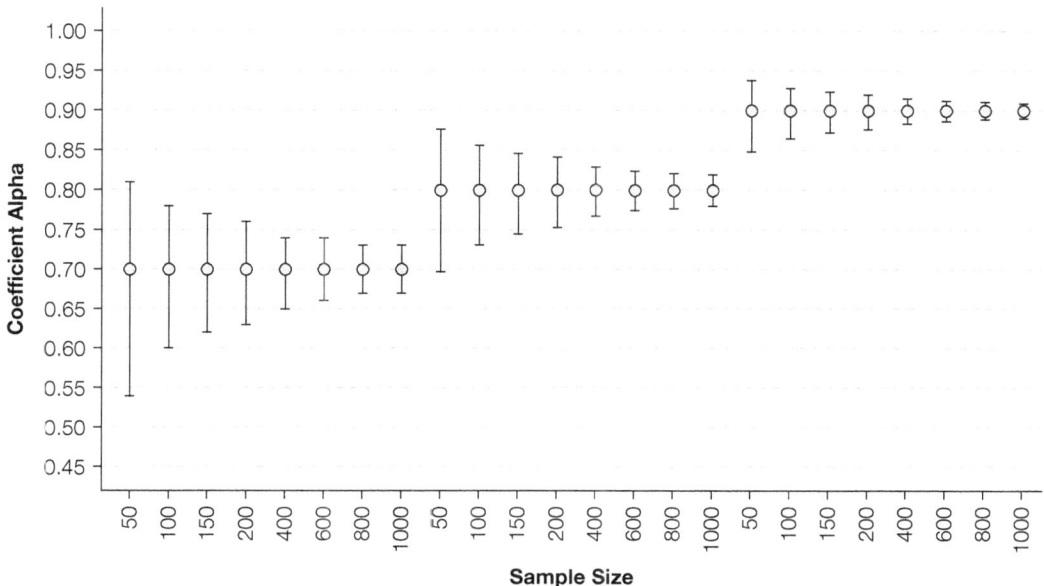

Figure 9.2. **95% Confidence Intervals Associated With Coefficient α Point-Estimates (.70, .80, and .90) Across Varying Sample Sizes (50 to 1,000) and a Hypothetical Scale of 5 Items.**

For example, for a sample size of 50, the lower-bound and upper-bound 95% confidence intervals corresponded to .540/.810 (range = .270), .697/.876 (range = .179), and .848/.938 (range = .090) for the .70, .80 and .90 coefficient α point-estimate conditions, respectively. Thus any non-normative coefficient α recommendation should probably take into consideration such an effect.

Finally, it will be noted that a point-estimate of .80 yielded a lower-bound 95% confidence interval of .70. Although one can only speculate, it is possible that Nunnally had in mind sampling variability when he shifted his guidelines (upward) from the first to second editions of his *Psychometric Theory* text. Either way, it should be emphasized that test developers should strive to develop measures that can be expected to on average yield estimates of internal consistency reliability of .70 as sampling variability will dictate that some researchers will obtain data for which the internal consistency reliability of the test scores is appreciably less than .70. A recommendation to require test developers to achieve internal consistency reliability of .80 for their measures would eliminate well-established and useful measures in differential psychology known to yield internal consistency reliabilities on average closer to .70 (e.g., Agreeableness; Caruso, 2000).

As stated in many sources, validity considerations should take precedence over reliability considerations (e.g., Nunnally & Bernstein, 1994). Therefore, increasing the degree of item homogeneity or adding more items to a measure simply to achieve higher levels of internal consistency reliability at the expense of validity is not recommendable psychometric practice. Instead, test developers should appreciate a minimum coefficient α of .70 as acceptable, and researchers .55 as acceptable, as such a lower value can be expected to occur simply by chance and does not have a great impact on statistical power, as discussed above.

Meaningful Interpretation of Observed Scores

A third, somewhat oblique approach by which a criterion-based guideline for minimum internal consistency reliability may be considered is basic visual perception identification. As stated earlier, internal consistency reliability may be defined as the ratio of true score variance to total variance (Nunnally & Bernstein, 1994). Given the correspondence between internal consistency reliability and factorial validity (Zinbarg et al., 2005),[6] an internal consistency reliability estimate derived from a well-fitting, single-factor model solution may be essentially considered a representation of the percentage of variance that is construct related variance (Hancock & Mueller, 2001). As argued by Gignac and Watkins (2013), any composite score with less than 50% true score variance would be difficult to interpret meaningfully as more than half the variance would be random variance (i.e., not construct variance). However, beyond 50% true score variance there is arguably the possibility of meaningful interpretation of composite scores. A question that arises pertains to how much more than 50% true score variance is required to achieve a sufficient amount of interpretability or clarity.

In the area of human perception and image resolution more broadly, research suggests that humans can identify an image correctly with 80% probability even when the image is substantially degraded (Torralba, 2009). Following on from this research, one relatively simple method to help generate a possible answer to the question is to generate pixelated images, whereby the percentage of randomly placed red pixels increases relative to non-red pixels. The point at which it becomes sufficiently clear that the overall square was intended to represent, say, red may be considered the point at which a sufficient amount of true score variance (i.e., reliability) is achieved.

As can be seen in Figure 9.3, in the condition in which 70% of the pixels are black, it is clear that black dominates the pattern, implying that within the context of this analogy, 70% true score variance

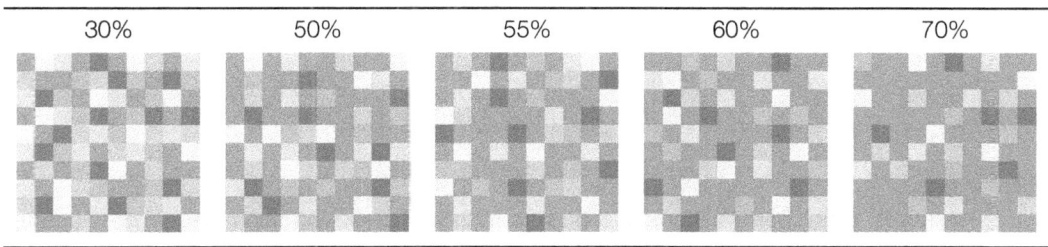

Figure 9.3. **Square Images with Pixels Represented by Various Colors.** *Note.* The number of black pixels (representing true score variance) increases from 30% of squares to 70% of squares. The non-black pixels (representing random variance) were placed randomly within each image; for a more compelling colored version of this figure, see http://tinyurl.com/4nr226p8.

is clearly adequate for interpretation purposes. By contrast, 30% black pixels (i.e., 30% true score variance) is clearly insufficient. Finally, between 55% and 60% appears to be about the minimum amount of signal one may consider for the purposes of reliable (and meaningful) interpretation. Thus, based on this approach, the Nunnally (1967) original minimum recommendation of between ".60 or .50" (p. 226) for internal consistency reliability appears to be further supported.

Estimating Test Score Reliability From Dichotomously Scored Items

Previous quantitative reviews of internal consistency reliability estimates have reported mean levels across various categories and types of reliability formulae (e.g., Greco et al., 2018; Charter, 2003; Peterson, 1994); however, to my knowledge no quantitative review of the empirical literature has examined the possibility that tests with items scored on a dichotomous scale may yield relatively lower levels of internal consistency reliability than tests measured on more informative scales. Theoretically it is plausible that tests with dichotomously scored items may yield relatively lower internal consistency reliability because dichotomous items tend to be associated with less variance than other types of items (Reise et al., 2000), and variance plays a central role in the magnitude of correlations between variables and, correspondingly, internal consistency reliability (Fife et al., 2012).

Dealing with the issue of dichotomously scored items, correlations, and internal consistency reliability is relevant to the purpose of this chapter as it is possible that tests with dichotomously scored items merit different internal consistency reliability guidelines. Additionally, it is possible that estimates of internal consistency reliability based on Pearson inter-item correlations (i.e., *phi*) between dichotomously scored items may be substantially underestimated. Correspondingly, if dichotomously scored item internal consistency reliability is appreciably underestimated in a particular sample, then the observation of an internal consistency reliability estimate substantially less than .70 may not be cause for concern for those who adhere strictly to the Nunnally (1978) guidelines.

It has been shown analytically that the maximum possible correlation between two dichotomously scored items (i.e., *phi*) is a function of the degree of disparity in the proportion of cases who score 1 and 0 (i.e., marginal distributions must be equal across items; Loevinger, 1954). Only when the proportion (π) of cases who score 1 across both items is exactly the same is a *phi* correlation of

|1.0| possible. The maximum possible correlation between two dichotomously scored items is known as *phi*-max (Lord & Novick, 1968) and may be formulated as

$$phi_{max} = \sqrt{\pi_j * \left(1 - \pi_i\right) / \pi_i * \left(1 - \pi_j\right)} \qquad (4)$$

where $\pi_i \geq \pi_j$.

Even relatively slight perturbations in the proportion of cases who score 1 across two items will impact the maximum possible *phi* correlation substantially. For example, if 84.4% and 72.9% of cases score 1 across two dichotomous items, the maximum possible *phi* correlation between those two items will be .71. Thus, from this perspective a hypothetical observed *phi* correlation of only .20 between those two items may be regarded as respectable, considering the maximum possible correlation may have been far from |1.0|.

Some researchers correct dichotomously scored correlations by dividing the observed *phi* correlation by *phi*-max in much the same way an observed correlation can be divided by r_{max} to obtain an ostensibly more accurate (i.e., true score) correlation estimate between two variables (early advocates include Johnson, 1945; Loevinger, 1948). In this context, the corrected *phi* correlation is known as upper-*phi* (Sun et al., 2007). Upper-*phi* is also known as the homogeneity coefficient (Mellenbergh, 2019). It is called the homogeneity coefficient as it facilitates less ambiguous comparisons between *phi* coefficients as they are placed on a common scale (i.e., a maximum *phi* coefficient of |1.0|). Molenaar (1997) developed formulae to estimate the equivalent of *phi*-max for items scored on 3, 4, and 5 point ordinal scales (e.g., Likert scale). These sorts of corrected correlations are essentially the same as the better-known tetrachoric and polychoric correlations (Mellenbergh, 2019).

Some have argued that it is permissible and even more appropriate to estimate coefficient α on a matrix of upper-*phi* rather than Pearson correlations when the items are scored dichotomously (e.g., Horst, 1953; Sun et al., 2007). Another similar application of coefficient α is known as *ordinal* α, a coefficient α estimated from a matrix of polychoric correlations (Zumbo et al., 2007). However, importantly, Gadermann et al. (2012, p. 2) noted that ordinal α pertains to "the reliability of the unobserved continuous variables underlying the observed item responses." Thus ordinal α pertains only to hypothetical scores (i.e., derived from hypothetical, unobserved continuously scored items) and not the actual, observed scores obtained from a particular test. From this perspective, ordinal α may be argued to be irrelevant to the responsibilities of psychometricians and researchers required to evaluate the amount of measurement error associated with the scores obtained from their test.

As noted earlier in this chapter, internal consistency reliability represents a ratio of true score variance to total variance (Nunnally & Bernstein, 1994). Curiously, procedures that eschew Pearson correlations to estimate coefficient α (i.e., upper-*phi* coefficient α; ordinal α) because, the argument goes, Pearson correlations underestimate the association between categorically scored items, appear to make no adjustment for the corresponding expected increase in the scale's total variance if the items were measured on a continuous scale. That is, theoretically, if the items were measured on a continuous scale, the scale's total variance would also increase, thus nullifying either substantially or entirely the benefits of the ostensible increase in true score variance estimation between the items via the upper-*phi*/polychoric correlations. Thus the apparent increase in coefficient α when estimated via upper-*phi* α and/or ordinal α is at the very least interpreted inappropriately in the context of the observed scores obtained from a test and is perhaps illusory even as a reliability estimate in a hypothetical scenario without a corresponding adjustment to hypothetical total scale variance.

Arguably the Horst (1953) suggestion to the estimation of a supposedly less biased underestimate of internal consistency reliability on the basis of a correction for the fact that dichotomously scored items have maximum values far from |1.0|, when the item proportions are unequal, is more plausibly valid in comparison to the Sun et al. (2007) procedure as the Horst (1953) method takes into consideration the maximum possible variance of the total scale. In an extreme example (i.e., substantial disparities in item proportions), Horst (1953) suggested that the internal consistency reliability of a scale may increase from .84 to .92 when the upper-*phi* correction is applied to coefficient α estimation (with corresponding total variance adjustment).

By comparison, based on a sample of 211 university students, Gignac et al. (2016) reported Pearson correlation-based coefficient α estimates of .28 and .31 for two subtests of the Culture Fair Intelligence Test (13 items each; Cattell, 1963). Furthermore, *phi*-max corrected coefficient α estimates based on upper-*phi* inter-item correlations but no adjustment to total variance (as described by Sun et al. 2007) were estimated at .89 and .90, respectively: a huge increase! On the one hand, such a large increase in the estimate of internal consistency reliability seems seriously implausible. However, based on a confirmatory factor analysis of a battery of cognitive ability tests, the CFIT subtests were found to load onto a fluid intelligence latent variable at .58 and .65, respectively, suggesting a reasonable amount of reliable variance associated with the CFIT subtest scores. Thus some underestimation in coefficient α as estimated from Pearson correlations may be possible. Based on the simulation of Lissitz and Green (1975), moving from essentially continuously scored items to dichotomously scored items impacted the coefficient α estimates by approximately .05: far less than the substantial increases suggested by some upper-*phi* α and ordinal α estimates observed in the literature but still non-trivial.

To confuse matters further, based on both analytical and simulation work, Cronbach and Azuma (1962) concluded that the adjusted coefficient α proposed by Horst (1953) as well as other similar adjustments suggested by others led to inaccurate estimates of internal consistency reliability. Furthermore, Cronbach and Azuma (1962) concluded that the original coefficient α, based on Pearson correlations, can be expected to yield valid estimates of internal consistency reliability in most cases even when applied to dichotomously scored items (assuming the test measures a single dimension). More recently, Revelle and Condon (2018, p. 728) conducted a simulation study to evaluate the validity of ordinal coefficient α and found that "using the tetrachoric or polychoric correlation inflates the reliability estimate."

Although the use of upper-*phi* and tetrachoric/polychoric correlations more generally may not have a place in the valid estimation of observed test score reliability, they have been argued more consistently to have a justifiable place in the evaluation of the dimensionality of scores derived from a test when analyzed via factor analysis (Dillon et al., 1981; Holgado-Tello et al., 2010; McDonald, 1965). That is, factor analyses based on dichotomous items have been argued to be susceptible to the production of purely statistical factors (e.g., difficulty factors or skew factors; Carlson & Jensen, 1980; Kubinger, 2003); therefore, researchers interested in uncovering the factorial validity associated with tests based on dichotomous/ordinal scores have been encouraged to conduct their dimension reduction analyses on tetrachoric/polychoric correlations (Gorsuch, 1974; Kubinger, 2003). However, a full review of this issue needs to acknowledge that a non-trivial amount of simulation research suggests that factor analyses based on *phi* coefficients can be expected to uncover more valid factor solutions than those based on tetrachoric correlations (e.g., Collins et al., 1986; Green, 1983). Additionally, in practice, correlation matrices based on tetrachoric/polychoric matrices (and likely upper-*phi*) can often be found to be non-positive definite, which causes different sorts of problems (Lorenzo-Seva & Ferrando, 2020). Thus the clear and entirely convincing case for the benefits of using upper-*phi* and/or tetrachoric correlations whether for test score reliability estimation and perhaps even factorial validity analyses remains to be made.

All things considered, the degree of observed test score internal consistency reliability underestimation when estimated from *phi* inter-item correlations is unlikely to be very appreciable. It may be best to simply acknowledge that tests based on dichotomously scored items will tend to yield somewhat lower levels of internal consistency reliability and, consequently, expectations of internal consistency reliability of .70 may be again too strict. As shown by Gignac et al. (2016), internal consistency reliabilities much lower than .70 derived from dichotomously scored tests can still yield theoretically plausible and statistically significant effects.

Limitations and Final Considerations

People familiar with the Nunnally (1978) guidelines will know that he distinguished between exploratory and basic research scenarios and recommended different reliability guidelines accordingly. I did not make such a distinction as I believe such a distinction is only applicable to test developers and not researchers using previously published measures.

Additionally, with respect to the criterion-based approach that involved the impact on a typical observed score correlation, I only considered r_{max} within the context of a single measure's imperfectly measured test scores and not two variable test score reliabilities even though no measure is likely to be associated with perfect measurement.[7] However, in practice it is unlikely that two measures will both be associated with relatively low reliability internal consistency reliability, and the impact on observed score correlations when reliability is .80 or greater is relatively negligible.

It will also be acknowledged that all three approaches considered in this work were focused entirely on coefficient α. There are potential approaches based on slightly different representations of test score reliability that may prove fruitful, including the stability of effects (Kretzschmar & Gignac, 2019). Correspondingly, I'll note that toward the end of Cronbach's life, he contended that coefficient α was not the most appropriate method to evaluate test score reliability: "I am convinced that the standard error of measurement . . . is the most important single piece of information to report regarding an instrument, and not a coefficient" (2004, p. 413).

Conclusion

My recommendation to reduce the minimum standard of internal consistency reliability for exploratory and basic research from .70 to .55 should not be interpreted to suggest that I believe test score reliability is less important than what Nunnally contended (see Nunnally & Bernstein, 1994, p. 221). In fact, next to validity, I also believe test score reliability to be the most important psychometric consideration in the evaluation of test scores. Furthermore, researchers should strive to conduct research in such a way as to help ensure the best chances of obtaining test scores with internal consistency reliability greater than .55. Thus a coefficient α of .55 should not be considered an aim for researchers and only a value obtained from a sample deemed acceptable for conducting research so long as the limitations are noted.

Researchers should seriously consider abandoning any statistical analyses with composite scores associated with test score reliability less than .50. Estimates of coefficient α (or coefficient ω) less than .50 imply that less than half of the test's scores are reliable variance, rendering interpretations difficult (Gignac & Watkins, 2013). Stated more simply, there is more noise than signal. In such a case, it would be best to consider the possibility that the participants either did not take the testing seriously or that there are serious problems with one or more items within the test. Either way, serious problems must be acknowledged. This recommendation does not necessarily apply to scales based on items scored dichotomously as I believe there are some issues that remain to be resolved in that context (as reviewed above).

Finally, in line with the comments of Pedhazur and Pedhazur Schmelkin (1991) on standards for reliability noted at the beginning of this chapter, it would be a disservice to the scientific community if the .55 minimum guideline derived from the outcomes described in this investigation were accepted and applied unthinkingly by researchers. Furthermore, some may disagree with one or more of the approaches used in this chapter to help derive a minimum acceptable level of test score internal consistency reliability. I would consider this a success as it may spur others into action to develop a more robust set of logically or empirically based considerations in the generation of a minimum internal consistency reliability guideline.

Notes

1 Cronbach encouraged people to refer to his estimate of internal consistency as "coefficient α" because he did not see it as entirely his invention ("It is an embarrassment to me that the formula became known as 'Cronbach's α'"; Cronbach & Shavelson, 2004, p. 397). That is, Cronbach acknowledged R. A. Fisher's work on the intra-class correlation as well as the previously developed Kuder-Richardson-21 internal consistency reliability formulation, which yielded an estimate of internal consistency reliability that represented the average of all possible split-halves. However, the KR-21 formula was limited to items scored dichotomously (proportion correct), whereas Cronbach's (1951) contribution was to demonstrate a method based on the inter-correlations between items, which could be applied to all items, whether they were scored dichotomously or not.

2 I used the pwr package for R (Champely et al., 2013) to calculate the sample size requirements in this chapter.

3 To demonstrate the calculations in more detail, a variable with test score reliability of .80 would be associated with an r_{max} of .894. Therefore, the maximum observed score correlation in this case would be .224 if the true score population correlation were .25 (i.e., .25*.894). Therefore, with the pwr package in R, the sample size required to detect an observed score correlation of .224 as significant statistically ($p <$ .05) with 80% probability was found to correspond to 153.

4 Johanson and Brooks (2010) recommended a minimum sample size of 30 for pilot studies.

5 That is, for experimental research with statistical analyses of composite scores.

6 The statement that there is a correspondence between internal consistency reliability and factorial validity does not presume that internal consistency values can inform the dimensionality of scores as it cannot do so validly (Gignac et al., 2019; Greer & Yang, 2015). Instead, the correspondence pertains to the fact that coefficient ω can be estimated from factor loadings (McDonald, 1999), and therefore a single-factor model with relatively larger factor loadings will yield a larger estimate of internal consistency reliability than the same single-factor model solution with smaller factor loadings (Gignac & Watkins, 2013). Additionally, there is a perfect, positive correlation between a principal component eigenvalue and coefficient α (Kaiser, 1991). It is on this basis that internal consistency reliability and factorial validity are considered to be closely related.

7 An exception would be the factor loadings within a latent variable model as reported for the Gignac et al. (2016) example with the CFIT.

References

Altman, D. G., & Bland, J. M. (2005). Standard deviations and standard errors. *BMJ, 331*(7521), 903. https://doi.org/10.1136/bmj.331.7521.903

Bartko, J. J. (1976). On various intraclass correlation reliability coefficients. *Psychological Bulletin, 83*(5), 762–765. https://doi.org/10.1037/0033-2909.83.5.762

Baugh, F. (2002). Correcting effect sizes for score reliability: A reminder that measurement and substantive issues are linked inextricably. *Educational and Psychological Measurement, 62*(2), 254–263. https://doi .org/10.1177/0013164402062002004

Baumgartner, T. A., & Chung, H. (2001). Confidence limits for intraclass reliability coefficients. *Measurement in Physical Education and Exercise Science, 5*(3), 179–188. https://doi.org/10.1207/ s15327841mpee0503_4

Beretvas, S. N., Meyers, J. L., & Leite, W. L. (2002). A reliability generalization study of the Marlowe-Crowne Social Desirability Scale. *Educational and Psychological Measurement, 62*(4), 570–589. https://doi.org /10.1177/0013164402062004003

Bonett, D. G., & Wright, T. A. (2015). Cronbach's alpha reliability: Interval estimation, hypothesis testing, and sample size planning. *Journal of Organizational Behavior, 36*(1), 3–15. https://doi.org/10.1002/job .1960

Bravo, G., & Potvin, L. (1991). Estimating the reliability of continuous measures with Cronbach's alpha or the intraclass correlation coefficient: Toward the integration of two traditions. *Journal of Clinical Epidemiology, 44*(4–5), 381–390. https://doi.org/10.1016/0895-4356(91)90076-I

Carlson, J. S., & Jensen, C. M. (1980). The factorial structure of the Raven Coloured Progressive Matrices test: A reanalysis. *Educational and Psychological Measurement, 40*(4), 1111–1116. https://doi.org/10 .1177/001316448004000440

Caruso, J. C. (2000). Reliability generalization of the NEO personality scales. *Educational and Psychological Measurement, 60*(2), 236–254. https://doi.org/10.1177/00131640021970484

Cattell, R. B. (1963). *The IPAT culture fair intelligence scales 1, 2 and 3* (2nd ed.). Institute for Personality and Ability Test.

Champely, A. S., Ekstrom, C., Dalgaard, P., Gill, J., Wunder, J., & De Rosario, H. (2013). Package "pwr," 1–21.

Charter, R. A. (2003). Study samples are too small to produce sufficiently precise reliability coefficients. *The Journal of General Psychology, 130*(2), 117–129. https://doi.org/10.1080/00221300309601280

Cicchetti, D. V. (1994). Guidelines, criteria, and rules of thumb for evaluating normed and standardized assessment instruments in psychology. *Psychological Assessment, 6*(4), 284–290. https://doi.org/10 .1037//1040-3590.6.4.284

Cicchetti, D. V., & Sparrow, S. A. (1981). Developing criteria for establishing interrater reliability of specific items: Applications to assessment of adaptive behavior. *American Journal of Mental Deficiency, 86*(2), 127. https://doi.org/10.1037/t15164-000

Clark, L. A., & Watson, D. (1995). Constructing validity: Basic issues in Objective Scale Development. *Psychological Assessment, 7*(3), 309–319. https://doi.org/10.1037//1040-3590.7.3.309

Cohen, J. (1960). A coefficient of agreement for nominal scales. *Educational and Psychological Measurement, 20*(1), 37–46. https://doi.org/10.1177/001316446002000104

Collins, L. M., Cliff, N., McCormick, D. J., & Zatkin, J. L. (1986). Factor recovery in binary data sets: A simulation. *Multivariate Behavioral Research, 21*(3), 377–391. https://doi.org/10.1207/ s15327906mbr2103_6

Cortina, J. M. (1993). What is coefficient alpha? An examination of theory and applications. *Psychological Bulletin, 78*, 98–104. https://doi.org/10.1037//0021-9010.78.1.98

Crocker, L. M., & Algina, J. (1986). *Introduction to classical and modern test theory*. Holt, Rinehart & Winston.

Cronbach, L. J. (1951). Coefficient alpha and the internal structure of tests. *Psychometrika, 16*(3), 297–334. https://doi.org/10.1007/bf02310555

Cronbach, L. J. (1990). *Essentials of psychological testing* (5th ed.). Harper & Row.

Cronbach, L. J., & Azuma, H. (1962). Internal-consistency reliability formulas applied to randomly sampled single-factor tests: an empirical comparison. *Educational and Psychological Measurement*, *22*(4), 645–665. https://doi.org/10.1177/001316446202200401

Cronbach, L. J., & Shavelson, R. J. (2004). My current thoughts on coefficient alpha and successor procedures. *Educational and Psychological Measurement*, *64*(3), 391–418. https://doi.org/10.1177/0013164404266386

Crowne, D. P., & Marlowe, D. (1960). A new scale of social desirability independent of psychopathology. *Journal of Consulting Psychology*, *24*, 349–354. https://doi.org/10.1037/h0047358

Cumming, G., Fidler, F., Kalinowski, P., & Lai, J. (2012). The statistical recommendations of the American Psychological Association Publication Manual: Effect sizes, confidence intervals, and meta-analysis. *Australian Journal of Psychology*, *64*(3), 138–146. https://doi.org/10.1111/j.1742-9536.2011.00037.x

Davis, F. B. (1964). *Educational measurements and their interpretation*. Wadsworth.

del Rosario, P. M., & White, R. M. (2005). The Narcissistic Personality Inventory: Test–retest stability and internal consistency. *Personality and Individual Differences*, *39*(6), 1075–1081. https://doi.org/10.1016/j.paid.2005.08.001

Diedenhofen, B., & Musch, J. (2016). cocron: A web interface and R package for the statistical comparison of Cronbach's alpha coefficients. *International Journal of Internet Science*, *11*, 51–60. https://doi.org/10.1371/journal.pone.0121945

Dillon, R. F., Pohlmann, J. T., & Lohman, D. F. (1981). A factor analysis of Raven's Advanced Progressive Matrices freed of difficulty factors. *Educational and Psychological Measurement*, *41*(4), 1295–1302 https://doi.org/10.1177/001316448104100438

Fan, X., & Thompson, B. (2001). Confidence intervals for effect sizes: Confidence intervals about score reliability coefficients, please: An EPM guidelines editorial. *Educational and Psychological Measurement*, *61*(4), 517–531. https://doi.org/10.1177/0013164401614001

Feldt, L. S., Woodruff, D. J., & Salih, F. A. (1987). Statistical inference for coefficient alpha. *Applied Psychological Measurement, 11*, 93–103. https://doi.org/10.1177/014662168701100107

Fife, D. A., Mendoza, J. L., & Terry, R. (2012). The assessment of reliability under range restriction: A comparison of α, ω, and test–retest reliability for dichotomous data. *Educational and Psychological Measurement*, *72*(5), 862–888. https://doi.org/10.1177/0013164411430225

Fleiss, J. L. (1971). Measuring nominal scale agreement among many raters. *Psychological Bulletin*, *76*, 378–382. https://doi.org/10.1037/h0031619

Gadermann, A. M., Guhn, M., & Zumbo, B. D. (2012). Estimating ordinal reliability for Likert-type and ordinal item response data: A conceptual, empirical, and practical guide. *Practical Assessment, Research, and Evaluation*, *17*(1), 3.

Gignac, G. E., Reynolds, M. R., & Kovacs K. (2019). Digit span subscale scores may be insufficiently reliable for clinical interpretation: Distinguishing between stratified coefficient alpha and omega hierarchical. *Assessment*, *26*(8), 1554–1563. https://doi.org/10.1177/1073191117748396

Gignac, G. E., Shankaralingam, M., Walker, K., & Kilpatrick, P. (2016). Short-term memory for faces relates to general intelligence moderately. *Intelligence*, *57*, 96–104. https://doi.org/10.1016/j.intell.2016.05.001

Gignac, G. E., & Szodorai, E. T. (2016). Effect size guidelines for individual differences researchers. *Personality and Individual Differences*, *102*, 74–78. https://doi.org/10.1016/j.paid.2016.06.069

Gignac, G. E., & Watkins, M. W. (2013). Bifactor modeling and the estimation of model-based reliability in the WAIS-IV. *Multivariate Behavioral Research*, *48*(5), 639–662. https://doi.org/10.1080/00273171.2013.804398

Gorsuch, R. L. (1974). *Factor analysis*. Saunders.

Graham, J. M. (2006). Congeneric and (essentially) tau-equivalent estimates of score reliability: What they are and how to use them. *Educational and Psychological Measurement*, *66*(6), 930–944. https://doi.org/10.1177/0013164406288165

Greco, L. M., O'Boyle, E. H., Cockburn, B. S., & Yuan, Z. (2018). Meta-analysis of coefficient alpha: A reliability generalization study. *Journal of Management Studies*, *55*(4), 583–618. https://doi.org/10.1111/joms.12328

Green, S. B. (1983). Identifiability of spurious factors using linear factor analysis with binary items. *Applied Psychological Measurement*, *7*(2), 139–147. https://doi.org/10.1177/014662168300700202

Green, S. B., & Yang, Y. (2015). Evaluation of dimensionality in the assessment of internal consistency reliability: Coefficient alpha and omega coefficients. *Educational Measurement: Issues and Practice*, *34*(4), 14–20. https://doi.org/10.1111/emip.12100

Hancock, G. R., & Mueller, R. O. (2001). Rethinking construct reliability within latent variable systems. In R. Cudeck, S. du Toit, & D. Sorbom (Eds.), *Structural equation modeling: Present and future—A festschrift in honor of Karl Jöreskog* (pp. 195–216). Scientific Software International.

Harding, B., Tremblay, C., & Cousineau, D. (2014). Standard errors: A review and evaluation of standard error estimators using Monte Carlo simulations. *The Quantitative Methods for Psychology*, *10*(2), 107–123. https://doi.org/10.20982/tqmp.10.2.p107

Henry, G. T. (2013). Practical sampling. In L. Bickman & D. Rog Eds., *The SAGE handbook of applied social research methods* (2nd ed., pp. 77–105). Sage Publications. https://doi.org/10.4135/9781483348858.n3

Holgado-Tello, F. P., Chacón-Moscoso, S., Barbero-García, I., & Vila-Abad, E. (2010). Polychoric versus Pearson correlations in exploratory and confirmatory factor analysis of ordinal variables. *Quality & Quantity*, *44*(1), 153–166. https://doi.org/10.1007/s11135-008-9190-y

Horst, P. (1953). Correcting the Kuder-Richardson reliability for dispersion of item difficulties. *Psychological Bulletin*, *50*(5), 371. https://doi.org/10.1037/h0062012

Iacobucci, D., & Duhachek, A. (2003). Advancing alpha: Measuring reliability with confidence. *Journal of Consumer Psychology*, *13*(4), 478–487. https://doi.org/10.1207/s15327663jcp1304_14

Johanson, G. A., & Brooks, G. P. (2010). Initial scale development: Sample size for pilot studies. *Educational and Psychological Measurement*, *70*(3), 394–400. https://doi.org/10.1177/0013164409355692

Johnson, H. M. (1945). Maximal selectivity, correctivity and correlation obtainable in 2× 2 contingency-tables. *The American Journal of Psychology*, *58*(1), 65–68. https://doi.org/10.2307/1417575

Kaiser, H. F. (1991). Coefficient alpha for a principal component and the Kaiser-Guttman rule. *Psychological Reports*, *68*(3), 855–858. https://doi.org/10.2466/pr0.1991.68.3.855

Kaplan, R. M., & Saccuzzo, D. P. (1982). *Psychological testing: Principles, applications, and issues*. Brooks/Cole.

Kaplan, R. M., & Saccuzzo, D. P. (2005). *Psychological testing: Principles, applications, and issues* (6th ed.). Wadsworth.

Kline, P. (1986). *A handbook of test construction: Introduction to psychometric design*. Methuen.

Koo, T. K., & Li, M. Y. (2016). A guideline of selecting and reporting intraclass correlation coefficients for reliability research. *Journal of Chiropractic Medicine*, *15*(2), 155–163. https://doi.org/10.1016/j.jcm.2016.02.012

Kretzschmar, A., & Gignac, G. E. (2019). At what sample size do latent variable correlation stabilize? *Journal of Research in Personality*, *80*, 17–22. https://doi.org/10.1016/j.jrp.2019.03.007

Kubinger, K. D. (2003). On artificial results due to using factor analysis for dichotomous variables. *Psychology Science*, *45*(1), 106–110.

Lance, C. E., Butts, M. M., & Michels, L. C. (2006). The sources of four commonly reported cutoff criteria: What did they really say? *Organizational Research Methods*, *9*(2), 202–220. https://doi.org/10.1177/1094428105284919

Landis, J. R., & Koch, G. G. (1977). The measurement of observer agreement for categorical data. *Biometrics*, 159–174. https://doi.org/10.2307/2529310

Lissitz, R. W., & Green, S. B. (1975). Effect of the number of scale points on reliability: A Monte Carlo approach. *Journal of Applied Psychology*, *60*(1), 10–13. https://doi.org/10.1037/h0076268

Loevinger, J. (1948). The technic of homogeneous tests compared with some aspects of "scale analysis" and factor analysis. *Psychological Bulletin*, *45*(6), 507–529. https://doi.org/10.1037/h0055827

Loevinger, J. (1954). The attenuation paradox in test theory. *Psychological Bulletin*, *51*(5), 493–504. https://doi.org/10.1037/h0058543

Lord, F. M., & Novick, M. R. (1968). *Statistical theories of mental test scores*. Addison-Wesley.

Lorenzo-Seva, U., & Ferrando, P. J. (2020). Not positive definite correlation matrices in exploratory item factor analysis: Causes, consequences and a proposed solution. *Structural Equation Modeling: A Multidisciplinary Journal*, 1–10. https://doi.org/10.1080/10705511.2020.1735393

McDonald, R. P. (1965). Difficulty factors and non-linear factor analysis. *British Journal of Mathematical and Statistical Psychology*, *18*(1), 11–23. https://doi.org/10.1111/j.2044-8317.1965.tb00690.x

McDonald, R. P. (1999). *Test theory: A unified treatment*. Mahwah, NJ: Lawrence Erlbaum.

McNeish, D. (2018). Thanks coefficient alpha, we'll take it from here. *Psychological Methods*, 23(3), 412–433. https://doi.org/10.1037/met0000144

Mellenbergh, G. J. (2019). Counteracting methodological errors in behavioral research. Springer.

Molenaar, I. W. (1997). Nonparametric models for polytomous responses. In W. J. van der Linden & R. K. Hambleton (Eds.), *Handbook of modern item response theory* (pp. 369–380). Springer-Verlag. https://doi .org/10.1007/978-1-4757-2691-6_21

Murphy, K. R. & Davidshofer, C. O. (1988). *Psychological testing: Principles and applications*. Prentice Hall.

Nunnally, J. C. (1967). *Psychometric theory*. McGraw-Hill.

Nunnally, J. C. (1978). *Psychometric theory* (2nd ed.). McGraw-Hill.

Nunnally, J. C. & Bernstein, I. H. (1994). *Psychometric theory* (3rd ed.). McGraw-Hill.

Pedhazur, E. J., & Pedhazur Schmelkin, L. (1991). *Measurement, design, and analysis: An integrated approach*. Lawrence Erlbaum & Associates. https://doi.org/10.4324/9780203726389

Peterson, R. A. (1994). A meta-analysis of Cronbach's coefficient alpha. *Journal of Consumer Research*, 21(2), 381–391. https://doi.org/10.1086/209405

Portney, L. G., & Watkins, M. P. (2009). *Foundations of clinical research: Applications to practice* (3rd ed.). Pearson/Prentice Hall.

Raykov, T. (1997) Scale reliability, Cronbach's coefficient alpha, and violations of essential tau-equivalence with fixed congeneric components. *Multivariate Behavioral Research*, 32, 329–353. https://doi.org/10 .1207/s15327906mbr3204_2

Raykov, T., & Marcoulides, G. A. (2019). Thanks coefficient alpha, we still need you! *Educational and Psychological Measurement*, 79(1), 200–210. https://doi.org/10.1177/0013164417725127

Reise, S. P., Waller, N. G., & Comrey, A. L. (2000). Factor analysis and scale revision. *Psychological Assessment*, 12(3), 287–297. https://doi.org/10.1037//1040-3590.12.3.287

Revelle, W., & Condon, D. M. (2018). Reliability. In P. Irwing, T. Booth, & D. J. Hughes (Eds.). *The Wiley handbook of psychometric testing: A multidisciplinary reference on survey, scale and test development* (Vols. 1–2) (pp. 709–749). Hoboken, NJ, EUA: John Wiley & Sons. https://doi.org/10.1002 /9781118489772.ch23

Savalei, V., & Reise, S. P. (2019). Don't forget the model in your model-based reliability coefficients: A reply to McNeish (2018). *Collabra: Psychology*, 5(1), 36. https://doi.org/10.1525/collabra.247

Segall, D. O. (1994). The reliability of linearly equated tests. *Psychometrika*, 59, 361–375. https://doi.org/10 .1007/bf02296129

Shepperd, J. A., Emanuel, A. S., Dodd, V. L., & Logan, H. L. (2016). The reliability of psychological instruments in community samples: A cautionary note. *Journal of Health Psychology*, 21(9), 2033–2041. https://doi.org/10.1177/1359105315569859

Sun, W., Chou, C. P., Stacy, A. W., Ma, H., Unger, J., & Gallaher, P. (2007). SAS and SPSS macros to calculate standardized Cronbach's alpha using the upper bound of the *phi* coefficient for dichotomous items. *Behavior Research Methods*, 39(1), 71–81. https://doi.org/10.3758/bf03192845

Thompson, B. (2007). Effect sizes, confidence intervals, and confidence intervals for effect sizes. *Psychology in the Schools*, 44(5), 423–432. https://doi.org/10.1002/pits.20234

Thompson, B., & Vacha-Haase, T. (2000). Psychometrics is datametrics: The test is not reliable. *Educational and Psychological Measurement*, 60(2), 174–195. https://doi.org/10.1177/0013164400602002

Torralba, A. (2009). How many pixels make an image? *Visual Neuroscience*, 26(1), 123–131. https://doi.org /10.1017/s0952523808080930

Vacha-Haase, T. (1998). Reliability generalization: Exploring variance in measurement error affecting score reliability across studies. *Educational and Psychological Measurement, 58*(1), 6–20. https://doi.org/10 .1177/0013164498058001002

Vacha-Haase, T., Ness, C., Nilsson, J., & Feetz, D. (1999). Practices regarding reporting of reliability coefficients: A review of three journals. *The Journal of Experimental Education*, 67(4), 335–341. https:// doi.org/10.1080/00220979909598487

Wasserman, J. D., & Bracken, B. A. (2003). Psychometric characteristics of assessment procedures. In J. R. Graham, J. A. Naglieri, & I. B. Weiner (Eds.), *Handbook of psychology: Volume 10: Assessment psychology* (pp. 43–66). John Wiley & Sons. https://doi.org/10.1002/0471264385.wei1003

Zinbarg, R. E., Revelle, W., Yovel, I., & Li, W. (2005). Cronbach's α, Revelle's β, and McDonald's ω H: Their relations with each other and two alternative conceptualizations of reliability. *Psychometrika, 70*(1), 123–133. https://doi.org/10.1007/s11336-003-0974-7

Zumbo, B. D., Gadermann, A. M., & Zeisser, C. (2007). Ordinal versions of coefficients alpha and theta for Likert rating scales. *Journal of Modern Applied Statistical Methods, 6*, 21–29. https://doi.org/10.22237/jmasm/1177992180

Chapter 10

The Incorporation of Inspection Time With Standardized Batteries of Intelligence

Joseph C. Kush

Overview

The definition and subsequent measurement of human intelligence remains one of the most elusive tasks for educational psychologists and psychometrists. Even aspects as basic as dimensionality remain unanswered; however, there s consensus that intelligence consists of an overarching ability that underlies all aspects of the construct (i.e., *g*, general mental ability) as well as smaller, component abilities such as verbal ability and abstract reasoning. While most commercially available tests of intelligence put forward claims that their instruments are grounded in established theory, all too often this is not the case. Rather, for the past half-century the vast majority of commercial IQ tests have had their theoretical framework defined in a post-hoc manner based on the results of psychometric analyses completed as part of the standardization procedure. Typically, a large number of subtests thought to be measuring a variety of discrete cognitive skills are developed and administered as part of the standardization process and are subsequently examined with factor analytic statistics. Not unlike the tail wagging the dog, the best-fitting outcome is then identified as the theoretical foundation of the instrument. Interestingly, across this past half-century, the number of identified subscale or component indices has increased with each revision of the test. Proponents of this process argue that IQ test revision is much like the upgrade from an iPhone 15 to an iPhone 16—more features and better stability—while critics point to commercial interests in that an IQ test that claims to measure five types of intelligence will sell better than one that only measures four. A second criticism of recent IQ scale development is that the tests are increasingly adding content that is better described as measures of learning rather than measures of intelligence. While the overwhelming diagnostic function of IQ tests is their predictive utility, the unfortunately current result is an artificially inflated correlation between tests of intelligence and tests of achievement. An increasingly appealing alternative to traditional IQ testing has been the recommendation to supplement the standard battery with physiologically based tasks termed *elementary tests of cognitive abilities*. In isolation these measures are significantly more theoretically grounded, producing improved face validity although predictive validity suffers slightly. This chapter presents one particular *elementary cognitive task* (ECT) measure, inspection time, and describes the process of how an inspection time task can be combined with individually selected IQ subtests to produce an assessment battery with improved diagnostic utility as well as better alignment with current theories of human intelligence. The combination of these approaches may offer the best of both worlds.

Much like modern-day civil service examinations, over 4,000 years ago applicants for public office in China were required to complete a variety of mental and physical tasks over a period of several days as part of a preliminary screening process. This initial screening process began at the provincial level, and successful applicants then traveled to Peking (now Beijing) for a second round of more intensive assessment. This practice continued until the Chinese revolution at the beginning of the 20th century and has been modeled extensively by Western countries up to the current time as intelligence tests continue to be strongly related to occupational, educational, economic, and social outcomes.

Fast forward two thousand years to Plato's argument that intelligence was housed in the soul rather than the body (Carpenter, 2008), and in his *Republic*, Plato wrote, "Then you see that this knowledge may be truly called necessary, necessitating as it clearly does the use of the pure intelligence in the attainment of pure truth" (Plato & Jowett 2019, p. 228). Specifically, Plato believed that God "could only create the fairest; and reflecting that of visible things the intelligent is superior to the unintelligent, he put intelligence in soul and soul in body, and framed the universe to be the best and fairest work in the order of nature, and the world became a living soul through the providence of God" (Plato & Jowett, 2019, p. 206).

These two historical references characterize an ongoing debate in the field of psychology between positions regarding the structure of intelligence and those that describe the structure of intelligence tests. The questions what is human intelligence and do IQ tests measure it have puzzled the intellectually curious throughout the course of history but almost always mention a professional discussion that occurred in 1921 where the editors of the *Journal of Educational Psychology* asked seventeen leading theorists to attempt to answer these questions. Surprisingly, at the time, no consensus was reached but rather produced the unfortunate, half-joking conclusion that "intelligence is what intelligence tests test" (Boring, 1923, p. 35).

We've long known that intelligence is one of the most important factors impacting success in job performance and educational achievement (Gottfredson, 1997a, 1997b; Jensen, 1998; Sackett et al., 2001; Schmidt & Hunter, 1981). It has also been established that the vast majority of commercially available tests of intelligence include content that is influenced by nonintellectual factors including reading ability, socioeconomic status, test-taking strategies, and cultural familiarity (Gould, 1996; Murdoch, 2007), and the inclusion of these components improves the predictive power of the scales because multiple domains as well as intelligence are being assessed (Watkins et al., 2006). Without doubt, when attempting to forecast future success, the inclusion of an individual's cognitive ability as well as other factors related to that outcome will improve the predictive utility over the sole predictive power of intellectual skills (Kush et al., 2011). And obviously any instrument claiming to accurately assess more types of intelligence will have greater commercial value than an instrument that can only measure a single dimension.

In most instances, at least for children, this prediction will be of academic achievement. And once again, a test battery that includes a knowledge of that student's cognitive functioning as well as their academic ability will offer a better prediction of school success than a measure of cognitive functioning in isolation. However, the circularity of this logic is problematic: the verbal content included in the measurement of intelligence often overlaps with the content used to measure achievement. A best practice approach would be to recognize that multiple predictive domains are being included as separate scales or tasks rather than making the claim that only intelligence is coming into play. The contamination of most major IQ tests with academic content (Naglieri & Bornstein, 2003; Naglieri & Das, 1997; Naglieri & Rojahn, 2004), while improving their predictive ability, confounds the interpretability of true intelligence.

Individual tests of intelligence were originally created to assist with the identification of children from the Paris school system who were at risk for school difficulties (Binet, 1905), and the earliest IQ measures included components that analyzed school examination scores for these children (Spearman, 1904). Millions of intelligence tests are administered each year to children in the United States as part of special education eligibility evaluations (Dombrowski et al., 2019; Gregory, 2022; Kamphaus et al., 2000) and are among the most common instruments used by psychologists in both clinical and educational settings (Wilson & Reschly, 1996). IQ tests are rarely administered in isolation and are typically used as part of a diagnostic battery primarily to predict occupational success or academic attainment such as school grades or standardized tests of academic achievement. An abundance of research has demonstrated typical IQ–academic correlations ranging from 0.50 to 0.80 (Deary et al., 2007; Mackintosh, 2011; Naglieri & Bornstein, 2003; Rohde & Thompson, 2007; Roth et al 2015). In fact, tests of intelligence often predict academic achievement with more accuracy than other tests of academic achievement. For example, STEM achievement has been shown to be better predicted by tests of cognitive ability than by achievement test scores in language or literacy (Deary et al., 2007; Lu et al., 2011). However, not all IQ tests measure the same thing (Mackintosh, 1998), and unfortunately, the tests that we commonly use have not substantially evolved since their inception (Thorndike, 1997).

Defining Human Intelligence

Over the past several centuries, psychologists have failed to agree upon a single definition of intelligence and as a result, there are many unresolved issues that remain (Neisser et al., 1996). Further, Wechsler (1975) posited that different fields have created different definitions of intelligence. For example, anthropology focuses on the ability to adapt to the environment whereas education focuses on the ability to learn. The British psychologist Charles Spearman (1904, 2010, 2022) established the psychometric approach to intelligence that focuses on a single factor underlying tests of cognitive ability, typically referred to as Spearman's g. In contrast, the American psychologist Louis Thurstone (1924, 1938) created a multi-faceted definition and posited seven independent factors that he termed *primary mental abilities*. While most 21st-century psychologists who study human intelligence acknowledge the existence of g, there remains a great disparity of thought considering the nature and structure of g. The debate focuses on the disagreement on how many kinds of intelligence exist. Is there simply one type of intelligence, a common factor that underlies all cognitive processes, or do multiple, discreet cognitive skills exist such as verbal ability, numerical ability, and spatial ability?

Most psychologists agree that the best contemporary definition of human intelligence was offered by a panel of 52 of the most influential researchers in the field of intelligence, coordinated by Linda Gottfredson (1997a).

Intelligence is a very general mental capability that, among other things, involves the ability to reason, plan, solve problems, think abstractly, comprehend complex ideas, learn quickly, and learn from experience. It is not merely book-learning, a narrow academic skill, or test-taking smarts. Rather, it reflects a broader and deeper capability for comprehending our surroundings— "catching on," "making sense" of things, or "figuring out" what to do. Intelligence, so defined, can be measured, and intelligence tests measure it well. They are among the most accurate (in technical terms, reliable and valid) of all psychological tests and assessments. (p. 13)

There is a further agreement today among psychologists that a hierarchical model with multiple factors or dimensions provides the most valid and comprehensive framework of intelligence (Beaujean & Benson, 2018, Deary, 2001; Neisser et al., 1996). The three most widely supported major models are Horn and Cattell's fluid-crystallized (Gf-Gc) model (Cattell, 1963; Horn & Noll, 1994, 1997); Carroll's Three-Stratum theory (3S; 1993), and the Cattell-Horn-Carroll model of intelligence (CHC; Benson et al., 2010; Schneider & McGrew, 2018). CHC is typically represented as a synthesis of Horn's extended Gf-Gc and 3S, and while not without its critics (e.g., Canivez & Youngstrom, 2019; Dombrowski & Watkins, 2013; Frazier & Youngstrom, 2007; Glutting et al., 2003; McGill, 2017; McGill et al., 2018), it is now associated with six major, commercial tests of intelligence.

Intelligence and IQ Tests

As a result, most contemporary intelligence tests have attempted to modify their structure to reflect CHC theory (e.g., the Wechsler Intelligence Scale for Children–Fifth Edition [WISC–V; Wechsler, 2014], the Wechsler Adult Intelligence Scale–Fourth Edition [WAIS–IV, Wechsler, 2008], the Stanford-Binet Intelligence Scales–Fifth Edition [SB–5; Roid, 2003], the Kaufman Assessment Battery for Children–Second Edition [KABC–II; Kaufman & Kaufman, 2004], the Reynolds Intellectual Assessment Scales [RIAS; Reynolds & Kamphaus, 2003], and the Wide Range Intelligence Test [WRIT; Glutting et al., 2000]. Often, despite the claims of the publishers, current research has consistently demonstrated that the overwhelming majority of IQ test variance is associated with higher-order g while substantially less variance is associated with first-order factors (Bodin et al., 2009; Canivez & Watkins, 2010; Watkins, 2006, 2010). Further, there is growing evidence across a number of scales, including the WISC–V, that the factor structures reported by the test publishers are often flawed and are better represented with a bifactor representation (Canivez et al., 2019; Dombrowski et al., 2015). Reise et al. (2010) have shown that a bifactor model containing a general factor yet allowing for multidimensionality is preferred to a higher-order model for determining the relative contribution of group factors independent of a general factor. These findings have led a number or researchers to conclude that the primary interpretation of IQ scores should occur at the g level rather than the factor index score level (Canivez & Kush, 2013; Canivez & Watkins, 2010; Watkins, 2006, 2010).

Increasingly however, commercial tests of intelligence are being criticized for their lack of a theoretical foundation or incongruence between the theory of intelligence and the corresponding IQ test (Canivez & Kush, 2013; Kush, 1996). This phenomenon is not necessarily new as Kaufman (2000, 2009) has argued that historically most tests designed to measure intelligence lack a solid theoretical foundation for their development. As one example, while the current Wechsler scales imply CHC constructs, it remains unclear whether a four- or five-factor CHC model best fits the data (Canivez, 2013; Niileksela et al., 2013; Keith, 2005; Watkins, 2010; Watkins et al., 2006). Relatedly, DiStefano and Dombrowski (2006) and Canivez (2008), using data from the Stanford-Binet–Fifth Edition (SB–5) standardization sample, obtained markedly different results for the SB–5 than the CFA results presented in its technical manual (Roid, 2003) and concluded that the SB–5 measured only one essential dimension (g). Similar findings exist for the WISC–V where Watkins and Canivez (2022) concluded that WISC–V group factors were not well defined and WISC–V index scores were contaminated with variance from other constructs making them insufficiently reliable for clinical decisions, and only the Full-Scale IQ (FSIQ) was found to be sufficiently reliable for clinical use.

Beyond an inability to demonstrate independent replication of factor structure (Canivez & Youngstrom, 2019), the continued accumulation of factors in CHC—from 10 broad abilities in 1997 to 17 in 2018—undermines its foundation (Wasserman, 2019). Further complicating CHC interpretation is the inability of the theory to accurately define and assess facets associated with cognitive speed. Schneider and McGrew (2018) have identified two broad speed factors—decision speed (Gt) and processing speed (Gs)—as well as two additional broad factors strongly associated with speed: psychomotor speed (Gps) and retrieval fluency (Gr). While this distinction is somewhat improved over Carrol's (1993) determination that narrow speed existed across four broad ability levels as well as two explicit broad speed factors (broad cognitive speediness, processing speed/decision speed), it remains a significant limitation. The recommendations for remediating some of these limitations (e.g., McGill & Dombrowski, 2019; Wasserman, 2019) cannot be underscored enough.

The prediction of academic achievement is perhaps the most important application of intelligence tests (Brown et al., 1999; Canivez, 2013; Weiss & Prifitera, 1995). In this aim, and perhaps originally unintentionally by the publishers, the content of contemporary IQ measures has evolved to include intelligence as well as other factors including personality (Chamorro-Premuzic et al., 2005), academic achievement (Kush, 2005; Sternberg, 1998, 1999), and the context of the learning environment (Ceci, 1991). It is this incremental validity that provides IQ tests with the "broad explanatory power" described by Jensen (1998), yet this same content detracts from the face validity of these measures as intellectual factors as well as non-intellectual factors are being assessed. Relatedly, it is important to remember Jensen's caution from over 40 years ago (1978) that intelligence must be distinguished from both learning and memory. In contrast, more focused or specialized measures of cognitive ability not only possess sound psychometric characteristics (Braden & Athanasiou, 2005) but also are sustained by well-articulated models of intelligence (Kranzler et al., 2010).

Criterion Validity: Using IQ Tests to Make Predictions

The ongoing debate regarding the nature of human intelligence must continue to collect data from both differential and experimental methodologies. However, as additional factor analytic studies continue to examine the construct validity of commercial IQ tests, it is critical to remember that the structure of *IQ* tests must not be equated with a discussion on the structure of intelligence. Factor analytic studies are valuable in ascertaining how many types of intelligence might be measured by an IQ test, but in isolation they provide no information about the diagnostic utility of the test (Canivez et al., 2009; Carroll, 1997). Empirical studies that examine the factor structure of IQ tests must therefore be extended to subsequently examine relations to external criteria to ascertain their clinical utility (Canivez, 2013).

Particularly for school psychologists, the prediction of academic achievement marks the primary use of intelligence tests (Brown et al., 1999; Weiss & Prifitera, 1995). Individual tests of intelligence were originally designed to assist with the identification of children who were at risk for school failure (Binet & Simon, 1904) and Binet's original IQ test included components that analyzed the school performance of children within the Paris school system (Spearman, 1904). Further, Piagetian tasks are also known for their high g loadings (Carroll 1993).

Intelligence tests are strong predictors of academic achievement (Brody, 2002; Carroll, 1993; Gottfredson, 2008; Naglieri & Bornstein, 2003) with median individually administered IQ–achievement correlations typically near .50 (Neisser et al., 1996; Brody, 2002). In cases where the IQ and achievement tests are co-normed on the same population, the correlation rises to near .70 (Elliott, 2007; Glutting et al., 2000; Kaufman & Kaufman, 2004; McGrew, 2009; Reynolds & Kamphaus, 2003; Roid, 2003; Wechsler, 2003, 2008; Woodcock et al., 2001). Finally, when individual and group IQ measures are included together, 85% to 90% of predictable criterion variable variance is accounted for by g (Thorndike, 1986).

However, with correlations in the .80 range, approximately two-thirds of the information contained on IQ tests and tests of academic achievement reflects shared variance or overlapping content, a figure that is simply too high for instruments thought to be measuring related yet discrete constructs (Kush, 2005). This view is supported by a number of researchers (e.g., Gardner, 1983; Gould, 1996; Murdoch, 2007; Naglieri & Bornstein, 2003; Sternberg, 1998, 1999, 2003) who point out that IQ tests are overly tainted by achievement, particularly vocabulary, information and arithmetic problem solving. These inflated IQ–achievement correlations would be reduced substantially if only the g portion of the test was used to predict achievement. For example, Glutting et al. (2006) demonstrated that the WISC–IV FSIQ predicted substantial portions of variance in reading and mathematics scores while the four-factor index scores did not contribute additional meaningful predictive power. This notion is further articulated by Ree and Carretta (2022), who concluded that research over the past 30 years has clearly demonstrated that specific cognitive abilities provide little or no incremental validity beyond general cognitive ability.

The practice of supplementing traditional, commercial batteries with auxiliary measures is becoming increasingly widespread. Perhaps the most common supplemental task is Raven's Progressive Matrices (RPM; Raven et al., 1998), a test of abstract reasoning ability that requires no verbal responses and minimizes the need for verbal instructions. Raven's Matrices present novel problems in a uniform visual format consisting of a matrix of visual patterns that must be solved by locating the missing piece among several provided choices. Items are presented in a matrix format and progress from relatively simple perceptual problems to more complex analytic problems that require high-level abstraction (Carpenter et al., 1990). In typical populations, Raven's and Wechsler scores provide comparable estimates of intellectual functioning although many current IQ tests now include matrix reasoning subtests.

An Alternative to Traditional IQ Tests and the Assessment of Basic Cognitive Processes

Because of the contamination of most commercial tests of intelligence, an alternative approach to the assessment of human intelligence has moved away from attempting to describe the underlying structure of intelligence and has focused instead on the direct measurement of the specific cognitive processes. This distinction is what Cronbach (1957) referred to as the "two disciplines of scientific psychology"—differential and experimental. The study of mental chronometry or the selection of more direct measures of cognitive ability, has led a growing number of researchers to the examination of ECTs (e.g., Deary, 1993, 2000; Jensen, 2006; Sheppard & Vernon, 2008). These tasks are seen as distinct from those found on traditional IQ tests; however, they are thought to assess the same features of cognition that underlie the performance of more complex intelligence test tasks (Partchev & de Boeck, 2012). To date most ECT research has focused on the constructs of working memory and processing speed (Conway et al., 2002; Jensen, 1998). While the theoretical rationale underlying mental chronometry is almost a century old, the sophistication and accuracy of empirical studies has only recently paralleled advances in technology and has been the result of cross-disciplinary collaboration.

Fast performance on elementary cognitive tasks requiring minimal reasoning effort, often termed *mental speed*, is known to correlate positively with general intelligence (Sheppard & Vernon, 2008). Examples of commonly used ECTs include those that measure processing speed, or reaction time (RT), and those that measure speed of information intake, or inspection time (IT; Jensen, 1998; Kush et al., 2011). However, recent models of intelligence offer a complex characterization of speed of processing abilities (Carroll, 1993; Horn, 1988; Roberts & Stankov, 1999). Speed of processing abilities are factorially complex, and IT provides a very specific measure of visualization speed. This type of mental processing speed should not be confused with the composite score consisting of several subtests typically found on most Wechsler scales.

The proposed hierarchical model of speed of processing offered by Roberts and Stankov (1999) identifies test-taking speed (correct-decision speed) at the apex, followed by perceptual speed as characterized by tests that, given enough time, almost anyone could complete correctly. At the third level of complexity, decision time represents the time required to make a simple sensory-based decision. At the lowest level in the hierarchy is movement time, characterized by psychomotor ability with minimal cognitive requirements. Roberts and Stankov (1999) included a general speed factor in their model. However, Horn (1988) and Carroll (1993) did not.

Current research has shown that measures of inspection time correlate with standardized measures of intelligence, typically near a value of -.50, after correcting for attenuation and range restriction (Burns & Nettelbeck, 2003; Deary, 2000; Grudnik & Kranzler, 2001; Kranzler & Jensen, 1989; Nettelbeck, 1987, 1998, 2001). Burns and colleagues (Burns & Nettelbeck, 2003; O'Conner & Burns, 2003) have demonstrated that IT correlates with one of the second-order factors from the Gf-Gc theory: general speed of processing (Gs), the cognitive factor that refers to the speed at which an individual is able to correctly perform simple or over-learned problems. These findings have been extended to the field of behavioral genetic studies (Luciano et al., 2001; Posthuma et al., 2001) where researchers have demonstrated that ECT measures are genetically correlated with IQ.

The speed at which a problem can be solved has commonly been thought of as an index related to overall cognitive ability (Nettelbeck, 1998, 2001). Jensen (2006) suggested that IT is a sensitive index of the "speed of perceptual intake" (p. 84) because participants have only to determine the difference in a visual stimulus, with no need for providing an immediate motor response as is required in reaction time tasks. Further, cognitive speed may not only determine the duration of processing but may also affect the quality of processing in complex tasks (Jensen, 2004). For example, Gottfredson (2000) has shown that individuals with higher levels of intelligence work more quickly and efficiently because they transmit electrical nerve impulses faster and use less glucose. Processing speed has also been shown to account for approximately one-third of the variance in academic performance (Carlson & Jensen, 1982; Petrill & Thompson, 1993). Differences in processing speed and efficiency have also been reported between groups of varying levels of mental ability including normal, intellectually disabled (Baumeister & Kellas, 1967), and gifted individuals (Cohn et al., 1985; Kranzler et al., 1994). Among ECTs, IT has produced the highest correlations with IQ and is related to overall perceptual speed (Deary & Stough, 1996, Mackintosh & Bennett, 2002). Additionally, Petrill et al. (2001) have shown that the variance IT tasks share with IQ is unique from the variance accounted for by other ECT measures and IQ.

Alternative approaches to the assessment of intelligence are showing much promise such as Jensen's (2006) work on mental chronometry, which focused on the speed with which the brain processes information (e.g., Haier, 2003; Prabhakaran et al., 2000). This research has attempted to directly measure activity in the brain using various neuroimaging procedures (e.g., electroencephalography, positron emission tomography, and functional magnetic resonance imaging) or the Higgins et al. (2007) neuropsychological measures of prefrontal cognitive ability.

Inspection Time

Vickers (1970; Vickers et al., 2014; Vickers et al., 1972) and his doctoral students conducted some of the earliest research on IT (Nettelbeck & Lally 1976) and have produced a large body of empirical findings since that time (Nettelbeck, 1987, 1998, 2001, 2003). Similar to the Raven's Matrices, IT eliminates the influences of verbal comprehension and expression. Within the typical inspection time paradigm, the task begins with participants focusing their attention on a simple visual cue, typically a large black dot in the center of the screen. Following a brief delay, subjects are briefly presented with a task requiring them to make decisions on multiple trials about which one of two legs of an inverted *u*-shaped, or *pi* figure (see Figure 10.1) is longer.

Stimuli are presented for a range of durations, from hundreds of milliseconds to very short durations in the range of several milliseconds. Immediately following the presentation of the figures, a large mask covers the stimuli to prevent any storage in iconic memory. The ability to determine which leg of the stimulus is longer is deemed to be so simple that given unlimited time, most subjects can make the correct response with 100% accuracy. The briefest stimulus duration at which a participant can achieve a given accuracy rate (typically between 70% and 95%) is defined as the participant's threshold IT. Inspection time is therefore "the time required by a subject to make a single observation or inspection of the sensory input on which a discrimination of relative magnitude is based" (Vickers & Smith, 1986, p. 609).

While the rationale for including a backward mask has been to prevent storage of the stimuli in iconic memory, the introduction of the mask has allowed some subjects to report that they are able to use the apparent movement of the mask as a cue or strategy to facilitate their performance (Chaiken & Young, 1993; Egan, 1986, 1994; Mackintosh, 1986; Nettelbeck, 1982). That is, when the larger mask is placed over the shorter leg of the *pi* stimulus, the shorter leg appears to grow in length, or move. This effect is referred to as priming and occurs when one visual stimulus influences the processing of a subsequent stimulus (Bar & Biederman, 1998; Kinoshita & Lupker, 2003). As a result, alternative stimuli and masks (see Figure 10.2) have been created that attempt to minimize the influence of possible movement cues (Frings & Neubauer, 2005; Kush, 2013).

The most important characteristic of the IT paradigm and the factor that distinguishes it from measures of reaction time is that the mental time needed to solve the task is recorded separately

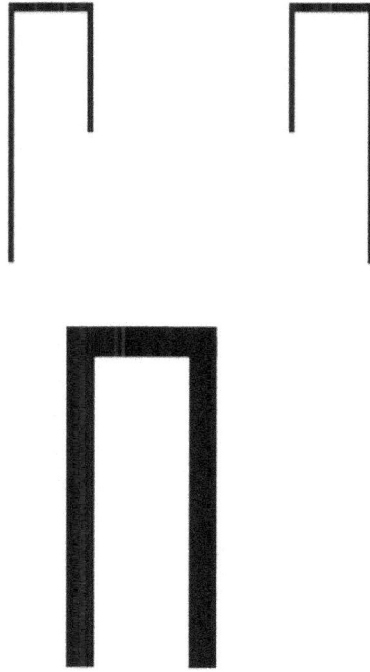

Figure 10.1. **Geometric *pi* Figures and Mask.**

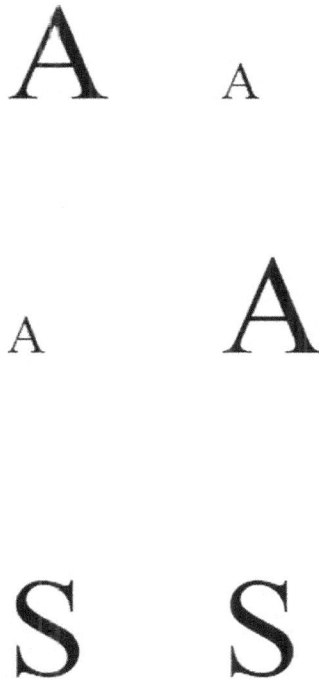

Figure 10.2. **Letter Stimuli and Mask.**

from the time needed to physically identify the correct answer. That is, participants need not make rapid responses as only the correctness of the response is noted; thus, inspection time tasks do not assess speed of reaction. Cognitive processing speed is comprised of distinct factors including movement time, decision time, and visualization speed (O'Connor & Burns, 2003). More specifically, Anderson and Miller (1998), have defined IT as "the stimulus exposure duration required by a subject to make a simple perceptual judgment, for example, the relative length of two lines" (p. 239). Because of the simplicity associated with IT measures, they reflect a stronger connection to biological processes than do traditional psychometric test scores (Jensen, 2006; Vernon & Mori, 1992). Many theorists (e.g., Burns & Nettelbeck, 2003, 2005; Deary, 2000; Jensen, 2006) consider IT to be a purer measure of intelligence than standardized IQ test batteries as the influences of verbal skills, memory, and socialization are minimized, making the results more culture fair. Inspection times have also been found to be significantly heritable (Luciano et al., 2001; Posthuma et al., 2001). Estimates of heritability of inspection time are obtained of between 26% (Luciano et al., 2001) and 56% (Posthuma et al., 2001); however, there appears to be a stronger genetic correlation between inspection time and Performance IQ (PIQ) than between inspection time and Verbal IQ (VIQ).

Faster IT is associated with higher intelligence in typical individuals (Burns & Nettelbeck, 2005; Sheppard & Vernon, 2008), and IT has been shown to be an estimate of perceptual processing speed or information processing efficiency (Burns et al., 1999; Deary et al., 2007; Waiter et al., 2008). Subjects who make a higher proportion of correct discriminations in inspection time tasks tend to score better on cognitive ability tests. This is true for children (Edmonds et al., 2008), healthy adults (Crawford et al., 1998), and healthy older adults (Nettelbeck & Rabbitt, 1992) as well as cognitively impaired older adults (Bonney et al., 2006). Additionally, there is no evidence that personality traits mediate the IT–IQ relationship (Bates & Eysenck, 1993; Luciano, Leisser et al., 2004; Stough et al., 1996).

It remains unclear, however, whether measures of IT are better characterized as an index of higher-level cognitive processes such as the speed and efficiency of cognitive processing (Anderson, 1992; Jensen, 2006; Nettelbeck, 1987, 1998, 2001; Nettelbeck & Wilson, 2005) or strategy use (Mackintosh, 1986), or if IT tasks reflect more specific cognitive processes such as attentional control (Fox et al., 2009) or task consistency (Bors et al., 1999). Two meta-analyses (Grudnik & Kranzler, 2001; Kranzler & Jensen, 1989) support the finding that general intelligence measures and IT are negatively correlated ($r = -.50$ after corrections for sampling error, attenuation, and range restriction) and that the relationship between IT and IQ is almost identical for adults and children (Grudnik & Kranzler, 2001). These IT–intelligence correlations have been observed in a variety of samples using instruments, including the Raven's Matrices (Hill et al., 2011) as well as with Wechsler scales, particularly with PIQ (Deary, 1993; 2000; Nettelbeck & Lally, 1976). Inspection time has a stronger relationship with Performance IQ (PIQ) than Verbal IQ (VIQ) (Deary, 1993; Deary & Stough, 1996).

There is evidence to suggest that the relationship between inspection time and IQ is causal, with individual differences in inspection time causing individual differences in IQ (Anderson, 1992; Brand, 1981; Brand & Deary, 1982; Neubauer, 1997). From a cognitive perspective this finding may be due to the influence of perceptual processing speed in PIQ subtests or from the indirect influence of processing speed on both IT and PIQ tasks. Relatedly, this influence may be the result of focused attention or response monitoring (Hill et al., 2011; Nettelbeck, 2001, 2003). From a physiological perspective, the confluence of IT and intelligence has been postulated to be deriving from ion channel density, speed of synaptic transmission, gene ensemble influences (Luciano,

Wright et al., 2004; Sheppard & Vernon, 2008), or perhaps a combination of all these influences. Further, Deary et al. (2001) found bilateral activation in the inferior fronto-opercular cortex, superior/medial frontal gyrus, and anterior cingulate gyrus, while bilateral deactivation was observed in the posterior cingulate gyrus and precuneus.

And while it has long been known that performance on neuropsychological tests, particularly tasks of memory and attention, improve with experience (Sullivan et al., 2017) the same cannot be concluded for IT tasks. There is evidence to suggest that participants may understand how to perform the task through self-monitoring of past and current performance (Nettelbeck, 2001), but it is not clear that this translates into increased performance. As a result, most IT protocols include familiarization trials (Deary et al., 2004; Duan et al., 2013); however, at the present time it is unknown how IT performance improves with practice.

Inspection time has been used to supplement the assessment of intelligence by several researchers studying samples of individuals with autism (Barbeau et al., 2013; Scheuffgen et al., 2000; Wallace et al., 2009) who found that IT performance was significantly better than predicted by Wechsler scores (e.g., WISC–IV; WAIS–III) although differences existed across the autism spectrum. Unfortunately, to date few studies have examined correlations between inspection time and specific cognitive abilities in children as well as with children with learning disabilities (Grudnik & Kranzler, 2001).

The Best of Both Worlds

The resulting Catch-22 poses both a theoretical as well as a practical dilemma for psychologists (Kush et al., 2011). Commercially published IQ tests are the most frequently used source for predicting academic achievement (Freberg et al., 2008; Parker & Benedict, 2002; Sattler, 2001) however, these tests include non-intellectual factors including academic achievement as well as test-taking strategies and cultural familiarity. Therefore, the inclusion of these components improves the predictive power of the instruments because intelligence and other factors are being assessed (Watkins et al., 2007).

Clearly intelligence is related to, but not identical with, academic achievement, and as Naglieri has convincingly demonstrated (Naglieri & Das, 1997; Naglieri & Rojahn, 2004), the contamination of IQ tests with achievement content confounds their interpretability. Unlike traditional indices of psychometric validity, (e.g., face, content, construct, predictive), the continued practice by publishers of commercial IQ tests of adding content that is overly laden with achievement content or adding spurious IQ subscales that fail to align with intellectual theory has been termed *cash validity* (Kush et al., 2011), that is, an attempt simply to increase the marketability of the IQ test.

As an alternative to commercial IQ tests, measures of mental chronometry, including inspection time, clearly align more obviously to psychometric g than almost all commercial IQ tests. However, their narrow focus, which has the advantage of minimizing memory and learned knowledge, also restricts their ability to predict occupational or academic performance (Kush et al., 2011). Hence the tradeoff: the focus on a single cognitive process provides a purer measure of g as well as greater theoretical tractability but at the same time offers less predictive power.

Neisser et al. (1996) opined that the study of intelligence needs self-restraint, reflection, and more cross-disciplinary research. New definitions of intelligence such as Fagan's (2000) view that intelligence should be seen as processing, and Schmidt's (2002) view that it should be seen as the ability to learn are two of the more promising examples. Unfortunately, however, the field of school psychology has embraced a psychometric definition of intelligence to the exclusion of other possibilities. There is little debate that intelligence test scores are good predictors of important life outcomes, but there is a considerable amount of variance that is unexplained.

The supplemental inclusion of an IT measure with traditional IQ test administration offers a promising approach going forward. For theoreticians, the IQ–IT relationship has already been well established. IT measures have been shown to make independent contributions to the prediction of IQ (Kranzler & Jensen, 1991; Nettelbeck & Rabbitt, 1992). However, IT is an elementary task free of the type of problem solving associated with the complex high-level demands of Raven's Matrices. Therefore, when combined with measures of problem solving, IT represents an additional and independent avenue for investigating approaches to measuring general intelligence. Additionally, as Nettelbeck (1987) has shown, measures of inspection time account for approximately 25% of the variance in IQ tests, a finding confirmed by meta-analysis findings from Kranzler and Jensen (1989). Further, the inclusion of an IT measure within a standard assessment battery may improve diagnostic utility. For example, IT has been shown to be an important biological marker in the diagnosis of anxiety disorders (In-Albon et al., 2009), Korsakoff's and Alzheimer's diseases (Deary et al., 1991), Parkinson's disease (Johnson et al., 2004), and major depression (Chase et al., 2009) as these populations demonstrate longer IT response times because of their impairment. Additionally, because IT has been shown to be stable across lifespan and free of gender differences, IT may serve as a biomarker to determine cognitive changes associated with aging (Burns & Nettelbeck, 2005). Finally, by using IT as a supplemental, individual measure rather than the less informative composite IQ index, a multivariate genetic analysis with IQ subtest scores will establish whether the IT–IQ relationship is influenced by the same or separate genetic factors (Luciano, Wright, et al., 2004). Further, it appears that most of the genetic variance in IT is better explained by genes influencing general ability rather than the perceptual speed/organization factor (Luciano, Wright, et al., 2004). For example, IT has demonstrated a strong phenotypic relationship with Wechsler's Digit Symbol (Crawford et al., 1998; Deary, 1993), although the relationship may be mediated by a general fluid ability factor rather than a factor characterizing perceptual speed (Luciano, Leisser, et al., 2004). Perceptual speed, as demonstrated by an inspection time task, has been shown to be an intermediate phenotype in studies attempting to determine genetic loci that determine variance in intelligence (Posthuma et al., 2001), accounting for approximately 10% of the genetic variance in VIQ and 20% of the genetic variance in PIQ. Based on fMRI studies, there is preliminary research to suggest that the patterns of brain activation during IT performance are surprisingly associated with complex cognitive tasks (Deary et al., 2001; Luciano et al., 2001, 2005; Luciano, Leisser, et al., 2004) with the areas of activation appearing to be the cingulate gyrus of the limbic lobe and the inferior, medial, and superior frontal gyri of the frontal lobes. And because IT is less cognitively complex than IQ, it may prove simpler to model biologically and as a result present an easier model for the selection of other candidate genes influencing cognitive ability (Luciano et al., 2005).

Finally, education and cultural factors have been shown to influence processing speed tasks less than other psychometric tasks, specifically those measuring verbal or nonverbal reasoning abilities (Rushton & Jensen, 2005). Future research should continue to include alternative and novel types of processing speed tasks, (e.g., McPherson & Burns, 2005, 2007, 2008) to better ascertain the influence of training and academic skills on performance.

It is also critical that the contribution of elemental tasks such as inspection time are included in batteries benchmarking machine learning and artificial intelligence. This discussion has already begun (e.g., Bringsjord & Schimanski, 2003; Detterman, 2011; Hernandez-Orall et al., 2016).

IQ test datasets have begun to emerge in the professional literature (e.g., Liu et al. 2019; Lynn & Vanhanen, 2009; Pietschnig & Voracek, 2015; Wang et al., 2016); however, most contain a small sample of questions or questions that are overly specific (e.g., analogies, number sequence, anonyms). Mirroring the danger of findings from studies examining IQ test factor structure subsequently leading to the creation or modification of a theory of intelligence, it would be equally incorrect for studies from artificial intelligence to dictate a definition of actual human intelligence.

References

Anderson, M. (1992). *Intelligence and development: A cognitive theory (Cognitive development).* Wiley-Blackwell.

Anderson, M., & Miller, K. L. (1998). Modularity, mental retardation and speed of processing. *Developmental Science, 1*(2), 239–245. https://doi.org/10.1111/1467-7687.00037

Barbeau, E. B., Soulières, I., Dawson, M., Zeffiro, T. A., & Mottron, L. (2013). The level and nature of autistic intelligence III: Inspection time. *Journal of Abnormal Psychology, 122*(1), 295–301. https://doi.org/10.1037/a0029984

Bates, T. C., & Eysenck, H. J. (1993). Intelligence, inspection time, and decision time. *Intelligence, 17*(4), 523–531. https://doi.org/10.1016/0160-2896(93)90016-x

Baumeister, A. A., & Kellas, G. A. (1967). Refractoriness in the reaction times of normals and retardates as a function of response-stimulus interval. *Journal of Experimental Psychology, 75*(1), 122–125. https://doi.org/10.1037/h0024939

Beaujean, A. A., & Benson, N. F. (2018). Theoretically-consistent cognitive ability test development and score interpretation. *Contemporary School Psychology, 23*(2), 126–137. https://doi.org/10.1007/s40688-018-0182-1

Benson, N., Hulac, D. M., & Kranzler, J. H. (2010). Independent examination of the Wechsler Adult Intelligence Scale–Fourth Edition (WAIS–IV): What does the WAIS–IV measure? *Psychological Assessment, 22*(1), 121–130. https://doi.org/10.1037/a0017767

Binet, A., & Simon, T. (1904). Méthodes nouvelles pour le diagnostic du niveau intellectuel des anormaux. *L'année Psychologique, 11*(1), 191–244. https://doi.org/10.3406/psy.1904.3675

Bodin, D., Pardini, D. A., Burns, T. G., & Stevens, A. B. (2009). Higher order factor structure of the WISC–IV in a clinical neuropsychological sample. *Child Neuropsychology, 15*(5), 417–424. https://doi.org/10.1080/09297040802603661

Bonney, K. R., Almeida, O. P., Flicker, L., Davies, S., Clarnette, R., Anderson, M., & Lautenschlager, N. T., (2006). Inspection time in non-demented older adults with mild cognitive impairment. *Neuropsychologia, 44*(8), 1452–1456. https://doi.org/10.1016/j.neuropsychologia.2005.12.002

Boring, E. G. (1923, June), Intelligence as the tests test it. *New Republic,* 35–37.

Bors, D., Stokes, T. L., Forrin, B., & Hodder, S. L. (1999). Inspection time and intelligence: Practice, strategies, and attention. *Intelligence, 27*(2), 111–129. https://doi.org/10.1016/s0160-2896(99)00010-0

Braden, J. P., & Athanasiou, M. S. (2005). A comparative review of nonverbal measures of intelligence. In D. P. Flanagan & P. L. Harrison (Eds.), *Contemporary intellectual assessment: Theories, tests, and issues* (pp. 557–577). Guilford Press.

Brand, C. (1981). General intelligence and mental speed: Their relationship and development. In M. P. Friedman, J. P. Das, & N. O'Connor (Eds.), *Intelligence and learning* (pp. 589–593). Springer. https://doi.org/10.1007/978-1-4684-1083-9_56

Brand, C. R., & Deary, I. J. (1982). Intelligence and "inspection time." In H. J. Eysenck (Ed.), *A model for intelligence* (pp. 133–148). Springer. https://doi.org/10.1007/978-3-642-68664-1_5

Bringsjord, S. & Schimanski, B. (2003). What is artificial intelligence? Psychometric AI as an answer. In *Proceedings of the 18th International Joint Conference on Artificial Intelligence,* IJCAI'03, 887–893.

Brody, N. (2002). *g* and the one-many problem: Is one enough? In *The nature of intelligence* (Novartis Foundation Symposium 233) (pp. 122–135). Wiley.

Brown, R. T., Reynolds, C. R., & Whitaker, J. S. (1999). Bias in mental testing since Bias in Mental Testing. *School Psychology Quarterly*, *14*(3), 208–238. https://doi.org/10.1037/h0089007

Burns, N. R., & Nettelbeck, T. (2003). Inspection time in the structure of cognitive abilities. *Intelligence*, *31*(3), 237–255. https://doi.org/10.1016/s0160–2896(02)00120-4

Burns, N. R., & Nettelbeck, T. (2005). Inspection time and speed of processing: Sex differences on perceptual speed but not IT. *Personality and Individual Differences*, *39*(2), 439–446. https://doi.org/10.1016/j.paid.2005.01.022

Burns, N. R., Nettelbeck, T., & Cooper, C. J. (1999). Inspection time correlates with general speed of processing but not with fluid ability. *Intelligence*, *27*(1), 37–44. https://doi.org/10.1016/s0160-2896(99)00013-6

Canivez, G. L. (2008). Orthogonal higher order factor structure of the Stanford-Binet Intelligence Scales–Fifth Edition for children and adolescents. *School Psychology Quarterly*, *23*(4), 533–541. https://doi.org/10.1037/a0012884

Canivez, G. L. (2013). Incremental criterion validity of WAIS–IV factor index scores: Relationships with WIAT–II and WIAT–III subtest and composite scores. *Psychological Assessment*, *25*(2), 484–495. https://doi.org/10.1037/a0032092

Canivez, G. L., Konold, T. R., Collins, J. M., & Wilson, G. (2009). Construct validity of the Wechsler Abbreviated Scale of Intelligence and Wide Range Intelligence Test: Convergent and structural validity. *School Psychology Quarterly*, *24*(4), 252–265. https://doi.org/10.1037/a0018030

Canivez, G. L., & Kush, J. C. (2013). WAIS–IV and WISC–IV structural validity: Alternate methods, alternate results. Commentary on Weiss et al. (2013a) and Weiss et al. (2013b). *Journal of Psychoeducational Assessment*, *31*(2), 157–169. https://doi.org/10.1177/0734282913478036

Canivez, G. L., & Watkins, M. W. (2010). Investigation of the factor structure of the Wechsler Adult Intelligence Scale—Fourth Edition (WAIS–IV): Exploratory and higher order factor analyses. *Psychological Assessment*, *22*(4), 827–836. https://doi.org/10.1037/a0020429

Canivez, G. L., Watkins, M. W., & Dombrowski, S. C. (2017). Structural validity of the Wechsler Intelligence Scale for Children–Fifth Edition: Confirmatory factor analyses with the 16 primary and secondary subtests. *Psychological Assessment*, *29*(4), 458–472. https://doi.org/10.1037/pas0000358

Canivez, G. L., & Youngstrom, E. A. (2019). Challenges to the Cattell-Horn-Carroll theory: Empirical, clinical, and policy implications. *Applied Measurement in Education*, *32*(3), 232–248. https://doi.org/10.1080/08957347.2019.1619562

Carlson, J. S., & Jensen, C. (1982). Reaction time, movement time, and intelligence: A replication and extension. *Intelligence*, *6*(3), 265–274. https://doi.org/10.1016/0160-2896(82)90003-4

Carpenter, A. D. (2008). Embodying intelligence: Animals and us in Plato's *Timaeus*. In M. Zovko & J. Dillon (Eds.), *Platonism and forms of intelligence* (pp. 39–58). Academie Verlag.

Carpenter, P. A., Just, M. A., & Shell, P. (1990). What one intelligence test measures: A theoretical account of the processing in the Raven Progressive Matrices Test. *Psychological Review*, *97*(3), 404–431. https://doi.org/10.1037/0033-295x.97.3.404

Carroll, J. B. (1993). *Human cognitive abilities: A survey of factor-analytic studies*. Cambridge University Press.

Carroll, J. B. (1997). Theoretical and technical issues in identifying a factor of general intelligence. In B. Devlin, S. E. Fienberg, D. P. Resnick, & K. Roeder (Eds.), *Intelligence, genes, and success: Scientists respond to the bell curve* (pp. 125–156). Springer-Verlag.

Cattell, R. B. (1963). Theory of fluid and crystallized intelligence: A critical experiment. *Journal of Educational Psychology*, *54*(1), 1–22. https://doi.org/10.1037/h0046743

Ceci, S. J. (1991). How much does schooling influence general intelligence and its cognitive components? A reassessment of the evidence. *Developmental Psychology*, *27*(5), 703–722. https://doi.org/10.1037/0012-1649.27.5.703

Chaiken, S. R., & Young, R. K. (1993). Inspection time and intelligence: Attempts to eliminate the apparent movement strategy. *The American Journal of Psychology*, *106*(2), 191. https://doi.org/10.2307/1423167

Chamorro-Premuzic, T., Moutafi, J., & Furnham, A. (2005). The relationship between personality traits, subjectively-assessed and fluid intelligence. *Personality and Individual Differences*, *38*(7), 1517–1528. https://doi.org/10.1016/j.paid.2004.09.018

Chase, H., Michael, A., Bullmore, E., Sahakian, B., & Robbins, T. (2009). Paradoxical enhancement of choice reaction time performance in patients with major depression. *Journal of Psychopharmacology*, *24*(4), 471–479. https://doi.org/10.1177/0269881109104883

Cohn, S. J., Carlson, J. S., & Jensen, A. R. (1985). Speed of information processing in academically gifted youths. *Personality and Individual Differences*, *6*(5), 621–629. https://doi.org/10.1016/0191-8869(85)90012-1

Conway, A. R., Cowan, N., Bunting, M. F., Therriault, D. J., & Minkoff, S. R. (2002). A latent variable analysis of working memory capacity, short-term memory capacity, processing speed, and general fluid intelligence. *Intelligence*, *30*(2), 163–183. https://doi.org/10.1016/s0160-2896(01)00096-4

Crawford, J., Deary, I. J., Allan, K. M., & Gustafsson, J. E. (1998). Evaluating competing models of the relationship between inspection time and psychometric intelligence. *Intelligence*, *26*(1), 27–42. https://doi.org/10.1016/s01602896(99)80050-6

Cronbach, L. J. (1957). The two disciplines of scientific psychology. *American Psychologist*, *12*(11), 671–684. https://doi.org/10.1037/h0043943

Deary, I. J. (1993). Inspection time and WAIS-R IQ subtypes: A confirmatory factor analysis study. *Intelligence*, *17*(2), 223–236. https://doi.org/10.1016/0160-2896(93)90029-5

Deary, I. J. (2000). *Looking Down on Human Intelligence: From psychometrics to the brain* (1st ed.). Oxford University Press.

Deary, I. J. (2001). Human intelligence differences: Towards a combined experimental–differential approach. *Trends in Cognitive Sciences*, *5*(4), 164–170. https://doi.org/10.1016/s1364-6613(00)01623-5

Deary, I. J., Hunter, R., Langan, S. J., & Goodwin, G. M. (1991). Inspection time, psychometric intelligence, and clinical estimates of cognitive ability in pre-senile Alzheimer's disease and Korsakoff's patients. *Brain*, *114*(6), 2543–2554. https://doi.org/10.1093/brain/114.6.2543

Deary, I. J., Simonotto, E., Marshall, A., Marshall, I., Goddard, N., & Wardlaw, J. M. (2001). The functional anatomy of inspection time: A pilot fMRI study. *Intelligence*, *29*(6), 497–510. https://doi.org/10.1016/S0160-2896(01)00076-9

Deary, I. J., Simonotto, E., Meyer, M., Marshall, A., Marshall, I., Goddard, N., & Wardlaw, J. M. (2004). The functional anatomy of inspection time: an event-related fMRI study. *NeuroImage*, *22*(4), 1466–1479. https://doi.org/10.1016/j.neuroimage.2004.03.047

Deary, I. J., & Stough, C. (1996). Intelligence and inspection time: Achievements, prospects, and problems. *American Psychologist*, *51*(6), 599–608. https://doi.org/10.1037/0003-066x.51.6.599

Deary, I. J., Strand, S., Smith, P., & Fernandes, C. (2007). Intelligence and educational achievement. *Intelligence*, *35*(1), 13–21. https://doi.org/10.1016/j.intell.2006.02.001

Detterman, D. K. (2011). A challenge to Watson. *Intelligence*, *39*(2–3), 77–78. https://doi.org/10.1016/j.intell.2011.02.006

DiStefano, C., & Dombrowski, S. C. (2006). Investigating the theoretical structure of the Stanford-Binet–Fifth Edition. *Journal of Psychoeducational Assessment*, *24*(2), 123–136. https://doi.org/10.1177/0734282905285244

Dombrowski, S. C., Canivez, G. L., Watkins, M. W., & Beaujean, A. (2015). Exploratory bifactor analysis of the Wechsler Intelligence Scale for Children—Fifth Edition with the 16 primary and secondary subtests. *Intelligence*, *53*, 194–201. https://doi.org/10.1016/j.intell.2015.10.009

Dombrowski, S. C., McGill, R. J., & Morgan, G. B. (2019). Monte Carlo modeling of contemporary intelligence test (IQ) factor structure: Implications for IQ assessment, interpretation, and theory. *Assessment*, *28*(3), 977–993. https://doi.org/10.1177/1073191119869828

Dombrowski, S. C., & Watkins, M. W. (2013). Exploratory and higher order factor analysis of the WJ-III full test battery: A school-aged analysis. *Psychological Assessment*, *25*(2), 442–455. https://doi.org/10.1037/a0031335

Duan, X., Dan, Z., & Shi, J. (2013). The speed of information processing of 9- to 13-year-old intellectually gifted children. *Psychological Reports*, *112*(1), 20–32. https://doi.org/10.2466/04.10.49.pr0.112.1.20-32

Edmonds, C. J., Isaacs, E. B., Visscher, P. M. Rogers, M., Lanigan, J., Singhal, A., Lucas, A., Gringras, P., Denton, J., & Deary, I. J. (2008). Inspection time and cognitive abilities in twins aged 7 to 17 years: Age-related changes, heritability and genetic covariance. *Intelligence*, *36*(3), 210–225. https://doi.org/10.1016/j.intell.2007.05.004

Egan, V. (1986). Intelligence and inspection time: Do high-IQ subjects use cognitive strategies? *Personality and Individual Differences*, 7(5), 695–700. https://doi.org/10.1016/0191-8869(86)90039-5

Egan, V. (1994). Intelligence, inspection time and cognitive strategies. *British Journal of Psychology*, 85(3), 305–315. https://doi.org/10.1111/j.2044-8295.1994.tb02526.x

Elliott, C. D. (2007). *Differential Ability Scales-Second Edition: Introductory and technical handbook.* Psychological Corporation.

Fagan, J. F. I. (2000). A theory of intelligence as processing: Implications for society. *Psychology, Public Policy, and Law*, 6(1), 168–179. https://doi.org/10.1037/1076-8971.6.1.168

Fox, M. C., Roring, R. W., & Mitchum, A. L. (2009). Reversing the speed–IQ correlation: Intra-individual variability and attentional control in the inspection time paradigm. *Intelligence*, 37(1), 76–80. https://doi.org/10.1016/j.intell.2008.08.002

Frazier, T. W., & Youngstrom, E. A. (2007). Historical increase in the number of factors measured by commercial tests of cognitive ability: Are we overfactoring? *Intelligence*, 35(2), 169–182. https://doi.org/10.1016/j.intell.2006.07.002

Freberg, M. E., Vandiver, B. J., Watkins, M. W., & Canivez, G. L. (2008). Significant factor score variability and the validity of the WISC–III full scale IQ in predicting later academic achievement. *Applied Neuropsychology*, 15(2), 131–139. https://doi.org/10.1080/09084280802084010

Frings, C., & Neubauer, A. (2005). Are masked-stimuli-discrimination-tests in masked priming studies measures of intelligence?—An alternative task for measuring inspection time. *Personality and Individual Differences*, 39(7), 1181–1191. https://doi.org/10.1016/j.paid.2005.02.024

Gardner, H. (1983). *Frames of mind: The theory of multiple intelligences.* Basic Books.

Glutting, J. J., Adams, W., & Sheslow, D. (2000). *Wide Range Intelligence Test: Manual.* Wide Range

Glutting, J. J., Watkins, M. W., Konold, T. R., & McDermott, P. A. (2006). Distinctions without a difference. *The Journal of Special Education*, 40(2), 103–114. https://doi.org/10.1177/00224669060400020101

Glutting, J. J., Watkins, M. W., & Youngstrom, E. A. (2003). Multifactored and cross-battery assessments: Are they worth the effort? In C. R. Reynolds & R. W. Kamphaus (Eds.), *Handbook of psychological and educational assessment of children: Intelligence aptitude, and achievement* (2nd ed., pp. 343–374). New York, NY: Guilford.

Gottfredson, L. S. (1997a). Mainstream science on intelligence: An editorial with 52 signatories, history, and bibliography. *Intelligence*, 24(1), 13–23. https://doi.org/10.1016/s0160-2896(97)90011-8

Gottfredson, L. S. (1997b). Why g matters: The complexity of everyday life. *Intelligence*, 24(1), 79–132. https://doi.org/10.1016/s0160-2896(97)90014-3

Gottfredson, L. S. (2000). Pretending that intelligence doesn't matter. *Cerebrum*, 2, 75–96.

Gottfredson, L. S. (2008). Of what value is intelligence? In A. Prifitera, D. Saklofske, & L. G. Weiss (Eds.), *WISC–IV clinical assessment and intervention* (2nd ed., pp. 545-564). Elsevier.

Gould, S. J. (1996). *The mismeasure of man* (Rev. ed.). W. W. Norton & Company.

Gregory, R. J. (2022). *Psychological testing: History, principles, and applications: International Edition* (6th edition). Robert J. Gregory.

Grudnik, J. L., & Kranzler, J. H. (2001). Meta-analysis of the relationship between intelligence and inspection time. *Intelligence*, 29(6), 523–535. https://doi.org/10.1016/s0160-2896(01)00078-2

Haier, R. J. (2003). Brain imaging studies of intelligence: Individual differences and neurobiology. In R. J. Sternberg, J. Lautrey, & T. I. Lubart (Eds.), *Models of intelligence: International perspectives*. American Psychological Association.

Higgins, D. M., Peterson, J. B., Pihl, R. O., & Lee, A. G. M. (2007). Prefrontal cognitive ability, intelligence, Big five personality, and the prediction of advanced academic and workplace performance. *Journal of Personality and Social Psychology*, 93(2), 298–319. https://doi.org/10.1037/0022-3514.93.2.298

Hill, D., Saville, C. W., Kiely, S., Roberts, M. V., Boehm, S. G., Haenschel, C., & Klein, C. (2011). Early electro-cortical correlates of inspection time task performance. *Intelligence*, 39(5), 370–377. https://doi.org/10.1016/j.intell.2011.06.005

Horn, J. (1988). Thinking about human abilities. In J. R. Nesselroade, & R. B. Cattell (Eds.), *Handbook of multivariate experimental psychology* (2nd ed., pp. 645–685). Plenum.

Horn, J. & Noll, J. (1994). A system for understanding cognitive capabilities: A theory and the evidence on which it is based. In D. K. Detterman (Ed.), *Current topics in human intelligence, Vol. 4: Theories of intelligence* (pp. 93-132). Springer-Verlag.

Horn, J. L., & Noll, J. (1997). Human cognitive abilities: Gf-Gc theory. In D. P. Flanagan, J. L. Genshaft, & P. L. Harrison (Eds.). *Contemporary intellectual assessment* (pp. 53-91). Guilford Press.

In-Albon, T., Dubi, K., Rapee, R. M., & Schneider, S. (2009). Forced choice reaction time paradigm in children with separation anxiety disorder, social phobia, and nonanxious controls. *Behaviour Research and Therapy*, 47(12), 1058–1065. https://doi.org/10.1016/j.brat.2009.08.003

Jensen, A. R. (1978). The nature of intelligence and its relation to learning. *Melbourne Studies in Education*, 20(1), 107–133. https://doi.org/10.1080/17508487809556119

Jensen, A. R. (1998). *The g Factor: The science of mental ability (Human evolution, behavior, and intelligence)*. Praeger.

Jensen, A. R. (2004). Mental chronometry and the unification of differential psychology. In R. J. Sternberg, & J. E. Pretz (Eds.), *Cognition and intelligence. Identifying the mechanisms of the mind* (pp. 26–50). Cambridge University Press.

Jensen, A. R. (2006). *Clocking the mind: Mental chronometry and individual differences*. Elsevier Science.

Johnson, A. M., Almeida, Q. J., Stough, C., Thompson, J. C., Singarayer, R., & Jog, M. S. (2004). Visual inspection time in Parkinson's disease: Deficits in early stages of cognitive processing. *Neuropsychologia*, 42(5), 577–583. https://doi.org/10.1016/j.neuropsychologia.2003.10.011

Kamphaus, R. W., Petoskey, M. D., & Rowe, E. W. (2000). Current trends in psychological testing of children. *Professional Psychology: Research and Practice*, 31(2), 155–164. https://doi.org/10.1037/0735-7028.31.2.155

Kaufman, A. S. (2000). Tests of intelligence. In R. J. Sternberg (Ed.), *Handbook of intelligence* (pp. 445–476). Cambridge University Press.

Kaufman, A. S. (2009). *IQ testing 101*. Springer Publishing.

Kaufman, A. S., & Kaufman, N. L. (2004). *Kaufman Assessment Battery for Children-Second Edition*. AGS Publishing.

Keith, T. Z. (2005). Using confirmatory factor analysis to aid in understanding the constructs measured by intelligence tests. In D. P. Flanagan & P. L. Harrison (Eds.), *Contemporary intellectual assessment: Theories, tests, and issues* (2nd ed., pp. 581–614). Guilford Press.

Kranzler, J. H., Flores, C. G., & Coady, M. (2010). Examination of the cross-battery approach for the cognitive assessment of children and youth from diverse linguistic and cultural backgrounds. *School Psychology Review*, 39(3), 431–446. https://doi.org/10.1080/02796015.2010.12087764

Kranzler, J. H., & Jensen, A. R. (1989). Inspection time and intelligence: A meta-analysis. *Intelligence*, 13(4), 329–347. https://doi.org/10.1016/s0160-2896(89)80006-6

Kranzler, J. H., & Jensen, A. R. (1991). The nature of psychometric g : Unitary process or a number of independent processes? *Intelligence, 15*, 397–422.

Kranzler, J. H., Whang, P. A., & Jensen, A. R. (1994). Task complexity and the speed and efficiency of elemental information processing: Another look at the nature of intellectual giftedness. *Contemporary Educational Psychology*, 19(4), 447–459. https://doi.org/10.1006/ceps.1994.1032

Kush, J. C. (1996). Factor structure of the WISC–III for students with learning disabilities. *Journal of Psychoeducational Assessment, 14*(1), 32–40. https://doi.org/10.1177/073428299601400103

Kush, J. C. (2005). Review of the Stanford-Binet Intelligence Scales–Fifth Edition. In R. S. Spies & B. S. Plake (Eds.), *The sixteenth mental measurements yearbook* (pp. 979–984). Buros Institute of Mental Measurements.

Kush, J. C. (2013). The utilization of inspection time as a supplement to standardized tests of intelligence. In J. Kush (Ed.), *Intelligence quotient: Testing, role of genetics and the environment and social outcomes*. Nova Science Publishers.

Kush, J. C., Spring, M. B., & Barkand, J. (2011). Advances in the assessment of cognitive skills using computer-based measurement. *Behavior Research Methods*, 44(1), 125–134. https://doi.org/10.3758/s13428-011-0136-2

Liu, Y., He, F., Zhang, H., Rao, G., Feng, Z, & Zhou, Y. (2019). How well do machines perform on IQ tests: A comparison study on a large-scale dataset. *Proceedings of the Twenty-Eighth International Joint Conference on Artificial Intelligence (IJCAI-19)*.

Lu, L., Weber, H. S., Spinath, F. M., & Shi, J. (2011). Predicting school achievement from cognitive and non-cognitive variables in a Chinese sample of elementary school children. *Intelligence*, *39*(2–3), 130–140. https://doi.org/10.1016/j.intell.2011.02.002

Luciano, M., Leisser, R., Wright, M. J., & Martin, N. G. (2004). Personality, arousal theory and the relationship to cognitive ability as measured by inspection time and IQ. *Personality and Individual Differences*, *37*(5), 1081–1089. https://doi.org/10.1016/j.paid.2003.11.016

Luciano, M., Posthuma, D., Wright, M. J., de Geus, E. J., Smith, G. A., Geffen, G. M., & Martin, N. G. (2005). Perceptual speed does not cause intelligence, and intelligence does not cause perceptual speed. *Biological Psychology*, *70*(1), 1–8. https://doi.org/10.1016/j.biopsycho.2004.11.011

Luciano, M., Smith, G. A., Wright, M. J., Geffen, G. M., Geffen, L. B., & Martin, N. G. (2001). On the heritability of inspection time and its covariance with IQ: A twin study. *Intelligence*, *29*(6), 443–457. https://doi.org/10.1016/s0160-2896(01)00071-x

Luciano, M., Wright, M. J., Geffen, G. M., Geffen, L. B., Smith, G. A., & Martin, N. G. (2004). A genetic investigation of the covariation among inspection time, choice reaction time, and IQ subtest scores. *Behavior Genetics*, *34*(1), 41–50. https://doi.org/10.1023/b:bege.0000009475.35287.9d

Lynn, R. & Vanhanen, T. (2009). *Intelligence and the wealth and poverty of nations*. Praeger.

Mackintosh, N. J. (1986). The biology of intelligence? *British Journal of Psychology*, *77*, 1–18.

Mackintosh, N. J. (1998). *IQ and human intelligence*. Oxford University Press.

Mackintosh, N. J. (2011). *IQ and human intelligence* (2nd ed.). Oxford University Press.

Mackintosh, N., & Bennett, E. (2002). IT, IQ and perceptual speed. *Personality and Individual Differences*, *32*(4), 685–693. https://doi.org/10.1016/s0191-8869(01)00069-1

McGill, R. J. (2017). Re(Examining) relations between CHC broad and narrow cognitive abilities and reading achievement. *Journal of Educational and Developmental Psychology*, *7*(1), 265. https://doi.org/10.5539/jedp.v7n1p265

McGill, R. J., & Dombrowski, S. C. (2019). Critically reflecting on the origins, evolution, and impact of the Cattell-Horn-Carroll (CHC) model. *Applied Measurement in Education*, *32*(3), 216–231. https://doi.org/10.1080/08957347.2019.1619561

McGill, R. J., Dombrowski, S. C., & Canivez, G. L. (2018). Cognitive profile analysis in school psychology: History, issues, and continued concerns. *Journal of School Psychology*, *71*, 108–121. https://doi.org/10.1016/j.jsp.2018.10.007

McGrew, K. S. (2009). CHC theory and the human cognitive abilities project: Standing on the shoulders of the giants of psychometric intelligence research. *Intelligence*, *37*(1), 1–10. https://doi.org/10.1016/j.intell.2008.08.004

McPherson, J., & Burns, N. R. (2005). A speeded coding task using a computer-based mouse response. *Behavior Research Methods*, *37*(3), 538–544. https://doi.org/10.3758/bf03192725

McPherson, J., & Burns, N. R. (2007). Gs Invaders: Assessing a computer game-like test of processing speed. *Behavior Research Methods*, *39*(4), 876–883. https://doi.org/10.3758/bf03192982

McPherson, J., & Burns, N. R. (2008). Assessing the validity of computer-game-like tests of processing speed and working memory. *Behavior Research Methods*, *40*(4), 969–981. https://doi.org/10.3758/brm.40.4.969

Murdoch, S. (2007). *IQ: A smart history of a failed idea* (1st ed.). Wiley.

Naglieri, J. A., & Bornstein, B. T. (2003). Intelligence and achievement: Just how correlated are they? *Journal of Psychoeducational Assessment*, *21*(3), 244–260. https://doi.org/10.1177/073428290302100302

Naglieri, J. A., & Das, J. P. (1997). *Cognitive Assessment System: Interpretive handbook*. Riverside Publishing.

Naglieri, J. A., & Rojahn, J. (2004). Construct validity of the PASS theory and CAS: Correlations with achievement. *Journal of Educational Psychology*, *96*(1), 174–181. https://doi.org/10.1037/0022-0663.96.1.174

Neisser, U., Boodoo, G., Bouchard, T. J., Jr., Boykin, A. W., Brody, N., Ceci, S. J., Halpern, D. F., Loehlin, J. C., Perloff, R., Sternberg, R. J., & Urbina, S. (1996). Intelligence: Knowns and unknowns. *American Psychologist*, *51*(2), 77–101. https://doi.org/10.1037//0003-066x.51.2.77

Nettelbeck, T. (1982). Inspection time: An index for intelligence? *Quarterly Journal of Experimental Psychology*, *34A*, 299–312. https://doi.org/10.1080/14640748208400843

Nettelbeck, T. (1987). Inspection time and intelligence. In P. A. Vernon (Ed.), *Speed of information processing and intelligence* (pp. 295–346). Ablex.

Nettelbeck, T. (1998). Jensen's chronometric research: Neither simple nor sufficient but a good place to start. *Intelligence, 26*(3), 233–241. https://doi.org/10.1016/s0160-2896(99)80006-3

Nettelbeck, T. (2001). Correlation between inspection time and psychometric abilities. *Intelligence, 29*(6), 459–474. https://doi.org/10.1016/s0160-2896(01)00072-1

Nettelbeck, T. (2003). Inspection time and *g*. In H. Nyborg (Ed.), *The scientific study of general intelligence: Tribute to Arthur R. Jensen* (pp. 77–91). Pergamon.

Nettelbeck, T., & Lally, M. (1976). Inspection time and measured intelligence. *British Journal of Psychology, 67*(1), 17–22. https://doi.org/10.1111/j.2044-8295.1976.tb01493.x

Nettelbeck, T., & Rabbitt, P. M. (1992). Aging, cognitive performance, and mental speed. *Intelligence, 16*(2), 189–205. https://doi.org/10.1016/0160-2896(92)90004-b

Nettelbeck, T., & Wilson, C. (2005). Uncertainty about the biology of intelligence: A role for a marker task. *Cortex, 41*(2), 234–235. https://doi.org/10.1016/s0010-9452(08)70904-3

Neubauer, A. C. (1997). The mental speed approach to the assessment of intelligence. In J. Kingma & W. Tomic (Eds.), *Advances in cognition and education: Reflections on the concept of intelligence*. JAI press.

Niileksela, C. R., Reynolds, M. R., & Kaufman, A. S. (2013). An alternative Cattell–Horn–Carroll (CHC) factor structure of the WAIS–IV: Age invariance of an alternative model for ages 70–90. *Psychological Assessment, 25*(2), 391–404. https://doi.org/10.1037/a0031175

O'Connor, T. A., & Burns, N. R. (2003). Inspection time and general speed of processing. *Personality and Individual Differences, 35*(3), 713–724. https://doi.org/10.1016/s0191-8869(02)00264-7

Parker, D. R., & Benedict, K. B. (2002). Assessment and intervention: Promoting successful transitions for college students with ADHD. *Assessment for Effective Intervention, 27*(3), 3–24. https://doi.org/10.1177/073724770202700302

Partchev, I., & de Boeck, P. (2012). Can fast and slow intelligence be differentiated? *Intelligence, 40*(1), 23–32. https://doi.org/10.1016/j.intell.2011.11.002

Petrill, S. A., Luo, D., Thompson, L. A., & Detterman, D. K. (2001). Inspection time and the relationship among elementary cognitive tasks, general intelligence, and specific cognitive abilities. *Intelligence, 29*(6), 487–496. https://doi.org/10.1016/s0160-2896(01)00074-5

Petrill, S. A., & Thompson, L. A. (1993). The phenotypic and genetic relationships among measures of cognitive ability, temperament, and scholastic achievement. *Behavior Genetics, 23*(6), 511–518. https://doi.org/10.1007/bf01068141

Plato, P., & Jowett, B. (2019). *The Republic*.

Posthuma, D., de Geus, E. J. C., & Boomsma, D. I. (2001). Perceptual speed and IQ are associated through common genetic factors. *Behavior Genetics, 31*(6), 593–602. https://doi.org/10.1023/a:1013349512683

Prabhakaran, V., Narayanan, K., Zhao, Z., & Gabrieli, J. D. E. (2000). Integration of diverse information in working memory within the frontal lobe. *Nature Neuroscience, 3*(1), 85–90. https://doi.org/10.1038/71156

Raven, J., Raven, J. C., & Court, J. H. (1998). *Standard Progressive Matrices Raven Manual: Section 3*. Oxford Psychologists Press.

Ree, M. J., & Carretta, T. R. (2022). Thirty years of research on general and specific abilities: Still not much more than g. *Intelligence, 91*, 101617. https://doi.org/10.1016/j.intell.2021.101617

Reise, S. P., Moore, T. M., & Haviland, M. G. (2010). Bifactor models and rotations: Exploring the extent to which multidimensional data yield univocal scale scores. *Journal of Personality Assessment, 92*(6), 544–559. https://doi.org/10.1080/00223891.2010.496477

Reynolds, C. R., & Kamphaus, R. W. (2003). *Reynolds Intellectual Assessment Scales*. Psychological Assessment Resources.

Roberts, R. D., & Stankov, L. (1999). Individual differences in speed of mental processing and human cognitive abilities: Toward a taxonomic model. *Learning and Individual Differences, 11*(1), 1–120. https://doi.org/10.1016/s1041-6080(00)80007-2

Rohde, T. E., & Thompson, L. A. (2007). Predicting academic achievement with cognitive ability. *Intelligence, 35*(1), 83–92. https://doi.org/10.1016/j.intell.2006.05.004

Roid, G. H. (2003). *Stanford-Binet Intelligence Scales–Fifth Edition: Technical manual*. Riverside Publishing.

Roth, B., Becker, N., Romeyke, S., Schäfer, S., Domnick, F., & Spinath, F. M. (2015). Intelligence and school grades: A meta-analysis. *Intelligence, 53*, 118–137. https://doi.org/10.1016/j.intell.2015.09.002

Rushton, J. P., & Jensen, A. R. (2005). Thirty years of research on race differences in cognitive ability. *Psychology, Public Policy, and Law*, *11*(2), 235–294. https://doi.org/10.1037/1076-8971.11.2.235

Sackett, P. R., Schmitt, N., Ellingson, J. E., & Kabin, M. B. (2001). High-stakes testing in employment, credentialing, and higher education: Prospects in a post-affirmative-action world. *American Psychologist*, *56*(4), 302–318. https://doi.org/10.1037/0003-066x.56.4.302

Sattler, J. M. (2001). *Assessment of children* (4th ed.). Jerome Sattler.

Scheuffgen, K., Happe, F., Anderson, M., & Frith, U. (2000). High "intelligence," low "IQ"? Speed of processing and measured IQ in children with autism. *Development and Psychopathology*, *12*(1), 83–90. https://doi.org/10.1017/s095457940000105x

Schmidt, F. L. (2002). The role of general cognitive ability and job performance: Why there cannot be a debate. *Human Performance*, *15*(1–2), 187–210. https://doi.org/10.1080/08959285.2002.9668091

Schmidt, F. L., & Hunter, J. E. (1981). Employment testing: Old theories and new research findings. *American Psychologist*, *36*(10), 1128–1137. https://doi.org/10.1037/0003-066x.36.10.1128

Schneider, W. J., & McGrew, K. S. (2018). The Cattell-Horn-Carroll theory of cognitive abilities. In D. P. Flanagan & E. M. McDonough (Eds.), *Contemporary intellectual assessment: Theories, tests, and issues* (4th ed., pp. 73–163). Guilford Press.

Sheppard, L. D., & Vernon, P. A. (2008). Intelligence and speed of information-processing: A review of 50 years of research. *Personality and Individual Differences*, *44*(3), 535–551. https://doi.org/10.1016/j.paid.2007.09.015

Spearman, C. (1904). "General Intelligence," Objectively determined and measured. *The American Journal of Psychology*, *15*(2), 201. https://doi.org/10.2307/1412107

Spearman, C. (2010). *The abilities of man: Their nature and measurement*. Kessinger Publishing.

Spearman, C. E. (2022). *The nature of "intelligence" and the principles of cognition* (2nd ed.). Macmillan.

Sternberg, R. J. (1998). Abilities are forms of developing expertise. *Educational Researcher*, *27*(3), 11. https://doi.org/10.2307/1176608

Sternberg, R. J. (1999). Intelligence as developing expertise. *Contemporary Educational Psychology*, *24*(4), 359–375. https://doi.org/10.1006/ceps.1998.0998

Sternberg, R. J. (2003). What is an "expert student?" *Educational Researcher*, *32*(8), 5–9. https://doi.org/10.3102/0013189x032008005

Stough, C., Brebner, J., Nettelbeck, T., Cooper, C. J., Bates, T., & Mangan, G. L. (1996). The relationship between intelligence, personality and inspection time. *British Journal of Psychology*, *87*(2), 255–268. https://doi.org/10.1111/j.2044-8295.1996.tb02589.x

Sullivan, E. V., Brumback, T., Tapert, S. F., Prouty, D., Fama, R., Thompson, W. K., Brown, S. A., Cummins, K., Colrain, I. M., Baker, F. C., Clark, D. B., Chung, T., de Bellis, M. D., Hooper, S. R., Nagel, B. J., Nichols, B. N., Chu, W., Kwon, D., Pohl, K. M., & Pfefferbaum, A. (2017). Effects of prior testing lasting a full year in NCANDA adolescents: Contributions from age, sex, socioeconomic status, ethnicity, site, family history of alcohol or drug abuse, and baseline performance. *Developmental Cognitive Neuroscience*, *24*, 72–83. https://doi.org/10.1016/j.dcn.2017.01.003

Thorndike, R. L. (1986). The role of general ability in prediction. *Journal of Vocational Behavior*, *29*(3), 332–339. https://doi.org/10.1016/0001-91(86)90012-6

Thorndike, R. M. (1997). The early history of intelligence testing. In D. P. Flanagan, J. L. Genshaft, & P. L. Harrison (Eds.), *Contemporary intellectual assessment: Theories, tests, and issues*. Riverside Publishing.

Thurstone, L. L. (1924). *The nature of intelligence*. Routledge.

Thurstone, L. L. (1938). *Primary mental abilities*. University of Chicago Press.

Vernon, P. A., & Mori, M. (1992). Intelligence, reaction times, and peripheral nerve conduction velocity. *Intelligence*, *16*(3–4), 273–288. https://doi.org/10.1016/0160-2896(92)90010-o

Vickers, D. (1970). Evidence for an accumulator model of psychophysical discrimination. *Ergonomics*, *13*(1), 37–58. https://doi.org/10.1080/00140137008931117

Vickers, D., Carterette, E. C., & Friedman, M. P. (2014). *Decision processes in visual perception (Academic Press series in cognition and perception)*. Academic Press.

Vickers, D., Nettelbeck, T., & Willson, R. J. (1972). Perceptual indices of performance: The measurement of "Inspection Time" and "Noise" in the visual system. *Perception*, *1*(3), 263–295. https://doi.org/10.1068/p010263

Vickers, D., & Smith, P. L. (1986). The rationale for the inspection time index. *Personality and Individual Differences*, 7(5), 609–623. https://doi.org/10.1016/0191-8869(86)90030-9

Waiter, G. D., Fox, H. C., Murray, A. D., Starr, J. M., Staff, R. T., Bourne, V. J., Whalley, L. J., & Deary, I. J. (2008). Is retaining the youthful functional anatomy underlying speed of information processing a signature of successful cognitive ageing? An event-related fMRI study of inspection time performance. *NeuroImage*, 41(2), 581–595. https://doi.org/10.1016/j.neuroimage.2008.02.045

Wallace, G. L., Anderson, M., & Happé, F. (2009). Brief report: Information processing speed is intact in autism but not correlated with measured intelligence. *Journal of Autism and Developmental Disorders*, 39(5), 809–814. https://doi.org/10.1007/s10803-008-0684-1

Wang, H., Tian, F., Gao, B., Bian, J., & Liu, T. (2016). Solving verbal questions in IQ test by knowledge-powered word embedding. *EMNLP'16*. 541–550.

Wasserman, J. D. (2019). Deconstructing CHC. *Applied Measurement in Education*, 32(3), 249–268. https://doi.org/10.1080/08957347.2019.1619563

Watkins, M. W. (2006). Orthogonal higher order structure of the Wechsler Intelligence Scale for Children–Fourth edition. *Psychological Assessment*, 18(1), 123–125. https://doi.org/10.1037/1040-3590.18.1.123

Watkins, M. W. (2010). Structure of the Wechsler Intelligence Scale for Children—Fourth Edition among a national sample of referred students. *Psychological Assessment*, 22(4), 782–787. https://doi.org/10.1037/a0020043

Watkins, M. W., & Canivez, G. L. (2022). Assessing the psychometric utility of IQ scores: A tutorial using the Wechsler Intelligence Scale for Children–Fifth Edition. *School Psychology Review*, 51(5), 619–633. https://doi.org/10.1080/2372966X.2020.1816804

Watkins, M. W., Lei, P. W., & Canivez, G. L. (2007). Psychometric intelligence and achievement: A cross-lagged panel analysis. *Intelligence*, 35(1), 59–68. https://doi.org/10.1016/j.intell.2006.04.005

Watkins, M. W., Wilson, S. M., Kotz, K. M., Carbone, M. C., & Babula, T. (2006). Factor structure of the Wechsler Intelligence Scale for Children–Fourth Edition among referred students. *Educational and Psychological Measurement*, 66(6), 975–983. https://doi.org/10.1177/0013164406288168

Wechsler, D. (1975). Intelligence defined and undefined: A relativistic appraisal. *American Psychologist*, 30(2), 135–139. https://doi.org/10.1037/h0076868

Wechsler, D. (2003). *Wechsler Intelligence Scale for Children-Fourth Edition technical and interpretive manual.* Psychological Corporation.

Wechsler, D. (2008). *Wechsler Adult Intelligence Scale-Fourth Edition: Technical and interpretive manual.* Pearson.

Wechsler, D. (2014). *Wechsler Intelligence Scale for Children* (5th ed.). NCS Pearson.

Weiss, L. G., & Prifitera, A. (1995). An evaluation of differential prediction of WIAT achievement scores from WISC–III FSIQ across ethnic and gender groups. *Journal of School Psychology*, 33(4), 297–304. https://doi.org/10.1016/0022-4405(95)00016-f

Wilson, M. S., & Reschly, D. J. (1996). Assessment in school psychology training and practice. *School Psychology Review*, 25(1), 9–23. https://doi.org/10.1080/02796015.1996.12085799

Woodcock, R. W., McGrew, K. S., & Mather, N. (2001). *Woodcock-Johnson III Tests of Cognitive Abilities.* Riverside Publishing.

Chapter 11

How Intelligence Tests Can Be Used to Predict Education and Assessed Through Education

Jonathan Wai and Frank C. Worrell

Intelligence tests have considerable overlap with standardized achievement tests, in part because both types of tests measure general intelligence, or g, to a large degree. Thus standardized achievement tests given to talented youths can be used to prospectively predict educational outcomes such as higher education degree completion even within the top 1% of ability. We illustrate this claim with evidence from two longitudinal databases, the Study of Mathematically Precocious Youth and Project Talent. Standardized achievement tests used for admission to universities can also be used, by proxy, as measures of intelligence. For example, one way to assess the general intelligence (g) level of a highly select occupational group is to retrospectively examine the educational selectivity—and, by proxy, average ability score—of people who are a part of that occupation. For this approach, we review evidence from numerous highly select occupational groups (including billionaires and Fortune 500 CEOs). One can also use the average and 25th to 75th percentile scores of a university to assess the ability level of the majority of students who attend that institution. The jangle fallacy—that is, the idea that two measures labeled differently may in fact measure the same thing—was introduced almost a century ago and was initially used to explain the significant overlap of traits measured by group intelligence tests and school achievement tests. We still see the jangle fallacy throughout many aspects of psychology and education. Though it is true that there is imprecision in exchanging one test for the other because both tests measure g to a large degree, this overlap can be leveraged to bring the concept of general intelligence more broadly into education research and education policy.

There is a large and robust literature linking g with numerous life outcomes (for summaries see Jensen, 1998; Kuncel et al., 2004; Lubinski, 2004; Schmidt & Hunter, 2004; Wai, Brown, et al., 2018; Wai, Worrell, et al., 2018). Another robust literature speaks to the importance of g across a wide variety of subgroups and settings (e.g., Canivez & Watkins, 2001; Watkins, 2006, 2010; Watkins et al., 2002, 2018a, 2018b; Watkins, Glutting, et al., 2007; Watkins, Lei, et al., 2007). This considerable literature has led some scholars to note that g is a Rosetta Stone across multiple areas of the sciences, linking seemingly disparate domains due to its centrality in the network of constructs that have consequence in everyday life (Jensen, 2006;

Wai, 2008). In this chapter, we draw from the centrality of *g* in the nomological network (Cronbach & Meehl, 1955) to illustrate how intelligence can be used to predict education (Tommasi et al., 2015; Watkins, Glutting, et al., 2007; Watkins, Lei, et al., 2007) and can be assessed through education. To make this argument, we first need to review a bit of history.

The Jangle Fallacy: Measurement Overlap Between Standardized Ability and Achievement Tests

The jangle fallacy was first defined nearly a century ago by Kelley (1927, p. 64) as "the use of two separate words or expressions covering in fact the same basic situation, but sounding different, as though they were in truth different" (cf., Coleman & Cureton, 1954, p. 347). Despite this information being known so long ago and numerous scholars pointing out the importance of *g* for education (e.g., Gottfredson, 2004; Jensen, 1981; Murray, 2008), the incorporation of *g* into education broadly but especially U.S. education in particular remains, to this day, a challenge (Maranto & Wai, 2020; Wai, Brown, et al., 2018; Wai, Worrell, et al., 2018).

Recent research has illustrated that numerous tests billed as and commonly thought of as achievement tests in fact largely measure *g*. These include the SAT (Frey & Detterman, 2004; Beaujean et al., 2006); ACT (Koenig et al., 2008); and GRE (Angoff & Johnson, 1990; Hsu & Schombert, 2010; also see Kuncel et al., 2004). This hypothesis goes back to Spearman (1927) in which he pointed out that because *g* enters into performance on any mental test, the specific content of the test is not particularly important. Instead, the *positive manifold* or *g* would very likely be found in any battery of mental tests. More recent research supports the idea that nearly any rigorous cognitive test in fact measures *g* even when techniques or items were intended for different purposes (Chabris, 2007; Johnson et al., 2004; Ree & Earles, 1991). Further, it turns out that from a measurement perspective, cognitive *g* and academic achievement *g* are essentially the same (Kauffman et al., 2012).

This finding does not mean that all tests measure the same set of constructs; it only indicates that all mental tests, including achievement tests, likely measure *g* to some degree. This finding also means that although there is imprecision in exchanging one type of test for another for different purposes, the Rosetta Stone of *g* can fruitfully link the literatures of intelligence to education research and policy (Wai, Brown, et al., 2018; Wai, Worrell, et al., 2018)

Prospective Prediction of General Mental Ability on Outcomes Within the Top 1% of Samples

In this section, we illustrate how intelligence tests can be used to predict educational outcomes prospectively. We focus on the top 1% in cognitive ability in two U.S. samples. The first nonrandom sample of the top 1% in ability comes from the Study of Mathematically Precocious Youth (SMPY; for a description of samples, see Lubinski & Benbow, 2006). The second random sample of the top 1% in ability comes from Project Talent (Wise et al., 1979).

Samples

SMPY Sample

The SMPY cohort in the top 1% of ability reviewed here consists of students who were identified prior to age 13 (Cohort 1) in 1972–1974 and were followed up two decades later at age 33 (N = 1,383). Summary data on the percentage earning bachelor's, master's, or doctoral degrees were drawn from Table 1 of Benbow et al. (2000, p. 475), and summary data on the percentage earning doctorate degrees within the top (Q4) and bottom (Q1) quartiles of the top 1% of ability were drawn from Table 1 of Wai et al. (2005, p. 485).

Project Talent (PT) Sample

The PT sample is a stratified random sample of roughly 400,000 U.S. high school students who were first identified in 1960 in four independent cohorts (Grades 9, 10, 11, and 12) and followed up 11 years after their high school graduation. These four cohorts took a number of cognitive ability tests and surveys that included a variety of variables including several related to life outcomes. For this study we use the math and verbal ability composites also used by Wai et al. (2009). The data are taken from Tables 1 and 2 of Wai (2014a, pp. 75–76).

Results and Discussion

The results in Table 11.1 are based on the nonrandom SMPY sample of the top 1% in ability and the random PT sample of the top 1% in ability and are used to examine what proportions within each highly selective sample earned a higher education degree and at what level. Much of the work published in the SMPY sample looks primarily at the math ability measure alone due to the focus of the study on mathematical, verbal, and spatial abilities; thus the top part of Table 11.1 illustrates the percentage of those earning a higher education degree for SMPY in comparison to each of the four independent cohorts of PT in relation to math reasoning. As can be seen, the percentages of degree earners are replicated in pattern across the two samples of the top 1%, indicating that the findings replicate and are robust.

The bottom part of Table 11.1 illustrates that the findings are also replicated for general ability (math + verbal). In 2012, the base rate in the general U.S. population was 19.8% for earning a bachelor's, 8.1% for a master's degree, and 1.6% for a doctorate. Comparing these top 1% samples with all cohorts combined to the base rate percentages for the general population indicated a relative risk (RR) of 4.57 for bachelor's—meaning the top 1% sample was 4.57 times as likely as the general population to earn a bachelor's degree. For a master's degree, the RR was 6.64, and for doctorates, this value was 15.31. Thus high-ability individuals identified on the basis of tests when they were still in elementary or middle school in the case of SMPY and high school in the case of PT end up earning higher education degrees at rates well above base rate expectations.

Table 11.2 is an assessment of what has come to be known as the *threshold hypothesis*—the idea that beyond a certain point, more ability no longer matters. We examine this hypothesis with a focus on differences within the top 1% in ability across these nonrandom and random samples using the relatively low base rate outcome of doctoral degree attainment. In the top

Table 11.1 Percentage of Individuals in the Top 1% of Ability in SMPY and PT Earning Undergraduate and Graduate Degrees

		SMPY	PT 9th grade	PT 10th grade	PT 11th grade	PT 12th grade
Top 1% in math ability	Bachelor's	1,216 of 1,383 **87.9%**	358 of 420 **85.2%**	339 of 379 **89.5%**	346 of 388 **89.2%**	330 of 349 **94.6%**
	Master's	505 of 1383 **36.5%**	216 of 420 **51.4%**	193 of 379 **50.9%**	203 of 388 **52.3%**	204 of 349 **58.5%**
	Doctorate	332 of 1,383 **24.0%**	97 of 420 **23.1%**	90 of 379 **23.8%**	90 of 388 **23.2%**	97 of 349 **27.8%**
Top 1 % in general ability (math + verbal)	Bachelor's		362 of 421 **86.0%**	342 of 378 **90.5%**	350 of 384 **91.1%**	336 of 353 **95.2%**
	Master's		214 of 421 **50.8%**	198 of 378 **52.4%**	209 of 384 **54.4%**	205 of 353 **58.1%**
	Doctorate	**23%**	90 of 421 **21.4%**	99 of 378 **26.2%**	91 of 384 **23.7%**	97 of 353 **27.5%**

Note. SMPY = Study of Mathematically Precocious Youth; PT = Project Talent. This table was adapted from Table 1 of Wai (2014a). Data on bachelor's and master's degree earners based on general ability were not available for the SMPY sample.

part of Table 11.2, focused on math ability, comparing the top quartile to the bottom quartile shows that a higher math ability predicts a significantly higher rate of earning doctorates and that across all samples these findings were significant. A similar pattern was found for general ability, but these comparisons were only significant for the 9th grade PT cohort. Taken together, these findings complement work by Ferriman-Robertson et al. (2010), who showed that within the SMPY sample, higher math ability predicts multiple and progressively more rarified long-term outcomes such as doctoral degrees, publications, patents, higher income, and even tenure at universities. A more recent study looking at three representative samples in the United States and one in the UK that span the last half century showed that across a wide range of educational, occupational, healthcare, and social outcomes, higher cognitive ability predicted more positive outcomes and was virtually never detrimental (Brown et al., 2020). The findings from all these samples suggest that there is no threshold beyond which more cognitive ability ceases to matter, thus falsifying the threshold hypothesis.

Retrospective Examination of Educational Selectivity of High-Achieving Occupational Groups

In the first part of this chapter, we reviewed how intelligence tests can be used to predict education. Now we pivot to one way in which intelligence can be assessed through education. This retrospective examination of educational selectivity draws from multiple prior data sources

Table 11.2 *Percentage of Individuals in the Top (Q4) and Bottom (Q1) Quarter of the Top 1% of Math and General Ability Earning Doctorates in SMPY and PT*

		SMPY	PT 9th grade	PT 10th grade	PT 11th grade	PT 12th grade
Math ability	Top 1% (Q4)	97 of 329 **29.5%**	30 of 109 **27.5%**	34 of 97 **35.1%**	35 of 97 **36.1%**	42 of 103 **40.8%**
	Top 1% (Q1)	63 of 361 **17.5%**	17 of 117 **14.5%**	12 of 85 **14.1%**	18 of 98 **18.4%**	13 of 87 **14.9%**
	95% CI around proportion differences	(0.06, 0.18) RR = **1.69**	(0.03, 0.24) RR = **1.89**	(0.09, 0.33) RR = **2.48**	(0.05, 0.30) RR = **1.96**	(0.14, 0.38) RR = **2.73**
General ability (math + verbal)	Top 1% (Q4)		34 of 102 **33.3%**	35 of 99 **34.5%**	29 of 99 **29.3%**	32 of 94 **34.0%**
	Top 1% (Q1)		14 of 99 **14.1%**	21 of 79 **26.6%**	20 of 99 **20.2%**	24 of 87 **27.6%**
	95% CI around proportion differences		(0.08, 0.31) RR = **2.36**	(−0.05, 0.22) RR = 1.33	(−0.03, 0.21) RR = 1.45	(−0.07, 0.20) RR = 1.23

Note. SMPY = Study of Mathematically Precocious Youth; PT = Project Talent; Q4 = the top quarter of the top 1% in ability; Q1 = the bottom quarter of the top 1% in ability; RR = relative risk of earning a doctorate of Q4 compared to Q1 within the top 1%. This table was adapted from Table 2 of Wai (2014a). Summary general ability data for the SMPY sample were not available. The percentages in bold indicate those who earned a doctorate degree (e.g., JD, MD, PhD) of ability. The RR value is also in bold when the 95% CI did not include zero.

including Wai et al. (2019, Table 2, p. 85). Table 2 in Wai et al. (2019) was compiled from data specific to that study and several published papers, including Wai (2013, Table 2, p. 206); Wai (2014b, Appendix A, p. 68); Wai and Perina (2018, Table 2, p. 6); and Wai and Lincoln (2016, Appendix A, p. 17, and Appendix H, p. 24).

The U.S. schools included in this study consisted of schools that reported average standardized test scores to *U.S. News & World Report* ("America's Best Colleges, 2013"). An elite school was considered one with average standardized test scores for graduate and undergraduate attendees in the top 1% in general ability (math + verbal scores). For a more in-depth account of the method used in this study to classify a school as elite, see the Method section in Wai et al. (2019, p. 81 and Appendix 1, p. 91). The full distribution of average test scores across all colleges and universities is reported in Wai, Brown, et al. (2018). As noted earlier, several studies (e.g., Frey & Detterman, 2004; Koenig et al., 2008) indicate that the SAT and ACT measure *g* to a large degree. This means that the mean test score of students attending a college or university can be used as a rough and indirect proxy of the ability level of students at that institution and by inference as an approximate indication of the ability level of someone who has been admitted there. For undergraduate institutions, this method results in a list of 29 schools in the United States: 21 national universities and 8 liberal arts colleges. Additionally, the method can be used to identify numerous other schools for which LSAT, GMAT, or GRE scores are at a similar benchmark.

Although this is only one method that can be used to identify an elite school and other metrics would be reasonable, this method is the strongest indicator relative to other school classifications of the g level required for admission to the school. Obviously this direct measure of educational selectivity is only by proxy a measure of g. Nonetheless, it is a reasonable approach to estimate aggregate ability level for groups as measurement noise in either direction may plausibly cancel out. For example, some students with high test scores may attend the honors college (which typically requires high test scores) of their home public institution for financial, scholarship, or other reasons (e.g., geographic) and thus will have been missed by this approach. On the flip side, other students may have attended an elite school but may have fallen into a group with typically lower average test scores relative to the average of the institution such as athletes, legacy admits, those with political connections, or affirmative action admissions (Espenshade & Radford, 2009; Golden, 2006; Sander, 2004). This method ultimately cannot tease apart the influence of numerous aspects such as school, family background, and wealth from g. Overall, these various limitations decrease the reliability of the method for approximating the ability of the individual through university attendance. Nonetheless, the method is a reasonable approach for assessing intelligence through educational selectivity relative to methods currently available.

Table 11.3 illustrates for 30 groups the percentage who attended various colleges and universities as a function of educational selectivity ranked from low to high as a function of the proportion who attended a U.S. school categorized as elite in some capacity. The Graduate School category indicates an individual who attended graduate school but not one of the schools categorized as elite. The College category indicates an individual attended college but not graduate school or an elite school. The NR/NC category represents students as Not Reported or No College if it was not clear from Internet searches if the individual attended a tertiary institution. Thus, these four categories are independent of one another and sum to 100%. Finally, the Harvard category indicates that an individual attended Harvard University in some capacity. Harvard was included as a separate category due to the influence of this particular school. Overall, the findings show that elite school attendance—and by proxy cognitive ability or g—varies quite widely across these various groups. The proportion attending elite schools and who are thus roughly in the top 1% in cognitive ability ranges from about 19% for Time100 artists and entertainers to 90% for Davos academics (see Wai et al., 2024, for the most up-to-date analysis using additional groups).

If the people in the top 1% in g are expected to be represented at about 1% in the base rate, this means that people who made it to one of these high-achieving groups are overrepresented by a factor of 19 to 90 times. Put another way, this is a relative risk (RR) ranging from 19 to 90, which is an enormous effect size. When combined with the average g level of various occupations (e.g., Gottfredson, 2003, Fig 15.1, p. 299) among the general population, ranging from packer (21st percentile) up through research analyst and attorney (91st percentile), Table 11.3 extends the g level distribution to the far right tail of occupations, illustrating that variation in how g-loaded an occupation is varies even in the extreme right tail of the achievement distribution.

Conclusion

In the first section of this chapter, we reviewed how intelligence tests can be used to predict education in two different samples of the top 1% in ability. These findings add to the vast literature showing that educational outcomes are largely predicted by student traits, especially cognitive

Table 11.3 Education and Inferred Cognitive Ability Among Groups of U.S. Expert High Achievers

	U.S. Elite School	Graduate School	College	NR/NC	Harvard
Time100 Artists/Entertainers	0.190	0.048	0.667	0.095	0.000
Time100 Leaders/Revolutionaries	0.200	0.500	0.150	0.150	0.100
U.S. House Members	0.206	0.475	0.308	0.009	0.066
Wealth-X[a] President	0.277	0.170	0.313	0.238	0.070
Time100 Heroes/Icons	0.300	0.200	0.300	0.200	0.050
Wealth-X[a] CEOs	0.309	0.196	0.319	0.175	0.076
Time100 Overall	0.317	0.221	0.365	0.096	0.087
Wealth-X[a] 30 million +	0.338	0.183	0.278	0.200	0.090
Wealth-X[a] Founders	0.338	0.183	0.274	0.203	0.082
Wealth-X Chairman	0.348	0.192	0.309	0.150	0.095
Wealth-X[a] self-made 30 million +	0.359	0.200	0.266	0.175	0.099
Time100 Builders/Titans	0.409	0.136	0.455	0.000	0.091
Federal Judges	0.409	0.591	0.000	0.000	0.119
Fortune 500 CEOs	0.410	0.262	0.268	0.058	0.116
U.S. Senators	0.410	0.420	0.160	0.010	0.120
Forbes Self-Made Billionaires	0.426	0.155	0.314	0.105	0.123
Wealth-X[a] Billionaires	0.434	0.129	0.338	0.099	0.122
Wealth-X[a] Self-Made Billionaires	0.437	0.161	0.316	0.086	0.134
New York Times Editors/Writers	0.439	0.129	0.376	0.056	0.044
Forbes Billionaires	0.448	0.122	0.321	0.109	0.113
Time100 Scientists/Thinkers	0.476	0.238	0.238	0.048	0.190
Wall Street Journal Editors/Writers	0.498	0.121	0.344	0.037	0.037
Davos[b] Overall	0.546	0.176	0.181	0.095	0.185
Davos[b] Media	0.556	0.111	0.256	0.078	0.133
Forbes Powerful Women	0.559	0.085	0.288	0.068	0.186
Davos[b] CEOs	0.599	0.194	0.171	0.036	0.153

(Continued)

Table 11.3 (Continued)

	U.S. Elite School	Graduate School	College	NR/NC	Harvard
The New Republic	0.642	0.000	0.316	0.042	0.189
Davos[b] Government & Policy	0.742	0.194	0.032	0.032	0.355
Forbes Powerful Men	0.852	0.037	0.111	0.000	0.407
Davos[b] Academics	0.901	0.088	0.011	0.000	0.275

Note. This table is adapted from Wai et al. (2019, Table 2, p. 85), which drew from several published papers including Wai (2013), Wai (2014b), Wai and Perina (2018), and Wai and Lincoln (2016). Time100 data from 2009 were used since matching categories were available.
[a]Wealth-X is a company that tracks individuals worth at least $30 million. [b]Davos indicates people who attended the World Economic Forum in Davos, Switzerland.

ability or intelligence (e.g., Detterman, 2016; Gottfredson, 2004; Wai, Worrell, et al., 2018). The second section of this chapter reversed the approach, using highly select samples to illustrate how educational selectivity—and by proxy cognitive ability through test scores of institutions—can be used to infer the *g* level of groups.

The literature on the association between intelligence and educational outcomes continues to advance via studies of genetics (e.g., Malanchini et al., 2020) and studies illustrating that education or schooling may indeed be one of the key levers to improving IQ or intelligence (Ceci, 1991; Ritchie & Tucker-Drob, 2018). At the same time, the role of intelligence is largely absent in education research and policy (Maranto & Wai, 2020; Wai, Worrell, et al., 2018). Given the long-standing knowledge about the jangle fallacy and how ability and achievement tests have always measured *g* to a large degree, perhaps the primary challenge going forward to help children is to uncover how these obviously connected research literatures can more fruitfully combine to help us understand how to find solutions to improve educational outcomes for all children and talent development for children with high cognitive ability. General intelligence or *g* remains a Rosetta Stone across numerous fields, and this chapter illustrates how it operates at the intersection of education and intelligence and should be taken into account.

References

Angoff, W. H., & Johnson, E. G. (1990). The differential impact of curriculum on aptitude test scores. *Journal of Educational Measurement, 27*(4), 291–305. https://doi.org/10.1111/j.1745-3984.1990.tb00750.x

Beaujean, A. A., Firmin, M. W., Knoop, J. D., Michonski, J. D., Berry, T. P., & Lowrie, R. E. (2006). Validation of the Frey and Detterman (2004) IQ prediction equations using the Reynolds Intellectual Assessment Scales. *Personality and Individual Differences, 41*(2), 353–357. https://doi.org/10.1016/j.paid.2006.01.014

Benbow, C. P., Lubinski, D., Shea, D. L., & Eftekhari-Sanjani, H. (2000). Sex differences in mathematical reasoning ability at age 13: Their status 20 years later. *Psychological Science, 11*(6), 474–480. https://doi.org/10.1111/1467-9280.00291

Brown, M. I., Wai, J., & Chabris, C. F. (2020). Can you ever be too smart for our own good? Linear and nonlinear effects of cognitive ability. *PsyArXiv Preprints.* https://doi.org/10.31234/osf.io/rpgea

Canivez, G. L., & Watkins, M. W. (2001). Long term stability of the Wechsler Intelligence Scale for Children–Third Edition among students with disabilities. *School Psychology Review*, *30*, 361–376. https://doi.org/10.1080/02796015.2001.12086125

Ceci, S. J. (1991). How much does schooling influence general intelligence and its cognitive components? A reassessment of the evidence. *Developmental Psychology*, *27*(5), 703–722. https://doi.org/10.1037/0012-1649.27.5.703

Chabris, C. F. (2007). Cognitive and neurobiological mechanisms of the law of general intelligence. In M. J. Roberts (Ed.), *Integrating the mind: Domain general versus domain specific processes in higher cognition* (pp. 449–491). Psychology Press. https://doi.org/10.4324/9780203926697

Coleman, W., & Cureton, E. E. (1954). Intelligence and achievement: the "jangle fallacy" again. *Educational and Psychological Measurement*, *14*(2), 347–351. https://doi.org/10.1177/001316445401400214

Cronbach, L. J., & Meehl, P. E. (1955). Construct validity in psychological tests. *Psychological Bulletin*, *52*(4), 281–302. https://doi.org/10.1037/h0040957

Detterman, D. K. (2016). Education an intelligence: Pity the poor teacher because student characteristics are more significant than teachers or schools. *Spanish Journal of Psychology*, *19*, 1–11. https://doi.org/10.1017/sjp.2016.88

Espenshade, T. J., & Radford, A. W. (2009). *No longer separate, not yet equal: Race and class in elite college admission and college life*. Princeton University Press. https://doi.org/10.1515/9781400831531

Ferriman-Robertson, K., Smeets, S., Lubinski, D., & Benbow, C. P. (2010). Beyond the threshold hypothesis: Even among the gifted and top math/science graduate students, cognitive abilities, vocational interests, and lifestyle preferences matter for career choice, performance, and persistence. *Current Directions in Psychological Science*, *19*(6), 346–351. https://doi.org/10.1177/0963721410391442

Frey, M. C., & Detterman, D. K. (2004). Scholastic assessment or *g*? The relationship between the Scholastic Assessment Test and general cognitive ability. *Psychological Science*, *15*(6), 373–378. https://doi.org/10.1111/j.0956-7976.2004.00687.x

Golden, D. (2006). *The price of admission*. Three Rivers Press.

Gottfredson, L. S. (2003). *g*, jobs, and life. In H. Nyborg (Ed.), *The scientific study of general intelligence: Tribute to Arthur R. Jensen* (pp. 293–342). Pergamon.

Gottfredson, L. S. (2004). Schools and the *g* factor. *Wilson Quarterly*, *28*, 35–45.

Hsu, S. D. H., & Schombert, J. (2010). Data mining the university: College GPA predictions from SAT scores. https://doi.org/10.2139/ssrn.1589792

Jensen, A. R. (1981). *Straight talk about mental tests*. Free Press.

Jensen, A. R. (1998). *The g factor*. Praeger.

Jensen, A. R. (2006). *Clocking the mind: Mental chronometry and individual differences*. Elsevier.

Johnson, W., Bouchard, T. J., Krueger, R. F., McGue, M., & Gottesman, I. I. (2004). Just one *g*: Consistent results from three test batteries *Intelligence*, *32*(1), 95–107. https://doi.org/10.1016/s0160-2896(03)00062-x

Kelley, T. L. (1927). *Interpretation of educational measurements*. World Book Company.

Koenig, K. A., Frey, M. C., & Detterman, D. K. (2008). ACT and general cognitive ability. *Intelligence*, *36*(2), 153–160. https://doi.org/10.1016/j.intell.2007.03.005

Kuncel, N. R., Hezlett, S. A., & Ones, D. S. (2004). Academic performance, career potential, creativity, and job performance: Can one construct predict them all? *Journal of Personality and Social Psychology*, *86*(1), 148–161. https://doi.org/10.1037/0022-3514.86.1.148

Lubinski, D. (2004). Introduction to the special section on cognitive abilities: 100 years after Spearman's (1904) "'General intelligence,' objectively determined and measured." *Journal of Personality and Social Psychology*, *86*(1), 96–111. https://doi.org/10.1037/0022-3514.86.1.96

Lubinski, D., & Benbow, C. P. (2006). Study of mathematically precocious youth after 35 years: Uncovering antecedents for the development of math-science expertise. *Perspectives on Psychological Science*, *1*(4), 316–345. https://doi.org/10.1111/j.1745-6916.2006.00019.x

Malanchini, M., Rimfeld, K., Allegrini, A. G., Ritchie, S. J., & Plomin, R. (2020). Cognitive ability and education: How behavioural genetic research has advanced our knowledge and understanding of their association. *Neuroscience and Biobehavioral Reviews*, *111*, 229–245. https://doi.org/10.1016/j.neubiorev.2020.01.016

Maranto, R., & Wai, J. (2020). Why intelligence is missing from American education policy and practice, and what can be done about it. *Journal of Intelligence*, *8*(1), 1–12. https://doi.org/10.3390/jintelligen ce8010002

Murray, C. (2008). *Real education: Four simple truths for bringing America's schools back to reality*. Crown Forum. https://doi.org/10.1016/j.intell.2008.10.006

Ree, M. J., & Earles, J. A. (1991). The stability of *g* across different methods of estimation. *Intelligence*, *15*(3), 271–278. https://doi.org/10.1016/0160-2896(91)90036-d

Ritchie, S. J., & Tucker-Drob, E. M. (2018). How much does education improve intelligence? A meta-analysis. *Psychological Science*, *29*(8), 1358–1369. https://doi.org/10.1177/0956797618774253

Sander, R. H. (2004). A systematic analysis of affirmative action in American law schools. *Stanford Law Review*, *57*, 367–483.

Schmidt, F. L., & Hunter, J. (2004). General mental ability in the world of work: Occupational attainment and job performance. *Journal of Personality and Social Psychology*, *86*(1), 162–173. https://doi.org/10.1037 /0022-3514.86.1.162

Spearman, C. (1927). *The abilities of man: Their nature and measurement*. Macmillan.

Tommasi, M., Watkins, M. W., Orsini, A., Pezzuti, L., Cianci, L., & Saggino, A. (2015). Gender differences in latent cognitive abilities and education links with *g* in Italian elders. *Learning and Individual Differences*, *37*, 276–282. https://doi.org/j.lindif.2014.10.020

U.S. News & World Report. (2013). America's best colleges. https://www.usnews.com/rankings.

Wai, J. (2008). A review of *Clocking the mind: Mental chronometry and individual differences*. *Gifted Child Quarterly*, *52*(1), 99–104. https://doi.org/10.1177/0016986207310434

Wai, J. (2013). Investigating America's elite: Cognitive ability, education, and sex differences. *Intelligence*, *41*(4), 203–211. https://doi.org/10.1016/j.intell.2013.03.005

Wai, J. (2014a). Experts are born, then made: Combining prospective and retrospective longitudinal data shows that cognitive ability matters. *Intelligence*, *45*, 74–80. https://doi.org/10.1016/j.intell.2013.08.009

Wai, J. (2014b). Investigating the world's rich and powerful: Education, cognitive ability, and sex differences. *Intelligence*, *46*, 54–72. https://doi.org/10.1016/j.intell.2014.05.002

Wai, J., Anderson, S. M., Perina, K., Worrell, F. C., & Chabris, C. F. (2024). The most successful and influential Americans come from a surprisingly narrow range of "elite" educational backgrounds. *Nature Humanities and Social Sciences Communications*, *11*, 1129. https://doi.org/10.1057/s41599-024 -03547-8

Wai, J., Brown, M. I., & Chabris, C. F. (2018). Using standardized test scores to include general cognitive ability in education research and policy. *Journal of Intelligence*, *6*(3), 37. https://doi.org/10.3390/jintelligen ce6030037

Wai, J., & Lincoln, D. (2016). Investigating the right tail of wealth: Education, cognitive ability, giving, network power, gender, ethnicity, leadership, and other characteristics. *Intelligence*, *54*, 1–32. https://doi.org/10 .1016/j.intell.2015.11.002

Wai, J., Lubinski, D., & Benbow, C. P. (2005). Creativity and occupational accomplishments among intellectually precocious youths: An age 13 to age 33 longitudinal study. *Journal of Educational Psychology*, *97*(3), 484–492. https://doi.org/10.1037/0022-0663.97.3.484

Wai, J., Lubinski, D., & Benbow, C. P. (2009). Spatial ability for STEM domains: Aligning over 50 years of cumulative psychological knowledge solidifies its importance. *Journal of Educational Psychology, 101*, 817–835. https://doi.org/10.1037/a0016127

Wai, J., Makel, M. C., & Gambrell, J. (2019). The role of elite education and inferred cognitive ability in eminent creative expertise: An historical analysis of the TIME 100. *Journal of Expertise, 2*(2), 77–91.

Wai, J., & Perina, K. (2018). Expertise in journalism: Factors shaping a cognitive and culturally elite profession. *Journal of Expertise, 1*, 57–78.

Wai, J., Worrell, F. C., & Chabris, C. F. (2018). The consistent influence of general cognitive ability in college, career, and lifetime achievement. In K. McClarty, K. Mattern, & M. Gaertner (Eds.), *Preparing students for college and careers: Theory, measurement, and educational practice*. Routledge. https://doi.org/10.4324 /9781315621975-5

Watkins, M. W. (2006). Orthogonal higher order structure of the Wechsler Intelligence Scale for Children–Fourth Edition among gifted students. *Psychological Assessment*, *18*(1), 123–125. https://doi.org/10 .1037/1040-3590.18.1.123

Watkins, M. W. (2010). Structure of the Wechsler Intelligence Scale for Children–Fourth Edition among a national sample of referred students. *Psychological Assessment*, *22*(4), 782–787. https://doi.org/10.1037/a0020043

Watkins, M. W., Dombrowski, S. C. & Canivez, G. L. (2018a). Construct validity of the WISC–IV[UK] with a large referred Irish sample. *International Journal of School and Educational Psychology*, *1*(2), 102–111. https://doi.org/10.1080/21683603.2013.794439

Watkins, M. W., Dombrowski, S. C. & Canivez, G. L. (2018b). Reliability and factorial validity of the Canadian Wechsler Intelligence Scale for Children–Fifth Edition. *International Journal of School and Educational Psychology*, *6*(4), 252–265. Https://doi.org/10.1080/21683603.2017.1342580

Watkins, M. W., Glutting, J. J., & Lei, P-W. (2007). Validity of the full-scale IQ when there is significant variability among WISC-III and WISC-IV factor scores. *Applied Neuropsychology*, *14*(1), 13–20. https://doi.org/10.1080/09084280701280353

Watkins, M. W., Greenawalt, C. G., & Marcell, C. M. (2002). Factor structure of the Wechsler Intelligence Scale for Children–Third Edition among gifted students. *Educational and Psychological Measurement*, *62*(1), 164–172. https://doi.org/10.1177/0013164402062001011

Watkins, M. W., Lei, P-W., & Canivez, G. L. (2007). Psychometric intelligence and achievement: A cross-lagged panel analysis. *Intelligence*, *35*(1), 59–68. https://doi.org/j.intell.2006.04.005

Wise, L. L., McLaughlin, D. H., & Steel, L. (1979). *The Project TALENT data bank*. American Institutes for Research.

Chapter 12

The Improper Use of IQ in Debates and Discussions About Race and Gender Differences on the Internet and in Mass Media

Marco Tommasi, Lina Pezzuti, and Aristide Saggino

In the years between 2014 and 2019 some episodes happened that had a strong resonance on the Internet and in mass media. All these episodes had as a common denominator the relationship between IQ and race. In particular, a White-Black IQ difference, with Blacks having lower IQ than Whites, was repeatedly proposed. However, the use of IQ difference as a justification of genetic differences between groups of people is untenable. In this chapter we explain why IQ measures and IQ differences cannot be valid arguments to explain differences between races or groups of people with biological differences such as male and female. IQ cannot be considered a direct measure of intelligence. IQs obtained with different intelligence tests are not equivalent because tests have different structure and validity. At the same time, IQ is affected by external factors, which increase or decrease its variability in space and time. In research only observed IQ is considered while the estimated true IQ, which takes into consideration reliability coefficient, that indicates the precision of the measure, should be preferred. Other problems are sample size and representativeness from which data are collected. IQ is used in correlational or quasi-experimental studies, which do not allow a clear definition of cause-effect relationships between variables, favoring different interpretation of the same experimental results. Last but not least, many researchers have prejudicial attitudes or have conflicts of interest that probably bias scientific works on intelligence. As a consequence of the combination of all these problems, IQ cannot be considered directly connected with intelligence. Scientists must limit their work in studying the phenotypic characteristics of people and in detecting the real causes of the variation of these characteristics. If these phenotypic characteristics are used by some researchers to judge the value of persons, this is a question pertinent to their ethics and morality, not to their scientific competence. The task of science is to explain phenomena, not to make moral or political judgments.

The Internet and the Debate Over the Relationship Between IQ and Race

In August 2014 Nicholas Wade published *A Troublesome Inheritance: Genes, Race and Human History* in which he stated that human races are a biological reality and that recent human evolution has led to racial differences in economic and social behavior. Geneticists opposed to Wade's statements said that he misinterpreted their works.[1] However, after the publication of the book, its resonance in mass media pushed many people to search for arguments on the Internet about the relationship between IQ and race. In March 2016 Charles Murray, one of the authors of the controversial book *The Bell Curve*, was invited for a seminar at Middlebury College in Vermont but he could not finish his speech because of a student protest.[2] In April 2017 Sam Harris, an American author and writer, posted on the Internet a podcast[3] in which he interviewed Charles Murray about *The Bell Curve*, a book that raised many reactions for his strong prejudicial attitude toward intelligence. The podcast was listened to by many people and had a strong impact on mass media. In February 2018, a student at McClatchy High School of Sacramento presented a poster[4] in which he stated that a Humanities and International Studies Program (HISP) was attended prevalently by Asians and Caucasians and to a lesser extent by Hispanic and Black people because the latter had a lower IQ.[5] HISP is a program managed by McClatchy High School to prepare high school students to be admitted to university courses. The program, obviously, follows an equal opportunity politic in recruiting students, but this politic is opposed by the idea that people of different races have different levels of intelligence and, therefore, cannot obtain advantages from programs aimed at social equality. Figure 12.1 reports Google trends for "IQ and race" between January 2014 and January 2019. It is possible to see a constant increasing trend in reaction to the previously mentioned events.

All these facts show that the debate about IQ race differences is not dead and still keeps a great interest in people. This interest pushed a journalist of the *Guardian*, Gavin Evans, to publish an

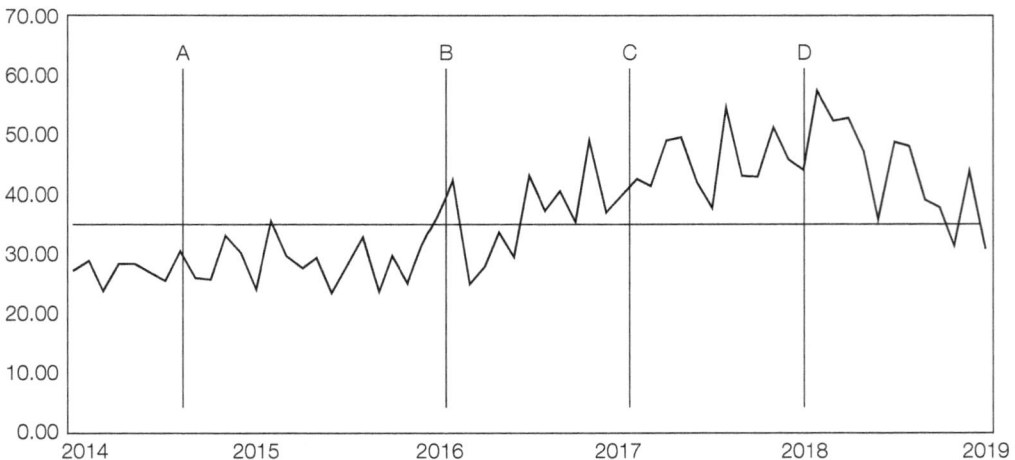

Figure 12.1. **Google Trends for the Terms "IQ" and "Race" Between January 2014 and January 2019.** *Note.* A: publication of Wade's book (August 2014); B: Murray's seminar in Vermont (March 2016); C: Harris's podcast publication (April 2017); D: student's poster in McClatchy High School (February 2018). Horizontal line represents the mean score of Google trends of the entire period.

article titled "The Unwelcome Revival of 'Race Science" in which he clearly stated that "a common theme in the rhetoric of race science is that its opponents are guilty of wishful thinking about the nature of human equality."[6] In other words, according to Evans, racists state that those who think that human beings are equal, or that there is not a real difference in races, are contradicted by science that has evidenced a real difference in IQ between races. If science confirms this racial difference in intelligence, therefore, it is stupid to defend political or economic equal opportunities programs for people belonging to different races.

In addition, there are web influencers such as Stefan Molyneux and Lauren Southern (Canadian podcasters and YouTubers) who have published a lot of videos on the Internet in which they say that race differences in intelligence have a genetic basis.[7] Molyneux, in particular, stated that Western nations can suffer from a strong decline in their level of civilization because the IQ of the population is lowering for the constant immigration of people from the third world, who have a low IQ, as showed by the book *IQ and the Wealth of Nations* (Lynn & Vanhanen, 2006) and also by the already cited book *The Bell Curve* (Herrnstein & Murray, 1994).

If people outside academia make mistaken or distorted statements about intelligence it is partly justifiable because they are not researchers; on the contrary there are expert scholars who sustain the biological nature of the connection between race and intelligence. This assertion is inadmissible because scientists must be intellectually honest and avoid confusing laypeople. In scientific papers many aspects about intelligence, IQ, and biological characteristics remain questionable, and the real nature of the connection between race and intelligence is not yet clear. We examine some of these aspects.

Interference of External Institutions on Intelligence Studies

The Pioneer Fund is a program to finance research about racial genetic differences. It was instituted in 1937 by Wickliffe Draper, a New England textile magnate. His purpose was the defense of pureness of the White race against the possible contamination of other races or ethnicities (Miller, 1994; Lombardo, 2002). The Pioneer Fund promoted eugenics and sterilization of individuals with low levels of intelligence. After World War II, the Pioneer Fund started funding researchers who worked in the field of intelligence. Some of them were famous researchers such as Jensen, Gottfredson, Lynn, and Rushton (Miller, 1994). As an example of the way these funds were used, we can cite the case of William Shockley, a professor at Stanford University, winner of the Nobel Prize in Physics in 1956, whose contribution to the field of intelligence was completely negligible (Miller, 1994; Lombardo, 2002). He used his funds above all for publicizing racial prejudices about human characteristics and abilities and his eugenic idea that people with low IQ should be sterilized. We do not want, in this work, to claim that all the works of the researchers included in the Pioneer Fund[8] have no scientific validity because they were funded by a racist institution; however, it is reasonable to raise some doubts about the existence of possible conflicts of interest. We regret that this external influence on the scientific activity has biased and retarded the progress of the research about intelligence, focusing all the efforts on the biological aspects of intelligence on IQ on the conviction that intelligence is only the manifestation of brain power by which it is possible to justify a disparity between races or ethnicities. One example was the paper published by Lynn on intelligence titled "In Italy, North-South Differences in IQ Predict Differences in Income, Education,

Infant Mortality, Stature, and Literacy" (2010). This paper generated many reactions in the Italian academic community with different published papers contesting the methodological validity of Lynn's work (Beraldo, 2010; Cornoldi et al., 2010; Robinson et al., 2011). These replies needed a lot of time and effort and it is not clear why researchers should waste their time to analyze studies that do not respect scientific rules and to reply to affirmations that are flawed in particular when partial or improper data were used to confirm an arbitrary hypothesis.[9]

Clear Definition of Intelligence, *g*, and IQ

The U.S. standardization of the adult version of Wechsler's scale, the WAIS–IV (Wechsler, 2008), clearly shows that the four principal races living today in the United States (Whites, Asians, Blacks, and Hispanics) have different IQs. The racial group with the highest IQ was the Asian group (IQ = 106.07), then the White (IQ = 103.21), the Hispanic (IQ = 91.63), and last the Black group (88.67). Therefore, there is an IQ difference equivalent to a one standard deviation between Whites and Blacks—the same previously found by Jensen (1998).[10]

Many wrong uses of racial IQ differences to justify racial biological differences are based on a mystification about the relation between intelligence and IQ. People think that intelligence and IQ are synonyms, but this is false. Intelligence is a problem-solving ability applied in different contexts (Neisser et al., 1996; Rindermann, 2007). There are different ways or scientific approaches to define intelligence and different models have been proposed to give a representation of intelligence. Sternberg (1985) proposed a triarchic theory of intelligence by which intelligence is composed by three components: analytic intelligence, practical intelligence, and creative intelligence. Gardner became famous after publishing his book *Formae Mentis* (Gardner & Sosio, 1987) in which he proposed that intelligence cannot be considered a unique factor but a composition of different factors: linguistic, musical, spatial, intrapersonal, interpersonal, logical-mathematical, bodily-kinesthetic, and naturalistic. Then there are cognitive and psychometric approaches to intelligence. The cognitive approach analyzes cognitive abilities in terms of components of the information processing (attentional resources, working memory, metacognition), while the psychometric approach defines the best methods to measure intelligence and its construct. In psychometrics there are different models of intelligence: Spearman's model of unique factor of intelligence (*g*); Thurstone's model of multiple factors of intelligence (primary mental abilities); Guilford's Structure of Intellect model; Vernon's Hierarchical Model of Intelligence; and the Three-Stratum model of Carroll (later incorporated into the CHC or Carrol-Horn-Cattell model), in which intelligence is articulated in specific and large cognitive skills all converging in the unique factor *g*. The latest model is currently the one most shared by researchers who deal with intelligence psychometrics (Carroll, 1993).[11]

Independently from these conceptualizations, intelligence is a biological trait, a component of human phenotype that increases human ability to survive in natural environments. Today human beings have no urgent necessity for survival thanks to the scientific and technological development of societies, but intelligence is always an important characteristic for the quality of life. Intelligence is correlated with good health and higher income (Deary et al., 2009). Therefore, research on intelligence is important for improving the welfare of individuals and societies.

Intelligence is a problem-solving ability applied in different contexts. A person who is able to memorize the content of an entire book but is not able to tie his or her shoes cannot be considered intelligent. Intelligence makes people versatile and flexible, able to deal with problems arising in different situations. Intelligence cannot be reduced to a narrow range of abilities; otherwise robots, which have very high but specialized abilities, could be considered intelligent. Because intelligence is pervasive and present in every cognitive task, it could be useful to define an index to summarize the level of global cognitive functioning. This index is IQ.

IQ is usually the sum of different measures of specific cognitive abilities. Intelligence is measured with different tests that compose a battery. The most famous test batteries for measuring intelligence are Wechsler's scales. The individual IQ is obtained by summing the individual scores in different subtests and then this sum is compared with the distribution of these sums in the population. IQ is a standardized index that represents the strength of the global cognitive performance. In conclusion, intelligence is the ability to solve problems connected with brain efficiency in information processing, while IQ is an index to summarize global individual performance in different intelligence tests or tasks. The nature of the connection between IQ and intelligence is still not completely clear. However, neuroscientific studies are showing that IQ is more related to efficiency in brain networks than to brain size (Neubauer & Fink, 2009). Therefore, IQ can be associated with the efficiency of information processing in the brain.

The *g* factor is the common general ability that is present in every cognitive task. As such, *g* represents the common variance in different test scores. This common variance is associated with intelligence. While IQ represents the quality of the global performance, *g* represents the association between the different specific performances. Factor analysis is used to estimate the association between specific performances and to estimate how each specific performance is associated with *g*. This association is given by *g* loadings. If a cognitive task or test has a high loading on *g*, this means that the scores in that task or test are above all affected by the intelligence of the individual. In the literature, *g* and IQ sometimes are confounded; however, they are very different indexes: the *g* factor indicates if the intelligence test is a valid measure of intelligence (valid tests have high loadings in *g*); IQ summarizes the global performance quality. IQ can be obtained from tests with high or low *g* loadings. IQs derived from tests with low loadings in *g* should be taken with extreme caution when describing the variation of intelligence in individuals (Carroll, 1993).

Which IQ?

IQ can be derived from many different intelligence tests such as, for example, Wechsler's scales for intelligence (WAIS, WISC, WPPSI), Raven's Progressive Matrices (SPM, CPM, and APM), Differential Ability Scales (DAS), Cattell's Culture Fair Test (CFT), and so on. Therefore, there is not a unique test for determining IQ. In many papers, however, IQ values are presented as a unique type of measure. But IQs obtained with different tests are not equivalent. An IQ obtained using Raven's Matrices is not the same as that obtained from Wechsler's scales. Probably there is a strong correlation between a Raven's and a Wechsler's IQ, but correlation is not synonymous with equivalence. Raven's Matrices measure a component of intelligence, fluid intelligence while Wechsler's scales are a more complete measure of global intelligence. Therefore, IQs obtained with different intelligence tests should be considered different kinds of indexes because some tests measure prevalently verbal aspects of intelligence, visual-spatial competencies, and working memory. Some tests include a measure of processing speed and others do not. These characteristics have an impact on IQ values. Table 12.1 shows the correlations between IQs obtained on intelligence tests with IQs obtained in different intelligence tests or with scores from

Table 12.1 Correlations Between Full-Scale IQs or Total Scores Derived From Intelligence and Achievement Tests

	WAIS–III	WAIS–IV	WISC–IV	WPPSI–IV	SAT	AFQT
WAIS–IV	.94		.91			
WISC–V		.89	.86	.83		
	Raven's Matrices	KABC–II†	CTONI–2	RIAS–2†		
WAIS	.67					
WAIS–IV				.31–.72		
WISC–III			.80–.81			
WISC–IV			.83	.58–.77		
WISC–V		.64–.81				
WPPSI–IV				.63–.74		
	KTEA–3†	WIAT–II	WIAT–III	Vineland–II†	SAT	AFQT
WAIS						.80¹ .77²
WAIS–IV		.88				
WISC–V	.52–.84	.80	.81	-.12–.27		
Raven's Matrices‡					.48	
Various Intelligence Tests‡					.53–.82	

Note. WAIS = Wechsler Adult Intelligence Scale; WAIS–III = Wechsler Adult Intelligence Scale–Third Edition; WAIS–IV = Wechsler Adult Intelligence Scale–Fourth Edition; WISC–III = Wechsler Intelligence Scale for Children–Third Edition; WISC–IV = Wechsler Intelligence Scale for Children–Fourth Edition; WISC–V = Wechsler Intelligence Scale for Children–Fifth Edition; WPPSI–IV = Wechsler Preschool and Primary Scale of Intelligence–Fourth Edition; KABC–II = Kaufman Assessment Battery for Children–Second Edition; CTONI–2 = Comprehensive Test of Nonverbal Intelligence–Second Edition; RIAS–2 = Reynolds Intellectual Assessment Scales–Second Edition. Achievement/Adaptive Behavior Tests: KTEA–3 = Kaufman Test of Educational Achievement–Third Edition; WIAT–II = Wechsler Individual Achievement Test–Second Edition; WIAT–III = Wechsler Individual Achievement Test–Third Edition; Vineland–II = Vineland Adaptive Behavior Scale–Second Edition; SAT = Scholastic Achievement Test; AFQT = Armed Forces Qualification Test

‡Total Score not included, correlations with principal test domains; Correlations for ¹White and ²Black men; †Data from Frey & Detterman.

Sources: McLeod & Rubin (1962); McGrevy et al. (1974); Frey & Detterman (2004); Wechsler et al. (2014); Wechsler (2003, 2008); Raines, Reynolds, & Kamphaus (2018); Hammill et al. (2009).

achievement or scholastic aptitude tests such as the SAT, Wechsler Individual Achievement Test (WIAT), and Kaufman Test of Educational Achievement (KTEA).

However, the most problematic point relative to IQ is that in scientific papers the difference between the observed and the true IQ is not specified. All researchers use observed IQs for their studies, but observed IQ contains measurement errors. True IQ is the value that also takes into consideration the component of measurement error. Every psychological test is affected by measurement error. The so-called gold-standard test is a pipe dream. For this reason, reliability is necessary to evaluate true scores. A true score is always an estimation; however, it allows us to be more confident in the validity of the measure obtained with the test. True IQ score, or IQ_v, can be obtained with the following equation:

$$IQ_v = IQ_m + r_{att} (IQ - IQ_m)$$

In the equation, IQ is the observed value, IQ_m is the mean of observed IQs, and r_{att} is the reliability of the test. Therefore, if a subject obtained an observed IQ of 105, both on WAIS–IV and on Raven's APM, and supposing that both WAIS and APM have a mean IQ of 100 and a standard deviation of 15, because WAIS–IV FSIQ has a reliability of .98 (Benson et al., 2010) and APM has a reliability of .84 (Raven et al., 1985), the IQ_v is 100 + .98(105 - 100) = 104.9 for the WAIS–IV and 100 + .85(105 - 100) = 104.2 for the APM.

Because true scores are an estimation, it is necessary to obtain their confidence interval to define the range in which there is 95% probability to find the true score. The formula for estimating the confidence interval (CI) of IQ_v is

$$IQ_{lim} = IQ_v \pm 1.96 \times s_v$$

in which IQ_{lim} is the inferior or superior limit of the CI and s_v the estimated variance of true score. In this case, s_v is equal to 2.1 for the WAIS–IV and 5.5 for the APM. Therefore, for the WAIS we have CI = (100.78, 109.02) while for the APM we have CI = (93.42, 114.98). The CI is larger in the APM than in the WAIS–IV as a consequence of less accuracy in APM measures.

Another problem is the IQ frequency distribution obtained with intelligence tests. It is assumed that IQ distributions should have a normal distribution because intelligence is considered a normative trait, but this is not always the case. For example, it is well known that IQ scores in Raven's Matrices are negatively skewed (many more scores are above the mean). For example, in the Italian standardization of Raven's SPM with a sample of 1,123 participants, the IQ distribution had a negative skewness of -0.703 (Raven, 2008); in a Peruvian study with 1,097 participants, SPM scores had a negative skewness of -1.114 (Millones et al., 2015); and in a sample of African students composed of 711 subjects, the SPM scores had a negative skewness of -0.936 (Vass, 1992). Score distributions are positively skewed if tests are very difficult because there are many scores under the mean while they are negatively skewed if tests are easy because there are many scores above the mean. Before comparing the IQs obtained in two different tests, it is necessary to estimate the level of difficulty of these tests and the impact of their difficulties on cognitive performance of examinees[12] because the scores may not necessarily have a normal distribution. The normality of score distributions is an abstract assumption, while the reality is that the IQ distribution depends on the performance quality of individuals and on test difficulty.

IQs derived from different intelligence tests are not equivalent and have not the same accuracy. This problem is not completely addressed in the literature but it should be because it increases the difficulty to compare results of different works in which IQ is measured with different tests. In addition, it is necessary to find a way to reduce the number of intelligence tests because different tests make difficult both the comparison of data of different researches (fundamental for meta-analyses) and the comparison of cognitive abilities of individuals in clinical practice or in personnel selection.

IQ Should Be Estimated Using Representative Samples

Lynn and Vanhanen (2006) analyzed the IQ of different nations. They found that nations of east Asia have the highest national IQ (Hong Kong = 107; Japan = 105; China = 106). Europe and North America obtained medium values (UK = 100; France = 98; Germany = 102; Italy = 102; U.S. = 98; Canada = 97), while African countries, particularly the sub-Saharan nations, obtained the lowest IQ values (the Congo = 73; Kenya = 72; Uganda = 73; Nigeria = 67; Ethiopia = 63). These results seem to confirm that African people are characterized by low intelligence. However, what were the sources used by authors to collect their data? The sources were different published works in which not only many different tests were used but also the samples were extremely various. In some cases, the samples were adults, in other cases, the samples were children, and, above all, in some cases the samples included hundreds or thousands of subjects while in others few subjects. Excluding the question of IQs obtained with different tests that we addressed in the previous section, how representative were the samples used in the studies cited by Lynn and Vanhanen?

In statistics, samples are representative if they are composed of numerous subjects. The De Moivre equation, or standard error, states that the variability of any statistic is affected by sample size. The larger the sample, the lower the variability. The lower the variability, the more reliable is the estimation of the statistical parameter in the population. But what is the minimum size of a sample to obtain reliable measures of IQ in the population? In addition, a sample, to be representative of the population, should have the same percentage of people on the basis of gender, educational level, race, and other characteristics.

If some characteristics can affect IQ value, then those characteristics should have the same percentage they have in population. For example, it is well known that IQ declines with age. Therefore, the sample should include people with different ages, but the percentage of people of different age must be equivalent to those of the population. In the same manner, if race affects IQ, the sample percentages of people of different races must be equal to those of the population. The percentage of Whites, Blacks, and Asians in the sample used for standardizing the WAIS–IV in the United States in relation to the entire sample ($N = 2,200$) was 70%, 11.81%, and 3.23%, respectively. According to the U.S. 2010 census, the percentages of different races were 72.4%, 12.6%, and 4.8% for Whites, Blacks and Asians, respectively. These values are compatible, but is the equivalence of sample-population valid also for other studies, researches, and standardizations?

If we want a low margin of error in our parameter estimation, in this case the mean IQ value of the entire population, we have to define an adequate sample size. For margins of error of 10%, 5%, 3%, and 1%, the sample must be composed by 96, 384, 1,067, and 9,604 subjects, respectively. For practical purposes, it is impossible to use samples with thousands of subjects. However, if we set the marginal error to 5%, a sample size of 384 is not difficult to achieve. Table 12.2 shows the number and the size of the samples used by Lynn to estimate the IQs of African, European, and East Asian nations (Lynn, 2006). According to Lynn (2006), the global IQ level for African, European,

Table 12.2 Number of Samples, Sample Size Range (Low to High), and Relative Range of Error Margins for Data Used to Estimate IQs of African, European, and East Asian Nations (Lynn, 2006) With Descriptive Statistics

Africa				Europe				East Asia			
Nation	N of samples	Range of Sample N	Range of Margin of Error	Nation	N of samples	Range of Sample N	Range of Margin of Error	Nation	N of samples	Range of Sample N	Range of Margin of Error
Cameroon	1	80	.11	Austria	2	67–187	.12–.07	China	10	60–5,108	.13–.01
Cent. African Rep.	1	1,149	.03	Belgium	3	247–944	.06–.03	Hong Kong	9	197–13,822	.07–.01
Congo	3	73–1,596	.11–.02	Britain	2	1,405–3,250	.03–.02	Japan	23	60–2,100	.13–.02
Congo-Zaire	5	47–222	.14–.07	Bulgaria	2	215–1,456	.07–.03	Singapore	2	147–159	.08–.05
Eq. Guinea	1	48	.14	Croatia	1	299	.06	South Korea	4	56–2,231	.13–.02
Ghana	2	225–1,693	.07–.02	Czech Rep.	3	64–832	.12–.03	Taiwan	10	118–4,3825	.09–.01
Guinea	2	50–1,144	.14–.03	Denmark	2	122–628	.09–.04				
Kenya	6	85–1,222	.11–.03	Estonia	2	1,835–2,689	.02–.02				
Madagascar	1	147	.08	Finland	2	122–755	.09–.04				
Mozambique	1	149	.08	France	4	328–1,320	.05–.03				
Nigeria	3	86–480	.11–.04	Germany	9	200–3,607	.07–.02				
Sierra Leone	2	33–122	.17–.09	Greece	5	220–990	.07–.03				
South Africa	16	26–1,726	.19–.02	Hungary	1	260	.06				
Sudan	4	80–293	.11–.06	Iceland	1	665	.04				

(Continued)

Table 12.2 (Continued)

	Africa			Europe				East Asia			
Nation	N of samples	Range of Sample N	Range of Margin of Error	Nation	N of samples	Range of Sample N	Range of Margin of Error	Nation	N of samples	Range of Sample N	Range of Margin of Error
Tanzania	3	179–2,959	.07–.02	Ireland	4	75–2,029	.11–.02				
Uganda	2	50–2,019	.14–.02	Italy	2	1,380–2,432	.03–.02				
Zambia	2	152–759	.08–.04	Lithuania	2	259–381	.06–.05				
Zimbabwe	1	204	.07	Malta	1	134	.08				
				Netherlands	4	333–4,032	.05–.02				
				Norway	1	333	.05				
				Poland	2	835–4,006	.03–.02				
				Portugal	2	242–807	.06–.03				
				Romania	1	300	.06				
				Russia	2	432–745	.05–.04				
				Serbia	1	76	.11				
				Slovakia	1	823	.03				
				Slovenia	2	1,080–1,556	.03–.02				
				Spain	3	854–3,271	.03–.02				
				Sweden	3	205–2,231	.07–.02				
				Switzerland	3	163–246	.08–.06				
M	3.11	471.88	.07		2.43	1,004.71	.05		9.67	1,717.84	.05
SD	3.53	596.90	.04		1.63	983.72	.03		7.34	6,068.79	.03
CV	113.45	126.49	54.30		67.12	97.91	56.48		75.92	353.28	55.71

and East Asian nations are 67, 99, and 105, respectively. Number of samples ranged from 1 to 16 for Africans (M = 3.11); 1 to 9 for Europeans (M = 2.43); and 2 to 23 for East Asians (M = 9.67). Sample sizes ranged from 26 to 2,959 for Africans (M = 471.88); 64 to 4,032 for Europeans (M = 1004.71); and 56 to 43,825 for East Asians (M = 1,717.84). Table 12.2 also shows the corresponding margins of error. The average margins of error were 7%, 5% and 5% for Africans, Europeans, and East Asians, respectively. In relation to Europeans and East Asians, the samples used to estimate IQ in Africans were less representative.

Coefficients of variation were very high for the number of samples, the size of samples, and for margin of errors, indicating a huge sample variability of these characteristics.[13] Therefore, there was not a homogeneous level of representativeness for each nation, especially in the number and dimension of samples. Lynn and Meisenberg (2010b) have recalculated the national IQs by weighting them with the relative sample size, but IQs were always presented as indexes with equivalent validity for each nation, which is a disputable question. Therefore, there are some doubts about the practical utility of estimating a global IQ for people living in different continents if national IQs have different levels of validity.

It is true that many studies on African samples converge to a mean IQ of 67 (Lynn & Meisenberg, 2010a, 2010b); however, IQ is not an absolute measure. IQ is an index constantly variable in space and time, and its variability is affected by the reliability of intelligence tests and by representativeness of samples. Some authors have argued that Lynn and Vanhanen used an arbitrary method to select African samples (Wicherts et al., 2010). According to these authors, Lynn and Vanhanen selected the samples with the lowest IQ levels. The authors stated that if the excluded samples were included, the mean IQ of African nations would increase to 80 instead of 67. Lynn and colleagues replied to this claim in another paper, asserting that Wicherts et al. used unrepresentative samples composed of high school students or by mixed-race people (Lynn & Meisenberg, 2010a). Irrespective of determining who is correct, these ongoing disputes thwart scientific progress and cast a shadow over researchers' efforts in the present societal discourse regarding the scientific validity of intelligence studies.

There is another point that is necessary to highlight. In Western societies, people have higher standards of life and they have the ability to study and to receive an education for obtaining profitable work. Intelligence tests measure capacity for abstraction and logical-formal reasoning that are the abilities developed by Western educational systems and required by Western professions. In many African countries people live in very poor conditions, and they cannot attend school because they have to survive in places and zones that do not require high levels of abstract reasoning, an important component required in intelligence tests. Therefore, their life conditions could be detrimental to their performance on intelligence tests, which were developed for people living in countries with a more developed economy. Some studies showed that intelligence tests, such as Raven's Matrices, which are generally considered culture fair, really are not culture or ethnic blind either (Owen, 1992; Zindi, 2013). Thus some authors propose new intelligence tests more suitable for African populations as, for example, the Zimbabwe Psychological Evaluation (ZIPE; Zindi, 2013).

Many Results in Studies of IQ Are Interpreted, Not Explained

Many studies on IQ are correlational studies. In these studies, the IQ measures are correlated with other measures (scholastic achievement, income, health, and so on). Correlation is not causation.

When two variables correlate with each other, probably there is a connection, but this connection is insufficient to determine if there is a cause-effect relationship between the two variables. Cause-effect connections can be determined only in true experimental designs in which people are randomly assigned to different groups, one group receiving an experimental treatment (the experimental group) and the other a false treatment (placebo) or no treatment at all (the control group). Before the beginning of the experiment, the two groups have to be as equal as possible, and if any difference appears between them after the experiment, then the scientist might conclude that the treatment was effective, establishing in this way the existence of a cause-effect relation between the treatment and the behavior.

Intelligence is the ability of our brain to solve problems. The functioning of our brain is affected both by genetic heritage and environment. The problem is that it is difficult to manipulate genetic or environmental characteristics to cause variations in intelligence. For example, height is affected by genes, (e.g., parents with high stature), and environment (e.g., food availability) as shown by scientific studies (Yang et al., 2015). However, it is difficult to force people to eat nothing, or to eat poor-quality food to determine the effect of food on height; or to force people with high or low stature to mate with people of the same height to see the effect of mating on offspring. Only with animals is this research possible. The same is true for intelligence. For the fact that it is practically or ethically impossible to manipulate many environmental factors that could have a possible effect on intelligence, researchers are forced to select individuals with certain characteristics (in the case of height, for example, people with low socioeconomic status for studying effect of food deprivation, or people with parents or relatives with high or low stature) to see if there is an association between these characteristics and the variable under investigation. However, when subjects' characteristics are selected, the probability of detecting a cause-effect connection is low in comparison to true experiments in which the researchers have the ability to control directly human characteristics or behaviors. And when the probability of finding a real cause-effect connection is low, the risk of interpreting, instead of explaining, experimental data increases.

In the next sections, we provide some examples in which data about individual characteristics and IQ are interpreted rather than explained. Explanation means that every time a specific characteristic appears, let say characteristic A, characteristic B also appears. The presence of B is determined by the presence of A. Interpretation means that every time the A characteristic appears, the B characteristic has a high probability to appear. However, the presence of A is not determinant for the presence of B because other factors can determine the presence of B. Interpretation can be considered a kind of probabilistic explanation. The difference between deterministic and probabilistic explanations is the ability to predict events. When you find a constant cause-effect connection, your predictions are very accurate; when you find that the appearance of both characteristics has not the same frequency, your predictions are less accurate. For example, there is a significant connection between IQ and income, but it is not possible to predict accurately the richness of people on the basis of their IQ level. Some people with low IQs are rich and some people with high IQ are beggars. But the most problematic point in correlational studies is the impossibility of attributing the role of cause and effect to the different characteristics. Is it A that causes B, or B that causes A? For example, is it intelligence that determines high socioeconomic status, or is it socioeconomic status that determines intelligence?

Nature or Nurture?

This is the never-ending question about intelligence. Is intelligence biologically determined or is it affected by environment and experience? We have researchers who are strongly convinced that intelligence is a biological matter and that it is connected to brain size. The connection between brain size and intelligence starts with the founder of psychometrics, Francis Galton, who discovered that the most prominent and talented students of Cambridge had larger heads (Galton, 1889). Since Galton there have been many researchers who evidenced that intelligence is related to brain size such as cortical volume or cortical thickness (Karama et al., 2011; McDaniel, 2005; Nave et al., 2019; Rushton & Ankney 1996; Wickett et al., 2000). Other researchers oppose this connection, maintaining that intelligence is related to efficiency in neural networks (Basten et al., 2015; Neubauer & Fink, 2009).

Regardless of whether one considers brain size or neural efficiency, it is widely acknowledged that intelligence is a biological trait (Deary et al., 2006; Erlenmeyer-Kimling & Jarvik, 1963; Hendrickson & Hendrickson, 1980; Hill et al., 2019). Many studies on monozygotic and dizygotic twins reared together or in different families have showed that intelligence is highly heritable (Bouchard, 2004; Erlenmeyer-Kimling & Jarvik, 1963; McCartney et al., 1990).

But intelligence is also affected by the environment. Schooling can affect intelligence. Some authors have reported an increment of intelligence proportionate to the increment of schooling (Brinch & Galloway, 2012; Falch & Sandgren Massih, 2011; Ritchie & Tucker-Drob, 2018). Other authors have found that socioeconomic status can affect intelligence. In other words, there is a combined effect of biological factors and socioeconomic status on cognitive abilities instead of a causal, linear connection from genes to intelligence to welfare (Tucker-Drob & Bates, 2016). Other studies have shown that the connection between intelligence and socioeconomic status is not linear but highly articulated with other individual characteristics (Zagorsky, 2007).

Reality is much more complex than some scientists imagine especially for the relationship between intelligence and individual characteristics. For example, people can select partners on the basis of their socioeconomic status. In this way, if genetics can have some effect on socioeconomic status, through intelligence, socioeconomic status can have some effects on genetics by partner selection. The new trend in studies about the effects of biological and environmental factors on intelligence considers intelligence partly genetically determined, partly environmentally affected, and partly affected by interaction between genes and environment (Plomin & Deary, 2015; Plomin & von Stumm, 2018; Richardson, 2017).

It is now sufficiently ascertained that intelligence is a consequence of genes, environment, and interaction between them. But the assertion that intelligence is determined both by genes and environment is not a valid explanation of IQ differences between groups. As highlighted by Block (1995), "in the case of IQ, no one has any idea how to separate out direct from indirect genetic effects because no one has much of an idea how genes and environment affect IQ" (p. 117). If IQ is heritable, this does not imply that IQ is genetically determined. Let us give two examples. In 1956, the inhabitants of Minamata, a small village in Japan, showed the symptoms of a pathology, called then Minamata disease, caused by the ingestion of great quantities of mercury. The inhabitants of Minamata were prevalently fishermen, and their diet was prevalently fish. However, a factory in the zone had poured a great amount of mercury into the sea around the village, contaminating all animals living in the water. The consequence of this pollution was an increase in fetus deformities.

In addition, the newborns showed strong cognitive impairment and a reduction of their level of intelligence (Yorifuji et al., 2015). The average IQ of Minamata people was 92 in relation to the national IQ level of 105 (Yorifuji et al., 2015). This difference, however, had a well-defined environmental cause and could not be considered as partly genetically determined. As regards the second example, it is known that phenylketonuria (PKU) is genetically determined and consists of an organism's inability to metabolize phenylalanine. This metabolic impairment can determine mental retardation, but if people affected by PKU have phenylalanine removed from their diet, they can have normal cognitive development (Block, 1995). Even if people with PKU tend to have a lower level of intelligence, and even if PKU is genetically determined, PKU is not a direct cause of mental retardation, and a variation of environmental conditions (in this case the diet) can change the phenotype of individuals. These examples show that IQ differences between groups can have different causes that could be genetic or environmental, that genes can have direct or indirect effects on intelligence, and that only a well-specified analysis of the characteristics of these causes allows a correct explanation of IQ differences. Therefore, White-Black IQ differences cannot be explained without the correct identification of the possible genetic or environmental factors, and Herrnstein and Murrays's declaration that 60% of intelligence is heritable is practically nonsense (Block, 1995; Herrnstein & Murray, 1994).

IQ and Gender

The mean IQ for females is about 4–5 points lower than that of males (Lynn, 1994b). Some authors are convinced that this difference is biologically determined (Lynn, 1994b; Lynn, 1998; Lynn & Irwing, 2002; Rushton & Jensen, 2005) while others consider this difference a result of cultural and social variations (Born et al., 1987) or educative system (Kaufman et al., 2009). The explanation of the gender difference in intelligence is the smaller brain size of women (Ankney, 1992; Lynn, 1994b; Rushton, 1992). However, other studies have showed that probably there are other causes of lower IQ in females. Some authors have proposed that it is a question of how subjects are recruited from population (Hunt & Madhyastha, 2008), others have proposed the level of education of parents (Andersson et al., 1998), and others have proposed a mix of biological and social characteristics in determining gender differences (Halpern, 1997).

However, over the last years another explanation has taken even more importance: the different performance of men and women in intelligence tests. There is much evidence that men outperform women in specific cognitive tasks such as mathematical, quantitative, or visual-spatial tasks, and women outperform men in processing speed tasks and verbal tasks (Abad et al., 2004; Born et al., 1987; Feingold, 1992). In particular, some researchers found that the contribution of g in intelligence tests is equivalent in males and females (Colom & García-López, 2002; Colom et al., 2002; Colom et al., 2000; Johnson & Bouchard, 2007; Keith et al., 2008; Saggino et al., 2014; Tommasi et al., 2015a, 2015b; Van der Sluis et al., 2006). In addition, male and female differences in cognitive performance have declined over the last years (Pezzuti et al., 2020). We are moving toward a society in which males and females are expected to have the same competencies and opportunities in the workplace and therefore this can promote an ever-decreasing difference in intelligence between sexes. However, there are still contradictory interpretations about gender differences in intelligence. Anyway, could 4–5 points of difference (admitting that Lynn is right) be considered really relevant? We highly doubt it.

The Minnesota Transracial Adoption Study

Some researchers conducted a longitudinal study of reared children to study the effect of adoption on IQ (Weinberg et al., 1992). In this study there were Black children reared by White parents. The authors found a significant increase of their IQ level in comparison to the IQ level in Black population (IQ = 87). At age 7 they showed an IQ of 109; at age 17 they showed an IQ of 98. The authors concluded that even if there was a reduction of about 11 points in IQ during years, Black children reared in White families showed an increment of intelligence. Other authors contrasted this affirmation by maintaining that the IQ between Blacks and Whites remained unchanged because the IQ level of Black adopted children was still lower than that of the corresponding adopted White children (White adopted children had an IQ of 106 at age of 17). The fact that the IQ of adopted Black children was halfway between the IQs of White and Black population was a confirmation of the biological origin of intelligence (Lynn, 1994a). So Black children adopted by White middle-class families have a level of intelligence that is intermediate between the lower intelligence of Blacks, living with people of their race and the higher intelligence of Whites. For Waldman et al. (1994) this was evidence of the effect of environment on intelligence. For other researchers, however, it was evidence of the genetic origin of intelligence (Lynn, 1994a). What can we say? Also in this case, it is a question of different interpretation of the same results by researchers with different political attitudes.

IQ Is Affected by Environmental Factors and by Individual Characteristics

Richard Flynn discovered that there is a continuous increment of IQ in intelligence tests (Flynn, 1987; te Nijenhuis & Van Der Flier, 2013). This increment is about 9 IQ points per generation (a generation lasts about 30 years). From the beginning of the use of intelligence tests, in early 20th century to today, IQ has increased about 30 points. Many explanations have been provided for the Flynn effect: increasing welfare, quality improvement of environmental conditions, reduced pollution (in countries that adopted anti-pollution provisions), and improvement of educational systems (Pietschnig & Voracek, 2015). Mingroni (2004) proposed the *heterosis* theory of the Flynn effect, that is, genetic selection resulting from matings between members of genetically distinct subpopulations, while Flynn (2007) himself explained the effect as a consequence of learning experiences of applying logic on a formal level rather than a concrete level through educational programs more centered on scientific reasoning and abstract logic. Flynn evidenced an increment of IQ level also in Black people (Dickens & Flynn, 2006). However this datum was criticized by other authors maintaining the racial gap in intelligence, arguing that even if there were a reduction of the gap, Black people still obtained a lower IQ level than Whites (Rushton, 1999; Rushton & Jensen, 2006). Again, the same datum is interpreted in opposite ways by scientists.

It is clear that the Flynn effect cannot be explained only on the basis of genetic factors because some studies show that in some countries in these last years the Flynn effect has stopped or it is reverting (Bratsberg & Rogeberg, 2018; Sundet et al., 2004). The Flynn effect most probably is environmentally determined and is related to IQ. Scores on intelligence tasks are reasonably affected by other factors not related to the biological characteristics of individuals. Therefore, if intelligence is mainly affected by biological characteristics (for Plomin and von Stumm [2018] the heritability of intelligence is about 80), IQ is prevalently determined by environmental factors and by other psychological characteristics of individuals.

There is much scientific evidence showing that IQ is affected by environment. Schooling and educational achievement affect individual IQ (Ceci & Williams, 1997; Ritchie et al., 2015). In particular, for one year of schooling there is an increment of about 1.9 IQ points in individuals (Tommasi et al., 2015a). Socioeconomic status affects cognitive performance in intelligence tests. Mani and colleagues showed that the variation of the welfare of people, determined by periods in which they were employed or unemployed, affects their performance on cognitive tasks (Mani et al., 2013). Other studies showed that adopted children reared by adoptive parents with high socioeconomic status can increase their IQ level about 12 points in relation to children adopted by parents with low socioeconomic status (Capron & Duyme, 1989).

Psychological characteristics such as motivation and anxiety can affect cognitive performance (Duckworth et al., 2011; Moutafi et al., 2006; Wicherts & Scholten 2010). Some studies also have shown a probable effect of personality traits on cognitive performance (Bartels et al., 2012; Djapo et al., 2011). Other studies have showed that the connection between race and IQ is affected by the presence of other cognitive abilities. Pesta and Poznanski (2008) pointed out that when elementary cognitive tasks such as processing speed and reaction time are taken into consideration as predictive factors of cognitive performance, the IQ gap between individuals of different races disappears. Probably, people with different race have different strategies in problem-solving tasks that have an effect on their performance in intelligence tests. Other authors have claimed that IQ is associated with literacy or people's ability to read and comprehend texts because the verbal subscales of intelligence tests show higher White-Black differences and a stronger Flynn effect (Marks, 2010).

Another important problem is that Black people have scored differently on an intelligence test depending on whether their examiner was co-racial or not. They obtained higher scores when the examiner was Black instead of White (Graziano et al., 1982; Terrell et al., 1981).

All these findings show that IQ is largely affected by external factors such as education, socioeconomic status, and individual differences such as motivation, anxiety, and personality. The effect of these factors increase measurement errors in assessment of intelligence. Therefore, IQ cannot be considered an unbiased estimator of intelligence. We think that other measures could be used to accurately measure intelligence, but these measures should be more connected with brain activity rather than performance in cognitive tests. For example, measures of efficiency of signal transmission in brain network could be a good candidate to estimate accurately the level of intelligence because there are empirical data showing that there is a positive correlation between IQ and the number of connections and the velocity of signal transmission in brain areas (Deco et al., 2008; Li et al., 2009; Neubauer & Fink, 2009; Van Den Heuvel et al., 2009).

In addition, we have to mention the fact that Rushton and Ankney (1996) declared that the correlation between intelligence and brain size was .44, which means that brain size can explain about 19% of variance in intelligence. A more recent study, instead, showed that the correlation between brain size and intelligence is .19, which is less than 4% of variance explained (Nave et al., 2019). On the basis of these results, we can make two possible conclusions: (a) in about 20 years the connection between intelligence and brain size has diminished, or, more probably, (b) the supposed connection between brain size and intelligence is an artifact created by researchers' expectations.

The Steve Jobs Paradox

Jason Richwine published a thesis titled "IQ and Immigration Policy" in which he declared that immigrants coming to the United States should be submitted to intelligence tests to accept only people with high level of intelligence (Richwine, 2009). The reason is that the national IQ of Mexico, a neighboring state, is about 87, which is lower than the mean U.S. IQ of 98 (Lynn & Vanhanen, 2006). Because people with low IQs hold low-paying jobs, according to Herrnstein and Murray (1994), Richwine claimed that indiscriminate immigration from Mexico meant a loss for the U.S. economy of about $8.8 billion. If intelligence tests were used to select immigrants from Mexico, this loss could be reduced to $3.5 billion. Even if Richwine used data about IQ levels of Mexican immigrants derived from ASVAB or PIAT–R Math tests, which are not canonical intelligence tests, his work seems to make a convincing argument in favor of more restrictive immigration politics.

However, this reasoning does not consider the fact that people are different and that they can change over time. As an example, we can consider the story of Steve Jobs, the founder of Apple and Pixar. Steve Jobs's father, Abdul Fattah Jandali, was an immigrant from Homs, Syria, a nation with a mean IQ of 83 (Lynn & Vanhanen, 2006). When he came to the United States, he attended Colombia University and the University of Wisconsin. Jandali dated Joanne Carol Schieble, a German-Swiss Catholic girl, who became the mother of Steve Jobs. Jadali and Schieble could not marry because of the opposition of her father. Therefore Steve was adopted by a Catholic couple, Paul and Clara Jobs. Then the story is known to everybody. In collaboration with Steve Wozniack, Jobs created Apple, which became a giant in computer hardware and software and in smartphones. Jobs also created Pixar, a company in which computer graphic animation is used to create movies for children. In October 2024, Apple had a global net worth of approximately $3.2 trillion.

The paradox here is in the fact that even if Steve Jobs was the son of an immigrant coming from a nation with lower IQ, he created a company that has largely increased the U.S. gross domestic product instead of working as a waiter or porter, according to Richwine's predictions. The paradox means that knowledge of the population characteristics cannot be used to predict the behavior of every single individual.

So what is the conclusion we can draw from these considerations? One important question is if reasonings based on abstract concepts, as national IQ, racial IQ, and so on have an important meaning in real economy. The economy of a country can be influenced by unpredictable and unknown events. Not one economist, for example, was able to predict the world financial crisis of 2008 generated by subprime home mortgages. Therefore IQ, as we have seen before, cannot be considered a valid predictor of economic national growth, which is affected by many external factors. The other point is that population characteristics cannot be used to hide individual behavior differences. Not all immigrants are equal or have the same behavior because individual differences are real. Moreover, selection of immigrants should be based on their behavior rather than on their characteristics. Criminal or aggressive behaviors are valid reasons for selecting people. Color of skin, religion, political orientation, country of origin, height, intelligence, or other individual differences are not valid reasons for imposing restrictions.

What We Can and Cannot Say About IQ

IQ cannot be used to justify racial gap or biological differences such as gender differences because IQ cannot be considered a precise measure of intelligence. IQs obtained with different intelligence tests are not equivalent because tests have different structure and validity. At the same time, IQ is affected by external factors, which increase or decrease its variability in space and time. In research, only observed IQ is considered while estimated true IQ, which takes into consideration measurement error, should be preferred. Other problems are sample size and representativeness from which data are collected. IQ is used in correlational or quasi-experimental studies that do not allow a clear definition of cause-effect relationship between variables, favoring different interpretation of the same experimental results. Last but not least, many researchers have showed prejudicial attitudes or conflicts of interest that probably biased their scientific works on intelligence. As a consequence of all these problems, IQ cannot be considered directly connected with intelligence. There is a lot of dark matter between the observed IQ and the latent construct of intelligence. This dark matter does not allow, for the moment, clear and precise affirmations of the difference in intelligence between races, ethnicities, or biologically different groups.

The scientific research about the genetic origin of the connection between race and intelligence is also obscure. Even if skin color and intelligence are genetically determined, they are not necessarily determined by the same gene or allele variants. This is an open question because there are no specific data, and scientists cannot debate questions for which there are no objective data. For this reason, Neisser and colleagues (1996) asserted that there is certainly no support for a genetic interpretation of intelligence difference between Blacks and Whites. Only 11%–23% of observed genetic variation is due to differences among populations, and this is mostly attributable to differences in allele frequencies, not all-or-nothing genetic differences. Therefore, race is more a social construct than a consequence of a real genetic difference.

But even if the IQ level of Blacks remains lower than that of Whites, where is the problem? Let us imagine two parents with two children, one smart, competent, and brilliant, the other clumsy and slow. What should the two parents do with the dumb one? Probably they will do the best they can to help the unlucky son or daughter. They will help them and provide all the means to give them the opportunity to have a good life and to be autonomous and motivated. This is the correct behavior. No parent will leave their child alone only because the child is not able or mediocre. In the same way, modern societies have an ethical duty to help their impaired members, offering them adequate educational systems and economic help in order to compensate for their limits or gaps. If some persons think that society must differentiate people because it is not possible to obtain anything good from persons with mediocre ability, they cannot use intelligence and, above all, its principal measure, IQ, to justify this discrimination.

A scientist can say that there are people with high and low IQ, but he or she cannot say that people with low IQs are bad and useless for the society. This is a moral judgment of persons, and judging the value of people is highly motivated by prejudice and racism. Racism has nothing to do with true science. While it may seem challenging to prevent individuals from leveraging IQ to rationalize their racial prejudices, it's crucial to underscore that they are manipulating data to serve their political agendas and reinforce social biases. Herrnstein and Murray (1994) wrote, "We urge generally that these policies, represented by the extensive network of cash and services for low-income women who have babies, be ended. The government should stop subsidizing births to anyone, rich or poor" (pp. 548–549). This is an undue interference of science (or, to be honest, pseudoscience) with politics. No scientist can affirm that people with low IQ must be discriminated against. If someone claims that immigrants must be blocked at frontiers or that people with different races cannot have equal opportunities because of their low IQ, he or she must have the courage and responsibility to admit that they are racist and intolerant instead of hiding their intolerance behind manipulated scientific concepts.

Scientists have to reduce the impact of their subjective attitudes or preferences in their scientific work and to speak with laymen to allow them to understand that there are no scientific justifications for discriminating against people and, above all, to judge some individuals better than others on the basis of their phenotypic characteristics. Equality or discrimination between persons are questions pertinent to ethics and morality, not to science.

Notes

1   https://www.sciencemag.org/news/2014/08/geneticists-decry-book-race-and-evolution

2   https://www.theguardian.com/books/2017/mar/06/bell-curve-author-charles-murray-speaks-out-after -speech-cut-short-by-protests

3   https://www.youtube.com/watch?v=1YfEoxU82us

4   The poster was presented during a science fair project organized by the school.

5   https://www.sacbee.com/news/local/article199440204.html

6   https://www.theguardian.com/news/2018/mar/02/the-unwelcome-revival-of-race-science

7   "Stefan Molyneux & Lauren Southern on *Sky News* About White Genocide and Race & IQ," https://www .facebook.com/watch/?v=661032477565152

8   The Pioneer Fund is still active.

9   For example, confusing human intelligence with school achievement as in Lynn (2010).

10 At the end of the last century (maybe in 1995) one of the authors of this chapter met with Arthur Jensen at Maudsley's cafeteria in London. Jensen asked him, "Can you tell me a valid reason why the color of your eyes is genetically determined and your intelligence shouldn't be?" He also said that he was against the laws of the State of California that some places in California universities had to be reserved for ethnic minorities. According to him, students with greater intelligence had to enter university regardless of their race. He also seemed genuinely sorry, even on a personal level, for the attacks he had suffered because of his studies of the differences in *g* between White people and Black people. His position was as follows: the difference of a standard deviation between White people and Black people is a scientific fact. Instead, its causes and consequences can be discussed. Unlike other scholars, Jensen opposed the existence of gender differences in intelligence. In conclusion, Jensen appears to be essentially an intellectually honest scholar although this does not mean we have to agree with all his scientific work.

11 We have to claim that Carroll based his analyses on 477 datasets collected from different parts of the world. Therefore, his work is based on a great amount of empirical data.

12 It is necessary to say that score distributions are affected also by examinee characteristics. For example, it is possible to have bimodal distribution of scores. Bimodality indicates the presence of two subpopulations with different characteristics. For example, a bimodal IQ distribution can be due to the presence of a high number of college students inside a sample composed by people of different educational levels.

13 Even if there is not a cut-off for coefficients of variation, however, a coefficient of less than 50% indicates an acceptable level of homogeneity in samples (Zinn et al., 2001; Henning & Jordaan, 2016).

References

Abad, F. J., Colom, R., Rebollo, I., & Escorial, S. (2004). Sex differential item functioning in the Raven's Advanced Progressive Matrices: Evidence for bias. *Personality and Individual Differences*, *36*(6), 1459–1470. https://doi.org/10.1016/s0191-8869(03)00241-1

Andersson, H. W., Sonnander, K., & Sommerfelt, K. (1998). Gender and its contribution to the prediction of cognitive abilities at five years. *Scandinavian Journal of Psychology*, *39*(4), 267–274. https://doi.org/10.1111/1467-9450.00086

Ankney, C. D. (1992). Sex differences in relative brain size: The mismeasure of woman, too? *Intelligence*, *16*(3–4), 329-336. https://doi.org/10.1016/0160-2896(92)90013-h

Born, M. P., Bleichrodt, N., & Van Der Flier, H. (1987). Cross-cultural comparison of sex-related differences on intelligence tests: A meta-analysis. *Journal of Cross-Cultural Psychology*, *18*(3), 283–314. https://doi.org/10.1177/0022002187018003002

Bouchard, T. J., Jr. (2004). Genetic influence on human psychological traits: A survey. *Current Directions in Psychological Science*, *13*(4), 148–151. https://doi.org/10.1111/j.0963-7214.2004.00295.x

Colom, R., García, L. F., Juan-Espinosa, M., & Abad, F. J. (2002). Null sex differences in general intelligence: Evidence from the WAIS–III. *The Spanish Journal of Psychology*, *5*(1), 29–35. https://doi.org/10.1017/s1138741600005801

Colom, R., & García-López, O. (2002). Sex differences in fluid intelligence among high school graduates. *Personality and Individual Differences*, *32*(3), 445–451. https://doi.org/10.1016/s0191-8869(01)00040-x

Colom, R., Juan-Espinosa, M., Abad, F., & García, L. F. (2000). Negligible sex differences in general intelligence. *Intelligence*, *28*(1), 57–68. https://doi.org/10.1016/s0160-2896(99)00035-5

Cornoldi, C., Belacchi, C., Giofrè, D., Martini, A., & Tressoldi, P. (2010). The mean Southern Italian children IQ is not particularly low: A reply to R. Lynn (2010). *Intelligence*, *38*(5), 462–470. https://doi.org/10.1016/j.intell.2010.06.003

Bartels, M., van Weegen, F. I., van Beijsterveldt, C. E., Carlier, M., Polderman, T. J., Hoekstra, R. A., & Boomsma, D. I. (2012). The five factor model of personality and intelligence: A twin study on the relationship between the two constructs. *Personality and Individual Differences*, *53*(4), 368–373. https://doi.org/10.1016/j.paid.2012.02.007

Basten, U., Hilger, K., & Fiebach, C. J. (2015). Where smart brains are different: A quantitative meta-analysis of functional and structural brain imaging studies on intelligence. *Intelligence*, *51*, 10–27. https://doi.org/10.1016/j.intell.2015.04.009

Benson, N., Hulac, D. M., & Kranzler, J. H. (2010). Independent examination of the Wechsler Adult Intelligence Scale–Fourth Edition (WAIS–IV): What does the WAIS–IV measure? *Psychological Assessment*, *22*(1), 121–130. https://doi.org/10.1037/a0017767

Beraldo, S. (2010). Do differences in IQ predict Italian north-south differences in income? A methodological critique to Lynn. *Intelligence*, *38*(5), 456–461. https://doi.org/10.1016/j.intell.2010.06.007

Block, N. (1995). How heritability misleads about race. *Cognition*, *56*(2), 99–128. https://doi.org/10.1016/0010-0277(95)00678-r

Bratsberg, B., & Rogeberg, O. (2018). The Flynn effect and its reversal are both environmentally caused. *Proceedings of the National Academy of Sciences*, *115*(26), 6674–6678. https://doi.org/10.1073/pnas.1718793115

Brinch, C. N., & Galloway, T. A. (2012). Schooling in adolescence raises IQ scores. *Proceedings of the National Academy of Sciences*, *109*(2), 425–430. https://doi.org/10.1073/pnas.1106077109

Capron, C., & Duyme, M. (1989). Assessment of effects of socio-economic status on IQ in a full cross-fostering study. *Nature*, *340*, 552–554. https://doi.org/10.1038/340552a0

Carroll, J. B. (1993). *Human cognitive abilities: A survey of factor-analytic studies*. Cambridge University Press. https://doi.org/10.1017/cbo9780511571312

Ceci, S. J., & Williams, W. M. (1997). Schooling, intelligence, and income. *American Psychologist*, *52*(10), 1051–1058. https://doi.org/10.1037//0003-066x.52.10.1051

Deary, I. J., Spinath, F. M., & Bates, T. C. (2006). Genetics of intelligence. *European Journal of Human Genetics*, *14*, 690–700. https://doi.org/10.1038/sj.ejhg.5201588

Deary, I. J., Whalley, L. J., & Starr, J. M. (2009). A lifetime of intelligence: Follow-up studies of the Scottish mental surveys of 1932 and 1947. *American Psychological Association*. https://doi.org/10.1037/11857-000

Deco, G., Jirsa, V. K., Robinson, P. A., Breakspear, M., & Friston, K. (2008). The dynamic brain: From spiking neurons to neural masses and cortical fields. *PLoS Computational Biology*, 4. https://doi.org/10.1371/journal.pcbi.1000092

Dickens, W. T., & Flynn, J. R. (2006). Black Americans reduce the racial IQ gap: Evidence from standardization samples. *Psychological Science*, 17(10), 913–920. https://doi.org/10.1111/j.1467-9280.2006.01802.x

Djapo, N., Kolenovic-Djapo, J., Djokic, R., & Fako, I. (2011). Relationship between Cattell's 16PF and fluid and crystallized intelligence. *Personality and Individual Differences*, 51(1), 63–67. https://doi.org/10.1016/j.paid.2011.03.014

Duckworth, A. L., Quinn, P. D., Lynam, D. R., Loeber, R., & Stouthamer-Loeber, M. (2011). Role of test motivation in intelligence testing. *Proceedings of the National Academy of Sciences*, 108(19), 7716–7720. https://doi.org/10.1073/pnas.1018601108

Erlenmeyer-Kimling, L., & Jarvik, L. F. (1963). Genetics and intelligence: A review. *Science*, 142(3598), 1477–1479. https://doi.org/10.1126/science.142.3598.1477

Falch, T., & Sandgren Massih, S. (2011). The effect of education on cognitive ability. *Economic Inquiry*, 49(3), 838–856. https://doi.org/10.1111/j.1465-7295.2010.00312.x

Feingold, A. (1992). Sex differences in variability in intellectual abilities: A new look at an old controversy. *Review of Educational Research*, 62(1), 61–84. https://doi.org/10.3102/00346543062001061

Flynn, J. R. (1987). Massive IQ gains in 14 nations: What IQ tests really measure. *Psychological Bulletin*, 101(2), 171–191. https://doi.org/10.1037//0033-2909.101.2.171

Flynn, J. R. (2007) *What is intelligence?* Cambridge University Press.

Frey, M. C., & Detterman, D. K. (2004). Scholastic assessment or *g*? The relationship between the scholastic assessment test and general cognitive ability. *Psychological Science*, 15(6), 373–378. https://doi.org/10.1111/j.0956-7976.2004.00687.x

Galton, F. (1889). Head growth in students at the University of Cambridge. *Nature*, 40, 318–318. https://doi.org/10.1038/040318a0

Gardner, H., & Sosio, L. (1987). *Formae mentis: Saggio sulla pluralità dell'intelligenza* [Formae mentis: Essay on the plurality of intelligence]. Feltrinelli.

Graziano, W. G., Varca, P. E., & Levy, J. C. (1982). Race of examiner effects and the validity of intelligence tests. *Review of Educational Research*, 52(4), 469–497. https://doi.org/10.3102/00346543052004469

Halpern, D. F. (1997). Sex differences in intelligence: Implications for education. *American Psychologist*, 52(10), 1091–1102. https://doi.org/10.1037//0003-066x.52.10.1091

Hammill, D. D., Pearson, N. A., & Wiederholt, J. L. (2009). *Comprehensive Test of Nonverbal Intelligence–Second Edition. Practitioner's guide to assessing intelligence and achievement.* PRO-ED.

Hendrickson, D. E., & Hendrickson, A. E. (1980). The biological basis of individual differences in intelligence. *Personality and Individual Differences*, 1(1), 3–33. https://doi.org/10.1016/0191-8869(80)90003-3

Henning, J. I., & Jordaan, H. (2016). Determinants of financial sustainability for farm credit applications—A Delphi study. *Sustainability*, 8, 77. https://doi.org/10.3390/su8010077

Herrnstein, R. J., & Murray, C. A. (1994). *The bell curve: Reshaping of American life by differences in intelligence.* Free Press.

Hill, W. D., Marioni, R. E., Maghzian, O., Ritchie, S. J., Hagenaars, S. P., McIntosh, A. M., Gale, C.R., Davies, G. & Deary, I. J. (2019). A combined analysis of genetically correlated traits identifies 187 loci and a role for neurogenesis and myelination in intelligence. *Molecular Psychiatry*, 24, 169–181. https://doi.org/10.1038/s41380-017-0001-5

Hunt, E., & Madhyastha, T. (2008). Recruitment modeling: An analysis and an application to the study of male-female differences in intelligence. *Intelligence*, 36(6), 653–663. https://doi.org/10.1016/j.intell.2008.03.002

Jensen, A. R. (1998). *The g factor: The science of mental ability.* Praeger.

Johnson, W., & Bouchard, T. J., Jr. (2007). Sex differences in mental abilities: *g* masks the dimensions on which they lie. *Intelligence*, 35(1), 23–39. https://doi.org/10.1016/j.intell.2006.03.012

Karama, S., Colom, R., Johnson, W., Deary, I. J., Haier, R., Waber, D. P., Lepage, C., Ganjavi, H., Jung, R., Evans, A. C., & Brain Development Cooperative Group. (2011). Cortical thickness correlates of specific cognitive performance accounted for by the general factor of intelligence in healthy children aged 6 to 18. *Neuroimage, 55*(4), 1443–1453. https://doi.org/10.1016/j.neuroimage.2011.01.016

Kaufman, A. S., Kaufman, J. C., Liu, X., & Johnson, C. K. (2009). How do educational attainment and gender relate to fluid intelligence, crystallized intelligence, and academic skills at ages 22–90 years? *Archives of Clinical Neuropsychology, 24*(2), 153–163. https://doi.org/10.1093/arclin/acp015

Keith, T. Z., Reynolds, M. R., Patel, P. G., Ridley, K. P. (2008). Sex differences in latent cognitive abilities ages 6 to 59: Evidence from the Woodcock–Johnson III tests of cognitive abilities. *Intelligence, 36*(8), 502–525. https://doi.org/10.1016/j.intell.2007.11.001

Li, Y., Liu, Y., Li, J., Qin, W., Li, K., Yu, C., & Jiang, T. (2009). Brain anatomical network and intelligence. *PLoS Computational Biology, 5*(5), e1000395. https://doi.org/10.1371/journal.pcbi.1000395

Lombardo, P. A. (2002). The American breed: Nazi eugenics and the origins of the Pioneer Fund. *Albany Law Review, 65*, 743–830.

Lynn, R. (1994a). Some reinterpretations of the Minnesota transracial adoption study. *Intelligence, 19*(1), 21–27. https://doi.org/10.1016/0160-2896(94)90050-7

Lynn, R. (1994b). Sex differences in intelligence and brain size: A paradox resolved. *Personality and Individual Differences, 17*(2), 257–271. https://doi.org/10.1016/0191-8869(94)90030-2

Lynn, R. (1998). Sex differences in intelligence: Data from a Scottish standardization of the WAIS–R. *Personality and Individual Differences, 24*(2), 289–290. https://doi.org/10.1016/s0191-8869(97)00165-7

Lynn, R. (2006). *Race differences in intelligence: An evolutionary analysis*. Washington Summit Publishers.

Lynn, R. (2010). In Italy, north-south differences in IQ predict differences in income, education, infant mortality, stature, and literacy. *Intelligence, 38*(1), 93–100. https://doi.org/10.1016/j.intell.2009.07.004

Lynn, R., & Irwing, P. (2002). Sex differences in general knowledge, semantic memory and reasoning ability. *British Journal of Psychology, 93*(4), 545–556. https://doi.org/10.1348/000712602761381394

Lynn, R., & Meisenberg, G. (2010a). The average IQ of sub-Saharan Africans: Comments on Wicherts, Dolan, and van der Maas. *Intelligence, 38*(1), 21–29. https://doi.org/10.1016/j.intell.2009.09.009

Lynn, R., & Meisenberg, G. (2010b). National IQs calculated and validated for 108 nations. *Intelligence, 38*(4), 353–360. https://doi.org/10.1016/j.intell.2010.04.007

Lynn, R., & Vanhanen, T. (2006). *IQ and global inequality*. Washington Summit Publishers.

Mani, A., Mullainathan, S., Shafir, E., & Zhao, J. (2013). Poverty impedes cognitive function. *Science, 341*(6149), 976–980. https://doi.org/10.1126/science.1238041

Marks, D. F. (2010). IQ variations across time, race, and nationality: An artifact of differences in literacy skills. *Psychological Reports, 106*(3), 643–664. https://doi.org/10.2466/pr0.106.3.643-664

McCartney, K., Harris, M. J., & Bernieri, F. (1990). Growing up and growing apart: A developmental meta-analysis of twin studies. *Psychological Bulletin, 107*(2), 226–237. https://doi.org/10.1037//0033-2909.107.2.226

McDaniel, M. A. (2005). Big-brained people are smarter: A meta-analysis of the relationship between in vivo brain volume and intelligence. *Intelligence, 33*(4), 337–346. https://doi.org/10.1016/j.intell.2004.11.005

McGrevy, D. F., Knouse, S. B., & Thompson, R. A. (1974). Relationships among an individual intelligence test and two Air Force screening and selection tests (No. AFHRL-TR-74-25). *Air Force Human Resources Lab Brooks AFB TX*, 5–15. https://doi.org/10.1037/e459972004-001

McLeod, H. N., & Rubin, J. (1962). Correlation between Raven Progressive Matrices and the WAIS. *Journal of Consulting Psychology, 26*(2), 190–191. https://doi.org/10.1037/h0040278

Miller, A. (1994). The Pioneer Fund: Bankrolling the professors of hate. *Journal of Blacks in Higher Education, 6*, 58–61. https://doi.org/10.2307/2962466

Mingroni, M. A. (2004). The secular rise in IQ: Giving heterosis a closer look. *Intelligence, 32*(1), 65–83. https://doi.org/10.1016/s0160-2896(03)00058-8

Moutafi, J., Furnham, A., & Tsaousis, I. (2006). Is the relationship between intelligence and trait neuroticism mediated by test anxiety? *Personality and Individual Differences, 40*(3), 587–597. https://doi.org/10.1016/j.paid.2005.08.004

Nave, G., Jung, W. H., Karlsson Linnér, R., Kable, J. W., & Koellinger, P. D. (2019). Are bigger brains smarter? Evidence from a large-scale preregistered study. *Psychological Science, 30*(1), 43–54. https://doi.org/10.1177/0956797618808470

Neisser, U., Boodoo, G., Bouchard, T. J., Jr. Boykin, A. W., Brody, N., Ceci, S. J., Halpern, D. F., Loehlin, J. C., Perloff, R., Sternberg, R. J. & Urbira, S. (1996). Intelligence: Knowns and unknowns. *American Psychologist*, 51(2), 77–101. https://doi.org/10.1037//0003-066x.51.2.77

Neubauer, A. C., & Fink, A. (2009). Intelligence and neural efficiency. *Neuroscience & Biobehavioral Reviews*, 33(7), 1004–1023. https://doi.org/10.1016/j.neubiorev.2009.04.001

Owen, K. (1992). The suitability of Raven's Standard Progressive Matrices for various groups in South Africa. *Personality and Individual Differences*, 13(2), 149–159. https://doi.org/10.1016/0191-8869(92)90037-p

Pesta, B. J., & Poznanski, P. J. (2008). Black-White differences on IQ and grades The mediating role of elementary cognitive tasks. *Intelligence*, 36(4), 323–329. https://doi.org/10.1016/j.intell.2007.07.004

Pezzuti, L., Tommasi, M., Saggino, A., Dawe, J., & Lauriola, M. (2020). Gender differences and measurement bias in the assessment of adult intelligence: Evidence from the talian WAIS–IV and WAIS–R standardizations. *Intelligence*, 79, https://doi.org/10.1016/j.intell.2020.101436.

Pietschnig, J., & Voracek, M. (2015). One century of global IQ gains: A formal meta-analysis of the Flynn effect (1909–2013). *Perspectives on Psychological Science*, 10(3), 282–306. https://doi.org/10.1177/1745691615577701

Plomin, R., & Deary, I. J. (2015). Genetics and intelligence differences: Five special findings. *Molecular Psychiatry*, 20, 98–108. https://doi.org/10.1038/mp.2014.105

Plomin, R., & von Stumm, S. (2018). The new genetics of intelligence. *Nature Reviews Genetics*, 19, 148–159. https://doi.org/10.1038/nrg.2017.104

Raines, T. C., Reynolds, C. R., & Kamphaus, R. W. (2018). The Reynolds Intellectual Assessment Scales, and the Reynolds Intellectual Screening Test. In D. P. Flanagan & E. M. McDonough (Eds.), *Contemporary intellectual assessment: Theories, tests, and issues* (4th ed., pp. 533–552). Guilford Press.

Raven, J. C. (2008). *SPM Standard Progressive Matrices: Standardizzazione italiana* [Standard Progressive Matrices: Italian standardization]. Giunt OS Organizzazioni Speciali, Firenze.

Raven, J. C., Court, J. H., & Raven, J. (1985). *A manual for Raven's Progressive Matrices and Vocabulary Scales*. H. K. Lewis.

Richardson, K. (2017). GWAS and cognitive abilities: Why correlations are inevitable and meaningless. *EMBO Reports*, 18(8), 1279–1283.

Richwine, J. (2009). *IQ and immigration policy*. Doctoral dissertation. Harvard University.

Rindermann, H. (2007). The *g*-factor of international cognitive ability comparisons: The homogeneity of results in PISA, TIMSS, PIRLS and IC-tests across nations. *European Journal of Personality*, 21(5), 667–706. https://doi.org/10.1002/per.634

Ritchie, S. J., Bates, T. C., & Deary, I. J. (2015). Is education associated with improvements in general cognitive ability, or in specific skills? *Developmental Psychology*, 51(5), 573–582. https://doi.org/10.1037/a0038981

Ritchie, S. J., & Tucker-Drob, E. M. (2018). How much does education improve intelligence? A meta-analysis. *Psychological Science*, 29(3), 1358–1369. https://doi.org/10.1177/0956797618774253

Robinson, D., Saggino, A., & Tommasi, M. (2011). The case against Lynn's doctrine that population IQ determines levels of socio-economic development and public health status. *Journal of Public Mental Health*, 10, 178–189. https://doi.org/10.1108/17465721111175056

Rushton, J. P. (1992). Cranial capacity related to sex, rank, and race in a stratified random sample of 6,325 U.S. military personnel. *Intelligence*, 16(3), 401–413. https://doi.org/10.1016/0160-2896(92)90017-I

Rushton, J. P. (1999). Secular gains in IQ not related to the g factor and inbreeding depression—Unlike Black-White differences: A reply to Flynn. *Personality and Individual Differences*, 26, 381–389.

Rushton, J. P., & Ankney, C. D. (1996). Brain size and cognitive ability: Correlations with age, sex, social class, and race. *Psychonomic Bulletin & Review*, 3, 21–36. https://doi.org/10.3758/bf03210739

Rushton, J. P., & Jensen, A. R. (2005). Thirty years of research on race differences in cognitive ability. *Psychology, Public Policy, and Law*, 11(2), 235–294. https://doi.org/10.1037/1076-8971.11.2.235

Rushton, J. P., & Jensen, A. R. (2006). The totality of available evidence shows the race IQ gap still remains. *Psychological Science*, 17(10), 921–922. https://doi.org/10.1111/j.1467-9280.2006.01803.x

Saggino, A., Pezzuti, L., Tommasi, M., Cianci, L., Colom, R., & Orsini, A. (2014). Null sex differences in general intelligence among elderly. *Personality and Individual Differences*, 63, 53–57. https://doi.org/10.1016/j.paid.2014.01.047

Sternberg, R. J. (1985). *Beyond IQ: A triarchic theory of human intelligence*. CUP Archive.

Sundet, J. M., Barlaug, D. G., & Torjussen, T. M. (2004). The end of the Flynn effect? A study of secular trends in mean intelligence test scores of Norwegian conscripts during half a century. *Intelligence, 32*(4), 349–362. https://doi.org/10.1016/s0160-2896(04)00052-2

te Nijenhuis, J., & Van Der Flier, H. (2013). Is the Flynn effect on *g*? A meta-analysis. *Intelligence, 41*(6), 802–807. https://doi.org/10.1016/j.intell.2013.03.001

Terrell, F., Terrell, S. L., & Taylor, J. (1981). Effects of race of examiner and cultural mistrust on the WAIS performance of Black students. *Journal of Consulting and Clinical Psychology, 49*(5), 750–751. https://doi.org/10.1037//0022-006x.49.5.750

Tommasi, M., Pezzuti, L., Colom, R., Abad, F. J., Saggino, A., & Orsini, A. (2015a). Increased educational level is related with higher IQ scores but lower *g*-variance: Evidence from the standardization of the WAIS–R for Italy. *Intelligence, 50*, 68–74. https://doi.org/10.1016/j.intell.2015.02.005

Tommasi, M., Watkins, M., Orsini, A., Pezzuti, L., Cianci, L., & Saggino, A. (2015b). Gender differences in latent cognitive abilities and education links with g in Italian elders. *Learning and Individual Differences, 37*, 276–282. https://doi.org/10.1016/j.lindif.2014.10.020

Tucker-Drob, E. M., & Bates, T. C. (2016). Large cross-national differences in gene × socioeconomic status interaction on intelligence. *Psychological Science, 27*(2), 138–149. https://doi.org/10.1177/0956797615612727

Van der Sluis, S., Posthuma, D., Dolan, C. V., de Geus, E. J., Colom, R., & Boomsma, D. I. (2006). Sex differences on the Dutch WAIS–III. *Intelligence, 34*(3), 273–289. https://doi.org/10.1016/j.intell.2005.08.002

Van Den Heuvel, M. P., Stam, C. J., Kahn, R. S., & Pol, H. E. H. (2009). Efficiency of functional brain networks and intellectual performance. *Journal of Neuroscience, 29*(23), 7619–7624. https://doi.org/10.1523/jneurosci.1443-09.2009

Vass, V. A. (1992). *Standardization of Raven's Standard Progressive Matrices for secondary school African pupils in the Grahamstown region*. Doctoral dissertation. Rhodes University.

Waldman, I. D., Weinberg, R. A., & Scarr, S. (1994). Racial-group differences in IQ in the Minnesota Transracial Adoption Study: A reply to Levin and Lynn. *Intelligence, 19*(1), 29–44. https://doi.org/10.1016/0160-2896(94)90051-5

Wechsler, D. (2003). *Wechsler Intelligence Scale for Children–Fourth Edition (WISC–IV)*. Psychological Corporation.

Wechsler, D. (2008). *Wechsler Adult Intelligence Scale–Fourth Edition (WAIS–IV)*. NCS Pearson.

Wechsler, D., Raiford, S. E., & Holdnack, J. A. (2014). *WISC–V technical and interpretive manual supplement: Special group validity studies with other measure and additional tables*. Pearson.

Weinberg, R. A., Scarr, S., & Waldman, I. D. (1992). The Minnesota Transracial Adoption Study: A follow-up of IQ test performance at adolescence. *Intelligence, 161*, 117–135. https://doi.org/10.1016/0160-2896(92)90028-p

Wicherts, J. M., Dolan, C. V., & van der Maas, H. L. (2010). The dangers of unsystematic selection methods and the representativeness of 46 samples of African test-takers. *Intelligence, 38*(1), 30–37. https://doi.org/10.1016/j.intell.2009.11.003

Wicherts, J. M., & Scholten, A. Z. (2010). Test anxiety and the validity of cognitive tests: A confirmatory factor analysis perspective and some empirical findings. *Intelligence, 38*(1), 169–178. https://doi.org/10.1016/j.intell.2009.09.008

Wickett, J. C., Vernon, P. A., & Lee, D. H. (2000). Relationships between factors of intelligence and brain volume. *Personality and Individual Differences, 29*(6), 1095–1122. https://doi.org/10.1016/s0191-8869(99)00258-5

Yang, J., Bakshi, A., Zhu, Z., Hemani, G., Vinkhuyzen, A. A. E., Lee, S. H., Robinson, M. R., Perry, J. R. B., Nolte, I. M., van Vliet-Ostaptchouk, J. V., Snieder, H., The LifeLines Cohort Study, Esko, T., Milani, L., Mägi, R., Metspalu, A., Hamsten, A., Magnusson, P. K. E., Pedersen, N. L., Ingelsson, E., Soranzo, N., Keller, M. C., Wray, N. R., Goddard, M. E. & Visscher, P. M. (2015). Genetic variance estimation with imputed variants finds negligible missing heritability for human height and body mass index. *Nature Genetics, 47*, 1114–1120. https://doi.org/10.1038/ng.3390

Yorifuji, T., Kato, T., Kado, Y., Tokinobu, A., Yamakawa, M., Tsuda, T., & Sanada, S. (2015). Intrauterine exposure to methylmercury and neurocognitive functions: Minamata disease. *Archives of Environmental & Occupational Health, 70*(5), 297–302. https://doi.org/10.1080/19338244.2014.904268

Zagorsky, J. L. (2007). Do you have to be smart to be rich? The impact of IQ on wealth, income, and financial distress. *Intelligence*, *35*(5), 489–501. https://doi.org/10.1016/j.intell.2007.02.003

Zindi, F. (2013). Towards the development of African psychometric tests. *Zimbabwe Journal of Educational Research*, *25*(1), 149–166. https://doi.org/10.4314/zjer.v16i1.26036

Zinn, J., Zalokowski, A., & Hunter, L. (2001) Identifying indicators of laboratory management performance: A multiple constituency approach. *Health Care Management Review*, *26*(1), 40–53. https://doi.org/10.1097/00004010-200101000-00004

Index

Page references for tables and figures are italicized.

About the Editor

Gary L. Canivez, PhD, is a professor of psychology at Eastern Illinois University and principally involved in the Specialist in School Psychology program. Before entering academia, he was a school psychologist for eight years in the Phoenix metropolitan area (Deer Valley Unified School District [three years] and Tempe Elementary School District [five years]), was on the adjunct faculty of Arizona State University and Northern Arizona University, and was president of the Arizona Association of School Psychologists. He presently serves as a senior editor for *School Psychology Review* and was formerly an associate editor for *Psychological Assessment* and *Archives of Scientific Psychology*. He serves on the editorial boards of *School Psychology* (formerly *School Psychology Quarterly*) and the *Journal of Psychoeducational Assessment*. Dr. Canivez is the author or coauthor of over 100 peer-reviewed articles and was coauthor of the 2018 *Journal of School Psychology* Best Article of the Year. Dr. Canivez is a Fellow of the American Psychological Association (Divisions 5 and 16), a Charter Fellow of the Midwestern Psychological Association, and an elected member of the Society for the Study of School Psychology. His research focuses on psychometric studies of tests of intelligence and psychopathology to help provide evidence necessary to guide evidence-based assessment. His research has been supported by the National Institutes of Health/National Institute of Mental Health and he was a Fulbright Specialist for the U.S. Department of State's Bureau of Educational and Cultural Affairs and World Learning from 2019 to 2024. Dr. Canivez has presented numerous continuing education workshops regarding ethics, test standards, test interpretation, and psychometric principles and research for the American Psychological Association, National Association of School Psychologists, the International Test Commission, the International School Psychology Association, state school psychology associations, and local school districts. In his spare time he has provided sport psychology services with a focus on prevention and training for peak performance in a variety of sports including cross-country, track, tennis, baseball, softball, golf, and wrestling, and he has worked with athletes who have competed at junior through elite levels. https://orcid.org/0000-0002-5347-6534.

About the Contributors

A. Alexander Beaujean, PhD, received PhDs in school psychology and educational psychology (methods emphasis) from the University of Missouri and is currently a professor of psychology at Baylor University. He has published extensively in the areas of individual differences and psychological assessment and is the author of two books on latent variable models. He earned a diplomate from the American Board of Assessment Psychology, is an elected member of the Society for the Study of School Psychology, and is a past president of the American Psychological Association's Division 5 (Quantitative and Qualitative Methods). https://orcid.org/0000-0001-7007-7968

Nicholas Benson, PhD, is an associate professor and director of the School Psychology PhD program at Baylor University. He is a licensed psychologist (Texas) and a nationally certified school psychologist. Dr. Benson's research interests focus broadly on psychological and educational assessment with emphasis on examining the validity of interpretations and uses of test scores. He has published extensively and has received awards for his work including elected membership in the Society for the Study of School Psychology and the Award for Excellence in Research from Mensa. He is an associate editor for the *Journal of School Psychology*. He also serves on the *Journal of Psychoeducational Assessment*, *Psychological Assessment*, *School Psychology*, and *School Psychology International* editorial boards. Dr. Benson earned his PhD from the University of Florida. https://orcid.org/0000-0001-8180-4243

Corinne J. Casey, EdS, is a nationally certified school psychologist and adjunct faculty member at Rider University in Lawrenceville, New Jersey. She serves as a full-time school psychologist and Child Study Team member at the high school level. She has published several scholarly articles and has presented twice at the National Association of School Psychologists annual convention. Her work has focused on contemporary topics including psychoeducational assessment, social-emotional learning, and postsecondary transitional planning.

Stefan C. Dombrowski, PhD, is a professor and director of the School Psychology program at Rider University in New Jersey. Professor Dombrowski completed his PhD in school psychology with a minor in counseling psychology at the University of Georgia. He also completed a post-doctoral fellowship in clinical psychology at the University of California, Davis Medical Center. Dr. Dombrowski is a licensed psychologist and certified school psychologist with primary research interests in psychological assessment and psychometrics. He has published five books and nearly 125 scholarly articles or chapters on assessment-related matters. https://orcid.org/0000-0002-8057-3751

Ryan L. Farmer, PhD, HSP, is director of the Psychological Services Center and coordinates the Master of Arts and Educational Specialist program in School Psychology at the University of Memphis. His research focuses on evaluating the effectiveness and utility of various practices within school psychology, aiming to distinguish empirically supported methods from those of lower value. He also investigates the factors that contribute to the persistence of low-value practices in educational and clinical settings. To date much of his work has focused on the psychometric properties of tests and the use of ineffective assessment practices. https://orcid .org/0000-0003-1409-7555

Randy G. Floyd, PhD, is a professor of psychology and department chair in the Department of Psychology at the University of Memphis. His research focuses on understanding the measurement properties of psychological assessment techniques including intelligence tests and behavior rating scales, and he is interested in understanding professional development processes supporting university-based faculty including engaging in the peer-review process.

Gilles Gignac, PhD, serves as an associate professor in the School of Psychological Science at the University of Western Australia. His research primarily focuses on individual differences especially in cognitive abilities and personality traits. He has also contributed to the fields of applied statistics and psychometrics, including reliability estimation. With over 110 peer-reviewed publications, Dr. Gignac has contributed extensively to these fields. Though he contends that standards for reliability in research may be lowered, he believes the opposite for personal reliability. He currently holds a position on the editorial board of *Intelligence* and serves as an associate editor for *Journal of Personality*. https://orcid.org/0000-0002-4900-6855

Samuel Y. Kim, PhD, is an associate professor and coordinator of the School Psychology PhD program at Texas Woman's University in Denton, Texas. His research interests include positive psychology as well as fostering relationships among youth and their families. In addition to being a licensed psychologist in both Colorado and Texas, he has worked in a variety of settings such as schools, community mental health clinics, and university clinics in Georgia, Michigan, Kentucky, Colorado, and Texas providing a range of psychological services including counseling, assessment, and consultation. https://orcid.org/0000-0002-3060-1961

John H. Kranzler, PhD, is a professor of school psychology and director of the APA–accredited and NASP–approved School Psychology Program in the School of Special Education, School Psychology, and Early Childhood Studies at the University of Florida. Dr. Kranzler's major area of scholarly interest concerns the nature, development, and assessment of human cognitive abilities. He has received awards for his teaching and research including the University of Florida Teaching Incentive Program award for undergraduate teaching; the Mensa Education and Research Foundation Award for Excellence in Research; and Article of the Year awards from *School Psychology Review* and *School Psychology Quarterly*. In 1997 and 2017, Dr. Kranzler received the University of Florida Research Foundation Professorship award for distinguished scholarship, and he was recently named a University of Florida Term Professor in 2019. He is a fellow of the American Psychological Association and an elected member of the Society for the Study of School Psychology. Dr. Kranzler has served as associate editor for *School Psychology Quarterly* and the *International Journal of School and Educational Psychology*, and he currently serves on the editorial board of the *Journal of School Psychology*. https://orcid.org/0000-0002 -6473-7410

Joseph C. Kush, PhD, is a Fulbright Scholar and professor of education at Duquesne University in Pittsburgh, Pennsylvania. He serves on the editorial boards of several school psychology and assessment journals. His research interests include topics related to intellectual assessment, issues of test bias and test fairness for children, and the use of technology and artificial intelligence to enhance learning. He is an accomplished guitarist and uses McIntosh computers exclusively. https://orcid.org/0000-0001-9614-6351

Ryan J. McGill, PhD, ABAP, is an associate professor of school psychology at the William & Mary School of Education in Virginia. Dr. McGill earned a Diplomate in Assessment Psychology from the American Board of Assessment Psychology (ABAP) and is a Board Certified Behavior Analyst (BCBA-D) as well as a Nationally Certified School Psychologist (NCSP). A fellow of the American Academy of Assessment Psychology, his research focuses on the applied validity and interpretation of psychological test scores, specifically on the use of intelligence tests for specific learning disability identification. In recognition of his scholarly contributions, he was recently named the Gerdleman Family Term Distinguished Associate Professor in Education, the first time that a member of the school psychology program has been awarded that distinction. https://orcid.org /0000-0002-5138-0694

Lina Pezzuti, PhD, is a professor of Theory and Techniques of Psychological Tests and Use and Interpretation of Psychological Tests at the Medicine and Psychology Faculty of the Sapienza University of Rome, Italy. She is also a teacher at the School of Specialization in Clinical Psychology of the Sapienza University of Rome. Her scientific interests are psychodiagnosis; cognitive processes across the life span; intelligence; the psychology of aging; construction, validation and standardization of psychological tests; and research methodologies and data analysis. She has authored 15 books or book chapters, she has authored 90 scientific papers in Italian and English journals, and she has been involved with and produced 13 validations and standardizations of psychological tests. https://orcid.org/0000-0001-5810-4185

Aristide Saggino, PhD, is a professor of psychometrics at the School of Medicine and Health Sciences of the Università di Chieti-Pescara, Italy and president of the Italian Association of Behavior Analysis and Modification and Behavioral-Cognitive Psychotherapy (AIAMC). His scientific interests are psychological assessment and individual differences, and evidence-based psychotherapy. He has authored 19 books and book chapters in Italian and English, and he is the author of 103 scientific publications indexed on Scopus. https://orcid.org/0000-0002-4903-9833

Marco Tommasi, PhD, is an assistant professor at the University of Chieti-Pescara, Italy. He took his PhD in scientific psychology at the University of Padua. He was a research assistant at the Justus Liebig University of Giessen, Germany. His areas of interest are psychophysics, psychometrics, and individual differences, in particular, intelligence, personality, emotions, psychological well-being, psychological testing, and data analysis. He currently teaches theory and techniques of psychological assessment and methodology of research and multivariate data analysis in psychology in psychological courses. His scientific productions include more than 60 papers published in indexed journals, books, and handbooks of psychological tests. He also has an expertise in programming and computerized adaptive testing. https://orcid.org/0000-0002-4876-0530

Jonathan Wai, PhD, is an associate professor of Education Policy and Psychology, 21st Century Endowed Chair in Education Policy at the University of Arkansas in the Department of Education

Reform. He holds a joint (courtesy) appointment in the Department of Psychology and is an affiliate faculty in Educational Psychology at the University of Alabama. Broadly, he studies education policy through the lens of psychology and multidisciplinary perspectives. His areas of expertise include education policy, psychology, gifted education, expertise, and talent development. Author of over 100 scholarly works, Dr. Wai has served on the board of directors of the MATHCOUNTS foundation, and he currently serves on the Research Advisory Board of the College Board Admissions Research Consortium; the Advisory Board of the Virtual Center for Advanced Potential at Schmidt Futures; the Advanced Education Working Group of the Thomas B. Fordham Institute; and as chair of the Education Working Group of the Association for Psychological Science Global Collaboration on COVID-19. He has received the AERA Michael Pyryt Collaboration Award and multiple international Mensa Awards for Research Excellence, and his work has been funded by the Institute of Education Sciences, the Walton Family Foundation, Schmidt Futures, the Educational Testing Service, and the American Psychological Foundation. He was named to the Education Week Education-Scholar Public Influence Ranking Top 200. https://orcid.org/0000-0002-7686-1312

Frank C. Worrell, PhD, is a distinguished professor at the Berkeley School of Education at the University of California, Berkeley, where he serves as the faculty director of the School Psychology Program and the Academic Talent Development Program and has an affiliate appointment in the Social and Personality Area in the Department of Psychology. His areas of expertise include at-risk youth, cultural identities, scale development, talent development, time perspective, and the translation of psychological research findings into practice. Author of over 300 scholarly works, Dr. Worrell is a fellow of the American Educational Research Association, the Association for Psychological Science, and of five divisions of the American Psychological Association (APA), and he is an elected member of the Society for the Study of School Psychology and the National Academy of Education. A former editor of *Review of Educational Research*, Dr. Worrell is a recipient of the Distinguished Scholar Award from the National Association for Gifted Children; the Distinguished Contributions to Research Award from Division 45 of the APA; the Nadine Lambert Outstanding School Psychologist Award (Region II) from the California Association of School Psychologists; the Outstanding International Psychologist Award from Division 52 of the APA; the Palmarium Award in Gifted Education from the University of Denver; the award for Outstanding Contributions to the Profession of School Psychology from the Council of Directors of School Psychology Programs; and an Honorary Doctorate from Heidelberg University. He was the 2022 president of the APA. https://orcid.org/0000-0002-7122-527X

9 7 8 1 5 3 8 1 4 5 7 2 2